POLITICAL PSYCHOLOGY

In recent decades, research in political psychology has illuminated the psychological processes underlying important political action, both by ordinary citizens and by political leaders. As the world has become increasingly engaged in thinking about politics, this volume reflects exciting new work by political psychologists to understand the psychological processes underlying Americans' political thinking and action.

In 13 chapters, world-class scholars present new in-depth work exploring public opinion, social movements, attitudes toward affirmative action, the behavior of political leaders, the impact of the 9/11 attacks, and scientists' statements about global warming and gasoline prices. Also included are studies of attitude strength that compare the causes and consequences of various strength-related constructs.

This volume will appeal to a wide range of researchers and students in political psychology and political science, and may be used as a text in upper-level courses requiring a scholarly and contemporary review of major issues in the field.

Jon A. Krosnick is Frederic O. Glover Professor in Humanities and Social Sciences and Professor of Communication, Political Science, and Psychology at Stanford University. His research interests include: attitude formation, change, and effects; the psychology of political behavior; and the optimal design of questionnaires used for laboratory experiments and surveys, and survey research methodology more generally.

I-Chant A. Chiang is Executive Vice President and Social Science Professor at Quest University Canada. Her research interests include how language influences thinking, the macro level of linguistic relativity, and the micro level of framing effects.

Tobias H. Stark is an Assistant Professor at the European Research Centre on Migration and Ethnic Relations at Utrecht University, The Netherlands. His research focuses on the link between social networks, interethnic relationships, and racial prejudice.

FRONTIERS OF SOCIAL PSYCHOLOGY

Series Editors:

Arie W. Kruglanski, *University of Maryland at College Park*
Joseph P. Forgas, *University of New South Wales*

Frontiers of Social Psychology is a series of domain-specific handbooks. Each volume provides readers with an overview of the most recent theoretical, methodological, and practical developments in a substantive area of social psychology, in greater depth than is possible in general social psychology handbooks. The editors and contributors are all internationally renowned scholars whose work is at the cutting edge of research.

Scholarly, yet accessible, the volumes in the *Frontiers* series are an essential resource for senior undergraduates, postgraduates, researchers, and practitioners and are suitable as texts in advanced courses in specific subareas of social psychology.

Published Titles

Aggression and Violence, Brad J. Bushman
Social Neuroscience, Harmon-Jones & Inzlicht
Addictions, Kopetz & Lejuez
Social Communication, Fiedler
Attitudes and Attitude Change, Crano
Negotiation Theory and Research, Thompson
The Self, Sedikides & Spencer
Social Psychology and the Unconscious, Bargh
Evolution and Social Psychology, Schaller, Simpson & Kenrick
The Science of Social Influence, Pratkanis
Close Relationships, Noller & Feeney
Affect in Social Thinking and Behavior, Forgas
Personality and Social Behavior, Rhodewalt
Stereotyping and Prejudice, Stangor & Crandall
Group Processes, Levine
Social Metacognition, Briñol & DeMarree
Goal-directed Behavior, Aarts & Elliot
Social Judgment and Decision Making, Krueger
Intergroup Conflicts and their Resolution, Bar-Tal
Social Motivation, Dunning
Social Cognition, Strack & Förster
Social Psychology of Consumer Behavior, Wänke

Forthcoming Titles

For continually updated information about published and forthcoming titles in the *Frontiers of Social Psychology* series, please visit: **https://www.routledge.com/psychology/series/FSP**

POLITICAL PSYCHOLOGY

New Explorations

Edited by Jon A. Krosnick, I-Chant A. Chiang, and Tobias H. Stark

Routledge
Taylor & Francis Group

NEW YORK AND LONDON

First published 2017
by Routledge
711 Third Avenue, New York, NY 10017

and by Routledge
2 Park Square, Milton Park, Abingdon, Oxon, OX14 4RN

Routledge is an imprint of the Taylor & Francis Group, an informa business

Library of Congress Cataloging in Publication Data
Names: Krosnick, Jon A., editor.
Title: Political psychology : new explorations / edited by Jon A. Krosnick, I-Chant A. Chiang, and Tobias H. Stark.
Description: New York, NY : Routledge, 2016. | Includes bibliographical references and index.
Identifiers: LCCN 2016019240| ISBN 9781841694450 (hb : alk. paper) | ISBN 9781138802018 (pb : alk. paper) | ISBN 9781315445687 (e)
Subjects: LCSH: Political psychology.Classification: LCC JA74.5 .P6375 2016 | DDC 320.01/9--dc23
LC record available at https://lccn.loc.gov/2016019240

ISBN: 978-1-84169-445-0 (hbk)
ISBN: 978-1-138-80201-8 (pbk)
ISBN: 978-1-315-44568-7 (ebk)

Typeset in Bembo
by HWA Text and Data Management, London

CONTENTS

FIGURES

TABLES

CONTRIBUTORS

Jonathan Bendor, Graduate School of Business, Stanford University

I-Chant A. Chiang, Quest University Canada

Faye Crosby, Cowell College, University of California – Santa Cruz

Amy Cuddy, Harvard Business School

Laura Dionne, Department of Behavioral and Social Sciences, Brown University

Leandre R. Fabrigar, Psychology Department, Queen's University

Laurel Harbridge, Department of Political Science, Northwestern University

Allyson Holbrook, Survey Research Laboratory, University of Illinois at Chicago

Roderick M. Kramer, Graduate School of Business, Stanford University

Jon A. Krosnick, Department of Communication, Stanford University

Bo MacInnis, Department of Communication, Stanford University

Douglas J. McAdam, Sociology Department, Stanford University

Joanne M. Miller, Department of Political Science, University of Minnesota

Gregory Mitchell, School of Law, University of Virginia

Catherine J. Norris, Department of Psychology, Swarthmore College

Natalie J. Shook, Department of Psychology, West Virginia University

Tobias H. Stark, European Research Centre on Migration and Ethnic Relations, Utrecht University

Alexander Tahk, Department of Political Science, University of Wisconsin – Madison

Philip E. Tetlock, Psychology Department and Wharton School, University of Pennsylvania

Randall K. Thomas, GfK Custom Research North America

Theresa K. Vescio, Department of Psychology, The Pennsylvania State University

Penny S. Visser, Department of Psychology, The University of Chicago

Kevin Weaver, Department of Psychology, The Pennsylvania State University

Jeffrey M. Wooldridge, Department of Economics, Michigan State University

1

THE TWO CORE GOALS OF POLITICAL PSYCHOLOGY

Jon A. Krosnick, Tobias H. Stark, and I-Chant A. Chiang

Defining Political Psychology

As a very broad definition, it is safe to say that the field of political psychology is concerned with explaining political phenomena from a psychological perspective. This means that political psychologists study political decision-making, political action, and political attitudes through the perspective of unobservable psychological processes unfolding in the minds of political actors. In doing so, scholars typically explain a political phenomenon with established psychological concepts. For most political psychologists, contributing to understanding the political context is the primary goal of their endeavor. Less frequently has work from political psychology also contributed to psychological theory formation in general (Krosnick, 2002).

Political psychology's focus on explaining political phenomena is partially due to the fact that political scientists have dominated the field for the last forty years. This is apparent in the ratio of political scientists compared to psychologists that have published in the seminal edited volumes in political psychology. For instance, ten of the 20 authors in Margaret Hermann's (1986) book (*Political Psychology: Contemporary Issues and Problems*) were political scientists whereas only five were psychologists. Similarly, Shanto Iyengar and William McGuire's (1993) book (*Explorations in Political Psychology*) has chapters from nine political scientists and only five psychologists and the *Oxford Handbook of Political Psychology* by David Sears, Leonie Huddy, and Robert Jervis (2003) has chapters from 18 political scientists and only seven psychologists. A similar trend can be observed among the participants of the Summer Institute in Political Psychology (SIPP) that was created at Ohio State University and is now at Stanford University.

Since 1991, when SIPP was founded, there have regularly been twice as many applicants and participants from political science than from psychology (with the exception of a few years when the ratio was closer to 1.5). In 2006 and 2008, more psychologists than political scientists participated, but since 2009, political scientists have again outnumbered psychologists.

This dominance of political scientists might explain why political psychology—very much unlike other fields in psychology—seems to be predominantly *not* concerned with identifying pan-contextual principles of how the human mind works. Even though psychological theories are typically applied to understand political phenomena, this research rarely has attempted to advance our understanding of these psychological theories. Instead, much political psychological research is based on a genuine interest in understanding the political context.

For instance, many scholars in the field have applied psychological theories about human cognition and behavior to political decision-making or voting behavior. This approach has yielded useful insights for political science, but the explicitly stated benefit for psychology—and for understanding of the human mind in general—has been more limited. Research in political psychology may quite easily serve both purposes if researchers begin their projects by aiming to produce findings with implications of two sorts: (1) implications for understanding of politics *and* (2) implications for basic psychological theory. Research that focuses only on the first outcome may be better described as psychological political science but not as political psychology (Krosnick, 2002). In fact, the term "political psychology" implies that it is a form of psychology. As such, the field can contribute to the larger psychological endeavor of studying behavioral and mental processes to discover general laws if researchers choose to do so from the outset of their efforts and take the time to explain those implications in publications.

Conducting political psychology in the hope of advancing basic psychological theory is especially likely to help psychology, because more often than not, political psychologists step out of the laboratory and conduct their research in the real world. This is valuable partly because it maximizes the external validity of research findings. This benefit may not seem especially valuable to psychologists who place higher importance on internal validity than on external validity and who believe that internal validity can be maximized in context-free lab settings created by researchers. But a mix of lab and field studies can maximize both internal and external validity, and studies of the real world often enrich basic psychological work by pointing to processes, mediators, and moderators that would not necessarily find their way into theorizing about impoverished, constructed context-free lab settings. Experimental research might be best viewed as suggestive about how people make decisions and behave in similar situations in the real world. To quote Roderick Kramer (Chapter 4, this volume), "the failure of most experimenters to ever step outside the cloistered confines of the psychological laboratory and into the booming, buzzing and messy world of the field has limited our knowledge about these important processes." Political psychology can fill this gap in psychology with its focus on real world behavior of humans in the political context.

In this light, it is interesting to note that this book spotlights political psychology done by psychologists or in the spirit of psychology. Thus, this book illustrates how the application of psychological theories to the political context can advance both our understanding of politics *and* our understanding of the underlying psychological processes. For instance, Laurel Harbridge and colleagues (Chapter 9, this volume) find that the application of theories of media priming enhances our understanding of people's approval of the U.S. president and yield new insights into the limits of media priming in general. Likewise, Joanne Miller and colleagues' (Chapter 6, this volume) study of political issue salience furthers our understanding of which political issues are relevant for whom and enhances more generally the psychological study of attitude strength. Penny Visser and colleagues (Chapter 8, this volume) improve our understanding of attitude-(in)congruent political behavior and, at the same time, of the multidimensionality of the psychological concept of attitude strength.

The book is organized in three part. The first part shows four examples of analyses beginning with psychological theories and yielding new perspectives on various political processes. The second part addresses the question of what determines political cognition and behavior, with a special focus on the importance of policy issues to individuals. The third part consists of three examples of how application of psychological theories can challenge conventional wisdom in the political domain. Despite addressing a large variety of political phenomena, every article in this volume ends with a clearly visible contribution to psychology in general.

Content of This Book

Part I: New Theoretical Perspectives on Political Science Questions

In Chapter 2, Jonathan Bendor discusses limitations of classical Rational Choice Theory in political science and presents ways in which ideas from the psychological study of bounded rationality may overcome or ameliorate these limitations. Virtually all rational choice models build on the premise that people compare different strategies to each other. But this procedure is cognitively demanding when choice problems are complex; hence it may not be used often in such situations. Instead, people may adopt a strategy if its expected outcome is better than their aspiration level (reference point). Such heuristics are also much more broadly applicable than rational choice procedures when people have only partially ordered preferences. The author further argues that models that build on aspiration levels instead of a conscious rational comparison of choice options offer new theoretical explanations of problems and puzzles that political science has faced.

With several examples, Bendor demonstrates how aspiration-based models offer new solutions to unresolved problems in political science (e.g., the paradox of voting). Along the way, the author shows how mathematical formalizations can help identify gaps in researchers' thinking, both in political science and psychology.

Importantly, Bendor concludes that both rational choice and aspiration-based models have their merits; neither should be used exclusively. The difficulty of the problem people are facing often determines whether they can decide rationally or not (i.e., whether the complexity of the task exceeds their cognitive constraints). It is the task of the political psychologist to identify whether ideas from rational choice theory or the bounded rationality research program are most applicable in the given situation. Bendor's chapter provides a great resource for making this decision.

In Chapter 3, Gregory Mitchell and Philip Tetlock present a so-far underutilized methodology that might advance theory formation in both political philosophy and social psychology. The so-called "hypothetical society paradigm" promises a solution to a problem both fields are regularly facing: that participants of real-world debates often invent facts to justify their opinions and conceal double standards. This prevents the possibility to disentangle value orientations from factual beliefs in people's ultimate assessment of a situation.

The hypothetical society paradigm combines the advantages of thought experiments with laboratory experiments to overcome this limitation. Participants are asked to react to concrete scenarios that describe hypothetical societies. Because all relevant facts are laid out in the description, participants cannot invent new facts to justify the scenario. Instead, they have to base their reaction purely on their value orientation, given the facts. By comparing, for example, different distributions of wealth and the relation between effort and pay-off, people's generic understanding of justice can be gauged. With this method, Mitchell and Tetlock show that people's attitude toward corrective justice is much less dependent on political ideology than previously assumed.

The authors also discuss how this method can be used to tease apart the underlying reasons for behaviors that are predicted by multiple social psychological theories. Psychologists sometimes face the problem that they have to deduce participants' psychological reasoning post hoc from their behavior. The authors discuss how the hypothetical society paradigm can be utilized to get a better understanding of the underlying psychological processes in order to advance psychological theories.

In Chapter 4, Roderick Kramer presents a psychological perspective on the decision-making of political and business leaders. In particular, he focuses on situations in which leaders, either through their own mistakes or through external events, are confronted with threats to the way these leaders see themselves and want to be seen by others (their identity). Kramer's psychological approach offers a new way to understand leaders' decision-making in such situations. He suggests that threats to leaders' identity create a state of identity dissonance, which these leaders are motivated to reduce through strategies of attention diversion.

In three qualitative case studies, Kramer presents evidence in line with his concept of identity-based (re-)categorization that explains decisions and behavior of leaders facing assaults on their authority or legitimacy. In such identity-threatening situations, leaders tend to employ cognitive strategies to divert the attention to alternative identities of the leadership or the organization. One strategy is to highlight positive dimensions of one's identity through generating social comparison groups that make the organization or the leader look more favorable on seemingly more relevant dimensions. Another strategy is to cognitively focus on more flattering dimensions of one's identity while downplaying those dimensions that have been threatened.

This psychological perspective on political decision-making offers a promising new perspective for political scientists trying to understand why leaders sometimes make the decision they do. Kramer illustrates in his analysis of Lyndon Johnson's unexpected reactions to developments in the Vietnam War how an identity-threat perspective can lead to a new understanding of political leaders' behavior. In fact, the author concludes that few activities of leaders are as consequential to the vitality of an organization or the legitimacy of his leadership as the re-categorization of the identity in focus.

In Chapter 5, Doug McAdam challenges three widely cited "facts" about the origins, the development, and consequences of social movements. In his overview of the history of research on social movements, the author points out that the field originally was very psychological and ignored the more structured organizational and political dimensions of social movements. The subsequent sociological and political science research, in contrast, focused almost exclusively on the social structure and overlooked important psychological processes. For instance, McAdam makes the compelling point that participation in a movement is contingent on existing social ties (structure) but only if such ties and participation in the movement reinforce an identity (psychological) that is important to the individual. This argument is in line with the findings of Visser and colleagues (Chapter 8, this volume) who show that attitude-congruent behavior, such as joining a social movement, depends on the personal importance people attribute to the goal of that movement.

McAdam points out several shortcomings in the social movements literature. Most provocative is his observation that several widely believed "facts" about movements are based on research that betrays the cardinal methodological sin of "selecting on the dependent variable." This approach has probably exaggerated the link between certain factors and participation in, or the consequences of, social movements. This does not necessarily mean that the widely believed facts are wrong, but that better research designs are needed to test these "facts" and to achieve a fuller understanding of the processes that might have led to the observed regularities. As such, this chapter is also meant as a call for more psychological research in social movements studies. McAdam suggests several promising paths that future research could follow.

Part II: Determinants of Political Cognition and Political Behavior – the Role of Personal Importance

In Chapter 6 at the beginning of Part II, Joanne Miller and colleagues build on psychological theories to improve our understanding of a widely used concept in political science: issue salience. Decades of research has shown that some people think more about certain issues than others and that people's attitudes toward these issues can affect their behavior. However, the literature has been divided about the question which issues are most influential. Are these the issues of national importance or those that are of personal importance to people?

Based on nine studies, Miller and colleagues argue that personal importance is the ultimate root of issue salience and present evidence of its psychological consequences. Surveys and a laboratory experiment show that voting, writing letters, and making phone calls to express policy preferences, contributing money to lobbying organizations, and attending group meetings are all inspired by personal importance but rarely by national importance. A deeper look at psychological consequences allows the authors to provide an explanation for this finding: Personal importance is behaviorally consequential because it instigates vigorous cognitive and emotional issue engagement.

Contrary to some earlier assertions, this chapter suggests that issue salience is relatively stable. Whereas political events or media attention may easily and quickly increase or decrease people's perception of the national importance of certain issues, this is not true for personal importance. People think deeply about issues they find personally important, store information in long-term memory, and experience strong emotions. An increase in media coverage might affect the appearance of the national importance of certain issues, but these fluctuations will not be especially consequential for people's own preferences.

In Chapter 7, Joanne Miller and colleagues extend Douglas McAdam's (Chapter 5, this volume) theoretical criticism of widely believed "facts" about social movements. The authors challenge the notion that political activism is predominantly motivated by people's dissatisfaction with the current life circumstances. Building on psychological insights from Prospect Theory (Kahneman & Tversky, 1979), the authors argue that much more motivating than dissatisfaction with the status quo is the threat of an undesirable policy change. The fear that things may get worse in the future should be a stronger motivator for social action than the possibility that things may get better in the future.

Evidence from three empirical studies, two of which include experimental manipulations in nationally representative samples, makes the case for the authors' argument. In contrast to earlier research that relied on macro-level analyses such as time-series analyses, the results in this chapter allow teasing apart different factors that might motivate people to political action (contributing money to interest groups in the present study). Threat of an undesirable policy change had a stronger and more consistent effect than dissatisfaction with the current situation. This effect was stronger for those with the necessary financial resources and for those who attached greater personal importance to the policy at stake. This latter finding links this chapter directly to the other chapter by Miller and colleagues (Chapter 6, this volume). In that chapter, the authors found that personal importance of an issue increased the likelihood of political action, but not everybody with high personal importance actually participates. The findings of the present chapter suggest that a second condition for political action might be the threat people perceive to the issue they care deeply about. Exploring this link further in research on social movements and political participation seems a promising path for future research in political psychology.

In Chapter 8, Penny Visser and colleagues give another spin to the question raised by Doug McAdam (Chapter 5, this volume) and Joanne Miller and colleagues (Chapter 7, this volume): Why do some social movements receive broad support but only few people take action? To answer this question, the authors address a much more fundamental problem that makes predictions in political science difficult: people often do not behave in accordance with their attitudes. Visser and co-authors point to the social-psychological concept of attitude strength as a possible explanation. Building on an ongoing debate in social psychology on the dimensionality of attitude strength, these authors assert that some strength-related features promote attitude-congruent behavior in distinct ways. In line with the research by Miller et al. (Chapter 6, this volume), the authors focus on the personal importance of an attitude as one of these features. The second feature examined is people's attitude-relevant knowledge. The authors of this chapter assert that both may be necessary to understand when attitude-congruent behavior occurs.

Visser and colleagues test their assertion in four studies that combine experimental research with survey research on nationally representative samples. They focus on particularly important topics for political science, such as attitudes toward capital punishment, legalization of abortion, and global warming. Results show that personal importance increases participants' motivation, which leads to better performance in attention tasks, and a higher likelihood to express and defend their attitudes. Although knowledge also increases attitude-congruent behavior, this link seems not to be due to increased motivation and is instead likely to reflect increased ability. Advancing psychological theory in general, the authors concluded that knowledge and importance exert their influence through distinct psychological processes. Simply increasing knowledge is not enough to promote a certain behavior. Building on these findings, the authors end the chapter with suggestions for future research and with guidelines on how to design more effective interventions.

In Chapter 9, Laurel Harbridge and colleagues consider the implications of theories of psychology by asking a typical political science question: How do prices of gasoline affect people's approval of the U.S. president? Gasoline prices may affect approval ratings because people are personally affected by rising or declining prices (pocketbook reasoning) or because they see the greater picture and take gasoline prices as indicators of current state of the economy (sociotropic reasoning). Each reasoning process has distinct implications for our understanding of the determinants of presidential approval, as well as for the focus of presidential election campaigns. Yet previous research on the influence of economic indicators on presidential approval struggled in teasing these two reasoning processes apart. To overcome this limitation, Harbridge and colleagues introduce psychological theories of media priming (Iyengar & Kinder, 1988; Miller & Krosnick, 2000) to the study of determinants of presidential approval. If sociotropic reasoning underlies the link between gasoline prices and presidential approval, people would use the amount of media coverage of the gasoline prices as an indicator of their societal importance. If people base their evaluation of the president only on their personal economic burden through the gasoline prices, priming through the media should not affect this link.

Using a database of more than 20 years of monthly presidential approval ratings, the authors find evidence consistent only with the notion of pocketbook reasoning. Media coverage of the gasoline prices did not moderate the effect of these prices on presidential approval and had no effect on their own. These results suggest that people's individual economic positions and not their perception of the national economy link gasoline prices to presidential approval. The dominance of the personal connection to gasoline prices over the national importance of those prices is in line with findings of Joanne Miller and colleagues (chapter 5, this volume). These authors found that personal importance more generally predicted policy attitudes, candidate preferences, and political behavior.

Importantly, Harbridge and colleagues' conclusions go beyond the initially raised political science question. They suggest that the results indicate a new limitation to the psychological concept of priming: media priming seems to have no consequence if concepts are readily accessible and personally impactful.

Chapter 10 by Bo MacInnis and Jon Krosnick fits both in this part on determinants of political behavior as well as in the next part on conventional wisdom about politics. Using various methodologies and an impressive number of data sources, the authors test opposing speculations in the literature on whether or not adopting a "green" position on global warming would help or harm political candidates in elections. Just as in the previous chapters, a special focus is on whether these effects might be particularly pronounced among people who attach greater personal importance to the issue of global warming.

Across eight studies, the authors use survey experiments, content analysis, and a traditional political science regression approach to examine the link between a green position on global warming and electoral success. On the one hand, the results suggest that political candidates—and in particular Democrats—can only gain votes by taking a green position. Moreover, a simulation building on an extensive content analysis of candidates' websites suggests that the outcomes of some races could have been flipped if candidates had spoken differently about global warming. On the other hand, the simulation also suggests that these changes would most likely not have altered which party controlled the U.S. Senate and House of Representatives. In line with the three previous chapters, particularly those people who attached greater personal importance to global warming were more strongly inclined to vote for candidates that took a green position.

In sum, this chapter provides an answer to the question of whether green positions help or harm political candidates and makes a more general contribution to political science, as it serves as an illustration on how the coordinated application of several research methods can illuminate the impact of a single issue on candidate choice.

Part III: Challenging Conventional Wisdom about Politics

In Chapter 11, Theresa Vescio and colleagues present an intriguing new perspective on prejudiced people's opposition to affirmative action. Prejudiced white people, the authors claim, derive their evaluation of black people from simplistic reasoning that is mainly based on dispositional expectations: the situational circumstances do not determine black people's fate but rather black people lack the necessary abilities to succeed. This reasoning makes it difficult to see the merits of affirmative action, which are complex policies that require the understanding of long causal chains from cause to consequence. In contrast, individuals who are not prejudiced tend to base their judgment of blacks on situational explanations that require more complex causal explanations. As such, these people are more willing to support affirmative action policies.

In their empirical studies, Vescio and colleagues present evidence in line with their arguments. Prejudiced participants made more dispositional attributions about black targets they had to evaluate and such participants spent more effort finding dispositional explanations than situational explanations for a black target's behavior. Importantly, prejudiced participants developed less complex dispositional explanations for blacks' fate or behavior than did less prejudiced participants who tended to develop more complex situational explanations.

The chapter concludes with an extensive overview of the origins, practices, and consequences of affirmative action in employment and education. Starting from Lyndon Johnson's vision of the "great society," that also lies at the heart of Kramer's analysis (Chapter 4, this volume), Vescio and colleagues make a compelling argument why understanding complex causal processes is needed to fairly judge affirmative action policies.

In Chapter 12, Randall K. Thomas and colleagues put a widely shared conventional wisdom to the test: that "everything has changed" in the U.S. following the terrorist attacks of September 11, 2001. Using a large database of 16 waves of online surveys that were spread out over eight years, the authors compared public opinion shortly after and a long time after 9/11 to the levels before the attacks. In line with results reported by Harbridge and colleagues (Chapter 9, this volume), the authors find an immediate increase in support for the government in general and for governmental measures related to the attacks right after 9/11. However, this support leveled off over time and then disappeared surprisingly quickly. Public opinion on other issues was unaffected. Only a few attitudes (e.g., about immigration) appeared to have permanently changed.

These results thus put bold question marks behind the conventional wisdom that "everything has changed." Importantly, these results challenge psychological theories about public opinion stability. The fact that some opinions snapped back to the original levels is in line with the notion of stable and durable opinions that only manifest temporary change (Cialdini, Levy, Herman, Kozlowski, & Petty, 1976). However, the finding that some opinions stayed at a higher level after the attacks challenges this notion and suggests that permanent opinion shifts can sometimes happen. Thomas and colleagues end their chapter with a call for two developments: (1) improved disconfirmability of theories of public opinion stability and change (current theories can be made to fit the observations making them difficult to disconfirm); and (2) more systematic research in political psychology that directly tests the specific predictions of the various theories of public opinion stability and change against each other.

Bo MacInnis and Jon Krosnick conclude the book in Chapter 13, in which they tackle a question of great political significance: what affects public perceptions of global warming? The focus of this chapter is on people's trust in climate scientists. Just as in the previous two chapters, the authors address an existing conventional wisdom—namely that controversies around the integrity of climate scientists have led to increasing disbelief in global warming among the general public. MacInnis and Krosnick build on several social psychological theories to address both the effect of trust in climate scientists and the accurateness of the conventional wisdom.

The authors employed a large database and an experimental design to rule out alternative explanations of their findings. The accumulating evidence suggests that the effect of the controversies about climate scientists' integrity on the public's trust in scientists has been exceedingly small at best. Interestingly, people who did not trust scientists were not affected by statements of climate experts that confirmed the existence of global warming, but they were also not affected by experts who were skeptical about global warming. Instead, these people seemed to have based their beliefs about global warming on their own experience with the weather.

Conversely, people who trusted scientists were more influenced by scientists of all types. Moreover, in line with evidence presented by Harbridge and colleagues (Chapter 9, this volume), trust in scientists was not influenced by media coverage of global warming. The chapter concludes with suggestions for future research in political psychology on the link between trust in scientists and the effect on the public's belief in global warming.

Final thoughts

Every chapter in this book represents political psychology true to its name. The chapters address important questions within political science from a psychological perspective, and they simultaneously advance psychological theories. In fact, the careful consideration of the political context leads to new and sometimes unexpected insights into the human mind. Some chapters discovered situational circumstances that prevent or intensify psychological effects; other chapters identified classes of people who are more or less likely to be affected by such processes. In some cases, it was the step outside of the laboratory and into the real world that brought about these important contributions to well-established psychological theories. We hope that the studies in this volume inspire more work in political psychology that keeps both goals of our field in mind from the start of the work, to contribute to our understanding of politics in particular as well as to psychological theory formation in general.

References

Cialdini, R. B., Levy, A., Herman, C. P., Kozlowski, L. T., & Petty, R. E. (1976). Elastic shifts of opinion: Determinants of direction and durability. *Journal of Personality and Social Psychology, 34*, 663–672.

Hermann, M. (1986). *Political Psychology: Contemporary Issues and Problems*. San Francisco, CA: Jossey-Bass.

Iyengar, S., & Kinder, D. R. (1988). *News That Matters*. Chicago, IL: University of Chicago Press.

Iyengar, S., & McGuire, W. (1993). *Explorations in Political Psychology*. Durham: Duke University Press.

Kahneman, D., & Tversky, A. (1979). Prospect theory: An analysis of decision under risk. *Econometrica, 47*, 263–291.

Krosnick, J. A. (2002). Is political psychology sufficiently psychological? Distinguishing political psychology from psychological political science. In J.H. Kuklinski (Ed.), *Thinking About Political Psychology*. New York: Cambridge University Press.

Miller, J. M., & Krosnick, J. A. (2000). News media impact on the ingredients of presidential evaluations: Politically knowledgeable citizens are guided by a trusted source. *American Journal of Political Science, 44*(2), 301–315.

Sears, D. O., Huddy, L., & Jervis, R. (2003). *Oxford Handbook of Political Psychology*. Oxford: University Press.

PART I

New Theoretical Perspectives on Political Science Questions

2

ASPIRATION-BASED MODELS OF POLITICS

Jonathan Bendor

Introduction

Political psychology is an intellectually rich subfield. It is invigorated by a steady stream of interesting ideas from psychology which are then challenged by being placed in political contexts. One of its valuable contributions to the discipline has been to present a richer view of human nature in general and decision making in particular than is typically put forth by rational choice theories (RCT).[1] Political psychology has been receptive to empirical regularities or hypotheses such as the following: imperfect rationality, decision making infused with emotion, stereotyping and more generally biased belief formation and revision, group orientation, altruism, and so forth. Consequently, political science has been treated to a vigorous debate between rational choice (RC) scholars and those with a different scientific background. This diversity has served the discipline well: RC theories (RCT) have been subjected to sharp empirical criticism and the discipline is accumulating a rich trove of empirical patterns.

Valuable as this is, the subfield could do even more: it could generate theoretical alternatives to RCT. This is important; as it is often said, you can't beat something with nothing (Shepsle, 1996). This is both an empirical pattern in the sociology of science and a sensible heuristic in normative theories of scientific decision making. Some scholars might agree with this recommendation but disagree with the preceding paragraph's diagnosis: they might contend that political psychology *does* offer theoretical alternatives. I concede the point. Formulations such as on-line processing by voters (Lodge, McGraw, & Stroh, 1989) are based on a coherent set of claims about (e.g.) how citizens store and update information; i.e., they are theories.

The point is somewhat subtler. Although political psychologists do offer (mostly verbal) theories, they rarely construct formal models; RC theorists do both. This is not the place to discuss the relative merits of these two kinds of representations. Here I will take it as a working hypothesis that both have scientific value.[2] And it is worth mentioning, given the recent flurry of enthusiasm in the social sciences for computational models, that there are sound methodological reasons for political psychologists to develop mathematical models with closed form solutions in addition to computational ones.[3]

This situation can be quickly rectified, however. Indeed, *it already has been rectified*; we just don't realize it.

Let's unpack that cryptic remark. It is easier to recognize that there is a serious alternative to the RC program if we see a forest and not just a group of trees. I believe that the main alternative research program is that of bounded rationality. The core of this program was well-stated by (of course) Herbert Simon: "[T] he capacity of the human mind for formulating and solving complex problems is very small compared with the size of the problems whose solution is required for objectively rational behavior in the real world—or even for a reasonable approximation to such objective rationality" (1957, p. 198).

Two points must be made about this statement.[4] First, Simon's idea of bounded rationality refers to a *relation* between a decision maker's mental abilities and the complexity of the problem she or he faces. It is *not* a proposition about the brilliance or stupidity of human beings, independent of their task environments. More than a few academics have missed this point and reified the notion of bounded rationality into an assertion about the absolute capacity of our species, as in the belief—just below the surface of many debates about rationality—that asserting that an agent is boundedly rational is roughly equivalent to claiming that s/he is dumb. On the contrary: these statements are *very* different.

Simon explicated his relational interpretation of bounded rationality via a homely metaphor: together "the structure of task environments and the computational capabilities of the actor" act as a "scissors [with] two blades" (Simon, 1990, p. 7). That is, because cognitive constraints "show through" (Simon, 1996) only when a problem is sufficiently difficult, theories of bounded rationality have more power than theories of complete rationality only when both blades of the scissors cut. Second, bounded rationality is a research program, not a theory. It contains many different theories; indeed, it contains more than a few families of theories.[5] In one such family the idea of *aspiration level* is central. In this chapter, an "aspiration level" or "reference point" (I use the terms interchangeably) is a threshold that a person uses as a standard of evaluation (Helson, 1964); it is a key part of how she or he mentally represents the choice problem at hand.[6] The object of evaluation varies across contexts. In some contexts the standard is used to evaluate action alternatives: options generating payoffs above the threshold are satisfactory; those below, unsatisfactory. In some contexts it is used to demarcate positive feedback ("this option should be tried more often in the future") from negative feedback ("that one should be tried less often"). In still others it is a boundary that distinguishes mental states: e.g., happiness from discontent.[7] In all cases, the theorist's premise is that the object of evaluation is significant for the decision maker: it matters what options are accepted and which rejected, which actions are reinforced and which inhibited, whether the agent is happy or sad, and so on.

It is vital to grasp the distinction between comparing outcomes *to each other*, as in classical utility theory, versus comparing an outcome to an aspiration level. Students find it hard to believe that canonical RC models do not contain the notion of a reference point: the idea, e.g., of a "gain"—an outcome better than one's reference point—is so intuitive that it strains credulity to hear that such a notion is not central to classical utility theory. But it isn't. The theory of revealed preferences assumes that options are compared (and ranked) only vis-a-vis each other. (Even colleagues sometimes find this hard to believe. Confusion on this point is partly due to the existence of *optimal search* theories [e.g., Kohn & Shavell, 1974] which bear some conceptual and empirical resemblance to one member of the aspiration-based family, satisficing. The basic thought is that an aspiration level is a stopping rule for a search process. This issue will be taken up in section 2.)

Members of this family of theories include satisficing (Simon, 1955, 1956), prospect theory (Kahneman & Tversky, 1979), and some versions of reinforcement learning (Bendor, Mookherjee, & Ray, 2001; Bendor, Diermeier, & Ting, 2003; Bendor et al., 2011). What all members of this family share is the concept of a threshold that partitions payoffs (etc.) into two disjoint subsets and the hypothesis that this partitioning has significant effects. (Some members of this family, e.g., prospect theory, presume that alternatives are compared to each other in addition to being compared to the evaluative threshold. Others, such as many variants of satisficing, assume that alternatives are compared only to the threshold.) As we will see, some of the implications generated by these theories are strikingly different from those of standard RC theories, and careful inspection reveals that many of these differences are due to the former's assumption that people compare alternatives to reference points, not only (as in RCT) to each other. Thus, the idea of aspiration level proves to be theoretically powerful, which justifies grouping the above theories together.

Many aspiration-based theories, including the most prominent ones, posit that at any given time a person has a single aspiration level; in these formulations the object of evaluation—alternatives, mental states, etc.—is partitioned into two subsets: good versus bad, gains versus losses. Although one can construct models with multiple aspiration levels, this chapter examines only those with a single level. These models have a clearer logic, and most of the intellectual contribution of aspiration-based theories is delivered by the simpler type.[8] (In particular, positing a single aspiration level suffices for generating predictions that differ in intriguing ways from RCT predictions.)

The rest of this chapter is organized as follows. Section 2 outlines some ways in which aspiration-based models differ from RC formulations. Section 3 examines some important properties of aspiration-based adaptive rules (ABARs). Section 4 summarizes some applications of satisficing, reinforcement learning, and prospect theory to the study of politics. Section 5 concludes with some comments about the rationality debates.

What's All the Fuss About?

In conversations about bounded rationality one sometimes hears the following claims: (1) satisficing is really optimizing (Jackman, 1993; Goodin, 2000); (2) bounded rationality boils down to satisficing; (3) hence, bounded rationality is not a rival to the RC program but only a special case of it.

This argument, usually presented more as bits and pieces than as an articulated whole, contains several major errors. Point (2) blurs the distinction between a research program and one of its theories. Satisficing is far from the only theory in its parent program. (Indeed, its family, aspiration-based theories, is not the only such group in the program.) So even if satisficing were a special case of optimizing, the conclusion—point (3)—wouldn't hold because point (2) fails.

But because satisficing is perhaps the best-known theory of bounded rationality in political science, it makes sense to assess point (1) directly. Two points are worth making. First, as we will see in section 3, satisficing is *not* observationally equivalent to optimizing, even if one takes informational constraints into account.[9] In particular, satisficing does not invariably guide decision makers to optimal actions even when people face the same choice problem over and over again.

Second, although satisficing and the closest RC formulation, optimal search theory, do make overlapping behavioral predictions,[10] their cognitive premises differ sharply. Psychologists do not presume that aspiration levels are consciously calculated: per dual-process theories of mind (Evans, 2003, 2008, 2010), they could be used automatically via a fast mental operation that is opaque to the decision maker. In contrast, an optimal stopping rule is *a conscious instrument* for maximizing expected utility: it is an exact solution to a clearly formulated problem. One can get this solution right or wrong. In my experience teaching this material, on their first try even good students don't always calculate optimal stopping rules correctly, even for fairly simple examples. Figuring out what the optimal stopping rule should be isn't easy: some students don't set the problem up correctly; others make computational errors. These observations suggest that optimal stopping is part of the slow, conscious and analytical cognitive processes that Stanovich and West (2000) and Kahneman (2011) call System 2; it must be learned.[11]

In contrast, people can satisfice without learning it in school and without consciously recognizing what they're doing. Indeed, some of the more interesting predictions of aspiration-based models arise when decision makers are unaware of the well-springs of their own aspirations, e.g., when peers influence aspirations, or when they're unaware that their aspirations are unrealistic (more on this shortly).

A more general answer to the question of what's all the fuss about can be stated provocatively: aspiration-based theories of adaptation do not presume that people have utility functions.

Constructing Preferences: When Do People Have Utility Functions?

Over the last few decades some psychologists (e.g., Slovic, 1995; Bettman, Luce, & Payne, 1998) have argued that people often don't have "look-up" tables of preferences stored in their minds. Instead, decision makers frequently must *construct* their preferences on the spot. This is an important part of the mental work involved in making some decisions—including some that matter most. Classical RC models ignore this possibility: they presume that agents in any choice situation come equipped with standard utility functions, i.e., complete and transitive preference orderings over alternatives. (See Austen-Smith & Banks, 2000, for a lucid statement of the classical position.)

If the psychologists are right then standard optimization procedures can be fragile in an important way: for some problems they demand inputs—complete and transitive preference orderings—that other parts of the mind won't deliver.[12] In contrast, aspiration-based choice procedures *generically don't require that people have utility functions*. This may sound heretical to RC scholars but it's true. Aspirational mechanisms can go to work on partially ordered preferences. Consider, for example, satisficing. Simon long ago asserted that "An organism that satisfices has no need of complete and consistent preference orderings of all possible alternatives of action, (Simon, 1957, p. 205; see also Simon 1955, 1956).[13] This is easily demonstrated. Suppose a decision maker has $k > 1$ goals, so a payoff vector can be represented as $(x_1, \ldots, x_k)$. Her aspiration levels are $(\overline{x}_1, \ldots, \overline{x}_k)$. An alternative is satisfactory if and only if it passes muster on all k dimensions, i.e., $x_j \geq \overline{x}_j$ for all $j = 1, \ldots, k$. (Figure 2.1 gives an example with two goals.)

This rule avoids making some (not all) trade-off comparisons: e.g., compare options A and B in figure 1. A is better vis-à-vis goal 1; B is better regarding goal 2. But B is acceptable whereas A, which fails goal 2's threshold, is not. Hence, although A and B embody trade-offs, this does not pose a problem for the decision maker: she is not forced to resolve the tension between her two objectives.

However, satisficing does not make *all* trade-offs irrelevant. Consider options C and D (Figure 2.2). Both are satisfactory on both goal-dimensions; hence, a satisficer wouldn't reject either out of hand.

Of course, a comparison between C and D might never arise: if the decision maker searched for alternatives sequentially then the order of search would

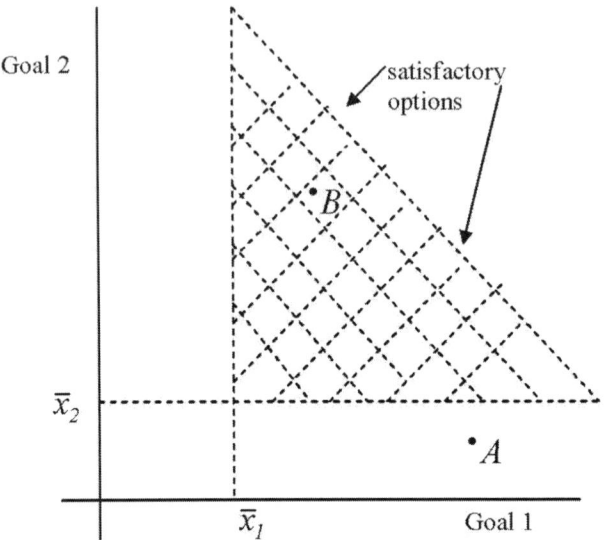

FIGURE 2.1 Aspirations without Utility Functions

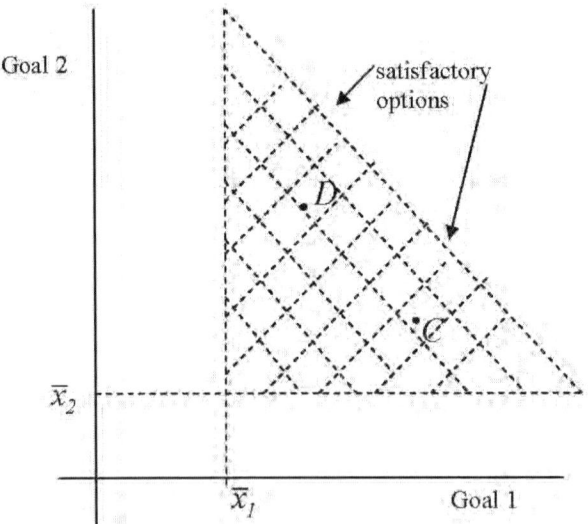

FIGURE 2.2 Trade-offs between Satisfactory Options

determine the outcome, and once again an aspiration-based rule would finesse the trade-off. But if both options came to the person's attention before a final choice was made then she would have to confront the trade-off.

It is worth noting that behavioral decision theorists are increasingly inclined to believe that decision makers often use a mix of noncompensatory and compensatory rules. (For an early statement of this view see Payne [1976].) The hypothesis is that first we deploy noncompensatory rules to cut a large set of options down to a manageable few and then use cognitively more demanding compensatory rules on the finalists.

This plausible claim provides a good reason for not rigidifying our view of the intellectual landscape. Academics may categorize themselves as behavioral decision theorists or RC theorists, but decision makers are free to be eclectic: they can use simple rules of thumb in some tasks, or in certain *phases* of a task, and optimize elsewhere. Indeed, Simon's scissors leads us to expect this (Bendor, 2003, p. 436).[14] If a problem is so simple that a decision maker can easily maximize expected utility then we expect this to happen. Consider, for example, the proverbial US$20 bill lying on a sidewalk in full view of a pedestrian. An obvious choice representation— "There is $20 on the sidewalk. It doesn't belong to anyone."—is tightly linked to an optimization-operation: "Bend over and pick it up."[15]

Thus, the claim that people will optimize when the choice problem is sufficiently easy is very plausible. We might disagree about exactly what kinds of problems *are* "sufficiently easy"; hence, identifying what makes certain problems hard for most humans (Kotovsky, Hayes, & Simon, 1985) is a vital empirical task for the bounded rationality research program. But the main points are clear: people have multiple choice representations, and associated operations, in their long-term memories, and although there is much evidence for believing that this set includes aspiration-based representations, what gets evoked in particular choice problems depends partly on whether cognitive constraints bind in the matter at hand.

Some General Properties of Aspiration-based Processes

Before we study common properties, it is important to mention a feature that differentiates some members of this family from others: the temporal orientation. Some of these theories are *prospective*: e.g., prospect theory assumes that agents know the payoffs or payoff distributions produced by different alternatives and choose accordingly. (Hence, in the most neoclassical versions of prospect theory [Munro & Sugden, 2003] decision makers maximize utility; the behavioral twist is that utility depends on reference points.[16]) Other members of this family—e.g., reinforcement learning—have a *retrospective* orientation: an agent finds out the worth of an option after selecting it.[17] Of course, even in the latter decision makers must be somewhat prospectively oriented—they have propensities toward options, which can be interpreted as expectations about the merits of alternatives—but the heart of the theory is how agents retrospectively evaluate options and then change action-propensities. Thus, in reinforcement learning models agents don't use the quintessentially prospective operation of maximizing *expected* utility; instead, they react to *experienced* utility.

1. Realistic Versus Unrealistic Aspirations

A natural question to ask about aspirations is, when are they realistic?[18]

Psychologists usually hypothesize that aspirations adjust to experience (e.g., Helson, 1964, pp. 395–400). This means, in the standard set-up, that they adjust to realized payoffs. A common functional form (e.g., Cyert & March, 1963) is the weighted average: $a_{i,t+1} = \lambda a_{i,t} + (1-\lambda)\pi_{i,t}$, where $a_{i,t}$ is i's aspiration level in t and $\pi_{i,t}$ is his payoff. (Note that this equation presumes that the agent adjusts only to her own experience. We return to this issue shortly.)

The weighted average assumption does reflect the idea that aspirations move toward payoffs. But it is much more specific than the general notion: the weighted average equation is deterministic and linear. That extra baggage is unnecessary. The following assumption about aspiration-adjustment is more general and closer to the qualitative spirit of the psychologists' conventional hypothesis.[19]

(A1) For all i and t,
If $\pi_{i,t} > a_{i,t}$ then $a_{i,t} < a_{i,t+1} \leq \pi_{i,t}$.
If $\pi_{i,t} = a_{i,t}$ then $a_{i,t+1} = a_{i,t}$.
If $\pi_{i,t} < a_{i,t}$ then $\pi_{i,t} \leq a_{i,t+1} < a_{i,t}$.

Observe that the weighted average model is a special case of this, for $0 < \lambda \leq 1$.

Now suppose that agent i plays a repeated game with $n-1$ other people. (The game need not be symmetric; players can have completely different roles, hence different action-sets and payoffs.) Then the following can be demonstrated. First, if player i's aspirations are ever in the feasible set of payoffs, i.e., in $[\underline{\pi}_i, \overline{\pi}_i]$, then there they will stay. (Call these *realistic aspirations*.) Second, if i's aspirations are outside the feasible set of payoffs then (a) in every period they move monotonically closer to that feasible set and (b) under plausible assumptions about the speed of adjustment, they will eventually become realistic.

However, the preceding adjustment process, with its conclusion of ultimately realistic aspirations, is purely individualistic. Sociologists have long argued (Merton & Rossi, 1950) that the experiences of relevant others—one's reference group—are influential. This probably holds for aspiration dynamics.

This doesn't destroy the above realism result if one's reference group is similarly situated—in the formalism of repeated games, everyone in i's reference group is playing the same stage game. But when this isn't so, when e.g., an impoverished youth aspires to a famous athlete's standard of living, then the former's aspirations may never become realistic in real time. (Most kids who want to make it to the NBA won't.) So let's consider some behavioral implications of unrealistic aspirations.

Mobilization, then Apathy. Consider a new democracy, say a country in Eastern Europe after the Iron Curtain's fall. Newly empowered citizens are often enthusiastic about participating in politics. However, their aspirations may initially be unrealistic: they may expect the new government to solve all their problems. If so, then one can show (Bendor, Diermeier, & Ting, 2003, proposition 7), given some additional assumptions about how vote-propensities adjust, that expected turnout will decrease. I believe this prediction is consistent with the evidence for most of the new democracies in Eastern Europe from 1990 to 2000.

Risky Behavior and Poor Young Men. Consider a poor 15 year-old male who wants to have the lifestyle of a famous athlete. However, although his aspirations are very high, this youth is puny and he accurately forecasts that his chances of becoming a professional athlete are nil. Crime is another option but it is risky: one might wind up a rich drug lord—or dead. His choice is either a low risk, low return path (a job flipping burgers), or crime.

Prospect Theory predicts, based on its premise that people are risk-seeking in the domain of bad (below-aspiration) payoffs, that the youth will be risk-seeking. This doesn't yet entail a prediction about behavior; more needs to be known about the person's opportunities and beliefs about expected return and risk. So assume for purposes of illustration that the expected payoff of crime equals the sure salary he'd earn at McDonald's. Hence a risk averse decision maker would turn it down. But a risk-seeking one would take the lottery, here, i.e., select the criminal path.[20] Further, this result is robust: as long as the expected payoff of crime is sufficiently close to that of the dead-end job, prospect theory implies that a youth with a high aspiration level will prefer crime.

The Utopian Aspirations of Revolutionaries. The preceding example presumes economic (insatiable) preferences, which is the standard context for prospect theory. However, this theory can be applied when utility is satiable (preferences with ideal points). Suppose a right-wing revolutionary group believes that it will create a utopia if it takes power. (Assume that people have single-peaked preferences in a unidimensional policy space, so the label of "right-wing" is meaningful.) If the group's ideal point is sufficiently extreme, compared to the incumbent government's policies, and the group is sufficiently ambitious—its aspiration level is close to its ideal point—then the revolutionaries will behave in a risk-seeking way.

All of these examples pertain to unrealistically high aspirations. There are also interesting effects of unrealistically *low* aspirations—e.g., being content with the short end of the socio-economic stick even though one's side has enough votes to win significant transfers. (This might be related to the puzzle that democracies don't redistribute income as much as certain baseline RC theories lead us to expect [Kenworthy & Pontusson, 2005, p. 456].) However, because modern media broadcasts how the rich and beautiful live to increasing numbers of poor people, one might hypothesize that unrealistically high aspirations are now more common than unrealistically low ones.

2. Aspiration-Based Adaptive Rules (ABARs) and Optimization

Enthusiastic proponents of RCT sometimes argue that satisficing and related adaptive rules are, as descriptive formulations, equivalent to optimization, given limited information (Jackman, 1993, p. 282) or cognitive constraints (Goodin, 2000). A dynamic version of this argument—which amounts to a defense of RCT as descriptive science (Conlisk, 1996)—is that adaptive rules will ultimately lead to optimal behavior, so we needn't study them: in equilibrium all is well.

But no matter how often these claims are repeated in hallways, they are conjectures, not established results. And on close examination they turn out not to hold in general. Typically, ABARs induce optimal behavior in the long-run in certain types of problems—those with features that make them especially well-matched to ABARs—but they do *not* lead to optimization, even in the long-run, when they encounter problems outside this special set. Bendor, Kumar, and Siegel (2009) show this in detail regarding satisficing.[21]

Because the relation between adaptation and optimization is often misunderstood, it is worth giving an example in which ABARs don't converge to optimal behavior. Consider an electorate with $n \geq 1$ voters. To keep things simple, assume that the government can generate only two payoffs: a high one, h, and a low one, l, with $h > l$. There are two parties, D and R. When in power each party consistently implements a particular policy, x_D and x_R, respectively. These two policies generate high and low payoffs to voters with different probabilities, so it matters which party is elected. (For example, D is better for voter i if $h_{i,D}$, the probability that i gets the high payoff when D is in power, exceeds $h_{i,R}$.) The voters don't understand the causal mechanisms connecting policies to outcomes. Instead, they vote retrospectively (Key, 1966; Bendor, Kumar, & Siegel, 2010) via the following aspiration-based rules. (Here the assumptions are specialized to voting. Later they'll be generalized so that they cover non-electoral contexts. The specialized versions, below, convey the sense of aspiration-based adaptation.)

(A2) (positive feedback): If $\pi_{i,t} > a_{i,t}$ then i's propensity to vote for the incumbent can't fall and it will increase if it isn't already one.

(A3) (negative feedback): If $\pi_{i,t} < a_{i,t}$ then i's propensity to vote for the incumbent can't rise and it will decrease if it isn't already zero.

We then get the following result. (We also assume, here and throughout this chapter, that there are finitely many players, each with finite action sets and finitely many possible payoffs. These are empirically innocuous.)

Proposition 2.1: Suppose payoffs are binary and voters' aspirations are between l and h. D is better for a majority of the voters. If $h_{i,D} < 1$ for all i and the voters adjust via (A2) and (A3), then the polity is never absorbed into the state of always electing D.

Hence, adaptive and optimal behavior remain distinct indefinitely in certain environments. Sweeping claims about convergence of the former to the latter are wrong. This is characteristic of heuristics, which suggests that some scholars have gone overboard in their enthusiasm for rules of thumb. Although simple heuristics can sometimes, in the words of Gigerenzer et al. (1999), "make us smart", they have limitations (Margolis, 2000).

3. The Matching of ABARs to Problems

Every ABAR is well-matched to some problems and ill-matched to others. This statement requires, of course, that we define "well-matched" and "ill-matched". In the following definition, $\underline{\pi}_i(X_{\text{optimal}})$ denotes player i's minimal payoff from the set of optimal outcomes and $\pi_i(x_{\text{suboptimal}})$ is a payoff to i in a particular suboptimal outcome. (To keep the discussion general, the set of optimal outcomes is intentionally left undefined. An example of a stipulation would be the Pareto optimal set.)

Definition 2.1: (after Bendor, Kumar, & Siegel, 2009) A choice problem is called **well-matched** to ABARs if $\pi_i(x_{\text{suboptimal}}) < \underline{\pi}_i(X_{\text{optimal}})$ for some player i in every suboptimal outcome. Otherwise it is called **ill-matched**.

To satisfy Occam's razor, this definition requires a justification. The next result, which shows that the performance of ABARs can be cleanly described via Definition 2.1's concepts, gives the needed justification.

The proposition refers to stable outcomes. An outcome is stable if it can be sustained by a self-replicating set of actions (or actions and aspirations). Thus, for the ABARs analyzed in this chapter—discrete-time Markov chains with stationary transition probabilities—if the system is in a stable state today then it will be in the same state tomorrow with probability one. (This is called an *absorbing state* in Markov terminology. See the appendix for a glossary of basic concepts of Markov processes and a brief introduction to Markov chains.)

Proposition 2.2: Suppose aspirations are exogenously fixed. Then there exists a set of aspiration levels such that every optimal outcome is stable and every suboptimal outcome is unstable if *and only if* the problem is well-matched to ABARs.

The intuition is as follows. (A formal proof is available upon request.) If the choice-problem is well-matched to aspiration-based adaptation, then there's a gap between the worst payoff in *all* the optimal outcomes and the worst payoff in any suboptimal one. *Aspiration-based rules are pre-adapted to such gaps*: it is precisely in these circumstances that ABARs can effectively distinguish good outcomes from bad ones. To see why, suppose that we, the omniscient observers, are wondering whether an aspiration-based rule can distinguish an optimal action x from a suboptimal one y. (As usual, we require here that the ABARs do this via only one aspiration level; nothing fancy here.) If there's a gap between the worst payoffs of x and y then the agents' rules can effectively discriminate: in the optimal outcome everybody's happy; in the suboptimal one someone is dissatisfied. If a person is content with an outcome then her propensity to re-try the corresponding action won't fall; if she is dissatisfied then it will. Since in a well-matched problem everyone is happy with any optimal outcome, if everyone is fully disposed to try their corresponding action today then so they'll be tomorrow. So the agents' action-propensities are collectively self-replicating; hence, x is stable. But if a person is dissatisfied then his propensity to re-try his current action will fall, so there's a chance he'll do something different tomorrow; hence, y is unstable.[22]

Proposition 2's combination of good and bad news is typical of heuristics more generally. Whether rules of thumb make us smart depends vitally on whether they are deployed on problems for which they are well-matched.[23]

4. ABARs Often Perform "Reasonably" Well

Although they are suboptimal when they encounter "hard" problems (i.e., those for which they are ill-matched), it can be shown that ABARs do behave sensibly in some of these difficult environments. Thus, if people use these heuristics in these contexts, they will do "pretty well", which accords with an important part of Simon's argument.[24] As V. O. Key famously said, voters aren't fools. But in some situations they can be fooled (Achen & Bartels, 2004).

For example, consider the above electoral context where the government generates high or low payoffs; different constituencies have different probabilities of getting h based on the relation between the policy of the party in power and their own interests. (Per Stokes' critique ([1963] of the Downsian formulation, voters need not have explicit or coherent ideologies. They do, however, have interests which governments can either advance or impede [Key, 1966; Fiorina, 1981].)

Suppose that voters 1, 2, and 3 live in the same district. Voter 1's political interests are the most liberal; voter 2 is relatively centrist while 3 is conservative. Hence, voter 1 is the most likely to get an h from D; voter 3 is the most likely one to get an h from R. Voter 2's chances of getting a high payoff from either party are in-between 1's and 3's. If they use the same retrospective voting rule and initially (i.e., at age 18) have the same propensity to vote (say) Democratic, then for a wide class of retrospective rules voter 1 will be the most likely to vote Democratic and voter 3, the least likely, in all subsequent elections (Bendor, Kumar & Siegel 2010, Proposition 1). Thus, ideologies are not necessary for party-based voting. Crude retrospective evaluation of the government's performance, and corresponding adjustment voting propensities, will endogenously generate party affiliation.

This example extends to a very large class of decision-making contexts. Although ABARs are often too crude to settle down on a person's optimal action, they commonly line up use-probabilities with payoff orderings: the more frequently an action generates high payoffs, the more likely an ABAR-guided agent will use it.[25]

5. ABARs and Dominance

The behavior and performance of ABARs is tightly connected to the existence of *dominance relations* among alternatives. The following property illustrates this link. Consider two alternatives that face the same n decision makers. Option 1 generates a payoff-vector of $(\pi_{1,1},\ldots,\pi_{1,n})$; option 2 yields $(\pi_{2,1},\ldots,\pi_{2,n})$. If the latter strictly Pareto-dominates the former then the following hold for all i, for *any* mix of ABARs: (a) if agent i's propensity to re-try the current action rises under payoff-vector 1 then it would rise given vector 2; (b) if agent i's propensity would fall given vector 2 then it must also fall given vector 1.[26]

Dominance is less important for RC solution concepts, especially strategic (i.e., game theoretic) ones. The main solution concept of noncooperative game theory is Nash equilibrium. As the Prisoners' Dilemma famously illustrates, an outcome (mutual defection) may be a Nash equilibrium even though one that Pareto-dominates it (mutual cooperation) isn't. In contrast, if aspiration-driven decision makers would be satisfied by mutual defection then they would also be satisfied by mutual cooperation. The explanation for the difference is subtle and important. (This follows Bendor, Kumar, & Siegel [2009].) A game theoretically rational player assesses an outcome via a counterfactual: she compares it to payoffs that she *could* get if she selected another action and all her partners continued using the same actions. Hence, although cooperation Pareto-dominates the Nash outcome of defection, the former isn't Nash because an agent in a cooperative outcome could do still better by unilaterally cheating. In contrast, ABAR-driven assessments don't involve the mentally demanding operation of counterfactual reasoning: they turn on direct comparisons between an alternative and the agent's evaluation-threshold. This is a fundamental cognitive difference between game theoretic and aspiration-based reasoning.

6. The Empirical Content of Aspiration-based Models[27]

A major methodological characteristic of a family of theories is their empirical content. Some predict that almost anything can happen; others predict a much smaller set of outcomes. One needn't be a strict Popperian to appreciate the latter's value.

Although it is well-known that standard game theoretic models of repeated interactions suffer from the problem of low empirical content (the folk theorems), it is not widely appreciated that similar problems plague many theories of adaptive behavior. For example, consider models of satisficing, defined as follows. (As before, $\pi_{i,t}$ is person i's payoffs in period t and $a_{i,t}$ are her aspirations.)

(A4): If $\pi_{i,t} \geq a_{i,t}$ then in $t+1$ player i will use the same action she used in t.

Given this straightforward definition of satisficing, we get the following folk-theorem result.

Proposition 2.3 (Bendor, Diermeier, & Ting, 2007): Consider any repeated game whose stage game has deterministic payoffs. Players satisfice-and-search by any arbitrary mix of adaptive rules that satisfy (A4) and adjust their aspirations by any arbitrary mix of rules that satisfy (A1). Then any outcome of the stage game can be sustained as a stable outcome by some self-replicating combination of actions and aspirations.

Thus, such models can be empirically vacuous.

Examples of Aspiration-based Models of Politics

1. Satisficing, Search, and Behavioral Models of Party Competition

The notion of satisficing was sufficiently clear in Simon's early work (1955, 1956) that little clarification or formalization is needed. Assumption (A5) just dots the i's and crosses the t's. (As Simon indicated, this assumption can be extended to multidimensional goals, but here unidimensional objectives suffice.)

(A5): Decision maker i has an aspiration level $a_{i,t}$ such that (i) if $\pi_{i,t} \geq a_{i,t}$ then she uses the same action in $t+1$ and (ii) if $\pi_{i,t} < a_{i,t}$ then she searches for a new option in $t+1$ with a probability above zero.

This idea has been used to develop behavioral models of two-party competition (Kollman, Miller, & Page, 1992, 1998 [henceforward KMP]; Bendor, Mookherjee, & Ray [BMR] 2006). In this work, winners satisfice: they keep the platform that won them office in the prior election.[28] Challengers, however, are treated differently by KMP and BMR; this produces some different predictions. Because this provides a useful illustration of how different behavioral models can yield distinct predictions, it is worth going into a bit of detail. (For brevity's sake this discussion is confined to unidimensional policy spaces; further, citizens have symmetric single-peaked preferences and so vote for the closer candidate.)

In KMP (1992) challengers use a variety of search rules to generate new platforms that they consider espousing. Office-oriented challengers select the one that maximizes votes against the incumbent's policy. Hence, if both parties are office-oriented then they converge to the median voter's ideal point (Page, personal communication, 1999).[29]

BMR uses a somewhat more general version of (A5), which implies that *losing is disappointing* (at least sometimes). To motivate this, think of Al Gore and the 2000 election. Gore got over half the popular vote but lost the election. It would be inhuman not to feel disappointed with the outcome—not only in the hedonic sense of unhappy, but also in the strategic sense of prompting the question "What should we have done differently?" Hence, (A5) implies that full Downsian convergence does not obtain, even in the long-run (BMR, proposition 4). (However, the *government's* policy will converge to the median voter's ideal point in this setting.) Thus, two quite weak behavioral premises— losing can be dissatisfying and dissatisfaction induces search—rule out permanent Tweedledee-Tweedledum outcomes.

A significant advantage of these behavioral formulations is that they extend easily into multidimensional policy spaces: the severe difficulties encountered by RC theories in multidimensional contexts simply do not arise for the satisficing-and-search models.

2. Reinforcement Learning and Turnout

The basic idea underlying reinforcement learning is that organisms respond to feedback: they become more inclined to try actions that succeed and less likely to try those which fail. Because it was originally part of behaviorist psychology, learning theorists initially hoped that "success" and "failure" could be defined solely by objective payoffs: e.g., cheese versus nothing for rats, money versus nothing for humans. This proved wrong: learning theorists discovered, despite their methodological commitment to behaviorism, that they needed to posit that organisms develop their own internal standards of evaluation.[30] People *code* experiences as successes or failures. Consequently, modern learning theory is a marriage between learning axioms and (sometimes implicit) assumptions about aspirations. Because the following assumptions parallel and generalize (A2) and (A3), which were specialized to the electoral context, they're called (A2´) and (A3´). (In what follows, α denotes an action.)

(A2´) (positive feedback): If $\pi_{i,t}(\alpha) \geq a_{i,t}$ then $p_{i,t+1}(\alpha) \geq p_{i,t}(\alpha)$, and this holds strictly if $\pi_{i,t} > a_{i,t}$ and $p_{i,t}(\alpha) < 1$.

(A3´) (negative feedback): If $\pi_{i,t}(\alpha) < a_{i,t}$ then $p_{i,t+1}(\alpha) \leq p_{i,t}$, and this holds strictly if $p_{i,t} > 0$.

Note that these assumptions allow aspirations to be exogenous or endogenous; if they're exogenous then $a_{i,t}$ is some constant a_i for all t.

The assumption about positive feedback, (A2´),says that if the agent codes the current payoff as a success, then her propensity to try the associated action cannot fall and it will rise if that's feasible (i.e., it's not already at 1.0) and payoffs strictly exceed aspirations. The negative feedback assumption says that if she codes the current payoff as a failure then her propensity to try the associated action cannot rise and it will fall if there's room for it to do so.

These are quite general learning axioms. Among other things, they allow agents to be responsive to *how much* payoffs differ from aspirations. For example, it would be natural to assume that propensity-change— $(p_{i,t+1} - p_{i,t})$ — is strictly increasing in ($\pi_{i,t} - a_{i,t}$), so that big pleasant surprises induce large increases in one's propensity to try the associated action and big unpleasant ones induce large decreases. But such extensions must be pursued elsewhere (e.g., Bendor, Diermeier, & Ting, 2014).

To see how reinforcement learning, formalized by (A2′) and (A3′) and the aspiration-adjustment assumption of (A1), can be used to study politics consider the turnout model of Bendor, Diermeier and Ting (2003). (Much of the following is taken from that paper.) The context for this model is the so-called paradox of voting. Turnout has been a vexing problem—indeed, a major anomaly—for rational choice theories of election for decades, as both critics (e.g., Green & Shapiro, 1994) and adherents to the RCT program have pointed out. Many of the latter have acknowledged the problem with admirable candor: e.g., "standard conceptions of rational behavior do not explain why anyone bothers to vote in a mass election. [Turnout is] the paradox that ate rational choice theory" (Fiorina, 1990, p. 334). The discrepancy between predictions of canonical RC models (negligible turnout in large electorates) and the evidence (over half the electorate votes in major elections in most stable democracies) is so large that it passes the ocular test: only eyeballing is needed. Sophisticated statistics are unnecessary.

What happens if, per (A2′) and (A3′), citizens learn to either vote or stay home based on their experiences? The answer depends—as it should—on how competitive the district is, so consider a competitive electorate with almost as many Democrats as Republicans. (We follow Palfrey and Rosenthal [1985] in constructing a simple strategic setting: people are fixed as D's or R's and whichever side turns out more citizens wins the election. All winners—shirkers as well as voters— get a payoff of $b>0$; losers get no electoral reward. Voting imposes a private cost of $c>0$.)

To cut to the chase, the outcome is that in the probabilistic steady state many citizens vote. (In Bendor et al.'s simulations, turnout ranged between 40 and 60 percent in the limiting distribution.) This effect is robust: among other parametric variations, it holds up in electorates as big as 1,000,000. The "paradox" disappears. More precisely, the anomaly that confronts standard RCTs does not confront this model of aspiration-based adaptation. Why?

The first part of the explanation is that citizens who adjust their turnout-propensities via ABARs are not thinking prospectively about the probability of being pivotal, and it is precisely the latter that produces the anomalously low predictions of standard RC models. Instead, citizens guided by ABARs ask themselves two backward-looking questions: (1) What did I do last time?; and (2) Did it work out? There is no compelling reason to believe that the collective answers to these questions will produce negligible turnout.

The second part of the explanation involves understanding in detail why citizens who ask questions (1) and (2) turn out in substantial numbers. This turns on an important class of aspiration levels: intermediate ones. In the context of a Palfrey-Rosenthal turnout game, aspirations are intermediate if they're in (0, b–c):

higher than two of the payoffs (losing and voting, losing and shirking) and lower than the other two (winning and voting, winning and shirking).[31] When aspirations are intermediate then losers are disgruntled and winners are happy. Hence, given the basic ABAR axioms, both losing shirkers and winning voters increase their propensity to vote. Then political demography kicks in: if the district is sufficiently competitive, these two groups form a majority of the electorate. Thus, when aspirations are intermediate more people are becoming more mobilized than less so. This, together with a bit more structure on the nature of propensity-adjustment, yields the implication that average turnout will rise (BDT, proposition 3, p. 272).

The computational model also yields the standard comparative statics of RC models: e.g., turnout falls if the cost of voting rises, ceteris paribus. This is important because these comparative statics—unlike RCT predictions about the fraction of the electorate that will turn out in a parametrically fixed setting—are empirically supported.

Hence, the comparison is striking: where canonical RC models do well, so does the aspiration-based model, *and* the latter performs well where the former does not. Regarding the underlying research programs this is all the more striking: whereas very able scholars in the RC program have been working on the paradox of voting for decades, the bounded rationality program has barely started. Since it is extremely unlikely that BDT somehow stumbled on the best turnout model in the latter program, we can expect improvements.

3. Aspirations, Reference Groups, and Collective Action

Sociologists are naturally inclined to study the impact of social structure on collective action (in, e.g., social movements; McAdam, 1986); in the last 20 years a few adventuresome political scientists have also pursued this theme.[32] In the context of aspiration-based choice, social structure can have influence via *reference groups* (Merton & Rossi, 1950): people in a focal actor's social environment who influence that actor's aspirations. Bendor, Diermeier and Ting (2007, 2014) examine a specific version of this general idea. As in their other work, actions are driven by ABARs. However, whereas aspiration-adjustment in the turnout model is purely individualistic, in the collective action theory agent i's aspiration level is a weighted average of the payoffs of people in her reference group as well as her own. Bendor et al. show that in games in which players who behave differently get different payoffs, in any stable outcome everyone who is connected by a series of overlapping reference groups will use the same action. This result is driven by the fact that in a sufficiently dense social network (e.g., person k is in j's reference group, j is in i's, and i is in k's), social comparisons of payoffs destabilize heterogeneous actions.

For example, consider n people in a village. Each person can contribute to some collective good or not. Suppose people get the same payoffs only in outcomes where everyone takes the same action, i.e., either everyone contributes or no one does. If the social network is sufficiently dense—technically, if it is *nondecomposable*—then in the long run everyone in the village will either contribute to the collective good or no one will.[33] On the way to either equilibrium, however, some people may contribute while others free ride. This pattern could persist for a substantial period of time if aspirations were heterogeneous and adjusted slowly.

Furthermore, heterogeneous behavior could persist indefinitely in sparse social networks. Consider a community divided into two groups, A and B, that have nonoverlapping reference groups: the reference group of every person in A is a subset of A and the reference group of everyone in B is a subset of B. In this case, it could be a stable outcome for all the As to contribute to the collective good while all Bs shirk. Thus, given aspiration-based adaptation, exploitation can be stable in sparse social networks.

4. Prospect Theory (PT)

In an important respect PT is the most complex of the three theories: not only is there a threshold, with payoffs being qualitatively defined (as gains versus losses) in comparison to that level, but in addition alternatives can then be compared to each other via the *value function* created (in part) by the reference point.

To see how PT models can consistently combine reference-dependence and a kind of value-maximization, it is helpful to analyze the simplest context: riskless choice by a single agent. (We can include contexts with a population of agents, as in voting, where people regard each other as fixed mechanisms. This decision theoretic mental model eliminates the cognitively taxing "how will my partner respond to my response to their move of...?".) Quattrone and Tversky (1988) studied this context experimentally; I will build on one of their most striking findings, pertaining to loss aversion.

Suppose at time t two countries, A and B, exhibit the same combination of employment and price stability (point v in Figure 2.3). Both of these are "goods": everyone wants them to rise, but people's intensities vary. Elections are occurring in both countries; in each, a liberal party is running on a platform of more employment at the expense of higher inflation, while a conservative party is running on the opposite combination (points x and y, respectively, in Figure 2.3). People in A and B have similar preference-distributions regarding economic policy. In the election at hand each country is evenly divided: half the citizens in each prefer x; the other half, y. Hence, this election cannot be won or lost on economic policy. Suppose, for reasons relating to different policy areas, the liberal party is elected in A; the conservative one, in B.

The governing policies implement their platforms and a new election is held in $t+1$. Enough time has passed so that x and y have become the reference points for people in A and B respectively. Now the liberal party in each country

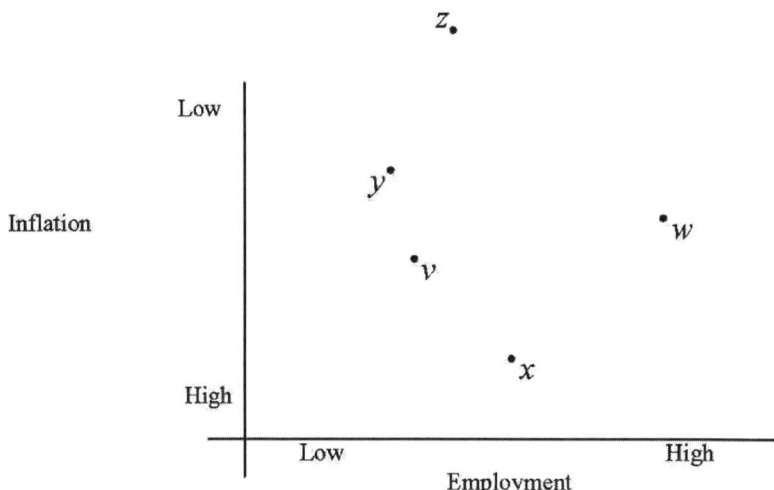

FIGURE 2.3   Policies and Path-Dependent Preferences

offers policy w and the conservatives offer z. Then PT predicts that more people in A than in B will prefer w over z, and more people in B than in A will prefer z over w. (If the countries would have been evenly split between w and z at date t then in the $t+1$ election a majority of As will prefer w and a majority of Bs, z.) This is true path-dependence in governmental policy: two countries that were initially alike diverge (for reasons unrelated to the policy in question), which produces further divergence.

This path-dependence (Pierson, 2000; Page, 2006) is due to a defining feature of classical PT—loss aversion—plus a property that extends the classical theory in a natural way: endogenous reference points. They work together as follows. Focus on voter A_j who with reference point v is indifferent between x and y. (From v he is also indifferent between w and z but these aren't on offer at t.) As assumed above, the liberal party wins in t in country A. After adjusting to x's combination of attributes A_j is presented with a choice of w versus z. Option w dominates x: it is better on both dimensions. But z would impose a *loss*, when viewed from the reference point of x, vis-à-vis employment. (This was *not* the case when w and z were compared from reference point v: both options are better than v on both inflation and unemployment.) Then loss aversion kicks in: since losses hurt more than gains help, if A_j had been indifferent between the w–z tradeoff when both dominated his old reference point then he will now prefer the option that continues to be an improvement in both respects over the alternative that now produces a mix of gains and losses.[34]

5. Applying Aspiration-based Models to Normative Issues: Happiness and Policy Evaluation[35]

Since Bentham, evaluations of public policies have had a strongly utilitarian cast. Yet modern applications of utilitarianism, such as cost-benefit analysis, are based not only on the classical theory's normative principles but also on a positive theory's descriptive axioms of utility—or, more informally, of human happiness. As noted earlier, these descriptive axioms *do not include the concept of an aspiration level*. Scholars working in the new field of hedonic psychology,[36] however, have found that concept very useful in explaining some intriguing empirical findings. (In this sense the largely empirical field of hedonic psychology is linking hands with the family of theories discussed in this chapter.) For example, although per capita GNP rose dramatically from 1946 to 1990 in France, Japan and the United States, "there was no increase in mean reports of [subjective well-being]" (Diener et al., 1999, p. 288). Endogenously rising aspirations explain this Faustian dynamic of doing well but feeling no better. (Note again the probably unintended and possibly unconscious effects of high aspiration levels. These probably do not arise from an RC calculation.)

The implications of these empirical findings and their aspiration-based explanation for policy evaluation could be profound. For example, if the subjective well-being of citizens is determined by their comparing a program's objective payoffs to their subjective aspiration levels, then cost-benefit analysis could be a seriously flawed method. Indeed, as the data reported by Diener et al. suggests, it could produce systematic biases: a better-grounded evaluation of the collective impact of our public policies is that though we're getting richer (on average) we're not becoming much happier.[37] (See, however, Deaton [2013] for a more upbeat interpretation of the evidence.)

More specific normative implications require a specific model of aspiration-based choice. Consider again prospect theory with endogenous aspirations. Given the axiom of loss aversion, plus the conventional assumption that aspirations adjust to bad payoffs with a substantial lag, such a model implies that a utilitarian measure of social welfare would be enhanced if public policies cushioned people against the short-term effects of sudden catastrophic losses. This is where we'd get a lot of happiness-bang for the buck.

Conclusions: From ABARs to Bounded Rationality

The preceding has shown that satisficing and other ABARs are sensible though often suboptimal. This dualistic conclusion is consistent with Simon's perspective on bounded rationality (e.g., 1990, p. 7). In his view the cup is *both* half-empty *and* half-full: it all depends on whether a task environment's complexity exceeds a person's cognitive constraints.

In contrast, in debates about rationality it is not uncommon to see the opposing sides described as optimists versus pessimists (e.g., Stanovich, 1999). The former emphasize how well human beings perform on various judgment and decision-making tasks; the latter, how badly. (For a lucid discussion of this debate from the perspective of one of its most thoughtful participants, see Kahneman [2011].)

Given how central rationality is to our self-esteem, these tendencies are understandable. But by the nature of our endeavor, political scientists do ourselves a disservice if we label ourselves or our work in this way. Instead, we should—of course!—strive to be realists, following Simon's dualistic perspective.[38] Our scientific obligation is to try to construct accurate theories, not those that flatter us ("See—we really *are* rational!"). This means building models that predict that humans are deft problem-solvers precisely in those domains where we are in fact competent. Good models should also predict that we do badly when we confront other kinds of problems. Or more subtly, that initially we do badly, but with proper training and experience normal adults can improve. Really good models will predict between-subjects variance when this is a robust empirical regularity. We are what we are: no more, no less.[39]

Given our special subject matter, it is especially easy for political scientists to get trapped into the dichotomous optimist-versus-pessimist framing of the rationality debate. To take a prominent example, we don't want to regard ordinary voters as fools. But 50 years of survey research make it hard for us to be optimists. Fortunately, our assessment of voters is not an answer to a forced-choice survey. We are not forced to code voters as either fools or geniuses; we are not forced to regard ourselves as either pessimists or optimists. We can be realists: most voters (a) are of ordinary intelligence and (b) don't specialize in politics or public policy. The combination of (a) and (b) has many implications. In particular, it immediately gives us a rough approximation of voters' problem-solving performance.

Intelligence is an attribute of a person. People with an IQ of 80 are unfortunate; they carry that degree of general intelligence around with them from domain to domain. But we haven't suddenly discovered that someone with a degree in civil engineering with an IQ of 110 is stupid just because he doesn't realize, when answering a survey in 1961 about the Berlin Wall, that that city was surrounded by large numbers of Soviet and East German troops, and so concludes that "vigorous military retaliation was the appropriate response" (Converse, 1975, p. 80) to the building of the Wall. Instead, we have learned that this ordinary human being—who is a competent civil engineer—knows little about foreign policy (duh!) and so would approve bad plans (duh!). Reverse the situation: let this engineer ask Philip Converse or other political scientists questions about how to build a bridge. We know little about this topic and we might approve bad plans. This wouldn't surprise us. Nor would it make us revise our images of ourselves ("argh! we're fools!") or of our basic cognitive abilities.

But, cry some political theorists, politics is different! More important! More central to who we are as human beings! Perhaps so. But the research program of bounded rationality tells us what to expect anyway.[40] We don't have to like it. More than a few people were displeased by the hypothesis that our planet is not the center of the solar system; many more were displeased by the hypothesis that, far from being the end product of a guided process, we are but one branch in a bushy evolutionary tree.

We aren't fools. Nor are we fully rational. We are clever but cognitively constrained problem-solvers.

Appendix: Markov Chains[41]

This is a brief glossary of key ideas and terms in the study of Markov processes and a *very* brief introduction to a few important results for discrete-time stationary Markov chains (MCs) with finitely many states. Readers who want a thorough understanding of formal models of aspiration-based adaptation should take at least one course on stochastic processes. Any introductory course will cover discrete-time finite-state MCs with stationary transition probabilities.

A fall-back option is self-study. A good introductory text is Taylor and Karlin (1998); if your background in this area is thin then it'd be sensible to read Moore and Siegel's lucid informal introduction to Markov chains (2013, pp. 340–350) first. If you pursue the self-study option then you should try to solve problems—preferably those for which the authors provide solutions—for every chapter. This is essential for getting a good grasp of the material.

Computational modeling is another useful—and increasingly accepted— tool for studying boundedly rational behavior.[42] It is, however, a technique rather than a body of theory, and use of this technique is greatly strengthened if one understands the relevant theories. Since many computational models turn out on inspection to be Markov chains, people interested in "agent-based" models would do well to study stochastic processes. Mathematical analysis and computational modeling complement each other.

Basic Concepts and Terms

State: A specification of the system in question at a given time. Examples: in a satisficing model, states are typically actions (if aspirations are exogenous) or actions and aspirations (for endogenous aspirations). There is usually more than one way to define a state in a given system; how to define states is an important modeling decision.

A system's set of states is often called its *state space*.

Transitions: A stochastic process moves the system from state to state based on some rule and the outcome of some random variable.

Markov Assumption: The probability distribution over the state space in $t+1$ depends only on what state the system is in at t (and the transition rules). It does *not* depend on the system's state prior to t.

Thus, MCs are one step—an important one—away from the simplest stochastic processes: those with independent events, e.g., a series of coin-tosses.

Discrete-state process: A stochastic process that has a finite or countably infinite number of states.

Discrete-time MC: States are defined only at discrete times, i.e., $t = 0, 1, 2, \ldots$.

Many of the extant models of adaptive behavior are discrete-time MCs with finitely many states.

State Vector: The probability distribution over the state space at a given time. (Hence, if there are k states then the state vector has k non-negative values that sum to one.)

Initial (Unconditional) Probability Distribution: The state vector at $t = 0$.

Probability Transition Matrix: A matrix representing the transition probabilities, e.g., the probability that the system goes from state i to state j. A matrix that is constant in time is called *stationary*. Stationary MCs are much more tractable than nonstationary ones and more is known (in the mathematical theory of MCs) about them.

Transition probabilities can be represented by a probability transition matrix, by a set of equations, e.g., Pr(system is in state i at date t | system was in state j at $t–1$), or by a diagram depicting states (circles) and their transitions (arrows).

Sample Path: A particular realization of the MC.

Limiting or *invariant* distribution: A stable or self-reproducing state vector, i.e., one that doesn't change when operated on by its probability transition matrix. Mathematically, this can be represented as $\tilde{p}P = \tilde{p}$, where $\tilde{p}$ is an invariant distribution.

Not all MCs have invariant distributions. However, all finite-state, discrete-time stationary MCs must have at least one such distribution. There are well-known theorems (see below for examples) that give sufficient or necessary and sufficient conditions for ensuring that a chain has a *unique* limiting distribution.

Pathwise or *dynamic* property: Something that is true not just in the long-run but along all sample paths that the system may take. Such a property is of course stronger than an equivalent one that holds only in the limit (i.e., for an invariant distribution).

Types of States and Their Properties

State k is *accessible* from state j if it is possible to go from j to k in finitely many steps, i.e. if the transition between them occurs in a finite number of steps with (strictly) positive probability.

States j and k *communicate* if each is accessible from the other.

Consider a state j and a transition matrix P. The *period* of state j is the greatest common divisor of all the integers n that satisfy $P_{j,j}^n > 0$; it is defined as zero if $P_{j,j}^n = 0$ for all n. Intuitively, it is the fastest frequency at which the system may return to state j after leaving it.

A MC in which all states have period 1 is called *aperiodic*. Most MCs studied in social science models are aperiodic. (Periodic MCs have an orderly "clockwork" temporal pattern that is rarely seen outside of tightly scheduled processes.) For an example of a periodic MC, consider a process with two states, i and j, and $p_{i,j} = p_{j,i} = 1$. If such a process is in state i in period 1, then it will return to i in all odd periods, hitting j in all even ones: perfect clockwork behavior with a periodicity of two. If, however, $p_{i,j}$ *and* $p_{j,i}$ were both in (0,1), then the process could be anywhere at any time—an aperiodic chain.

A state is **transient** if the system's probability of being in it vanishes in the long run. Because these states occur with zero probability in any limiting distribution, they may be ignored if one cares only about a system's long run properties.

A state is **recurring** if it isn't transient.

A recurring state is **absorbing** if, once reached, the system remains in it forever.

A system with multiple absorbing states does not have a unique limiting distribution. Such systems generally exhibit more history- and path-dependence than do those with a unique long run distribution. MCs that have the least history- and path-dependence are known as ergodic ones, as defined below.

Definition: A MC is called *ergodic* if the following two conditions hold:

1   It has a unique limiting distribution.
2   It converges to that limiting distribution from all initial state vectors.

A few useful theorems for discrete-time stationary MCs with finitely many states:

Theorem 2.1: If all states communicate then the MC has a unique limiting distribution.

Note: the process needn't converge to the unique invariant distribution from all possible initial state vectors.

Theorem 2.2: If all states communicate and the process is aperiodic then the MC is ergodic: it has a unique invariant distribution and it must converge to that state vector from all initial state vectors.

Note: This is sufficient for ergodicity. It isn't necessary. Theorem 2.3 is both.

Theorem 2.3: A stationary (etc.) MC is ergodic if and only if (1) it is aperiodic and (2) there is at least one state that is accessible from all other states.

Empirical Connections

Pathwise properties are the most desirable, as they tell you not only where the system will eventually end up (after enough time) but also how it is likely to get there and what happens along the way. Thus, pathwise results should be sought actively, though they are generally harder to pin down analytically than are descriptions of what happens in the limit.

Limiting distributions can also yield important results, however, and allow for close comparisons with equilibrium solutions of rational choice models.

One can analyze comparative statics or dynamics by varying a parameter's value and studying its impact on either the limiting distribution or the system's pathwise behavior, respectively. Comparative dynamics are often more difficult to analyze, but inductive proofs or even educated guesses can lead to insight.

Notes

1 Lest this remark be misunderstood, I should add that much of my work is squarely in the RC tradition and that this chapter's criticisms of that tradition are friendly ones.
2 One piece of evidence can be stated tersely and so is worth noting here: scholars in the most highly developed scientific fields take both theories and formal models seriously. This suggests, under even a mildly (Mertonian) functionalist view of scientific practice, that both types of formulations are valuable.
3 Practices in the natural sciences are again illuminating. For example, physicists often first try to get analytical results; if unable to do so they fall back on computation.
4 Much of this paragraph is from Bendor (2010, p. 14).
5 Most of these are descriptive formulations. (Not all however: Lindblom's disjointed incrementalism is an applied theory, designed to improve policy making [Bendor, 2014].) This chapter focuses mostly on descriptive theories.
6 Some readers, believing that a person's reference point is his status quo endowment whereas aspirations need not be, may object to using the terms as synonyms. But a careful reading of Kahneman and Tversky's seminal 1979 article shows that the idea that reference points are status quo endowments was an auxiliary hypothesis; it was not part of the theory's axiomatic core. Abstractly, a reference point in prospect theory is simply a payoff that is assigned the value of zero, so that higher payoffs are positive, lower ones are negative, and the other axioms (e.g., loss aversion) hold. The *source* of the reference point—the status quo, peers' payoffs, etc.—is not specified by the axiomatic core. (Many scholars following in Kahneman and Tversky's footsteps now seem to think that the status quo property is fundamental but the 1979 article draws a clear distinction between the theory's core and auxiliary hypotheses.) Hence, I think it is reasonable to use both terms as labels for the underlying idea of a threshold that serves as a standard of evaluation. (For further discussion of this issue see Heath, Larrick, & Wu (1999, p. 104).)
7 These contextual differences may have masked the underlying similarities of aspiration based models.
8 Positing a single aspiration level is not without empirical justification. Anthropologists have found that binary evaluation codes (good versus bad, etc.) occur in many human societies—e.g., Brown (1991, p. 90) says that this dualistic thinking is an extremely strong empirical regularity, indeed, one with no known exceptions (Brown, email, January 11, 2006)—and such codes are generated by a single evaluation threshold.
9 Whether it is optimal given *cognitive* constraints is a more subtle, and still open, question. But it is a mistake to focus so much on the question "do people optimize?" The much more important questions are "when do cognitive constraints bind, and

when they do what are the consequences?" E.g., if a person's mental representation of a problem has reduced its complexity enough so s/he can implement an optimization rule, then cognitive constraints obviously matter; they shouldn't be overlooked just because they occurred in the problem-editing phase (March, 1994).

10 For example, simple satisficing and optimal search models both predict that we will observe the following qualitative sequence of actions by decision makers: reject an alternative, reject an alternative, …, accept an alternative and stop searching.

11 Some may dismiss this as irrelevant to empirical assessments of rival theories, but such a stance is blatantly inconsistent with our conduct as teachers. We are committed to believing that tests and problem sets can measure a student's understanding of, e.g., optimal search. Hence, responses to instructions such as "show your work" are relevant data.

12 The caveat of "for some problems" matters. In some choice situations—e.g., when the present author walks into an ice cream parlor—optimization does not require a complete preference ordering: chocolate ice cream is always best. Always.

13 This is also true of satisficing's cousin, elimination by aspects (Tversky, 1972). More generally, *noncompensatory* rules don't require complete preference orderings. For a comparison of noncompensatory to compensatory rules see Hogarth (1987). Most aspiration-based decision rules are noncompensatory.

14 Some of the following is taken from Bendor et al. (2011, p. 13).

15 This is not an "as if" claim. It is a "realist" view, in the philosophy of science sense: it involves a theoretical commitment to a computational interpretation of optimization, as a procedure that actually occurs in people's heads, for certain classes of problems.

16 Munro and Sugden (2003) establish the intriguing fact that many standard axioms of RC consumer behavior are consistent with the assumption of reference-dependent preferences. It is therefore possible to construct models of choice which are aspiration-based *and* in which the agents maximize utility. Scholars who like neat (disjoint) categorizations of research programs may find it disturbing that these two different intellectual traditions can mate and produce viable offspring, but that's life.

17 Economists sometimes call these *inspection* goods and *experience* goods, respectively. This distinction arises naturally in the study of consumer behavior: the quality of some goods is well known prior to purchase (an inspection good); for others it isn't (an experience good).

18 There is no need to prejudge this issue; commitments to a particular side in the "rationality wars" (Samuels, Stich, & Bishop, 2002) shouldn't contaminate our empirical understanding. A plausible descriptive theory could be built on an assumption that sometimes people have wildly unrealistic aspirations. This could generate very interesting predictions; more on this shortly.

19 Throughout this chapter all adjustment rules are assumed to be Markovian and stationary, unless it is explicitly stated otherwise. (See the appendix for an explanation of these terms.) Many of the ideas and results extend to adaptive behavior that isn't stationary or even Markovian. But the extensions involve complications of a mostly technical nature; hence, they are distractions in this type of chapter.

20 This argument is consistent with Merton's theory about opportunity structures and criminal behavior: young criminals haven't rejected the American Dream; they've embraced it. His argument is complemented by prospect theory's premise that people will be risk-seeking in the domain of bad (below-aspiration) payoffs.

21 Interestingly, Simon himself never argued that satisficing is equivalent to optimizing. Indeed, he made rather modest claims about satisficing's objective performance properties, asserting that it belongs to a class of *weak* (though general) heuristics. (See Newell [1969, pp. 377–380; 1980, pp. 184–187] for enlightening discussions of

the relation between the power of heuristics and their generality. He argues that no problem-solving method is both general and powerful.)

22 It should be kept in mind that like the other results described in this chapter, proposition two presumes ABARs that are Markovian and stationary. Some non-stationary ABARs can become stoic in the face of failures (Bendor & Kumar, 2005).

23 Optimists in the rationality debate, to use Stanovich's categorization (1999), might argue that humans have large repertoires of heuristics and switch among them effectively, deploying appropriate rules in different problem-environments (Cosimides & Tooby, 1992; Payne, Bettman, & Johnson, 1988, 1993; Todd & Gigerenzer, 2000, p. 740). But this "adaptive toolbox" (Gigerenzer & Selten, 2001) perspective leads to questions that are still wide-open: (1) How large are our rule-repertoires?; (2) How effectively do we code problems and match solutions to them?; and (3) How stable are our problem-environments? These are far from settled matters: e.g., see the spirited set of criticisms on Todd and Gigerenzer (2000) in that issue of *Behavioral and Brain Sciences*.

24 See Lupia (1994) for a statement of this view in political science, and Gigerenzer et al. (1999) for a more general statement. The latter in particular is too optimistic about the performance of garden-variety heuristics. In political science see Lau and Redlawsk (2001) and Tetlock (2005, pp. 119–120) for criticisms of unvarnished optimism; more generally see a fascinating exchange in the symposium led off by Todd and Gigerenzer (2000).

25 This result—use-probabilities are ordered just as success-probabilities are—is more likely to hold in the probabilistic steady state (i.e., in the limiting distribution) than dynamically. For circumstances in which the result holds for satisficing in the limit but not dynamically, see Bendor, Kumar, & Siegel (2009).

26 This property need *not* hold over time. Suppose that the group first encounters option 1. They adopt it and then stumble onto alternative 3, which gives some people payoffs that exceed anything they could get from options 1 or 2. If aspirations adjust sufficiently quickly—and there is some evidence that good times rapidly boost aspirations (Kahneman, Knetsch, & Thaler, 1990)—then these people will regard the payoffs they later get from option 2 as disappointing.

27 The following is adapted from Bendor, Diermeier, and Ting (2007).

28 Winners satisfice in Kramer (1977). Though he didn't base this assumption on bounded rationality, Kramer's unusual model can in some ways be regarded as an ancestor of KMP and BMR.

29 Note that this would not hold if challengers' polls were noisy—an interesting extension of their model. Just as with Downsian models (Grofman, 2004), one can get a variety of predictions from different behavioral models. One must understand a model in detail in order to grasp what it predicts.

30 Two eminent learning theorists described the finding as follows: "[I]n studies of learned performance, a given reward for a response may have either an incremental or decremental effect upon performance depending on what reward the subject expects or on the range of alternative rewards the subject has been receiving in similar contexts. If a person is expecting a one cent payoff, getting ten cents is going to be positively rewarding; if he is expecting a dollar payoff, the ten cents is frustrating and may have the effect of a punishment. Effects such as these have been observed with animals as well as men ... They can all be interpreted in terms of Helson's concept of adaptation level. The rewards obtained over the past trials in a given context determine, by some averaging process, an internal standard or norm called the adaptation level. *Each new reward is evaluated in relation to this adaptation level, having a positive influence on behavior if it is above the norm, a negative influence if it is below*" (Hilgard & Bower, 1966, p. 486; emphasis added).

31 Payoffs in the BDT model are stochastic, to ensure that the model has empirical content. So specifying intermediate aspirations in that model is more complicated. But the basic idea is the same.

32 For an illuminating formal analysis of the effect of social networks on political participation, see Siegel (2007).

33 Bendor et al. define a set of players as nondecomposable if, for every partition of the set into two disjoint and nonempty subsets, at least one person in each subset has someone in the other subset in his or her reference group.

34 More generally, PT predicts the following about the combined effect of loss aversion and endogenous reference points. (1) Any A who preferred w to z given a reference point (rp) of v will keep that preference given a new rp of x. (2) Any A who was indifferent between w and z, given rp$=v$, prefers w over z given rp$=x$. (3) Of the As who preferred z to w given rp$=v$, any who were "sufficiently" close to indifference will prefer w to z given rp$=x$. (Analogous predictions hold for the Bs, given a shift of their reference point from v to y.) Hence, except for unusual knife-edge cases, a move from v to x will reduce the percentage of As who favor w, while the move from v to y will make fewer Bs favor w.

35 Most of this is taken from Bendor (2010, pp. 8–9).

36 For an excellent introduction to this field, see Kahneman, Diener, and Schwarz (1999).

37 Some may feel that this line of reasoning would lead to a dangerous degree of subjectivity in policy evaluation; better to rely on objective proxies such as dollars gained and spent. But this response reflects a kind of goal-displacement. If one is a utilitarian then the fundamental object of interest should be human happiness—an *intrinsically* subjective variable. If human beings are so constructed that they are content when payoffs exceed aspirations and dissatisfied otherwise, then that is a fact about the world that normative theories should take into account.

38 When the totality of his work is considered, it is clear that Simon was a realist. On the one hand he famously criticized economists for being too optimistic; on the other, his work on expertise contains an important though implicit criticism of the heuristics-and-biases approach for being too pessimistic. It was probably no coincidence that his father was an engineer.

39 Of course, the "are" in this claim includes statements about capacities, not just current behavior (e.g., a normal infant has the capacity to learn its native tongue). Less obviously, it also includes predictions about what humans *could* learn to do that they don't presently and counter-factuals about what humans could have done in the past (e.g., with the proper education most people in medieval Europe could have come to understand elementary statistics) though in fact they didn't.

40 That is, apart from domains such as language acquisition in which hominids have been subject to persistent selective forces and domains where an individual homo sapiens studies hard for many years, most humans don't know much and use general heuristics that are weak—they don't exploit powerful domain-specific knowledge. (How could they?)

41 This is adapted from Bendor and Siegel (2005).

42 For an excellent overview of computational models of politics see Kollman and Page (2006).

References

Achen, Christopher, & Larry Bartels. 2004. "Blind Retrospection: Electoral Responses to Drought, Flu, and Shark Attacks." Unpublished manuscript (January 27). Princeton University, New Jersey.

Austen-Smith, David, & Jeffrey Banks. 2000. *Positive Political Theory I: Collective Preference*. Ann Arbor, MI: University of Michigan Press.

Bendor, Jonathan. 2003. "Herbert A. Simon: Political Scientist." In N. Polsby (Ed.), *Annual Review of Political Science* (Vol. 6). Palo Alto, CA: Annual Reviews, 433–471.

Bendor, Jonathan. 2010. *Bounded Rationality and Politics*. Berkeley, CA: University of California Press.

Bendor, Jonathan. 2014. "Incrementalism: Dead but Flourishing." Prepared for presentation at the Annual Conference of the American Society of Public Administration, Washington, D.C., March 16–19, 2014.

Bendor, Jonathan, Daniel Diermeier, & Michael Ting. 2003. "A Behavioral Model of Turnout." *American Political Science Review* 97(2): 261–280.

Bendor, Jonathan, Daniel Diermeier, & Michael Ting. 2007. "Comment: Adaptive Models in Sociology and the Problem of Empirical Content." *American Journal of Sociology* 112(5): 1534–1545.

Bendor, Jonathan, Daniel Diermeier, & Michael Ting. 2014. "Inequality, Aspirations, and Social Comparisons." Unpublished ms., Columbia University, New York.

Bendor, Jonathan, Daniel Diermeier, David Siegel, & Michael Ting. 2011. *A Behavioral Theory of Elections*. Princeton, NJ: Princeton University Press.

Bendor, Jonathan, & Sunil Kumar. 2005. "The Perfect Is the Enemy of the Best." *Journal of Theoretical Politics* 17(1): 5–39.

Bendor, Jonathan, Sunil Kumar, & David Siegel. 2009. "Satisficing: A 'Pretty Good' Heuristic." *The B.E. Journal of Theoretical Economics (Advances)* 9(1): Article 9.

Bendor, Jonathan, Sunil Kumar, & David Siegel. 2010. "Adaptively Rational Retrospective Voting." *Journal of Theoretical Politics* 22(1): 26–63.

Bendor, Jonathan, Dilip Mookherjee, & Debraj Ray. 2001. "Aspiration-Based Reinforcement Learning in Repeated Interaction Games: An Overview." *International Journal of Game Theory Review* 3:159–174.

Bendor, Jonathan, Dilip Mookherjee, & Debraj Ray. 2006. "Satisficing and Selection in Electoral Competition." *Quarterly Journal of Political Science* 1(2): 171–200.

Bendor, Jonathan, & David Siegel. 2005. "Notes on Markov Chains." Unpublished ms. Graduate School of Business, Stanford University, California.

Bettman, James, Mary Frances Luce, & John Payne. 1998. "Constructive Consumer Choice Processes." *Journal of Consumer Research* 25 (December): 187–217.

Brown, Donald. 1991. *Human Universals*. Boston, MA: McGraw-Hill.

Conlisk, John. 1996. "Why Bounded Rationality?" *Journal of Economic Literature* 34: 669–700.

Converse, Philip. 1975. "Public Opinion and Voting Behavior." In Fred Greenstein & Nelson Polsby (Eds.), *Handbook of Political Science* (Vol. 4). Reading, MA: Addison-Wesley, 75–169.

Cosmides, Leda, & John Tooby. 1992. "Cognitive Adaptations for Social Exchange." In J. Barkow, L. Cosmides, & J. Tooby (Eds.), *The Adapted Mind: Evolutionary Psychology and the Generation of Culture* (pp. 163–228). New York: Oxford University Press.

Cyert, Richard, & James March. 1992. *A Behavioral Theory of the Firm* (2nd ed.). Cambridge, MA: Blackwell Business.

Deaton, Angus. 2013. *The Great Escape: Health, Wealth, and the Origins of Inequality*. Princeton, NJ: Princeton University Press.

Diener, Ed, & Eunkook Suh. 1999. "National Differences in Subjective Well-Being." In D. Kahneman, E. Diener and N. Schwarz (Eds.), *Well-Being: The Foundations of Hedonic Psychology*. New York: Russell Sage Foundation, 434–452.

Evans, J. St. B. T. 2003. "In Two Minds: Dual Process Accounts of Reasoning." *Trends in Cognitive Science* 7: 454–459.

Evans, J. St. B. T. 2008. "Dual-Processing Accounts of Reasoning, Judgment, and Social Cognition." *Annual Review of Psychology*, 59: 255–278.

Evans, J. St. B. T. 2010. *Thinking Twice: Two Minds in One Brain*. Oxford: Oxford University Press.

Fiorina, Morris. 1981. *Retrospective Voting in American National Elections*. New Haven, CT: Yale University Press.

Fiorina, Morris. 1990. "Information and Rationality in Elections." In John Ferejohn & James Kuklinski (Eds.), *Information and Democratic Processes*. Urbana, IL: University of Illinois Press, 329–42.

Gigerenzer, Gerd, & Reinhard Selten, Eds. 2001. *Bounded Rationality: The Adaptive Toolbox*. Cambridge, MA: The MIT Press.

Gigerenzer, Gerd, P. Todd, & the ABC Group. Eds. 1999. *Simple Heuristics That Make Us Smart*. Oxford: Oxford University Press.

Goodin, Robert. 2000. "Rationality Redux: Reflections on Herbert Simon's Vision of Politics." In James Alt, Margaret Levi, & Elinor Ostrom (Eds.), *Competition and Cooperation: Conversations with Nobelists about Economics and Political Science*. New York: Russell Sage, 60–84.

Green, Donald, & Ian Shapiro. 1994. *Pathologies of Rational Choice Theory*. New Haven, CT: Yale University Press.

Grofman, Bernard. 2004. "Downs and Two-Party Convergence." *Annual Review of Political Science* 7: 25–46.

Heath, Chip, Richard Larrick, & George Wu. 1999. "Goals as Reference Points." *Cognitive Psychology* 38: 79–109.

Helson, Harry. 1964. *Adaptation-Level Theory*. New York: Harper & Row.

Hilgard, Ernest, & Gordon Bower. 1966. *Theories of Learning*. New York: Appleton-Century-Croft.

Hogarth, Robin. 1987. *Judgment and Choice* (2nd ed.). New York: Wiley.

Jackman, Robert. 1993. "Rationality and Political Participation." *American Journal of Political Science* 37: 279–290.

Kahneman, Daniel. 2011. *Thinking, Fast and Slow*. New York: Farrar, Straus and Giroux.

Kahneman, Daniel, Edward Diener, & Norbert Schwarz. Eds. 1999. *Well-Being: The Foundations of Hedonic Psychology*. New York: Russell Sage Foundation.

Kahneman, Daniel, Jack Knetsch, & Richard Thaler. 1990. "Experimental Tests of the Endowment Effect and the Coase Theorem." *Journal of Political Economy* 98: 1325–1348.

Kahneman, Daniel, & Amos Tversky. 1979. "Prospect Theory: An Analysis of Decision under Risk." *Econometrica* 47: 263–291.

Kenworthy, Lane, & Jonas Pontusson. 2005. "Rising Inequality and the Politics of Redistribution in Affluent Countries." *Perspectives on Politics* 3: 449–472.

Key, V. O. 1966. *The Responsible Electorate: Rationality in Presidential Voting 1936–1960*. Cambridge, MA: Belknap Press.

Kohn, Meier, & Steven Shavell. 1974. "The Theory of Search." *Journal of Economic Theory* 9(2): 93–123.

Kollman, Ken, & Scott Page. 2006. "Computational Methods and Models of Politics." In Leigh Tesfatsion and Kenneth Judd (Eds.), *Handbook of Computational Economics* (Vol. 2) (pp. 1433–1463). Amsterdam: North-Holland.

Kollman, Ken, John Miller, & Scott Page. 1992. "Adaptive Parties in Spatial Elections." *American Political Science Review* 86: 929–937.

Kollman, Ken, John Miller, & Scott Page. 1998. "Political Parties and Electoral Landscapes." *British Journal of Political Science* 28: 139–158.

Kotovsky, Kenneth, John Hayes, & Herbert Simon. 1985. "Why Are Some Problems Hard?" *Cognitive Psychology* 17: 248–294.

Kramer, Gerald. 1977. "A Dynamical Model of Political Equilibrium." *Journal of Economic Theory* 16: 310–334.

Lau, Richard, & David Redlawsk. 2001. "Advantages and Disadvantages of Cognitive Heuristics in Political Decision Making." *American Journal of Political Science* 45: 951–971.

Lodge, Milton, Kathleen McGraw, & Patrick Stroh. 1989. "An Impression-Driven Model of Candidate Evaluation." *American Political Science Review* 83: 399–420.

Lupia, Arthur. 1994. "Shortcuts versus Encyclopedias: Information and Voting Behavior in California Insurance Reform Elections." *American Political Science Review* 88: 63–76.

March, James. 1994. *A Primer on Decision Making: How Decisions Happen*. New York: The Free Press.

Margolis, Howard. 2000. "Simple Heuristics That Make Us Dumb." *Behavioral and Brain Sciences* 23: 758.

McAdam, Doug. 1986. "Recruitment to High-Risk Activism—The Case of Freedom Summer." *American Journal of Sociology* 92(1): 64–90.

Merton, Robert, & A. Rossi. 1950. "Contributions to the Theory of Reference Group Behavior." In R. Merton and P. Lazarsfeld (Eds.), *Continuities in Social Research*. Glencoe, IL: Free Press, 40–105.

Moore, Will, & David Siegel. 2013. *A Mathematics Course for Political and Social Research*. Princeton, NJ: Princeton University Press.

Munro, Alistair, & Robert Sugden. 2003. "On the Theory of Reference-Dependent Preferences." *Journal of Economic Behavior and Organization* 50: 407–428.

Newell, Allen. 1969. "Heuristic Programming: Ill-Structured Problems." In Julius Aronofsky (Ed.), *Progress in Operations Research* (Vol. 3). New York: Wiley.

Newell, Allen. 1980. "One Final Word." In D. Tuma & F. Reif (Eds.), *Problem-Solving and Education: Issues in Teaching and Research*. Hillsdale, NJ: Lawrence Erlbaum Associates, 175–189.

Page, Scott. 2006. "Path Dependence." *Quarterly Journal of Political Science* 1: 87–115.

Palfrey, Thomas, & Howard Rosenthal. 1985. "Voter Participation and Strategic Uncertainty." *American Political Science Review* 79: 62–78.

Payne, John. 1976. "Task Complexity and contingent Processing in Decision Making: An Information Search and Protocol Analysis." *Organizational Behavior and Human Decision Processes* 16(2): 366–387.

Payne, John, James Bettman, & Eric Johnson. 1988. "Adaptive Strategy Selection in Decision Making." *Journal of Experimental Psychology: Learning, Memory, and Cognition* 14(3): 534–552.

Payne, John, James Bettman, & Eric Johnson. 1993. *The Adaptive Decision Maker*. Cambridge MA: Cambridge University Press.

Pierson, Paul. 2000. "Increasing Returns, Path Dependence, and the Study of Politics." *American Political Science Review* 94(2): 251–267.

Quattrone, George, & Amos Tversky. 1988. "Contrasting Rational and Psychological Analyses of Political Choice." *American Political Science Review* 82: 719–736.

Samuels, Richard, Stephen Stich, & Michael Bishop. 2002. "Ending the Rationality Wars: How to Make Disputes about Human Rationality Disappear." In R. Elio (Ed.), *Common Sense, Reasoning and Rationality*, Vancouver Studies in Cognitive Science (Vol. 11). New York: Oxford University Press, 236–268.

Shepsle, Kenneth. 1996. "Statistical Political Philosophy and Positive Political Theory." In Jeffrey Friedman (Ed.), *The Rational Choice Controversy*. New Haven, CT: Yale University Press, 213–222.

Siegel, David. 2007. "Social Networks and Collective Action." *American Journal of Political Science* 53 (January): 122–138.

Simon, Herbert. 1955. "A Behavioral Model of Rational Choice." *Quarterly Journal of Economics* 69 (February): 99–118.

Simon, Herbert. 1956. "Rational Choice and the Structure of the Environment." *Psychological Review* 63: 129–138.

Simon, Herbert. 1957. *Models of Man: Social and Rational*. New York: Wiley.

Simon, Herbert. 1990. "Invariants of Human Behavior." In *Annual Review of Psychology* 41: 1–19, M. Rosenzweig & L. Porter (Eds.). Palo Alto, CA: Annual Reviews.

Simon, Herbert. 1996. *The Sciences of the Artificial* (3rd ed.). Cambridge, MA: MIT Press.

Slovic, Paul. 1995. "The Construction of Preference." *American Psychologist* 50: 364–371.

Stanovich, Keith. 1999. *Who Is Rational? Studies of Individual Differences in Reasoning*. Mahwah, NJ: Lawrence Erlbaum.

Stanovich, K., & R. West. 2000. "Individual Differences in Reasoning: Implications for the Rationality Debate." *Behavioral and Brain Sciences* 23: 645–665.

Stokes, Donald. 1963. "Spatial Models of Party Competition." *American Political Science Review* 57(2): 368–377.

Taylor, Howard, & Samuel Karlin. 1998. *An Introduction to Stochastic Modeling* (3rd ed). New York: Academic Press.

Tetlock, Philip. 2005. *Expert Political Judgment*. Princeton, NJ: Princeton University Press.

Todd, Peter, & Gerd Gigerenzer. 2000. "Simple Heuristics that Make Us Smart." *Behavioral and Brain Sciences* 23(5): 727–741.

Tversky, Amos. 1972. "Elimination by Aspects: A Theory of Choice." *Psychological Review* 79: 281–299.

Tversky, Amos, & Daniel Kahneman. 1991. "Loss Aversion in Riskless Choice: A Reference-Dependent Model." *Quarterly Journal of Economics* 106: 1039–1061.

3

EXPERIMENTAL POLITICAL PHILOSOPHY

Justice Judgments in the Hypothetical Society Paradigm

Gregory Mitchell and Philip E. Tetlock

Political philosophers often employ thought experiments in developing their normative accounts of justice. Most famously within modern political philosophy, Rawls (1971) develops his theory of justice by reflecting on the principles of justice to which people would consent if they made their choices behind a "veil of ignorance" that blinded them to their likely standing in a future society. Almost as famously, Nozick (1974) advances his competing, libertarian conception of justice with a hypothetical about Wilt Chamberlain's entitlement to the fruits of his labor obtained through free exchange. Ackerman (1980) imagines a society in which a "perfect technology of justice" removes all practical impediments to achieving social justice—all for the express purpose of providing "a clean-cut thought experiment to test the claim that liberalism is bankrupt" (p. 21). Several other examples of prominent thought experiments in modern political philosophy could be given, for "[r]ecent liberal theory has been distinctive for its thought experiments" (Fishkin, 1992, p. 50).

As empiricists, social scientists tend to be skeptical of thought experiments (suspecting great potential for experimenter bias when $N = 1$—and the experimenter is the sole subject), and, as positivists, social scientists tend to be skeptical of the normative theories of justice that percolate out of thought experiments (suspecting that clashing "ought" claims boil down to pre-existing ideological preferences of the thought experimenters). Social scientists prefer to employ their own distinctive research tools: laboratory experiments, surveys, and historical and econometric studies to develop descriptive and explanatory accounts of justice.[1] By examining how experimental participants divide rewards among members of a small group engaged in a collective task, how survey participants respond to questions about the distribution of wealth, or how different groups react to different welfare policies or institutions distribute scarce resources, social scientists try to shift the spotlight from the unanswerable question "What is just?" to the answerable question "Who finds what to be just—and why?"

Mutual suspicion is likely to persist for a long time. It is hard to persuade philosophers that empirical studies can produce findings about justice *per se*, due to self-interest contaminants and insufficient conceptual care in formulating public opinion questions and answers (Liebig, 2001; Swift, 1999), and it is perhaps even harder to persuade social scientists that thought experiments can produce theories of justice uncontaminated by pet theories (Barber, 1975) or cultural biases (Okin, 1989).

In this chapter, however, we argue for a partial rapprochement: we advocate blending thought experiments with laboratory experiments via a technique we call "the hypothetical society paradigm" designed to bring out the inferential advantages of both approaches while minimizing the disadvantages. We divide the chapter into three sections. In the first section, we discuss the primary benefits of this technique; in the second section, we survey the principal empirical findings thus far obtained using this technique; in the third section, we discuss two categories of fruitful future applications of this and related techniques: (1) isolating sources of support and resistance to particular policy proposals with potentially profound societal implications; and (2) helping to clarify boundary conditions for the applicability of competing and complementary psychological theories of justice.

Turning Thought Experiments into Lab Experiments

Thought experiments help philosophers isolate and clarify the role of different principles and assumptions in their normative arguments, to see what is essential and what is not to a theory, much like laboratory experiments help to identify the role of different variables in cause–effect relationships. In the mind of a philosopher committed to working out the logical implications of propositions in alternative worlds, the thought experiment can be a rigorous means to an end: "She follows through all the relevant implications of altering one part of her worldview and attempts to construct a coherent model of the situation she is imagining. The rigor with which thought experimenters attempt to answer 'what if' questions is what differentiates thought experiments from daydreams and much fiction. ... The thought experimenter is committed to rigorously considering all relevant consequences in answering the 'what if' questions" (Cooper, 2005, p. 337).

Thought experiments, however, even when conducted by philosophers who faithfully report their mental simulations and conclusions, lack the transparency and replicability deemed essential to scientific research (Bunge, 1961), and suspicions about the accuracy and reliability of self-reports on introspection lead many to dismiss the thought experiment as a path to reliable knowledge (see Sorenson, 1992, Chapter 2). Thus, when scientists employ thought experiments, as Galileo, Newton and Einstein did with some success, the resulting theories must ultimately be couched in publicly testable terms to qualify as scientific (Dennett, 2003).

Thought experiments also suffer from an extreme version of the external validity complaint often lodged against laboratory studies. Whereas laboratory researchers can make some claim that their findings represent the views of a cross-section of college students reacting to real, if simulated, situations, thought experimenters can make no claim that their findings represent the views of people in general, or even philosophers specifically, reacting to realistic simulations. Indeed, many philosophical debates persist because philosophers reach different conclusions about hypothetical cases or the validity of background assumptions in these cases (e.g., the philosophical study of personal identity has been particularly plagued by competing hypotheticals and competing conclusions; see S. Coleman, 2000), and the very purpose of many thought experiments is to create *unreal* situations that can exist only in the imagination (Souder, 2003).

For the empiricist who finds a thought experiment interesting but doubts the reliability and generalizability of its product, a simple solution exists: reduce the thought experiment to concrete terms that can be reproduced as written scenarios and ask subjects to react to the scenarios to see what trends emerge (e.g., Machery et al., 2004). The emerging field of experimental philosophy seeks to do just this with a variety of philosophical conundrums (see Knobe, 2004). But that view emphasizes what laboratory studies can do for thought experiments. In our view, thought experiments can do much for laboratory studies of justice.

Empirical studies of justice pose their own difficulties, some of which may be alleviated by incorporating elements of thought experiments into these studies. First, and virtually impossible to control within empirical studies, is the problem that public opinion on matters of justice often depends on mixtures of emotionally charged political values (such as liberty, equality, religious purity, and national sovereignty) and technically complex matters of fact (such as whether individual or societal conditions are greater determinants of economic outcomes or whether tying welfare benefits to work requirements—"workfare"—will encourage self-sufficiency or whether intergenerational mobility is rising or declining). When causal relations and policy effects are difficult to determine, there is a powerful temptation to bring one's beliefs about the facts into convenient alignments that minimize dissonance and mental strain (e.g., Herrmann et al., 2001; Mitchell et al., 1993; Skitka, 1999). For instance, Skitka and Tetlock (1992, 1993) and Christiansen and Lavine (1997) found that liberals and conservatives held different pre-existing beliefs about the causes of public assistance and, as a result, made different trade-offs in a mock public aid allocation task. Thus, surveys that find different views about distributive justice between liberals and conservatives but fail to check for differences in background beliefs may mistakenly attribute response differences to value differences. Conversely, surveys that find agreement across groups regarding distributive justice and the propriety of redistribution may simply reflect widespread mistaken beliefs about important underlying facts, such as the degree of economic mobility present within a society (see Ferrie, 2005; Fong, 2005) or the proportion of families within different socioeconomic categories (see Kluegel et al., 1995). These problems are particularly acute when one tries to study the impact of macroeconomic variables and system-level conditions on individual judgments of justice, but informational problems can arise in any setting where important facts are vague or disputed (as, for example, in the bargaining studies conducted by Babcock et al., 1995).

In order to overcome factual disagreements and avoid factual confusion, we took a page from the philosopher's book on thought experiments and developed a "hypothetical society paradigm" in which experimental participants judge the justice of different distributions of wealth within hypothetical societies (see Mitchell et al., 1993). This paradigm capitalizes on the unreality of thought experiments: because the experimenter designs the hypothetical societies, the experimenter controls the structure of these hypothetical societies, including the location of the poverty line and percentage of persons below it, mean income and income variance within the society, levels of redistribution and welfare services available, the level of meritocracy (i.e., the degree to which individual merit versus other factors determine economic outcomes), and whether the hypothetical society is in the "original position" or considering changes to existing procedures and distributions. Using the hypothetical society approach, one is able to examine which features of societies are most important to people's judgments of social justice and able to examine how these judgments change as features of the societies change. In short, the hypothetical society paradigm allows researchers to unconfound the role of factual beliefs from the influence of value orientations in judgments of justice. Because individuals tend to avoid value trade-offs, often by arguing facts (see, e.g., Tetlock & McGuire, 1986), this ability to manipulate value conflict provides considerable experimental advantages.

Thus, one main benefit of importing hypothetical societies into the laboratory is the control one gains over otherwise complex and debatable matters of fact.[2] A second benefit involves the control one gains over the influence of selfish interests. A problem commonly confronted in empirical studies of justice is that of disentangling biased from unbiased judgments (see Fong et al., 2006; Konow, 2005; Liebig, 2001). The hypothetical society paradigm allows researchers to place participants in the position of impartial spectator: researchers who want to eliminate or minimize the role of material self-interest and social influence on judgments ask participants to make anonymous judgments about hypothetical societies with no material implications for themselves. Alternatively, researchers interested in the role of social influences can ask participants to explain or justify their judgments under various accountability conditions or can manipulate the group identities involved, while researchers interested in the influence of material self-interest can alter the method to have participants imagine themselves inside the society or ask them to allocate resources within the society (using either hypothetical or real pay-offs).

In our studies using the hypothetical society paradigm, we have favored experimental manipulations that place the participant in the position of impartial spectator because arguably judgments from that position best represent unbiased judgments of justice.[3] As a number of studies have shown, when participants have a stake in the distribution at hand, egocentric and in-group biases will often influence participants' judgments about the fairness of these distributions (Bar-Hillel & Yaari, 1993; Epley & Caruso, 2004; Frohlich & Oppenheimer, 1997, 2000; Greenberg, 1983; Konow, 2005; Messick & Sentis, 1983; Pillutla & Murnighan, 2003). We cannot trust that unbiased judgments of justice will be given when individuals judge their own situations, and so, if we seek to know what justice ideally requires, "thought experiments trump real experiments" (Cooper, 2005, p. 344).[4] While the experience of injustice from the first-person perspective is an important subject of inquiry in its own right (Lerner, 2003; Miller, 2001), individualized appeals to justice always invoke moral norms or principles of general application that the individual claims are or should be endorsed by the polity or community. The notion of justice principles idiosyncratic to the individual, as opposed to there being individual differences in phenomenological experiences of injustice in subjective claims about what social justice requires in a particular case, is oxymoronic from a philosophical perspective. For the philosopher, a judgment about a distribution or procedure qualifies as a justice judgment only if the judgment is made from an impartial point of view, such as by third-party observers to hypothetical societies, and reflects the ethical preferences of those impartial spectators (Liebig, 2001; Lerner, 1974, likewise argues that non-self-involved persons are more likely to base their judgments on moral values than self-involved persons).

Judgments about justice made by detached observers of hypothetical societies may nevertheless be useful guides about justice in real societies. Most obviously, to the extent hypothetical societies and real societies possess common features important to participants' judgments of justice, judgments about justice in the hypothetical societies may generalize to real societies. But even with highly artificial scenarios, judgments about hypothetical societies can identify areas of agreement and disagreement on topics of economic policy and social justice and explain how factual beliefs and value differences combine to produce either consensus or dissension. For instance, in our first hypothetical society studies (Mitchell et al., 1993), we found a surprising degree of agreement across political groups on the importance of providing a minimum safety net, even in perfect meritocracies in which the poor controlled their economic fates. And perhaps most ambitiously, to the extent that the judgments individuals reach as impartial spectators cause individuals to reflect on just distributions in their own societies, the hypothetical society paradigm could be used as a device to foster deliberation about social policy (e.g., Fishkin, 1991). If used in this sense, the hypothetical society paradigm may perform a "reflective equilibrium" function (Rawls, 1971; see Daniels, 1996), possibly leading persons to give up their initial intuitions or change their views about what justice requires once they are confronted with a series of controlled thought experiments.

Although our focus has been on how thought experiments can aid empirical studies of justice, it is worth pausing to note that the hypothetical society paradigm may also aid philosophical studies of justice. Elster (1995) notes that one of the problems for Rawls' (1971) theory of justice is deciding what arrangements agreed to in the original position are likely to have the greatest "psychological stability." For instance, when will people be more concerned about wastefulness or unfairness in the original position? The hypothetical society paradigm is well-positioned to answer such robustness questions, because different hypothetical policies varying in efficiency and fairness can be systematically compared and evaluated in this paradigm. In fact, we conducted a comparison of this sort in one of our studies, and we found that conservatives were more sensitive to waste in redistributive policies than liberals when the redistribution was meant for deserving recipients (Mitchell et al., 2003), suggesting that the psychological stability of arrangements depends on the mix of liberals and conservatives among respondents and the mix of deserving and undeserving recipients in the applicant pool. Further, philosophers may use empirical data on fairness intuitions about hypothetical societies "as a heuristic in selecting which intuitions to scrutinize most intensely" (Elster, 1995, p. 94), or as a disturbance to the philosopher's reflective equilibrium that can lead to a wider reflective equilibrium. For instance, if the great majority of considered judgments of well-educated participants in a controlled thought experiment indicate that corrective justice operates independently of distributive justice under most conditions (Mitchell & Tetlock, 2006), is this not a finding that philosophers pressing the view that corrective justice depends on distributive justice should take into account?

Our hypothetical society paradigm is not the first attempt to wed political philosophy and experimental design. Most notably, Brickman (1977) and Frohlich and Oppenheimer (1992) approximated Rawls' original position in small-group experiments, with Brickman finding support for Rawls' maximin principle and Frohlich and Oppenheimer finding support for a modified utilitarianism in which utility was maximized above a floor constraint that the worst-off receive a guaranteed minimum income. But we do believe that the hypothetical society paradigm weds political philosophy and experimentation in a unique way that makes the experimental study of interactions between macro-

and micro-level variables more manageable and opens to direct testing a range of questions that would otherwise be subject only to indirect testing. In the next section we describe some of the discoveries made using this unique approach, and in the third section we describe a sampling of controversial questions that the hypothetical society paradigm is uniquely situated to answer.

In sum, an empirical perspective on thought experiments suggests ways to overcome the replication and "idiosyncratic intuition" problems that plague many philosophical thought experiments on justice. A thought-experiment perspective on empirical studies suggests ways to overcome the partiality problems, both with respect to facts and motivations, that plague many empirical studies of justice. The hypothetical society paradigm combines elements of thought experiments and laboratory experiments in an effort to avoid both sets of problems.[5]

Justice in Hypothetical Societies

The benefits of the hypothetical society paradigm are better appreciated by examining the empirical pay-offs of this approach to date. The general descriptive message from the hypothetical society studies is that, above a safety-net floor constraint, normative agreement about distributive justice varies greatly, depending on participants' political ideology and how ambiguous the relationship is between merit and outcomes, but agreement about corrective justice is quite context-insensitive and appears to be less ideology-sensitive than agreement about distributive justice. The general methodological message from these studies is that the hypothetical society paradigm can easily be adapted to address a range of foundational questions.

Most studies using the hypothetical society paradigm examine the justice of societal-level patterns of distribution or rules for distributing resources within a society, and so we begin with findings from these studies on social justice. We first utilized the hypothetical society paradigm to examine how people make macro-level trade-offs between equality and efficiency. Specifically, we described for participants three different societies that differed in their levels of meritocracy, with the correlation between effort and outcome being high, medium, or low, and we displayed income distributions within each society that varied in terms of their equality (income variance) and efficiency (average income) (for a full description of the hypothetical society instructions and stimuli, see the Appendix to Mitchell et al., 1993). Participants were asked to imagine themselves as outside observers to the societies and to make pair-wise comparisons of all possible income distributions for one of the societies, choosing which distribution within each pair was more fair, so that a fairness ranking of income distributions could be derived for each individual within a society and for groups of individuals across all three hypothetical societies. These fairness rankings were then compared to a variety of ideal-type fairness rankings for the income distributions derived from competing theories of distributive justice, namely, egalitarianism (emphasizing equality), utilitarianism (emphasizing efficiency), a Rawlsian maximin principle (emphasizing a quality subject to efficiency constraints), and Boulding's (1962) compromise theory (emphasizing efficiency subject to equality constraints—in which minimum equality is required by government ensuring a safety net for the poor but the goal of prosperity is encouraged by rewarding individual effort above this social safety net).

We found that, consistent with Boulding's compromise theory, both liberals and conservatives were willing to accept considerable inequality of wealth in high meritocracy societies but with the reservation that distributions allowing persons to fall below the poverty line remained unpopular for both ideological groups even in high meritocracy societies (a finding somewhat consistent with choices by Frohlich and Oppenheimer's experimental groups favoring utilitarianism above a floor constraint). However, a majority of liberals *and* conservatives favored a Rawlsian "maximin" approach (Rawls, 1971) to the distribution of wealth in low and moderate meritocracy societies (a finding at odds with Frohlich and Oppenheimer, 1992, and which suggests that implicit assumptions of meritocracy may have driven Frohlich and Oppenheimer's experimental groups to favor a modified utilitarianism). Liberals and conservatives disagree most sharply when the reward structure in the hypothetical society was most ambiguous (i.e., in the moderate meritocracy society), with liberals tending toward greater equality and conservatives toward greater efficiency in such societies. Thus, we found that for both ideological groups beliefs about the level of meritocracy in the hypothetical society moderated value trade-offs, suggesting that ideological disagreements about social justice may arise just as often from different views about the reward structure in society as from value differences (compare Fong, 2004, reporting that target-specific beliefs regarding individual responsibility for economic outcomes drove attitudes toward redistributive policies).

In a subsequent hypothetical society study using similar experimental stimuli (Mitchell et al., 2003), we again found that the perceived level of meritocracy in a society greatly affected judgments about the justice of distributions in that society, with support for greater equality (and less prosperity) strongest at low levels of meritocracy and support for greater prosperity (and less equality) strongest at high levels of meritocracy. In this study, we also manipulated whether participants were judging the fairness of income distributions as if they were alternative *original distributions* for each society versus as if they were *redistributions* of income from an existing distribution in each society. When participants judged *re*distributions (i.e., when it was clear that income would be taken from one group and redistributed to another), both liberals and conservatives became more sensitive to the level of meritocracy in the society and considered redistributions in the moderate and high meritocracy societies to be significantly less fair than equivalent distributions viewed as alternative starting distributions in the same societies. Further, for all three societies, including a "no meritocracy" society where there was no relation between effort and outcomes, participants judged redistributions that led to losses in equality or losses in prosperity to be less fair than when they simply judged the fairness of these distributions as possible "original positions," suggesting a vicarious type of loss aversion at work even in judgments about hypothetical redistributions. This finding that detached observers of imaginary societies found the fact of redistribution normatively significant, and generally distasteful, points out the practical problems faced by politicians who argue for redistributive policies, and points out the need for philosophical theories of distributive justice to consider whether (or when) the different normative concerns primed by distributive versus redistributive mindsets should count in normative theories of justice.

Providing further empirical evidence against a unidimensional conception of distributive justice such as utilitarianism and in favor of a multidimensional conception such as in Boulding's compromise theory, Ordóñez and Mellers (1993) utilized the hypothetical society paradigm to examine whether individuals make trade-offs when judging social fairness. They found that the great majority of participants did make trade-offs between different principles, but the principles that most concerned their participants were need and desert, with participants wanting to ensure a minimum salary for all members of the hypothetical society but also wanting to provide just deserts to those who worked hard in the society; equality and efficiency were of little concern to participants in this study. This study is also interesting because Ordóñez and Mellers asked participants to make judgments about the fairness of societies but also to express preferences for societies as places to live. They found that most participants rated high meritocracy societies as fair, but they preferred to live in societies with high minimum incomes (a finding that applied particularly to participants who self-reported low socioeconomic status). This finding is consistent with the view that the hypothetical society paradigm can be used to elicit both refined justice judgments and preference judgments that may be contaminated by self-interested concerns.

Scott and his colleagues (Scott et al., 2001) employed a variant of the hypothetical society paradigm to compare the role of equality, efficiency, merit, and need in people's judgments of distributive justice, finding that each principle proved influential to some extent except that merit considerations only influenced women's judgments of justice in this study. In a second study, this research group (Michelbach et al., 2003) replicated their finding that individuals try to balance equality, efficiency, need, and merit in their justice judgments, but they failed to replicate the "gender gap" in meritocracy concerns found in their first study. However, this second study did find a "racial gap" in meritocracy concerns, with the nature of equality-efficiency trade-offs by White participants dependent on their merit assumptions but not for racial minorities. Also, Michelbach and colleagues (2003), with a refinement to the hypothetical society paradigm that arguably provided a cleaner test between egalitarianism and Rawls' maximin principle than used in our original study (Mitchell et al., 1993), found that a significant number of participants endorsed the maximin principle, but many other participants deemed merit an important principle and deviated from a strict adherence to the maximin principle.

These studies by Scott and his colleagues support our original finding (Mitchell et al., 1993) that impartial spectators often place considerable weight on equality and the maximin principle when making justice judgments, especially when meritocracy is lacking within a society. However, these studies and their findings of gender and racial gaps in the weight placed on meritocracy in justice judgments also caution against making generalizations about the role of meritocracy in justice judgments and suggest that White men, women, and minorities, who are likely to have had very different experiences with meritocracy in the United States, may have difficulty divesting themselves of their life experiences and placing themselves into the position of impartial observer.

We also used the hypothetical society paradigm to examine the long-standing debate within legal theory on the relationship between corrective justice and distributive justice (Mitchell & Tetlock, 2006).[6] Some legal philosophers claim that corrective justice is parasitic on distributive justice, with a tortfeasor having a duty only to repair a harm imposed on another if the underlying distribution of goods disturbed was just, whereas others claim that corrective justice and distributive justice impose independent moral demands on members of a society that cannot be traded-off against one another. To test the competing views, we constructed distributively just and unjust hypothetical societies—with distributive justice operationalized in terms of meeting needs, equality, and desert—and told participants of intentional and unintentional torts occurring in these societies that upset the distribution of resources in these just and unjust societies. The task for participants was to determine whether justice required the tortfeasor to make the victim of the tort whole, as a norm of corrective justice would require.

We found, somewhat to our surprise in light of much empirical research showing the context-sensitivity of competing norms of justice (see Miller, 1999), that the norm of corrective justice consistently trumped distributive justice norms, even where enforcing the norm of corrective justice would lead to a more unjust distribution of resources in the community (i.e., in a society with no meritocracy, where an undeserving poor man had to compensate an undeserving rich man for harm negligently done by the poor man, leading to greater inequality and greater unmet needs). Indeed, in many conditions there was near unanimity that corrective justice required that the tortfeasor make the victim whole regardless of distributive justice conditions in the society and regardless of whether the victim had insurance that would otherwise cover the harm done.

Only under conditions of extreme injustice in the distribution of resources did a majority of participants deem it just that a tort go unrepaired. Thus, in a hypothetical society in which a racial minority perpetuated its hold over power and wealth through discriminatory policies that kept the racial majority in poverty, a majority of participants felt that justice did not require that an impoverished member of the racially oppressed majority compensate a wealthy member of the racially-oppressive minority for a negligent tort (and with a great majority of this majority being liberals). However, in this same society where the tort was the intentional tort of conversion of a valuable watch owned by the rich man, a majority of participants judged this action out of bounds as a matter of justice even though it arguably is a form of self-help that would lead to a more just distribution of wealth in this racially unjust society (with half of the liberal participants and more than half of the conservative participants judging justice to require compensation for this intentional tort).

The findings of this study are significant in at least two ways. First, they demonstrate the importance of adding corrective justice norms to the list of justice concerns that may be triggered by context (see Konow, 2003), and they illustrate that this norm will be potent, and likely dominant, in contexts that emphasize transactional harms. These findings emphasize the importance placed on personal responsibility for rectifying harms done, at least among our sample of Americans, and cast into doubt the popularity of social compensation schemes for accidents, such as New Zealand's taxpayer-funded, no-fault accident fund. To date, there has been little experimental research into corrective justice, but our findings point out the need to better understand the scope, source, and function of the norm of corrective justice and its relation to the norm of retributive justice, which has received much more empirical attention (e.g., Darley and Pittman, 2003), but both of which have received considerably less attention than distributive and procedural justice.

Second, these findings further illustrate the malleability of the hypothetical society paradigm. Outside of an experimental setting such as that supplied by the hypothetical society paradigm, it would be very difficult to conduct an empirical test of the different theoretical positions on the relationship between norms of distributive and corrective justice. And unlike much analysis within political philosophy, which argues for what societies should do to be moral and just, conceptual analysis within the law is concerned with making sense of why legal systems operate as they do (e.g., J. Coleman, 2001). Thus, empirical studies such as ours may shed considerable light on the psychological forces that give rise to or sustain a norm of corrective justice that ultimately finds expression within the law.

Although we believe that there is much to gain from using the hypothetical society paradigm to study judgments of justice in all their richness, and our study shows that this paradigm can shed light on more than just judgments about social justice (Mitchell & Tetlock, 2006), there are also other promising applications of this method. We discuss a sampling of these in the next section.

Future Directions

We divide this final section into two subsections. The first focuses on the challenges of teasing apart the complex mixtures of factual and value differences underlying disagreements on foundational policy issues, including: the criteria that society should use in judging the degree to which equality of opportunity has been satisfied and in deciding what, if any, additional policy interventions are warranted to promote equality of opportunity; the criteria that society should use in judging the wisdom of entering into trade-liberalization agreements that facilitate the free flow of capital, people, goods, and services across national borders; the criteria that society should use in judging whether it has struck the right balance among competing stakeholders in formulating rules for corporate governance. In pursuing these lines of inquiry, we suspect it will also be possible to bring into sharper focus how these policy debates are likely to evolve in response to new evidence (requiring the updating of our beliefs about the facts) and in response to shifting perceptions of societal needs (requiring updating of moral-political values).

The second subsection explores the potential of the hypothetical society paradigm to distinguish competing psychological theories of justice, in particular, those theories that we designate here as transparent-functionalist theories (which posit that the motives and goals the people openly endorse are the key drivers of their justice judgments) and subterranean-motivational theories (which posit that people are largely or entirely unaware of the functionalist motives driving their justice judgments).

Policy Controversies

(1) The Links Between Intergenerational Mobility and Meritocracy

In the first-generation of hypothetical society research, we were content with simple operational definitions of meritocracy that highlighted the relative causal importance of hard work versus luck in determining income. But many people find it difficult to view a society as meritocratic if the children of the relatively poor have virtually no chance of rising into a higher socio-economic class whereas the children of the relatively wealthy are virtually guaranteed of remaining in that class (Rawls, 1971; Fishkin, 1983). It follows that social science research on intergenerational mobility has relatively high political stakes. As we saw in the earlier hypothetical-society studies, virtually everyone moves in a more egalitarian or leftward direction on income transfers when they believe they are confronted with a low meritocracy society.

This raises an interesting question of applied cognitive-dissonance theory: what should one do if one is a conservative in early 21st century America who learns that the best scientific estimates now are that: (1) inequality is growing in the United States (the distance between the economic cellar and economic penthouse); and (2) it is becoming increasingly difficult for people to rise from poverty to prosperity in one or even two generations (more difficult than it used to be and more difficult than it is in Western Europe or Canada)?

In the real world, there is an obvious and, from a conservative perspective, plausible dissonance reduction strategy, namely, to argue that richer children have better prospects than poorer children because they have genetic endowments better suited to facilitate success in competitive market economies (more intelligent, higher energy levels, optimism, etc.). The list of possible DNA suspects is long so it is difficult to rule out this hypothesis with great confidence in the real world (which may be one reason why some egalitarians simply prefer to suppress such arguments with political correctness codes). It is easy, however, to rule out this alternative explanation in the hypothetical society paradigm: we need simply to stipulate that there are no genetically heritable differences in abilities or personalities or temperaments across social strata. We suspect that this stipulation would drive many conservatives to an alternative dissonance reduction strategy: namely, to argue that richer children have better prospects because their parents do a better job bringing them up and inculcating the character traits conducive to success in competitive market economies. Again, it is difficult to rule out this hypothesis in the real world but it is easy to do so in the hypothetical society paradigm. We can simply stipulate that rich and poor parents raise their children in remarkably similar ways.

We have now narrowed the range of plausible explanations for social inequality in the hypothetical society to two salient candidates: better schools for the rich and better networking opportunities for the rich. We suspect that some hard-core conservatives will still resist egalitarian policy interventions designed to improve schooling opportunities and networking opportunities for the poor (e.g., generous vouchers and affirmative action incentives). These conservatives might argue that previous generations of parents must have worked hard to ensure that their descendants would have advantages—and it is a bad idea to destabilize that societal expectation. But we also suspect that many moderate conservatives at this juncture will make some policy concesssions—and accept the need for egalitarian interventions of some form.

Of course, the hypothetical society paradigm can also be used to subject liberals to various forms of cognitive-dissonance torture. For instance, what should one do if one is a liberal confronted with a hypothetical society in which: (1) inequality, the distance between the economic cellar and economic penthouse, is large and growing; (2) there is, however, a very high safety net which guarantees that even the poorest of the poor receive very high quality schooling and medical care that is not appreciably different from that available to the wealthy; (3) there is virtually no intergenerational mobility but the best scientific evidence is that this is because children from wealthier families have genetic endowments better adapted for success in competitive market economies; (4) raising taxes any more on the wealthy will have disincentive effects that slow economic growth and, in the long run, reduce the absolute standard of living of the poor more than that of the wealthy; and (5) new recombinant DNA technologies make it possible to level the genetic playing field for the poor. We might call this the Herrnstein scenario in which a true meritocracy perpetuates itself genetically—and the only viable policy intervention becomes swallowing a pair of bitter ideological pills for egalitarians: acknowledging the importance of genetic determinants of social class and abandoning a visceral distaste for "eugenics."

The potential experimental manipulations of "fact situations" are obviously numerous. If we put aside manipulations of the heritability of intelligence and character traits, and of the availability of currently-science-fiction technologies to equalize opportunity at the level of DNA, we suspect that much of the policy tension will ultimately focus on the value trade-offs between family autonomy and social equality. Egalitarian philosophers—from Rousseau to Marx to Cohen—have long recognized that, as long as the family is the social unit primarily responsible for socializing children and as long as some families are (holding income constant) prepared to make much greater sacrifices to ensure the success of their children, it is logically impossible to achieve equality of opportunity. Socializing the task of socializing children becomes an attractive option from this egalitarian point of view—and many socialist governments have indeed pursued this "it-takes-a-village" option (from Israeli kibbutzim to Scandinavian day care to Chinese communes). Conservative and libertarian philosophers suspect that transferring the task of socializing children to the state is a dangerous step toward totalitarianism and collective mind control. Rejecting a prominent state role in childcare is an equally easy choice from these points of view.

We suspect that most people are deeply torn by this value conflict and will oscillate somewhat erratically between favoring family autonomy versus equality of opportunity as a function of horror stories of child neglect and abuse (favoring the left) and horror stories of state mind control and parents losing parental rights for "trivial" reasons (favoring the right). Building on earlier work on the value pluralism model (Tetlock, 1986; Tetlock et al., 1996), our prediction would be that people will develop integratively complex policy solutions to the dilemma (solutions that acknowledge and reason through trade-offs) only to the degree that simple modes of dissonance resolution have been blocked off in the hypothetical societies. These simpler modes of dissonance reduction include challenging the "fact situation" posited in the hypothetical society (e.g., "that is just too absurd to contemplate") and the classic spreading of the alternatives response (denial of weaker political value and bolstering of the stronger value). Previous research also suggests the importance of blocking off decision evasion tactics such as obfuscation, buck-passing, and procrastination by communicating clearly to subjects that they are accountable for taking a stand. If integratively complex policy reasoning is one's ideal outcome from a process of deliberative democracy (Fishkin, 1992), this would be how to achieve it via the hypothetical society paradigm.

(2) The Links Between Absolute and Relative Wealth Within and Across Societies

In the first generation of hypothetical society research, we were content to rely on crude operational definitions of the poverty line, assuming that everyone shared an understanding of what poverty was and that poverty was bad. What counts as poor, however, in one society at one point in history may count as quite wealthy for that same society at previous point in history or for other societies at the same point in history. Middle-class societies in sub-Saharan Africa in the early 21st century have per capita incomes substantially lower (even using a purchasing-power-parity standard) than the average factory worker in Western Europe or the United States.

For orthodox free-market theorists, the solution is surgically simple: the logic of comparative advantage in international trade holds that the surest method of reducing large income gaps across societies is by promoting the free flow of goods, services, capital, and human beings across borders. If rich countries would quit erecting protectionist barriers that prevent poor people from working their way out of poverty, there would be much less poverty in the world today.

Of course, this surgically simple solution can be painful. International trade can produce major dislocations within societies. American blue-collar workers who were accustomed to earning US$25 per hour run the risk of losing their jobs to Mexican workers who are rapidly becoming as efficient and were glad to make US$5 per hour—and these Mexican workers, in turn, run the risk of losing their jobs to Chinese workers who were glad to make US$2 per hour.

How should one respond if one is an egalitarian who is asked to judge the acceptability of a trade agreement that will increase inequality within one's own wealthy society (because the pay checks of one's "own" working-class are in decline) and even increase inequality within poor societies (because the well-off in those societies gain more rapidly than do the poor) but also raise the absolute standard of living of the poorest people in poor societies as well as decrease inequality between societies (by raising the overall per capita income of poorer societies closer to that of wealthier societies)? Much depends on the degree to which one is a cosmopolitan egalitarian, who is concerned more with inequality on a global scale, versus a parochial egalitarian, who is concerned solely with inequality within one's own society. Much also depends on the escape routes one is offered from this dissonance-inducing problem (escape routes such as reserving some of the wealth generated by free trade for transfer payments to help those in one's own wealthy society who are most adversely affected by free trade).

The maximum-value-conflict dilemmas probably take somewhat different forms for more conservative observers—those who are less concerned about equality (either within or across borders) and more concerned about national sovereignty and relative national power. For instance, how should one respond if one is a conservative confronted by a trade agreement that will increase the GDP of one's own society by 2% but increase the GDP of the other society by 5%? Much may depend here on whether that other society is perceived to be a potential geopolitical threat (Herrmann et al., 2001). Or how should conservatives respond when confronted by patterns of labor migration into one's own country that increase net wealth but threaten the traditional ethnic or racial or religious or linguistic identity of the society?

Again, it is worth emphasizing that the hypothetical society paradigm is uniquely well-suited to disentangle causality in these types of controversies. It is too easy for policy advocates in the real world to make up facts that obscure the underlying trade-offs: "No, those migrants are not making our society wealthier" or "No, a trade agreement will not really make our society wealthier," and so on. It is also worth emphasizing that we would expect people to engage in the hard mental work of crafting integratively complex trade-offs only when we have successfully foreclosed all of the simpler dissonance-reduction options, such as redefining the facts, spreading the alternatives by bolstering and denial, and slipping into decision-evasion mode.

(3) The Links Between Corporate Governance, Profits, and Other Social Objectives

Corporations can be viewed as mini-societies of their own. Corporations also raise unique challenges of governance because of the complex principal-agency relationships connecting the formal owners of the corporation, the principals or stockholders, and the agents responsible for the daily operations of the corporation, the top executive team and the employees. The shareholders obviously want to maximize their return on their investments whereas the top executive team obviously wants as large a fraction of the profits as possible for themselves (either directly via salary and stock options or indirectly via managerial perks such as lavish offices, chauffeurs, and private planes).

The now conventional solution to this principal-agent problem—formally articulated by Jensen and Meckling (1976)—is stock options. By linking managerial compensation to the price of the stock—the same index that determines returns to shareholders—the idea was to transform an adversarial relationship into a collaborative one. But, the devil as always lurks in the details and much hinges on how such stock-option agreements are written. If the agreements are written by members of Boards of Directors who are cronies of the CEO, there is a good chance that the agreements will guarantee massive rewards for relatively mediocre performance (e.g., Khurana and Pick, 2005).

The hypothetical society paradigm can be used to explore how tolerant people are of inequality within the corporate world under various business and regulatory conditions. One libertarian reaction is that any pay package is acceptable as long as it is a contract freely entered into by the shareholders (or their representatives on the Board of Directors) and the CEO. But even some libertarians have difficulty when the corporation is functioning under a regulatory regime that makes shareholder democracy difficult and the extraction of large managerial rents easy. (Hard-line libertarians tend to be unrelenting: they argue that if someone does not like the ground rules in one capitalist economy, move on to another.)

To create maximum value conflict for libertarians and many conservatives, one would describe corporations in hypothetical societies that have created regulatory ground rules that favor managers over shareholders and one would describe pay packages that reward CEOs lavishly even for relatively poorer mediocre performance. These would be ideal conditions for pressuring anti-regulation observers to make integratively complex concessions and trade-offs in response to pro-regulation arguments. To create maximum value conflict for egalitarians, the hypothetical societies would need to stipulate that the CEOs make enormous amounts of money only when they are playing a key causal role in generating massive wealth for the shareholders and that significant amounts of that wealth trickle down to the employees, that the ratio between highest-paid and lowest paid workers is staggeringly large (say, 500:1) and growing, and that these super-incentives for top executives are indeed necessary causes for stimulating rapid-based entrepreneurial growth that makes pay increases for the lowest-paid possible. These would be ideal conditions for pressuring critics of CEO compensation to make integratively complex concessions in response to anti-regulation arguments.[7]

Exploring Further Theoretical Implications

Skeptics of the hypothetical society paradigm could argue that it is equipped to tap into only relatively superficial psychological processes to which people have ready conscious access and which people are not embarrassed about revealing. The skeptics are correct that we have thus far tended to take the political values and intuitive philosophies of our respondents at face value. If respondents say that they are Rawlsian egalitarians or Nozickian libertarians and respond in that spirit to our instruments, we classify them accordingly. These ideal-type belief-system models are best classified as transparent-motivational theories that make the working assumption that people are intuitive political philosophers making good-faith efforts to understand the world around them and reach defensible conclusions about what constitutes a fair social order. From the skeptics' perspective, we have yet to seriously explore the possibility that motives to which our respondents do not have conscious access (or might be embarrassed to admit) are systematically influencing judgments of macro-social fairness.

It is not difficult, however, to adapt the hypothetical society paradigm to test less transparent, more subterranean-motivational theories that posit that people have very limited access to the true functionalist forces driving their judgments. Over the last century and a half, behavioral and social scientists have advanced an extraordinarily ingenious array of such theories. We would include under this rubric the work of psychodynamic scholars who have argued that insecure authoritarian personalities derived psychic gratification from exercising symbolic dominance over those below them in the societal pecking order; the work of social-dominance theorists who have drawn on evolutionary and other speculation to reach a strikingly similar conclusion about high scorers on their measure of social-dominance orientation; and the work of system-justification theorists who have posited a deep-rooted psychological tendency to justify existing status hierarchies (a tendency that there's a marked family resemblance to the classic Marxist notion of false consciousness).

In our view, the hypothetical society paradigm is the optimal context for testing the relative merits of more transparent-motivational and more subterranean-motivational theories. It is instructive, for instance, to examine the deep indeterminacy problems that arise in testing a formulation such as system-justification in the real world. We repeatedly run into a problem that one person's reason for holding a belief (say, about social-class differences in intelligence) can often be viewed by others as a mere rationalization (say, as a means of justifying existing inequality—or, to flip it around, as a means of justifying proposals to redistribute income). Commenting on indeterminacy problems of this nature, Rubin and Hewstone (2004) note that system-justification theorists should not get explanatory credit for phenomena, such as attributional favoritism toward higher-status groups, that could simply be the result of people observing depressing patterns of covariation between group membership and outcomes in society at large (e.g., the higher levels of crime, family breakdown, drug abuse, school failure, etc., among the poor). To use their analogy to a football game, do we feel comfortable concluding that members of the losing team who attribute their defeat to their own shortcomings are guilty of outgroup favoritism and system justification? Or should we conclude that they are engaging in highly adaptive forms of self-criticism?

The list of reason-rationalization indeterminacy problems is a long one. For instance, if one believes that prosperity and economic efficiency require creating incentives for hard work and risk-taking (incentives that inevitably create inequality), does that belief count as evidence for the operation of a system-justification motive (one's belief that the wealthy are being rewarded for merit) or as evidence simply that one understands a fundamental scientific principle of economics? If one believes that a social system with stable, secure property rights is essential for promoting prosperity and economic efficiency, does that count as evidence of my desire for unequal relations among social groups or does it count as evidence that one has drawn correct lessons from history—at least according to Douglass North (1981, 2005)? If one believes that intelligence, the capacity to delay need gratification, and other positively charged traits conducive to economic success are found more often among the economically successful, does that count as evidence of system-justifying cognition or as evidence that I am in touch with sociological reality?

To the best of our knowledge, no social psychologist has yet discovered a method of answering these questions by asking people questions about the social world they actually inhabit. There are simply too many sources of uncertainty, too many historical confounds, to permit investigators to draw strong functionalist conclusions about whose opinions are serving subterranean versus more transparent motivational forces.

If we want to escape these indeterminacy dilemmas, we need to explore human judgment in imaginary social worlds that we can experimentally manipulate in precise, conceptually targeted ways.

Using the hypothetical society paradigm, it should be possible to answer questions of the following sorts:

1 Are people so committed to defending traditional status hierarchies that they would rather preside over a shrinking economic pie to which their group continues to enjoy a high priority claim over expanding an economic pie to which their group enjoys a lower priority claim (but is still, in absolute terms, better off)? If so, we should find that high scorers on measures of system justification and social dominance and perhaps authoritarianism should be especially likely to reject societal reforms that simultaneously make everyone wealthier and reduce inequality and blur traditional status distinctions.

2 Do people become more punitive toward norm violators not simply as a function of the severity of the violation of the collective conscience of society (as Durkheimian theories suggest; see Tetlock et al., 2007) but also as a function of the degree to which norm violations destabilize existing patterns of social dominance? If the latter, we should expect stronger activation of the punitive prosecutorial mindset when people are led to believe (holding absolute amount of crime constant) that patterns of criminal behavior are breaking down the boundaries between the rich and poor, as opposed to having no net effect or even perpetuating them.

3 Does tolerance of inequality reflect conscious consideration of existing societal circumstances or unconscious system-justifying motives? How much do people feel that they should change their minds when they learn not just about the distribution of objective wealth in a society but also about the distribution of subjective well-being (the extent to which people

feel they are living fulfilling and happy lives)? One hypothesis—which we view as being in the spirit of social-dominance and system-justification theories—is that observers, especially those who score highly on measures of social dominance and system justification, will latch onto evidence that the poor are as happy as the rich (or even happier) as grounds for dismissing the need for redistribution. An alternative hypothesis—which we prefer— is that support for redistribution may indeed fall when people learn that the poor are as happy as, or more happy than, the well-off but that this shift in policy preferences should not be treated as a mere rhetorical cloak for social-dominance or system-justification goals but rather as based on a reasoned reappraisal of the degree to which:

a the poor have serious unsatisfied basic human needs,
a the rich have privileged access to resources that greatly enhance human experience,
a the poor may have opted for lower incomes in order to gain more leisure or family time, and
a the rich may have opted for higher income and the sacrifice of leisure and family time.

These questions are unanswerable in real-world debates because it is so easy for advocates—motivated reasoners that they are (see Kunda, 1999)—to invent facts that conceal potential trade-offs and double standards (an invention process that, if it is to serve its subterranean-motivational function, needs to occur automatically, outside of awareness). But these questions become answerable in the hypothetical society paradigm because it is so difficult for advocates to conceal the same trade-offs and double standards in a world in which all of the key factual parameters have been pre-specified by experimental fiat. The hypothetical society paradigm then becomes the platform for previously impossible conversations between theorists. For instance, if transparent-motivational theories outperform subterranean-motivational theories in the starkly simplistic hypothetical society environment, subterranean-motivational theorists can argue that more socially undesirable motivational forces only come into play when people have rationalization covers (or attributional ambiguity). We do not automatically dismiss this argument as a desperate patch-up operation of a degenerating research program. This theoretical defense may be defensible—and the best way to determine whether this is so is by gradually adding complexity to the hypothetical society paradigm so that we can identify more precisely exactly how much attributional ambiguity we need to create for subterranean-motivational theories to gain explanatory traction.

To put our argument in a nutshell, the hypothetical society paradigm reveals a paradox: we have to step into imaginary social worlds if we want to understand how we understand our own social world.

Notes

1 Some political philosophers and political theorists do rely on empirical research to develop their theories of justice. For instance, Miller (1999) relies heavily on empirical studies of justice, and Elster (1992) relies heavily on actual practices of institutions.

2 We speak here in terms of laboratory studies, but with innovations in web-based surveys, the hypothetical society paradigm could also be employed in large-scale experimental surveys using the Internet (see Skitka & Sargis, 2006), or in more traditional questionnaire surveys (e.g., Jasso and Opp, 1997, conducted a factorial questionnaire survey with hypothetical vignettes). In simplified form, hypothetical society manipulations may also be candidates for inclusion in telephone surveys.

3 In fact, the inspiration for the hypothetical society paradigm was Rawls' impartial-reasoning device, the "veil of ignorance," which seeks to "nullify the effects of specific contingencies which put men at odds and tempt them to exploit social and natural circumstances to their own advantage" (Rawls, 1971, p. 136). Behind the veil, "no one knows his place in society, his class position or social status; nor does he know his fortune in the distribution of natural assets and abilities, his intelligence and strength, and the like" (Rawls, 1971, p. 137). Because we cannot divest participants of the self-knowledge required by a true veil of ignorance, we chose instead to remove narrow self-interests as an influence on judgments by having participants disinterestedly evaluate hypothetical societies.

4 Cooper (2005) makes this point in the context of thought experiments involving trade-offs between avoiding torture to oneself versus avoiding harm to others, where what we seek to know is not what the tortured person would actually do but what a rational person should do in such a situation: "The judgments of people contemplating what should be done under torture are more reliable than the judgments of people actually being tortured" (p. 344).

5 A closely related device for studying justice judgments is the vignette study (e.g., Bukszar & Knetsch, 1997; Konow, 2003). Vignette studies typically ask experimental or survey participants to judge whether justice occurred in some realistic but imaginary event (e.g., pay distribution in a hypothetical work setting). The advantage of a vignette study over a hypothetical society study is that the former possesses greater external validity. The disadvantage of the vignette study relative to the hypothetical society study is that, because the participant may find the vignette more realistic and familiar, the participant may find it more difficult to imagine or accept the stipulated facts and detach herself from the situation about which she is supposed to be an impartial judge and the researcher has less freedom when creating hypothetical situations.

6 Corrective justice provides, roughly, that a person who wrongfully causes harm to another has a duty to repair the harm (see Forde-Mazrui, 2004). The concept of corrective justice goes back to Aristotle and his distinction between justice in transactions, or arithmetic forms of justice, and justice in overall distributions within a polity, or geometric forms of justice (see Weinrib, 2002).

7 The questions we explore in the text are meant only to illustrate the types of policy controversies that may be explored using the hypothetical society paradigm. Other examples include the criteria that society should use in judging how far to take advances in biotechnology that have the potential to transform the nature of human nature and how society should deal with intergenerational externalities such as global warming and deficit spending. Although we have yet to collect data on most of these questions, one question that we have explored in some pilot research is the degree to which people do or do not look hard at surface appearances when

looking harder has the potential either to reinforce or undercut their belief systems (and either make trade-offs easier or harder). For instance, if one is a libertarian who is motivated to believe that corporate capitalism is functioning as it should, then one should be quite willing to take at face value the information that CEO compensation is linked to a stock option plan whereas if one is in egalitarian who is motivated to perceive corporate capitalism as malign, then one should be more suspicious of the stock option plan (suspecting cronyism and corruption).

References

Ackerman, B. A. (1980). *Social Justice in the Liberal State*. New Haven, CT: Yale University Press.

Babcock, L., G. Loewenstein, S. Issacharoff, & C. Camerer. (1995). Biased judgments of fairness in bargaining. *American Economic Review, 85*, 1337–1343.

Bar-Hillel, M., & M. Yaari. (1993). Judgments of distributive justice. In B. A. Mellers, & J. Baron (Eds.), *Psychological Perspectives on Justice*. Cambridge: Cambridge University Press, 55–86.

Barber, B. R. (1975). Justifying justice: Problems of psychology, politics and measurement in Rawls. In N. Daniels (Ed.), *Reading Rawls*. Stanford, CA: Stanford University Press, 292–318.

Boulding, K. E. (1962). Social justice in social dynamics. In R. B. Brandt (Ed.), *Social Justice*. Englewood Cliffs, NJ: Prentice Hall, 73–92.

Brickman, P. (1977). Preference for inequality. *Sociometry, 40*, 303–310.

Bukszar, E., & J. L. Knetsch. (1997). Fragile redistribution choices behind a veil of ignorance. *Journal of Risk and Uncertainty, 14*, 63–74.

Bunge, M. (1961). The weight of simplicity in the construction and assaying of scientific theories. *Philosophy of Science, 28*, 120–149.

Christiansen, N. D., & H. Lavine. (1997). Need-efficiency trade-offs in the allocation of resources: Ideological and attributional differences in public aid decision making. *Social Justice Research, 10*, 289–310.

Coleman, J. (2001). *The Practice of Principle*. New York: Oxford University Press.

Coleman, S. (2000). Thought experiments and personal identity. *Philosophical Studies, 98*, 53–69.

Cooper, R. (2005). Thought experiments. *Metaphilosophy, 36*, 328–347.

Daniels, N. (1996). *Justice and Justification*. Cambridge: Cambridge University Press.

Darley, J. M., & T. S. Pittman. (2003). The psychology of compensatory and retributive justice. *Personality and Social Psychology Review, 7*, 324–336.

Dennett, D. C. (2003). Who's on first? Heterophenomenology explained. *Journal of Consciousness Studies, 10*, 19–30.

Elster, J. (1992). *Local Justice*. Cambridge: Cambridge University Press.

Elster, J. (1995). The empirical study of justice. In D. Miller, & M. Walzer (Eds.), *Pluralism, Justice, and Equality*. Oxford: Oxford University Press, 81–98.

Epley, N., & E. M. Caruso. (2004). Egocentric ethics. *Social Justice Research, 17*, 171–187.

Ferrie, J. P. (2005). The end of American exceptionalism? Mobility in the United States since 1850. *Journal of Economic Perspectives, 19*, 199–215.

Fishkin, J. S. (1983). *Justice, Equal Opportunity, and the Family*. New Haven, CT: Yale University Press.

Fishkin, J. S. (1991). *Democracy and Deliberation*. New Haven, CT: Yale University Press.

Fishkin, J. S. (1992). *The Dialogue of Justice*. New Haven, CT: Yale University Press.

Fong, C. M. (2004). *Which Beliefs Matter for Redistributive Politics? Target-specific Versus General Beliefs About the Causes of Income*. Unpublished manuscript.

Fong, C. M. (2005). *Prospective Mobility, Fairness, and the Demand for Redistribution*. Unpublished manuscript.

Fong, C. M., S. Bowles, & H. Gintis. (2006). Strong reciprocity and the welfare state. In J. Mercier-Ythier, S. Kolm, and L. A. Gerard-Varet, *Handbook on the Economics of Giving, Reciprocity and Altruism*. Amsterdam: Elsevier.

Forde-Mazrui, K. (2004). Taking conservatives seriously: A moral justification for affirmative action and reparations. *California Law Review, 92*, 683–754.

Frohlich, N., & J. A. Oppenheimer. (1992). *Choosing Justice: An Experimental Approach to Ethical Theory*. Berkeley, CA: University of California Press.

Frohlich, N., & J. A. Oppenheimer. (1997). A role for structured observations in ethics. *Social Justice Research, 10*, 1–21.

Frohlich, N., & J. A. Oppenheimer. (2000). How people reason about ethics. In A. Lupia, M.D. McCubbins, & S. L. Popkin, *Elements of Reason*. Cambridge: Cambridge University Press.

Greenberg, J. (1983). Overcoming egocentric bias in perceived fairness through self-awareness. *Social Psychology Quarterly, 46*, 152–156.

Herrmann, R., P. E.Tetlock, & M. Diascro. (2001). How Americans think about trade: Resolving conflicts among money, power, and principles. *International Studies Quarterly, 45*, 191–218.

Jasso, G., & K. D. Opp. (1997). Probing the character of norms: A factorial survey of the norms of political action. *American Sociological Review*, 947–964.

Jensen, M. C., & W. H. Meckling. (1976). Theory of the firm, managerial behavior, agency costs and capital structure. *Journal of Financial Economics, 3*, 305–360.

Kahneman, D., & A. B. Krueger. (2006). Developments in the measurement of subjective well-being. *Journal of Economic Perspectives, 20*, 3–24.

Khurana, R., & K. Pick. (2005). The social nature of boards. *Brooklyn Law Review, 70*, 1259–1285.

Kluegel, J. R., G. Csepeli, T. Kolosi, A. Orkney, & M. Nemenyi. (1995). Accounting for the rich and the poor: Existential justice in comparative perspective. In J. R. Kluegel, D.S. Mason, and B. Wegener (Eds.), *Social Justice and Political Change: Public Opinion in Capitalist and Post-communist States*. New York: Aldine de Gruyter, 179–207.

Knobe, J. (2004). What is experimental philosophy? *The Philosophers' Magazine, 28*.

Konow, J. (2003). Which is the fairest one of all? A positive analysis of justice theories. *Journal of Economic Literature, 41*, 1188–1239.

Konow, J. (2005). Blind spots: The effects of information and stakes on fairness bias and dispersion. *Social Justice Research, 18*, 349–390.

Kunda, Z. (1999). *Social Cognition*. Cambridge, MA: MIT Press.

Lerner, M. J. (1974). The justice motive: Equity and parity among children. *Journal of Personality and Social Psychology, 29*, 539–550.

Lerner, M.J. (2003). The justice motive: Where social psychologists found it, why they lost it, and why they may not find it again. *Personality and Social Psychology Review, 7*, 388–399.

Liebig, S. (2001). Lessons from philosophy? Interdisciplinary justice research and two classes of justice judgments. *Social Justice Research*, *14*, 265–287.

Machery, E., R. Mallon, S. Nichols, & S.P. Stich. (2004). Semantics, cross-cultural style. *Cognition*, *92*, B1–B12.

Messick, D. M., & K. P. Sentis. (1983). Fairness, preference, and fairness biases. In D. M. Messick, & K. S. Cook (Eds.), *Equity Theory*. New York: Praeger, 61–94.

Michelbach, P., J. T. Scott, R. E. Matland, & B. Bornstein. (2003). Doing justice to Rawls: An experimental study of norms concerning income distribution. *American Journal of Political Science*, *47*, 523–539.

Miller, D. (1999). *Principles of Social Justice*. Cambridge, MA: Harvard University Press.

Miller, D. T. (2001). Disrespect and the experience of injustice. *Annual Review of Psychology*, *52*, 527–553.

Mitchell, G., & P. E. Tetlock. (2006). An empirical inquiry into the relation of corrective justice to distributive justice. *Journal of Empirical Legal Studies*, *3*, 421–466.

Mitchell, G., P. E. Tetlock, B. A. Mellers, & L. D. Ordóñez. (1993). Judgments of social justice: Compromises between equality and efficiency. *Journal of Personality and Social Psychology*, *65*, 629–639.

Mitchell, G., P. E. Tetlock, D. G. Newman, & J. S. Lerner. (2003). Experiments behind the veil: Structural influences on judgments of social justice. *Political Psychology*, *24*, 519–547.

North, D. C. (1981). *Structure and Change in Economic History*. New York: Norton.

North, D. C. (2005). *Understanding the Process of Economic Change*. Princeton, NJ: Princeton University Press.

Nozick, R. (1974). *Anarchy, State, and Utopia*. New York: Basic Books.

Okin, S. M. (1989). *Justice, Gender, and the Family*. New York: Basic Books.

Ordóñez, L. D., & Mellers, B. A. (1993). Tradeoffs in fairness and preference judgments. In B. A. Mellers and J. Baron (Eds.), *Psychological Perspectives on Justice: Theory and Applications*. New York: Cambridge University Press.

Pillutla, M. M., & J. K. Murnighan. (2003). Fairness in bargaining. *Social Justice Research*, *16*, 241–262.

Rawls, J. (1971). *A Theory of Justice*. Cambridge, MA: Belknap.

Rubin, M., & M. Hewstone. (2004). Social identity, system justification, and social dominance: Commentary on Reicher, Jost et al., & Sidanius et al. *Political Psychology*, *25*, 823–844.

Scott, J. T., R. E. Matland, P. A. Michelbach, & B. H. Bornstein. (2001). Just deserts: An experimental study of distributive justice norms. *American Journal of Political Science*, *45*, 749–767.

Skitka, L. J. (1999). Ideological and attributional boundaries on public compassion: Reactions to individuals and communities affected by a natural disaster. *Personality and Social Psychology Bulletin*, *25*, 792–808.

Skitka, L. J. & E. G. Sargis. (2006). The internet as psychological laboratory. *Annual Review of Psychology*, *57*, 529–555.

Skitka, L. J., & P. E. Tetlock. (1992). Allocating scarce resources: A contingency model of distributive justice. *Journal of Experimental Social Psychology*, *28*, 491–522.

Skitka, L. J., & P. E. Tetlock. (1993). Of ants and grasshoppers: The political psychology of allocating public assistance. In B. A. Mellers, & J. Baron (Eds.), *Psychological Perspectives on Justice*. Cambridge: Cambridge University Press, 205–233.

Sorenson, R. A. (1992). *Thought experiments*. Oxford: Oxford University Press.

Souder, L. (2003). What are we to think about thought experiments? *Argumentation, 17*, 203–217.

Swift, A. (1999). Public opinion and political philosophy: The relation between social-scientific and philosophical analyses of distributive justice. *Ethical Theory and Moral Practice, 2*, 337–363.

Tetlock, P. E. (1986). A value pluralism model of ideological reasoning. *Journal of Personality and Social Psychology, 50*, 819–827.

Tetlock, P. E., & C. McGuire. (1986). Cognitive perspectives on foreign policy. In R. White (Ed.), *Psychology and the Prevention of Nuclear War*. New York: Free Press, 255–273.

Tetlock, P. E., R. Peterson, & J. Lerner. (1996). Revising the value pluralism model: Incorporating social content and context postulates. In C. Seligman, J. Olson, and M. Zanna (Eds.), *Ontario Symposium on Social and Personality Psychology: Values*. Hillsdale, NJ: Erlbaum, 255–273.

Tetlock, P. E., P. Visser, R. Singh, M. Polifroni, A. Scott, S.B. Elson, P. Mazzocco, & P. Rescober. (2007). People as intuitive prosecutors: The impact of social control motives on attributions of responsibility. *Journal of Experimental Social Psychology, 43*, 195–209.

Weinrib, E. J. (2002) Corrective justice in a nutshell. *University of Toronto Law Journal, 52*, 349–356.

4

IDENTITY THREATS AND IDENTITY REPAIRS

How Leaders Construe and Respond to Identity-Threatening Predicaments[1]

Roderick M. Kramer

> The president saw the various attacks on him as part of a vast plot by intellectual snobs to destroy a president who was representative of the man on the street ... he perceived himself as a fighter – involved in mortal battle with the forces of evil.
>
> Admiral Elmo Zumwalt, Chief of Naval Operations, describing President Richard Nixon's perceptions of the attacks on his presidency (cited in Ambrose, 1991, p. 285)

The portrayal of leaders as "sensemakers" whose task it is to help both organizational members and external observers interpret events that impact the perceived credibility, legitimacy, and authority of an organization or its leadership has gained considerable currency in recent years (e.g., Ginzel, Kramer, & Sutton, 1993; Haslam, Reicher, & Platow, 2010; Hickey & Essid, 2014; Kramer & Lewicki, 2010; Podolny, Khurana & Hill-Popper, 2005; Sutton & Kramer, 1990; Weick, 1993). Such perspectives can be viewed as contemporary versions of a long tradition in leadership theory and research that construes leaders as "managers of meaning" (Meindl, Ehrlich, & Dukerich, 1985; Pfeffer, 1981). In an early and influential articulation of this perspective, Weick and Daft (1983) went so far as to assert that the primary job of the organizational leader is "to interpret, not to get the work of the organization done" (pp. 90–91).

While perhaps hyperbolic, Weick and Daft's claim serves to remind us that perceptions of leaders' abilities to explain their own performance or that of their organization often matters as much as the actual performances themselves. Leaders are expected to not only make decisions that benefit their organizations, but also are expected to be adept at explaining and justifying those decisions.

Yet, successfully maintaining positive images of their leadership can be difficult and problematic because of the high levels of scrutiny directed at many leaders today (Sutton & Galunic, 1996). Leaders find their decisions endlessly dissected and debated by various organizational stakeholders and interpreters. As Pfeffer (1992) succinctly observed, "To be in power is to be watched more closely, and this surveillance affords one the luxury of few mistakes" (p. 302).

When leaders do make mistakes—or are perceived to have made mistakes—they are likely to find their leadership ability or competence called into question. Indeed, the list of public and business leaders who have recently found themselves under the harsh limelight of public scrutiny is a long and impressive one. Presidents Barack Obama, George Bush and William Clinton frequently found the White House to be a fishbowl, surrounded by a relentlessly intrusive and demanding press driven to feed 24/7 news cycles. Similarly, JPMorgan Chase's Jamie Dimon, Microsoft's Steve Balmer and Apple's Tim Cook are just a few examples of business leaders repeatedly forced to defend their credibility and competence, or the wisdom of their decisions. Whether coming from within their organizations or from external constituencies without, such assaults on leaders' authority and legitimacy constitute potentially severe *identity-threatening predicaments*. In other words, to the extent such events call into question central aspects of a leader's desired sense of self, they constitute a threat to that coveted self-conception.

A primary aim of the present chapter is to more systematically explore two important questions pertaining to the impact of identity-threatening predicaments on leaders. First, how do leaders *construe* identity-threatening predicaments? Secondly, what tactics do they use when *responding* strategically to such predicaments? Specifically, I investigate some of the cognitive categories leaders use when trying to make sense of identity-threatening predicaments. I then examine some of the cognitive strategies leaders use when attempting to repair those threatened identities.

In pursuing these two issues, I should note at the outset of this chapter that the focus of my analysis differs somewhat from prior work in this area. For the most part, previous work related on this topic has focused on the use of explanatory accounts that decision makers use to mitigate the deleterious effects of identity threats, including specifically the use of such tactics as apologies, excuses, and justifications (e.g., Elsbach, 1994; Elsbach & Sutton, 1992; Ginzel, Kramer, & Sutton, 1993; Salancik & Meindl, 1984). In the present research, in contrast, I investigate the role of what I will term *strategic categorization* (and also *re-categorization*) processes to repair threatened leader identities. In particular, I present results from three studies that were designed to explore how leaders construe identity-threatening predicaments that befall them, and how they attempt, in turn, to repair the damage to their tarnished identities.

To achieve these aims, the chapter is organized as follows. First, I provide a brief conceptualization of what I mean by a leader's psychological identity. I elaborate on how various kinds of organizational events, including both external events beyond a leader's control, as well as events arising from leaders' own deliberate decisions, can threaten such identities. Next, I discuss approaches to studying leader responses to identity threats. I then present some findings from three studies that explored leaders' responses to identity-threatening predicaments over three different domains. Using the results from these studies, I conclude the chapter by discussing some theoretical and practical implications of the findings.

Conceptualizing Leader Identity and Identity-Threatening Predicaments

For the purposes of the present analysis, I define *psychological identity* in terms of the attributes individuals use to describe themselves. From this perspective, leaders' identities constitute the set of self-perceived attributes they use to characterize themselves and/or their leadership. These self-ascribed attributes include those unique or distinctive individual personal qualities leaders associate with themselves. Leaders might, for example, consider themselves intelligent, competent, trustworthy, competitive, visionary, or resilient leaders. These self-ascriptions also include references to various social and political categories they might use to categorize themselves. Thus, a leader might describe herself as a feminist, a centrist democrat, a neo-conservative, or a radical environmentalist.

As with other forms of psychological identity, leader identities are presumed to be highly differentiated cognitive constructs that characteristically include multiple identity components. Thus, when asked to describe themselves, most leaders will experience little difficulty invoking a variety of different attributes and categories. To be sure, leaders may vary with respect to the richness or complexity of their self-representations. Some may describe themselves in terms of a very few, closely related attributes; others may describe themselves in terms of numerous attributes, some of which may seem inconsistent with, and not easily integrated into, a single, coherent sense of self. Leaders may display, similarly, varying degrees of comfort versus ambivalence about their attributes. Martin Luther King Jr., for example, was acutely sensitive to what he perceived as his personal moral weaknesses and failings, especially those related to his "womanizing" activities. Nonetheless, he engaged these critical self-perceptions to sharpen his thinking regarding his role in the leadership of the civil rights movement (Branch, 2006).

Identity attributes vary also in terms of how important or central they are to a leader's sense of self. Obviously, some of a leader's self-perceived attributes will pertain to more central and enduring components of his or her psychological identity. For example, some leaders might define themselves first and foremost in terms of their ability to manifest grace under pressure (an attribute President John F. Kennedy highly valued). Reagan valued his optimism and deep faith in himself and the wisdom of his judgment. Other leaders may view as central their ability to bounce back from personal or political crises, as did Presidents Richard Nixon and William Jefferson Clinton. Clinton, for instance, famously referred to himself as "The Comeback Kid," drawing attention to his impressive ability, manifested time and time again, to snatch victory from the jaws of scandal. Similarly, Nixon perceived himself as a scrappy, street-tough fighter who was often underestimated by the Harvard-trained intellectuals and media critics. Other attributes, in contrast, will be considered secondary or peripheral to how a leader sees him or herself. For President Kennedy, his religious affiliation was a matter of low personal importance relative to other attributes he expressed considerable concern about.

I characterize those attributes and categories which leaders view as central to their self-conceptions as *core identity* attributes or categories. From a functional perspective, all of the various self-ascriptions and self-categorizations leaders employ when describing themselves can be viewed as helping them define who they are, how they should interpret situations, and how they should act in those situations (March, 1994). Threats to these central and cherished core identity attributes, however, are presumably particularly salient and threatening to leaders.

A few other points merit mention at this juncture in the analysis. First, as with other forms of identity, leader identities are to some extent socially constructed and socially validated. Leaders create, for example, identities of trustworthiness and credibility through their actions. Their ability to sustain these perceptions is, in no small measure, however, influenced by the reactions of various observers of the leader's actions. Second, allies, constituents, shareholders, employees, board members, pundits, and critics constitute a broad, diverse organizational audience that plays a major role in the cultivation, shaping and maintenance of leader identities. Because of this interdependence, leaders' success or failure at constructing and sustaining a valued or desired identity depends, at least in part, on others' reactions to their identity affirmations and claims. Thus, the extent to which a given identity aspiration or claim can be registered convincingly depends, at least in part, on the reactions of important organizational constituents and audiences to that claim. In this sense, leaders' identities emerge and are sustained through their interactions with other people, including especially those audiences to whom those leaders feel particularly accountable. Stated differently, identity management can be viewed as a reciprocal influence process, involving dynamic interactions between leaders and their audiences (Ginzel, Kramer, & Sutton, 1993).

Because leaders' identities are socially constructed and negotiated, the success or failure of a leader's attempt at identity restoration or repair is likely to hinge, therefore, upon a perceptive reading of the organizational audience and a deft negotiation of that audience's concerns, interpretations, beliefs, etc. And this brings the leader's skills at self-presentation and impression management to the fore.[2] Leader repair processes are linked to the leader's skill at persuasion, influence, and negotiation.

With these general ideas and assumptions as a backdrop, I turn now to talking about the problem of studying leader identity threat and repair processes. As used in the present context, the term *identity-threatening predicament* refers to any event that calls into question or challenges a leader's cherished or valued identity attributes (Tedeschi, 1981). For example, if a leader considers him or herself to be a moral and trustworthy leader, and highly values those attributes, then an event that calls into question those attributes is likely to constitute an identity threat. Such threats constitute self-presentational predicaments for leaders because they create an expectation of some sort of response or reaction from the leader. In other words, leaders recognize that they must do something to respond to the external event. Audiences expect a response. Even apart from audience expectations, leaders might themselves feel a need for closure or constructive resolution in trying to make sense of the event.

Studying Leader Identity Threat and Repair Processes

A number of approaches have been used to study how individuals respond to identity threats. Some social psychologists, for instance, have employed experimental methods to investigate antecedents and consequences of identity threats. Steele's (1988) programmatic studies on self-affirmation are illustrative of this approach. His experiments demonstrate that when individuals experience a threat to one aspect of their social identities, they can sometimes mitigate the severity of that threat by affirming other positive social identities. Thus, if a student's competence in mathematics is called into question or challenged, the student might affirm other compensatory attributes, including their writing ability or knowledge of art.

Laboratory studies of this sort, involving inexperienced undergraduate students responding to abstract and artificial social stimuli, are quite valuable when exploring the basic psychological processes associated with common social identity threat and repair processes. They are less useful, however, for investigating how real-world organizational or political leaders respond to identity threats. It's hard to bring a president, senator or corporate CEO into the experimental laboratory and measure their response to some hypothetical contrived and transient threat. At best, experimental investigations are merely suggestive of how real-world decision makers might perform in similar situations. The failure of most experimenters to ever step outside the cloistered confines of the psychological laboratory and into the booming, buzzing and messy world of the field has limited our knowledge about these important processes.

Accordingly, to explore how real-world leaders think about their core identities and how they respond to naturally occurring threats to those identities requires a different approach. Accordingly, the approach I've taken in the research described below is to use qualitative data to inductively investigate how leaders respond to identity threats. There is, I should hasten to add, an impressive body of knowledge and insight accumulating from such qualitative studies (see Hatch & Schultz, 2004, for a representative sample). I report the results of three qualitative studies in this vein. The first study explored how business school leaders respond to threats to their business school leadership. The second study explored how President Lyndon Johnson responded to threats to his presidential performance. The third study investigated how President Reagan and his aides responded to threats to his presidential leadership.

Study 1: Countering the Business Week Rankings: Using Selective Categorization and Strategic Social Comparisons to Mitigate Identity Threats

Organizational behavior researcher Kimberly Elsbach and I explored the use of identity construal and repair tactics by business school deans and other administrative leaders in responding to organizational identity threats posed by the *Business Week* rankings of U.S. business schools (Elsbach & Kramer, 1996).

Business Week (*BW*) magazine began ranking U.S. business schools in 1988. The survey evaluated business schools on two primary criteria. The first criterion was Master of Business Administration (MBA) graduates' satisfaction with their school, including the quality of the educational experience and support for career placement. The second criterion was recruiters' satisfaction with recent graduates of the school. A composite score based on these two dimensions was then used to rank business schools, resulting in a list of the supposed "top twenty" schools in the country. By way of background, I should point out that, during the period when we collected the data for this study, competition among business schools for the best students was fierce. Reputations and rankings were viewed as important drivers of prospective MBA students' selection of schools. Thus these rankings constituted a new but also very serious threat to business schools and also the deans and other administrators leading them.

Another reason the *BW* rankings constituted such a novel threat to business schools is that they essentially changed "the name of the game" for many schools. Prior to the rankings, many top business schools had carved out distinct reputational niches for themselves. Harvard, for example, was renowned for producing top-flight management-oriented leaders. Northwestern was considered the most prominent marketing program. Wharton was famous for its finance program. Stanford was widely perceived as the premier "basic research-oriented" business school. MIT and Berkeley were high-tech, entrepreneurial-oriented schools. Other schools enjoyed regional reputations that helped them attract students. One school, for example, was widely known as the "Harvard of the South."

Because of these distinctive niches, it was possible for many schools to consider themselves quite outstanding, claiming high status even while avoiding invidious comparisons. By suggesting a single, common and purportedly objective metric for evaluating all schools, the *BW* ranking forced schools to respond to its criteria. The "live and let live" feeling pervasive among schools prior to the rankings was replaced by a potential "winner-take-all" mindset among schools competing for the best students. In the future, potential students would select schools on the basis of their absolute ranking, rather than on the basis of fit or other reasonable considerations.

In trying to examine how business school leaders construed the threat posed by the *BW* rankings, and how they responded to that perceived threat, Elsbach and I collected a variety of different kinds of evidence. First, we collected and content analyzed documents produced by the schools, including official press releases and published interviews. We also collected newspaper articles from campus, regional, and national newspapers. Finally, we conducted extensive interviews ourselves with business school deans, associate deans, and administrators involved in media relations.

Content analyses of these various interview and archival materials revealed strong evidence that the *BW* rankings constituted a serious threat to many business schools in at least two distinct ways. First, the rankings in many instances devalued, or ignored altogether important core identity dimensions of those schools and, by implication, their leadership. For example, by emphasizing only MBA students' satisfaction with teaching as a primary evaluative criterion, *BW* implicitly called into question the value of research-oriented schools, such as Berkeley, MIT, and Stanford associated with their basic research missions.

Second, by "force ranking" the schools on the basis of its narrow criteria, the *BW* rankings effectively called into question many schools' claims regarding their strong positional status relative to business schools, both nationally and regionally. As John Byrne, the creator and editor of the *BW* survey noted,

> For years and years there were probably 50 business schools that claimed that they were in the top 20 and probably hundreds that claimed they were in the top 40 … What the *Business Week* survey [did] is eliminate the ability of some schools to claim that they [were] in a top group.
>
> (Elsbach & Kramer, 1996, p. 445)

Business school leaders and their administrative spokespersons are expected to protect the status and prestige of their schools and its leadership. Students want their schools to be ranked highly because job placement and starting salaries are clearly tied to the prestige and reputation of a school. Alumni pressure deans to keep rankings high to preserve the value of their degree and the status it confers. As one dean from an Ivy League school put it, when asked why he couldn't just choose to ignore the rankings if their validity was so suspect, "Regardless of my personal views, I wouldn't be dean of this institution for very long if I did nothing to respond to even the *perception* that our school was slipping in its national standing."

Having established the nature and severity of the perceived threat posed by the rankings to business school leaders in our sample, Elsbach and I then sought evidence regarding how these leaders responded to those threats. Accordingly, we again studied formal press releases, formal interviews in campus, regional, and national newspapers. We searched for and coded every statement made by any administrative leader in response to the *BW* rankings pertaining to the threats and/or institutional interpretations and responses to them. We also conducted intensive, semi-structured interviews with a select number of leaders from each of the schools in our sample.

Our research identified the following tactics as prevalent. First, we found extensive evidence that leaders used what we labeled *strategic re-categorization tactics* to challenge *BW*'s implicit characterization of the value of their core identity and/ or their positional status. Leaders appeared to use these categorization tactics for two purposes. The first purpose was to help them make sense of and explain to important constituents why their schools had achieved a specific, disappointing ranking. The second was to affirm positive aspects of their school's identity that the rankings had neglected or minimized.

The first kind of re-categorization entailed highlighting or increasing the salience of positive identity attributes not emphasized by the rankings. Some examples will illustrate the use of selective categorizations for these purposes. One administrator from Berkeley's Haas Business School categorized his school as a "public management, entrepreneurial-oriented" program implying it was different from and should not be compared with other general purpose, private business schools. In noting the importance of this identity attribute, he emphasized to us, "We *really value* our entrepreneurial culture around here. It's central to how we see ourselves." He then went on to elaborate, "If the Haas emphasis on high-tech and entrepreneurship were to change, the school would lose its identity and competitive advantage." He further noted that the identity of the school was complex because, "As a public institution, we have numerous missions private schools don't have."

In a similar vein, a Stanford Business School associate dean observed that Stanford had a distinctly entrepreneur-oriented program that catered to the career aspirations of its students, the majority of whom hoped to found their own start-ups in the Silicon Valley, rather than work for more traditional, large corporations. "More Stanford MBAs have non-Fortune 1000 interests, choosing instead, smaller and entrepreneurial ventures." As a consequence, he noted, "Some of the things that improve rankings are part of what we don't want to change [about our school]."

A Texas business school administrator, similarly, emphasized that his business school "catered to regional labor markets" better than other schools, and that regional standing was a "more important" and salient metric for evaluating his effectiveness as a school leader, since students were seeking jobs within the region rather than heading necessarily to the West or East coast. "I feel responsible for making sure our students get the jobs they want locally, so much of our focus is on that goal," he asserted.

The second re-categorization tactic, strategic social comparisons, entailed highlighting or increasing the salience of *favorable social comparisons* not emphasized by the rankings. In discussing the functionality of this tactic, Hogg and Abrams noted,

> By differentiating ingroup and outgroup on dimensions on which the ingroup is at the evaluatively positive pole, the ingroup acquires a positive distinctiveness, and thus a relatively positive social identity in comparison to the outgroup.
>
> (1998, p. 23)

As the social psychological literature has shown, following unfavorable social comparisons, people may invoke comparisons based on other, more flattering dimensions which they appear to have an advantage (see Wood & Wilson, 2003 for a review of this evidence). In much the same way, Elsbach and I found that following the *BW* rankings, many business school leaders selectively categorized their schools in ways that placed them in more favorable inter-organizational comparison groups. This tactic seemed to serve the dual purpose of both affirming their perceptions of valued core identity dimensions and their perceptions of their school's positional status. Thus, in this vein, we found that many business school leaders used categorizations that increased the salience of identity dimensions that were also held by well-respected and highly ranked schools, but were neglected or devalued by *BW*. For example, in categorizing her school as a regional leader, one Texas business school administrator noted:

> We're in a similar situation as highly-ranked University of Michigan Business School ... [In fact] we are considered to be the best in our region ... like Michigan, which is a very powerful regional school, and is also of national stature with Stanford, Harvard, and Wharton. So that's how we'd like to be seen. We'd like to be a school that totally dominates a region.

A University of Chicago business school associate dean indicated, "We're a top research institution. I think of us in the same academic league as Harvard or Stanford."

One Berkeley administrator was particularly articulate in implying the unfairness and illogic of employing a single metric as did *BW* in its rankings.

> In its market, Berkeley does a better job than most schools. But *BW* is throwing the Fords and the Chevys and the Porsches in the same mix ... It's really not fair. It's like judging apples and oranges, and we're not the same type of school as many others.

As these examples illustrate, business school leaders used this tactic not only to affirm positive aspects of their school's identity that the rankings had minimized or neglected, but also to deflect attention away from the attributes the rankings emphasized.

These tactics were also used to help constituents make sense of and/or explain why their school had achieved a particularly low or disappointing ranking. By directing attention away from the ranking itself, they showed how it was misleading or incomplete in its representation of the school, because it ignored aspects of the school's identity that were more important than the criteria used in the survey. The categorization tactics observed in this second study change the perceived field of salient or available comparisons. Our study re-affirms the potency of such tactics not just for making sense of where one stands in the social order or how well one is doing on some standard, but also in helping leaders repair threats to their core identity or the core identifies of the ongoing actions they represent.

Elsbach and I used the metaphor of a microscope, as it is used to view material on a slide, to visualize how these identity repair tactics function. Using this metaphor of evaluators peering through the lens of a microscope, selective categorization processes can be likened to manipulating the field of view available to the perceiver and, by implication, the inclusiveness or exclusiveness of comparisons. Thus, the first strategy of highlighting cherished or valued identity attributes is like using a high level of magnification to focus down on the focal organization only, and moving the slide around to highlight or make salient positive attributes or facets of that focal organization. Focusing down only on positive identity attributes, and excluding from the field of view those tainted or tarnished attributes, helps perceivers establish a more positive overall perception of the organization and its leadership.

The second strategy is akin to using a lower powered or reduced magnification to selectively enlarge the field of view to include a set of comparison organizations that reflect favorably on the focal organization and its leadership. This strategy of highlighting alternate comparison groups in the field of view involves, metaphorically, moving the slide around to focus on different subsets of organizations and their inter-relationships or similarities. By placing the organization in a more diffuse, broader visual field, its relationship to other organizations (e.g., its perceived similarity and distinctiveness) can be manipulated. By focusing, for example, narrowly on a specific region or subset of schools, leaders can generate a social comparison group in which the organization enjoys high status. In this fashion, leaders affirm the organization's relative value and prestige within that salient reference group.

To summarize, this first study identified a number of cognitive tactics organizational leaders use to make sense of and manage external threats to their organizations and its leadership. In some sense, the threat posed by the *BW* rankings was an external threat, largely beyond the control of any individual business school or its leadership. However, identity-threatening predicaments sometimes arise when leaders make decisions themselves that create a threatening predicament. In the next study, accordingly, I explored how the actual decisions leaders make can themselves constitute identity-threatening predicaments. In contrast to the sort of external threats from rankings, decisions are interesting because leaders are more clearly responsible for them, and thus must find some way of making sense of them to constituents who challenge their quality, legitimacy, etc.

Study 2: Leader Decisions as Identity-Threatening Predicaments: Lyndon Johnson and the Vietnam Decisions

Leaders are not only expected to explain and make sense of their organization's performance, they are also responsible for making the decisions that influence that performance. A swift, sure, and effective decisiveness may even be regarded as one of the *sine qua non*'s of the true leader. Such, at least, would be one conclusion that readily emerges from the voluminous leadership literature that characterizes effective leaders in terms of bold decisions rendered in moments of great crisis or opportunity (e.g., Janis, 1989; Useem, 1999).

Obviously, the decisions leaders make have important identity-relevant consequences for leaders. For example, decisions can constitute identity-enhancing opportunities when they enable leaders to project valued or desired identities through their decisions. President John F. Kennedy received rave reviews by American journalists and political pundits following his successful management of the Cuban Missile Crisis. On the other hand, decisions can constitute identity-threatening predicaments when their consequences call into question or undermine leaders' valued or desired identities. Thus, President Kennedy was roundly criticized for his indecisive handling of the Bay of Pigs invasion. More recently, President George W. Bush was widely criticized by the media for his slow and indecisive handling of emergency relief and federal intervention in the wake of Hurricane *Katrina*.

To investigate how leaders' own decisions might constitute identity-threatening predicaments and how they might respond to such identity threats, I wanted to find an example of a leader decision that met several criteria. First, I thought it would be ideal if the nature of the perceived identity threat was quite severe, throwing into bold relief the psychological stresses operating upon the leader as he or she wrestled with the perceived threat. Second, I thought it would be instructive to examine the cognitive tactics of a leader widely regarded for his or her political acumen and leadership skills. In other words, it would be ideal to find a leader who had previously demonstrated skill with respect to his or her self-presentational abilities and impression management skills. Such a leader might be expected to be particularly effective and resourceful at parrying such a threat. Third, and for purely practical reasons, I thought it would be ideal to identify a decision where extensive evidence was available as to how the leader him or herself had personally construed the threat.

Fortunately, a candidate case meeting these criteria presented itself in the form of the presidential leadership of Lyndon Johnson and his Vietnam decisions. Few instances of leader decision making have attracted the level of sustained attention from historians, political scientists, psychologists, and organizational theorists that Johnson's Vietnam decisions have received. These decisions have been the focus of enormous scholarly scrutiny—not only because of their intrinsic historical importance, but also because of their perplexing character (see Kramer, 1995 and 1998 for overviews).

The perplexing character of Johnson's Vietnam decisions stems, in part, from the seeming disjunction between the attributes of the decision maker and the decisions he made in this instance. Few U.S. presidents have entered the Oval Office with a clearer perception of his ultimate goals and ambitions. Moreover, few of the individuals who have assumed the duties of President have seemed better positioned to implement those goals and achieve those ambitions. Lyndon Johnson was widely regarded as one of the most capable wielders of power ever to have assumed the presidency. He was a master politician who understood better than almost anyone else in his time how Washington worked.

Johnson's performance in his first months in office, following the unexpected death of President Kennedy, only contributed to scholars' perplexity regarding his subsequent Vietnam decisions. Shortly after assuming the presidency, Johnson performed flawlessly as the nation's leader, winning over a wary Congress and a skeptical public as he sought to enact both President Kennedy's stalled legislation and his own initiatives. After only a few months in office, he was elected to the Presidency on his own in 1964 with the then-largest popular mandate in U.S. history. He displayed considerable clarity regarding his priorities and confidence in pursuing them.

Indeed, on the basis of his early White House performance, it looked as if Lyndon Johnson might well be on his way to achieving his aim of being remembered in history as one of the great activist presidents, especially if judged primarily by his legislative accomplishments with respect to domestic advances in civil rights, health care, education, and the war against poverty.

Additionally, Johnson's initial assessments of the Vietnam situation seemed remarkably prescient. He clearly foresaw, for example, the prospect of becoming mired in a costly, fruitless escalating conflict with little upside for America (see, e.g., Johnson's remarks, recorded in his taped conversations; Beschloss, 1997, 2001). Relatedly, early in his presidency he confessed to his mentor Richard Russell and others that he saw no way such a war might be won. He believed that the conflict itself was not worth the shedding of a single American youth's blood. He begged his advisors to show great caution and care, suggesting that future historians will dissect these decisions with the same critical scrutiny as the Bay of Pigs decisions.

Relative to these initial, rather perceptive assessments of the conflict in Vietnam, Johnson's subsequent presidential decisions between 1964 and 1968 remain a conundrum to scholars. These decisions, all too obviously, dramatically escalated the conflict and, in the end, went terribly awry, undoing first Johnson's beloved domestic programs, then his presidency, and ultimately the legacy he had fought for so long and so hard to create. Perhaps it is for this reason that these decisions have attracted so much scholarly scrutiny.

Previous psychological research on the Johnson Vietnam decisions, I should note, has taken several approaches, mostly centered on issues of decision quality. Janis's groupthink remains one of the more influential social psychological interpretations (Janis, 1983), explaining Johnson's flawed performance largely in terms of defective group dynamics. Another approach has been escalation of commitment (Staw, 1976). These accounts have emphasized the psychological pressures toward private and public consistency in actions that operate on leaders.

In contrast to these prior theoretical efforts, I approached the Vietnam decisions from an identity perspective (Kramer, 2004). To explicate how identity and decision collided dramatically and with devastating consequence, I first provide a brief characterization of how Lyndon Johnson "self-categorized" himself as president. I then examine in detail his cognitive responses to the identity-threatening predicament posed by his Vietnam decisions.

In order to suggest an intimate link between Johnson's core identity as a political leader and his Vietnam decisions, it is necessary first to attempt to characterize that identity. Fortunately, Lyndon Johnson was fairly articulate about the core identity that he cherished and energetically sought to project as president, describing his aspirations and goals to many people (e.g., Henggeler, 1991; Kearns-Goodwin, 1976; Valenti, 1977). His views surfaced frequently also in both his public pronouncements and his private ruminations with close confidantes and aides. Always foremost in his mind was furthering his ambition of becoming one of the greatest presidents in American history. As his aide Jack Valenti put it, "He had one goal: to be the greatest president doing the greatest good in the history of the nation" (quoted in Middleton, 1990, p. 24). He wanted, in his own words, to be "the greatest father the country had ever had" (quoted in Gruber, 1991). He once expressed the view that he aspired—figuratively at least—to have his visage placed alongside the other great figures looking out from Mount Rushmore.

In Johnson's eyes, presidential greatness had two cornerstones. The first was a record of historic domestic achievement. Here Johnson sought, as Nicholas Lemann once aptly commented, to "set world records in politics the way a star athlete would in sports" (quoted in Dallek, 1999, p. 109). In pursuit of this goal, Johnson displayed a breath-taking legislative genius, passing more sweeping domestic legislation than any president in history. He was determined to rival the record of Franklin Roosevelt as a president, who knew how to throw the great machinery of government into high gear in pursuit of great if difficult aims.

In this spirit, Johnson embarked on a broad set of initiatives that he brought together under the umbrella of his Great Society program. In large measure, he felt this historic domestic program would be the capstone of his presidency. This would be the banner on which he would hang his legacy as a great democratic president. The second cornerstone to presidential greatness in Johnson's eyes was the ability of a president to keep the nation out of harm's way. No U.S. president, Johnson knew, had achieved greatness without successfully waging war against its adversaries. In Johnson's eyes, Lincoln and Roosevelt were the two premier examples of great war-time presidents.

If Johnson entertained a clearly defined vision of the identity he sought as President, he knew just as clearly how he would achieve that identity. He knew from his reading of history and his intense study of the presidency the kind of president it would take to achieve such stunning accomplishments. As Kearns-Goodwin (1976) put it, Johnson believed that, "If you had the energy and drive to work harder than everyone else you would achieve what you set out to accomplish." Johnson, she went on to note, "held before him the image of the daring cowboy, the man with the capacity to outrun the wild herd, riding at a dead run in the dark of the night" (pp. 343–344). He drew a distinction between those leaders who were the "doers" and those he dismissed as the "thinkers" and "talkers" of the world. Thus, Johnson's identity was just as sharply defined in the realm of means as it was with respect to the ends he would pursue.

It is within the context of this finely and sharply drawn identity portrait that the Vietnam decisions of the Johnson presidency can—and should—be placed. With respect to his Vietnam decisions, Johnson saw little upside. In his view, he had inherited the dilemma of Vietnam just as he had inherited his presidency—on a tragic moment's notice on November 22, 1963. From the instant of that assumed presidency, Johnson clearly recognized the threat that Vietnam posed to his legacy (Beschloss, 1997, 2001). In terms of furthering his ambitions, unfortunately, none of the alternatives presented to Johnson regarding Vietnam seemed attractive or viable. "I feel like a hound bitch in heat in the country," he poignantly complained. "If you run, they chew your tail off. If you stand still, they slip it to you" (Berman, 1989, p. 183). The thought of "cutting and running," as he once put it, was anathema to a man with such a keenly developed image of what great, activist presidents need to do in moments of crisis or challenge.

In Johnson's eyes, the Vietnam decisions also directly threatened his ability to implement his broad Great Society initiatives. In his view, it was these Great Society decisions that would enable Johnson to demonstrate to the American public the sweep and grandeur of his presidential vision. He envisioned a revitalized and eventually completed America, where people would be judged by the "quality of their minds," and not merely by the "quantity of their goods" (Gruber, 1991). He described the program as being like a beautiful woman that the

American people would love (Kearns-Goodwin, 1976). Thus, the Great Society decisions constituted, in Johnson's eyes, an identity-enhancing opportunity.

The intensity of the conflict between the identity Johnson hoped to affirm to himself and project to others through his Vietnam decisions intensified as the war drained economic and attentional resources from the Great Society. The program that he earlier had characterized as a young and beautiful woman now withered in Johnson's eye under the economic hardships imposed by the Vietnam War:

> She's getting thinner and thinner and uglier and uglier all the time … Soon she'll be so ugly the American people will refuse to look at her; they'll stick her in a closet to hide her away and there she'll die. And when she dies, I, too, will die.
> (quoted in Kearns-Goodwin, 1976, pp. 286–287)

In Johnson's mind, the threat to his identity was intensified by the sudden disaffection of large segments of the American public—the same public that, only months ago, had made Lyndon Johnson one of the most popular and beloved presidents in U.S. history. As Berman (1989) noted, "It pained him that those he believed had been helped most by his presidency [e.g., students, blacks, and educators] were leading the opposition to his war" (p. 183).

How did Johnson respond to the identity-threatening predicament he perceived in his Vietnam decisions? Initially, his response was characterized by extremely vigilant and mindful information processing of the sort described by Janis (1989) in his classic work on high quality decision making. Johnson studied all of the details of the decisions and vigorously pressed his Secretary of Defense Robert McNamara and his other advisors to consider every implication of every decision:

> What I would like to know is what has happened in recent months that requires this kind of decision on my part. What are the alternatives? I want this discussed in full detail, from everyone around this table … what are the compelling reasons [for this decision]? What results can we expect? Again, I ask you, what are the alternatives? I don't want us to make snap judgments. I want us to consider all our options …
> (Valenti, 1975, pp. 259–260)

As the escalating conflict in Vietnam continued to defy resolution, Johnson increasingly displayed two less adaptive cognitive responses. The first cognitive response is what Janis (1989) identified as hyper-vigilant information processing.

> If Ronald Reagan was the Teflon president, to whom nothing stuck, Johnson was the flypaper president, to whom everything clung. A compulsive reader, viewer, and listener who took every criticism personally

and to heart, he was at first intent on, and then obsessed with, answering every accusation, responding to every charge.

(Herring, 1993, p. 95)

A second dysfunctional cognitive response evidenced by Johnson was intense and intrusive dysphoric rumination about Vietnam. "If Johnson was unhappy thinking about Vietnam," Kearns-Goodwin (1976) once noted, "he was even less happy not thinking about it" (p. 299). Johnson often

> consciously and deliberately decided not to think another thought about Vietnam, yet discussions that started on poverty or education invariably ended up on Vietnam … he found himself unwilling, and soon unable, to break loose from what had become an obsession.
>
> (Kearns-Goodwin, 1976, p. 299)

In particular, he tended to ruminate at length about his deteriorating image as a leader and as president. This led Johnson to begin to imagine a vast web of conspiracy by powerful forces, including his many perceived political enemies, who he felt were lined up against him with the common aim of denying him the presidential legacy he sought (see, e.g., Califano, 1991; Dallek, 1991; Goodwin, 1988). As he put it, even years later, "They'll get me anyhow, no matter how hard I try … the reviews are in the hands of my enemies—the *New York Times* and my enemies—so I don't have a chance" (quoted in Kearns-Goodwin, 1976, p. 357).

In terms of repairing Johnson's threatened presidential identity, there were two interesting cognitive responses evidenced in the archival data that parallel the results obtained in the study of business school responses to the *BW* rankings. Both of these cognitive responses constitute attempts by Lyndon Johnson at re-categorizing himself as president and the decisions he was making in that role. The first pattern evident in these data was use of *selective self-categorizations* used to cognitively focus on self-enhancing facets of Johnson's identity, while downplaying or minimizing attention to less flattering facets. For example, when challenged by the Vietnam critics and advisors about the wisdom of his military policy, Johnson would remind them of all he had done for civil rights, poverty, education, and healthcare reform (Beschloss, 2001). According to his friend Governor John Connally he carried in his breast pocket a list of all his legislative accomplishments, which he would pull out and read off as if it were a baseball score card (Gruber, 1991). By highlighting alternative accomplishments in the domestic realm, Johnson could identity-enhance.

A second cognitive tactic much in evidence in the archival data is selective self-categorization through the sort of strategic (i.e., motivated or self-enhancing) social comparisons observed in the *BW* study. Thus, in framing the choice dilemmas he faced as president, Johnson continually compared himself to other U.S. presidents, particularly Franklin Roosevelt and Woodrow Wilson. For example, in justifying his persistence in Vietnam, despite evidence that the war was not progressing favorably, Johnson argued that, "You see, I deeply believe we are quarantining aggressors over there ... Just like FDR [did with] Hitler, just like Wilson [did] with Kaiser. You've simply got to see this thing in historical perspective" (quoted in Kearns-Goodwin, 1976, p. 313).

Similarly, when friends, aides, advisors, and critics suggested to him that he might be perceived as a greater president if he decisively ended such an unpopular conflict, Johnson recoiled. "Everything I know about history," he asserted, "proves this absolutely wrong. It was our lack of strength and failure to show stamina, our hesitancy, vacillation, and love of peace being paraded so much that caused all our problems before World War I, World War II, and Korea" (Kearns-Goodwin, 1976, p. 313).

Johnson also drew solace in comparisons with Abraham Lincoln and the unpopular decisions he had confronted as president, "I read all about the troubles Lincoln had in conducting the Civil War. Yet he persevered and history rewarded him for his perseverance" (Kearns-Goodwin, 1976, p. 314). "We're going to have our troubles," Johnson acknowledged at another point, but "we're not running from nothing ... And remember old Abraham Lincoln ..." (quoted in Beschloss, 2001, p. 136). As he admonished his confidantes, "They [the public] don't ever remember many of these Presidents from Jackson to Lincoln. They don't remember many from Lincoln to Roosevelt. The ones they remember are those that stood up ..." (quoted in Beschloss, 2001, p. 136).

To summarize, the results of this second study replicate and extend the findings from the study of business school leaders' responses to identity threats. First, the analysis suggests that decisions can constitute identity-threatening predicaments in at least two ways. First, decisions can challenge or invalidate leaders' self-perceptions of their core identities. Leader decisions can create, in this sense, an internal "credibility gap" in so far as they call into question desired or cherished self-categorizations. Second, decisions can threaten or call into question a leader's public or social claims regarding their core identities. Leaders care not only about their private identities, but also by the social images they project to others. When decisions cause important constituents to question a leader's intentions, motives, actions, or competence then the leader may feel he or she is in a crisis management situation.

As the data revealed, Johnson utilized both of the tactics observed in the *BW* study. Recall that the first cognitive tactic, which entails the use of *selective self-categorizations*, is used by leaders to highlight alternate identity attributes. The second cognitive tactic, involving the use of *selective social comparisons*, helps a leader highlight alternate comparison groups to invoke when trying to make sense of the predicament. Selective social comparison can be viewed as a form of "re-categorization" in terms of a selective subset of comparison with others within one's perceived social identity group. In discussing the adaptive value of this psychological tactic, Frey and Ruble (1990) proposed that, "healthy [psychological] functioning may depend on the ability to exhibit flexibility in the choice of evaluative comparisons in order to maintain a sense of competence and high self-esteem" (p. 169). Both of these tactical responses can be thought of as re-categorization efforts in the service of identity maintenance and repair.

An identity perspective also provides a somewhat novel perspective on leader decision making. The study of leader decision making has taken a variety of approaches. For example, some studies have examined the role of power in decision making (Neustadt, 1990; Pfeffer, 1992). Other studies have explored the role that leaders' advisory systems play in decision making (Burke & Greenstein, 1989; George, 1980; Janis, 1983). Still others have investigated the impact of various accountability mechanisms and structures on leader judgment and choice (Allison, 1971; Tetlock, 1992). Approaching leader decision making from an identity perspective contributes to our understanding of how leaders' perceived core identities influence the manner in which they frame or construe the decisions they confront. Leaders' decisions, in turn, have important implications for leaders' identity claims and aspirations. In particular, the ability of leaders to construct and sustain valued or desired identities clearly depends on the favorable or unfavorable consequences of the decisions they make. The research described above indicates some of the ways in which decisions represent important routes of leader identity construction and maintenance through either identity-enhancement or identity threat.

An identity perspective on leader decision making also helps illuminate some of the particular and often idiosyncratic reasons why leaders sometimes make the decisions they do. Such a perspective suggests, further, why leaders might persist with a chosen course of action even when the consequences of their decisions seem flawed and self-defeating from the perspective of a rational calculation of advantage. Thus, although intended to resolve an identity-threat, leaders' responses sometimes only serve instead to increase threat, as the leaders' responses invite further hostile or critical scrutiny.

Study 3: Transforming Failure into Success in the Iceland Arms Control Talks: Reagan as Confident Cold Warrior and Master Negotiator

The third study I will describe investigated attempts by the Reagan administration to address threats to the perception of President Reagan as a competent negotiator when dealing with the Soviet Union. In particular, organizational researcher Robert Sutton and I conducted a qualitative study of "spin control" efforts in the historic 1986 Iceland Arms Control talks between President Ronald Reagan and Soviet Premier Mikhail Gorbachev (Sutton & Kramer, 1990).

To set the stage, it may be useful to briefly recall the events precipitating this incident. On September 19, 1986, Soviet Foreign Minister Eduard Shevardnadze delivered a letter from Soviet Premier Mikhail Gorbachev to President Ronald Reagan proposing that the two of them meet prior to their official summit for some informal pre-summit discussion. Reagan responded affirmatively to this proposal, suggesting such a meeting might indeed prove productive. Accordingly, the two leaders met in Reykjavik, Iceland for two days on October 11 and 12, 1986. They discussed a wide range of issues at this historic meeting, including the strategic arms postures and nuclear policies of their respective countries.

Almost immediately following completion of the talks, post-mortems by print journalists and media pundits presented a grim, almost universally negative assessment of what the talks had accomplished. Perhaps even more importantly, what they had failed to accomplish. *Newsweek* (October 27, 1986, p. 31) summarized the widespread initial perception of failure in a particularly scathing characterization of the talks:

> The dejection in the President's carriage as he walked out of Hofdi house, the disappointment etched into every line of Secretary of State George Shultz's face as he briefed the press, had flashed an unmistakable message to TV watchers around the world: the summit meeting with Mikhail Gorbachev had ended in failure. Moreover, the blame was placed squarely at Reagan's feet.

As *Newsweek* put it:

> Worse, headlines were spreading the impression that Reagan had thrown away the promise of a nuclear-free world by clinging to his vision of a space-based defense—even if there might be no missiles to defend against.
> (*Newsweek*, October 27, 1986, p. 31)

The perceived failure of these talks constituted a serious identity threat to Reagan along several fronts. First, Reagan considered himself a masterful negotiator: competent and tough. He thus felt both confident and comfortable in his face-to-face meeting with Gorbachev and apparently entertained little fear or doubt regarding his ability to measure up. When aides expressed concern about Reagan's ability to talk nuclear strategy with Gorbachev, Reagan dismissed their concerns by saying simply that Gorbachev didn't really understand all that stuff either. As his speechwriter Peggy Noonan once observed,

> When he first met with Gorbachev and had to negotiate arms control, he had no great anxiety because, as he put it, he'd been president of the Screen Actor's Guild, he'd negotiated with Sam Goldwyn and Jack Warner, and Gorbachev was nothing compared to those guys.
> (1995, p. 218)

Second, Reagan believed it was his responsibility to secure our safety and, if necessary, to stand up to communist leaders and contain the menace of communism. In his view, the leaders of one of the world's most evil empires should not be appeased or allowed to expand their influence. Moreover, Reagan had a sense of destiny—he had a strong view about his place in American history, and that place included helping to restore America's confidence and strength. In short, Reagan considered himself America's lifeguard.

Therefore, the initial construal of the talks as failures, and the characterization that historic gains in arms reductions had been within grasp, only to be unrealized, left Reagan and his team scrambling for a better storyline. They were not long in finding one.[3] White House Communications Director Patrick Buchanan suggested one alternative framing of the situation (and his language is instructive), "Basically, our story is this. The President made the most sweeping, far-reaching arms control proposal in history" (*New York Times*, October 15, 1986, A1). It was Gorbachev, he asserted, who said, "No." Buchanan further contended that press analyses suggesting the talks were a failure were simply "mistaken." One White House aide put it this way, "We weren't focusing on the one yard we didn't gain … what about the ninety-nine yards we did? We kept saying, 'Let's focus on that'" (cited in Sutton & Kramer, 1990, p. 240).

In putting these efforts by the Reagan administration to respond to this identity-threatening predicament in perspective, it is important to note that the level of effort expended was unusually extensive even by White House standards. Efforts included 44 "on the record" briefings and interviews in the first week following the talks. One White House reporter I interviewed for this study stated, "It was impossible to even use the restroom without some White House aide following you into the bathroom trying to tell you more about 'what really happened.'" Buchanan himself acknowledged that their efforts constituted "the most extensive and intensive communications plan I've ever been associated with in the White House" (*New York Times*, October 15, 1986, A1).

Even Secretary of State Shultz acknowledged there was an active effort underway to "reshape perceptions" of the Reykjavik meeting. Shultz, initially dispirited immediately following the end of the talks, now characterized the discussions as a "watershed" because "for the first time the two sides agree to dramatic agreements in nuclear and strategic arms" (cited in Sutton & Kramer, 1990, p. 240).

In an attempt to echo a Churchillian note on the encounter, the White House Communications Office released a statement characterizing the meeting between the two leaders as "Reagan's finest hour." President Reagan himself argued, "We prefer no agreement than to bring home a bad agreement to the United States" (*New York Times*, October 13, 1986).

Donald Regan suggested to a *New York Times* reporter only a few days later that these efforts at explaining what had really transpired had paid off handsomely:

> Look at the polls. The American people are behind us. The point was we wanted to tell people what happened inside, so the outsiders will understand the enormity of the accomplishments that the President made. It wasn't a defeat at all, but it might have been characterized that way if we had sat still ... Why not tell what happened? Why not let it all hang out? We have nothing to be ashamed of.
>
> (*New York Times*, October 16, 1986, A1)

Data from several independent polls support Regan's contention that their efforts had borne fruit. Over the course of several months, for example, the perception of the talks changed from an outright failure to a dramatic success. Indeed, as time passed and the event was re-assessed, Americans reported *greater* confidence in President Reagan's ability to successfully negotiate an effective arms control agreement with the Soviets. In a perceptive (if perhaps unintentionally disparaging) appraisal of their success, Donald Regan offered a colorful image of just what they had accomplished. "Some of us [in the administration] were like a shovel brigade that follows a parade down Main Street cleaning up," he noted with a laugh. "We took Reykjavik and turned what was a sour situation into something that turned out pretty well," he bragged to a *New York Times* reporter.

The results of this third study further illustrate the efficacy of cognitive repair tactics in helping a leader weather an identity-threatening predicament. In particular, by re-categorizing the outcome in terms of American resolve and avoidance of losses, Reagan was able to suggest he had effectively avoided making undesirable concessions or retreating from his avowed firm posture. He even suggested he had avoided being lulled by Gorbachev into a public relations trap. In short, he maintained his identity as a tough, vigilant negotiator who had stood up to and faced down his opponent.

Implications and Conclusions

Viewed in concert, the findings from these three studies converge on several insights regarding how leaders initially construe identity threats, as well as some of the cognitive tactics they use to respond to those perceived threats.[4]

With respect to the first question—how leaders construe identity-threatening predicaments—one way of thinking about the results of these studies is that they suggest threats to a leader's sense of self create a psychological state we might characterize as *identity dissonance*. The magnitude or level of dissonance leaders experience reflects the perceived discrepancy or disparity between the leader's desired or claimed identity and the identity they perceive is held by important or powerful members of the organizational audience. Thus, if a leader desires or likes to be perceived as trustworthy, and believes important audiences do not perceive them to be trustworthy, the result is highly dissonant.

As with other forms of cognitive dissonance, identity dissonance is assumed to be an aversive psychological state that individuals are motivated to reduce or eliminate. Threats to core identity attributes, it should be noted, are assumed to be especially aversive, and thus leaders will be particularly motivated to reduce dissonance involving these attributes.

To reduce identity dissonance, these studies suggest, leaders may use a variety of identity repair tactics. The particular tactic leaders select will depend upon their assessment of the likelihood that a given tactic will be effective. Leaders' estimates of effectiveness will be influenced by their perceptions of the audience and their own assessment of the credibility or validity of the claim. As the results of these studies further suggest, identity repair should be viewed as a dynamic, iterative process. Leader identities are negotiated identities: they are constructed and maintained through a series of identity claims and responses by identity stakeholders to those claims.

In addition to their theoretical implications and contributions, the findings from these studies have several practical implications for organizational and political leaders. First, identity-based categorization (and re-categorization) tactics constitute potent tools for leaders to use when trying to help not only themselves, but other individuals—both inside and outside the organization—make sense of the organization's values, decisions, purpose, etc. As March (1994) has observed generally, "Organizations [and their leaders] shape individual action both by providing the *content* of identities … and by providing *appropriate cues* for invoking them" (p. 71). Such identity cues enable leaders to focus members' attention on what they should be thinking, about. They provide broad cognitive frames for action. Few leader activities are more consequential to the vitality of an organization or the legitimacy of his leadership. As Pfeffer (1981) noted, "Every organization has an interest in seeing its definition of reality accepted … for such acceptance is an integral part of the legitimization of the organization and the development of assured resources" (p. 26). The same is true for organizational leaders—their authority and credibility clearly hinge, at least in part, on their ability to proffer identities that others view as legitimate, valuable, efficacious, etc.

The results from these studies suggest also that identity-based re-categorization processes may help leaders change or reshape not only their own identities, but also the identities of their organizations. Along these lines, Burgelman and Grove (1996) proposed a model of what they termed "strategic dissonance" whereby leaders purposefully take advantage of distress related to perceived incongruities or discrepancies between an organization's avowed strategic intent and leader's strategic actions. They suggest that leaders might use information generated by such strategic dissonance "when trying to discern the true shape of the company" (p. 20). The authors go on to argue, however, that "it must be a realistic picture grounded in the company's distinctive competencies—existing ones or new ones that are already being developed

… Getting through that period of immense change requires reinventing the company's identity" (p. 20).

In a similar way, leaders may transition from "old" identities to new ones by positively construing changes or apparent "flip flops" as President Reagan did when he did what amounted to an "about face" in his rapprochement and constructive engagement with Soviet leaders toward the end of his administration (cf., Kramer, 2005). The tactics described in this chapter suggest some of the creative ways leaders can invent and re-invent themselves in response to changing realities.

Notes

1 I am extremely grateful to Jonathan Bendor, Phil Tetlock, and Gregory Mitchell for their helpful comments on an earlier draft of this chapter. I am grateful also to the William Kimball family for funds supporting this research. I thank the librarians at the John F. Kennedy and Lyndon Baines Johnson presidential libraries for their assistance in locating relevant documents and responding to my inquiries. The first draft of this chapter was written while I was a visiting scholar at the Center for Public Leadership, John F. Kennedy School of Government, Harvard University. I am grateful for its generous support.

2 There is a large literature on self-presentation and impression management in organizations (see Leary, 1995 and Elsbach, 2006 for thorough overviews of these respective literatures). For the purposes of this analysis, impression management strategies are viewed as consciously chosen methods to mitigate or attenuate perceived threats to a leader's identity. In other words, perception of an identity threat is presumed to activate impression management concerns, resulting in a search for, and selection of, those strategies deemed most appropriate and effective.

3 It is important to note that not all of the identity repair processes Sutton and I observed occurred retrospectively. In our analysis of statements released by the White House prior to the meetings in Reykjavik, interestingly, we found some evidence of efforts to pre-emptively frame blame for anticipated failure or setback. President Reagan, for instance, responded to reporters' questions about the potential for the upcoming talks by noting, "Success is not guaranteed. But, if Mr. Gorbachev comes to Iceland in a truly cooperative spirit, I think we can make some progress" (*New York Times*, October 9, 1986). The President further allowed that he entertained only "cautious optimism" regarding the prospects for the talks, given previous Soviet intransigence. Moreover, Reagan's advisors worked to dampen "heightened expectations" prior to the talks. There were, in some instances, almost comical elements in these initial attempts by the Reagan administration to deflect blame and also share credit for the upcoming talks. In an article entitled "Keeping Score," the New York Times suggested that Mr. Gorbachev deserved credit for arranging this face-to-face meeting between the two Superpower leaders. Mr. Reagan responded to this point by noting that, although the idea for the talks had been Gorbachev's, the United States had proposed the dates for the meeting!

4 Although these repair tactics can be regarded as simply impression management strategies designed to placate or counter adversarial or questioning audience members (press critics, media, critics, political enemies, etc.), I wish to emphasize here the use of such tactics to cognitively repair perceived threats to the self system. The two motives are not incompatible, of course.

References

Allison, G. T. (1971). *Essence of Decision: Explaining the Cuban Missile Crisis*. Boston, MA: Little, Brown.

Ambrose, S. (1991). *Nixon: Ruin and Recovery, 1973–1990*. New York: Simon & Schuster.

Berman, L. (1989). *Lyndon Johnson's War*. New York: Norton.

Beschloss, M. R. (1997). *Taking charge: The Johnson White House Tapes, 1963–1964*. New York: Simon & Schuster.

Beschloss, M. (2001). *Reaching for Glory: Lyndon Johnson's Secret White House Tapes, 1964–1965*. New York: Simon and Schuster.

Branch, T. (2006). *At Canaan's Edge: America in the King Years, 1965–1968*. New York: Simon and Schuster.

Burgelman, R. A., & Grove, A. S. (1996). Strategic dissonance. *California Management Review, 38*, 8–28.

Burke, J. P., & Greenstein, F. I. (1989). *How Presidents Test Reality: Decisions on Vietnam, 1954 and 1965*. New York: Russell Sage Foundation.

Califano, J. A. (1991). *The Triumph and Tragedy of Lyndon Johnson*. New York: Simon & Schuster.

Dallek, R. (1991). *Lone Star Rising: Lyndon Baines Johnson*. New York: Oxford University Press.

Dallek, R. (1999). *Flawed giant: Lyndon Johnson and his times: 1961–1973*. New York: Oxford University Press.

Elsbach, K. D. (1994). Managing organizational legitimacy in the California cattle industry: The construction and effectiveness of verbal accounts. *Administrative Science Quarterly, 39*, 57–88.

Elsbach, K. D. (2006). *Organizational Perception Management*. Mahwah, NJ: Erlbaum.

Elsbach, K. D., & Kramer, R. M. (1996). Members' responses to organizational identity threats: Encountering and countering the *Business Week* rankings. *Administrative Science Quarterly, 41*, 442–476.

Elsbach, K. D., & Sutton, R. (1992). Acquiring organizational legitimacy through illegitimate actions: A marriage of institutional and impression management theories. *Academy of Management Journal, 35*, 699–738.

Frey, K. S., & Ruble, D. N. (1990). Strategies for comparative evaluation: Maintaining a sense of competence across the life span. In R. J. Sternberg, & J. Kolligian (Eds.), *Competence Considered*. New Haven, NJ: Yale University Press.

George, A. (1980). *Presidential Decisionmaking in Foreign Policy: The Effective Use of Information and Advice*. Boulder, CO: Westview.

Ginzel, L. E., Kramer, R. M., & Sutton, R. I. (1993). Organizational impression management as a reciprocal influence process: The neglected role of the organizational audience. In L. L. Cummings, & B. M. Staw (Eds.), *Research in Organizational Behavior, 15*, 227–266. Greenwich, CT: JAI Press.

Goodwin, R. N. (1988). *Remembering America: A Voice from the Sixties*. New York: Harper & Row.

Gruber, D. (1991). *LBJ: A Biography* (video). Dallas, TX: North Texas Public Broadcasting.

Haslam, S. A., Reicher, S. D., & Platow, M. J. (2010). *The New psychology of Leadership: Identity, Influence and Power*. New York: Psychology Press.

Hatch, M. J., & Schultz, M. (2004). *Organizational Identity: A Reader*. New York: Oxford University Press.

Henggeler, P. R. (1991). *In Yis Steps: Lyndon Johnson and the Kennedy Mystique*. Chicago, IL: Dee.

Herring, G. C. (1993). The reluctant warrior: Lyndon Johnson as Commander in Chief. In D. L. Anderson (Ed.), *Shadow on the White House: Presidents and the Vietnam War, 1945–1975* (pp. 87–112). Kansas, MI: University of Kansas Press.

Hickey, D. J., & Essid, J. (2014). *Identity and Leadership in Virtual Communities: Establishing Credibility and Influence*. New York: IGI Global.

Hogg, M. A., & Abrams, D. (1988). *Social identifications: A social psychology of intergroup relations and processes*. New York: Routledge.

Janis, I. L. (1983). *Groupthink* (2nd ed.). Boston, MA: Houghton Mifflin.

Janis, I. L. (1989). *Crucial Decisions*. New York: Free Press.

Kearns-Goodwin, D. (1976). *Lyndon Johnson and the American Dream*. New York: New American Library.

Kramer, R. M. (1995). In dubious battle: Heightened accountability, dysphoric cognition and self-defeating bargaining behavior. In Roderick M. Kramer, & David M. Messick (Eds.), *Negotiation as a Social Process* (pp. 95–120). Thousand Oaks, CA: Sage Publications.

Kramer, R. M. (1998). Revisiting the Bay of Pigs and Vietnam decisions 25 years later: How well has the groupthink hypothesis stood the test of time? *Organizational Behavior and Human Decision Processes*, *73*, 236–271.

Kramer, R. M. (2004). The imperatives of identity: The role of identity in leader judgment and decision making. In D. van Knippenberg, & M. A. Hogg (Eds.), *Leadership and Power* (pp. 184–196). Thousand Oaks, CA: Sage.

Kramer, R. M. (2005). Flipping without flopping. *Harvard Business Review*, *83*, 18.

Kramer, R. M., & Lewicki, R. J. (2010). Repairing and enhancing trust: Approaches to reducing organizational trust deficits. In J. P. Walsh, & A. P. Brief (Eds.), *Academy of Management Annals* (Vol. 4) (pp. 245–278). New York: Routledge.

Leary, M. R. (1995). *Self-presentation: Impression Management and Interpersonal Behavior*. New York: Westview.

March, J. G. (1994). *A Primer on Decision Making*. New York: Free Press.

Meindl, J. R., Ehrlich, S.B., & Dukerich, J. M. (1985). The romance of leadership. *Administrative Science Quarterly*, 30, 78–102.

Middleton, H. J. (1990). *LBJ: The White House Years*. New York: Harry N. Abrams Publishing.

Neustadt, R. E. (1990). *Presidential Power and the Modern Presidents*. New York: Free Press.

Noonan, P. (1995). Ronald Reagan, 1981–1989. In R. Wilson (Ed.), *Character Above All: Ten Presidents from FDR to George Bush* (pp. 202–223). New York: Simon & Shuster.

Pfeffer, J. (1981). Management as symbolic action. In L. L. Cummings, & B. M. Staw (Eds.), *Research in Organizational Behavior, 3*, 1–52. Greenwich, CT: JAI Press.

Pfeffer, J. (1992). *Managing with Power*. Cambridge, MA: Harvard Business School Press.

Podolny, J. Khurana, R., & Hill-Popper, M. (2005). Revisiting the meaning of leadership. In B. M. Staw, & R. M. Kramer (Eds.), *Research in Organizational Behavior* (Vol. 26) (pp. 1–36). New York: Elsevier.

Salancik, G. R., & Meindl, J. R. (1984). Corporate attributions as strategic illusions of management control. *Administrative Science Quarterly*, *29*, 238–254.

Staw, B. M. (1976). Knee-deep in the big muddy: A study of escalating commitment to a chosen course of action. *Organizational Behavior and Human Performance*, *16*, 27–44.

Steele, C. M. (1988). The psychology of self-affirmation: Sustaining the integrity of the self. In L. Berkowitz (Ed.), *Advances in Experimental Social Psychology, 21,* 261–302. New York: Academic Press.

Sutton, R. I., & Galunic, D. C. (1996). Consequences of public scrutiny for leaders and their organizations. In B. M. Staw, & L. L. Cummings (Eds.), *Research in Organizational Behavior* (Vol. 18) (pp. 201–250). Greenwich, CT: JAI Press.

Sutton, R. I., & Kramer, R. M. (1990). Transforming failure into success: Spin control in the Iceland arms control talks. In R. L. Kahn, & M. Zald (Eds.), *Organizations and Nation States: New Perspectives on Conflict and Cooperation* (pp. 221–248). San Francisco, CA: Jossey-Bass.

Tedeschi, J. T. (1981). *Impression Management Theory and Social Psychological Research.* New York: Academic Press.

Tetlock, P. E. (1992). The impact of accountability on judgment and choice: Toward a social contingency model. In L. Berkowitz (Ed.), *Advances in Experimental Social Psychology* (Vol. 25) (pp. 331–376). New York: Academic Press.

Useem, M. (1999). *The Leadership Moment.* New York: Crown Business Books.

Valenti, J. (1975). *A Very Human President.* New York: W. W. Norton.

Weick, K. E. (1993). Sensemaking in organizations. In J. K. Murnighan (Ed.), *Social Psychology in Organizations: Advances in Theory and Practice* (pp. 10–37). Englewood Cliffs, NJ: Prentice-Hall.

Weick, K. E., & Daft, R. L. (1983). The effectiveness of interpretation systems. In K. S. Cameron, & D. A. Whetten (Eds.), *Organizational Effectiveness* (pp. 71–93). New York: Academic Press.

*Wood, J. V. and Wilson, A. E. (2003). How important is social comparison? In M. R. Leary and J. P. Tangney (Eds.), *Handbook of Self and Identity* (pp. 344–366). New York: The Guilford Press.

5

TOWARD A SOCIAL PSYCHOLOGY OF SOCIAL MOVEMENTS

Douglas J. McAdam

Forty-five years ago the thought of trying to fashion a viable social psychology of social movements would have seemed laughable. Why, because the dominant perspectives on social movements and collective action were already overwhelmingly psychological and social psychological in their focus and proposed causal dynamics. This was true at both the micro and macro levels of analysis.

At the micro level, the emphasis was more psychological than social psychological, with various personality traits or psychological dynamics stressed as the catalyst for individual activism. A complete survey is beyond the scope of this chapter, but a sampling of these theories will convey the general tenor of the accounts. For example, the idea that the cluster of personality traits known as *authoritarianism* disposed people to participate in movements—especially right-wing movements—gained wide currency in the 1950s and 60s (Adorno & Frenkel-Brunswick, 1950; Hoffer, 1951; Lipset & Rabb, 1973). Another influential theory from the 1960s held that people were motivated to achieve *cognitive consistency* in their beliefs and behaviors (Rokeach, 1969). When applied to social movement participation the logic was straightforward: as people become aware of fundamental contradictions between deeply held beliefs and features of society they are psychologically compelled to participate in efforts to resolve the inconsistency. In contrast, *mass society* theorists argued that it was the alienation and sense of disconnection characteristic of modern society that accounted for movement participation (Aberle, 1966; Klapp, 1969; Kornhauser, 1959). In this view it is the individual's desire to overcome his/her feelings of alienation and achieve the sense of belonging they lack in their life that draws them to the "substitute community" of the social movement. In another influential work from the period, Lewis Feuer (1969) sought to explain student activism on the basis of unresolved Oedipal conflicts between male activists and their fathers.

Of all the psychologically oriented theories, however, perhaps none generated as much interest or empirical attention as *relative deprivation* theory. The central premise was that activism is motivated by an unfavorable gap between what a person feels he or she is entitled to and what, in fact, they are receiving. The underlying impulse to action, however, is not so much the substantive desire to close the gap. Whether framed as an extension of the *frustration-aggression* hypothesis (Davies, 1963, 1969; Feieraband, Feieraband, & Nesvold, 1969; Gurr, 1970), or grounded in the *cognitive balance* literature (Geschwender, 1968; Morrison, 1973), the theory "assumes an underlying state of individual psychological tension that is relieved by SM [social movement] participation" (Gurney & Tierney, 1982: 36).

For all their apparent theoretical sophistication, empirical support for all of these individually based psychological accounts of movement participation has proven elusive. Summarizing their exhaustive survey of the literature on the relationship between activism and various personality traits and/or psychological factors, Wilson and Orum (1976: 189) concluded "that the many analyses … of collective actions during the past decade, impress upon us the poverty of psychology; or, at the very least, the limitations of psychology."

But it was not simply at the micro level that psychological perspectives held sway in the study of social movements. At the macro level the dominance of *collective behavior theory* presumed psychological explanations for the "when" and "how" of movements as well. Like all forms of collective behavior (e.g. panics, crazes, fads), movements were held to emerge *when* rapid social change occasioned a generalized breakdown of the social order. So Nazism emerged out of the social and economic chaos of Weimar Germany. The 19th Century Temperance Movement in the U.S. was a "symbolic crusade" by New England Protestants rendered politically and culturally anxious by immigrant "hordes" from Italy and Ireland and the threat they were seen to pose to the traditional small town Yankee way of life (Gusfield, 1963). Cargo cults and other millenary movements emerged out of native people's attempts to cope with the massive dislocations occasioned by colonial conquest (Kobben, 1960; Wallace, 1966; Worsley, 1968).

Neil Smelser, one of the most influential of the collective behavior theorists, sought to explain the *how* of social movements. According to Smelser, the stress and sense of dislocation occasioned by rapid social change "excites feelings of anxiety, fantasy [and] hostility" (1962: 11). In turn these feelings motivate those affected to fashion "generalized beliefs" to restore the normative order destroyed by social change. These "generalized beliefs" serve as the ideational basis of the movement and its adherents. But Smelser's description of these "generalized beliefs" makes it clear what function he believes they play for movement adherents. "These beliefs," he writes,

> differ … from those which guide other types of behavior. They involve a belief in the existence of extraordinary forces—threats, conspiracies,

etc.—which are at work in the universe. They also involve an assessment of the extraordinary consequences which will follow if the collective attempt to reconstitute social action is successful. The beliefs on which collective behavior is based ... are thus akin to magical beliefs.

(1962: 8)

In short, movements function not as a form of rational, instrumental political behavior, but like all collective behavior, as a seductive, but ultimately ineffective group psychological response to a social system under stress.

Resource Mobilization, Political Process and the Retreat from Psychology

A central tenet of the sociology of knowledge is that academic work is always shaped by the specific social/historical context in which it is produced. And so it was for both the classic social theorists who gave us *collective behavior, mass society theory*, and the like and for the newer generation of social movement scholars who challenged the existing psychological perspectives. Both groups sought to understand the most consequential movements of their eras. Those movements could not, however, have been more different. For the earlier generation of scholars, Nazism, and Soviet-style Communism were the touchstone movements demanding explanation. And without lapsing into a simplistic functionalism, it should be clear that highlighting the psychological elements inherent in these movements had the effect of discrediting them for an academic audience whose sympathies were decidedly anti-authoritarian.

Political sensibilities certainly figured in the rejection of the classic psychological perspectives as well. These theories were challenged, at least in part, because they did not accord with the experiences of a whole new generation of scholars who came of age in the 1960s. To this generation, the touchstone struggles of the era—civil rights, anti-war, the women's movement—were simply incompatible with and poorly explained by models that emphasized social disorganization and abnormal psychology as the keys to understanding collective action. In turn, this perceived lack of fit sparked something of a paradigm shift in the social scientific study of social movements. The net effect of the new scholarship was to shift the focus of analysis from psychological and "breakdown" models to more political and organizational accounts of movement emergence. Chief among these newer perspectives were *resource mobilization* and *political process.*

As formulated by its chief proponents, John McCarthy and Mayer Zald (1973, 1977), *resource mobilization* was conceived as a response to those who saw movements as the product of strain and social disorganization. McCarthy and Zald argued that there was always sufficient strain or discontent in society to motivate collective action. What varied, they asserted, was not the motivation to mobilize but the organizational capacity to do so. In advancing this argument, McCarthy and Zald explicitly asserted the rational instrumental nature of social movements and sought to reclaim the field for organizational scholars. Their goal was to understand the social processes and factors that allowed aggrieved groups to mobilize and sustain the organizations necessary for effective movement action.

While agreeing that movements should be seen as another form of rational, instrumental action, *political process* theorists focused not on their organizational, but political, dimensions and dynamics (Gamson, 1990[1975]; McAdam, 1999[1982]; Tarrow, 1982; Tilly, 1978). Movements, in this conception, are politics by other means, practiced primarily by groups who typically lack the necessary leverage to pursue their goals through "proper channels." Society, in this view, is seen as an elaborate system of power relations that grants some groups— "members" in Gamson's (1990[1975]) phraseology—routine access to power while denying it to others (e.g., "challengers"). But this set of power relations is not immutable. Accordingly, movements are expected to emerge when those in power are more vulnerable or receptive to the demands of challenging groups. The analytic focus was squarely on the ways in which developing "political opportunities" shaped the emergence and ongoing fate of social movements.

The more or less exclusive stress on the organizational and political dimensions of social movements tended to crowd out any focus on the more psychological or social psychological aspects of collective action. More to the point, the stress on irrationality and abnormality in the earlier perspectives had served to discredit the psychological in the study of social movements. If the older theories had been biased toward the psychological and the irrational, the newer perspectives were equally narrow in their stress on "structure" and rationality.

Fortunately, while the "newer" (now quite "old") perspectives have remained generally dominant, an awareness of their limits has developed within the field, accompanied by increasing calls for more systematic empirical work and theory on the cultural, emotional, and social psychological dynamics of social movements (Aminzade & McAdam, 2001; Einwohner, 2006; Emirbayr & Goodwin, 1994; Gamson, 1992; Goodwin, Jasper, & Polletta, 2004; Klandermans, 1997, 2004; Sherkat, 1998; Snow & McAdam, 2000; Snow & Oliver, 1995; Stryker, Owens, & White, 2000). In truth, however, attention to these aspects of collective action has never been truly absent from the field. Some examples will help make the point. In 1985, Ferree and Miller published an influential article in *Sociological Inquiry* that explicitly called for an integration of social psychological and the newer structural perspectives on social movements.

Beginning with the pioneering work of Snow et al. in 1986, the study of "framing processes" has been a central focus of social movement research (Snow & Benford, 1988, 1992; Ellingson, 1995; Noonan, 1995). Framing processes refer to the efforts of movement actors (and their opponents) to fashion especially resonant and persuasive accounts of the movement to attract new recruits, generate media attention and ultimately convince the general public and policymakers of the rightness of their cause. Attention to these dynamics invariably includes an interest in such standard social psychological topics as social construction, social influence, and media effects.

In similar fashion, groundbreaking work in the 1980s by Alberto Melucci (1980, 1984, 1985) and other European *new social movement* theorists criticized the structural bias in the resource mobilization and political process perspectives and called for more attention to cultural processes in movements. Of special interest to Melucci was the creative potential for movements to give rise to new and enduring "collective identities." Indeed, for Melucci, fluid network dynamics and collective identity processes were the defining features of social movements.

Most recently a number of movement analysts have asserted the powerful influence of emotions and emotion processes in the origins, development and decline of social movements (Aminzade & McAdam, 2001; Goodwin, Jasper, & Polletta, 2001, 2004; D. Gould, 2009). In doing so, they have explicitly critiqued the rationalist bias inherent in the "newer" perspectives, while steering clear of a return to the classic collective behavior and/or "breakdown" frameworks.

This last point is important. Rather than a rejection of the resource mobilization and political process "revolution," these fragments of more cultural and social psychological analysis represent "friendly amendments" to these perspectives. The plea is for a broader set of perspectives on collective action and, in the context of this volume, specifically for a viable social psychology of social movements. Space constraints—to say nothing of my own academic limitations—will not allow for anything approaching that ambitious goal here. My aims are much more modest. In the spirit of theoretical synthesis, I intend to: (1) review three consistent empirical findings that have come out of the structural research program of the past 35–40 years; and (2) discuss the social psychological processes that appear to inform these stylized structural "facts." The aim is to begin to suggest the convergent lines of research and theory that might eventually yield the broader understanding of social movements for which analysts are calling.

Three Structural "Facts" and Their Social Psychological Implications[1]

I use the balance of the chapter to illustrate the approach advocated here. I take three recurrent findings about social movements and, drawing on other work, speculate a bit about the social psychological processes that appear to be implicated in the results. I begin by simply stating the "facts."

- *Fact 1*: prior social ties are the principal means of movement recruitment.
- *Fact 2*: the great majority of social movements tend to develop within established social settings (e.g. existing organizations or networks).

- *Fact 3*: participation in social movements (read: immersion in social movement networks) has enduring effects on the lives of activists.

For the most part, these findings have been represented as recurring structural features of movements, with insufficient attention to the complex social and cultural processes that account for their persistence. Here I want to focus, in particular, on the social psychological processes that may be implicated in each.

Prior Social Ties as a Basis for Movement Recruitment

In one of his last published pieces, the influential network and social movement analyst, Roger Gould (2003: 236) noted that "one of the first and most frequently cited facts about social ties and activism is that activists are frequently drawn into a movement by the people they know." But, as he went on to say, "simply observing that social ties affect mobilization is not much of a contribution. It is a bit like noticing that people who are stricken with plague have had contact with other plague victims" (p. 237). To their credit, network analysts have not simply hypothesized these effects. Indeed, they have produced a large volume of work attesting to the consistency of the relationship (Anheier, 2003; Diani, 1995; Dixon & Roscigno, 2003; R. Gould, 1993, 1995; Kitts, 2000; Klandermans & Oegema, 1987; McAdam, 1986, 1988; McAdam & Paulsen, 1993; Nepstad & Smith, 1999; Passy, 2003; Snow, Zurcher, & Ekland-Olson, 1980). But the social processes that account for the finding remain surprisingly opaque. As another movement scholar has observed: "[W]e are now aware that social ties are important for collective action, but we still need to theorize …the actual role of networks" (Passy, 2003: 22). Without specifying the mechanisms that account for the effect, movement researchers are guilty of assaying a structurally determinist explanation of movement recruitment. We are left with the unfortunate impression that any individual who is linked to a movement by prior social ties is somehow compelled to join the struggle. There are at least three reasons why we should reject this simple structural imperative.

First, the above account skirts the important question of origins. That is, to say that people join movements because they know others who are involved ignores the obvious point that on the eve of a movement, there are no salient alters already involved to pull ego into activism. Second, the structural account fails to acknowledge conceptually or address empirically the fact that potential recruits invariably possess a multitude of "prior social ties" that are likely to expose them to conflicting behavioral influences. Here we confront the hoary problem of sampling on the dependent variable. Overwhelmingly, the studies of movement recruitment start by surveying activists after their entrance into a movement. But showing that these activists were linked to the movement by some prior tie does not prove the causal potency of the connection. No doubt there are also many nonactivists with ties to the movement who did not participate, perhaps because salient others outside the movement put pressure on them to remain on the sidelines.

The final shortcoming of the simplistic structural account of movement recruitment is the very general one mentioned above. Quite simply, movement analysts have generally failed to identify the mediating social processes that might account for the network effects they observe. In contrast, rational choice theorists have assayed such an account, though one that is notably void of social psychology (Hardin, 1995; Lichbach, 1998; Olson, 1965; Opp, 2009). Rooted in game theory, the account holds for the more general class of "iterated social dilemmas;" that is, situations in which individuals are making behavioral decisions based on the expectation that they will have ongoing interaction with others confronting the same decision. When applied to movement recruitment, the formal implications of the iterated social dilemma game are clear.

> People who expect future interaction with movement participants should be more likely, all else equal … to join. Such people, the reasoning goes, are more likely to view joining as beneficial to themselves because their 'ties' to other joiners give the latter an opportunity to reward (or punish) their decision to join (or not to join).
>
> (R. Gould, 2003: 241)

This is especially true if the early joiners have the capacity to carefully monitor the actions of those potential recruits to whom they are tied (Hechter, 1987; Taylor, 1988).

As with all rational choice models, the causal connection between the prior social tie and later activism is held to follow from what might be thought of as an individual cognitive mechanism. There is little conventional social influence here. It is not that salient alters have persuaded ego to join the movement. Rather ego has come to view this as the rational course of action, based on: (1) the behaviors of others; (2) the expectation of future interaction; and (3) the capacity of alters to monitor his/her actions.

For all the appealing clarity and parsimony of the rational choice perspective, you will not be surprised to learn that I find it lacking. Owing to its impoverished view of *the social* and social influence in particular, the rational choice perspective proffers a highly truncated account of individual motivation and action. That said, I take very seriously the need for just this kind of motivational model of activism and for the identification of dynamic mechanisms and processes that can bridge the micro and meso dimensions of social movements. I do not pretend to deliver on the full promise of such a model here. But drawing on some previous work by the author as well as recent work by others (R. Gould, 2003; Passy, 2003; Uhlaner, 1989), I think we can begin to move in this direction. I begin by making a single foundational point. Any viable model of human action must take account of the fundamentally social/relational nature of human existence (Uhlaner, 1989). This is not to embrace the over socialized conception of the individual implicit in the work of most structural network analysts (and curiously many culturalists as well). Consistent with the rationalists, I too stress the potential for individual autonomy and choice. Where I part company with the rationalists is in the central importance I attach to one powerful motivator of human action. I think most individuals act routinely to safeguard and sustain the central sources of meaning and identity in their lives. As a practical matter, this typically means prizing solidary incentives over all others and, in particular, conforming to the behavioral dictates of those whose approval and emotional sustenance are central to our most salient identities.

How might this foundational tenet translate into a specific account of movement recruitment? In 1993, I coauthored an article with Ronnelle Paulsen in which we offered a sequential account of the onset of individual activism. We argued (p. 647) that:

> [t]he ultimate decision to participate in a movement would depend on four ...[mechanisms]: (1) the occurrence of a specific recruiting attempt, (2) the successful linkage of movement and [salient] identity, (3) support for that linkage from persons who normally serve to sustain the identity in question, and (4) the absence of strong opposition from others on whom other salient identities depend.

Echoing the central theme of this chapter, we then closed the article with the following plea (p. 663):

> the most important implication of this research is as much social psychological as structural. Network analysts of movement recruitment have been overly concerned with assessing the structure of the subject's relationship to the movement without paying sufficient attention to the social psychological processes that mediate the link between structure and activism ... [P]rior ties would appear to encourage activism only when they (a) reinforce the potential recruit's strong identification with a particular identity and (b) help to establish a strong linkage between that identity and the movement in question. When these processes of *identity amplification* and *identity/movement linkage* take place, activism is likely to follow ... Movement analysts then, need to be as attuned to the *content* of network processes as to the *structures* themselves (emphases in original).

The provisional model outlined in the 1993 article is sketched schematically in Figure 5.1.

The process sketched here, and the empirical results reported in McAdam and Paulsen, accord nicely with the central themes and conclusions of recent

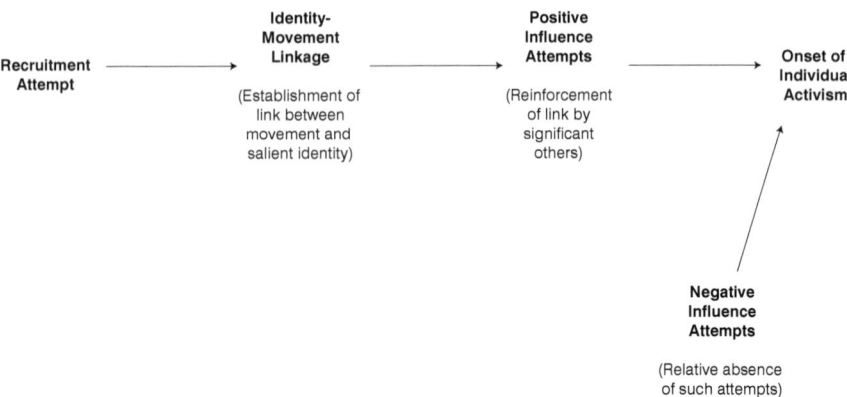

FIGURE 5.1 The Process of Individual Recruitment

work by Passy (2003), R. Gould (2003) and Nepstad and Smith (1999). In her effort to better specify the structural account of recruitment, Passy ascribes three crucial functions to network ties. These she terms the "structural-connection," "socialization," and "decision-shaping" functions. These three functions bear a striking similarity to three of the four mechanisms identified in Figure 5.1. Passy's "structural-connection" function is essentially the same as the "recruitment attempt" in Figure 5.1. That is, prior ties can connect a potential activist to a movement through a concrete recruitment attempt. What Paulsen and I termed "identity-movement linkage," Passy calls the "socialization" function of networks. Finally, Passy's "decision-shaping" function is more or less synonymous with the "positive influence" mechanism shown in Figure 5.1. The important point for McAdam and Paulsen was that although these various mechanisms could occur independently, the likelihood of successful recruitment was dramatically increased when they occurred sequentially through the efforts of a single, highly salient prior tie. So if, for example, a very close friend asked you to take part in a demonstration ("recruitment attempt"), and worked both to create a plausible link between the action and an identity s/he knew you prized ("identity-movement linkage") and to argue for the correctness of the action in general terms ("positive influence attempt"), I think it is very likely that you would take part, especially if you encountered little or no opposition to the action from others ("negative influence attempts").

This hypothetical example is very close to the one that Roger Gould (1993) models in his work. The unique, and I think entirely justified, supposition that Gould builds into his model is that a recruitment attempt by a prior tie works, not because of any anticipated punishment for nonparticipation (which is what rationalists argue), but because shared involvement comes to be viewed as a way of enhancing the existing relationship. But this, as Gould notes, will only work if the two individuals are very close to begin with. Indeed, the model predicts that the closer, more emotionally salient the tie, the more likely the recruitment effort will succeed. This is entirely consistent with what McAdam and Paulsen argue. To the extent that a single, highly salient (in Gould's term "strong") tie orchestrates the three mechanisms identified in Figure 5.1, the likelihood of a successful recruitment attempt is very high.

Established Social Settings as the Locus of Movement Emergence

It has become part of the received wisdom that movements almost always develop within established social settings. Besides the classic studies that helped establish the "fact" (Freeman, 1973; Tilly et al., 1975; Margadant, 1979; Evans, 1980; Aminzade, 1981; Morris, 1984; McAdam, 1999[1982]), a host of more recent works have served to confirm it. In his research on the 1989 Chinese student movement, Zhao (1998, 2001) shows how the dense ecological concentration of college campuses in Beijing served to facilitate initial mobilization. Glenn (2001), among others, documents the role that a network of independent theatre companies played in the origins of Civic Forum in Czechoslovakia. Osa's research (1997, 2003) highlights the critical role that the Catholic Church played in nurturing Solidarity and the broader dissident movement in Poland in the 1980s. Finally, in keeping with a long line of research, recent work by Polletta (1999) and Futrell and Simi (2004) reinforces the longstanding interest in the role of "free spaces"—localized social spaces that are insulated from official scrutiny and control—in nurturing and sustaining embryonic movements.

Consistent with these studies, proponents of the political process model have long emphasized the role of indigenous organizations or associational networks in the emergence of a movement. Absent any extant "mobilizing structure," incipient movements are held to lack the capacity to act even when afforded the opportunity to do so. As straightforward and seemingly self-evident as this proposition would appear to be, it must be remembered that, when first voiced, it contradicted the emphasis on social breakdown and disorganization so central to the collective behavior tradition. Since this particular debate was joined, it seems clear that the weight of empirical evidence favors the political process camp over the breakdown school. All well and good, but, as with the notion of "prior tie," the "mobilizing structure" concept has too often been treated as an objective structural facilitator of protest, rather than a contested site of interaction that can give rise to opposite lines of action. The point is, like prior ties, existing groups or networks are more apt to discourage than to facilitate insurgent action. Bottom line: it is *not* prior ties or indigenous organization per se that enable protest, but rather the interactive dynamics and group level processes that take place in these settings and which, on occasion, give rise to the new frames and identities that legitimate emergent collective action.

The point can be made more concretely by revisiting the case that helped establish this "fact" in the first place. Movement scholars have thoroughly documented the central role played by the black church in helping to launch the civil rights movement (Oberschall, 1973; Morris, 1984; McAdam, 1999[1982]). But while the movement's debt to the black church is widely acknowledged, the standard narrative account obscures cultural and social psychological processes of great importance. Until the rise of the movement, it was common for observers—black no less than white—to depict the black church as a generally conservative institution with a decided emphasis, not on the "social gospel in action," but rather on the realization of rewards in the afterlife (Johnson, 1941; Mays and Nicholson, 1969; Myrdal, 1944). Nor did the traditional conservatism of the institution entirely disappear during the movement. Charles Payne's (1996) exceptional book on the movement in Mississippi makes it clear that the conservative nature of local black clergy remained a significant obstacle to local organizing even during the movement's heyday.

Given this more complicated portrait of the black church, the highly contingent nature of initial mobilization attempts should be clear. To turn even some black congregations into vehicles of collective protest, movement leaders had to engage in a lot of creative cultural work, through which the aims of the church and its animating collective identity were redefined to accord with the goals of the emerging struggle. This is, first and foremost, a social psychological process that has far more to do with social construction, collective attribution and re-socialization than with any kind of objective inventory of organizational resources. Organization and resources matter little if their use is not governed by shared meanings and identities legitimating contention.

This discussion brings us, inevitably, back to the limits of the dominant structural perspective in social movement studies. By starting from the accomplished fact of collective action, and then working back in time to note that movements tend to arise in established social settings, structural analysts exaggerated the link between organization and action. By, once again, selecting on the dependent variable—in this case, successful social movements—analysts inevitably focused on the exceptional cases where existing groups birthed movements, but not the far more numerous examples where established groups constrain action. Moreover their methods—principally case study and event research—were essentially those of the outsider, making it impossible for them to observe the group level dynamics—cultural and social psychological—that shaped the exceptional cases.

But were we to invest in more observational or experimental methods, on what concrete social processes would we want researchers to focus? What are the social psychological mechanisms that appear to key the transformation of an established social setting into a site of emergent mobilization? Based on some earlier work (McAdam, 1999[1982], McAdam, Tarrow, & Tilly, 2001), I stress the two mechanisms shown in Figure 5.2.

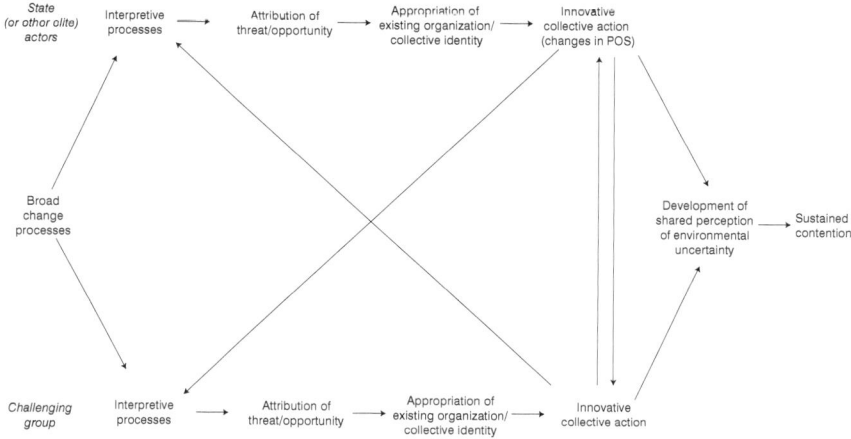

FIGURE 5.2 A Dynamic, Interactive Framework for Analyzing the Emergence of Contentious Politics

1 Attribution of Threat or Opportunity

Human beings are voracious meaning makers. The routine monitoring and interpretation of events and environmental conditions is the foundation for all social life, routine no less than contentious. Consistent with this view, initial movement mobilization depends upon an emerging collective account of some new threat to, or opportunity for, the realization of group interests. Normally this account is a response to objective change processes. In rare cases, these changes are so dramatic as to virtually compel their own interpretation. The 9/11 terrorist attacks are a good case in point. Far more often, however, the emerging accounts of threat/opportunity are highly contingent social constructions that are in no simple sense determined by the change processes themselves. Indeed, in rare instances such interpretations may even arise in the absence of any objective changes in the life circumstances of the group in question (Kurzman, 1996). But, as Goodwin and Jasper (1999) note, rather than emphasize the constructed nature of *perceived* opportunities (or threats), the tendency has been to assert a deterministic link between objective change processes and movement mobilization. What is glossed in this are the critically important processes of social construction and attribution that shape the collective response to objective events.

In their 1982 book *Encounters with Unjust Authority*, Gamson, Fireman and Rytina report the results of an ingenious study designed to better understand these crucial mediating processes. The researchers began by placing an ad in a local paper inviting individuals to participate for pay in "research involving group discussion of community standards." When each of the 33 groups of participants assembled they were told the discussion they were going to have would establish the "community standards" that would determine the guilt or innocence of a gas station owner who was being stripped of his station by a national oil company for failure to live up to the "moral turpitude" clause of his contract. They were further told that the firm running the videotaped discussion session was working for the oil company, but were simply gathering information to aid the trial process. But as the session unfolded the person in charge became increasingly coercive in his efforts to elicit statements supporting the oil company's position in the case. By session's end it was all too apparent that the "research" project was little more than a front for the interests of the oil company. The group was clearly being used to subvert the criminal justice system. Surely these groups resisted this transparent injustice. In point of fact, slightly fewer than half did so, reminding us again that "objective" grievances are not sufficient to produce collective action. Key to the transformation of these "objective" grievances into a shared resolve to act was the social construction of an "injustice frame" (Gamson et al., 1982: chapter 10).

2 Social Appropriation

But as Gamson et al. (1982) go on to show, the emergence of this shared frame is not sufficient for collective action. For collective attributions to key emergent action the interpreters must share enough of a sense of "we-ness" to make conjoint action viable. This is almost certainly why movements develop within established groups or networks, settings in which a well-defined collective identity already exists. The point is, as a prerequisite for action, would-be insurgents must either create an embryonic collective identity or *appropriate* an existing one. Without minimizing the difficulties inherent in the process, *social appropriation* is far easier than creating a sense of "we-ness" from scratch. No doubt much of the difficulty Gamson's would-be insurgents faced owed to the absence of any pre-existing collective identity.

But incipient movements require much more than a shared sense of identity to be successful. They also require some sort of action vehicle. Again, these can be created from whole cloth. But it is much more efficient to have access to an existing structure. The other virtue of appropriation is that it typically affords the burgeoning movement a ready-made mobilizing structure. That is, *social appropriation* typically involves the transformation of an established social setting (including the redefinition of its animating collective identity) into a legitimate site of emergent contentious action.

This brings us to the key explanatory question: what factors make successful social appropriation more likely? The question takes on added force in the face of the powerful inertial force of most social settings. That is, with few exceptions, established groups, institutions, and networks are geared to reproducing (or at least accommodating), rather than challenging, the status quo. Religious institutions are houses of worship, colleges are learning and credential mills, etc. To transform any routine social setting into a site of incipient rebellion poses a distinct challenge to any whom would make the attempt. What factors or processes give some hope of successfully engaging the challenge? Alas, the structural bias in social movement studies means we have almost no empirical work to draw upon in answering this question. For now, informed speculation will have to fill the void. I close this section by briefly discussing two factors that would appear to facilitate social appropriation.

The first factor is what Snow and Benford (1988) refer to as "frame resonance." By "frame resonance," they mean system critical interpretative schema that resonate with deeply held cultural beliefs and values. It makes sense to hypothesize that, all things equal, attempts at appropriation are more likely to succeed if they are framed in especially resonant terms. But if the message is important, I am inclined to believe the messenger is even more important. That is, the single most important factor shaping the prospects for successful appropriation may well be the social status of the would-be "appropriator." This is little more than an extension of years of diffusion research. The success and speed with which innovations diffuse depends centrally on the social status of the innovators and initial adopters. If we regard appropriation attempts as *social* innovations, it makes sense to assume the same pattern would hold. So, for example, I would expect the established leaders of an organization to have an easier time redefining its purposes than I would an ordinary rank and file member of the group. For example, much of the stunning and immediate success of the Montgomery Bus Boycott owed to the vocal support—sponsorship really—it received from the town's established ministerial elite. Redefining the Christian duties of their congregations to include staying off the busses, the ministers effectively appropriated their churches in the service of the burgeoning movement.

Social Movements as a Powerful Vehicle of Personal Transformation

Though perhaps less developed than the study of movement origins and movement recruitment, there is also a considerable body of research on the individual impact of movement participation. The results of that research have been interpreted as supporting a clear conclusion: movement participation has enduring effects on the political and personal lives of activists. Though my own work (1988, 1989, 1999) has been cited frequently in support of this conclusion, I am increasingly convinced that the effects of activism are actually quite varied and critical of our failure to more closely interrogate the social psychological processes that might account for this variation in impact.

To illustrate the variable effects of sustained activism and to speculate a bit about the causes of that variation, I begin by summarizing the results of two ambitious follow-up studies of activists. The first is the study I conducted of applicants to the 1964 Mississippi Summer Project (better known as "Freedom Summer"). The other is some recent research I conducted looking at the enduring "civic effects" of participation in Teach for America (TFA) during the program's first six years. The Freedom Summer project brought roughly 1,000 primarily white college students to Mississippi during the summer of 1964 to register black voters, teach in "Freedom Schools," and generally dramatize the continued denial of civil rights to African-Americans in the Deep South. Teach for America asks a large number of graduating college seniors (roughly 2,000 in 2004) to commit to teaching for two years in resource poor urban and rural schools. While different in many respects, Freedom Summer and Teach for America are alike in that they require (or required in the case of Freedom Summer) intense, sustained commitment by those involved. They also expose (or exposed) participants to the marked economic inequality and racism that shape the lives of all too many in this country. And yet, for all these similarities, the aggregate impact of the experience appears to be very different in the two cases.

The Freedom Summer research yielded consistent evidence of striking differences in the subsequent personal and political lives of the two groups of applicants studied. Twenty years after the summer project, the volunteers remained much more active politically than the "no-shows" (applicants who were accepted by project organizers, but never made it to Mississippi), especially in movement, as opposed to institutional, politics. They also remained more resolutely "leftist" in their political views than the no-shows, who scored out as more conventionally liberal in orientation.

The personal differences were just as striking, and perhaps more surprising. While no less likely to have ever married, only half of the volunteers were married at the time of the study. This compared to 72 percent of the no-shows and 79 percent of a matched group of their age and educational peers within the U.S. (McAdam, 1988: 219). The volunteers had also experienced much more episodic work histories and, partly as a result of that, had significantly lower incomes on average than either the no-shows or the national comparison group (McAdam, 1988: 225–227). Nor were any of these (and other) findings explained by group differences evident before the Freedom Summer project. In short, while the biographies of the two groups look remarkably similar going into the summer, they diverge sharply afterwards. The conclusion seems unmistakable: in the aggregate, participation in the project transformed the lives of the volunteers.

Do we see something similar in the case of TFA? Certainly proponents of the program assert that this kind of life-changing impact is very common (Kopp, 2001). In particular, they argue that, besides the valuable educational service the program provides, TFA also serves to "make life-long citizens." The principal goal of the TFA study was to test these claims by comparing the long-term civic attitudes and behaviors of three groups of applicants: "graduates" (those who fulfill their two year teaching commitment); "dropouts" (those who leave the program before completing their teaching assignment); and "non-matriculants" (those who are offered, but turn down, a teaching assignment). If one adopts the "clinical trials" analogy that is common to this literature, the expectation is clear. Having had two full years of the TFA "treatment," the graduates should exceed the other two groups in their embrace of civic attitudes and actual rates of subsequent service. Deprived of the treatment, non-matriculants should presumably rank lowest on both measures, with the dropouts arrayed in between. This is not at all what we find.

We find little evidence of positive attitudinal or behavioral effects of participation in TFA. While graduates do score consistently higher on a broad range of attitudinal items measuring civic commitment, these differences appear to be less a byproduct of the experience, than a reflection of the ongoing participation of roughly a third of program alumni in TFA. When these TFA activists are removed from the analysis, the current attitudes of the remaining graduates are indistinguishable from those of the dropouts and non-matriculants.

The behavioral impact of TFA participation is clearer still. There are two parts to the story. First, graduates lag significantly behind the non-matriculants in their aggregate level of current service. Just as important, instead of emerging as the broadly engaged citizens depicted by program proponents, the graduates become more narrowly attuned to education, with special attention to ongoing involvement in TFA activities. Indeed, in *all* forms of service—save for TFA participation—both the non-matriculants and dropouts outpace graduates.

Needless to say, the study of the TFA applicants fails to confirm the citizenship-conferring effects of this kind of activist youth service. Should we be surprised by these findings? I think not. Going into the study I was skeptical about the received wisdom embodied in the clinical trials image of the impact of TFA or similar youth service programs. This skepticism was rooted in two hunches. The first was that the extreme selection inherent in programs like TFA made claims about the life-transforming effects of participation implausible. If applicants are already strongly committed to, and experienced in, service activities, how could their subsequent civic commitments be attributed to the intervening service experience? For such a highly select group, it makes more sense to assume continuity in civic involvement, rather than the "before" and "after" transformation implied in the popular and scholarly accounts of such experiences. This is, in fact, what we see in our findings. Even acknowledging the "channeling" effect of TFA participation, the overwhelming majority of our subjects remain attitudinally committed to, and engaged in, civic service of some kind.

The second assumption was that variation in the actual service experience strained the credibility of the clinical trials analogy. While such trials are carefully designed experiments that effectively control the effects of other possible explanatory factors, the real world service/activist experiences studied by social scientists are inevitably messy affairs, characterized by lots of differences in the nature of the experience.

Why shouldn't we expect this variation to produce interesting within-group differences in the effects of the experience? Going beyond the current study, we also suspect that these kinds of experiential differences hold the key to understanding the starkly different outcomes we see in the TFA and Freedom Summer studies. What specific mechanisms *not* in evidence in TFA might help explain these highly divergent effects? We see three such mechanisms as key in this regard.

1 Gap Between Expectation and Reality

Over and over again the Freedom Summer volunteers talked about how their idealized views of the U.S. were contradicted by the stark reality of poverty, state-sanctioned violence, and atavistic racism they witnessed in Mississippi. This chasm between expectation and reality left many volunteers unwilling or unable to "go home" at the close of the summer. They simply had seen too much, experienced too much, to return to the sheltered lives they had lived before. Without discounting the intensity of the TFA experience, few of our subjects appear to have experienced a reality starkly different from the one they had anticipated when they headed off to begin their teaching assignment. Some of this credit goes to TFA for preparing participants for the experience. But most of the difference probably owes to the very different eras in which the projects took place. The early 1960s was a highly idealized period in the U.S., especially for the white, upper-middle and upper class youth who accounted for the vast majority of Freedom Summer volunteers. By contrast, contemporary college students have a much more realistic, perhaps even jaundiced, view of the U.S. than did the typical Freedom Summer volunteer. While this no doubt better prepared them for their activist experience, it probably also muted its impact relative to their Freedom Summer counterparts.

2 Radical Re-socialization

As powerful as the Freedom Summer experience was for most of the volunteers, the impact of that experience was greatly magnified by their interaction with the veteran fieldworkers from the Student Non-violent Coordinating Committee (SNCC) who served as project staff. The SNCC staff afforded the volunteers a radical new lens through which to view and interpret the disturbing things they were seeing in Mississippi. As one project participant put it:

> Lots of the volunteers sort of sat at the feet of the SNCC guys ... It was sort of pathetic, everybody trying to out SNCC each other. But it was also hard not to. They were tremendously charismatic ... very forceful and frankly, their rap made sense. It was hard not to start seeing the world through their eyes.
>
> (McAdam, 1988: 131)

There is no question that the TFA participants were also exposed to a form of re-socialization at the hands of Teach for America staff. But the worldview espoused by the TFA staffers was nowhere near as radical as the one expressed by the SNCC veterans. In a very real sense, SNCC was the cutting edge of the New Left protest cycle that would dominate American activism well into the 1970s. By contrast, the TFA perspective, while critical of inequality and enduring racism, is essentially ameliorative in its focus and laudatory in its celebration of the role TFA participants play in redressing these problems. In short, there is little in the perspective to challenge the fundamental beliefs of the modal TFA applicant.

3 Movement Versus Organizational "Capture"

The final critical factor that differentiates the experiences of those involved in TFA and Freedom Summer are the very different loyalties encouraged by the two projects. As noted earlier, TFA has substantially captured the loyalties of many of its graduates. There is nothing wrong with this. At the same time, this capture has clearly narrowed and institutionalized the activist/civic commitments of the TFA alumni. Needless to say, this did not happen in the case of Freedom Summer, even though SNCC was ideally positioned at the close of the summer to co-opt the activist energies of the volunteers. Because of tensions engendered by the project and growing separatist sentiments with the organization, SNCC rebuffed most of the volunteers who asked to stay on after the summer. Instead the SNCC fieldworkers explicitly called on the volunteers to "organize against the sources of oppression in your own lives" (McAdam, 1988: chapter 4).

The practical effect of these two organizational strategies could not have been more different. If the effect of TFA's ongoing efforts to command the loyalties of their graduates has been to narrow and institutionalize their activist commitments, SNCC's general call to arms had the opposite effect. Encouraged to organize on their own and to draw connections between what was happening in Mississippi and elsewhere, many of the volunteers did just that, setting in motion various strands of New Left activism including the student movement, women's liberation, and the anti-war movement (McAdam, 1988: chapter 5). In the end it was "the Movement" rather than any specific organization that captured the loyalties of the Freedom Summer volunteers.

I offer these comparisons not as a definitive accounting of the critical mechanisms that inevitably mediate the long-term impact of intensive service or activist experiences, but rather to encourage those interested in the general topic of civic education to move beyond the simplistic assumption of life-transforming effects to search for the factors and processes that may lead to enduring patterns of civic engagement. Reflecting on these two cases, I suspect the impact of most service or activist experiences is likely to resemble the modest effects of TFA rather than the dramatic biographical alterations characteristic of Freedom Summer. But only by doing careful empirical work on a broad range of activist and service experiences will we be able to confirm this speculation and, in the context of this volume, identify those social psychological processes that help account for variation in the long term effects of such experiences.

Conclusion

I have sought in this chapter to suggest the limits of our current understanding of three widely cited "facts" about social movements. Not only do I think that in some instances (e.g. the assumption of life-transforming effects of movement participation) the "fact" in question is false, but that in all three cases, we know very little about the underlying social processes that may account for the finding. In particular, I have tried to identify those social psychological mechanisms I see implicated in each of the three topics at issue here. However, in focusing on these three—individual recruitment, initial mobilization, and the effects of sustained activism—I do not mean to suggest that these are the only aspects of social movements that would benefit from a closer social psychological "reading." In fact, there are many other lines of movement research—including, for example, the woefully neglected topic of "leadership"—that I am certain would be enriched by such a treatment. But rather than simply offer up a patchwork list of such topics, I thought it better to explore in depth some of the issues that have most concerned movement researchers and for which consistent empirical results have been produced. For if in these "mature" areas of research the limits of what we know can be demonstrated, it should be obvious that we will need to move well beyond the structural program of theory and research that has dominated the field over the past forty years if we are to move closer to a fuller understanding of social movement dynamics. Social psychology will necessarily play a central role in this effort.

Note

1   This section draws on some earlier thinking on this topic which was published as "Beyond Structural Analysis: Toward a More Dynamic Understanding of Social Movements," in Diani & McAdam (Eds.), *Social Movements and Networks* (Oxford University Press, 2003).

References

Aberle, David. 1966. *The Peyote Religion Among the Navajo*. Chicago, IL: Aldine.
Adorno, T. W., E. Frenkel-Brunswick, D.J. Levinson, & R.N. Sanford. 1950. *The Authoritarian Personality*. New York: Harper & Brothers.

Aminzade, Ron A. 1981. *Class, Politics, and Early Industrial Capitalism: A Study of Mid-Nineteenth Century Toulouse*. Albany, NY: State University of New York Press.

Aminzade, Ron A., & Doug McAdam. 2001. "Emotions and Contentious Politics." In Ron Aminzade, Jack Goldstone, Doug McAdam, Elizabeth J. Perry, William H. Sewell, Jr., Sidney Tarrow, & Charles Tilly (Eds.), *Silence and Voice in the Study of Contentious Politics* (pp. 14–50). Cambridge: Cambridge University Press.

Anheier, Helmut. 2003. "Movement Development and Organizational Networks: The Role of 'Single Members' in the German Nazi Party, 1925–1930." In Mario Diani, & Doug McAdam (Eds.) *Social Movements and Networks* (pp. 49–74). Oxford: Oxford University Press.

Davies, James C. 1963. *Human Nature in Politics: The Dynamics of Political Behavior*. New York: John Wiley.

Davies, James C. 1969. "The J-curve of Rising and Declining Satisfaction as a Cause of Some Great Revolutions and a Contained Rebellion." In Hugh David Graham, & Ted Robert Gurr (Eds.), *Violence in America: Historical and Comparative Perspectives* (pp. 690–730). Washington, DC: Government Printing Office.

Diani, Mario. 1995. *Green Networks: A Structural Analysis of the Italian Environmental Movement*. Edinburgh: Edinburgh University Press.

Dixon, Marc, & Vincent J. Roscigno. 2003. "Status, Networks, and Social Movement Participation: The Case of Striking Workers." *American Journal of Sociology* 108: 1292–1327.

Einwohner, Rachel L. 2006. "Identity Work and Collective Action in a Repressive Context: Jewish Resistance on the 'Aryan Side' of the Warsaw Ghetto." *Social Problems* 53: 38–56.

Ellingson, Stephen. 1995. "Understanding the Dialectic of Discourse and Collective Action: Public Debate and Rioting in Antebellum Cincinnati." *American Journal of Sociology* 101: 100–144.

Emirbayer, Mustafa, & Jeff Goodwin. 1994. "Network Analysis, Culture, and the Problem of Agency." *American Journal of Sociology* 99: 1411–1454.

Evans, Sara. 1980. *Personal Politics: The Roots of Women's Liberation in the Civil Rights Movement and the New Left*. New York: Vintage Books.

Feieraband, Ivo, Rosalind Feieraband, & Betty Nesvold. 1969. "Social Change and Political Violence: Cross National Patterns." In Hugh David Graham, & Ted Robert Gurr (Eds.), *Violence in America: Historical and Comparative Perspectives* (pp. 497–595). Washington, DC: Government Printing Office.

Ferree, Myra Marx, & Frederick Miller. 1985. "Mobilization and Meaning: Toward an Integration of Social Psychological and Resource Mobilization Perspectives on Social Movements." *Sociological Inquiry* 55: 38–61.

Feuer, Lewis. 1969. *The Conflict of Generations: The Character and Significance of Student Movements*. New York: Basic Books.

Futrell, Robert, & Pete Simi. 2004. "Free Spaces, Collective Identity, and the Persistence of U.S. White Power Activism." *Social Problems* 51: 16–42.

Gamson, William A. 1990 [1975]. *The Strategy of Social Protest*. Second Edition. Belmont, CA: Wadsworth.

Gamson, William A. 1992. "The Social Psychology of Collective Action." In Aldon D. Morris, & Carol McClurg Mueller (Eds.), *Frontiers in Social Movement Theory* (pp. 53–76). New Haven, CT and London: Yale University Press.

Gamson, William A., Bruce Fireman, & Steven Rytina. 1982. *Encounters with Unjust Authority*. Homewood, IL: Dorsey Press.

Geschwender, James. 1968. "Explorations in the Theory of Social Movements and Revolution." *Social Forces* 47: 127–135.

Glenn, John K., III. 2001. *Framing Democracy: Civil Society and Civic Movements in Eastern Europe*. Stanford, CA: Stanford University Press.

Goodwin, Jeff, & James M. Jasper. 1999. "Caught in a Winding, Snarling Vine: The Structural Bias of Political Process Theory." *Sociological Forum* 14: 27–54.

Goodwin Jeff, James M. Jasper, & Francesca Polletta (Eds.). 2001. *Passionate Politics*. Chicago, IL: University of Chicago Press.

Goodwin Jeff, James M. Jasper, & Francesca Polletta (Eds.). 2004. "Emotional Dimensions of Social Movements." In David A. Snow, Sarah A. Soule, & Hanspeter Kriesi (Eds.), *The Blackwell Companion to Social Movements* (pp. 413–432). Malden, MA: Blackwell Publishing Co.

Gould, Deborah B. 2009. *Moving Politics*. Chicago, IL: University of Chicago Press.

Gould, Roger. 1995. *Insurgent Identities: Class, Community and Protest in Paris from 1848 to the Commune*. Chicago: University of Chicago Press.

Gould, Roger. 2003. "Why Do Networks Matter? Rationalist and Structuralist Interpretations." In Mario Diani, & Doug McAdam (Eds.), *Social Movements and Networks* (pp. 233–257). Oxford and New York: Oxford University Press.

Gurney, J. N., & Kathleen T. Tierney. 1982. "Relative Deprivation and Social Movements: A Critical Look at Twenty Years of Theory and Research." *Sociological Quarterly* 23: 33–47.

Gurr, Ted. 1970. *Why Men Rebel*. Princeton, NJ: Princeton University Press.

Gusfield, Joseph R. 1963. *Symbolic Crusade: Status Politics and the American Temperance Movement*. Urbana, IL: University of Illinois Press.

Hardin, Russell. 1995. *One for All: The Logic of Group Conflict*. Princeton, NJ: Princeton University Press.

Hechter, Michael. 1987. *Principles of Group Solidarity*. Berkeley, CA: University of California Press.

Hoffer, Eric. 1951. *The True Believer: Thoughts on the Nature of Mass Movements*. New York: New American Library.

Johnson, Charles S. 1941. *Growing Up in the Black Belt*. Washington, DC: American Council on Education.

Kitts, James. 2000. "Mobilizing in Black Boxes: Social Networks and SMO Participation." *Mobilization* 5: 241–257.

Klandermans, Bert. 1997. *The Social Psychology of Protest*. Oxford: Blackwell.

Klandermans, Bert. 2004. "The Demand and Supply of Participation: Social-Psychological Correlates of Participation in Social Movements." In David A. Snow, Sarah A. Soule, & Hanspeter Kriesi (Eds.), *The Blackwell Companion to Social Movements* (pp. 360–379). Malden, MA: Blackwell Publishing Co.

Klandermans, Bert, & Dirk Oegema. 1987. "Potentials, Networks, Motivations, and Barriers: Steps toward Participation in Social Movements." *American Sociological Review* 52: 519–531.

Klapp, Orrin. 1969. *Collective Search for Identity*. New York: Holt, Rinehart and Winston.

Kobben, A.J.F. 1960. "Prophetic Movements as an Expression of Social Protest." *International Archives of Ethnography* 44: 117–164.

Kopp, Wendy. 2001. *One Day All Children: The Unlikely Triumph of Teach for America and What I Learned Along the Way*. New York: Public Affairs.

Kornhauser, William. 1959. *The Politics of Mass Society*. Glencoe, IL: Free Press.

Kurzman, Charles. 1996. "Structural Opportunity and Perceived Opportunity in Social Movement Theory: The Iranian Revolution of 1979." *American Sociological Review* 61: 153–170.

Lichbach, Mark I. 1998. *The Rebel's Dilemma*. Ann Arbor, MI: University of Michigan Press.

Lipset, Seymour M., & Earl Rabb. 1973. *The Politics of Unreason: Right-Wing Extremism in America, 1790–1970*. New York: Harper & Row.

Margadant, T. W. 1979. *French Peasants in Revolt: The Insurrection of 1851*. Princeton, NJ: Princeton University Press.

Mays, Benjamin and Joseph W. Nicholson. 1969. *The Negro's Church*. New York: Arno Press and The New York Times.

McAdam, Doug. 1986. "Recruitment to High Risk Activism: The Case of Freedom Summer." *American Journal of Sociology* 92: 64–90.

McAdam, Doug. 1988. *Freedom Summer*. New York: Oxford University Press.

McAdam, Doug. 1989. "The Biographical Consequences of Activism." *American Sociological Review* 54: 744–760.

McAdam, Doug. 1999. "The Biographical Impact of Activism." In Marco Giugni, Doug McAdam, & Charles Tilly (Eds.), *How Social Movements Matter* (pp. 117–146). Minneapolis, MN: University of Minnesota Press.

McAdam, Doug. 1999[1982]. *Political Process and the Development of Black Insurgency, 1930–1970*. Chicago, IL: University of Chicago Press.

McAdam, Doug. 2003. "Beyond Structural Analysis: Toward a More Dynamic Understanding of Social Movements." In Mario Diani, & Doug McAdam (Eds.), *Social Movements and Networks* (pp. 281–298). Oxford and New York: Oxford University Press.

McAdam, Doug, & Ronnelle Paulsen. 1993. "Specifying the Relationship between Social Ties and Activism." *American Journal of Sociology* 99: 640–667.

McAdam, Doug, Sidney Tarrow, & Charles Tilly. 2001. *Dynamics of Contention*. New York: Cambridge University Press.

McCarthy, John D., & Mayer N. Zald. 1973. *The Trend of Social Movements in America: Professionalization and Resource Mobilization*. Morristown, NJ: General Learning Press.

McCarthy, John D., & Mayer N. Zald. 1977. "Resource Mobilization and Social Movements: A Partial Theory." *American Journal of Sociology* 82: 1212–1241.

Melucci, Alberto. 1980. "The New Social Movements: A Theoretical Approach." *Social Science Information* 19: 199–226.

Melucci, Alberto. 1984. "An End to Social Movements?" *Social Science Information* 23: 819–835.

Melucci, Alberto. 1985. "The Symbolic Challenge of Social Movements." *Social Research* 52: 789–816.

Morris, Aldon D. 1984. *The Origins of the Civil Rights Movement: Black Communities Organizing for Change*. New York: The Free Press.

Morrison, Denton. 1973. "Some Notes Toward Theory on Relative Deprivation, Social Movements, and Social Change." In Robert R. Evans (Ed.), *Social Movements: A Reader and Sourcebook* (pp. 103–116). Chicago, IL: Rand McNally.

Myrdal, Gunnar. 1944. *An American Dilemma*. New York: Harper & Brothers.

Nepstad, Sharon E., & Christian Smith. 1999. "Rethinking Recruitment to High-Risk/ Cost Activism: The Case of Nicaragua Exchange." *Mobilization* 4: 25–40.

Noonan, Rita K. 1995. "Women Against the State: Political Opportunities and Collective Action Frames in Chile's Transitions to Democracy." *Sociological Forum* 10: 81–111.

Oberschall, Anthony. 1973. *Social Conflict and Social Movements*. Englewood Cliffs, NJ: Prentice-Hall.

Olson, Mancur. 1965. *The Logic of Collective Action*. Cambridge, MA: Harvard University Press.

Opp, Karl-Dieter. 1989. *The Rationality of Political Protest: A Comparative Analysis of Rational Choice Theory*. Boulder, CO: Westview Press.

Opp, Karl-Dieter. 2009. *Theories of Political Protest and Social Movements*. New York: Routledge.

Osa, Maryjane. 1997. "Creating Solidarity: The Religious Foundations of the Polish Social Movement." *East European Politics and Societies* 11: 339–365.

Osa, Maryjane. 2003. *Solidarity and Contention: The Networks of Polish Opposition, 1954–1981*. Minneapolis, MN: University of Minnesota Press.

Passy, Florence. 2003. "Social Networks Matter. But How?" In Mario Diani, & Doug McAdam (Eds.), *Social Movements and Networks* (pp. 21–48). Oxford and New York: Oxford University Press.

Payne, Charles. 1996. *I've Got the Light of Freedom*. Berkeley, CA: University of California Press.

Polletta, Francesca. 1999. "'Free Spaces' in Collective Action." *Theory and Society* 28: 1–38.

Rokeach, Milton. 1969. *Beliefs, Attitudes, and Values*. San Francisco, CA: Jossey-Bass.

Sherkat, Darren E. 1998. "What's in a Frame: Toward an Integrated Social Psychology of Social Movements." Paper presented at the Annual Meetings of the American Sociological Association, Montreal, Quebec, Canada.

Smelser, Neil. 1962. *Theory of Collective Behavior*. New York: Free Press.

Snow, David A., & Robert D. Benford. 1988. "Ideology, Frame Resonance, and Participant Mobilization." In Bert Klandermans, Hanspeter Kriesi, & Sidney Tarrow (Eds.), *From Structure to Action: Social Movement Participation across Cultures* (pp. 197–217). Greenwich, CT: JAI Press.

Snow, David A., & Robert D. Benford. 1992. "Master Frames and Cycles of Protest." In Aldon D. Morris, & Carol McClurg Mueller (Eds.), *Frontiers in Social Movement Theory* (pp. 133–155). New Haven, CT and London: Yale University Press.

Snow, David A., & Doug McAdam. 2000. "Identity Work Processes in the Context of Social Movements: Clarifying the Movement/Identity Nexus." In Sheldon Stryker, Timothy J. Owens, & Robert W. White (Eds.), *Self, Identity, and Social Movements* (pp. 41–67). Minneapolis: University of Minnesota Press.

Snow, David A., & Pamela E. Oliver. 1995. "Social Movements and Collective Behavior: Social Psychological Dimensions and Considerations." In Karen S. Cook, Gary Alan Fine, & James S. House (Eds.), *Sociological Perspectives on Social Psychology* (pp. 571–599). Boston, MA: Allyn and Bacon.

Snow, David A., E. Burke Rochford, Jr., Steven K. Worden, & Robert D. Benford. 1986. "Frame Alignment Process, Micromobilization, and Movement Participation." *American Sociological Review* 51: 464–481.

Snow, David A., Louis A. Zurcher, & Sheldon Ekland-Olson. 1980. "Social Networks and Social Movements: A Microstructural Approach to Differential Recruitment." *American Sociological Review* 45: 464–481.

Stryker, Sheldon, Timothy J. Owens, & Robert W. White (Eds). 2000. *Self, Identity, and Social Movements*. Minneapolis, MN: University of Minnesota Press.

Tarrow, Sidney. 1982. "Social Movements, Resource Mobilization and Reform during Cycles of Protest." Western Studies Program Project, Social Protest and Policy Innovative Work, Paper 1. Ithaca, NY: Cornell University.

Taylor, Michael. 1988. "Rationality and Revolutionary Collective Action." In Michael Taylor (Ed.), *Rationality and Revolution* (pp. 63–97). Cambridge: Cambridge University Press.

Tilly, Charles. 1978. *From Mobilization to Revolution*. Reading, MA: Addison-Wesley.

Tilly, Charles, Louise Tilly, & Richard Tilly. 1975. *The Rebellious Century, 1830–1930*. Cambridge, MA: Harvard University Press.

Uhlaner, Carole Jean. 1989. "'Relational Goods' and Participation: Incorporating Sociability into a Theory of Rational Action." *Public Choice* 62: 253–285.

Wallace, Anthony. 1966. *Religion: An Anthropological View*. New York: Random House.

Wilson, Kenneth L., & Anthony M. Orum. 1976. "Mobilizing People for Collective Political Action." *Journal of Political and Military Sociology* 4: 187–202.

Worsley, Peter. 1968. *The Trumpet Shall Sound: A Study of "Cargo" Cults*. 2nd edition. New York: Schocken Books.

Zhao, Dingxin. 1998. "Ecologies of Social Movements: Student Mobilization during The 1989 Prodemocracy Movement in Beijing." *American Journal of Sociology* 103: 1493–1529.

Zhao, Dingxin. 2001. *Power of Tiananmen*. Chicago, IL: University of Chicago Press.

PART II

Determinants of Political Cognition and Behavior—the Role of Importance

6

THE ORIGINS OF POLICY ISSUE SALIENCE

Personal and National Importance Impact on Behavioral, Cognitive, and Emotional Issue Engagement[1]

Joanne M. Miller, Jon A. Krosnick, and Leandre R. Fabrigar

Most scholars of American mass political behavior feel comfortable using and reading the term "issue salience." It has been used for decades to illustrate that any given policy issue (abortion, gun control, etc.) may be a focus of thinking for some citizens while being ignored by others at the same time. Heinz Eulau (1955) used the term for the first time in the *American Political Science Review*, and it has appeared in 1273 articles in the *APSR*, the *American Journal of Political Science*, the *British Journal of Political Science*, the *Journal of Politics*, *Political Behavior*, and *Public Opinion Quarterly*.[2]

Despite its frequent use in the literature, policy issue salience has more often been a vague metaphor than a precisely defined scientific concept with an accepted operationalization. The majority (62%) of articles that focused on policy issue salience provided no conceptual definition of the term at all. Among the remaining articles, salience was defined in a variety of different ways. Some assumed that salient policy issues are those that are prominent in the minds of citizens, frequently the subject of thought (Edwards, Mitchell, & Welch, 1995; Feldman & Sigelman, 1985; Fleishman, 1986; Lau, Brown, & Sears, 1978; RePass, 1971; Schuman, Ludwig, & Krosnick, 1986). Others said that policy issue salience is the amount of importance that an individual citizen attaches to an issue (Adams, 1997; Chaney, Alvarez, & Nagler, 1998; Edwards, Mitchell, & Welch, 1995; Erbring, Goldenberg, & Miller, 1980; Feldman & Sigelman, 1985; Hutchings, 2001; Kaufman & Petrocik, 1999; Kerr, 1978; Lau, Brown, & Sears, 1978; Monroe, 1998; Mutz & Soss, 1997; Niemi & Bartels, 1985; Rabinowitz, Prothro, & Jacoby, 1982; Stewart, Warhola, & Blough, 1984; Wright, 1976). And still others provided different definitions.

Likewise, scholars have measured issue salience in many different ways. Some scholars presumed that the more often political elites or the news media mention an issue, the more salient it is to everyone in a population (elites: Stewart, Warhola, & Blough, 1984; media: Canes-Wrone & de Marchi, 2002; Edwards et al., 1995; Hardin, 1998). One author assumed that the higher the price of electricity, the more salient electricity-related issues were to people (Berry, 1979). Some authors presumed that the amount of weight voters place on an issue in evaluating political candidates indicates the salience of the issue (Adams, 1997; Bernstein, 1995; Chaney, Alvarez, & Nagler, 1998; Kaufmann & Petrocik, 1999). Some authors presumed that salience is indicated by membership in a social group or groups for which the issue is directly relevant (Conover, 1984; Hutchings, 2001). Still others viewed issue salience as indicated by the amount of time citizens said they spent thinking about the issue (Beck & Parker, 1985). And other articles presumed that the more respondents in a survey sample say they "don't know" their opinion on an issue, the less salient it is to everyone in a population (Petry, 1999; Pierce, 1975; Shapiro & Mahajan, 1986).

The most popular measurement approach has been to gauge the amount of importance citizens ascribe to the issue, but through two principal and different ways. The most common has been to ask people to report the importance of a policy issue for the country (Best, 1999; Campbell, 1983; Erbring et al., 1980; Flanagan, 1980; Green & Guth, 1988; Lau et al., 1978; Monroe, 1998; RePass, 1971; Schuman et al., 1986) or for their community (Mutz & Soss, 1997). Less common has been to ask people to report how important the issue is to them personally, without mention of the country (Niemi & Bartels, 1985; Rabinowitz et al., 1982; Tedin, 1979; Wright, 1976). Some authors have combined measures of national and personal importance into an aggregated measure of salience (e.g., Lau et al., 1978), and others have measured issue importance without telling respondents whether to gauge the importance to them personally, to the country, or to some other aggregation (Feldman & Sigelman, 1985).

If research conclusions about the origins and consequences of salience were the same regardless of how the construct is measured, then these operational distinctions would have little practical importance. But in fact, a large literature suggests that the choice between measuring personal importance vs. national important may have substantial impact on research findings. Citizens' judgments of the national economy have much more impact on presidential evaluations and voting than do those citizens' personal economic circumstances (Kinder & Kiewiet, 1979, 1981; Lau & Sears, 1981), and people's policy preferences and participation in social protests is driven minimally by their own self-interest and instead is driven more by perceptions of the best interest of people around them (see Birt & Dion, 1987; Bobo, 1988; Sears & Funk, 1990, 162). Thus, self-interest seems to have little effect on the valence of political attitudes.

But is the same true of issue salience? Do citizens think about and act mostly on the policy issues they think are important for the nation as a whole? Or do citizens focus their thinking and actions on issues that are important to them personally? To answer these questions, we begin by offering a formal definition of issue salience and reviewing the existing findings of research that measured salience via personal and national importance. Finally, we describe the results of nine studies gauging the impact of personal and national importance judgments on citizens' cognitive, emotional, and behavioral engagement in a policy issue domain. This evidence makes the case that salience operationalization should not be done arbitrarily, because different measures produce very different results in a way that casts light on the core nature of salience and on popular political judgment.

Defining Policy Issue Salience

The work that we describe here is premised on the notion that the more salient a particular policy issue is to a citizen, the more he or she is cognitively and behaviorally engaged in that issue. That is, if an issue is salient to a person, he or she thinks frequently and deeply about it, gathers information about it to accumulate in long-term memory, and uses the issue as a basis for making voting decisions and charting other courses of political action. This definition is faithful to the spirit of most past work on policy issue salience and also resonates with work in psychology on attitude strength (see, e.g., Petty & Krosnick, 1995).

Past Studies of National Issue Importance Judgments

A great deal of research has explored the dynamics of judgments of the national importance of policy issues in the U.S. Not surprisingly, judgments of the national importance of an issue rise and fall according to changes in the objective seriousness of national problems (e.g., Behr & Iyengar, 1985; Erbring et al., 1980; Iyengar & Kinder, 1987; MacKuen, 1984b; MacKuen & Coombs, 1981; McCombs & Shaw, 1972; Schuman et al., 1986; Wlezien, 2005). In addition, national importance judgments rise and fall with the volume of media attention to that issue, an effect dubbed "agenda-setting" (e.g., Behr & Iyengar, 1985; Erbring et al., 1980; MacKuen 1984a, 1984b; MacKuen & Coombs, 1981; Miller & Wanta, 1996).

Cohen (1963) characterized the latter effect this way:

> The press ... is stunningly successful in telling readers what to think *about* ... The editor may believe he is only printing the things that people want to read, but he is thereby putting a claim on their attention, powerfully determining what they will be thinking about, and talking about.
>
> (p. 13)

Thus, he presumed that if citizens say an issue is nationally important, then they are presumably thinking and talking about it. Consistent with this logic, McCombs and Reynolds (2002) said that agenda-setting is "establishing [issue] salience among the public so that an issue becomes the focus of public attention, thought, and perhaps even action" (p. 1). Other agenda-setting work has presumed that by causing people to view an issue as nationally important, news media attention to it leads people to place more weight on the issue when evaluating candidates (Iyengar, 1979) and when deciding for whom to vote (Weaver, 1987, 1994).

However, very few studies have actually tested the presumption that national importance judgments are cognitively and behaviorally consequential, and the evidence from these studies is quite mixed. Ostrom and Simon (1985) found that evaluations of the state of the economy and of foreign policy decision-making affected presidential approval to the extent that the issues were said to be nationally important by the public (see also Miller & Krosnick, 2000). And Flanagan (1980) found that voter occupation (a proxy for economic self-interest) had more impact on vote choice among citizens who considered economic issues to be more important for the nation. But contrary to the sociotropic perspective, Maggiotto and Piereson (1978) and Johns (2008) found that candidate preferences were *not* shaped more powerfully by issues that voters believed were more important for the nation. Natchez and Bupp (1968) found that issues people cited as more important for the nation had *less* impact on voting. And Wlezien (2005) found that attaching more national importance to defense spending was not associated with more impact of general defense spending preferences on support for specific changes in defense spending policy.

Macro-level work on government responsiveness has also assumed that people's national importance judgments are politically consequential (e.g., Hibbs, 1979; Monroe, 1998), and some studies have offered empirical support for the presumption. For example, Jones (1994) found that policy attitudes predicted government policies better when more citizens said the issue was nationally important. From this evidence, he concluded that, "where policies are salient, it is likely that [government] responsiveness is more forthcoming" (p. 128).

Macro-level national importance judgments have also been shown to affect candidates' campaign strategies. For example, Burden and Sandberg (2003) found that when more Americans cited the federal budget as one of the nation's most important issues, candidates were more likely to address the budget during subsequent campaign speeches. Therefore, Burden and Sandberg concluded that issue salience causes attention to an issue by candidates. Campbell (1983) found that although national importance judgments had no direct effect on the specificity with which candidates describe their issue positions to the public, more national importance attached to an issue by the public "causes candidates to move closer to the median position of the public. This greater proximity, in turn, reduces the candidates' fear of voter disaffection, thus allowing them to clarify their positions" (p. 290).

Past Studies of Personal Issue Importance Judgments

Another research tradition, with its roots in psychology, suggests the possibility that cognitive and behavioral engagement in a policy issue may be motivated differently, by personal importance rather than national importance judgments (see, e.g., Boninger, Krosnick, & Berent, 1995). To attach personal importance to an issue is to care tremendously about the issue and to be deeply concerned about it. Such personal concern has been posited to come from one of three sources: (1) material self-interest (because a policy issue is thought to have direct implications for a person's behavioral rights and privileges); (2) identification with reference groups or reference individuals (when they are affected directly by the issue or attach great personal importance to it); and (3) values (when they are seen as linked to the issue; Boninger et al., 1995). People presumably know very well when they are deeply concerned about an issue, and they know just as well when they have no special concern about one. Deep concern about an issue is presumably not fleeting—it is thought to be much like taking a new job or getting married, entailing a long-term connection and commitment. And this personal concern, emanating from very personal considerations closely linked to self-concepts, may be what makes a policy issue psychologically salient to a citizen (i.e., cognitively and behaviorally consequential).

If this is true, then citizens do not shift their personal issue priorities easily or often. Once a person gets attached to a policy issue, that attachment is likely to last over time and to be self-reinforcing—thinking about an issue breeds more thinking; knowledge gain breeds more knowledge gain; and attitude-expressive action breeds more action. So even as the objective conditions of the country change and people see changes in the most important problem facing the country, their personal connections to issues may remain relatively fixed.

A number of studies have provided evidence consistent with these presumptions about personal importance. People for whom a policy issue is highly personally important have been shown to place great weight on it when deciding how to vote (Aldrich & McKelvey, 1977; Bélanger & Meguid, 2008; Fournier, Blais, Nadeau, Gidengil, & Nevitte, 2003; Granberg & Holmberg, 1986; Krosnick, 1988a; Rabinowitz et al., 1982; Schuman & Presser, 1981; Shapiro, 1969; Visser, Krosnick, & Simons, 2003).[3] Citizens for whom an issue is highly personally important are the most likely to write letters to the media and to public officials expressing their views on the issue (Krosnick, 1986; Schuman & Presser, 1981). Financial contributions to and memberships in interest groups come mostly from people for whom the issue is highly personally important (Krosnick, 1986; Schuman & Presser, 1981; Visser et al., 2003). And people for whom an issue is personally important selectively expose themselves to information on the issue, attend closely to that information, think carefully about its implications, have more accessible attitudes toward the issue, remember it accurately long after exposure, see extensive linkages between the issue and others, and hold stable opinions on the issue (see, e.g., Holbrook, Berent, Krosnick, Visser, & Boninger, 2005; Bizer & Krosnick, 2001; Howard-Pitney, Borgida, & Omoto, 1986; Jackman, 1977; Krosnick, 1988b, 1991; Lavine, Sullivan, Borgida, & Thomsen, 1996; Visser et al., 2003).

One possible reason for the power of personal importance judgments involves the cognitive demands of political information processing. A great deal of psychological research suggests that people are cognitive misers who seek to minimize information processing whenever possible (e.g., see Fiske & Taylor, 1990). Understanding the importance of issues for the nation as a whole may require large-scale understanding of the country. In contrast, a person can decide to attach personal importance to an issue despite having very little information about that issue, based on idiosyncratic considerations. As a result, people may form judgments of personal importance with great confidence, whereas judgments about the importance of issues for the nation may be formed more tentatively. Therefore, these latter judgments may be less consequential in guiding thinking and action.

If all these speculations are true, they have a number of important implications. For example, the dynamics of national importance judgments caused by media agenda-setting and real-world cues may have no substantial, real, lasting effects on the political behavior of the citizenry of a nation. Ups and downs in the public's agenda documented by public opinion polls surely have some effects on the conduct of elite politics, because answers to the "most important problem" question are widely reported in the news media and call legislators' attention to some problems while deflecting their attention from others (Cohen, 1973; Kingdon, 1981, 1995; Peters & Hogwood, 1985; Wlezien, 2005). But this may be the only political consequence of agenda-setting and real-world cue effects on national importance judgments.

This Investigation

Before we jump to this conclusion, however, it is important to recognize that it is too early to reject the notion that national importance judgments indicate individual-level policy issue salience. We have found very few studies exploring this question, and they are quite limited in scope. Indeed, these studies are so idiosyncratic that they seem to provide no basis at all for drawing broad conclusions in this regard. More research seems to be needed before we should conclude that national importance judgments are inconsequential in the minds of citizens.

The studies described below attempted to explore these issues by investigating six questions. The *first question* is: Are personal importance and national importance judgments empirically distinct from one another? These two types of judgments are obviously conceptually distinct, and citizens have been shown to distinguish between individual and collective political judgments in other domains (e.g.,

Conover, 1984). However, cognitive consistency theories argue that people are motivated to maintain consistency among cognitions (e.g., Festinger, 1957). This motivation could lead people to perceive issues that are important to them personally as also important for the country and vice versa. If this is so, there would be no point in any further comparisons of these two judgments. We found that these two types of judgments are distinct from one another, which suggests merit in comparing the political effects of personal and national importance.

The *second question* is: Which is more consequential in shaping issue-relevant political behavior—personal importance or national importance? We gauged whether attaching personal or national importance to an issue inspired citizens to express their policy preferences to public officials or the news media, to contribute money to a political lobbying organization attempting to influence policy on the issue, and to attend meetings or do other work with grassroots organizations trying to influence policy on the issue. Such actions turned out to be driven more by personal importance than by national importance.

Our *third question* is: Which is more consequential in shaping candidate preferences—personal importance or national importance? If a policy issue is genuinely salient for a member of a democratic polity, and if that salience has real and meaningful cognitive consequences, he or she should use the issue to choose candidates. We gauged the extent to which personal importance and national importance judgments moderated the impact of policy preferences on candidate preferences and vote choices, and found personal importance to have strong impact in this regard, whereas national importance did not.

The *fourth question*, inspired by Converse's (1964) instincts about issue public membership, asks: Is personal importance more consequential than national importance because the former is more effective at inspiring cognitive and emotional engagement in an issue? Specifically, attaching importance to a policy issue may motivate people to seek exposure to information on the issue and store lots of such information in their long-term memories, to think extensively about that information, to develop a sense of certainty about their opinions on the issue, and for those opinions to become very accessible in memory and therefore easy to retrieve and use (see, e.g., Boninger, Krosnick, Berent, & Fabrigar, 1995). In addition, attaching importance to an issue may activate and engage a person's emotion systems (e.g., Lazarus & Smith, 1988; Smith, Haynes, Lazarus, & Pope, 1993), thus directing and inspiring action (see Zajonc, 1998 for a review). We therefore explored whether personal importance and national importance inspire knowledge accumulation, thought, certainty, attitude accessibility, and emotional reactions to issue-relevant information. Personal importance turned out to be the primary instigator, and national importance had almost no effects at all.

Fifth, we formally tested the mediational question implicit in the logic offered above: Does cognitive and emotional issue engagement mediate the effect of personal importance on political behavior? That is, we explored whether personal importance leads to increases in attitude-expressive behavior by first increasing cognitive and emotional issue engagement. We found evidence of such mediation.

Finally, we ask a *sixth question*: Is national importance more consequential than it appeared to be in the analyses outlined above because it is a cause of personal importance? Boninger, Krosnick, and Berent (1995) speculated that if a policy issue is important to a social group with which a person identifies, that issue will become personally important to the person as a result. Although Boninger et al. (1995) reported evidence consistent with this claim, none of their studies examined identification with the nation as a whole, instead focusing on other, smaller, social groups. It is therefore possible that national importance judgments shape personal importance judgments. The reverse is also possible: if attaching personal importance to an issue leads people to gather information about it and to think carefully about the implications of that information, a consequence of that process may be recognition of many reasons why the issue is truly important for the nation as a whole. We therefore gauged the causal impact of personal importance judgments on national importance judgments and vice versa.

Description of Studies

To explore these questions, we analyzed nine sets of data, described briefly below (and in more detail in the Appendix).

Study 1 and 2

Studies 1 and 2 assessed the relation between personal and national issue importance judgments. For Study 1, telephone interviews were conducted by trained telephone interviewers with 400 18–24 year-old students from a large Midwest university. For Study 2, data were collected via self-administered questionnaires with 471 18–24 year-old students from a large Midwest university who participated for course credit. Respondents reported how important each of a series of policy issues were to them personally and how important each issue was for the U.S. as a whole.

Study 3

Study 3 examined the impact of personal and national importance judgments on candidate preferences and vote choice using the 1980, 1984, and 1996 American National Election Study (NES) surveys. The 1980 NES involved interviewing three separate, nationally representative samples, and we combined all of the data from interviews done just before and after the election with 3,136 American adults. For the 1984 NES, 1,989 Americans were interviewed in September/October and again in November/December. For the 1996 NES, 1,534 Americans were interviewed in September/October and again in November/December. In each of these surveys, respondents reported their attitudes on a series of policy issues, their perceptions of the presidential candidates' stands on the issues, the personal and national importance of the issues, their attitudes toward the presidential candidates, and their vote choices.

Study 4

Study 4 used a different method to test whether more important policy attitudes have more impact on candidate preferences and to gauge the impact of personal and national importance on direct expression of policy preferences to public officials and the news media. A national sample of 512 American adults was contacted via random-digit dialing and interviewed by telephone by International Communications Research, Inc., in December, 1988. Respondents were asked about the personal and national importance of the Arab–Israeli conflict, the impact of that issue on their candidate preferences, and whether they had expressed their views on the issue to a public official or the media.

Study 5

Studies 3 and 4 involved only single measures of personal and national importance judgments, so the statistical parameters estimated with those data were attenuated by measurement error in responses to those questions. Study 5 measured personal and national importance judgments with multiple items, permitting correction of parameter estimates for random and systematic measurement error. A representative sample of 148 adult residents of a large Midwest city, was contacted via random-digit dialing and interviewed by telephone by staff at a major Midwest university. Respondents reported the personal and national importance of four issues (abortion, gun control, health care, and trade with Mexico) and described the impact of each issue on their presidential candidate preferences and whether they had expressed their attitudes on any of the issues to elected officials or the news media.

Study 6

Study 6 focused on the issue of global warming and assessed the impact of personal and national importance on an index of policy-relevant political behaviors. In addition, Study 6 gauged the impact of personal and national importance on an index of cognitive issue engagement. This study also explored whether cognitive issue engagement mediated the effect of personal importance on behavioral issue engagement.

Computer-assisted telephone interviews were conducted with a representative sample of 1,413 American adults (generated by RDD) by the survey research center at a major Midwest university between September 1997 and February 1998. Respondents reported the personal and national importance of the issue of global warming. They also reported on whether they had expressed their opinions about the issue to politicians or the news media, whether they had made a financial contribution to a political organization concerned with global warming, and whether they had attended a group meeting to discuss the issue (these measures were averaged to form an overall index of issue-relevant political behavior). Finally, respondents reported how much they felt they knew about global warming, how much they had thought about the issue, and how certain they were of their opinions about the issue (these three measures were averaged to form an overall index of cognitive issue engagement).

Study 7

Study 7 explored whether personal and national importance affected a new indicator of cognitive issue engagement (attitude accessibility), a second operationalization of knowledge accumulation (memory for issue information), and affective issue engagement (emotional reactions to issue-relevant information).

Three-hundred-and-eighty-five 18–25 year-old students from a large Midwest university participated in this experiment for course credit. The experiment employed a procedure developed by Iyengar and Kinder (1987). Respondents watched a 20-minute videotape containing seven stories taken from ABC, CBS, and NBC national evening news broadcasts. Five of the stories were fillers that all respondents watched. One-third of the respondents (selected randomly) saw two additional stories about crime. Another one-third of the respondents instead saw two additional stories about unemployment. And the final one-third saw two additional stories about pollution instead.

After viewing the videotape, respondents answered questions on a computer (which measured attitude accessibility via reaction time to attitude report questions) and on a paper-and-pencil questionnaire (which measured the personal and national importance of crime, unemployment, and pollution, memory for the news stories they had watched, and the emotional reactions they had to the news stories).

Study 8

Of the 1,413 respondents interviewed for Study 6, 497 were reinterviewed between December 1997 and February 1998. Study 8 was of the 446 panel respondents (who were interviewed in both December 1997 and February 1988) with valid data on all the variables needed to estimate the effects of personal and national importance on one another. These respondents reported the personal and national importance of the issue of global warming during both interviews.

Study 9

Study 9 used data from Wave 22 of the 2008–2009 ANES panel study (focusing on the issues of the war in Iraq and global warming) to explore the impact of personal and national importance on issue-relevant behavior, cognitive issue engagement, and emotional issue engagement, as well as whether cognitive or emotional engagement mediated the effect of personal importance on political behavior.

A representative sample of 2,270 U.S. citizens aged 18 or older completed the survey via online computers between October 22 and November 30, 2009. Respondents reported the personal and national importance of the issues of global warming and the Iraq war. They also reported whether they had expressed their attitude on each issue to a government official or a news organization, contributed money to an organization working on each of the issues, worked with an organization focused on each of the issues, or attended a group meeting to talk about each of the issues (combined to form separate indices of behavior regarding global warming and Iraq war). In addition, respondents reported how much they felt they knew about global warming and the Iraq war (in separate questions), how much they had thought about each issue, and how certain they were of their opinions about each issue (these three measures were averaged to form an overall index of cognitive issue engagement). Finally, respondents were asked to report how angry, hopeful, afraid, and proud they felt when they thought about what people have been doing and saying in recent years about the issues of global warming and the Iraq war (the four emotions were averaged to form indices of emotional arousal for the two issues).

Results

Question 1: Are Personal and National Importance Judgments Empirically Distinct?

To explore whether people's judgments of the extent to which an issue is important to them personally differ from the extent to which they perceive the issue to be important for the nation, we estimated the parameters of multiple indicator covariance structure models and corrected for random and systematic measurement error using data from Studies 1 and 2.[4] Both studies' models fit the data well (Study 1: $\chi^2(74) = 129.90$, p<.001; RMSEA = .046; standardized RMR = .029; non-normed fit index = .95; Study 2: $\chi^2(184) = 347.41$, $p<.001$; RMSEA = .044; standardized RMR = .023; non-normed fit index = .95).[5]

Corrected correlations between personal importance and national importance ranged from .49 to .73 and averaged .61 (see Table 6.1). This means that only 37% of the variance was shared between personal and national importance on average. Not surprisingly, constraining the correlations between personal and

TABLE 6.1 Corrected Correlations Between Personal Importance and National Importance—Studies 1 and 2

Issue	Study 1	Study 2
Capital punishment	.56	
Central america	.63	
Abortion	.73	
Defense spending	.55	.51
Environment		.66
Unemployment		.60
Drug abuse		.63
Taxes		.49
School bussing		.72

Note: All correlations are statistically significant ($p < .001$).

national importance for each issue to be 1.0 significantly worsened the fit of covariance structure models (Study 1: $\Delta\chi^2(4) = 235.11$, $p<.001$; Study 2: $\Delta\chi^2(6) = 457.67$, $p<.001$). Thus, respondents' personal and national importance judgments appeared to be distinct.

Using the data from representative national samples from Studies 4 and 6, we found that correlations between personal and national importance regarding the Arab–Israeli conflict and global warming were .30 ($p<.001$), and .42 ($p<.001$), respectively. When we disattenuated these correlations for measurement error using the average reliability of the importance measures generated with data from Studies 1 and 2, we found them to be .48 and .67, respectively, which average .58, reinforcing the findings from Studies 1 and 2.

This evidence clearly challenges the assumption that personal and national importance judgments are isomorphic. But from this evidence alone, we cannot tell which of these constructs is worth spotlighting in theories of political cognition and action. Perhaps one construct is consequential, whereas the other is not. But perhaps both are consequential and deserve theoretical attention.

Question 2: Which is More Consequential in Shaping Issue Specific Political Behavior—Personal or National Importance?

Using data from Studies 4 and 5, we examined the impact of personal and national importance on the decision to express one's policy preferences to politicians or the news media. For Study 4, logistic regression coefficients were estimated, predicting attitude expression on the issue of the Arab–Israeli conflict with the variables listed in Table 6.2. As column 1 shows, personal importance was a significant instigator of policy preference expression ($b = 1.70, p < .05$), but national importance was not ($b = 1.04$, *n.s.*). The data from Study 5 permitted gauging the impact of personal and national importance on policy preference expression for four issues (abortion, gun control, health care, and trade with

TABLE 6.2 Personal and National Importance Predicting Issue Impact on Policy Preference Expression, Financial Contributions, Working with an Organization, and Attending a Group Meeting—Studies 4, 5, 6, and 9

	Policy preference	Policy preference	Environment behavior	Iraq behavior	Global warming behavior
	Expression	Expression	Index	Index	Index
Predictor	(Study 4)	(Study 5)	(Study 6)	(Study 9)	(Study 9)
Personal importance	1.70★ (.76)	.38★★★ (.12)	.11★★ (.02)	.15★★★ (.02)	.19★★★ (.02)
National importance	1.04 (.83)	.06 (.14)	.01 (.01)	.01 (.02)	−.05+ (.02)
Male	.49 (.47)	−.05 (.03)	.01 (.01)	.02★ (.01)	.03★★★ (.02)
Age	−1.14 (.74)	.00 (.07)	−.02 (.02)	−.01 (.02)	−.01 (.02)
White	.12 (.70)		.02+ (.01)	.01 (.01)	−.01 (0.1)
Income	−1.14 (.83)		−.03★ (.01)	−.04★★★ (.01)	−.14★★ (.01)
Education	2.79★★★ (.82)	.10 (.06)	.04★★ (.01)	.06★★★ (.02)	.11★★★ (.02)
Democrat			−.01 (.01)	−.01 (.02)	−.01 (.02)
Republican			−.03★★ (.01)	−.02 (.02)	−.02 (.02)
R^2	.06	.08	.06	.06	.08
N	386	111	1270	1931	1911

Note: Table entries in column 1 are logistic regression coefficients. Table entries in column 2 are unstandardized coefficients obtained from LISREL. Table entries in columns 3–5 are unstandardized regression coefficents. Standard errors appear in parentheses.
$+p < .10$, ★$p < .05$, ★★$p < .01$, ★★★$p < .001$

Mexico) using multiple measures by estimating the parameters of a covariance structure model.[6] The model fit the data well (χ^2 (70) = 102.76, $p < .05$; RMSEA = .07; standardized RMR = .07; non-normed fit index = .94). Personal importance was a significant predictor of attitude expression ($b = .38$, $p < .001$), but national importance was not ($b = .06$, $n.s.$; see column 2 of Table 6.2).

Study 6's data permitted estimating OLS regression coefficients predicting an index of behaviors (attitude expression, financial contributions, and group meeting attendance) with personal and national importance. Personal importance was a significant positive predictor of the behavioral index ($b = .11$, $p < .01$), whereas national importance was not ($b = .01$, $n.s.$; see column 3 of Table 6.2).[7]

Study 9's data replicate the findings from Study 6. As columns 4 and 5 of Table 6.2 show, personal importance was a positive, statistically significant predictor of the behavior index for both the Iraq war ($p = .15$, $p < .001$) and the global warming issues ($b = .19$, $p < .001$). National importance was not a significant predictor for the Iraq war issue, and was a marginally significantly *negative* predictor of issue relevant behavior regarding global warming.[8]

Question 3: Which is More Consequential in Shaping Candidate Preferences—Personal or National Importance?

Next, we examined the extent to which personal and national importance determine the degree to which citizens' policy preferences influence their attitudes towards candidates. In the OLS regressions shown in Table 6.3 (which use the data from Study 3, in which candidate preference is coded such that larger numbers represent a greater preference for the Republican candidate), a positive, statistically significant interaction between issue distance and personal importance would mean that people who attached more personal importance to the issue placed greater weight on it when formulating attitudes toward the candidates. Likewise, a positive, statistically significant Issue Distance × National Importance interaction would mean that people who considered the issue to be more nationally important weighed the issue more heavily.

The expected positive and statistically significant Issue Distance × Personal Importance interaction appeared in nine of the twelve analyses (see Table 6.3). In contrast, only two marginally significant, positive interactions between issue distance and national importance appeared, and the remaining coefficients were non-significant. Thus, it appears that a policy issue had more impact on candidate attitudes among people who attached more personal importance to the issue, but attaching national importance to an issue did not enhance its impact on candidate attitudes (logistic regressions predicting vote choice yielded similar results).[9]

Likewise, using Study 4's data (which assessed personal and national importance of the Arab–Israeli conflict and the impact of the issue on candidate preferences), personal importance was a significant predictor of the degree to which

TABLE 6.3 Personal and National Importance Moderating the Impact of Policy Issue Distance on Candidate Preference (Study 3)

| | 1980 | | | | | | | 1984 | | | 1996 | |
Predictor	Unemp.	Defense spending	Gov't services	Guar. Jobs	Soviet union	Aid to minorities	Taxes	Gov't services	Guar. Jobs	Central america	Gov't services	Aid to minorities
Issue proximity × personal importance	1.53*** (.39)	.20 (.13)	.49*** (.12)	.35** (.13)	.45*** (.12)	.46*** (.13)	.05 (.12)	.39*** (.12)	.47*** (.13)	.45** (.15)	.54* (.25)	−.14 (.22)
Issue distance × national importance	.15 (.24)	.22+ (.12)	.04 (.08)	.07 (.08)	.33+ (.19)	−.16 (.14)	.30 (.22)	.06 (.07)	−.01 (.07)	.03 (.14)	−.13 (.12)	.06 (.11)
Personal importance	.01 (.03)	−.01 (.03)	.07** (.03)	.03 (.03)	.02 (.02)	−.02 (.03)	.09* (.04)	−.07* (.03)	−.07* (.03)	−.03 (.04)	.14* (.06)	.05 (.05)
National importance	.00 (.02)	.02 (.03)	−.02 (.02)	−.01 (.02)	−.07+ (.04)	.01 (.03)	−.10 (.07)	−.05* (.02)	−.01 (.02)	−.07* (.03)	−.03 (.03)	−.03 (.03)
Issue distance	−.23 (.26)	.13+ (.07)	.05 (.08)	.13+ (.03)	−.05 (.07)	.12+ (.07)	.17* (.07)	−.01 (.09)	.03 (.09)	−.01 (.10)	.05 (.22)	−.27+ (.16)
Male	.02 (.02)	.00 (.02)	.00 (.02)	.01 (.02)	.01 (.02)	.01 (.02)	.02 (.03)	.02 (.02)	.03 (.02)	.03+ (.02)	.08** (.02)	.07** (.03)
Age	.05 (.05)	.03 (.04)	−.02 (.04)	.01 (.04)	.01 (.04)	.04 (.04)	.10 (.07)	.03 (.05)	.04 (.05)	.08 (.05)	.03 (.06)	.03 (.06)

continued…

Table 6.3 continued...

Predictor	1980							1984			1996	
	Unemp.	Defense spending	Gov't services	Guar. Jobs	Soviet union	Aid to minorities	Taxes	Gov't services	Guar. Jobs	Central america	Gov't services	Aid to minorities
White	.14*** (.03)	.18*** (.03)	.16*** (.03)	.17*** (.03)	.16*** (.03)	.12*** (.03)	.19*** (.05)	.15*** (.03)	.16*** (.03)	.18*** (.03)	.07+ (.04)	.06 (.04)
Income	.08* (.04)	.07* (.03)	.07* (.03)	.06+ (.03)	.07* (.03)	.07* (.03)	.07 (.05)	.04 (.04)	.05 (.04)	.07+ (.04)	.00 (.05)	.01 (.05)
Education	-.10*** (.03)	-.04+ (.03)	-.07* (.03)	-.06* (.03)	-.05+ (.03)	-.02 (.02)	-.04 (.04)	-.03 (.03)	-.05+ (.03)	-.03 (.03)	-.03 (.04)	.03 (.04)
Democrat	-.20*** (.02)	-.20*** (.02)	-.19*** (.02)	-.21*** (.02)	-.21*** (.02)	-.22*** (.02)	-.20*** (.03)	-.24*** (.02)	-.25*** (.02)	-.26*** (.02)	-.30*** (.03)	-.30*** (.03)
Republican	.26*** (.02)	.24*** (.02)	.23*** (.02)	.23*** (.02)	.25*** (.02)	.24*** (0.3)	.28*** (.03)	.26*** (.02)	.26*** (.02)	.29*** (.02)	.34*** (.03)	.35*** (.03)
R^2	.29	.28	.29	.30	.27	.30	.31	.39	.38	.38	.50	.49
N	1540	2066	2034	1981	2045	2097	870	1464	1478	1330	668	664

Note: Table entries are unstandardized OLS regression coefficients. Standard errors appear in parentheses.

$+p < .10$, $*p < .05$, $**p < .01$, $***p < .001$

TABLE 6.4 Personal and National Importance Predicting Issue Impact on Candidate Preference—Studies 4 and 5

Predictor	Study 4	Study 5
Personal importance	.47***	.47***
	(.05)	(.09)
National importance	.07	.19
	(.04)	(.11)
Male	.00	−.01
	(.03)	(.02)
Age	.06	.04
	(.04)	(.05)
White	.10*	
	(.04)	
Income	−.06	
	(.05)	
Education	−.12**	.04
	(.05)	(.05)
R^2	.29	.25
N	373	111

Note: Table entries in column 1 are unstandardized OLS regression coefficients and in column 2 are unstandardized coefficients obtained from LISREL. Standard errors appear in parentheses.
$\star p < .05$, $\star\star p < .01$, $\star\star\star p < .00$

which respondents said the issue impacted their candidate preferences ($b = .47$, $p<.001$), but national importance was not ($b = .07$, n.s.; see column 1 of Table 6.4). And using the data from Study 5 (which assessed personal and national importance and issue impact on candidate preferences for abortion, gun control, health care, and trade with Mexico), personal importance was a significant predictor of issue impact on candidate preferences ($b = .47, p<.001$), but national importance was not ($b = .19$, n.s.; see column 2 of Table 6.4). These findings therefore replicate Study 3's evidence that national importance judgments are not significant moderators of issue impact on candidate preferences.

Question 4: Which is More Cognitively and Affectively Consequential— Personal or National Importance?

The data from Studies 6, 7, and 9 allowed assessing the impact of personal and national importance on cognitive issue engagement (indicated by an index of the amount of thought a person gave to issue-relevant information, the amount of issue-relevant knowledge a person had and the certainty of issue attitudes), memory for attitude-relevant information, emotional reactions to information about the issue, and the cognitive accessibility of issue-relevant information.

As can be seen in Column 1 of Table 6.5, the effect of personal importance on cognitive issue engagement in Study 6 was positive and statistically significant (b = .32, $p<.001$), as was the impact of national importance (b = .04, $p<.05$), although personal importance was a much stronger predictor than national importance. The data from Study 9 replicate the personal importance finding, for both the Iraq war and global warming issues. In contrast to Study 6, national importance of the Iraq war was not a significant predictor of cognitive issue engagement (b = .01, *n.s.*), whereas national importance of global warming was significantly *negatively* associated with cognitive issue engagement (b = $-.12$, $p<.001$).[10]

Data from Study 7 allowed examining whether personal and national importance were related to knowledge accumulation and to emotional reactions by estimating the parameters of a covariance structure model that corrected for random and systematic measurement error.[11] The model fit the data well (χ^2 (9) = 8.39, *n.s.*; RMSEA = .00; standardized RMR = .02; non-normed fit index = 1.01).

The effect of personal importance on memory for the news stories was positive and marginally significant (b = .67, $p<.10$), whereas the effect of national importance was not significant (b = $-.60$, *n.s.*; see column 4 of Table 6.5). And personal importance was a positive predictor of the extent of emotional reactions to a news story (b = .39, $p<.05$), but national importance was not (b = $-.18$, *n.s.*; see column 5 of Table 6.5).

Data from Study 9 confirms the emotion findings from Study 6. As columns 6 and 7 of Table 6.5 show, the effects of personal importance of both the Iraq war and global warming were positive and statistically significant (b = .18 and b = .21, respectively, $p<.001$ for both). Also consistent with Study 6, national importance was not significantly related to emotional reactions for either issue.

Finally, Study 7's data allowed estimating the parameters of a covariance structure model predicting accessibility with personal and national importance.[12] This model fit the data well (χ^2 (31) = 36.51, n.s.; RMSEA = .03; standardized RMR = .03; non-normed fit index = .97). As column 8 of Table 6.5 shows, the effect of personal importance on accessibility was significant and positive (b = .29, $p<.01$), but the effect of national importance was not significant (b = $-.10$, *n.s.*).

The differential effect of personal and national importance on accessibility means that issues that are personally important to an individual are more likely to be at the top of his/her head and therefore more likely to be used when making political judgments (Zaller, 1992) than issues that are perceived to be nationally important. Personal importance is therefore likely to have more effects on other types of attitudes in addition to those we have explored, including policy preferences, attitudes toward government institutions, attitudes toward value tradeoffs, and more (Zaller, 1992).

TABLE 6.5 Personal and National Importance Predicting Cognitive and Affective Issue Engagement—Studies 6, 7, and 9

	Study 6	Study 9		Study 7		Study 9		Study 7
Predictor	Cognitive engagement index	Cognitive engagement index (Iraq)	Cognitive engagement index (GW)	Issue memory	Emotion	Iraq emotion	GW emotion	Accessibility
Personal Importance	.32*** (.02)	.29*** (.02)	.30*** (.02)	.67+ (.38)	.39* (.16)	.18*** (.01)	.21*** (.02)	.29*** (.11)
National Importance	.04* (.02)	.01 (.02)	-.11*** (.02)	-.60 (.43)	-.18 (.17)	.02 (.02)	.01 (.02)	-.10 (.11)
Male	.07*** (.01)	.08*** (.01)	.07*** (.01)	-.07 (.01)	-.08*** (.02)	-.01 (.01)	.02** (.01)	.00 (.01)
Age	-.04 (.03)	.03 (.02)	-.02 (.02)	.03 (.06)	.03 (.06)	-.00 (.02)	.00 (.02)	-.02 (.04)
White	.03* (.01)	-.01 (.06)	-.01 (.01)	.07*** (.02)	.07** (.02)	.01 (.01)	.01 (.01)	-.01 (.01)
Income	.05* (.02)	.02* (.01)	.02 (.01)			.00 (.01)	-.01 (.01)	
Education	.13*** (.02)	.09*** (.02)	.16*** (.02)			-.03** (.01)	.01 (.01)	

continued…

Table 6.5 continued...

Predictor	Study 6 Cognitive engagement index	Study 9 Cognitive engagement index (Iraq)	Cognitive engagement index (GW)	Study 7 Issue memory	Emotion	Study 9 Iraq emotion	GW emotion	Study 7 Accessibility
Democrat	.00 (.01)	-.01 (.01)	-.03 (.02)			.01 (.01)	.01 (.01)	
Republican	-.01 (.01)	.01 (.01)	.03* (.02)			.03* (.01)	.01 (.01)	
R^2	.22	.23	.16	.02	.09	.14	.18	.04
N	1270	1931	1911	297	297	1934	1903	297

Note: Table entries in columns 1, 2, 3, 6, and 7 are unstandardized OLS regression coefficients. Table entries in columns 4, 5, and 8 are unstandardized coefficients obtained from LISREL. Standard errors are in parentheses.
+ $p < .10$, * $p < .05$, ** $p < .01$, *** $p < .001$

TABLE 6.6 Personal and National Importance Predicting Political Behavior Controlling for Cognitive and Affective Issue Engagement—Studies 6 and 9

Predictor	Environment behavior index (Study 6)	Iraq behavior index (Study 9)	Iraq behavior index (Study 9)	Global warming behavior index (Study 9)	Global warming behavior index (Study 9)
Personal importance	.07*** (.02)	.06*** (.02)	.13*** (.02)	.10*** (.02)	.15*** (.02)
National importance	-.01 (.01)	.00 (.02)	.00 (.02)	-.01 (.02)	-.05* (.02)
Cognitive issue engagement	.12*** (.02)	.30*** (.03)		.29*** (.02)	
Emotion			.16*** (.03)		.21*** (.03)
Male	.00 (.01)	-.01 (.01)	.02* (.01)	.01 (.01)	.03 (.01)
Age	-.01 (.02)	-.02 (.02)	-.01 (.02)	-.00 (.02)	-.01 (.02)
White	.02 (.01)	.02 (.01)	.01 (.01)	-.00 (.01)	-.01 (.01)
Income	.02+ (.01)	.05*** (.01)	-.04*** (.01)	-.04*** (.02)	-.04*** (.01)
Education	.03* (.01)	.03* (.02)	.06*** (.02)	.06*** (.02)	.10*** (.02)

continued…

Table 6.6 continued...

Predictor	Environment behavior index (Study 6)	Iraq behavior index (Study 9)	Iraq behavior index (Study 9)	Global warming behavior index (Study 9)	Global warming behavior index (Study 9)
Democrat	-.01 (.01)	-.01 (.02)	-.02 (.02)	-.00 (.02)	-.01 (.02)
Republican	-.03** (.01)	-.02 (.02)	-.02 (.02)	-.03+ (.02)	-.02 (.02)
R^2	.09	.12	.06	.16	.10
N	1270	1931	1924	1911	1903

Note: Table entries are unstandardized regression coefficients. Standard errors are in parentheses.
★ $p < .05$, ★★ $p < .01$, ★★★ $p < .001$

Question 5: Do Cognitive or Affective Issue Engagement Mediate the Effects of Personal Importance on Political Behavior?

Cognitive and/or affective issue engagement may mediate the effect of personal importance on political behavior. Study 6 and Study 9 permitted tests of these hypotheses. Table 6.6 reports the results of OLS regressions predicting political behavior with personal importance, national importance, cognitive issue engagement (Columns 1, 2, and 4), affective issue engagement (Columns 3 and 5) and the control variables. In all models, the direct effect of personal importance is statistically significant, as is the proposed mediator (cognitive or affective engagement). To test whether cognitive/affective engagement is a statistically significant mediator of the effect of personal importance on political behavior, we analyzed the indirect effects using a bootstrap method with bias corrected confidence intervals (95%) developed by Preacher and Hayes (2008) using the program PROCESS created by Hayes (2013; see also Hayes, 2009). As Table 6.7 shows, in all cases, the indirect effect was statistically significant (i.e., the confidence intervals do not contain 0). These results are consistent with the conclusion that personal importance impacted all three types of behavioral issue engagement through its impact on cognitive or affective issue engagement.[13]

TABLE 6.7 Does Cognitive and/or Affective Issue Engagement Mediate the Effect of Personal Importance on Political Behavior?

Study / mediator	Effect	Bootstrap standard error	Bootstrap lower level confidence interval	Bootstrap lower level confidence interval
Study 6 / Cognitive	0.04	0.01	0.02	0.05
Study 9 Iraq / Cognitive	0.09	0.01	0.07	0.11
Study 9 GW / Cognitive	0.09	0.01	0.07	0.11
Study 9 Iraq / Affective	0.03	0.01	0.02	0.05
Study 9 GW / Affective	0.04	0.01	0.03	0.06

Question 6: Does Personal Importance Cause National Importance or Vice Versa?

Does personal importance cause national importance, or vice versa? Data from Study 8 permitted estimating the parameters of a covariance structure model to gauge the lagged causal impact of personal importance on national importance and the lagged causal impact of national importance on personal importance. This model allowed time 1 personal importance to predict time 2 personal importance and allowed time 1 national importance to predict time 2 national importance, reflecting the stability in the constructs over time. After controlling for the stability of the constructs, the only unexplained variance in time 2 personal and national importance judgments represented change in these importance judgments between time 1 and time 2. Therefore, we allowed time 1 personal importance to predict time 2 national importance, and we allowed time 1 national importance to predict time 2 personal importance, in order to estimate the amount of change in the time 2 variables attributable to the time 1 variables. Such lagged effects are consistent with the hypothesis that the time 1 variable caused changes in the time 2 variable (see Kenny, 1979; Kessler & Greenberg, 1981). The model also allowed for correlated errors between time 1 personal and national importance and between the residuals of time 2 personal and national importance.

Time 1 personal importance was a significant predictor of time 2 personal importance ($b = .42$, SE $= .04$, $p<.001$), indicating over-time stability. Likewise, time 1 national importance was a significant predictor of time 2 national importance ($b = .33$, SE $= .04$, $p<.001$). Time 1 personal importance was also a significant, positive predictor of time 2 national importance ($b = .26$, SE $= .05$, $p<.001$), and national importance at time 1 was a positive and significant but weaker predictor of personal importance at time 2 ($b = .13$, SE$= .03$, $p<.001$), indicating reciprocal causality. Thus, although national importance was a cause of personal importance, national importance was much more a *result* of personal importance.

Note also that the stability over time of personal importance ($b = .42$) is larger than the stability of national importance ($b = .33$). When the parameters of the model were re-estimated constraining these coefficients to be equal, goodness of fit declined marginally significantly ($\Delta\chi^2 = 2.10$, $p<.10$). This reinforces the notion that personal importance assessments are more crystallized than national importance judgments.

The standardized effect of national importance on personal importance was .17, which means that only 3% of the effect of personal importance on behavioral, cognitive, and emotional issue engagement can be attributed to national importance. But it is still possible that personal importance mediates the effect of national importance on behavioral, cognitive, and emotional issue engagement. That is, it is possible that national importance causes personal importance, which, in turn, affects issue engagement. If this were the case, then our analyses, because they include both personal and national importance in the same equation, might mask potential effects of national importance. To test this possibility, we re-estimated the effects of national importance not controlling for personal importance (i.e., in the equations reported in Tables 6.2–6.5). National importance had statistically significant effects in only 8 of the 27 equations (plus 1 marginally significant effect), compared to the 23 of 27 statistically significant personal importance coefficients (plus 1 marginally significant effect).

Discussion

The Power of Personal Importance

When evaluating candidates for public office, making vote choices, and expressing policy preferences directly to elected officials and the news media, citizens are apparently focused primarily on policy issues they consider to be personally important rather than issues they consider to be nationally important (in 74% of our tests of the effect of personal and national importance on political behavior, the personal importance coefficient was statistically significantly larger than the national importance coefficient). Personal importance was a statistically significant predictor of behavioral, affective, and cognitive issue engagement in our tests, whereas national importance rarely was. These results are consistent across a variety of political issues and behaviors, using both open-ended and closed-ended questions to measure importance, and for both representative samples of adults and convenience samples of college students. Had the results of our studies with representative samples of adults been different from the results obtained from convenience samples of college students, more weight should presumably be placed on the studies of general public samples. But since the results are consistent across the two types of samples, we do not need to choose. And our results indicate that the process of conferring cognitive, affective, and behavioral engagement on some issues over others is similar for students and non-students alike.

The primacy of personal importance occurs for three reasons. Attaching personal importance to an issue apparently leads people to think extensively about relevant information, to store it in long-term memory, and therefore remember it better. Furthermore, information on personally important issues evokes stronger emotions. And attitudes on more personally important policy issues are held with greater certainty and are more accessible in memory (for a similar finding regarding accessibility, see Lavine et al. 1996). Thus, the roots of policy issue engagement for democratic citizens appear to be in personal importance assessments.

One interesting implication of this conclusion has to do with the political consequences of media agenda-setting and real-world cues indicating problem seriousness. Although these forces can apparently alter judgments of the national importance of issues, the resulting ups and downs of issues on the public's national problem agenda are not especially consequential in the citizens' own thinking or action. Another implication of our findings is that in future research, scholars should rely on personal importance measures to identify citizens who are highly engaged in an issue, rather than assuming that saying an issue is nationally important indicates engagement.

The Roots of Personal Importance

The superiority of personal importance judgments in driving political thinking and action seems especially understandable in light of the differences between the causes of national importance judgments (media agenda-setting and real-world cues) and the causes of personal importance judgments (material self-interest, identification with a reference group or reference individual whose material interests are at stake in an issue or who care deeply about it, or the relevance of a person's core abstract values about how life should be lived; Boninger et al., 1995). Thus, instead of being quickly and sensitively responsive to shifts in news media content and recent events, personal issue importance appears to be rooted in more enduring and thoughtfully generated links between an issue and key elements of a citizen's self-concept and place in the social structure. In this light, it is not surprising that the amount of personal importance an individual attaches to a particular policy issue appears to be much more stable over time (Krosnick, Berent, & Boninger, 1994) than are judgments of the national importance of issues (e.g., Behr & Iyengar, 1985). This sort of evidence is also consistent with the notion that national importance judgments are formed tentatively, change easily, and are not especially psychologically consequential, whereas personal importance judgments are crystallized and revised thoughtfully and gradually and have more potential to shape political cognition and action.

When Might National Importance Be Consequential?

National importance judgments might be less consequential because citizens form them with only limited confidence, given the complexity of national circumstances and the information burdens inherent in becoming informed about those circumstances. To explore this possibility, we examined the impact of personal and national importance judgments on issue engagement among citizens of differing levels of political sophistication. More sophisticated individuals are more exposed to a range of political information from the media and may therefore be more equipped to form national importance judgments with confidence. More politically sophisticated citizens may also be socialized to focus their political thinking on national considerations when deciding how to think about and participate in politics. Thus, a positive relation between political sophistication and impact of national importance judgments would not definitively support the "difficulty" explanation, but such a result could lend some initial support to it.

Study 6's data permitted testing this notion using educational attainment as a surrogate for political sophistication and testing interactions of education with each type of importance when predicting policy preference expression, contributing money, attending a meeting, knowledge, thought, and certainty. None of the six interactions involving national importance was statistically significant, meaning that the effect of national importance judgments did not vary with education. One interaction between education and personal importance was statistically significant: personal importance had more impact on knowledge accumulation among less educated citizens. Although education is not an optimal index of political sophistication (Zaller, 1990), no evidence suggests that national importance judgments are more consequential among political sophisticates compared to the less sophisticated.

Theories of group processes suggest that perceptions of a group's circumstances should only be consequential among individuals who identify with the group in some way (e.g., Conover, 1984, 1988; Kramer & Brewer, 1984) and that identification with the nation is likely to be more powerful in some situations than in others (e.g., Brewer & Gardner, 1996; Smith & Spears, 1996). Therefore, the generally weak effects of national importance judgments we observed might be traceable to relatively weak identification with the nation for most Americans most of the time, perhaps because it is too heterogeneous a group. If this is so, national importance might have a sizable impact on issue engagement among citizens who do closely identify with the nation (e.g., highly patriotic individuals), or in situations when unifying characteristics of the nation are spotlighted (e.g., under circumstances of a national crisis such as a war; see Mueller, 1994).

Perhaps national issue importance judgments do have consequences, but on different outcomes than examined here. For example, perhaps citizens want government to put more effort into addressing nationally important issues, not issues they attach importance to personally. And perhaps aggregations of national importance judgments, measured in widely publicized national surveys, lead politicians to devote more effort to working on a particular issue (see, e.g., Jones, 1994). We look forward to future research exploring these possibilities.

Conflict with Evidence on Economic Voting?

Some readers might think that the findings reported here are in conflict with those in the literature on the impact of economic beliefs on vote choices, which has shown that people do not use their own personal economic circumstances to decide whether to vote for or against an incumbent (see Anderson, 2007). Instead, people seem to use their perceptions of the nation's economy when deciding how to vote in presidential elections. But the apparent reason for this is applicable only in that context: whereas citizens hold presidents responsible for national-level economic conditions, they see little connection between a president's actions and their own personal economic situations (Feldman, 1982; Lau and Sears, 1981). This reasoning has no clear implications for whether policy issue engagement should result from judgments of national or personal issue importance, so we see no conflict between our findings and those on economic voting.

Put simply, the studies reported here are of a very different phenomenon. Personal importance does not solely reflect material self-interest and instead also reflects values and the concerns of groups with which the individual identifies. Thus, personal importance should not be equated with self-interest. As such, our findings do not contradict evidence that retrospective and concurrent judgments of national economic conditions are much more consequential than such judgments of personal economic circumstances. Likewise, our results do not conflict with Tyler's (1990), which showed that people obey the law not because they fear being personally punished but rather because they perceive the legal system to be legitimate. And our results do not conflict with Mutz's (1998) evidence that an individual's personal experiences of life events have much less impact on political judgments than do perceptions of the collected opinions and experiences of others. Unlike all of these scholars, we are focused on citizens' attitudes toward specific government policy options and the amount of personal importance attached to those attitudes (whether that importance is derived from self-interest, values, or group identity concerns). And in this domain, personal trumps national.

Coda

In 1983, Sheila Rowbotham wrote, "It is still a vexed question as to when the personal is political or the personal remains personal, and how the personal connects with the political" (p. 44). Many years later, much is still left to be understood on this matter. The findings offered here suggest that, at least with regard to policy issue engagement, the personal *is* political. But this is clearly not always the case in politics. We look forward to future research on other aspects of political cognition and action to see how and when the personal connects with the political and when these two arenas remain separate and unconnected.

Appendix: Measures and Variable Coding

Studies 1 and 2

Personal Importance

Respondents were asked two questions to assess the personal importance of a series of issues (Study 1: capital punishment, Central America, abortion, and defense spending; Study 2: defense spending, the environment, drug abuse, taxes, and school bussing): 1) How important to you personally is the issue of (x)? (Not at all important, not too important, somewhat important, very important, extremely important); and 2) How concerned are you personally about the issue of (x)? (Not at all concerned, not too concerned, somewhat concerned, very concerned, extremely concerned). Responses were coded to range from 1–5, where 1 = not at all and 5 = extremely.

National Importance

Respondents were asked two questions to assess the national importance of the same issues about which personal importance was gauged: 1) How important for the country as a whole is the issue of (x)? (Not at all important, not too important, somewhat important, very important, extremely important); and 2) How concerned should the country as a whole be about the issue of (x)? (Not at all concerned, not too concerned, somewhat concerned, very concerned, extremely concerned). Responses were coded to range from 1–5, where 1 = not at all and 5 = extremely.

Study 3

Respondents' Policy Attitudes

In the NES surveys, respondents were asked to report their attitudes on many policy issues, and on some issues, respondents were also asked how important the issue was to them personally, measures that were required for our analyses. In 1980, suitable data were collected on the issues of defense spending, spending on government services, guaranteed full employment, relations with the Soviet Union, aid to minorities, taxes, and the tradeoff between combating inflation and combating unemployment. In 1984, suitable data were collected on the issues of spending on government services, guaranteed full employment, and U.S. policy in Central America. The policy issues suitably addressed in the 1996 NES were spending on government services and aid to minorities. All policy attitudes were coded to range from 0–1.

The labels on the end points of these policy attitude rating scales were: Defense spending: 0 = greatly decrease, 1 = greatly increase; government services: 0 = reduce spending a lot, 1 = no reduction in spending; guaranteed employment: 0 = government should assure a job and good standard of living for everyone, 1 = government should let each person get ahead on his own; Soviet Union: 0 = try very hard to get along with Russia, 1 = do not try too hard to get along with Russia; aid to minorities: 0 = government should help minority groups, 1 = minority groups should help themselves; taxes: 0 = no tax cut, and 1 = cut taxes by 30%. Inflation/unemployment: 0 = reduce inflation even if it means large increases in unemployment, 1 = reduce unemployment even if it means large increases in inflation; Central America: 0 = much more U.S. involvement in Central America, 1 = much less U.S. involvement in Central America.

Perceptions of Candidates' Policy Attitudes

After reporting their attitudes toward each policy, respondents were asked to report their perceptions of the two major presidential candidates' policy attitudes on the issue. The response options for these questions were the same as those used to gauge respondents' attitudes and were coded to range from 0 to 1.

Personal Importance

In 1980, respondents were asked how important it was to them that the federal government continue what it was doing or change what it was doing so that it stayed close to or came closer to their own position on the issue, on a 0–100 scale. Following Krosnick (1988a), we rescaled this variable such that 0–59 = 0, 60–89 = .33, 90–99 = .66, and 100 = 1. In 1984, respondents were asked how important it was to them that the federal government do what they thought was best on the issue—not important at all, somewhat important, very important, or extremely important (coded 0, .33, .66, and 1, respectively). In 1996, respondents were asked how important the issue was to them—not important at all, not too important, somewhat important, very important, or extremely important (coded 0, .25, .5, .75, and 1, respectively).

National Importance

All respondents were asked to list what they thought were the most important problems facing the country. Up to three responses were recorded from each respondent in 1980 and 1984, and in 1996, up to four responses were recorded. A respondent was coded 1 if he or she considered an issue to be nationally important and was coded 0 otherwise.

Responses to the open-ended most important problem questions were coded into a series of standard categories in the NES datasets. In 1980, the unemployment codes were 10, 11, 12, 19, 400, 401, and 402; defense spending codes were 700, 710, 711, 712, 713, and 719; government services codes were 10, 11, 12,119, 20, 21, 22, 29, 30, 31, 32, 39, 40, 41, 42, 50, 51, 52, 54, 55, 56, 59, 60, 61, 62, 63, 64, 69, 90, 91, 92, 414, 415, and 837; guaranteed jobs codes were 10, 11, 12, 19, 60, 61, 62, 63, 64, 69, 90, 91, 92, and 405; Soviet Union codes were 530, 531, 532, 533, and 539; aid to minorities codes were 60, 61, 62, 63, 64, 69, 90, 91, 92, 300, 301, 302, 303, 304, 310, 311, 312, 317, 318, and 319; taxes codes were 416, 417, and 418 (see Miller, 1980). In 1984, government services and guaranteed jobs codes were the same as in 1980; Central America codes were 514, 550, 551, 552, 559, 560, 561, 562, and 569 (see Miller, 1984). In 1996, government services and aid to minorities codes were the same as in 1980 (see Rosenstone et al., 1996).

Although NES questions measured policy preferences and personal importance regarding abortion in 1980, women's rights in 1984, and abortion, defense spending, and the environment in 1996, we could not use these issues for our analyses, because too few people listed these issues as nationally important. In 1980, only 6 people mentioned abortion. In 1984, only 18 people listed women's rights. And in 1996, only 35 people listed defense spending, 13 people listed abortion, and 98 people listed the environment.

Candidate Preference

Respondents were asked to report their attitudes toward the two major presidential candidates on 101-point feeling thermometers. Preferences were indexed by subtracting ratings of the Democratic candidate from ratings of the Republican candidate and rescaling the resulting variable to range from −1 (meaning a respondent strongly favored the Democratic candidate) to +1 (meaning the respondent strongly favored the Republican candidate). Respondents with no preference between the candidates were coded 0.

Control Variables

Interviewers recorded respondents' gender (coded $1 = $ male, $0 = $ female). Respondents reported their race (coded $1 = $ white, $0 = $ nonwhite), age (coded in years to range from 0 to 1), education ($0 = $ no high school diploma, $.33 = $ high school diploma, $.66 = $ some college, and $1 = $ at least a BA degree), and their total household income from the previous year (in 21 income categories, coded to range from 0 to 1). Party identification was represented by two variables, one coded 1 for Democrats and 0 for everyone else, and the other coded 1 for Republicans and 0 for everyone else.

Issue Proximity

To represent the relative distance between each respondent's attitude toward a policy and the candidates' attitudes toward the policy while avoiding confounding due to projection, we computed net spatial distances using each national sample's average perception of each candidate's attitude to approximate his or her true attitude (see Krosnick, 1988a; Markus, 1982; Markus, & Converse, 1979; Page, 1978) as follows:

$$|\text{R's attitude} - \text{mean Democratic candidate attitude}| - |\text{R's attitude} - \text{mean Republican candidate}| \quad (1)$$

The resulting issue distance scores ranged from −1 to +1. Positive numbers indicated that the respondent's issue position was closer to the Republican candidate's, and negative numbers indicated that the respondent's position was closer to the Democratic candidate's. Respondents whose attitudes were equidistant from the two candidates received scores of 0 on this measure.

Study 4

Personal Importance

Respondents reported how important the Arab–Israeli conflict was to them personally, as compared to other political issues (not among the five issues they personally considered most important, one of the five most important issues, one of the two or three most important issues, or the single most important issue, coded 0, .33, .66, and 1, respectively).

National Importance

Respondents were asked how important the Arab–Israeli conflict was for the security and welfare of the United States as a whole (not too important, somewhat important, very important, or extremely important, coded 0, .33, .66, and 1, respectively).

Issue Impact on Candidate Preferences

Respondents were asked to identify their favorite presidential candidate during the 1988 primary season. Then, they were asked how important their views on the Arab–Israeli conflict were in determining which of the candidates was their favorite (not among the five most important issues, one of the five most important issues, one of the two or three most important issues, or the single most important issue, coded 0, .33, .66, and 1, respectively).

Expressing Policy Preferences to Politicians or the News Media

Respondents were asked if they had ever written a letter, made a telephone call, or done anything else to express their views on the Arab–Israeli conflict directly to a government official, newspaper, or magazine. People who had were coded 1, and people who had not were coded 0.

Control Variables

Interviewers recorded respondents' gender (coded 1 = male, 0 = female). Respondents reported their race (coded 1 = whites and 0 = nonwhites), age (coded to range from 0 to 1 from the youngest to oldest), education (0 = no high school diploma, .25 = high school diploma, .50 = some college, and .75 = college graduate, 1 = at least some postgraduate education), and total household income (9 categories, coded to range from 0 to 1 from lowest to highest income).

Study 5

Personal Importance

Respondents were asked two questions for each of four issues (abortion, gun control, health care, and trade with Mexico) to assess personal importance: how important the issue was to them personally (not at all important, not too important, somewhat important, very important, or extremely important) and how personally concerned they were about the issue (not at all concerned, not too concerned, somewhat concerned, very concerned, or extremely concerned). Answers to both questions were coded to range from 0 to 1, with higher numbers meaning more importance.

National Importance

Respondents were asked two national importance questions for each issue: how important the issue was for the country as a whole (not at all important, not too important, somewhat important, very important, or extremely important), and how concerned the country as a whole should be about the issue (not at all concerned, not too concerned, somewhat concerned, very concerned, or extremely concerned). Again, answers to these questions were coded to range from 0 to 1, with higher numbers meaning more importance.

Issue Impact on Candidate Preferences

Respondents were asked to identify their favorite presidential candidate during the 1992 campaign. They were then asked how important their opinions on each of the issues were in determining which of the candidates was their favorite (not among the five most important issues, one of the five most important issues, one of the two or three most important issues, or the single most important issue, coded from 0 to 1).

Expressing Policy Preferences to Politicians or the News Media

Respondents were asked if they had ever written a letter, made a telephone call, or done anything else to express their views on each of the four issues directly to a government official, newspaper, or magazine. Respondents who said they had were then asked how many times they had done so. People who said they had never expressed their attitudes were coded 0; people who had done so once were coded .5; and people who had done so more than once were coded 1.

Other Variables

Interviewers recorded respondents' gender (coded 1 = male, 0 = female), and respondents reported their education (coded 0 = not a high school graduate, .25 = high school graduate, .5 = some college, .75 = college graduate, 1 = post-college) and their age (coded to range from 0 to 1).

Study 6

Personal Importance

Respondents were asked how important global warming was to them personally (not at all important, not too important, somewhat important, very important, or extremely important, coded from 0 to 1).

National Importance

Respondents were asked how serious of a problem they thought change in the world's climate is likely to be for the country (no problem at all, slightly serious, pretty serious, very serious, or extremely serious, coded from 0 to 1).

Expressing Policy Preferences to Politicians or the News Media

Respondents were asked whether, during the four months prior to the interview, they had written a letter to a public official expressing their views about global warming. People who had were coded 1, and those who had not were coded 0.

Financial Contributions to Lobbying Organizations and Attending Group Meetings

Respondents were asked whether, during the four months prior to the interview, they had given money to an organization that was concerned with global warming (coded 1 for yes and 0 for no) and whether, during the four months prior to the interview, they had attended a group meeting to discuss global warming (coded 1 for yes and 0 for no).

Knowledge Accumulation, Prior Thought, and Opinion Certainty

Respondents were asked how much they felt they knew about global warming (nothing, a little, a moderate amount, or a lot, coded from 0 to 1), how much thinking they had done about global warming before the interview (none at all, hardly any, a moderate amount, or a lot, coded from 0 to 1), and how sure they were of their opinions about global warming (not sure at all, slightly sure, somewhat sure, very sure, or extremely sure, coded from 0 to 1).

Control Variables

Interviewers recorded respondents' gender (coded 1 = male, 0 = female). Respondents reported their race (coded 1 = whites and 0 = nonwhites), age (coded in years to range from 0 to 1), education (0 = no high school diploma, .33 = high school diploma, .66 = some college, and 1 = at least a BA level degree) and total household income (using 9 categories that were coded to range from 0 to 1). Party identification was represented by two variables, one coded 1 for Democrats and 0 for everyone else, and the other coded 1 for Republicans and 0 for everyone else.

Study 7

Personal Importance

Respondents were asked two questions to assess personal importance. First, they were asked to list up to three policy issues that were most important to them personally. A coder who had no other information about the respondents read their answers and recorded whether they mentioned each of the target issues (crime, unemployment, and pollution). For each target issue, we then created a dichotomous variable indicating whether the respondent had mentioned the issue (coded 1) or had not (coded 0).

Respondents also reported the importance of each target issue to them personally (not at all important, not too important, somewhat important, very important, or extremely important, coded from 0–1).

National Importance

Respondents were asked both an open-ended and a closed-ended question to assess the national importance of the target issues in the respondents' opinions. First, they were asked to list up to three policy issues that were the most important for the country. Second, they were asked to rate how important each issue was for the country as a whole (not at all important, not too important, somewhat important, very important, or extremely important). Answers to these questions were coded in the same fashion as were answers to the personal importance questions.

Attitude Accessibility

Accessibility was gauged using procedures developed by Fazio (1990). When seated at the computer, respondents evaluated President Bill Clinton's handling of each target issue twice and evaluated his handling of nine other issues once each. On each trial, the name of an issue appeared in the middle of the screen, and respondents pressed one of two buttons, labeled "approve" and "disapprove." The length of time between the appearance of each issue name and the pressing of a button was recorded by the computer.

Response times less than 501 milliseconds (so fast that respondents probably accidentally pressed a button or did not read the issue name) and greater than 7000 milliseconds (so slow that respondents probably were not concentrating exclusively on the task) were considered to be invalid measurements. We therefore treated these as instances of missing data and created our measures of accessibility using the remaining valid measurements from each respondent (see Fazio, 1990). On average, only 7 respondents out of the total of 385 failed to provide valid accessibility data on each item.

After subjecting the response times to a reciprocal transformation (to normalize the distributions), the response times of the two evaluations of presidential performance on each target issue were averaged. To control for differences between people in the speed with which they made all judgments, the mean response time for the nine filler issues was subtracted from the mean response time for each target issue (Fazio, 1990). The resulting three scores were then standardized to place them all on a common metric (unconfounded by differences in the familiarity of the issue labels); larger numbers indicated greater accessibility.

Knowledge Accumulation

The paper-and-pencil questionnaire asked respondents to think back to the news stories they saw and to describe the stories that stood out most in their minds. A coder who had no other information about the respondents counted the number of stories about the target issue that each respondent correctly recalled. Virtually all respondents were able to recall one of the two target stories he or she saw, so we classified people who remembered both target stories as having evidenced better memory (coded 1) than those who remembered either one or none (coded 0).

Emotions

Respondents were given a list of eight emotions (angry, sad, disgusted, proud, hopeful, happy, afraid, and sympathetic) and were asked to indicate which they had felt while watching the two target stories. To create an index of the volume of emotional reactions a respondent had, we summed the number of emotional reactions each respondent reported feeling during the two target stories (ranging from 0 to 16) and rescaled the resulting index to range from 0 to 1.

Control Variables

Respondents reported their gender (coded 1 = male, 0 = female), age (coded to range from 0 to 1), and race (coded 1 = whites, 0 = nonwhites).

Study 9

Personal Importance

Respondents were asked how important the issues of global warming and the Iraq war were to them personally, in separate questions (not at all important, slightly important, moderately important, very important, or extremely important, coded from 0 to 1).

National Importance

Respondents were asked how important the issues of global warming and the Iraq war were for the country as a whole, in separate questions (not at all important, slightly important, moderately important, very important, or extremely important, coded from 0 to 1).

Expressing Policy Preferences to Politicians or the News Media

For each of the two issues (Iraq war and global warming), respondents were asked how many times during the last year they wrote a letter, made a telephone call, or did anything else to express their opinion about the issue to a government official, newspaper, magazine, or on a webpage on the internet. People who responded "0 times" were coded 0. All other respondents were coded 1.

Financial Contributions to Organizations

Respondents were asked how much money they had contributed to an organization working on the issues of the war in Iraq and global warming during the last year (in separate questions). Respondents who said that they had not contributed any money were coded 0, and respondents who had contributed money, regardless of amount, were coded 1.

Working with Organizations

Respondents reported how many hours during the last year they worked with an organization that is working on the issues of the war in Iraq and global warming (in separate questions). Responses were coded such that 0 = 0 hours and 1 = 1 or more hours.

Attending Group Meetings

Respondents reported how many times during the last year they attended a group meeting to talk about the Iraq war and global warming issues (in separate questions). Responses were coded such that 0 = 0 time and 1 = 1 or more times.

Knowledge Accumulation, Prior Thought, and Opinion Certainty

For each of the two issues, respondents were asked how much they felt they knew about the issue (nothing, a little, a moderate amount, a lot, or a great deal, coded from 0 to 1), how much thinking they had done about the issue (none, a little, a moderate amount, a lot, or a great deal, coded from 0 to 1), and how sure they were of their opinions about the issue (not sure at all, slightly sure, somewhat sure, very sure, or extremely sure, coded from 0 to 1).

Emotions

Respondents were asked: When you think about what people have been doing and saying in recent years about the issue of the war in Iraq [global warming], how angry [hopeful, afraid, proud] do you feel (not at all, slightly, moderately, very, or extremely)? Responses were coded to range from 0 to 1.

Control Variables

Gender was coded such that 1 = male and 0 = female. Respondents reported their race (coded 1 = whites and 0 = nonwhites), age (coded in years to range from 0 to 1), education (0 = no high school diploma, .25 = high school diploma, .50 = some college, .75 = BA degree, and 1 = graduate or professional degree) and total household income (coded such that 0 = below US$35,000 and 1 = US$35,000 or above). Party identification was represented by two variables: one coded 1 for Democrats and 0 for everyone else, and the other coded 1 for Republicans and 0 for everyone else.

Notes

1 This research was conducted partly while the second author was a fellow at the Center for Advanced Study in the Behavioral Sciences, funded by NSF Grant SBR-9022192. The study of public opinion on global warming was supported by grants from the National Science Foundation (Grant SBR-9731532), the National Oceanic and Atmospheric Administration, the U.S. Environmental Protection Agency, and the Ohio State University and was sponsored by Resources for the Future. Jon Krosnick is University Fellow at Resources for the Future. The authors would like to thank Paul Beck for his encouragement and advice and Paul Goren, John Bullock, Neil Malhotra, Daniel Schneider, and Lori Gauthier for their helpful comments and suggestions.

2 These figures come from a search using www.jstor.org of the *AJPS* between 1973 and 2002, the *APSR* between 1906 and 2000, the *BJPS* between 1971 and 1998, the *JoP* between 1939 and 2000, *PB* between 1979–1998, and *POQ* between 1937 and 1999. "Salience" appeared in the title or abstract of 76 of these articles, and 47 of them dealt specifically with the salience of policy issues in the minds of citizens, which is our current focus.

3 Some studies failed to find effects of personal importance in regulating issue impact on vote choice (e.g., Aldrich, Niemi, Rabinowitz, & Rohde, 1979; Beardsley, 1973; Grynaviski & Corrigan, 2006; Hinckley, Hofstetter, & Kessel, 1974; Jackson, 1979; Niemi & Bartels, 1985), but Krosnick (1988a) identified a series of aspects of the analytic methods used in those studies that are likely to have masked the importance effects.

4 For each issue, we specified two latent substantive factors: personal importance (how personally important the issue was and how personally concerned the respondent was about it) and national importance (how important the issue was for the nation and how concerned the country should be about it). The latent factors were permitted to correlate freely with one another. To account for correlated measurement error shared by pairs of questions involving the same response scale (due to people's idiosyncratic interpretations of the response options; see, e.g., Ostrom & Upshaw, 1968), two method factors are included (see Alwin & Krosnick, 1985; Boruch & Wolins, 1970). The Importance Method Factor was a cause of answers to the questions with a response scale ranging from "not at all important" to "extremely important" (both were constrained to load 1.0 on that factor). The Concern Method Factor was a cause of answers to the questions with a response scale ranging from "not at all concerned" to "extremely concerned" (both were constrained to load 1.0 on that factor). Since LISREL analyzed a variance-covariance matrix, constraining the method factor loadings to be equal and estimating the variances of those factors amounts to assuming that each method factor creates a constant amount of variance in all indicators it affects. The method factors were not allowed to correlate with each other or with the substantive latent factors (see Judd & Krosnick, 1982; Krosnick & Alwin, 1988; Widaman, 1985). The metric of each substantive latent factor was set by fixing at 1.0 the loading of the question using the word "importance," and estimating all other loadings.

5 An RMSEA of .05 or less indicates the model is a good fit to the data; .051–.08 indicates acceptable fit (Browne & Cudeck, 1992). A non-normed fit index of .95 or more indicates good fit, as does a standardized RMR of .08 or less (Hu & Bentler, 1998).

6 The two personal importance questions were treated as indicators of a personal importance latent factor for each issue, and the two national importance questions were indicators of a national importance latent factor for each issue. To correct for systematic measurement error, we allowed for correlated error between the

personal and national importance questions that asked about *importance* of the issue, and between the personal and national importance questions that addressed *concern* about the issue. The latent personal and national importance factors, along with the demographic control variables, were allowed to be correlated with one another, and were used to predict the issue's impact on expressing preferences on the issues to politicians or the news media. To obtain single coefficients for the effects of personal and national importance on each outcome variable, we constrained the effects of personal and national importance to be equal across issues.

7 Results are similar when we examine each behavior separately—personal importance is a significant predictor and national importance is not.

8 Results are consistent when we examine each behavior separately.

9 In this study, the personal importance measure was a closed-ended question, and the national importance measure was an open-ended question, so the use of an open-ended question might have handicapped the performance of national importance here. But other studies here used closed-ended measures of national importance, and they fared no better.

10 Results are similar when we examine the cognitive engagement variables separately.

11 The two personal importance questions for the issue about which each person viewed target news stories (because the memory and emotion measures asked them only about the target news stories they had viewed) were treated as indicators of a latent personal importance variable for the issue, and the two national importance questions were treated as indicators of a latent national importance variable. Thus, for each respondent, only the personal and national importance questions regarding their randomly assigned target issue were used to predict memory and emotions. The latent personal and national importance factors and the demographic controls were allowed to be correlated with one another. To correct for systematic measurement error, we allowed for correlated error between the open-ended personal and national importance questions and between the closed-ended personal and national importance questions.

12 This analysis focuses on all three issues for each respondent. The two personal importance questions for each issue were treated as indicators of a latent personal importance variable for each issue, and the two national importance questions for each issue were treated as indicators of a latent national importance variable for each issue. The latent personal and national importance factors and the demographic controls were allowed to correlate with one another. The effects of personal importance and national importance on accessibility were constrained to be equal across issues to yield single, efficient tests. To correct for systematic measurement error, we allowed for correlated error between the open-ended personal and national importance questions and between the closed-ended personal and national importance questions.

13 We also estimated the parameters of less theoretically plausible models changing the causal sequence. For example, one model proposed that personal importance was the independent variable, behavior was the mediator, and cognitive issue engagement was the outcome variable. Another model proposed that behavior was the independent variable, personal importance was the mediator, and cognitive issue engagement was the outcome variable. These and all other such models produced evidence of significant mediation. The available data do not provide a basis for discriminating among these various models in terms of their plausibility.

References

Adams, James. 1997. "Condorcet Efficiency and the Behavioral Model of the Vote." *The Journal of Politics* 59(4): 1252–1263.

Aldrich, John H., & Richard D. McKelvey. 1977. "A Method of Scaling with Applications to the 1968 and 1972 Presidential Elections." *American Political Science Review* 71: 111–130.

Aldrich, John, Richard Niemi, George Rabinowitz, & David Rohde. 1979. "Memorandum on Analysis of the 1979 Pilot Study Issue Questions." Unpublished manuscript, University of Michigan, The Institute for Social Research, Center for Political Studies, Ann Arbor, MI.

Aldrich, John H., John L. Sullivan, & Eugene Borgida. 1989. "Foreign Affairs and Issue Voting: Do Presidential Candidates 'Waltz Before A Blind Audience?'" *American Political Science Review* 83: 123–141.

Alwin, Duane F., & Jon A. Krosnick. 1985. "The Measurement of Values in Surveys: A Comparison of Ratings and Rankings." *Public Opinion Quarterly* 49: 535–552.

Anderson, Christopher J. 2007. "The End of Economic Voting? Contingency Dilemmas and the Limits of Democratic Accountability." *Annual Review of Political Science* 10: 271–96.

Baron, Robert M., & David A. Kenny. 1986. "The Moderator-Mediator Variable Distinction in Social Psychological Research: Conceptual, Strategic, and Statistical Considerations." *Journal of Personality and Social Psychology* 51: 1173–1182.

Barry, Brian M. 1965. *Political Argument*. New York: Humanities Press.

Beardsley, Philip L. 1973. "The Methodology of the Electoral Analysis: Models and Measurement." In David M. Kovenoek, & James W. Prothro (Eds.), *Explaining the Vote: Presidential Choices in the Nation and the States, 1968* (pp. 30–92). Chapel Hill, NC: Institute for Research in Social Science.

Beck, Paul Allen, & Suzanne Parker. 1985. "Consistency in Political Thinking." *Political Behavior* 7(1): 37–56.

Behr, Roy L., & Shanto Iyengar. 1985. "Television News, Real-World Cues, and Changes in the Public Agenda." *Public Opinion Quarterly* 49: 38–57.

Bélanger, Eric, & Bonnie M. Meguid. 2008. "Issue Salience, Issue Ownership, and Issue-Based Vote Choice: Evidence from Canada." *Electoral Studies* 27: 477–491.

Bellah, Robert N., Richard Madsen, William M. Sullivan, Ann Swidler, & Steven M. Tipton. 1985. *Habits of the Heart*. New York: Harper and Row.

Bernstein, Robert A. 1995. "Directing Electoral Appeals Away from the Center: Issue Positions and Issue Salience." *Political Research Quarterly* 48(3): 479–505.

Berry, William D. 1979. "Utility Regulation in the States: The Policy Effects of Professionalism and Salience to the Consumer." *American Journal of Political Science* 23(2): 263–277.

Best, Samuel J. 1999. "The Sampling Problem in Measuring Policy Mood: An Alternative Solution." *Journal of Politics* 61: 721–740.

Birt, Catherine M., & Kenneth L. Dion. 1987. "Relative Deprivation Theory and Responses to Discrimination in a Gay Male and Lesbian Sample." *British Journal of Social Psychology* 26: 139–145.

Bizer, George Y., & Jon A. Krosnick. 2001. "Exploring the Structure of Strength-related Attitude Features." *Journal of Personality and Social Psychology* 81: 566–586.

Bobo, Lawrence. 1988. "Attitudes Toward the Black Political Movement." *Social Psychology Quarterly* 51: 287–302.

Boninger, David S., Jon A. Krosnick, & Matthew K. Berent. 1995. "The Origins of Attitude Importance." *Journal of Personality and Social Psychology* 68: 61–80.

Boninger, David S., Jon A. Krosnick, Matthew K. Berent, & Leandre R. Fabrigar. 1995. "The Causes and Consequences of Attitude Importance." In Richard E. Petty, & Jon A. Krosnick (Eds.) *Attitude Strength: Antecedents and Consequences* (pp. 159–189). Hillsdale, NJ: Erlbaum.

Boruch, Robert. F., & Leroy Wolins. 1970. "A Procedure for Estimation of Trait, Method, and Error Variances Attributable to a Measure." *Educational and Psychological Measurement* 30: 547–574.

Brewer, Marilynn, & Wendi Gardner. 1996. "Who Is This 'We'? Levels of Collective Identity and Self Representations." *Journal of Personality and Social Psychology* 71: 83–93.

Browne, Michael W., & Robert Cudeck. 1992. "Alternative Ways of Assessing Model Fit." *Sociological Methods and Research* 21: 23–258.

Burden, Barry C., & Joseph Neal Rice Sandberg. 2003. "Budget Rhetoric in Presidential Campaigns from 1952 to 2000." *Political Behavior* 25(2): 92–118.

Campbell, James E. 1983. "Ambiguity in the Issue Positions of Presidential Candidates: A Causal Analysis." *American Journal of Political Science* 27(2): 284–293.

Canes-Wrone, Brandice, & Scott de Marchi. 2002. "Presidential Approval and Legislative Success." *Journal of Politics* 64(2): 491–509.

Chaney, Carole Kennedy, R. Michael Alvarez, & Jonathan Nagler. 1998. "Explaining the Gender Gap in U.S. Presidential Elections, 1980–1992." *Political Research Quarterly* 51(2): 311–339.

Cohen, Bernard C. 1963. *The Press and Foreign Policy*. Princeton, NJ: Princeton University Press.

Cohen, Bernard C. 1973. *The Public's Impact on Foreign Policy*. Boston, MA: Little, Brown, and Company.

Conover, Pamela J. 1984. "The Influence of Group Identifications on Political Perception and Evaluation." *American Journal of Political Science* 46: 760–785.

Conover, Pamela J. 1988. "The Role of Social Groups in Political Thinking." *British Journal of Political Science* 18: 51–76.

Converse, Philip E. 1964. "The Nature of Belief Systems in Mass Publics." In D. E. Apter (Ed.) *Ideology and Discontent*. New York: Free Press.

Cook, Fay Lomax, Tom R. Tyler, Edward G. Goetz, Margaret T. Gordon, David Protess, Donna R. Leff, & Harvey L. Molotch. 1983. "Media Agenda-Setting: Effects on the Public, Interest Group Leaders, Policy Makers, and Policy." *Public Opinion Quarterly* 47: 16–35.

Downs, Anthony. 1957. *An Economic Theory of Democracy*. New York: Harper.

Edwards, George C. III, William Mitchell, & Reed Welch. 1995. "Explaining Presidential Approval: The Significance of Issue Salience." *American Journal of Political Science* 39(1): 108–134.

Erbring, Lutz, Edie N. Goldenberg, & Arthur H. Miller. 1980. "Front-Page News and Real-World Cues: A New Look at Agenda-Setting by the Media." *American Journal of Political Science* 24: 16–49.

Eulau, Heinz. 1955. "Perceptions of Class and Party in Voting Behavior: 1952." *American Political Science Review* 49: 364–384.

Fazio, Russell H. 1990. "A Practical Guide to the Use of Response Latency in Social Psychological Research." In Clyde Hendrick, & Margaret Clark (Eds.) *Research Methods in Personality and Social Psychology* (pp. 74–97). London: Sage Publications.

Feldman, Stanley. 1982. "Economic Self-Interest and Political Behavior." *American Journal of Political Science* 26: 446–466.

Feldman, Stanley, & Lee Sigelman. 1985. "The Political Impact of Prime-Time Television: 'The Day After.'" *The Journal of Politics* 47(2): 556–578.

Festinger, Leon. 1957. *A Theory of Cognitive Dissonance.* Stanford, CA: Stanford University Press.

Fiorina, Morris P. 1978. "Economic Retrospective Voting in American National Elections: A Micro-Analysis." *American Journal of Political Science* 22: 426–443.

Fiske, Susan T., & Shelley E. Taylor. 1990. *Social Cognition.* NY: McGraw Hill.

Flanagan, Scott C. 1980. "Value Cleavages, Economic Cleavages, and the Japanese Voter." *American Journal of Political Science* 24: 177–206.

Fleishman, John A. 1986. "Trends in Self-Identified Ideology from 1972–1982: No Support for the Salience Hypothesis." *American Journal of Political Science* 30(3): 517–541.

Fournier, Patrick, André Blais, Richard Nadeau, Elisabeth Gidengil, & Neil Nevitte. 2003. "Issue Importance and Performance Voting." *Political Behavior* 25(1): 51–67.

Granberg, Donald, & Soren Holmberg. 1986. "Political Perception among Voters in Sweden and the U.S.: Analyses of Issues with Explicit Alternatives." *Western Political Quarterly* 39: 7–28.

Green, John C., & James L. Guth. 1988. "The Christian Right in the Republican Party: The Case of Pat Robertson's Supporters." *The Journal of Politics* 50(1): 150–165.

Grynaviski, Jeffrey D., & Bryce E. Corrigan. 2006. "Specification Issues in Proximity Models of Candidate Evaluation (with Issue Importance)." *Political Analysis* 14(4): 393–420.

Hardin, John W. 1998. "Advocacy versus Certainty: The Dynamics of Committee Jurisdiction Concentration." *The Journal of Politics* 60(2): 374–397.

Hayes, Andrew F. 2009. "Beyond Baron and Kenny: Statistical Mediation Analysis in the New Millennium." *Communication Monographs* 76: 408–420.

Hayes, Andrew F. 2013. *Introduction to Mediation, Moderation, and Conditional Process Analysis.* New York: The Guilford Press.

Hibbs, Douglas A. 1979. "The Mass Public and Macroeconomic Performance: The Dynamics of Public Opinion Toward Unemployment and Inflation." *American Journal of Political Science* 23(4): 705–731.

Hinckley, Barbara, Richard Hofstetter, & John Kessel. 1974. "Information and the Vote: A Comparative Election Study." *American Politics Quarterly* 2: 131–158.

Holbrook, Allyson L., Matthew K. Berent, Jon A. Krosnick, Penny S. Visser, & David S. Boninger. 2005. "Attitude Importance and the Accumulation of Attitude-Relevant Knowledge in Memory." *Journal of Personality and Social Psychology* 88: 749–769.

Howard-Pitney, B., Eugene Borgida, & A. M. Omoto. 1986. "Personal Involvement: An Examination of Processing Differences." *Social Cognition* 4: 39–57.

Hu, Litze, & Peter M. Bentler. 1998. "Fit Indices in Covariance Structure Modeling: Sensitivity to Underparameterized Model Misspecification." *Psychological Methods* 3: 424–453.

Hutchings, Vincent L. 2001. "Political Context, Issue Salience, and Selective Attentiveness: Constituent Knowledge of the Clarence Thomas Conference Vote." *Journal of Politics* 63(3): 846–868.

Iyengar, Shanto. 1979. "Television News and Issue Salience: A Reexamination of the Agenda-Setting Hypothesis." *American Politics Quarterly* 7: 395–426.

Iyengar, Shanto, & Donald R. Kinder. 1987. *News that Matters.* Chicago, IL: University of Chicago Press.

Jackman, Mary R. 1977. "Prejudice, Tolerance, and Attitudes Toward Ethnic Groups." *Social Science Research* 6: 145–169.

Jackson, John E. 1979. "Analysis of Pilot Study Issue Questions." Unpublished manuscript, University of Michigan, The Institute for Social Research, Center for Political Studies, Ann Arbor, MI.

Johns, Robert. 2008. "Measuring Issues Salience in British Elections: Competing Interpretations of 'Most Important Issue.'" *Political Research Quarterly*, 63(1), 143–158.

Jones, Bryan. 1994. *Reconceiving Decision-Making in Democratic Politics: Attention, Choice, and Public Policy.* Chicago, IL: University of Chicago Press.

Judd, Charles M., & Jon A. Krosnick. 1982. "Attitude Centrality, Organization, and Measurement." *Journal of Personality and Social Psychology* 42: 436–447.

Kaufman, Karen M., & John R. Petrocik. 1999. "The Changing Politics of American Men." *American Journal of Political Science* 43: 864–887.

Kenny, David A. 1979. *Correlation and Causality.* New York: Wiley.

Kerr, Henry H. Jr. 1978. "The Structure of Opposition in the Swiss Parliament." *Legislative Studies Quarterly* 3(1): 51–62.

Kessler, Ronald C., & David F. Greenberg. 1981. *Linear Panel Analysis: Models of Quantitative Change.* New York: Academic Press.

Key, V. O. 1961. *Public Opinion and American Democracy.* New York: Knopf.

Kinder, Donald R., & D. Roderick Kiewiet. 1979. "Economic Discontent and Political Behavior: The Role of Personal Grievances and Collective Economic Judgments in Congressional Voting." *American Journal of Political Science* 23: 495–517.

Kinder, Donald R., & D. Roderick Kiewiet. 1981. "Sociotropic Politics: The American Case." *British Journal of Political Science* 11: 129–161.

Kingdon, John W. 1981. *Congressmen's Voting Decisions.* New York: Harper & Row.

Kingdon, John W. 1995. *Agendas, Alternatives, and Public Policies.* New York: Harper Collins.

Kramer, Gerald H. 1983. "The Ecological Fallacy Revisited: Aggregate Versus Individual-Level Findings on Economics and Elections, and Sociotropic Voting." *American Political Science Review* 77: 92–111.

Kramer, Roderick M., & Marilyn B. Brewer. 1984. "Effects of Group Identity on Resource Use in a Simulated Commons Dilemma." *Journal of Personality and Social Psychology* 46: 1044–1057.

Krosnick, Jon A. 1986. "Policy Voting in American Presidential Elections: An Application of Psychological Theory to American Politics." Ph.D. Diss. University of Michigan.

Krosnick, Jon A. 1988a. "The Role of Attitude Importance in Social Evaluation." *Journal of Personality and Social Psychology* 55: 196–210.

Krosnick, Jon A. 1988b. "Attitude Importance and Attitude Change." *Journal of Experimental Social Psychology* 24: 240–255.

Krosnick, Jon A. 1990. "Government Policy and Citizen Passion: A Study of Issue Publics in Contemporary America." *Political Behavior* 12: 59–92.

Krosnick, Jon A., & Duane F. Alwin. 1988. "A Test of the Form-Resistant Correlation Hypothesis: Ratings, Rankings, and the Measurement of Values." *Public Opinion Quarterly* 52: 526–538.

Krosnick, Jon A., Matthew K. Berent, & David S. Boninger. 1994. "Pockets of Responsibility in the American Electorate: Findings of a Research Program on Attitude Importance." *Political Communication* 11: 391–411.

Lau, Richard R., & David O. Sears. 1981. "Cognitive Links Between Economic Grievances and Political Responses." *Political Behavior* 3: 279–302.

Lau, Richard R., Thad A. Brown, & David O. Sears. 1978. "Self-Interest and Civilians' Attitudes Toward the Vietnam War." *Public Opinion Quarterly* 42: 464–483.

Lavine, Howard, John L. Sullivan, Eugene Borgida, & Cynthia J. Thomsen. 1996. "The Relationship of National and Personal Issue Salience to Attitude Accessibility on Foreign and Domestic Policy Issues." *Political Psychology* 17: 293–316.

Lazarus, Richard S., & Craig A. Smith. 1988. "Knowledge and Appraisal in the Cognition-Emotion Relationship." *Cognition and Emotion* 2: 281–300.

Lewis-Beck, Michael S. 1988. *Economics and Elections*. Ann Arbor, MI: University of Michigan.

MacKuen, Michael. 1984a. "Exposure to Information, Belief Integration, and Individual Responsiveness to Agenda Change." *American Political Science Review* 78: 372–391.

MacKuen, Michael. 1984b. "Reality, the Press, and Citizen's Political Agendas." In Charles F. Turner, & Elizabeth Martin (Eds.) *Surveying Subjective Phenomena* (Vol. 2). New York: Russell Sage.

MacKuen, Michael, & Steven L. Coombs. 1981. *More than News: Media Power in Public Affairs*. Beverly Hills, CA: Sage.

Maggiotto, Michael A., & James E. Piereson. 1978. "Issue Publics and Voter Choice." *American Politics Quarterly* 6: 407–429.

Markus, Gregory B. 1982. "Political Attitudes During an Election Year: A Report on the 1980 NES Panel Study." *American Political Science Review* 76: 538–560.

Markus, Gregory B., & Philip E. Converse. 1979. "A Dynamic Simultaneous Equation Model of Electoral Choice." *American Political Science Review* 73: 1055–1070.

Markus, Hazel R., & Shinobu Kitayama. 1991. "Culture and the Self: Implications for Cognition, Emotion, and Motivation." *Psychological Review* 98: 224–253.

McCombs, Maxwell, & Amy Reynolds. 2002. "News Influence on Our Pictures of the World." In Jennings Bryant, & Dolf Zillman (Eds.) *Media Effects. Advances in Theory and Research* (2nd ed.). Mahwah, NJ: Lawrence Erlbaum Associates.

McCombs, Maxwell, & Donald Shaw. 1972. "The Agenda-Setting Function of the Mass Media." *Public Opinion Quarterly* 36:176–187.

McCombs, Maxwell, & Jian-Hua Zhu. 1995. "Capacity, Diversity, and Volatility of the Public Agenda: Trends from 1954 to 1994." *Public Opinion Quarterly* 59: 495–525.

Melzer, Alan H., & Mark Vellrath. 1975. "The Effects of Economic Policies on Votes for the Presidency." *Journal of Law and Economics* 18: 781–798.

Miller, Joanne M., & Jon A. Krosnick. 2000. "News Media Impact on the Ingredients of Presidential Evaluations: Politically Knowledgeable Citizens are Guided by a Trusted Source." *American Journal of Political Science* 44: 295–309.

Miller, Randy E., & Wayne Wanta. 1996. "Sources of the Public Agenda: The President-Press-Public Relationship." *International Journal of Public Opinion Research* 8: 390–402.

Miller, Warren E. 1980. *American National Election Study, 1980: Integrated File Codebook*. Ann Arbor, MI: University of Michigan, Center for Political Studies.

Miller, Warren E. 1984. *American National Election Study, 1984: Pre-Post Election Study Codebook*. Ann Arbor, MI: University of Michigan, Center for Political Studies.

Modigliani, Andre, & William A. Gamson. 1979. "Thinking about Politics." *Political Behavior* 1: 5–30.

Monroe, Alan D. 1998. "Public Opinion and Public Policy, 1980–1993." *Public Opinion Quarterly* 62: 6–28.

Mueller, John. 1994. *Policy and Opinion in the Gulf War*. Chicago, IL: University of Chicago Press.

Mutz, Diana C. 1998. *Impersonal Influence*. New York: Cambridge University Press.

Mutz, Diana C., & Joe Soss. 1997. "Reading Public Opinion." *Public Opinion Quarterly* 61(3): 431–451.

Natchez, Peter B., & Irvin C. Bupp. 1968. "Candidates, Issues, and Voters." *Public Policy* 18: 409–437.

Niemi, Richard G., & Larry M. Bartels. 1985. "New Measures of Issue Salience: An Evaluation." *Journal of Politics* 47: 1212–1220.

Ostrom, Charles W., & Dennis M. Simon. 1985. "Promise and Performance: A Dynamic Model of Presidential Popularity." *American Political Science Review* 79: 334–358.

Ostrom, Thomas M., & H. S. Upshaw. 1968. "Psychological Perspective and Attitude Change." In Anthony G. Greenwald, Timothy C. Brock, & Thomas M. Ostrom (Eds.) *Psychological Foundations of Attitudes* (pp. 217–242). New York: Academic Press.

Page, Benjamin I. 1978. *Choices and Echoes in Presidential Elections: Rational Man and Electoral Democracy*. Chicago, IL: Chicago University Press.

Page, Benjamin, & Robert Shapiro. 1983. "Effects of Public Opinion on Policy." *American Political Science Review* 77: 23–43.

Page, Benjamin, & Robert Shapiro. 1992. *The Rational Public*. Chicago, IL: University of Chicago Press.

Peters, B. Guy, & Brian W. Hogwood. 1985. "In Search of the Issue-Attention Cycle." *Journal of Politics* 47: 239–253.

Petry, François. 1999. "The Opinion-Policy Relationship in Canada." *The Journal of Politics* 61(2): 540–550.

Petty, Richard E., & Jon A. Krosnick 1995. *Attitude Strength*. Hillsdale, NJ: Erlbaum.

Pierce, John C. 1975. "The Relationship Between Linkage Salience and Linkage Organization in Mass Belief Systems." *Public Opinion Quarterly* 39: 102–110.

Preacher, Kristopher J., & Andrew F. Hayes. 2008. "Asymptotic and Resampling Strategies for Assessing and Comparing Indirect Effects in Multiple Mediator Models." *Behavior Research Methods 40*: 879–891.

Rabinowitz, George, James W. Prothro, & William Jacoby. 1982. "Salience as a Factor in the Impact of Issues on Candidate Evaluation." *Journal of Politics* 44: 41–63.

RePass, David E. 1971. "Issue Salience and Party Choice." *American Political Science Review* 65: 389–400.

Rokeach, Milton. 1968. *Beliefs, Attitudes, and Values*. San Francisco, CA: Jossey-Bass.

Rokeach, Milton. 1973. *The Nature of Human Values*. New York: Free Press.

Rosenstone, Steven S., Donald R. Kinder, & Warren E. Miller. 1996. *American National Election Study, 1996: Pre-Post Election Study Codebook*. Ann Arbor, MI: University of Michigan.

Rowbotham, Sheila. 1983. *Dreams and Dilemmas*. London: Virago Press.

Schuman, Howard, & Stanley Presser. 1981. *Questions and Answers: Experiments on Question Form, Wording and Context in Attitude Surveys*. New York: Academic Press.

Schuman, Howard, Jacob Ludwig, & Jon A. Krosnick. 1986. "Perceived Threat of Nuclear War, Salience, & Open Questions." *Public Opinion Quarterly* 50: 519–536.

Sears, David O., & Carolyn L. Funk. 1990. "Self-Interest in Americans' Political Opinions." In Jane J. Mansbridge (Ed.) *Beyond Self-Interest* (pp. 147–170). Chicago, IL: University of Chicago Press.

Shapiro, Michael J. 1969. "Rational Political Man." *American Political Science Review* 63: 1106–1119.

Shapiro, Robert Y., & Harpreet Mahajan. 1986. "Gender Differences in Policy Preferences: A Summary of Trends from the 1960s to the 1980s." *Public Opinion Quarterly* 50(1): 42–61.

Sherif, Muzafer, & Carl I. Hovland. 1961. *Social Judgment*. New Haven, CT: Yale University Press.

Sigelman, Lee, & T. Tsai. 1981. "Personal Finances and Voting Behavior." *American Politics Quarterly* 9: 371–400.

Smith, Craig A., Kelly N. Haynes, Richard S. Lazarus, & Lois K. Pope. 1993. "In Search of 'Hot' Cognitions." *Journal of Personality and Social Psychology* 65: 916–929.

Smith, Heather J., & Russell Spears. 1996. "Ability and Outcome Evaluations as a Function of Personal and Collective (Dis)advantage." *Personality and Social Psychology Bulletin* 22: 690–704.

Smith, Tom W. 1980. "America's Most Important Problem—A Trend Analysis, 1946–1976." *Public Opinion Quarterly* 44: 164–180.

Sobel, Michael E. 1982. "Asymptotic Confidence Intervals for Indirect Effects in Structural Equation Modeling." In S. Leinhart (Ed.) *Sociological Methodology 1982* (pp. 290–312). San Francisco, CA: Jossey-Bass.

Stewart, Philip D., James W. Warhola, & Roger A. Blough. 1984. "Issue Salience and Foreign Policy Role Specialization in the Soviet Politburo of the 1970s." *American Journal of Political Science* 28: 1–22.

Tedin, Kent L. 1979. "Political Variables in Political Socialization: Reply to 'The Dynamics of Interpersonal Attitudinal Influence.'" *Political Behavior* 1(3): 285–293.

Triandis, Harry C. 1990. "Cross-Cultural Studies of Individualism and Collectivism." In J. Berman (Ed.) *Nebraska Symposium on Motivation*. Lincoln, NE: University of Nebraska Press.

Tufte, Edward R. 1978. *Political Control of the Economy*. Princeton, NJ: Princeton University Press.

Tyler, Tom R. 1990. *Why People Obey the Law*. New Haven, CT: Yale University Press.

Visser, Penny S., Jon A. Krosnick, & Joseph P. Simmons. 2003. "Distinguishing the Cognitive and Behavioral Consequences of Attitude Importance and Certainty." *Journal of Experimental Social Psychology* 39(March): 118–141.

Weaver, David. 1987. "Media Agenda Setting and Elections: Assumptions and Implications." In David L. Paletz (Ed.) *Political Communication Research*. Norwood, NJ: Ablex Publishing Corp.

Weaver, David. 1994. "Media Agenda-Setting and Elections: Voter Involvement or Alienation?" *Political Communication* 11: 347–356.

Widaman, Keith F. 1985. "Hierarchically Nested Covariance Structure Models for Multitrait-Multimethod Data." *Applied Psychological Measurement* 9: 1–26.

Wlezien, Christopher. 2005. "On the Salience of Policy Issues." *Electoral Studies* 24(4): 555–579.

Wright, Gerald C. 1976. "Community Structure and Voting in the South." *Public Opinion Quarterly* 40(2): 201–215.

Yankelovich, Daniel. 1981. *New Rules: Searching for Self-Fulfillment in a World Turned Upside Down*. New York: Random House.

Zajonc, Robert B. 1998. "Emotions." In Daniel T. Gilbert, Susan T. Fiske, & Gardner Lindzey (Eds.) *The Handbook of Social Psychology*. Boston, MA: McGraw Hill.

Zaller, John R. 1990. "Political Awareness, Elite Opinion Leadership, and the Mass Survey Response." *Social Cognition* 8: 125–153.

Zaller, John R. 1992. *The Nature and Origins of Mass Opinion*. Cambridge: Cambridge University Press.

7

THE IMPACT OF POLICY CHANGE THREAT ON FINANCIAL CONTRIBUTIONS TO INTEREST GROUPS[1]

Joanne M. Miller, Jon A. Krosnick,
Allyson Holbrook, Alexander Tahk, and
Laura Dionne

Citizen activism in democratic societies can guide government policy-making in numerous ways. People can work to help elect candidates with whom they agree on policy issues (Milbrath & Goel, 1977; Verba, Schlozman, & Brady, 1995). They can support interest groups that lobby legislators on particular issues (Cigler & Loomis, 1995; Hansen, 1991). In the extreme, they can join together and catalyze social movements to demand more radical social change (Smelser, 1962; Tarrow, 1998).

Why do citizens choose to join particular groups in order to try to influence government in particular ways? Underlying research on this question is the notion that people who share a common interest have an incentive to work with one another to pursue and/or protect that interest. However, many people who share common interests with one another do not collaborate as activists. Therefore, driven by Olson's (1965) landmark work, scholars have sought to identify the costs and benefits of participating, presuming that action occurs only when the latter outweigh the former (e.g., Salisbury, 1969). The benefits that have received the most attention include selective incentives, solidary and purposive rewards, beliefs about a group's ability to succeed, and the individual's access to necessary resources (e.g., Finkel, Muller, & Opp, 1989; Milbrath & Goel, 1977; Olson, 1965).

We put the spotlight on another potential motivator of activism: perceiving a threat of a change in public policy that an individual would consider undesirable. We use data from three representative sample surveys (two with experiments built in) to test the hypothesis that the threat of an undesirable policy change will motivate one form of issue-focused activism aimed at influencing government action: making financial contributions to interest groups working to prevent the policy change. We also explore the conditions under which this sort of threat is most likely to inspire this sort of activism.

Documented Determinants of Issue-Focused Activism

Among citizens who share the desire to see a particular public policy enacted, the most effort would presumably come from staff members of interest groups devoted to lobbying elected representatives. Somewhat less effort would be expected from members of the "active public," people who voluntarily give their time and money to groups, attend rallies, and write letters. Other citizens may be called "passive sympathizers," people supportive of groups' efforts but who do nothing to help.

We focus on the factors that determine whether a person will be among the active public or the passive sympathizers at any given moment in time. Prior research on activism points to a number of important determining factors, some of which are attributes of the individual. For example, people with more requisite resources (e.g., free time and disposable income) are less taxed by participation (Rosenstone & Hansen, 2002; Verba et al., 1995; see Leighley, 1995, for a review of the socioeconomic status model). Highly educated people are better equipped with civic skills, which presumably confer a sense of confidence that their efforts can make a difference (Verba et al., 1995; see also Gore & Rotter, 1963; Klandermans, 1983). People who care deeply about a particular policy issue or who link their own identities to a group affected by the issue are most likely to participate (Finkel & Opp, 1991; Krosnick & Telhami, 1995; Morris & Mueller, 1992).

The behavior of interest group coordinators also helps determine when people will be politically active. For example, people are much more likely to participate when they have been invited to do so than when they must invest the effort to locate a group to join and devise a strategy for doing so (Gamson, 1975; Walker, 1991). Groups can offer selective incentives, tangible rewards (e.g., discounted goods or services) that only active members can receive (Gamson, 1975; Olson, 1965; Salisbury, 1969). Groups can also take steps to demonstrate their effectiveness in influencing policy (Moe, 1980; Opp, 1986; Roseneau, 1974) and to convince people that their participation will enhance the group's chances of success (Muller, Dietz, & Finkel, 1991).

Changes in real-world conditions can inspire activism as well. As Truman (1951) outlined, societies evolve into comfortable states of equilibrium that are punctuated by occasional disturbances. When a disturbance causes a decline in people's quality of life, they are motivated to rectify the situation, at times through political activism. Thus, an important motivator is the sense of dissatisfaction with undesirable current life circumstances and the concomitant desire to change them (Gamson, 1975; Gurr, 1970; Loomis & Cigler, 1995).

This theme is especially prominent in the social movements literature. The French Revolution, the Civil Rights movement, and other such movements (and perhaps the recent Tea Party Movement) emerged in response to dissatisfaction with governmental policies or social structures that appeared to treat people unfairly (e.g., Smelser, 1962). As Smelser (1995, p. 409) put it, "All social movements begin with some feeling of discontent with the existing social order—with things the way they are." Likewise, interest groups have often formed to oppose newly created government programs that disadvantaged the group or to oppose other citizen groups that took actions with which the group disagreed (Baumgartner & Leech, 1998; Loomis & Cigler, 1995; Walker, 1991), and Hansen (1985) demonstrated that when people suffered serious economic hardships, they were especially likely to join groups that could help alleviate the hardships.

Threat

Less prominent, but nonetheless present in this literature, is the somewhat different notion that *satisfaction* with current circumstances and the desire to defend them can also motivate activism. Various scholars have argued that when people face threats of undesirable economic, social, or political changes in the future, they are especially likely to join others to protect the status quo (Gusfield, 1963; Hansen, 1985; Loomis & Cigler, 1995). People may also be motivated by the threat of undesirable future policy change even if they are not especially happy with the current circumstances. As such, it may not be necessary for life circumstances to take a turn for the worse before people will become active. The *appearance* that things may become worse in the future may be effectively motivating as well, regardless of satisfaction with the status quo.

When it comes to democratic politics, citizens can experience various types of threats. Our focus here is on what we call "policy change threat"—a citizen's perception that a politically powerful individual or individuals are mobilizing to change public policy in a way that the citizen opposes. Perceptions of policy change threat may come about whenever a person surveys the political landscape and becomes aware that an agent or agents are taking such steps. For example, a newly elected President may express a commitment to changing an existing law or passing a new one. An election can shift the leadership of the Congress from one political party to the other, thereby giving special legislative power to a group that places priority on changing a law or passing a new one. Or powerful social groups outside of government can initiate public efforts to change laws. By their actions, these agents threaten losses to citizens who disagree with the proposed change. The Tea Party Movement might be an instance of citizens mobilizing to prevent undesirable changes in the status quo.

Two aspects of this definition of policy change threat are especially important. First, it is the onset or emergence of efforts to *change* public policy that are perceived as threatening. Although some conceptualizations of threat have presumed that an undesirable *current* situation can be threatening (e.g., Hansen, 1985), we view threat instead as a future-oriented perception of possibility.[2] A second key aspect of this hypothesis focuses on agent effort: policy change threat exists only if people perceive that a group or individual is working *hard* to enact an undesired change in public policy.

The notion that threat motivates action is compelling from many perspectives. For example, Prospect Theory (Kahneman & Tversky, 1979) describes how the threat of a loss is especially motivating, even more so than the possibility of a gain. And much psychological research has shown that fear of a loss powerfully inspires behavior to avert the loss (Leventhal, 1970; Meyerowitz & Chaiken, 1987; Rothman & Salovey, 1997).

In a similar fashion, threat of a loss seems likely to inspire citizen political activism to prevent the loss, a notion that various scholars have entertained. For example, Marcus, Neuman, and MacKuen (2000) have argued that perceiving a political candidate as threatening inspires citizens to engage in electoral activism. Likewise, King and Walker (1991, p. 93) argued that "when persons face a threat to their livelihood or to rights they already enjoy, they are more likely to engage in collective actions to protect these gains ..." (see also Diamond, 1995; Loomis & Cigler, 1995; Walker, 1991). This notion has also been suggested in a number of historical analyses of social movements (e.g., Moen, 1992) and appears to be endorsed by interest group fundraisers, whose direct mail solicitations routinely point out threats of undesirable policy changes to motivate people to join their organizations (Godwin, 1988; Mitchell, 1979).

Existing Evidence

Indirect evidence that policy change threat may inspire activism comes from studies documenting other political consequences of threat. Threat plays an important role in inspiring the "rally-round-the-flag" effect (Brody, 1991; Mueller, 1973, 1994). And threats increase authoritarianism (Altemeyer, 1996; Doty, Peterson, & Winter, 1991; Rokeach, 1960), intolerance (Marcus et al., 1995), ethnocentrism (Feldman & Stenner, 1997), and support for energetic, active, and determined presidential candidates (McCann, 1997).

Coming a bit closer to the phenomenon of interest here, Gusfield (1963) documented how the temperance movement emerged because the Protestant middle-class perceived lower-class urban immigrants to have compromised the moral character of society and threatened to do so further. The threat of nuclear war inspired political activism among people who perceived that threat most powerfully (Fiske, Pratto, & Pavelchak, 1983; Tyler & McGraw, 1983). Environmental activism has been inspired partly by the perception that the quality of the environment was threatened and was likely to decline in the future (McKenzie-Mohr et al., 1995). Feeling anxious about the candidates in an election leads to increased political participation (Brader, 2006; Marcus et al., 2000), and post 9/11 policy threat resulted in greater political participation among some Arab Americans (Cho, Gimpel, & Wu, 2006).

Other evidence suggesting the impact of policy change threat on activism involves trends over time in public support for environmental lobbying groups. Controlling for many factors (including aspects of interest group behavior) and correcting for inflation, financial contributions to such groups were higher during the Reagan and Bush administrations than during the Carter administration or during the first two years of the Clinton administration (Lowry, 1997; Richer, 1995). And membership in the Sierra Club and the Audubon Society grew much less rapidly during the Kennedy and Johnson administrations than during the Nixon and Ford administrations (Mitchell, 1979). Higher levels of activism during Republican administrations may have reflected environmentalists' perceptions of greater threat of undesirable policy change at those times.

However, these trends are consistent with two alternate interpretations. First, it is possible that support grew during Republican administrations not because of the threats they posed but rather in response to damage that environmentalists might have perceived these administrations to have done already (Bosso, 1997; Mitchell, 1990). This would then be activism in response to dissatisfaction with current life conditions (e.g., Hansen, 1985).

Alternatively, it is possible that opportunities for desirable policy change posed by the arrival of Democratic presidents may actually have inhibited activism and inspired passivity instead. When people see a powerful individual or group advocating a policy change they favor, this could conceivably be viewed as offering an *opportunity* to join with him, her, or them to bring about such desirable changes.[3] Without such powerful advocates, social movements and interest groups stand little chance of success. But ordinary citizens may presume that their own efforts on behalf of the same cause are no longer needed when a powerful ally joins the fight.

This potential inhibiting effect of what we call "policy change opportunity" would be consistent with the well-documented "social loafing effect" described by Social Impact Theory (Latane, 1981): people devote less effort to pursuing a desired common goal when they believe others are working with them toward the same goal (e.g., Ingham et al., 1974; Sweeney, 1973). This is very much like the free-rider phenomenon identified by Olson (1965): when people believe that they will be able to reap the benefits of others' efforts without having to work toward the goal themselves, they will likely slack off and let others do the work for them. So if a person believes that others are working to change a public policy in a desired direction, he or she may decide to allocate his or her limited resources elsewhere, knowing that if the policy is indeed changed, he or she would benefit from it just as much as those who worked toward that end.

Because perceived policy change opportunities created by the appearance of a powerful ally may inhibit activism, aggregate-level time series analyses (e.g., Lowry, 1997; Mitchell, 1979; Richer, 1995) cannot provide clear evidence of the psychological mechanisms at work. That is, higher levels of environmental activism during Republican administrations could reflect the motivating effect of policy change threat then, or the stultifying effect of policy change opportunity during Democratic administrations. Clear insight can only come from quantitative studies of individual citizens, testing the impact of perceived policy change threat on activism and identifying the conditions under which such an effect is most likely to occur, while simultaneously controlling for the impact of perceived policy change opportunities and dissatisfaction with current conditions. The three studies described here did so, focusing on monetary contributions to political organizations.[4]

Moderators of the Effect of Policy Change Threat on Financial Contributions

In exploring the conditions under which policy change threat is most likely to inspire this form of activism, we focused on two potential moderators: income and attitude importance.

Income

No matter how much people may want to become politically active, whether or not they actually do is determined in part by whether they have the resources necessary to do so (e.g., Rosenstone & Hansen, 2002; Verba et al., 1995). Those who want to volunteer their time to help an interest group will not be able to do so if they are single parents who work 60 hours a week, and those who want to make a financial contribution to an interest group will not be able to do so if they barely make enough money to cover their basic living costs. Therefore, the effects of threat on political activism may be moderated by the amount of necessary resources people have at their disposal.

Income seems likely to be the primary necessary resource for financial contributions to interest groups. Past research offers some support for this notion—one predictor of whether people make financial contributions to a political organization is how much disposable income they have (Rosenstone & Hansen, 2002; Verba et al., 1995). However, past studies have not tested the hypothesis examined here: that resource availability *moderates* the impact of perceptions of the political context (in this case, policy change threat) on contributions.

Importance

A second potential moderator is issue public membership. Converse (1964) coined the term "issue publics" to refer to small segments of society, each composed of people who care deeply about a single issue, while most members of the polity attach far less significance to it (see Krosnick, 1990). For issue public members, an undesirable policy change would presumably be personally devastating. The deeply committed feminist who has spent her adult life advocating legalized abortion would find the overturning of Roe vs. Wade disastrous. But to another citizen whose political passions focus on gun control instead, a change in abortion laws, though perhaps undesirable, would not be nearly as personally significant. Therefore, the threat of an undesirable policy change regarding abortion seems more likely to activate the former individual than the latter.

One might imagine that personal importance would be so powerful a motivator of activism in itself that everyone who attaches great significance to an issue would be perpetually active, regardless of whether threats are present or not. But this turns out not to be so: many people who view an issue as extremely personally important do not always engage in relevant political activism (Gilbert, 1988; Krosnick & Telhami, 1995; Roseneau, 1974). Nonetheless, these people may be the most readily mobilizable among the passive sympathizers when a credible threat does appear. Therefore, we tested whether policy change threat has a stronger impact on financial contributions to interest groups among people for whom the issue is more personally important.

Mediators of the Effect of Policy Change Threat on Financial Contributions

Importance

Nadeau, Niemi, and Amato (1995) suggested another possible effect of policy change threat involving issue importance. They reported evidence that they interpreted as showing that threat of an undesirable policy change increased the personal importance that people attached to an issue. This raises the possibility that importance may *mediate* the effect of threat we observed. That is, threat may increase importance, which in turn may inspire activism.

Upon close inspection, the measure of personal importance Nadeau et al. (1995) used appears not to have tapped personal importance of the issue but instead tapped support for public debate on the issue and a personal inclination toward activism on the issue. Respondents were asked how much they agreed or disagreed with the following statement: "I think that all the debates about French in Quebec are useless," and they were asked, "How do you react in general when, in convenience stores, restaurants, and shops, you are served only in English?" and answered "Indifferent, prefer but won't insist, or prefer and insist." Because Nadeau et al.'s (1995) study did not offer a direct test of whether threat increases importance, we tested this meditational hypothesis directly.

Anxiety

Marcus et al. (2000) suggested another possible mediator of our threat effects: anxiety. People who report higher levels of anxiety about presidential candidates (which Marcus and colleagues called "threat") are more likely to vote and contribute money to political candidates (Marcus et al., 2000), presumably because anxiety causes electoral activism (see also Brader, 2006). Perhaps policy change threat causes anxiety about an issue, which then inspires issue-focused activism. We tested the notion that threat causes an increase in financial contributions through its impact on anxiety.

This Investigation

The three studies described below are either measured or experimentally manipulated perceived policy change threat, perceived policy change opportunity, and dissatisfaction, and assessed their impact on financial activism with regard to a specific issue (the environment, gun control, and abortion respectively). The studies tested five hypotheses: (1) threat will increase the amount of money respondents have contributed, or are willing to contribute; (2) the effect of threat will be larger among respondents with more income; (3) the effect of threat will be larger among respondents for whom the issue is more important, (4) the effect of threat on activism is mediated by importance, and (5) the effect of threat on activism is mediated by anxiety.

Description of Studies

The methodologies of the three studies are described briefly below and in more detail in the Appendix. Study 1 was correlational, using data from a representative survey sample to examine the relations of policy change threat, policy change opportunity, and dissatisfaction to financial contributions to environmental organizations. Studies 2 and 3 implemented experimental manipulations in representative sample surveys to examine the causal impact of policy change threat, policy change opportunity, and dissatisfaction on financial contributions to groups working for or against increased gun control laws or abortion laws. The third study also permitted testing the two mediational hypotheses regarding importance and anxiety.

Study 1: Survey on Environmental Activism

The first investigation used data from a survey asking people about their attitudes and perceptions regarding the environment and financial contributions to organizations advocating environmental protection. Computer-assisted telephone interviews were conducted with a representative sample of adult residents of Ohio by the Ohio State University Polimetrics Laboratory. The sample of households with landline telephones was generated by random digit dialing, and the adult member of each contacted household who had the next birthday was selected to be interviewed (Salmon & Nichols, 1983). Completed interviews were obtained from 758 individuals; the cooperation rate for the survey was 57%. Interviewing began in December, 1995 and ended in January, 1996. One-third of the respondents ($N = 221$) were selected at random to receive the questions designed to test our hypotheses.[5]

Study 2: Survey Experiment on Gun Control Activism

Study 2 used an experimental design to provide stronger evidence of causality. This study sought to simulate the process of learning about changes in the political world in an experiment embedded in a representative sample survey. People can become aware of policy change threats or opportunities through conversations with friends or relatives, through the news media, or through information provided by politicians or interest groups. Study 2 attempted to simulate this sort of information acquisition, taking cues from past experiments that manipulated the content of information received to mirror real world learning (e.g., Kinder & Sanders, 1990; Nelson & Kinder, 1988). Thus, Study 2 provided different respondents with different information about impending changes in policy to see the effects of the information on inclination toward activism.

The manipulations were designed to alter perceptions of policy change threat and opportunity with regard to gun control. Respondents were randomly assigned to receive information about one of various different legislative initiatives that were being pursued in Congress at the time the data were collected. Some respondents were told about Congressional efforts to *increase* restrictions on gun access, and other respondents were told about Congressional efforts to *decrease* restrictions. A third group was not told anything about gun control legislative efforts. We tested the effects of policy change threat and policy change opportunity on willingness to contribute money to pro- or anti-gun control organizations by comparing these groups to one another.

Therefore, Study 2 complemented Study 1 by assessing the robustness of the effect of policy change threat for a different issue (gun control) and by examining activism on both sides of the gun control controversy—pro-gun control and anti-gun control, rather than on only one side of an issue (pro-environmental protection).

This survey experiment was conducted by Knowledge Networks (now GfK), who assembled a representative sample of American households via random digit dialing telephone interviews. Panel members completed a short survey each week in exchange for being given free WebTV equipment and free internet access. For this study, a random sample of 2,763 panel participants was drawn and were sent an email notification inviting them to complete the survey; 2,164 people completed it via the internet between January 3 and January 24, 2003 (completion rate = 78%; response rate 2 = 11.53%; see Callegaro & DiSogra, 2008).

Study 3: Survey Experiment on Abortion Activism

Study 3 was a survey experiment similar to Study 2, this time focused on abortion. As with Study 2, Study 3 implemented manipulations to alter perceptions of policy change threat and opportunity. Respondents were randomly assigned to be given information about one of various different legislative initiatives currently being pursued. Some respondents were told about efforts being made in Congress to *increase* restrictions on abortion, and other respondents were told about efforts in Congress being made to *decrease* restrictions. Some respondents were told that Congress members were working hard to accomplish the legislative changes we described, and other respondents were not told the agents were working hard. A final group of respondents was not told anything about current legislative efforts.

This study combined data from two surveys done via computer-assisted telephone interviewing by the Center for Survey Research at the Ohio State University. The first involved adult residents of the United States ($N = 300$). A representative sample of private households was generated by random digit dialing, and the first adult member of each contacted household who was willing to participate was interviewed. Interviewing was conducted between August 4 and 19, 1999. The cooperation rate for the survey was 39%. The second survey involved a sample of adult residents of Franklin County, Ohio ($N = 217$). Telephone numbers were also generated by random digit dialing, and the first adult member of each contacted household who was willing to participate was interviewed. Interviewing was conducted between August 19 and 30, 1999. The cooperation rate for the survey was 49%.[6]

In both surveys, respondents were first asked to report their attitudes on the issue of abortion and to describe how important the issue was to them personally. After answering a series of questions about other political topics, respondents were then given information aimed at instigating perceptions of policy change threat or policy change opportunity or were given no information. Then, respondents reported how much money they would be willing to contribute to an organization with which they agreed and that was concerned with the issue of abortion. They reported how anxious and worried they were when they thought about abortion laws in this country (on 5-point scales ranging from not at all anxious/worried to extremely anxious/worried); these reports were averaged to yield a single index of anxiety. Finally, respondents reported their demographics and political ideology, as well as how personally important the issue of abortion was to them, and interviewers recorded respondents' gender. Thus, in Study 3, respondents were asked to report the personal importance of the issue of abortion both before *and* after the manipulation was implemented.

Results

Mean reported contribution amounts conformed to our hypotheses about the effects of threat, income, and importance. Table 7.1 displays the mean reported contributions (for Study 1) and mean amounts of money that respondents said they were willing to contribute (for Studies 2 and 3) in U.S. dollars. The first column in each panel shows the mean contributions for the full sample of respondents divided into two groups, people who perceived (in Study 1) or were assigned to perceive (in Studies 2 and 3) little policy change threat (row 1) and people who perceived high policy change threat (row 2).[7] The third row in each panel shows the effect of threat: the difference between the low threat and the high threat means.

As expected, increasing threat was associated with more financial contributions in every study. Also as expected, the difference between the high and low threat groups was larger among the high income respondents (greater than US$75,000) than among the low income respondents (less than or equal to US$75,000). Likewise, the difference between the high and low threat groups was larger among the high importance respondents (those for whom the issue was extremely important) than among the low importance respondents (all others). Thus, all three studies' observed data conform to our predictions.

Hypothesis 1: The Effect of Threat on Financial Contributions

For each of the three studies, we conducted OLS regressions predicting contributions (past or future, depending on the study) using policy change threat, policy change opportunity, dissatisfaction, agent preferences (for Study 1 only), education, gender, race, age, and the liberal [Democrat] and conservative [Republican] dummy variables. As the first column of Table 7.2 shows, as expected, policy change threat was positively associated with contributions in Studies 1 and 2. In other words, people who thought that politicians were trying to weaken environmental laws reported contributing more money to environmental groups than those who did not perceive such policy change threats. And people for whom gun control policy change threats (either pro- or anti-, depending on their prior attitudes) were made salient expressed a greater willingness to contribute money to like-minded interest groups than those for whom policy change threats were not made salient. There was no main effect of policy change threat in Study 3.

TABLE 7.1 Average Amounts People Said They Did Contribute or Would Contribute in U.S. dollars

Policy change threat	All respondents	High income respondents	Low income respondents	High importance respondents	Low importance respondents
Study 1					
Low threat	$10.40	$7.31	$10.27	$20.29	$8.35
High threat	$13.78	$16.00	$12.72	$17.89	$8.32
Difference	$3.38	$8.69	$2.45	$17.60	–$0.03
Study 2					
Low threat	$17.76	$24.17	$16.28	$27.83	$15.92
High threat	$22.69	$35.22	$20.43	$41.14	$19.50
Difference	$4.93	$11.05	$4.15	$13.31	$3.58
Study 3					
Low threat	$55.68	$49.44	$56.79	$47.33	$58.49
High threat	$96.81	$125.17	$90.00	$132.36	$77.25
Difference	$41.13	$75.73	$33.21	$85.03	$18.76

TABLE 7.2 Main Effect of Threat and Opportunity on Financial Contributions

Predictor	Study 1	Study 2	Study 3
Policy change threat	.22* (.08)	.02+ (.01)	.00 (.02)
Policy change opportunity	−.05 (.09)	−.01 (.01)	−.01 (.03)
Dissatisfaction	.06* (.03)	.01 (.01)	.06*** (.02)
Agent preferences	.15 (.10)		
Education	.04 (.03)	.02* (.01)	−.05 (.02)
Male	.03 (.02)	.02*** (.01)	.02 (.02)
Caucasian	−.04 (.03)	.02*** (.01)	.01 (.02)
Age	.05 (.05)	.01 (.01)	−.16*** (.04)
Liberal/Democrat	.01 (.03)	−.01 (.01)	.03 (.02)
Conservative/ Republican	.04+ (.02)	.01 (.01)	.03 (.02)
Constant	−.18* (.08)	.01 (.01)	.12*** (.03)
R^2	.09	.02	.11
N	220	2052	335

Note: Standard errors appear in parentheses below OLS unstandardized regression coefficients.
+ $p<.10$, *$p<.05$, ***$p<.00$

The effect of policy change opportunity was not significant in any of the three studies. As expected, dissatisfaction was associated with larger contributions in Studies 1 and 3 (but not in Study 2). That is, people who wanted environmental protection laws strengthened contributed more money to environmental groups than people who were satisfied with the status quo or wanted these laws weakened (Study 1). And people who were dissatisfied with current abortion laws expressed greater willingness to contribute money to like-minded interest groups in the near future than those who were satisfied with current abortion laws (Study 3).

Hypotheses 2 and 3: Is the Effect of Threat on Financial Contributions Moderated by Income or Importance?

To test whether income or importance moderated the effect of policy change threat on contributions, we added interactions between income/importance and policy change threat, policy change opportunity, and dissatisfaction (as well as the main effects of income and importance) to all three OLS regressions reported in Table 7.2 (for Study 3 we used the pre-manipulation measure of importance).

The policy change opportunity × income interaction was not statistically significant in any of the studies, and the dissatisfaction × income interaction was marginally statistically significant in Study 3. Consistent with expectations, the interaction between policy change threat and income was positive and statistically or marginally statistically significant in all three studies (see Row 6 of Table 7.3). To illustrate the shape of the policy change threat × income interactions, we regressed contributions on policy change threat, policy change opportunity, dissatisfaction, and the control variables separately for respondents in the low, moderate, and high income categories for each of the three studies.

TABLE 7.3 Is the Effect of Threat on Financial Contributions Moderated by Income or Importance?

Predictor	Study 1	Study 2	Study 3
Policy change threat	−.22	.01	−.09★
	(.13)	(.01)	(04)
Policy change opportunity	−.19	−.01	−.06
	(.19)	(.01)	(.06)
Dissatisfaction	.03	.01+	.02
	(.05)	(.01)	(.04)
Income	−.05	.01	−.06
	(.05)	(.02)	(.04)
Importance	−.06	.03★	.04
	(.06)	(.02)	(.04)
Policy change threat × Income	.27★	.03+	.13★
	(.12)	(.02)	(.05)
Policy change opportunity × Income	−.01	.01	.07
	(.18)	(.02)	(.08)
Dissatisfaction × Income	−.01	−.01	.08+
	(.06)	(.02)	(.05)
Policy change threat × Importance	.61★★★	.02	.09+
	(.18)	(.01)	(.06)

continued…

Table 7.3 continued…

Predictor	Study 1	Study 2	Study 3
Policy change opportunity × Importance	.26 (.27)	.01 (.02)	.06 (.08)
Dissatisfaction × Importance	.03 (.08)	−.02 (.02)	−.04 (.06)
Agent Preferences	.18+ (.11)		
Education	.07+ (.03)	.02★ (.01)	−.06+ (.03)
Male	.03 (.02)	.02★★★ (.01)	.03 (.02)
Caucasian	−.05 (.03)	.02★★★ (.01)	.02 (.03)
Age	.05 (.05)	−.01 (.01)	−.16★★★ (.04)
Liberal/Democrat	.03 (.03)	−.01 (.01)	.02 (.03)
Conservative/Republican	.05★ (.02)	.01 (.01)	.03 (.02)
Constant	−.18★ (.08)	.01 (.01)	.12★★★ (.03)
R^2	.09	.02	.11
N	220	2052	335

Note: Standard errors appear in parentheses below OLS unstandardized regression coefficients.
+ $p<.10$, ★$p<.05$, ★★★$p<.001$

With regard to Study 1, the effect of threat was not significant among low or moderate income respondents ($b = -.03$, n.s. and $b = .18$, n.s., respectively), but it was significant and positive among high income respondents ($b = .26$, $p<.01$), confirming the hypothesis that threat only motivated financial contributions among people who had the requisite financial resources. With regard to Study 2, the effect of threat was also not significant among low or moderate income respondents, ($b = .01$, n.s. and $b = .01$, n.s., respectively). Among high income respondents, the impact of threat was positive and marginally significant ($b = .04$, $p<.09$), consistent with our hypothesis. Similar results obtain for Study 3— no effect of threat on willingness to contribute among low or moderate income respondents ($b = -.06$, *n.s.*, and $b = .00$, *n.s.*), but a positive, significant effect among high income respondents ($b = .07$, $p < .05$).

Rows 9, 10, and 11 of Table 7.3 show the results of the importance interactions. As expected, the policy change threat × importance interaction was positive and statistically significant or marginally significant in two of the three studies (1 and 3); it was not statistically significant in Study 2. None of the importance interactions with policy change opportunity or dissatisfaction were statistically significant.

To illustrate the shape of the (policy change threat × importance) interactions in Studies 1 and 3, we regressed contributions on policy change threat, policy change opportunity, dissatisfaction, and the control variables separately for respondents in the low, moderate, and high importance categories. With regard to Study 1, the effect of threat was not significant among low and moderate importance respondents ($b = .00$, *n.s.*, and $b = .07$, n.s., respectively), but it was positive and significant among high importance respondents ($b = .66$, $p < .05$). Thus, policy change threat motivated contributions among people who cared a great deal about the issue of the environment, but not among people who cared less about it. With regard to Study 3, the effect of threat was not significant among low and moderate importance respondents ($b = .00$, *n.s.*, and $b = -.06$, *n.s.*, respectively), but it was positive and significant among respondents high in importance ($b = .14$, $p < .05$). As with Study 1, policy change threat motivated an increased willingness to contribute to like-minded abortion interest groups among respondents for whom the issue was highly personally important, but not among respondents for whom the issue was less personally important.[8]

Hypotheses 4 and 5: Is the Effect of Threat on Financial Contributions Mediated by Importance or Anxiety?

Study 3 allowed us to test whether importance mediates the impact of threat on contributions. We examined whether policy change threat caused an increase in personal importance by regressing the post-manipulation importance measure on pre-manipulation importance, policy change threat, policy change opportunity, dissatisfaction, ideology, and the demographic control variables. Contrary to the mediational hypothesis, increased threat did not yield increased personal importance ($b = .03$, *n.s.*). This suggests that importance could not be a mediator of the effect of threat on activism, reinforcing our confidence that importance moderates threat's impact. In other words, threat does not appear to affect activism by increasing the amount of importance a person attaches to the issue. Rather, threat instigates activism *among people for whom the issue is already important.*

We also used Study 3's data to test whether anxiety mediated the threat effect on contributions. Specifically, we regressed anxiety on policy change threat, policy change opportunity, dissatisfaction, ideology, and the demographic control variables. Dissatisfaction was a significant positive predictor of anxiety ($b = .23$,

$p<.001$), meaning that people who were less satisfied with current policy were more likely to be worried when thinking about the issue. Also, policy change opportunity was a significant negative predictor ($b = -.10$, $p<.05$), meaning that seeing opportunity for desirable policy change was associated with less worrying. But policy change threat had no impact on anxiety ($b = .02$, *n.s.*). This disconfirms the hypothesis that threat inspires activism by enhancing anxiety.[9]

One might argue that policy change threat, policy change opportunity, and dissatisfaction might affect anxiety especially powerfully among people who attached great importance to the issue, so we tested these interactions. Whereas the dissatisfaction × importance interaction was positive and significant (indicating that dissatisfaction was a stronger predictor of anxiety among people for whom abortion was personally important, $b = .13$, $p<.05$), the policy change threat × importance and policy change opportunity × importance interactions were not significant ($b = .03$, *n.s.*, and $b = .06$, *n.s.*, respectively). Thus, the impact of policy change threat on activism seems to be the result of "cold" cognition (meaning unemotional mental calculations) rather than "hot" cognition (Abelson, 1963; Lodge & Taber, 2013), at least with regard to anxiety.

Discussion

Threat of Undesirable Policy Changes

These studies suggest that policy change threat inspires financial contributions to interest groups. We can have particular confidence in this conclusion because of the methodological triangulation employed in the present array of studies. Positive effects of policy change threat appeared in three representative sample surveys of adults—using both correlational and experimental designs. In addition, the effect of policy change threat was observed for three issues, environmental protection, gun control, and abortion, and with various different sorts of measures. The appearance of the effect across studies points to its robustness.

Our results are the first to confirm an implication of Prospect Theory (Kahneman & Tversky, 1979) noted by Hansen (1985)—that policy change threat should be more motivating than policy change opportunity. In addition, the evidence reported here documents *when* policy change threat instigates activism. In doing so, this work links research on the conditions under which activism occurs to research on the core psychological motivators of activism. The impact of policy change threat turned out to be regulated both by the availability of financial resources and the personal importance of the issue. Therefore, this research contributes to the broader political participation literature by showing how attributes of an individual (his or her ability and motivation to become active) interact with attributes of the political context (perceptions of threat) to influence activism.

Whereas past research has blurred the distinction between threat and dissatisfaction (Hansen, 1985), the current research attests to the value of distinguishing between these variables. We observed individual-level evidence that dissatisfaction with the status quo *and* the threat of future undesirable policy change can both instigate activism. Because these variables are closely related conceptually and empirically, our findings suggest that future studies should distinguish their effects and their overlap.

Although past research has presumed that issue-focused activism is primarily aimed at *inducing* social change in response to undesirable conditions, the evidence presented here shows that activism can also be aimed at *preventing* social change. And according to Ornstein and Elder (1978), taking action to undermine policy change threats is a sensible strategy. In their words, "in a political system geared toward slow change and with numerous decision points and checks and balances, a group's likelihood of success is enhanced if it focuses on blocking rather than initiating action" (Ornstein & Elder, 1978, p. 58). In this light, the evidence reported here documents a tendency of human nature that may be quite practical.

Income

The demonstration here of a moderating effect of income also adds to the literature on activism. A great deal of research on participation has examined the effect of income, viewed as an indicator of the cost of participation. For example, Verba et al. (1995) showed that people with more money were more likely to make financial contributions to lobbying organizations. This sort of result suggests that the more income people have, the more they will contribute to all groups—period. Although scholars have at times implied that resource variables should interact with other variables that motivate activism, this notion had yet to be tested directly. Our findings suggest that, not surprisingly, people who have a lot of money do not contribute indiscriminately—they choose where to allocate their resources, and it appears that policy change threat guides those choices, at least in part.

Importance

Policy change threat helps to explain when and why attitude importance is translated into activism. Although people who attach more personal importance to an issue are more likely to become active, many more people attach tremendous importance to an issue than act (e.g., Gilbert, 1988; Krosnick & Telhami, 1995). The potential benefits of action are presumably quite high for people for whom an issue is important, but these benefits are apparently not sufficiently substantial to motivate the majority of these people to act at all times. Therefore, research that examines the effect of importance on political participation (Gilbert, 1988; Krosnick & Telhami, 1995; Verba et al., 1995) may not capture the full effect of the variable.

By identifying the impact of political context, the present research shows how perceptions of threat can help to differentiate people who care deeply about an issue and are politically active from those who care deeply but remain passive. Threat may change the cost/benefit calculus by making the potential for the loss of something valued more salient or costly, thus causing people to be more willing to make the sacrifices entailed by activism.

Coda

Our research illustrates the value of psychological analysis of political actors for the enterprise of political science. To some scholars, it is enough to link time-series evidence on the ebbs and flows of interest group membership to broad political changes that are presumed to be threatening or reassuring (e.g., Richer, 1995) or to content-analyze fundraising letters and assume that interest groups use certain appeals most often because they effectively resonate with potential members (e.g., Godwin, 1988). From this perspective, the consequences of changes in the political context are revealed at the macro level of analysis, not the micro level.

Although we have learned a lot from the macro-level approach, much can be learned from the micro level as well. Peering into the minds of citizens has led to a refined picture of the motivators of political activism. Our evidence illustrates the consequences of people's perceptions and thereby documents processes about which macro-level analyses can only speculate. Therefore, macro and micro approaches to the same problem can complement one another, and we look forward to more such concerted scholarly efforts.

Appendix: Measures and Variable Coding

Study 1: Environmental Activism

Policy Change Threat and Opportunity

Perceptions of policy change threat and opportunity are presumably derived from a series of ingredient beliefs and attitudes: (1) a person's support of or opposition to a current policy; (2) perceptions of whether powerful political agents are trying to change the policy; (3) perceptions of the types of changes being advocated by agents who are believed to be pursuing change; and (4) perceptions of the amount of effort these agents are devoting to bringing about such change. To maximize measurement precision, we asked respondents to report each of these ingredient attitudes and perceptions separately.[10] Responses were then combined into measures of policy change threat and policy change opportunity for each respondent.

Specifically, respondents were asked whether they wanted to see environmental protection laws strengthened, kept the same, or weakened. Respondents were also asked whether they perceived that President Bill Clinton, the U.S. Congress, and U.S. businesses wanted environmental protection laws to be stronger, kept the same, or weakened, and respondents who said they thought a political agent wanted to make environmental laws stronger or less strong were asked: "How hard do you think [President Clinton/the U.S. Congress/U.S. businesses] will try to make environmental laws [stronger/less strong]? Very hard, somewhat hard, not too hard, or not hard at all?"

Using these measures, two variables were created for each agent to describe the extent of policy change threat and opportunity perceived by each respondent. Because only pro-environmental activism was assessed, the only sort of policy change threat that could inspire it would come from an agent who was perceived to want environmental laws weakened. And the only policy change opportunities that would inspire such activism would come from agents who were perceived to want to strengthen those laws. Therefore, the 18 respondents who said they wanted to see environmental laws weakened were excluded from the analyses.[11]

The overall measure of policy change threat was therefore built as follows. Among respondents who wanted environmental protection laws to remain as they were or be strengthened and thought a political agent wanted to weaken those laws, people who said the agent would try "very hard" were coded 1, and people who said the agent would try "somewhat hard," "not too hard," or "not hard at all" were coded .5. Respondents who wanted environmental protection laws to be weakened were coded 0, because they could not perceive a policy change threat from an agent in a way that would inspire pro-environmental activism. Respondents who wanted environmental laws to remain as they were or be strengthened and thought a political agent wanted those laws kept as they were or strengthened were also coded 0. The mean computed across the three agents was treated as the overall index of policy change threat.[12] Forty-six percent of the sample perceived at least some policy change threat.

To create an overall measure of policy change opportunity, we followed the same sort of procedure. Among respondents who could experience opportunity (because they wanted environmental protection laws to be strengthened and thought a political agent also wanted to strengthen those laws), people who said the agent would try "very hard" were coded 1, and people who said the agent would try "somewhat hard," "not too hard," or "not hard at all" were coded .5. Respondents who wanted environmental laws to remain as they were or weakened were coded 0, because they could not perceive a policy change opportunity from an agent in a way that would inspire pro-environmental activism. Respondents who wanted environmental laws strengthened and thought political agents wanted those laws kept as they were or weakened were also coded 0. The mean computed across the three agents was treated as the overall index of policy change opportunity.[13] Thirty-nine percent of the sample perceived at least some policy change opportunity.

- **Dissatisfaction with current policy.** Respondents who said they wanted to see environmental protection laws kept as they were or weakened were coded 0 on "dissatisfaction," and respondents who said they wanted to see these laws strengthened were coded 1, because these were the only people whose dissatisfaction could cause pro-environmental activism.
- **Importance.** Respondents were asked "How serious of a problem do you think the state of the environment is likely to be in the future?" Importance was coded 0 for respondents who said "no problem" or "slightly serious," .5 for respondents who said "pretty serious" or "very serious," and 1 for respondents who said "extremely serious."[14]
- **Income.** Respondents were asked to report their family's total income before taxes. People with incomes less than US$30,001 were coded 0, people with incomes between US$30,001 and US$50,000 were coded .5, and people with incomes of US$50,001 or more were coded 1.
- **Activism.** Respondents reported the amount of money they had contributed to an environmental organization since January 1, 1995, that is, during approximately the one year prior to their interviews. Eighty-one percent of respondents said they had made no contributions during this period, and the remaining 19% of respondents contributed amounts ranging as high as US$300.[15] The mean contribution amount was US$12, and the standard deviation was US$45. The contribution variable was rescaled to range from 0 (meaning US$0) to 1 (meaning US$300).
- **Ideology.** Two dummy variables were created to represent ideology, one coded 1 for people who said they were liberals and 0 for everyone else. The other dummy variable was coded 1 for people who said they were conservatives and 0 for everyone else.
- **Other demographics.** Education was coded 0 for people with less than a high school education, .5 for high school graduates, and 1 for people with at least some college education. Gender was coded 0 females and 1 for males, and race was coded 0 for whites and 1 for non-whites. Age was rescaled to range from 0 to 1, with 0 representing the youngest age (18) and 1 representing the oldest age (86).

Study 2: Gun Control Activism

Manipulation

One-third of the respondents, chosen randomly, were given no information about gun control legislation and therefore served as the experiment's control group. The remaining two-thirds of the respondents were given legislation information, beginning with the following introduction:

Members of the U.S. Congress often introduce bills to change existing laws or create new laws. We are interested in what you know about Congress members' activities these days with regard to gun control. Please read this brief description of what members of Congress are doing on gun control laws and then answer the questions that follow.

After clicking the "continue" button on the computer screen, respondents read one of two statements (determined randomly):[16]

- **Decrease restrictions.** "Many members of the U.S. Congress are currently working hard to pass two laws. One law would make it legal for people convicted of a misdemeanor crime of domestic violence to buy a handgun. The other law would make it legal for people to buy, sell, or possess a semiautomatic weapon."
- **Increase restrictions.** "Many members of the U.S. Congress are currently working hard to pass two laws. One law would make it illegal to sell or possess a 50-caliber rifle, which is a type of rifle originally built to be used in the military. The other law would make it illegal for a person to buy more than one handgun during a 30-day period."

Measures

- **Gun control attitude.** Before reading the manipulation information, respondents reported whether they thought laws concerning gun control should be changed so it would be easier for people to obtain guns, more difficult for people to obtain guns, or kept as they were.
- **Policy change threat and opportunity.** Whether the policy descriptions some respondents heard should have instigated perceptions of policy change threat or opportunity depended on whether the respondents favored or opposed the policies described. Disliking the policies and thinking that members of Congress were working to get them passed would be threatening. Therefore, respondents in the "increase restrictions" group who wanted it to be easier to obtain guns or who wanted gun laws to be kept as they were were coded 1 on the threat variable. Respondents in the "decrease restrictions" group who wanted it to be more difficult to obtain guns or who wanted gun laws to be kept as they were were also coded 1 on the threat variable. All other respondents were coded 0 on this variable. Forty-five percent (N = 973) of respondents experienced some threat, and 55% (N = 1187) did not.

  The policy change opportunity variable was coded 1 for respondents in the "decrease restrictions" group who wanted it to be easier to obtain guns and for respondents in the "increase restrictions" group who wanted it to be more difficult to obtain guns. All other respondents were coded 0 on this variable.[17] Twenty-one percent (N = 464) of respondents experienced some opportunity, and 78% (N = 1696) did not.

- **Dissatisfaction.** Respondents who said that gun control laws should be kept as they were were coded 0 on the dissatisfaction variable, and respondents who wanted it to be easier or more difficult for people to obtain guns were coded 1. Sixty-two percent (N = 1346) of respondents were dissatisfied with the status quo, and 38% (N = 814) were not.

- **Income.** Respondents with total household incomes for the previous twelve months of US$85,000 or more were coded 1 on income, and everyone else was coded 0.

- **Importance**. Before reading the manipulation, respondents were asked how important the issue of gun control was to them personally. Importance was coded 1 for respondents who said "extremely important" and 0 for respondents who said "very important," "somewhat important," "slightly important," or "not at all important."

- **Willingness to contribute.** Respondents were asked how willing they would be to give money to an organization that they agreed with and that was concerned with the issue of gun control—not at all willing, slightly willing, somewhat willing, very willing, or extremely willing. If they said they were at least slightly willing to contribute money (43% of the sample), they were asked how much money they would be willing to contribute within the next year. Respondents who said they were not at all willing to contribute money (57% of the sample) were coded 0. The remaining respondents' projected contribution amounts ranged as high as US$500, with a mean of US$20 and a standard deviation of US$52.[18]

- **Party identification.** Measures of political ideology were not available in this study, so party identification was used instead. Two dummy variables were created to represent party identification, one coded 1 for people who said they were *Democrats* and 0 for everyone else. The other dummy variable was coded 1 for people who said they were *Republicans* and 0 for everyone else.

- **Other demographics.** Education, gender, race, and age were coded as in Study 1.

Study 3: Abortion Activism

Manipulation

One-fifth of the respondents, chosen randomly, were given no information about abortion legislation and therefore served as the experiment's control group. The remaining four-fifths of the respondents were given legislation information, beginning with the following introduction:

Now, I'd like to switch to a different issue. Members of the U.S. Congress often introduce bills to change existing laws or create new laws. We are interested in what you know about Congress members' activities these days with regard to the issue of abortion. I'm going to read you a statement that briefly describes what members of Congress are currently doing about specific pieces of abortion legislation and ask you some questions about it.

These respondents then heard one of the following four statements (determined randomly):

- **Increase restrictions, high effort.** "Many members of the U.S. Congress favor enacting the following two laws. One would ban all abortions, except when there is a threat to a woman's life caused by the pregnancy, and the other would prevent women in the U.S. military from being able to use their own money to pay for abortion services abroad. And many members of Congress are currently working hard to pass these two laws."
- **Increase restrictions, low effort.** "Many members of the U.S. Congress favor enacting the following two laws. One would ban all abortions, except when there is a threat to a woman's life caused by the pregnancy, and the other would prevent women in the U.S. military from being able to use their own money to pay for abortion services abroad. However, none of the members of Congress are currently working to get either of these laws passed."
- **Decrease restrictions, high effort.** "Many members of the U.S. Congress favor enacting the following two laws. One would allow women to obtain an abortion without mandatory waiting periods, and the other would allow women on Medicaid and federal employees to receive health insurance coverage for abortion services. And many members of Congress are currently working hard to pass these two laws."
- **Decrease restrictions, low effort.** "Many members of the U.S. Congress favor enacting the following two laws. One would allow women to obtain an abortion without mandatory waiting periods, and the other would allow women on Medicaid and federal employees to receive health insurance coverage for abortion services. However, none of the members of Congress are currently working to get either of these laws passed."

Measures

- **Abortion attitude.** Respondents were asked whether they thought laws concerning abortion should be changed so it would be easier for women to obtain an abortion, changed so it would be harder for women to obtain an abortion, or kept as they were.

- **Policy change threat and opportunity.** Whether the policy descriptions some respondents heard should have instigated perceptions of policy change threat or opportunity depended upon on whether the respondents favored or opposed the policies described. Disagreeing with the policies and thinking that Congress members were working hard to get them passed would be threatening. Therefore, respondents in the increase restrictions, high effort condition who wanted it to be easier to obtain an abortion were coded 1 on the threat variable. Respondents in the decrease restrictions, high effort condition who wanted it to be more difficult to obtain an abortion were coded 1 on the threat variable. Respondents in the increase restrictions, high effort and decrease restrictions, high effort conditions who wanted abortion laws kept as they were were also coded 1 on the policy change threat variable. All other respondents were coded 0 on this variable.

  The policy change opportunity variable was coded 1 for respondents in the decrease restrictions, high effort condition who wanted it to be easier to obtain an abortion and for respondents in the increase restrictions, high effort condition who wanted it to be more difficult for women to obtain an abortion. All other respondents were coded 0 on this variable.

- **Dissatisfaction.** Respondents who said that abortion laws should be kept as they were coded 0 on the dissatisfaction variable, and respondents who wanted it to be easier or harder for women to obtain an abortion were coded 1.

- **Importance.** Respondents were asked how important the issue of abortion was to them personally. Importance was coded 0 for respondents who said "not at all important" or "slightly important," .5 for respondents who said "somewhat important" or "very important," and 1 for respondents who said "extremely important."

- **Income.** Respondents reported their total household income before taxes for 1998. If they refused to answer this question, they were asked whether their income was more than US$10,000, more than US$20,000, more than US$30,000, more than US$40,000, more than US$50,000, more than US$60,000, more than US$75,000, more than US$100,000, or more than US$150,000. People with incomes less than US$30,001 were coded 0, people with incomes between US$30,001 and US$50,000 were coded .5, and people with incomes of US$50,001 or more were coded 1.

- **Activism.** Respondents were asked how willing they would be to give money to an organization that they agreed with and that was concerned with the issue of abortion—not at all willing, slightly willing, somewhat willing, very willing, or extremely willing. If they said they were at least slightly willing to contribute money (52% of the sample), they were asked how much money they would be willing to contribute within the next year. Respondents who said they were not at all willing to contribute money (48% of the sample) were coded 0. The remaining respondents' projected contribution amounts ranged as high as US$520, with a mean of US$39 and a standard deviation of US$81.[19] The amount was rescaled to range from 0 (meaning US$0) to 1 (meaning US$520).

- **Ideology.** Ideology was measured and coded as in Study 1.
- **Other demographics.** Education, gender, race, and age were measured and coded as in Studies 1 and 2.

Notes

1 We thank Robert Unsworth, Sarah Malloy, Mark Hansen, Sidney Verba, Morris Fiorina, Catherine Heaney, Russell Hardin, Robert Mitchell, Robert Mendelson, Daniel Kahneman, David Schkade, Karen Stenner, Kathleen Carr, Anne Smith, Paul Beck, Richard Timpone, Dean Lacy, Marilynn Brewer, Robert Arkin, Roger Tourangeau, Nora Cate Schaeffer, Seymour Sudman, Simon Jackman, John Bullock, Laura Lowe, and the members of the Ohio State University Political Psychology Interest Group for their help and advice during the course of this project. This chapter is based on the first author's Ph.D. dissertation and was written partly while the second author was a Fellow at the Center for Advanced Study in the Behavioral Sciences (supported by a grant from the National Science Foundation, SBR-9022192). Financial support for Study 1 was provided by a grant from the Electric Power Research Institute to Industrial Economics, Inc. Correspondence regarding this chapter should be addressed to Joanne M. Miller at jomiller@umn.edu.

2 Hansen (1985) described evidence he said shows that threat instigates activism. But in fact, he documented effects of undesirable changes that had already occurred, not prospects of undesirable future changes. Consequently, despite the terminology to the contrary, this evidence documents how dissatisfaction with the present influences participation aimed at changing the current state of affairs.

3 The activism literature has traditionally viewed "opportunity" as being created by any changes in social or life circumstances that genuinely enhance the likelihood of a group succeeding in causing political change (McAdam, 1985). We use the term more specifically, to refer to the emergence of a powerful ally who offers a new opportunity for collaborative efforts and enhances the apparent probability of success in instigating desirable political change.

4 In a field experiment in which people received a letter from an interest group soliciting donations and signed postcards to be mailed to the President, Miller and Krosnick (2004) found that policy change threat was a significant predictor of financial contributions, whereas policy change opportunity significantly predicted postcard returns. However, given the constraints of field experiments, the study focused only on one side of one issue (pro-choice) and could not control for alternative explanations or explore the conditions under which the effects were most likely to obtain.

5 With a few exceptions, the subsample's demographic characteristics closely matched those of all adults in the state, as ascertained via the March 1994 Current Population Survey. People over age 60 were under-represented (comprising 22% of the population but 13% of our sample), as were people with less than a high school education (comprising 18% of the population but 7% of our sample). People who had obtained a Bachelor's degree or more education were over-represented (comprising 19% of the population but 31% of our sample).

6 Refusal conversions were not attempted for the two surveys that comprise Study 3, which partly accounts for the lower cooperation rates.

7 Respondents who received a score of 1 on the continuous threat variable in Study 1 were categorized as "high threat," and all others were coded as "low threat" for this analysis.

8 The dependent variable in our analyses is visibly skewed in all three datasets, with a very large number of zeros, and the OLS residuals are quite skewed as well. Moreover, although the dependent variable takes on many possible values, a sizeable percentage of the observations take on a smaller set of "round" numbers. Therefore, we conducted robustness checks on our tests of hypotheses 1–3 by replicating the OLS regressions again with bootstrap standard errors in place of their normal-theory counterparts. The bootstrap (Efron & Tibshirani, 1993) provides a non-parametric method for estimating standard errors and performing hypothesis tests that makes no distributional assumptions, and treats the independent variables as random (Freedman 1981; Efron & Tibshirani, 1993). We used 10,000 bootstrap Monte Carlo-based samples, a number sufficiently large to eliminate virtually any variance in the estimates of the standard error. We relied upon the bootstrap for estimates of the standard errors as well as hypothesis tests. The results of the bootstrap analyses are consistent with the parametric tests reported here (results available from the authors.)

9 Anxiety was positively related to willingness to contribute (b = .10, se = .04), controlling for threat, opportunity, and dissatisfaction.

10 We took this approach because psychological research suggests direct reports of such complex beliefs will be less valid than respondents' reports of components of such judgments (e.g., Armstrong, Denniston, & Gordon, 1975).

11 Including these respondents does not change the results we report.

12 Analyses comparable to those reported here but assessing the impact of threat from the three agents separately yielded results consistent with the more parsimonious approach of combining across the three agents.

13 As with threat, analyses comparable to those reported here but assessing the impact of policy change opportunity from the three agents separately yielded results consistent with those reported here.

14 We would normally have preferred that respondents be asked directly how important the issue was to them personally. But because we sought to predict pro-environmental activism, and the importance of people's pro-environmental attitudes is likely to be determined principally by perceptions of environmental problem seriousness (Boninger, Krosnick, & Berent, 1995), this seemed like an acceptable proxy measure.

15 One respondent who reported having contributed US$7,000 was dropped from our analyses to prevent distortion due to this outlying value. The finding that 19% of Ohioans reported having contributed to an environmental group during the prior year is quite in line with other survey results documenting this sort of percentage for the nation as a whole. A 1997 national survey done by the Gallup Organization for the National Center for Charitable Donations found that 12% of American households had contributed to an environmental organization during the prior year. And a 1996 national survey done by Belden and Russonello for the Consultative Group on Biological Diversity found this figure to be 13%.

16 Both statements described legislation that had been introduced in Congress at the time of the survey.

17 In order to determine whether the manipulations had the desired effects, respondents were asked two manipulation check questions at the end of the survey, the order of which was randomly determined for each respondent. One question asked respondents how many members of Congress they thought were working hard to get laws passed that would make it *easier* for people to obtain guns in this country (coded such that 0 = none, .25 = a few, .50 = some, .75 = many, and 1 = most). The mean

response offered by people in the "increase restrictions" group was significantly higher than the mean response among all other respondents (t(2153) = 3.10, p<.01). Another question asked respondents how many members of Congress they thought were working hard to get laws passed that would make it *more difficult* for people to obtain guns in this country (coded the same). The mean response offered by people in the "decrease restrictions" group was significantly higher than the mean response among all other respondents (t(2152) = 6.90, p<.001).

18 Sixteen respondents said they would contribute between US$1000 and US$9000; these outliers (.6% of the sample) were dropped from the analyses.

19 One respondent said he would be willing to contribute US$800, five said they would contribute US$1000, and one said she would contribute US$4000; these individuals were dropped from the analyses to prevent distortion due to outlying values.

References

Abelson, Robert P. 1963. "Computer Simulation of 'hot' Cognition." In Silvan S. Tomkins, & Samuel Messick (Eds.), *Computer Simulation of Personality* (pp. 277–298). New York: Wiley.

Altemeyer, Robert. 1996. *The Authoritarian Specter*. Cambridge, MA: Harvard University Press.

Armstrong, J. Scott, William B. Denniston, & Matt M. Gordon. 1975. "The Use of the Decomposition Principle in Making Judgments." *Organizational Behavior and Human Performance* 14 (October): 257–263.

Baumgartner, Frank R., & Beth L. Leech. 1998. *Basic Interests: The Importance of Groups in Politics and in Political Science*. Princeton, NJ: Princeton University Press.

Belden, Nancy, & John Russonello. 1996. *Human Values and Nature's Future: Americans' Attitudes on Biological Diversity*. Conducted for the Consultative Group on Biological Diversity.

Boninger, David S., Jon A. Krosnick, & Matthew K. Berent. 1995. "The Origins of Attitude Importance: Self-Interest, Social Identification, and Value-Relevance." *Journal of Personality and Social Psychology* 68(1): 61–80.

Bosso, Christopher J. 1997. "Seizing Back the Day: The Challenge to Environmental Activism in the 1990s." In Norman J. Vig, & Michael E. Kraft (Eds.), *Environmental Policy in the 1990s* (pp. 53–74). Washington, DC: CQ Press.

Brader, Ted. 2006. *Campaigning for Hearts and Minds: How Emotional Appeals in Political Ads Work*. Chicago, IL: University of Chicago Press.

Brody, Richard A. 1991. *Assessing the President*. Stanford, CA: Stanford University Press.

Callegaro, Mario, & Charles DiSogra. 2008. "Computing Response Metrics for Online Panels." *Public Opinion Quarterly* 72(5): 1008–1032.

Cho, Wendy K. Tam, James G. Gimpel, & Tony Wu. 2006. "Clarifying the Role of SES in Political Participation: Policy Threat and Arab American Mobilization." *Journal of Politics* 68: 977–991.

Cigler, Allan J., & Burdett A. Loomis. 1995. *Interest Group Politics*. Washington, DC: CQ Press.

Converse, Philip E. 1964. "The Nature of Belief Systems in Mass Publics." In David E. Apter (Ed.), *Ideology and Discontent* (pp. 206–261). New York: Free Press.

Diamond, Sara. 1995. *Roads to Dominion: Right-Wing Movements and Political Power in the United States*. New York: Guilford Press.

Doty, Richard M., Bill E. Peterson, & David G. Winter. 1991. "Threat and Authoritarianism in the United States, 1978–1987." *Journal of Personality and Social Psychology* 61(4): 629–640.

Efron, Bradley, & Robert Tibshirani. 1993. *An Introduction to the Bootstrap*. New York: Chapman & Hall.

Feldman, Stanley, & Karen Stenner. 1997. "Perceived Threat and Authoritarianism." *Political Psychology* 18 (December): 741–770.

Finkel, Steven E., & Karl-Dieter Opp. 1991. "Party Identification and Participation in Collective Political Action." *Journal of Politics* 53 (May): 339–371.

Finkel, Steven, Edward N. Muller, & Karl-Dieter Opp. 1989. "Personal Influence, Collective Rationality and Mass Political Action." *American Political Science Review* 83 (September): 885–904.

Fiske, Susan T., Felicia Pratto, & Mark A. Pavelchak. 1983. "Citizen's Images of Nuclear War: Contents and Consequences." *Journal of Social Issues* 39 (Spring): 41–66.

Freedman, David A. 1981. "Bootstrapping Regression Models." *The Annals of Statistics* 9(6): 1218–1228.

Gamson, William A. 1975. *The Strategy of Social Protest.* Homewood, IL: The Dorsey Press.

Gilbert, Richard Karman. 1988. "The Dynamics of Inaction: Psychological Factors Inhibiting Arms Control Activism." *American Psychologist* 43 (October): 755–764.

Godwin, Kenneth R. 1988. *One Billion Dollars of Influence: The Direct Marketing of Politics.* Chatham, NJ: Chatham House Publishers.

Gore, Pearl M., & Julian B. Rotter. 1963. "A Personality Correlate of Social Action." *Journal of Personality* 31(1): 58–64.

Gurr, Theodore R. 1970. *Why Men Rebel.* Princeton, NJ: Princeton University Press.

Gusfield, Joseph E. 1963. *Symbolic Crusade: Status Politics and the American Temperance Movement.* Urbana, IL: University of Illinois Press.

Hansen, John Mark. 1985. "The Political Economy of Group Membership." *American Political Science Review* 79 (March): 79–96.

Hansen, John Mark. 1991. *Gaining Access: Congress and the Farm Lobby, 1919–1981.* Chicago, IL: University of Chicago Press.

Ingham, Alan G., George Levinger, James Graves, & Vaughn Peckman. 1974. "The Ringelmann Effect: Studies of Group Size and Group Performance." *Journal of Experimental Social Psychology* 10 (July): 371–384.

Kahneman, Daniel, & Amos Tversky. 1979. "Prospect Theory: An Analysis of Decision Under Risk." *Econometrica* 47 (March): 263–291.

Kinder, Donald R., & Lynn M. Sanders. 1990. "Mimicking Political Debate with Survey Questions: The Case of White Opinion on Affirmative Action for Blacks." *Social Cognition* 8(1): 73–103.

King, David C., & Jack L. Walker. 1991. "An Ecology of Interest Groups in America." In Jack L. Walker (Ed.), *Mobilizing Interest Groups in America* (pp. 57–73). Ann Arbor, MI: University of Michigan Press.

Klandermans, Bert. 1983. "Rotter's I.E. Scale and Socio-Political Action-Taking: The Balance of 20 Years of Research." *European Journal of Social Psychology* 13(4): 399–415.

Krosnick, Jon A. 1990. "Government Policy and Citizen Passion: A Study of Issue Publics in Contemporary America." *Political Behavior* 12(1): 59–92.

Krosnick, Jon A., & Shibley Telhami. 1995. "Public Attitudes Toward Israel: A Study of the Attentive and Issue Publics." *International Studies Quarterly* 59 (December): 535–554.

Latane, Bibb. 1981. "The Psychology of Social Impact." *American Psychologist* 36 (April): 343–356.

Leighley, Jan E. 1995. "Attitudes, Opportunities and Incentives: A Field Essay on Political Participation." *Political Research Quarterly* 48(1): 181–209.

Leventhal, Howard. 1970. "Findings and Theory in the Study of Fear Communications." In Leonard Berkowitz (Ed.), *Advances in Experimental Social Psychology* (Vol. 5) (pp. 119–186). New York: Academic Press.

Lodge, Milton, & Charles Taber. 2013. *The Rationalizing Voter*. New York: Cambridge University Press.

Loomis, Burdett A., & Allan J. Cigler. 1995. "Introduction: The Changing Nature of Interest Group Politics." In Allan J. Cigler, & Burdett A. Loomis (Eds.), *Interest Group Politics* (pp. 1–34). Washington, DC: CQ Press.

Lowry, Robert C. 1997. "The Private Production of Public Goods: Organizational Maintenance, Managers' Objectives, and Collective Goals." *American Political Science Review* 91 (June): 308–323.

Marcus, George E., W. Russell Neuman, & Michael B. MacKuen. 2000. *Affective Intelligence and Political Judgment*. Chicago, IL: University of Chicago Press.

Marcus, George E., John L. Sullivan, Elizabeth Theiss-Morse, & Sandra L. Wood. 1995. *With Malice Toward Some: How People Make Civil Liberties Judgments*. New York: Cambridge University Press.

McAdam, Doug. 1985. *Political Process and the Development of Black Insurgency, 1930–1970*. Chicago, IL: University of Chicago Press.

McCann, Stewart J. H. 1997. "Threatening Times, 'Strong' Presidential Popular Vote Winners, and the Victory Margin, 1824–1964." *Journal of Personality and Social Psychology* 73 (1): 160–170.

McKenzie-Mohr, Doug, Lisa Sara Nemiroff, Laurie Beers, & Serge Desmarais. 1995. "Determinants of Responsible Environmental Behavior." *Journal of Social Issues* 51: 139–156.

Meyerowitz, Beth E., & Shelly Chaiken. 1987. "The Effect of Message Framing on Breast Self-Examination Attitudes, Intentions, and Behavior." *Journal of Personality and Social Psychology* 52(3): 500–510.

Milbrath, Lester W., & Madan L. Goel. 1977. *Political Participation: How and Why do People Get Involved in Politics?* Chicago, IL: Rand McNally.

Miller, Joanne M. and Jon A. Krosnick. 2004. "Threat as a Motivator of Political Activism: A Field Experiment." *Political Psychology* 25: 507–524.

Mitchell, Robert Cameron. 1979. "National Environmental Lobbies and the Apparent Illogic of Collective Action." In Clifford S. Russell (Ed.), *Collective Decision Making: Applications from Public Choice Theory* (pp. 87–121). Baltimore, MD: Johns Hopkins University Press.

Mitchell, Robert Cameron. 1990. "Public Opinion and the Green Lobby: Poised for the 1990s?" In Norman J. Vig, & Michael E. Kraft (Eds.), *Environmental Policy in the 1990s* (pp. 81–99). Washington, DC: Congressional Quarterly Press.

Moe, Terry M. 1980. *The Organization of Interests: Incentives and the Internal Dynamics of Political Interest Groups*. Chicago, IL: The University of Chicago Press.

Moen, Matthew C. 1992. *The Transformation of the Christian Right*. Tuscaloosa, AL: The University of Alabama Press.

Morris, Aldon D., & Carol McClurg Mueller. 1992. *Frontiers in Social Movement Theory*. New Haven, CT: Yale University Press.

Mueller, John. 1973. *War, Presidents, and Public Opinion*. NY: Wiley.

Mueller, John. 1994. *Policy and Opinion in the Gulf War*. Chicago, IL: University of Chicago Press.

Muller, Edward N., Henry A. Dietz, & Steven E. Finkel. 1991. "Discontent and the Expected Utility of Rebellion: The Case of Peru." *American Political Science Review* 85 (December): 1261–1282.

Nadeau, Richard, Richard G. Niemi, & Timothy Amato. 1995. "Emotions, Issue Importance, and Political Learning." *American Journal of Political Science* 39 (August): 558–574.

Nelson, Thomas E., & Donald R. Kinder. 1988. "Issue Frames and Group-Centrism in American Public Opinion." *Journal of Politics* 58 (November): 1055–1078.

Olson, Mancur. 1965. *The Logic of Collective Action*. Cambridge, MA: Harvard University Press.

Opp, Karl-Dieter. 1986. "Soft Incentives and Collective Action: Participation in the Anti-Nuclear Movement." *British Journal of Political Science* 16 (January): 87–112.

Ornstein, Norman J., & Shirley Elder. 1978. *Interest Groups, Lobbying, and Policymaking*. Washington, DC: CQ Press.

Richer, Jerrell. 1995. "Green Giving: An Analysis of Contributions to Major U.S. Environmental Groups." *Discussion Paper 95–139*. Washington, DC: Resources for the Future.

Rokeach, Milton. 1960. *The Open and Closed Mind*. NY: Basic Books.

Roseneau, James N. 1974. *Citizenship Between Elections: An Inquiry into the Mobilizable American*. New York: The Free Press.

Rosenstone, Steven J., & John Mark Hansen. 2002. *Mobilization, Participation, and Democracy in America (Longman Classics Edition)*. New York: Longman.

Rothman, Alexander J., & Peter Salovey. 1997. "Shaping Perceptions to Motivate Healthy Behavior: The Role of Message Framing." *Psychological Bulletin* 121 (1): 3–19.

Salisbury, Robert H. 1969. "An Exchange Theory of Interest Groups." *Midwest Journal of Political Science* 13 (February): 1–32.

Salmon, Charles T., & John Spicer Nichols. 1983. "The Next-Birthday Method of Respondent Selection." *Public Opinion Quarterly* 47 (Summer): 270–276.

Smelser, Neil J. 1962. *Theory of Collective Behavior*. NY: Free Press.

Smelser, Neil J. 1995. *Sociology*. Englewood Cliffs, NJ: Prentice-Hall.

Sweeney, John W. 1973. "An Experimental Investigation of the Free Rider Problem." *Social Science Research* 2: 277–292.

Tarrow, Sidney. 1998. *Power in Movement*. New York: Cambridge University Press.

Truman, David B. 1951. *The Governmental Process: Political Interests and Public Opinion*. New York: Alfred A Knopf.

Tyler, Tom R., & Kathleen M. McGraw. 1983. "The Threat of Nuclear War: Risk Interpretation and Behavioral Response." *Journal of Social Issues* 39 (Spring): 25–40.

Verba, Sidney, Kay Lehman Schlozman, & Henry E. Brady. 1995. *Voice and Equality: Civic Volunteerism in American Politics*. Cambridge, MA: Harvard University Press.

Walker, Jack L. 1991. *Mobilizing Interest Groups in America: Patrons, Professions, and Social Movements*. Ann Arbor, MI: The University of Michigan Press.

8

ATTITUDE IMPORTANCE AND ATTITUDE-RELEVANT KNOWLEDGE

Motivator and Enabler[1]

Penny S. Visser, Jon A. Krosnick, and Catherine J. Norris

Public health officials have increasingly come to recognize that many of the leading causes of death in the United States can be traced to the everyday behavioral choices that people make. In fact, an investigation published in the Journal of the American Medical Association in 2004 concluded that approximately half of the deaths in the U.S. can be attributed to a small number of preventable behaviors, such as smoking, inactivity, poor diet, and alcohol consumption (Mokdad, Marks, Stroup, & Gerberding, 2004). Consequently, public heath advocates have increasingly turned to the social and behavioral sciences for insights into behavior modification.

Changing behavior sometimes requires changes in relevant attitudes. But in many cases, people already possess positive attitudes toward healthy behaviors and negative attitudes toward unhealthy behaviors, yet those health-promoting attitudes do not inspire appropriate health behaviors (see, e.g., Fisher & Fisher, 1992). The challenge for public health advocates, then, is to strengthen existing attitudes so that they motivate and guide behavior, shape the way new information is processed, resist change in the face of challenges, and persist over time (Krosnick & Petty, 1995).

Public health officials' efforts to strengthen attitudes have usually focused on increasing people's knowledge about various threats to their health, a strategy that appears eminently sensible in light of evidence from the attitude strength literature. A large store of attitude-supportive knowledge is a well-established correlate of attitude strength. More attitude-relevant knowledge is associated with greater consistency between attitudes and behavior, greater resistance to attitude change, and greater attitude stability (e.g., Biek, Wood, & Chaiken, 1996; Davidson, 1995; Wilson, Dunn, Kraft, & Lisle, 1989; Wood, 1982; Wood

& Kallgren, 1988; Wood, Kallgren, & Preisler, 1985; Wood, Rhodes, & Biek, 1995). And yet interventions that have successfully increased the public's attitude-relevant knowledge have often failed to bring about increases in attitude-behavior correspondence.

The case of AIDS in the United States provides an excellent illustration. Initially, public health officials assumed that if they could educate people about the disease and how to avoid it, the appropriate behaviors would follow (Helweg-Larsen & Collins, 1997). So the government launched a massive public education campaign to increase people's knowledge about the disease (for review, see Fisher & Fisher, 1992). This effort was tremendously successful—virtually all U.S. adults soon knew what AIDS is, had a basic understanding of how it is transmitted, and knew what steps can be taken to avoid exposure (DiClemente, Forrest, Mickler, & Principal Site Investigators, 1990; Rogers, Singer, & Imperio, 1993). Yet such educational campaigns have most often yielded no reliable effects on behavior (e.g., Mann, Tarantola, & Netter, 1992). Knowledge, in and of itself, seems not to have been sufficient to instigate attitude-congruent behavior.

Similar large-scale efforts to increase the public's knowledge about the health consequences of obesity have been initiated during the last decades. For example, the U.S. Department of Health and Human Services launched a webpage to be a "source of credible, accurate information to help Americans choose to live healthier lives," arguing that "accurate scientific information on nutrition and dietary guidance is critical to the public's ability to make the right choices in the effort to curb obesity and other food related diseases" (www.healthierus.gov). Unfortunately, however, as with AIDS awareness, such information campaigns seem not to be having their intended effect—data from the National Center for Health Statistics indicate that the proportion of U.S. adults who are overweight or obese has risen steadily, reaching a startling 66% in the early 2000s (Hedley et al., 2004).

Why have these well-funded, apparently sound interventions had so little success in enhancing the correspondence between people's attitudes toward healthy living and their relevant behaviors? We propose that these failures are due in part to insufficient attention, not only among public health officials but also in the attitude literature more generally, to the basic processes through which various strength-related attitude features exert their impact. More specifically, we propose that some strength-related features exert their influence by conferring particular abilities—the ability, for example, to effectively plan and execute attitude-congruent behaviors. In our view, attitude-relevant knowledge is the quintessential example of this type of strength-related feature. Other features exert their influence through motivational processes, providing the impetus, for example, to initiate, persist in, and successfully carry out attitude-congruent behavior. We nominate personal importance as an exemplar of this type of strength-related attitude feature. Furthermore, we propose that both of these elements are essential for promoting attitude-congruent behavior. Without adequate motivation, increases in ability may have modest impact on behavior. Similarly, if relevant abilities are lacking, even dramatic increases in motivation may be unlikely to lead to attitude-appropriate behavior. Our claim, therefore, is that both ability and motivation—conferred, for example, by the co-presence of attitude-relevant knowledge and personal importance—may be necessary for maximal attitude-behavior correspondence.

Overview

This proposition rests on the assumption that various strength-related attitude features, including attitude importance and attitude-relevant knowledge, are distinct psychological constructs rather than redundant reflections of a common underlying construct. We begin, therefore, by briefly reviewing evidence suggesting that strength-related attitude features are indeed multidimensional (e.g., Bizer & Krosnick, 2001; Visser, Bizer, & Krosnick, 2006; Visser & Krosnick, 1998; Visser, Krosnick, & Simmons, 2003). We then extend this work by building the case that not only are various strength-related attitude features distinct, but also they may have effects on thought and behavior through fundamentally different psychological mechanisms. Specifically, we advocate distinguishing between strength-related features that operate by conferring abilities and those that operate through motivational processes, and we present four studies examining attitude-relevant knowledge and personal importance to illustrate the utility of this distinction. We then consider the implications of this distinction for understanding the disparate array of findings that have emerged in the attitude strength literature. Finally, we return to the issue with which we began and consider how this new conceptualization of attitude strength may account for the disappointing results of many public health information campaigns and may provide the bases for theoretically derived interventions that are more likely to be effective.

Attitude Strength

Psychologists have long recognized that some attitudes are durable and consequential, whereas others are not. The term "attitude strength" is often used to capture this distinction. More specifically, strong attitudes are those that: (1) resist change; (2) persist over time; (3) guide information processing; and (4) motivate and direct behavior (Krosnick & Petty, 1995). Over the last few decades, roughly a dozen attitude features have been identified that are associated with the strength of an attitude. Among these are: *knowledge*, the volume of information people have about the object (e.g., Wood, 1982); *attitude importance*, the amount of psychological significance people attach to an attitude object (e.g., Krosnick, 1988a, 1988b); *certainty*, the degree to which people are sure of their attitudes (e.g., Budd, 1986); *elaboration*, the amount of thinking people have done about the attitude object (e.g., Petty & Cacioppo, 1986); *extremity*, how far from the midpoint the attitude is on a negative-positive continuum (e.g., Osgood, Suci, & Tannenbaum, 1957); *accessibility*, the speed and ease with which the attitude comes to mind (e.g., Fazio, 1990); *ambivalence*, how conflicted people feel about the attitude object (e.g., Kaplan, 1972); *intensity*, the strength of the emotional reaction provoked by the attitude object (Cantril, 1944, 1946; Stouffer et al., 1950); and a handful of others. In separate programs of research, each of these features has been shown to correlate with one or more of the four defining properties of attitude strength (see Petty & Krosnick, 1995).

Relations Among Strength-Related Attitude Features

Because these various features all relate in similar ways to the defining properties of strong attitudes, many researchers have assumed that they are largely overlapping reflections of a small number of underlying latent constructs. And in a number of studies, exploratory factor analyses or related techniques have yielded evidence consistent with the notion that the various strength-related attitude features do in fact reflect a small number of underlying psychological constructs (for a review, see Visser, Bizer, & Krosnick, 2006). On the basis of these findings, many investigators have combined measures of different strength-related features into composite indices of attitude strength (e.g., Bassili, 1996; Bassili & Roy, 1998; Eagly et al., 2000; Hodson, Maio, & Esses, 2001; Holland et al., 2001; Pomerantz et al., 1995; Prislin, 1996; Theodorakis, 1994; Thompson & Zanna, 1995; Verplanken, 1989, 1991). Of course, if various strength-related features reflect a common underlying construct, distinguishing among them is unnecessary—interventions that bring about increases in one of the features will necessarily bring about changes in the others.

Distinct Constructs?

The results of the exploratory factor analyses are quite surprising in light of what seem to be sharp differences in the conceptual nature of the various strength-related features. Take the case of attitude importance and attitude-relevant knowledge. Nineteen published exploratory factor analyses included measures of both features, and they loaded on the same factor in 14 (74%) of these studies (Visser et al., 2006). And yet attaching a great deal of personal importance to an attitude seems to be quite different from simply possessing a large store of knowledge about the attitude object. To attach great importance to an attitude is to care tremendously about it and to be deeply concerned about it. In contrast, knowledge is simply a cache of information stored in memory. Differences of this sort in the psychological nature of the various strength-related attitude features have led some scholars to question the wisdom of treating them as interchangeable indices of attitude strength.

And indeed, investigations using confirmatory rather than exploratory factor analyses have posed a strong challenge to the notion that various strength-related attitude features reflect a few underlying constructs (e.g. Krosnick et al., 1993; Krosnick, Jarvis, Strathman, & Petty, 1994; Lavine, Huff, Wagner, & Sweeney, 1998; Visser, 1998). These studies have consistently found that although a few pairs of features are quite strongly correlated, most are weakly or not at all correlated. And explicit tests of the notion that a common underlying construct could account for covariation among pairs or sets of strength-related features have consistently contradicted this view. Specifically, models that treat the various strength-related features as distinct (albeit correlated) constructs routinely yield better fit to data than models that treat pairs or sets of the features as reflections of a single underlying construct.

Corroborating these findings, investigations have isolated pairs of strength-related attitude features and documented divergences in their antecedents and consequences, reinforcing the notion that the features are distinct psychological constructs. For example, Bizer and Krosnick (2001) explored the potential overlap between attitude accessibility and attitude importance. Some scholars have suggested that accessibility and importance are redundant, the latter being simply a vague subjective judgment derived from the former. This would require that accessibility and importance share common antecedents— factors that increase accessibility must necessarily increase importance as well. In fact, in two studies, Bizer and Krosnick (2001) demonstrated that repeated attitude expression increases the accessibility of people's attitudes but does not increase the importance they attach to these attitudes. They also found that material self-interest in an issue caused importance to increase but did not affect accessibility, whereas exposure to issue-relevant information increased accessibility but not importance.

Visser, Krosnick, and Simmons (2003) explored the ways in which attitude importance and attitude certainty regulated the cognitive and behavioral consequences of attitudes. Although importance and certainty have loaded together on the same factor in many previous exploratory factor analyses, Visser et al. (2003) found many divergences in consequences. For example, people who attached more importance to their policy attitudes were more likely to try to convince other people how to vote, whereas people who held their policy attitudes with more certainty were no more likely to do so. The amount of importance people attached to their policy attitudes was unrelated to the degree to which they found one of their non-preferred Presidential candidates acceptable, but people higher in attitude certainty were much less likely to find any of their non-preferred candidates acceptable. And whereas importance and certainty were both related to pre-election intentions to vote, only importance predicted whether people actually voted.

Distinct Processes

Findings of this sort reinforce the notion that various strength-related features are separate constructs with distinct consequences for thought and behavior. In so doing, these findings raise interesting new questions about the processes by which these constructs regulate cognition and action. Although these various strength-related attributes may all lead to many of the same cognitive and behavioral consequences, they may do so through different psychological processes. In our view, this represents the next challenge for attitude researchers: clarifying precisely how the various strength-related attitude features exert their influence. A fruitful first step toward that end may therefore be to explore the distinction between motivation and ability.

Motivation and Ability

The performance of virtually any deliberate behavior requires sufficient levels of both ability and motivation. In the public health domain, for example, the simple act of using a condom to prevent exposure to a sexually transmitted disease requires a range of specific abilities. At a minimum, an individual must recognize the link between condom use and disease prevention, know how to go about procuring a condom and have the means to do so, be able to anticipate situations where a condom might be needed and have one on hand, be able to successfully negotiate condom use with one's partner, and be able to use a condom effectively. But of course, the presence of each of these abilities does not ensure that condom use will occur. Individuals must also be sufficiently motivated to engage in this health-promoting behavior. Acute fear of contracting a sexually transmitted disease, for example, may provide a powerful impetus to use condoms during all sexual encounters. Motives of this sort exert an energizing influence, instigating, directing, and sustaining actions aimed at achieving currently salient goals.

As this illustration makes clear, the combination of motivation and ability is critical to the performance of deliberate behaviors. The absence of any one of a number of relevant abilities renders condom use unlikely, even among people who are highly motivated to protect themselves against disease. Similarly, individuals who lack the motivation to protect themselves are unlikely to use condoms, even if they possess all of the relevant abilities for doing so. Interventions that increase one but not both of these factors, then, are likely to have modest effects on behavior.

Enablers of Attitude-Congruent Behavior

The claim that knowledge operates by conferring various abilities is hardly controversial. A wealth of existing evidence attests to this notion. For example, prior knowledge on a particular topic has been shown to enhance people's ability to store new information on that topic and retrieve the information later (e.g., Cooke, Atlas, Lane, & Berger, 1993; Fiske, Lau, & Smith, 1990; Hambrick, 2003; McGraw & Pinney, 1990; Recht & Leslie, 1988; Schneider, Gruber, Gold, & Opwis, 1993). Prior knowledge also improves comprehension of new information, enabling people to extract the central elements of a passage and draw appropriate inferences (Eckhardt, Wood, & Jacobvitz, 1991; Recht & Leslie, 1988). And knowledge increases the speed of relevant judgments (e.g., Fiske et al., 1990; Paull & Glencross, 1997) and improves cue utilization in decision tasks (Paull & Glencross, 1997).

With regard to attitudes in particular, knowledge has been shown to enhance recall of the arguments contained in a persuasive appeal (Wood, Rhodes, & Biek, 1995). Knowledge also improves people's ability to critically evaluate the cogency of persuasive messages (Ratneshwar & Chaiken, 1991; Wood, Kallgren, & Preisler, 1985), and it enables them to generate effective counter-arguments to a persuasive appeal, presumably yielding resistance to attitude change (Wood, 1982; Wood, Rhodes, & Biek, 1995).

Evidence also indicates that knowledge equips people with the requisite information to plan and execute effective behavioral strategies, enabling them to efficiently engage in attitude-expressive behaviors. For example, political scientists have demonstrated people are much more likely to perform behaviors expressive of their political views if they have gained procedural knowledge for doing so through previous participation in non-political organizations (e.g., Ayala, 2000; Brady, Verba, & Schlozman, 1995; Verba, Schlozman, & Brady, 1995). Knowledge about politics enables people to make political decisions that are in line with their attitudes and core values (e.g., Delli Carpini & Keeter, 1996). Knowledge about environmental conservation has been shown to enable people with pro-environmental attitudes to successfully plan and execute attitude-congruent behaviors (e.g., Meinhold & Malkus, 2005). And knowledge about child development enables young mothers to engage in stimulating play with their infants (e.g., Fry, 1985). Taken together, a large and diverse body of evidence suggests that knowledge confers cognitive and behavioral abilities.

Motivators of Attitude-Congruent Behavior

Other strength-related attitude features seem likely to enhance attitude-behavior correspondence not by increasing people's ability to act in accordance with their attitudes but by boosting their motivation to do so. And attitude importance may operate in precisely this way. Attitude importance is defined as the subjective sense of concern, caring, and significance that an individual attaches to an attitude (e.g., Krosnick, 1988a). To attach great personal importance to an attitude is to care passionately about it and to be deeply concerned about it. There is nothing subtle about attitude importance, particularly at its highest levels: people know very well when they are deeply invested in an attitude, and they know just as well when they have no special investment in one. In short, attitude importance is a belief (see Fishbein & Ajzen, 1975) linking an attitude to an attribute (i.e., high, moderate, or low psychological significance or investment).

Perceiving an attitude to be personally important may motivate people in four ways: (1) to nurture the attitude by bolstering it with relevant information; (2) to protect the attitude from change; (3) to use the attitude in processing information and making decisions; and (4) to express the attitude to others. These outcomes are most likely to be apparent when people are in consequential situations that demand they plan out their courses of thought and action carefully. This could include situations ranging from choosing a spouse to choosing which presidential candidate to support to deciding whether to experiment with cigarette smoking. In this sense, attitude importance is most likely to be helpful for understanding situations that entail what Fazio (1990) called "deliberative processing." Importance may also have automatic motivational effects on information processing and behavior as well, outside of awareness, but these effects are likely to evolve over time as the result of deliberate choices that people make based upon how much personal importance they attach to an attitude (see Boninger, Krosnick, Berent, & Fabrigar, 1995).

Thus, to attach personal importance to an attitude is to commit oneself to think about the object, to gather information about it, to use that information as well as one's attitude in making relevant decisions, and to design one's actions in accord with the attitude. In this sense, attaching personal importance to an attitude represents a substantial motivational commitment, in some ways analogous to making a long-term commitment to an interpersonal relationship. Consequently, we suspect, people are not likely to attach personal importance to an attitude lightly, in response to relatively trivial events. Just as people are "misers" with regard to cognitive processing (e.g., Fiske & Taylor, 1991), they are probably also miserly with their attachments of psychological significance and value to attitudes: Only clear and compelling reasons seem likely to motivate such a psychological investment. Because of this, high levels of importance are unlikely to emerge unnoticed over time. Rather, deep and lasting concern is likely to be instigated by significant events of which people are well aware.

In particular, past research points to three general classes of factors that inspire attitude importance (Boninger, Krosnick, & Berent, 1995). First, an attitude may become important to individuals who perceive it to be linked to their material self-interest. Self-interest based importance develops when one perceives an attitude to be instrumental to one's tangible rights, privileges, or lifestyle (or what Johnson & Eagly, 1989, referred to as relevant "outcomes"). That is, attitudes that are related to the attainment of desired material goods or behavioral opportunities are likely to be perceived as relevant to an individual's self-interest.

A second basis for an attitude to become personally important is social identification with reference groups or reference individuals. This may occur in a number of ways. First, identification with a social group may lead an attitude to become important to a person if the group's rights or privileges are perceived to be at stake (Key, 1961; Modigliani & Gamson, 1979). Strong identification with a group that consensually considers an attitude to be important can also serve as an impetus for importance, independent of whether tangible rewards or punishments for the group are in question (Sherif & Hovland, 1961). Similarly, attitude importance may develop as a result of identification with reference individuals whose interests are perceived to be at stake or who are perceived to care deeply about a particular attitude.

Third, an attitude may become personally important to an individual if he or she comes to view the object as relevant to his or her basic social or personal values (which are abstract beliefs "about how [people] ought or ought not to behave, or about some end-state of existence worth or not worth attaining" Rokeach, 1968, p. 124). The stronger the perceived linkage between an attitude object and an individual's values and the more important the values, the more important the attitude is likely to be to him or her (Campbell, Converse, Miller, & Stokes, 1960; Johnson & Eagly, 1989; Katz, 1960; Rosenberg, 1956). All three of these classes of causes of importance seem motivational in character, and we believe importance itself is motivational as well.

Some published evidence appears to be consistent with this assertion. For example, higher attitude importance appears to inspire people to devote careful thought to attitude-relevant information (Berent, 1990; Berent & Krosnick, 1993; Celsi & Olson, 1988; Holbrook, Berent, Krosnick, Visser, & Bonninger, 2005; Howard-Pitney, Borgida, & Omoto, 1986). More important attitudes are also more consequential in determining people's liking or disliking of other people (Byrne, London, & Griffitt, 1968; Clore & Baldridge, 1968; Granberg & Holmberg, 1986; Krosnick, 1988b; McGraw, Lodge, & Stroh, 1990), perhaps reflecting increased motivation to form attitude-congruent judgments of others. And higher attitude importance is associated with more frequent performance of some behaviors: seeking attitude-relevant information (Berent & Krosnick, 1993; Holbrook et al., 2005; Zaichkowsky, 1985) and expressing one's attitudes to others via letter-writing or telephone calls to newspapers or congressional representatives (Krosnick & Telhami, 1995; Schuman & Presser, 1981). All of these correlations could reflect the fact that importance is motivational in character, inspiring people to think and act in these ways. But no direct evidence yet exists confirming this motivational quality of importance.

The Current Research

The goals of the current research are therefore two-fold. First, we set out to directly test the notion that attitude importance operates through motivational channels, inspiring people to use and protect their cherished attitudes. These tests employed a diverse set of paradigms in an effort to provide a broad base of empirical evidence on this point.

Second, we explored the possibility that knowledge, too, may operate through motivational channels. As our review of the literature illustrated, it is fairly well established that knowledge confers a host of cognitive and behavioral abilities. And we see no strong theoretical basis for believing that shear knowledge volume will inspire action. To date, however, no research has directly explored the possibility that having a large cache of knowledge stored in memory motivates particular cognitive and behavioral outcomes. Evidence of this sort would challenge the utility of distinguishing between ability-based and motivationally based determinants of attitude strength.

To pursue these two goals, we examined the relation of attitude importance with a range of outcomes known to reflect motivational processes. And simultaneously, we examined the relation of attitude-relevant knowledge with the same outcomes, permitting us to explore potential dissociations between importance and knowledge. We predicted that importance would be related to these various motivational outcomes, whereas knowledge would not.

Our first study used a modified version of the Wason selection task (Wason, 1966, 1968) to test the hypothesis that people who attach more importance to their attitudes are more motivated to disconfirm counter-attitudinal assertions, whereas people who simply possess a great deal of attitude-relevant information have no particular motivation to do so. Our second study explored the relations of importance and knowledge with one of the hallmarks of motivation: the experience of negative affect when one's goals are blocked by impediments in the environment. Study 3 expanded the scope of our investigation, examining the relations of importance and knowledge with a broad set of outcomes reflecting motivational processes and explored the joint impact of motivation and ability on attitude-expressive behavior, explicitly testing whether the co-presence of importance and knowledge leads to a pronounced surge of attitude-congruent action. Finally, our fourth study replicated this latter finding with a representative sample of U.S. adults.

Study 1

The Wason selection task was originally designed to explore confirmatory biases in people's reasoning processes. In this study, we used a modified version of the task to assess people's motivation to disconfirm assertions that challenge their attitudes.

The Original Wason Selection Task

In the original version of the Wason task, participants are presented with four cards, each with a letter printed on one side and a number printed on the other side. The cards are arrayed in front of participants so they can see one side of each card. Participants are asked to use the cards to test a conditional assertion presented to them, such as "If a card has a vowel on one side, it has an even number on the other side." The participants' task is to select those cards (and only those cards) that must be turned over (revealing the number or letter on the reverse side) to determine whether or not the assertion is true. For example, the cards in front of a participant may display an "A," a "T," a "4," and a "9." To correctly test the assertion above, participants must select "A" (to determine if it has an even number on the reverse side) and "9" (to make sure that it does not have a vowel on the reverse side).

Although the task appears quite simple, participants do surprisingly poorly at it. In most studies, only about 20% of participants select the correct cards. The most common mistakes (using the current example as an illustration) involve selecting the "4" and failing to select the "9." Wason argued that these errors reflect a confirmatory bias, or the tendency to seek evidence that confirms the hypothesis one has set out to test and neglect information that could disconfirm the hypothesis (e.g., Wason & Johnson-Laird, 1972). Specifically, participants often select the "4" because it could yield evidence that would seem to confirm the assertion (if it reveals a vowel on the reverse side). In fact, however, the card is entirely nondiagnostic regarding the validity of the assertion: the discovery of a vowel on the reverse side would not prove that the assertion is true (because the presence of one card with a vowel on one side and an even number on the other side does not prove that *all* cards with vowels on one side have even numbers on the reverse), nor would the discovery of a consonant prove that the assertion is false (because the assertion does not require that *only* cards with vowels on one side have even numbers on the reverse). In addition, a tendency to neglect information that could disconfirm the hypothesis renders participants unlikely to select the "9" card, despite the fact that this card *must* not have a vowel on the reverse for the assertion to be true.

Modifications to the Wason Selection Task

Follow-up studies have reinforced the notion that poor performance on the Wason selection task is due to a confirmatory bias. For example, a number of studies have demonstrated that performance on the task can be improved by explicitly instructing participants to adopt a falsification strategy when testing the hypothesis (e.g., Fiedler & Hertel, 1994; Griggs, 1984; Valentine, 1985; Yachanin, 1986; Yachanin & Tweney, 1982). When they are motivated to disconfirm the hypothesis, participants are significantly less likely to neglect the card that could enable them to do so.

Dawson, Gilovich, and Regan (2002) demonstrated that such motivation can spring from internal as well as external sources. That is, even without being explicitly instructed to do so, participants often spontaneously strive to falsify hypotheses that they find personally disagreeable. For example, Dawson et al. (2002) found that participants performed substantially better on the task when the hypothesis to be tested implied that they were at risk of an early death, a hypothesis that participants were clearly motivated to refute. Similarly, participants performed substantially better when the hypothesis to be tested involved a negative stereotype about their own group that participants were motivated to falsify.

In the current study, we adapted the procedures developed by Dawson et al. (2002) to test the hypothesis that attitude importance is an inherently motivational construct, inspiring people to defend their attitudes. Specifically, participants performed the Wason selection task to test a counter-attitudinal assertion. We expected that participants who attached importance to the target attitude would be especially motivated to refute the assertion, and this motivation would cause them to perform better on the task than participants who attached less importance to the attitude. We did not expect one's volume of attitude-relevant knowledge to determine performance on the task because the cognitive abilities that it confers are irrelevant to participants' performance on this particular task.

Method

Overview

Participants completed a brief questionnaire that measured their attitudes toward capital punishment and several other policies. They also reported how important each issue was to them personally and how knowledgeable they were on each issue. In an ostensibly unrelated study, participants then completed a modified version of the Wason selection task that required them to test a counter-attitudinal assertion.

Participants

Forty-eight undergraduate students at the University of Chicago participated in this study in exchange for extra credit in a psychology course or for payment. These participants were selected from a larger set of undergraduates on the basis of their responses to items in the initial questionnaire regarding capital punishment: only people who expressed opposition to capital punishment were selected for inclusion, rendering the assertion to be tested counter-attitudinal for all participants.

Measures

Attitudes

Embedded in a set of items about other political issues, participants reported their attitudes toward the target issue of capital punishment on a fully labeled 7-point bipolar scale.

Importance

Participants indicated how important the issue of capital punishment was to them personally on a fully labeled 5-point unipolar scale. Responses were coded to range from 0 to 1 (with higher numbers reflecting more importance).

Knowledge

Participants indicated how knowledgeable they were about capital punishment on a fully labeled 5-point unipolar scale. Responses were coded to range from 0 to 1 (with higher numbers reflecting more knowledge).

Wason selection task

Participants were told that a separate study would explore how individuals solve problems. They were told that they would be asked to test one of several different statements about social issues, and that the evidence they would use to test these statements would be presented on double-sided cards. Participants were told that each card represented one observation (e.g., one state in the U.S., or one country in the world, or one high school in the U.S.), and that each side of the card would provide information about that observation. They were told that they would first view one side of each of four cards and then select the two cards that they would need to turn over in order to test the statement.[2] To make sure that they understood the instructions, participants were then presented with an example of the Wason selection task and were guided through a step-by-step explanation of what the task involved.

Participants then proceeded to the card selection task. They were presented with the following statement to test: "All states that allow capital punishment have lower murder rates than the national average." They were presented with four cards, which ostensibly contained information about particular states. The cards were labeled "State A," "State B," "State C," and "State D," and the front of each card contained information about whether or not that particular state allows the death penalty, whereas the back of each card contained information about whether the state's murder rate is *lower* than the national average or *higher* than the national average. The cards were arrayed such that two of the cards presented information about the states' death penalty laws (one state allowed capital punishment and one state did not) and two of the cards presented information about the states' murder rates (one state had a murder rate above the national average, and the other had a murder rate below the national average). Participants indicated which two of the four cards they would need to turn over to test the assertion. Overall task performance was coded 1 for participants who selected the correct cards and 0 for participants who failed to do so.

Results

Relation Between Importance and Knowledge

Importance and knowledge were moderately positively associated, $r = .48$, $N = 48$, $p < .001$.

Overall Task Performance

Consistent with past findings, participants performed quite poorly on the task: only 31% of participants selected the correct cards. And as in past studies, the most common mistakes involved selecting the card indicating that the state had a lower murder rate than the national average (51% of participants selected this card) and failing to select the card indicating that the state had a higher-than-average murder rate (55% of participants failed to select this card).

Attitude Importance, Attitude-Relevant Knowledge, and Task Performance

We conducted a series of logistic regressions using attitude importance and attitude-relevant knowledge to predict whether participants chose the correct cards. As predicted, importance was positively associated with task performance, $b = 2.75$, $SE = 1.14$, $p < .02$. Fifty-three percent of people who said capital punishment was extremely or very important to them selected the correct cards, whereas only 19% of the remaining participants did so. And as expected, the biggest performance gap involved selection of the card that could potentially disconfirm the counter-attitudinal assertion—whereas 37% of the low importance participants correctly selected this card, nearly 60% of the high importance participants did so.

Also as predicted, knowledge was unrelated to task performance, suggesting that participants high in knowledge were not more motivated than those low in knowledge to disconfirm the counter-attitudinal assertion, $b = -1.77$, $SE = 1.15$, n.s. The proportion of participants who selected the correct cards was virtually identical among participants who said that they were extremely or highly knowledgeable about capital punishment and those who said they were not at all, slightly, or quite knowledgeable about this issue: 31% and 32%, respectively. No significant differences emerged in selection rates for any of the four cards.

Knowledge and importance did not interact to predict performance, $b = -.19$, SE $= .41$, n.s., indicating that the relation between importance and task performance did not vary across levels of knowledge.

Discussion

A great deal of evidence attests to the pervasiveness of confirmation bias, the tendency to seek out evidence that would confirm a hypothesis being tested and to neglect evidence that may disconfirm it (for a review, see Klayman & Ha, 1987). This tendency causes people to perform poorly on the Wason selection task, which requires the pursuit of disconfirming evidence. But performance is improved when people are intrinsically motivated to disconfirm the hypothesis to be tested, such as when the hypothesis runs counter to one's preferred beliefs or attitudes (Dawson et al., 2002). This internal motivation appears to override the confirmation bias, leading people to actively seek out evidence that would discredit the hypothesis under consideration.

Study 1's results indicate that people are not always motivated to disconfirm counter-attitudinal assertions. Instead, this motivation depends on the degree to which an attitude is deemed personally important. The participants all opposed capital punishment, so the assertion to be tested was counter-attitudinal for all of them. But only when the attitude was personally important were participants motivated to actively seek out evidence that would debunk a counter-attitudinal assertion. In contrast, participants who attached no special significance to their attitudes seem not to have been particularly motivated to defend them. Presented with an opportunity to test a counter-attitudinal assertion, people low in attitude importance exhibited the typical confirmatory bias.

Possessing a large store of information about an attitude object seems not to have engendered the motivation to defend the attitude: people who were highly knowledgeable about capital punishment were no more likely than those who possessed relatively little knowledge on this issue to seek out evidence that could disconfirm the counter-attitudinal assertion. These findings are consistent with the notion that importance and knowledge operate through distinct psychological processes—whereas importance appears to arouse the motivation to protect an attitude, knowledge seems not to do so.

Study 2

One of the hallmarks of striving is the experience of negative affect when one's goals are blocked by impediments in the environment. If importance motivates people to use and protect their attitudes, they should experience negative affect when these goals are thwarted. For example, people who attach importance to a particular political attitude should feel upset if the government enacts laws that are contrary to their position. In contrast, if attitude-relevant knowledge confers abilities but does not ignite any particular motives, people who simply possess a great deal of information about an issue should be less likely to experience a negative affective reaction of this sort. We tested these ideas in our second study.

Method

Participants

Fifty-six undergraduates enrolled in a psychology course participated in this study in partial fulfillment of a course requirement.

Measures

ATTITUDES

Embedded in a set of items about other political issues, participants reported their attitudes toward abortion being legal on a fully labeled 7-point bipolar scale and three 7-point bipolar semantic differential scales. Responses were coded to range from 0 to 1, with higher numbers reflecting more favorable attitudes, and were averaged together (Cronbach's alpha = .95).

IMPORTANCE

Participants indicated how important the issue of legalized abortion was to them personally, how much they personally cared about the issue, and how much they cared about this issue relative to other issues on fully labeled 5-point unipolar scales. Responses were coded to range from 0 to 1 (with higher numbers reflecting greater importance) and averaged (Cronbach's alpha = .89).

KNOWLEDGE

Participants indicated how knowledgeable they were about the issue of abortion, how much information they had on this issue, and the extent to which they considered themselves experts on this issue on fully labeled 5-point unipolar scales. Responses were coded to range from 0 to 1 (with higher numbers reflecting greater knowledge) and averaged (Cronbach's alpha = .82).

AFFECTIVE REACTIONS TO COUNTER-ATTITUDINAL LAWS

Participants reported the degree to which they would be upset if the government enacted a new law on the issue of abortion that was contradictory to their own views on the issue using a fully labeled five point unipolar scale. Responses were coded to range from 0 to 1 (with higher numbers reflecting greater distress).

AFFECTIVE REACTIONS TO COUNTER-ATTITUDINAL SPEECH

Participants were asked to imagine that they were listening to a speech on the issue of abortion containing a number of very compelling arguments. They were asked to imagine how they would feel if they found it difficult to refute these counter-attitudinal arguments. Participants were asked to report the degree to which they would experience each of a series of negative emotional states (anxious, frustrated, angry, uncomfortable, upset) on a fully labeled 5-point unipolar scale. Responses were coded to range from 0 to 1 (with higher numbers reflecting more intense experiences of each emotion) and averaged (Cronbach's alpha = .82).

MOTIVATION TO OBTAIN ADDITIONAL INFORMATION

Participants indicated how interested they were in obtaining additional information on each of a series of contemporary social and political issues (e.g., legalized abortion, the Arab–Israeli conflict, global warming, legalization of marijuana) using a fully labeled 5-point unipolar scale. Responses were coded to range from 0 to 1 (with higher numbers reflecting greater interest).

Results

Relation Between Importance and Knowledge

As in Study 1, importance and knowledge were moderately positively associated, $r = .55, N = 56, p < .001$.

Affective Reactions to Counter-Attitudinal Law

We conducted a series of ordinary least squares regressions predicting participants' affective reactions to the enactment of a law that runs contrary to their own views on abortion. As expected, people who attached more importance to the issue of abortion reported greater levels of distress, $b = .56$, SE = .15, $p = .001$.[3] In contrast, knowledge explained no variance in negative affect, $b = .01$, SE = .16, n.s. Importance and knowledge did not interact to predict distress, $b = -.20$, SE = .66, n.s.

Affective Reactions to Counter-Attitudinal Speech

As expected, people who attached greater importance to the issue of abortion anticipated more negative affect when they encountered a compelling counter-attitudinal speech that they found difficult to refute, $b = .33$, SE $= .13$, $p < .02$. Knowledge volume was unrelated to negative affect, $b = -.14$, SE $= .14$, n.s. Once again, importance and knowledge did not interact to predict negative affect, $b = -.60$, SE $= .56$, n.s.

Motivation to Obtain Additional Information

As expected, importance was a significant predictor of participants' motivation to gain additional information on this topic, $b = .67$, SE $= .19$, $p = .001$, whereas knowledge was unrelated to this motivation, and $b = .02$, SE $= .21$, n.s.[4] Importance and knowledge did not interact to predict this motivation, $b = -.57$, SE $= .86$, n.s.

Discussion

Reinforcing the results of Study 1, people who attached a great deal of importance to the issue of abortion reported that they would be very upset if the government enacted a law that contradicted their position on this issue, that they would experience a range of negative emotions if they encountered a counter-attitudinal speech that they found difficult to dispute, and that they were highly motivated to learn more about the issue of legalized abortion. Each of these findings suggests that attaching importance to an attitude motivates people to express, defend, and bolster their position. In contrast, more knowledgeable people were no more likely to exhibit this motivation. These findings are consistent with the notion that importance and knowledge operate through distinct psychological mechanisms.

Study 3

In Study 3, we expanded the scope of our investigation in two ways. First, we tested some of the hypotheses explored in Study 1 using different measures. Second, we assessed the degree to which importance and knowledge predict several new strength-related outcomes. And third, we introduced a gap of several weeks between the measurement of attitude importance and knowledge and the collection of several of the outcome measures.

Information Gathering

In Study 2, we examined a meta-attitudinal measure of interest in attitude-relevant information. Here, we examined the same phenomenon, but using an operative measure of effort to gather attitude-relevant information for use in a subsequent judgment instead. When given access to a diverse array of information, we expected that people who attached more importance to their attitudes would be motivated to selectively gather information that would enable them to make attitude-congruent judgments in an upcoming task. And we expected that possessing a large store of attitude-congruent information would be unrelated to this sort of selective information seeking.

Attitude-Expressive Behavior

Second, we tested the hypothesis that the performance of attitude-expressive behavior may be facilitated by the co-presence of ability and motivation. We expected both importance and knowledge to predict the frequency of attitude-expressive behavior, but we also anticipated that attitude-expressive behavior would be especially frequent among people who attach importance to an issue *and* possess a large cache of issue-relevant knowledge.

Resistance to Attitude Change

To explore whether importance and knowledge confer resistance to attitude change, we employed an experimental paradigm developed by Lord, Ross, and Lepper (1979). In this procedure, participants are shown descriptions of a set of scientific studies on a controversial political issue, some of which claim to support the efficacy of a policy and others of which refute it. As a result, the counter-attitudinal findings cause people's attitudes to become more moderate (see Miller, McHoskey, Bane, & Dowd, 1993). Empirical evidence contradicting people's own views is apparently effective at inducing attitude change in this context.

Previous studies have shown that more important attitudes change less in response to a persuasive message (e.g., Fine, 1957; Gorn, 1975), presumably because importance motivates people to defend their attitudes. So we expected attitude change to be more prevalent among people who attached less importance to their attitudes. We posited that knowledge would enable people to identify flaws in the attitude-challenging studies, but would also enable them to recognize compelling aspects of those studies. These tendencies might cancel each other out, leaving no net effect of knowledge on real change. So we were uncertain about how knowledge volume might moderate attitude change.

Perceived attitude change

When asked to report the impact of the empirical evidence on their attitude, participants in Lord et al.'s (1979) study claimed that those attitudes had become more extreme in response to the mixed evidence. This presumably occurred because the conflicting empirical evidence was threatening to people, motivating them to minimize or dismiss its impact on their views. In doing so, people apparently overcorrected, coming to see themselves as even more staunchly committed to their original views.

Based on the results of our Study 2, we expected that people who attached more importance to their attitudes would find the attitude-challenging evidence more distressing and would therefore be especially motivated to defend and protect their attitudes. When these people were asked about the impact of the empirical evidence on their own views, we expected them to be especially likely to overcorrect, reporting particularly strong attitude polarization. Knowledge would not be helpful in critiquing this evidence, because Lord, Ross, and Lepper's (1979) procedure entailed providing participants' with explicit criticisms of each study and rebuttals of those criticisms. So we did not expect knowledge to moderate perceived attitude change.

Temporal Delay

We introduced a three-week delay between the time when attitude importance and knowledge were measured and the time when three of the four dependent measures were collected. This delay was intended to reduce the likelihood that the heightened salience of participants' attitudes on the target issues induced by the lengthy process of completing the battery of attitude-related measures during the first session would influence the measures collected during the second session. The delay also minimized the likelihood that rationalization of the importance and knowledge ratings could account for any observed relations of these measures with the dependent measures. And because importance and knowledge were measured three weeks before participants were given the opportunity to selectively gather information about the issues, an observed relation between attitude importance and selective information gathering cannot plausibly be attributed to the impact of information gathering on the attitude importance reports.

Method

Participants

Undergraduates enrolled in an introductory psychology course participated in this study in partial fulfillment of a course requirement. Participants visited the laboratory on two occasions separated by three weeks. One hundred fifty-nine students participated in the first session, and 138 returned for the second.

Procedure and Measures

In the first session, participants completed a questionnaire that measured their attitudes on two target issues, abortion and capital punishment, as well as attitude importance, knowledge volume, and frequency of attitude-expressive behaviors. During the second session, participants completed tasks that enabled us to assess efforts to gather attitude-relevant information and to assess actual and perceived attitude change in response to conflicting empirical evidence. Each construct was assessed with multiple questions of differing formats and scale lengths. Responses to all questions were coded to range from 0 to 1 (with higher numbers reflecting higher levels of each construct), and responses to the constituent items were averaged to yield composite indices of each construct.

ATTITUDES

Attitudes on each issue were assessed via five bipolar rating scales. These scales were of differing length (ranging from seven to eleven scale points) and were differentially labeled (for one scale, all scale points were verbally labeled and for four scales, only the endpoints were labeled; Cronbach's alpha = .95 and .93 for abortion and capital punishment, respectively).

IMPORTANCE

Participants reported how important each issue was to them personally, how much they personally cared about the issue, and how important they considered the issue compared to other issues on unipolar scales of differing length (ranging from five to eleven scale points) that were differentially labeled (for one scale, all scale points were verbally labeled and for the remaining scales, only the endpoints were labeled; Cronbach's alpha = .85 and .83 for abortion and capital punishment, respectively).

KNOWLEDGE

Participants indicated how knowledgeable they were on each issue, how much information they had on the issues, and the extent to which they considered themselves experts on each issue on unipolar scales of differing length (ranging from five to eleven scale points) that were differentially labeled (for one scale, all scale points were verbally labeled and for the remaining scales, only the endpoints were labeled; Cronbach's alpha = .77 and .79 for abortion and capital punishment, respectively).

SELECTIVE INFORMATION-GATHERING

During the second session, we assessed participants' motivation to use their attitudes in a subsequent judgment using a procedure developed by Holbrook et al. (2005). Participants were told that they would receive information about 12 different political candidates and would be asked to evaluate each one. Participants were told that for each candidate, they could choose to learn about his or her position on three of six political issues. The six available issues differed across candidates, requiring participants to consider each candidate individually and choose three issues from the six that were available for that particular candidate. The issue of abortion was available for six of the 12 candidates, and the issue of capital punishment was available for a different set of six candidates. Thus, the number of times participants requested a candidate's position on legalized abortion and capital punishment could be used as an index of participants' drive to use their attitudes on these issues to evaluate the candidates.

ATTITUDE-EXPRESSIVE BEHAVIOR

During the first session, participants reported whether they had ever performed seven specific behaviors expressing their attitudes toward legalized abortion (e.g., contacting a public official about the issue, giving money to an organization concerned with the issue, wearing a button or t-shirt indicating their views on the issue). Participants also reported their overall level of involvement in activities related to the issue of legalized abortion on an 11-point unipolar scale with verbally labeled endpoints.

SELECTIVE JUDGMENT

During the second session, participants engaged in a task designed to assess their reactions to a set of balanced and self-critical information on abortion. Following Lord, Ross, and Lepper's (1979) procedures, participants evaluated two scientific studies, one that yielded evidence of negative psychological consequences for women who obtained an abortion, and the other offering evidence of positive psychological consequences. Each study's description outlined its methodology, findings (including a graphic presentation of the data), criticisms from other researchers, and a rebuttal of the criticism. The order of presentation of the two studies (negative vs. positive consequences) was randomly counterbalanced across participants. The methodologies of the two studies were also counterbalanced, so that each methodology suggested negative consequences for approximately half of the participants and positive consequences for the other half of the participants.

After reading about each study, participants summarized its conclusions and evaluated how well conducted the study was, and how convincing it was. In each case, participants made these ratings on bipolar scales ranging from –8 to +8 with endpoints labeled "very poorly conducted"/"very well-conducted" and "completely unconvincing"/"completely convincing." These measures were highly correlated for each study (correlations ranging from .74 to .85) and were combined to create indices of participants' evaluations of each study. An index of selective judgment was computed by subtracting the perceived convincingness of the studies reporting negative consequences of abortion from the perceived convincingness of the studies reporting positive consequences.

ACTUAL AND PERCEIVED ATTITUDE CHANGE

After they had read about all of the studies, participants reported their attitudes toward legalized abortion on the same rating scales they had used during the first session. Attitude change was assessed by comparing the two sets of attitudes. Also, following Lord et al.'s (1979) procedure, participants reported their perceptions of how their attitudes toward abortion had changed, if at all, since the beginning of the study (on a 17-point bipolar rating scale, ranging from "much more opposed" to "much more in favor").

Results

Relation Between Importance and Knowledge

The correlations between importance and knowledge were comparable to those observed in Studies 1 and 2: $r = .46, p < .01$ and $r = .57, p < .01$ for abortion and capital punishment, respectively.

Selective Information Gathering

As expected, people who attached more importance to an issue requested candidates' positions on the issue significantly more often, $b = .55$, SE $= .16$, $p = .001$, and $b = .48$, SE $= .15$, $p = .002$ for abortion and capital punishment, respectively. However, possessing more knowledge was not related to information selection on either issue, $b = .05$, SE $= .16$, n.s., and $b = -.20$, SE $= .16$, n.s. Attaching importance to an issue apparently motivated participants to seek information that enabled them to use their attitudes when evaluating candidates, but possessing knowledge did not. Importance and knowledge did not interact to predict selective information gathering for either issue, $b = .09$, SE $= .61$, n.s. and $b = .11$, SE $= .60$, n.s., for abortion and capital punishment, respectively.

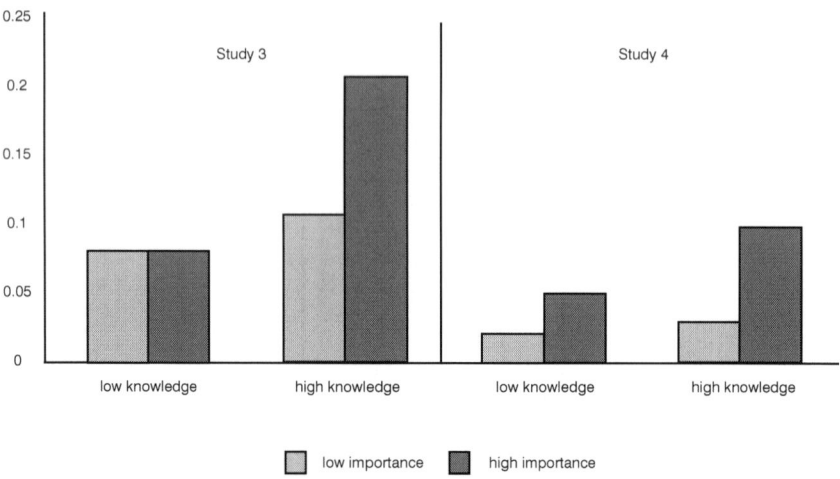

FIGURE 8.1 Performance of Attitude-Expressive Behaviors as a Function of Attitude Importance and Attitude-Relevant Knowledge (Studies 3 and 4)

Attitude-Expressive Behavior

As expected, importance and knowledge were both positively associated with increases in attitude-expressive behavior, $b = .16$, SE $= .06$, $p < .01$ and $b = .22$, SE $= .06$, $p < .001$, respectively. And importance and knowledge interacted significantly, $b = .46$, SE $= .22$, $p < .05$. As the left panel in Figure 8.1 illustrates, participants who were above the median in importance for abortion *and* were above the median in their knowledge volume on this issue performed an especially large number of attitude-expressive behaviors.

Selective Judgment

Consistent with past findings, the valence of participants' initial attitudes was strongly associated with selective judgment, $b = .24$, SE $= .09$, $p < .01$. Thus, participants who initially favored legalized abortion were inclined to find more convincing those studies that revealed positive consequences of abortion, whereas participants who initially opposed legalized abortion were inclined to find more convincing those studies that revealed negative consequences of abortion. And as expected, this relation was moderated by attitude importance. When attitude importance was added to the regression equation, along with a term reflecting the interaction between importance and participants' initial attitudes, both were significant predictors of selective judgment, $b = -.54$, SE $= .27$, $p < .05$, $b = .87$, SE $= .39$, $p < .05$, respectively. Thus, people who attached great importance to the issue of abortion were especially likely to selectively interpret the mixed evidence.

In contrast, the relation between participants' initial attitudes and selective judgment was not moderated by attitude-relevant knowledge. When knowledge and the product of knowledge and initial attitudes were added to the regression equation, neither significantly predicted selective judgment, $b = -.05$, SE $= .28$, n.s., $b = .41$, SE $= .40$, n.s., respectively. Thus, participants with a large store of attitude-relevant knowledge were no more likely than their less knowledgeable counterparts to selectively evaluate the studies in attitude-congruent ways. The three-way interaction between knowledge, importance, and initial attitudes was also not significant, $b = 1.48$, SE $= 1.25$, n.s.

Actual Attitude Change

Replicating previous findings (e.g., Miller, McHoskey, Bane, & Dowd, 1993), the mixed scientific evidence caused attitude moderation. People who were initially favorable toward legalized abortion became less so after reading the material, $t(56) = 2.24$, $p < .03$, and people who were initially unfavorable toward abortion became less so as well, $t(60) = 2.68, p = .01$.

As expected, participants who attached more importance to their attitudes changed less, $b = -.17$, SE $= .07$, $p = .02$. Knowledge volume was positively but non-significantly associated with attitude change: people who were more knowledgeable about the issue of legalized abortion exhibited slightly more attitude moderation in response to the mixed evidence, $b = .12$, SE $= .07, p = .10$. If reliable, this trend would be consistent with some prior research (for a review, see Wood, Rhodes, & Biek, 1995) suggesting that knowledge equipped people to see flaws in the study that supported their own views and to recognize the validity of the study that contradicted their views, making them more likely to adopt a more moderate stance. Importance and knowledge did not interact when predicting attitude change, $b = .03$, SE $= .03$, n.s.

Perceived Attitude Change

Replicating Lord, Ross, and Lepper (1979), participants perceived their attitudes to have polarized. Participants who were initially favorable toward legalized abortion perceived themselves to have become more favorable after reading the mixed evidence, $t(55) = 5.02$, $p < .001$, and participants who were initially unfavorable toward legalized abortion perceived themselves to have become less favorable toward it, $t(60) = 3.71$, $p < .001$. And as expected, participants who attached more importance to the issue perceived marginally significantly more polarization, $b = .29$, SE $= .17$, p $< .10$. Knowledge was unrelated to perceived attitude change, $b = -.09$, SE $= .17$, n.s., and importance and knowledge did not interact in predicting perceived attitude change, $b = .07$, SE $= .65$, n.s.

Mediation

The findings for selective judgment parallel the findings regarding perceived polarization: people who attached more importance to their attitudes were especially likely to show attitude-congruent biases in their evaluations of the studies, but people who possessed a great deal of knowledge were no more likely than those who possessed little knowledge to exhibit this bias. This raises the possibility that selective judgment may mediate the relation between attitude importance and perceived attitude polarization. That is, attitude importance may have increased the attitude-congruent bias in participants' assessments of the studies, and on the basis of these biased judgments, participants with importance attitudes may have inferred that their attitudes had become more extreme. Surprisingly, however, this appears not to be the case. The degree to which participants evaluated the studies in attitude-congruent ways was unrelated to perceptions that their attitudes had polarized in response to the mixed evidence, $b = -.02$, SE $= .03$, n.s.

Discussion

These results provide further evidence that importance and knowledge operate in fundamentally different ways—the former by motivating and the latter by enabling. Importance motivated people to selectively seek out attitude-relevant information for use in an upcoming judgment, but knowledge volume was unrelated to selective information seeking. Both importance and knowledge were associated with greater attitude-expressive behavior, but as expected, the co-presence of importance and knowledge was associated with an especially pronounced increase in attitude-expressive behavior. This is consistent with the notion that knowledge provides the ability to plan and execute attitude-expressive behavior, whereas importance provides the motivation to do so.

Differential motivation to bolster and defend their views was also evident in participants' responses to a set of mixed empirical evidence. People who attached a great deal of importance to their attitudes exhibited greater commitment to their original views and were less prone to adopt more moderate attitudes. In contrast, people who possessed more attitude-relevant knowledge might have been more likely to adopt more moderate attitudes (though this effect was not significant), perhaps because knowledge enabled them to recognize the validity of the attitude-incongruent evidence.

In response to the mixed empirical evidence, people who attached more importance to their attitudes also perceived their attitudes to have become more extreme, presumably the result of a strong motivation among these participants to express their resoluteness in the face of conflicting evidence. And they were more likely to selectively evaluate the quality of the evidence, judging attitude-congruent studies to be of higher quality than attitude-challenging studies. People who possessed more attitude-relevant knowledge were no more likely to perceive their attitudes to have polarized, suggesting that knowledge did not motivate people to present themselves as especially resolute in the face of conflicting evidence. Nor were knowledgeable participants especially motivated to discredit attitude-challenging studies and endorse attitude-congruent studies.

Interestingly, selective judgment did not mediate the relation between attitude importance and perceived polarization. That is, people who attached great importance to their abortion attitudes were especially likely to selectively judge the studies they read about, and they perceived especially strong attitude polarization, but selective judgment and perceived polarization were unrelated. Thus, in the current investigation importance appears to have inspired two independent motivational processes.

The observed independence of these two outcomes may seem surprising— selective judgment has often been presumed to be causally responsible for perceived attitude polarization in the Lord, Ross, and Lepper (1979) paradigm. In fact, however, there is little direct evidence for this mechanism. In their own investigation, Lord et al. (1979) relied on correlations between selective judgment and perceived polarization to make the case that the former was the driving force behind the latter. Subsequent investigations have often replicated those correlations (e.g., Miller et al., 1993), but they have not directly tested for mediation. And the magnitude of these investigations has often been quite modest (in the range of .2 – .3 in Miller et al.'s [1993] studies).

Further, other investigations have documented the independence of these outcomes. For example, people have sometimes been shown to exhibit strong attitude-driven biases in their evaluations of studies and yet not perceive their attitudes to have polarized in response to the studies (Miller et al., 1993, Study 3). Thus, together with some past findings, the current results suggest that selective judgment is not necessary for perceived polarization in the Lord, Ross, and Lepper (1979) paradigm, nor is it always sufficient to produce perceived polarization.

Across all of these diverse outcomes, importance appears to have motivated people to protect and express their views, whereas knowledge appears to have enabled them to do so. Because importance and knowledge were measured several weeks before most of the dependent measures were collected, we can be confident that these relations do not reflect rationalization of those initial ratings.

Study 4

Overview

In our final study, we sought to replicate one of the findings from Study 3, this time with a representative sample of adults. In particular, we tested the notion that the combination of ability and motivation leads to a particularly pronounced surge in attitude-behavior correspondence. We did so by interviewing a large, representative sample of American adults about the issue of global warming.

Method

Participants

A representative national sample of 688 English-speaking adults living in private households in the U.S. were interviewed by telephone by the Ohio State University Center for Survey Research during September and the first six days of October in 1997. The sample was generated via random digit dialing (see, e.g., Waksberg, 1978), and the cooperation rate was 67.3%. To assure representativeness of the sample, within household sampling was done by asking the adult resident with the most recent birthday to participate, a convenient quasi-random selection device (Salmon & Nichols, 1983). And the sample did in fact appear to be representative of the nation: the demographic characteristics of the sample closely matched the distributions of race, education, age, gender, and region of residence, as gauged by the March 1997 Current Population Survey, done by the U.S. Census Bureau. To offset the small demographic discrepancies that did emerge, the data from each sample were weighted to match current census statistics for race, education, age, gender, and region of the country (for description of procedures, see Lavrakas, 1993).

Measures

ATTITUDE IMPORTANCE

Participants reported the degree to which they attached personal importance to the issue of global warming using a fully labeled 5-point scale. Responses were coded to range from 0 to 1 (with higher numbers reflecting greater importance).

KNOWLEDGE

Participants reported how knowledgeable they were about this issue on a fully labeled 4-point scale. Responses were coded to range from 0 to 1 (with higher numbers reflecting greater knowledge).

ATTITUDE-EXPRESSIVE BEHAVIOR

Participants reported whether they had performed three behaviors expressing their views about global warming during the prior four months: writing a letter to a public official about global warming or air pollution, giving money to an organization concerned with this issue, and attending a meeting to discuss the issue. Each participant was assigned a score reflecting the total number of activities performed, which was then rescaled to range from 0 to 1.

Results

Relation Between Importance and Knowledge

Importance and knowledge were positively correlated: $r = .26$, $N = 688$, $p < .001$, though more weakly than we saw in the previous studies of student samples and well-known issues.

Attitude-Expressive Behavior

Replicating the results of Study 3, importance and knowledge were both positively associated with attitude-expressive behavior, $b = .29$, $SE = .06$, $p < .001$ and, $b = .24$, $SE = .06$, $p < .001$, respectively. And as in Study 3, these main effects were qualified by an interaction between importance and knowledge, $b = .50$, $SE = .19$, $p = .01$. Once again, participants who were above the median in both importance and knowledge were especially likely to have performed attitude-expressive behaviors (see the right side of Figure 8.1).

Discussion

Replicating our earlier findings, Study 4 suggests that the combination of importance and knowledge is associated with a pronounced increase in attitude-expressive behavior in a representative sample of adults. These findings reinforce the notions that attitude importance provides the motivation and that knowledge confers the ability to plan and successfully execute attitude-expressive behaviors. Alone, each is associated with modest increases in attitude-congruent behavior, but acting in concert, these two factors appear to produce a surge in attitude-behavior correspondence.

General Discussion

At the beginning of the twentieth century, attitude was considered by many to be the single most important construct in social psychology. Indeed, some went so far as to *define* social psychology as the scientific study of attitudes (e.g., Thomas & Znaniecki, 1918). In 1935, Gordon Allport famously described attitude as "the most distinctive and indispensable concept in contemporary American social psychology" (Allport, 1935, p. 198). According to Allport, attitudes provide order and structure to the social and physical environment, powerfully shaping virtually all aspects of thought and behavior.

And indeed, in the years since Allport's bold claim, a great deal of empirical evidence has accumulated suggesting that attitudes often do resemble the robust and powerful constructs that Allport described. Equally clear from this literature, however, is that attitudes do not always manifest these properties. In fact, although some attitudes powerfully motivate and guide behavior, others seem entirely unrelated to behavior. And whereas some attitudes are durable and unyielding, others are quite elastic, fluctuating greatly over time. In fact, by the late 1960s, the literature was so inconsistent that some prominent scholars questioned the very existence of attitudes, sending the field into a period of crisis.

Since then, social psychologists have made great progress toward identifying the conditions under which attitudes influence thoughts and behavior. It is now clear, for example, that attitudes are consequential for some types of people more than others, and in some situations more than others (for a review, see Eagly & Chaiken, 1993). More recently, social psychologists have also come to recognize that some attitudes are *inherently* more powerful than others. That is, even within the same individual and across situations, some attitudes exert a pronounced impact on thinking and on behavior, whereas others are largely inconsequential. Similarly, some attitudes are tremendously durable, resisting change in the face of strong challenges and remaining stable over long spans of time, whereas others are highly malleable and fluctuate greatly over time.

This distinction between strong and weak attitudes has provided scholars with tremendously useful conceptual leverage, bringing clarity and order to a seemingly incoherent literature. And this distinction has to a large extent set the agenda for attitude research in recent decades. A high priority has identifying factors that determine the strength and durability of an attitude. In this regard, attitude researchers have been tremendously successful, identifying and cataloguing a diverse set of attitude features that are each related to the hallmarks of attitude strength (e.g., resistance to change, attitude-behavior correspondence; for a review, see Petty & Krosnick, 1995).

More recently, attitude researchers have extended these initial advances by clarifying the relations among the various strength-related attitude features and the underlying latent structure governing these relations (for a review see Visser, Bizer, & Krosnick, 2006). Whereas scholars once assumed that the various strength-related features were largely interchangeable indicators of one or a few latent constructs, it is now fairly well-established that instead, the strength-related features each appear to represent distinct constructs in their own right, perhaps arising from different sets of antecedents and setting into motion at least partially distinct cognitive and behavioral consequences.

This recent advance has opened the door to an exciting new set of questions about the nature of attitude strength and the processes by which it functions.

Specifically, this "multidimensional" view of attitude strength encourages attitude researchers to explore the psychological processes by which these distinct features operate, clarifying their workings, alone and in combination. The work reported here represents an initial step in that direction. Whereas knowledge appears to operate by conferring particular cognitive and behavioral abilities, attitude importance appears to operate through motivational processes, inspiring people to protect and use their attitudes. And the combination of ability and motivation conferred by the co-presence of knowledge and importance leads uniquely to a pronounced rise in attitude-expressive behavior.

These findings represent an important advance, clearing a path for the development of much more refined predictions regarding attitude strength based on the psychological nature of particular strength-related attitude features. That is, rather than declaring an attitude "strong" and attributing to it all of the myriad qualities associated with strength, we may be able to anticipate the particular ways in which an attitude will influence thought and behavior by identifying the basis of its strength. If an attitude is strong because it is based on a great deal of knowledge, for example, we can anticipate specific cognitive and behavioral abilities, and we can make predictions about the precise implications of these abilities for particular outcomes. If an attitude is strong because it is deemed personally important, we can anticipate specific motivational processes, which suggest that particular cognitive and behavioral outcomes will be observed. And if an attitude is strong because of the co-presence of knowledge and importance, we can make other predictions based on the joint influence of ability and motivation. In this way, the current research leads us one step closer to the establishment of a more precise, integrative theory of attitude strength based on a full understanding of the psychological processes by which the various strength-related attitude features operate.

Does Knowledge Sometimes Act as a Motivator?

Although knowledge volume in general seems to have operated here by conferring abilities, gaining particular pieces of new information might seem likely to motivate people. For example, gaining the knowledge that unprotected sex can cause AIDS may seem to inspire people to take appropriate precautions. In fact, however, we believe that in such instances, new information enables people to recognize a link between the attitude object (i.e., unprotected sex) and their own material self-interest (i.e., preservation of their health and longevity). A wealth of existing evidence suggests that the recognition of such a link causes people to attach importance to the attitude (for a review, see Boninger et al., 1995), and the evidence we have presented here suggests that attaching importance to an attitude motivates action. Thus, it is the new ability to recognize a link between an attitude object and one's self-interest, and not the new information itself, that inspires attitude-congruent behavior (see Figure 8.2).

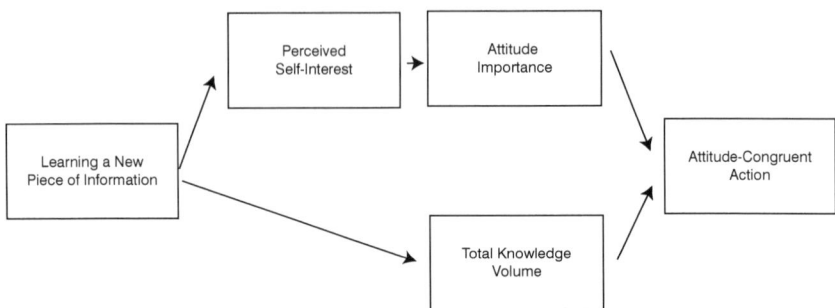

FIGURE 8.2 Model of the Impact of Learning on Attitude-Congruent Action

Consider a man who places little value on maintaining his health and promoting his longevity. For this person, learning that unprotected sex can cause AIDS does not reveal a link between the attitude object and his material self-interest—unprotected sex has no implications for his valued outcomes. For such an individual, gaining this new piece of information is unlikely to motivate any particular action.

As this example illustrates, knowledge volume per se seems unlikely to motivate behavior. But knowledge may sometimes confer the ability to recognize links between an attitude object and one's material self-interest, core values, or social identities. To the extent that new information leads to the recognition of such links, attitude importance is likely to increase, setting into motion a host of motivational processes.

Measurement of Knowledge: Meta-attitudinal or Operative?

Because attitude importance is defined as a "subjective sense of the concern, caring, and significance that [a person] attaches to an attitude" (Boninger, Krosnick, Berent, & Fabrigar, 1995, p. 160), its inherent nature suggests that assessment of it through self-report measures is optimal. In contrast, knowledge simply refers to the amount of attitude-relevant information people have stored in memory, and a number of different possible measures of this construct have been employed in past research, each justifiable.

Many researchers have used meta-attitudinal self-report measures similar to the ones we used (e.g., Davidson, Yantis, Norwood, & Montano, 1985; Krosnick et al., 1993; Pomerantz et al., 1995; Prislin, 1996). Others have asked people to list everything they know about an attitude object (e.g., Davidson et al., 1985; Krosnick et al., 1993; Prislin, 1996; Wood, 1982; Wood & Kallgren, 1988; Wood et al., 1985). And still others have assessed attitude-relevant knowledge via people's performance on quizzes (e.g., Wilson, Kraft, & Dunn, 1989).

Each measure of attitude-relevant knowledge has advantages and disadvantages. Quizzes provide objective, standardized metrics for assessing the relative knowledge levels of a group of people. However, because items on a quiz will almost always represent only a small subset of the information available on any given topic, it is possible for people to possess large stores of knowledge and still score poorly. Furthermore, the use of quizzes hinges on the assumption that only factually correct information is legitimately considered knowledge. In keeping with the bulk of prior research on attitude-relevant knowledge (e.g., Davidson et al., 1985; Krosnick et al., 1993; Pomerantz et al., 1995; Prislin, 1996; Wood, 1982; Wood & Kallgren, 1988; Wood et al., 1985), we view knowledge as the quantity of information that people believe to be true about an attitude object, regardless of the accuracy of those beliefs. This makes quizzes less desirable measures.

Both self-reports and knowledge-listing tasks offer the advantage of being able to assess all of the information stored in people's memories, not just factually correct information. But both are subject to limitations as well. In addition to random measurement error, perceived knowledge volume is subject to systematic measurement error, because some people may experience social desirability pressure to report or even to genuinely perceive that they are more knowledgeable than they truly are. Counting the number of responses to a knowledge-listing task may also provide a distorted portrait of relative knowledge levels because individual responses may differ in the richness of knowledge lying behind a single comment, and individuals may differ in the extent to which they "unpack" a given statement to explicate the beliefs embedded within it. People also differ in overall verbosity, so some of the between-person differences in the amount of information that people list may reflect differences in communication styles rather than actual differences in knowledge volumes. Therefore, people with a lot of knowledge may sometimes appear to possess relatively little knowledge on a knowledge-listing task, and those who are not particularly knowledgeable may appear to be.

We used measures of perceived amount of knowledge in part because doing so allowed us to use the same method to assess knowledge that we used to gauge importance (i.e., both are meta-attitudinal), thereby eliminating a potential confound when comparing the relations between the two strength-related attributes and the various attitude effects. And steps were taken to minimize the impact of random and systematic measurement error in our knowledge assessment. To reduce the effects of random error, knowledge was assessed with multiple indicators that were averaged to form a more reliable index. And in an effort to reduce social desirability pressures, the questions assessing knowledge volume were prefaced with a statement explicitly acknowledging that people often know quite a bit about some topics but not very much about other topics, to assure participants that it was perfectly acceptable to concede that they were not especially knowledgeable on this particular topic.

Furthermore, some existing evidence indicates that meta-attitudinal self-reports and knowledge-listing measures of attitude-relevant knowledge tap the same underlying construct (e.g., Krosnick et al., 1993). Nevertheless, it remains possible that measures of attitude-relevant knowledge derived from knowledge-listing tasks would have exhibited different associations with the various attitude effects than those observed in the current investigation. Future investigations exploring this possibility therefore seem warranted.

Moving Beyond Attitude Importance and Attitude-relevant Knowledge

Although the studies reported here focused on importance and knowledge, the implications of this work are much broader. Just as for attitude importance and attitude-relevant knowledge, the unique qualities of other strength-related attitude features may suggest the distinct causal mechanisms through which they operate.

This is not to suggest, of course, that every strength-related attitude feature operates via a unique set of psychological mechanisms. To the contrary, there is likely to be overlap in the mechanisms by which different strength-related features exert their effects. It may therefore be possible to identify clusters of strength-related features that lead to the same outcomes through the same processes, providing a parsimonious way of conceptualizing attitude strength and organizing the various strength-related attitude features.

The distinction between motivation and ability that we have explored may be a sensible starting point. Just as importance operates through motivational channels, so may other strength-related features (e.g., intensity). And just as knowledge operates by conferring abilities, so may other strength-related features (e.g., elaboration). This basic distinction, therefore, may provide one way of organizing sets of strength-related attitude features. The pursuit of other conceptual distinctions of this sort will surely yield new insights regarding the nature and functioning of attitude strength. In our view, this pursuit represents an important and promising challenge for attitude researchers.

Practical Implications

We began this chapter with a question: Why have so many well-funded, apparently sound public health interventions had so little success in improving the correspondence between people's attitudes toward healthy living and their relevant behaviors? We suggested that the problem may lie in the fact that many public health interventions have focused primarily on increasing knowledge volume and have not directly targeted the importance that people attach to the attitude object. It seems worthwhile to return to this question in light of the current findings.

When one approaches this problem from the attitude strength perspective, it becomes apparent that an optimal strategy for improving health behavior would involve three steps: (1) creating the needed attitudes through targeted persuasive efforts (e.g., negative attitudes toward unsafe sex); (2) making those attitudes personally important to people (and thus cementing them and inspiring motivation to express those attitudes behaviorally); and (3) educating people to give them the specific knowledge they need to be able to successfully express those attitudes behaviorally. Steps 1 and 3 are common components of public health education campaigns, but the middle step is not.

By following this strategy, interventionists would foster the co-presence of the desired attitude, attitude importance, and needed knowledge, which our results indicate will yield greater attitude-behavior correspondence than either the attitude or importance or knowledge in isolation. To be sure, we found that people who possessed lots of information about an issue were more likely to engage in attitude-expressive behaviors than were people who knew little about the issue. And people who cared deeply about an issue were more likely to take action than were people who attached little importance to it. But people who were highly knowledgeable and also attached great importance to the issue exhibited the surge of attitude-congruent behavior that interventionists want to see.

It is especially important to recognize that the three steps should be taken in the above order rather than in a different order. If importance or knowledge volume are increased before the necessary attitudes are in place, then one will have cemented just the attitudes one wants to change, making Step 1 even more difficult to accomplish. This sort of time sequence is also rare if ever a part of public attitude change campaigns.

The literature on attitude importance provides guidance regarding how to increase the degree of psychological significance people attach to an attitude. As we have noted already, one determinant of importance is the extent to which people recognize a link between the attitude object and their own material self-interest (Boninger et al., 1995). In this regard, current intervention practices may seem to be quite appropriate. For example, the website launched by the U.S. Department of Health and Human Services that we discussed earlier not only provides information about how to engage in healthier behavior, but it also lists a battery of benefits, including increased strength and aerobic fitness, stress relief, greater motivation, relaxation, improved sleep, and reduced risk of coronary heart disease, colon cancer, diabetes, and high blood pressure (www.healthierus.gov). These all appear to be outcomes that most Americans would deem desirable.

Nonetheless, the attitude literature suggests that a number of important improvements can be made in this approach. First, it is not clear that presenting people with a laundry list of potential benefits that may accrue is an effective way of leading individuals to draw a connection between a desired behavior and their own material interests. In fact, although this approach appears likely to increase knowledge levels, it may do little to increase the importance people attach to particular outcomes or behaviors. Instead, messages that prompt individuals to affirm their desires for fitness, stress relief, relaxation, improved sleep, and so on may be more effective at leading people to recognize personal benefits that they value. Stimulating people to reflect upon the specific ways in which their *own* lives would be better may produce links between the target behavior and people's material interests, inspiring them to attach importance to the behavior.

Second, interventions often focus primarily or exclusively on the material benefits that people can expect if they behave in particular ways. Efforts to increase people's motivation to act in attitude-congruent ways may be more effective if they simultaneously address the other antecedents of attitude importance as well (see Boninger, Krosnick, & Berent, 1995). Drawing people's attention to the links between their personal values and an attitude object may lead them to increase the importance attached to the attitude, motivating them to act in accordance with it. And efforts to increase the value that people place on their own personal health may be effective in this regard as well (see, e.g., Krosnick et al., 2006). Messages that focus on the interests or identities of reference groups or individuals with whom they identify may also increase the importance people attach to their attitudes.

Third, it is clearly worth exploring the possibility that messages targeting other strength-related attitude features will further improve the correspondence between people's health-relevant attitudes and their behavior. For example, people who are knowledgeable about the issue of global warming and care deeply about it might be particularly likely to act in accordance with their attitude if they also hold the attitude with great certainty, or if the attitude is minimally ambivalent, or if it possesses other strength-related features. As with attitude importance, the antecedents of these and other strength-related features are fairly well documented, providing guidance for interventions geared toward increasing them (see Petty & Krosnick, 1995).

Acknowledging that the various strength-related attitude features are distinct constructs that operate through different mechanisms alerts us to the fact that there are multiple avenues by which attitudes can be strengthened, and it also suggests that there are many ways to *reduce* attitude strength. Surprisingly, public health advocates may sometimes be more effective in changing people's attitudes if they first devote effort to reducing strength-related features of those attitudes. For example, calling into question the links people perceive between a target attitude and their own material interests may reduce the importance people attach to the attitude. Challenging the factual validity of people's beliefs may reduce their confidence in their attitudes. Implementing these and other such techniques before attempting to change counter-productive attitudes may be a necessary first step in some cases if a public education campaign is to be effective. We therefore look forward to future research seeking to enhance our understanding of the psychological mechanisms by which strength-related attitude features can be reduced, thus weakening the attitude itself and opening it up to the possibility of subsequent change.

Conclusion

Although psychologists have long recognized that some attitudes are strong and others are weak, only recently have we come to recognize that strength is multi-dimensional. With that recognition in hand, theory development must move ahead by documenting the independent, overlapping, and interactive causes and effects of the array of strength-related attitude features. The research reported here represents a step in that direction, focused on importance and knowledge volume. We look forward to more such work exploring other strength-related features in the quest for a general theory of attitude potency.

Notes

1 This research is based in part on a doctoral dissertation submitted by the first author to the graduate school at Ohio State University and was conducted partly while the second author was a Fellow at the Center for Advanced Study in the Behavioral Sciences, supported by a grant from the National Science Foundation (SBR-9022192). The authors are grateful for thoughtful comments from Richard Petty and Philip Tetlock and from the members of the Group for Attitudes and Persuasion and the Political Psychology Research Team at Ohio State University. Study 4 was funded by the National Science Foundation (grant SBR-9731532), the U.S. Environmental Protection Agency, the National Oceanic and Atmospheric Administration, and the Ohio State University, and it was sponsored by Resources for the Future. Jon Krosnick is University Fellow at Resources for the Future. Correspondence regarding this manuscript should be addressed to Penny S. Visser, Department of Psychology, University of Chicago, 5848 S. University Avenue, Chicago, IL 60637; email: pvisser@uchicago.edu.

2 The original Wason selection task instructions did not constrain participants to select two cards. This constraint has often been used in subsequent studies, however, to help participants perform the task correctly.

3 Included in this and all subsequent regressions was a dummy variable contrasting participants who favored abortion and those who opposed abortion to account for potential differences between the two groups.

4 To control for individual differences in general political interest, we included the measures of participants' interest in receiving additional information about the other political issues as control variables.

References

Allport, G. W. (1935). Attitudes. In C. Murchison (Ed.), *A handbook of social psychology* (pp. 798–844). Worcester, MA: Clark University Press.

Ayala, L. J. (2000). Trained for democracy: The differing effects of voluntary and involuntary organizations on political participation. *Political Research Quarterly, 53,* 99–115.

Bassili, J. N. (1996). Meta-judgmental versus operative indexes of psychological features: The case of measures of attitude strength. *Journal of Personality and Social Psychology, 71*, 637–653.

Bassili, J. N., & Roy, J. P. (1998). On the representation of strong and weak attitudes about policy in memory. *Political Psychology, 19*, 669–681.

Berent, M. K. (1990). *Attitude importance and the recall of attitude-relevant information.* Unpublished Master's thesis. The Ohio State University, Columbus.

Berent, M. K., & Krosnick, J. A. (1993). *Attitude importance and selective exposure to attitude-relevant information.* Unpublished manuscript. The Ohio State University, Columbus.

Biek, M., Wood, W., & Chaiken, S. (1996). Working knowledge, cognitive processing, and attitudes: On the determinants of bias. *Personality and Social Psychology Bulletin, 22*, 547–556.

Bizer, G. Y., & Krosnick, J. A. (2001). Exploring the structure of strength-related attitude features: The relation between attitude importance and attitude accessibility. *Journal of Personality and Social Psychology, 81*, 566–586.

Boninger, D. S., Krosnick, J. A., & Berent, M. K. (1995). Origins of attitude importance: Self-interest, social identification, and value relevance. *Journal of Personality & Social Psychology, 68*, 61–80.

Boninger, D. S., Krosnick, J. A., Berent, M. K., & Fabrigar, L. R. (1995). The causes and consequences of attitude importance. In R. E. Petty & J. A. Krosnick (Eds.), *Attitude strength: Antecedents and consequences* (pp. 159–189). Mahwah, NJ: Erlbaum.

Brady, H. E., Verba, S., & Schlozman, K. L. (1995). Beyond ses: A resource model of political participation. *American Political Science Review, 89*(2), 271–294.

Budd, R. J. (1986). Predicting cigarette use: The need to incorporate measures of salience in the theory of reasoned action. *Journal of Applied Social Psychology, 16*, 663–685.

Byrne, D. E., London, O., & Griffitt, W. (1968). The effect of topic importance and attitude similarity–dissimilarity on attraction in an intrastranger design. *Psychonomic Science, 11*, 303–304.

Campbell, A., Converse, P. E., Miller, W. A., & Stokes, D. E. (1960). *The American voter.* Chicago, IL: University of Chicago Press.

Cantril, H. (1944). *Gauging public opinion.* Princeton, NJ: Princeton University Press.

Cantril, H. (1946). The intensity of attitude. *Journal of Abnormal and Social Psychology, 41*, 1–12.

Celsi, R. L., & Olson, J. C. (1988). The role of involvement in attention and comprehension processes. *Journal of Consumer Research, 15*, 210–224.

Clore, G. L., & Baldridge, B. (1968). Interpersonal attraction: The role of agreement and topic interest. *Journal of Personality and Social Psychology, 9*, 340–346.

Cooke, N. J., Atlas, R. S., Lane, D. M., & Berger, R. C. (1993). Role of high-level knowledge in memory for chess positions. *American Journal of Psychology, 106*, 321–351.

Cronbach, L. J. (1995). Giving method variance its due. In P. E. Shrout & S. T. Fiske (Eds.), *Personality research, methods, and theory: A festschrift honoring Donald W. Fiske* (pp. 145–157). Hillsdale, NJ: Lawrence Erlbaum Associates.

Davidson, A. R. (1995). From attitudes to actions to attitude change: The effects of amount and accuracy of information. In R. E. Petty & J. A. Krosnick (Eds.), *Attitude strength: Antecedents and consequences* (pp. 315–336). Mahwah, NJ: Lawrence Erlbaum Associates.

Davidson, A. R., Yantis, S., Norwood, M., & Montano, D. E. (1985). Amount of information about the attitude object and attitude-behavior consistency. *Journal of Personality and Social Psychology, 49*, 1184–1198.

Dawson, E., Gilovich, T., & Regan, D. T. (2002). Motivated reasoning and performance on the Wason selection task. *Personality and Social Psychology Bulletin, 28,* 1379–1387.

DiClemente, R. J., Forrest, K. A., Mickler, S., & Principal Site Investigators. (1990). College students' knowledge about AIDS and changes in HIV-preventative behaviors. *AIDS Education and Prevention, 2,* 201–212.

Delli Carpini, M., & Keeter, S. (1996). *What Americans know about politics and why it matters.* New Haven, CT: Yale University Press.

Eagly, A. H., Kulesa, P., Brannon, L. A., Shaw, K., & Hutson-Comeaux, S. (2000). Why counterattitudinal messages are as memorable as proattitudinal messages: The importance of active defense against attack. *Personality and Social Psychology Bulletin, 26,* 1392–1408.

Eagly, A. H., & Chaiken, S. (1993). *The psychology of attitudes.* Fort Worth, TX: Harcourt Brace Jovanovich.

Eckhardt, B. B., Wood, M. R., & Jacobvitz, R. S. (1991). Verbal ability and prior knowledge: Contributions to adults' comprehension of television. *Communication Research, 18,* 636–649.

Fazio, R. H. (1990). Multiple processes by which attitudes guide behavior: The MODE model as an integrative framework. In M. P. Zanna (Ed.), *Advances in experimental social psychology* (Vol. 23, pp. 75–109). San Diego, CA: Academic Press.

Fiedler, K., & Hertel, G. (1994). Content-related schemata versus verbal framing effects in deductive reasoning. *Social Cognition, 12,* 129–147.

Fine, B. J. (1957). Conclusion-drawing, communicator credibility, and anxiety as factors in opinion change. *Journal of Abnormal and Social Psychology, 5,* 369–374.

Fishbein, M., & Ajzen, I. (1975). *Belief, attitude, intention, and behavior: An introduction to theory and research.* Reading, MA: Addison-Wesley.

Fisher, J. D., & Fisher, W. A. (1992). Changing AIDS-risk behavior. *Psychological Bulletin, 11,* 455–474.

Fiske, S. T., Lau, R. R., & Smith, R. A. (1990). On the varieties and utilities of political expertise. *Social Cognition, 8,* 31–48.

Fiske, S. T., & Taylor, S. E. (1991). *Social Cognition* (2nd ed.). New York: McGraw Hill.

Fry, P. S. (1985). Relations between teenagers' age, knowledge, expectations, and maternal behavior. *British Journal of Developmental Psychology, 3,* 47–55.

Gorn, G. J. (1975). The effects of personal involvement, communication discrepancy, and source prestige on reactions to communications on separatism. *Canadian Journal of Behavioral Science, 7,* 369–386.

Granberg, D., & Holmberg, S. (1986). Political perception among voters in Sweden and the U.S.: Analyses of issues with specific alternatives. *Western Political Quarterly, 39,* 7–28.

Griggs, R. A. (1984). Memory cueing and instructional effects on Wason's selection task. *Current Psychological Research and Reviews, 3*(4), 3–10.

Hambrick, D. Z. (2003). Why are some people more knowledgeable than others? A longitudinal study of knowledge acquisition. *Memory and Cognition, 31,* 902–917.

Hedley, A. A., Ogden, C. L., Johnson, C. L., Carroll, M. D., Curtin, L. R., & Flegal, K. M. (2004). Overweight and obesity among US children, adolescents, and adults, 1999–2002. *Journal of the American Medical Association, 291,* 2847–2850.

Helweg-Larsen, M., & Collins, B. E. (1997). A social psychological perspective on the role of knowledge about AIDS in AIDS prevention. *Current Directions in Psychological Science, 6,* 23–26.

Hodson, G., Maio, G. R., & Esses, V. M. (2001). The role of attitudinal ambivalence in susceptibility to consensus information. *Basic and Applied Social Psychology*, *23*, 197–205.

Holbrook, A. L., Berent, M. K., Krosnick, J. A., Visser, P. S., & Bonninger, D. (2005). Attitude importance and the accumulation of attitude-relevant knowledge in memory. *Journal of Personality and Social Psychology*, *88*, 749–769.

Holland, R. W., Verplanken, B., Smeets, R., & van Knippenberg, A.(2001). *Attitude strength and value-expressive behavior.* Unpublished manuscript, University of Nijmegen, Nijmegen, the Netherlands.

Howard-Pitney, B., Borgida, E., & Omoto, A. M. (1986). Personal involvement: An examination of processing differences. *Social Cognition*, *4*, 39–57.

Johnson, B., T., & Eagly, A., H. (1989). Effects of involvement on persuasion: A meta-analysis. *Psychological Bulletin*, *106*, 290–314.

Kaplan, K. J. (1972). On the ambivalence–indifference problem in attitude theory and measurement: A suggested modification of the semantic differential technique. *Psychological Bulletin*, *77*, 361–372.

Katz, D. (1960). The functional approach to the study of attitudes. *Public Opinion Quarterly, 24,* 163–204.

Key, V. O. (1961). *Public Opinion and American Democracy.* New York: Knopf.

Klayman J., & Ha, Y-M. (1987). Confirmation, disconfirmation, and information in hypothesis testing. *Psychological Review*, *94,* 211–228.

Krosnick, J. A. (1988a). Attitude importance and attitude change. *Journal of Experimental Social Psychology*, *24*, 240–255.

Krosnick, J. A. (1988b). The role of attitude importance in social evaluations: A study of policy preferences, presidential candidate evaluations, and voting behavior. *Journal of Personality and Social Psychology*, *55*, 196–210.

Krosnick, J. A., & Petty, R. E. (1995). Attitude strength: An overview. In R. E. Petty & J. A. Krosnick (Eds.), *Attitude strength: Antecedents and consequences* (pp. 1–24). Mahwah, NJ: Erlbaum.

Krosnick, J. A., & Telhami, S. (1995). Public attitudes toward Israel: A study of the attentive and issue publics. *International Studies Quarterly*, *39*, 535–554.

Krosnick, J. A., Jarvis, B., Strathman, A., & Petty, R. E. (1994). *Relations among dimensions of attitude strength: Insights from induced variable models.* Unpublished manuscript, Ohio State University, Columbus.

Krosnick, J. A., Boninger, D. S., Chuang, Y. C., Berent, M. K., & Carnot, C. G. (1993). Attitude strength: One construct or many related constructs? *Journal of Personality and Social Psychology*, *65*, 1132–1151.

Krosnick, J. A., Chang, L., Sherman, S. J., Chassin, L., & Presson, C. (2006). The effects of beliefs about the health consequences of cigarette smoking on smoking onset. *Journal of Communication*, *56*, 518–537.

Lavine, H., Huff, J. W., Wagner, S. H., & Sweeney, D. (1998). The moderating influence of attitude strength on the susceptibility to context effects in attitude surveys. *Journal of Personality and Social Psychology*, *75*, 359–373.

Lavrakas, P. J. (1993). *Telephone survey methods: Sampling, selection, and supervision* (2nd ed.). Newbury Park, CA: Sage.

Lord, C. G., Ross, L., & Lepper, M. R. (1979). Biased assimilation and attitude polarization: The effects of prior theories on subsequently considered evidence. *Journal of Personality and Social Psychology*, *37*, 2098–2109.

Mann, J. M., Tarantola, D. J. M., & Netter, T. W. (1992). *AIDS in the world*. Cambridge, MA: Harvard University Press.

McGraw, K. M., & Pinney, N. (1990). The effects of general and domain-specific expertise on political memory and judgment. *Social Cognition, 8*, 9–30.

McGraw, K. M., Lodge, M., & Stroh, P. K. (1990). On-line processing in candidate evaluation: The effects of issue order, issue salience, and sophistication. *Political Behavior, 12*, 41–58.

Meinhold, J. L., & Malkus, A. J. (2005). Adolescent environmental behaviors: Can knowledge, attitudes, and self-efficacy make a difference? *Environment and Behavior, 37*, 511–532.

Miller, A. G., McHoskey, J. W., Bane, C. M., & Dowd, T. G. (1993). The attitude polarization phenomenon: Role of response measure, attitude extremity, and behavioral consequences of reported attitude change. *Journal of Personality and Social Psychology, 64*, 561–574.

Modigliani, A., & Gamson, W. A. (1979). Thinking about politics. *Political Behavior, 1*, 5–30.

Mokdad, A. H., Marks, J. S., Stroup, D. F., & Gerberding, J. L. (2004). Actual causes of death in the U. S., 2000. *Journal of the American Medical Association, 291*, 1238–1245.

Osgood, C. E., Suci, G. J., & Tannenbaum, P. H. (1957). *The measurement of meaning*. Urana, IL: University of Illinois Press.

Paull, G., & Glencross, D. (1997). Expert perception and decision making in baseball. *International Journal of Sport Psychology, 28*, 35–56.

Petty, R. E., & Cacioppo, J. T. (1986). *Communication and persuasion: Central and peripheral routes to attitude change*. New York: Springer-Verlag.

Petty, R. E., & Krosnick, J. A. (1995). *Attitude strength: Antecedents and consequences*. Mahwah, NJ: Erlbaum.

Pomerantz, E. M., Chaiken, S., & Tordesillas, R. S. (1995). Attitude strength and resistance processes. *Journal of Personality and Social Psychology, 69*, 408–419.

Prislin, R. (1996). Attitude stability and attitude strength: One is enough to make it stable. *European Journal of Social Psychology, 26*, 447–477

Ratneshwar, S., & Chaiken, S. (1991). Comprehension's role in persuasion: The case of its moderating effect on the persuasive impact of source cues. *Journal of Consumer Research, 18*, 52–62.

Recht, D. R., & Leslie, L. (1988). Effect of prior knowledge on good and poor readers' memory of text. *Journal of Educational Psychology, 80*, 16–20.

Rogers, T. F., Singer, E., & Imperio, J. (1993). AIDS—An update. *Public Opinion Quarterly, 57*, 92–114.

Rokeach, M. (1968). *Beliefs, Attitudes, and Values*. San Francisco, CA: Jossey-Bass.

Rosenberg, M. J. (1956). Cognitive structure and attitudinal affect. *Journal of Abnormal and Social Psychology, 53*, 367–372.

Salmon, C. T., & Nichols, J. S. (1983). The next-birthday method of respondent selection. *Public Opinion Quarterly, 47*, 270–276.

Schneider, W., Gruber, H., Gold, A., & Opwis, K. (1993). Chess expertise and memory for chess positions in children and adults. *Journal of Experimental Child Psychology, 56*, 328–349.

Schuman, H., & Presser, S. (1981). *Questions and answers: Experiments on question form, wording, and context in attitude surveys*. New York: Academic Press.

Sherif, M., & Hovland, C. I. (1961). *Social judgement: Assimilation and contrast effects in communication and attitude change*. New Haven, CT: Yale University Press.

Stouffer, S. A., Guttman, L., Suchman, E. A., Lazarsfeld, P. F., Star, S. A., & Clausen, J. A. (1950). *Measurement and prediction*. Princeton, NJ: Princeton University Press.

Theodorakis, Y. (1994). Planned behavior, attitude strength, role identity, and the prediction of exercise behavior. *The Sports Psychologist, 8,* 149–165.

Thomas, W. I., & Znaniecki, F. (1918). *The Polish peasant in Europe and America: Monograph of an immigrant group*. Boston, MA: Badger.

Thompson, M. T., & Zanna, M. P. (1995). The conflicted individual: Personality-based and domain-specific antecedents of ambivalent social attitudes. *Journal of Personality, 63,* 259–288.

U.S. Department of Health and Human Services. (1990). *Healthy people 2000: National health promotion and disease prevention objectives*. Washington, DC: Author.

Valentine, E. R. (1985). The effect of instructions on performance in the Wason selection task. *Current Psychological Research and Reviews, 4,* 214–223.

Verba, S., Schlozman, K. L., & Brady, H. (1995). *Voice and equality: Civic voluntarism in American politics*. Cambridge, MA: Harvard University Press.

Verplanken, B. (1989). Involvement and need for cognition as moderators of beliefs-attitude-intention consistency. *British Journal of Social Psychology, 28,* 115–122.

Verplanken, B. (1991). Persuasive communication of risk information: A test of cue versus message processing effects in a field experiment. *Personality and Social Psychology Bulletin, 17,* 188–193.

Visser, P. S. (1998). *Assessing the structure and function of attitude strength: Insights from a new approach*. Unpublished doctoral dissertation. The Ohio State University, Columbus.

Visser, P. S., & Krosnick, J. A. (1998). The development of attitude strength over the life cycle: Surge and decline. *Journal of Personality and Social Psychology, 75,* 1389–1410.

Visser, P. S., Bizer, G., & Krosnick, J. A. (2006). Exploring the latent structure of strength-related attitude attributes. In M. Zanna (Ed.), *Advances in experimental social psychology, 38,* (pp. 1–67). San Diego, CA: Academic Press.

Visser, P. S., Krosnick, J. A., & Simmons, J. P. (2003). Distinguishing the cognitive and behavioral consequences of attitude importance and certainty: A new approach to testing the common-factor hypothesis. *Journal of Experimental Social Psychology, 39,* 118–141.

Waksberg J. S. (1978). Sampling methods for random digit dialing. *Journal of the American Statistical Association, 73,* 40–46.

Wason, P. C. (1966). Reasoning. In B. M. Foss (Ed.), *New horizons in Psychology* (pp. 135–151). Harmondsworth, Middlesex, UK: Penguin Books.

Wason, P. C. (1968). Reasoning about a rule. *The Quarterly Journal of Experimental Psychology, 20,* 273–281.

Wason, P. C., & Johnson-Laird, P. N. (1972). *Psychology of Reasoning: Structure and Content*. Cambridge, MA: Harvard University Press.

Wilson, T. D., Kraft, D., & Dunn, D. S. (1989). The disruptive effects of explaining attitudes: The moderating effect of knowledge about the attitude object. *Journal of Personality and Social Psychology, 25,* 379–400.

Wilson, T. D., Dunn, D. S., Kraft, D., & Lisle, D. J. (1989). Introspection, attitude change, and attitude-behavior consistency: The disruptive effects of explaining why we feel the way we do. *Advances in Experimental Social Psychology, 22,* 287–343.

Wood, W. (1982). Retrieval of attitude-relevant information from memory: Effects on susceptibility to persuasion and on intrinsic motivation. *Journal of Personality & Social Psychology, 42*, 798–810.

Wood, W., & Kallgren, C. A. (1988). Communicator features and persuasion: Recipients' access to attitude-relevant information in memory. *Personality and Social Psychology Bulletin, 14*, 172–182.

Wood, W., Kallgren, C. A., & Preisler, R. M. (1985). Access to attitude-relevant information in memory as a determinant of persuasion: The role of message features. *Journal of Experimental Social Psychology, 21*, 73–85.

Wood, W., Rhodes, N., & Biek, M. (1995). Working knowledge and attitude strength: An information-processing analysis. In R. E. Petty & J. A. Krosnick (Eds.), *Attitude strength: Antecedents and consequences* (pp. 283–313). Mahwah, NJ: Lawrence Erlbaum Associates.

Yachanin, S. A. (1986). Facilitation in Wason's selection task: Content and instructions. *Current Psychological Research & Reviews, 5*, 20–29.

Yachanin, S. A., & Tweney, R. D. (1982). The effect of thematic content on cognitive strategies in the four-card selection task. *Bulletin of the Psychonomic Society, 19*, 87–90.

Zaichkowsky, J. L. (1985). Measuring the involvement construct. *Journal of Consumer Research, 12*, 341–352.

9

PRESIDENTIAL APPROVAL AND GAS PRICES

Sociotropic or Pocketbook Influence?[1]

Laurel Harbridge, Jon A. Krosnick, and Jeffrey M. Wooldridge

The democratic nature of American politics hinges on the relation between those who govern and those who are governed. This social contract, dating back to the writings of Hobbes and Locke (Locke, 1948; Hobbes, 2002), is the basis of our political system. And that social contract is founded on the notion that the legitimacy of government is based on the consent of the governed.

The American public's approval of their president's performance is an especially important component of system legitimacy. Beyond its normative importance, presidential approval is an important determinant of a president's power to govern. Public approval affects a president's ability to arouse popular support for his agenda and his ability to push members of Congress, in his own party and in the opposing party, to go along with his plans (Bond & Fleisher, 1990; Bond & Fleisher, 2000; Canes-Wrone, 2001; Neustadt, 1990). A president enjoying more popular support has greater potential to make legislative headway. Furthermore, approval ratings of a president predict the likelihood that the president or the president's party will win subsequent elections.

Given the importance of presidential approval as a normative democratic signal and as a determinant of a president's efficacy in policy making, understanding the determinants of presidential approval is critical. And this issue has been of great interest to political psychologists. During the last half-century, a number of factors have been heralded as important for understanding how individuals form opinions about presidential performance and how these judgments aggregate into approval figures for the nation. These factors include international affairs, rally events, honeymoon periods, economic conditions, and more.

The impact of economic conditions has been of special interest over the years and has been a matter of significant controversy in the scholarly literature.

Kramer's (1971) early work demonstrated that macro-economic indicators predicted election outcomes, and many scholars assumed that the mechanism was individuals' focus on their own pocketbooks. But direct tests of this assumption discredited it and demonstrated that individuals' evaluations of national political actors are affected instead by their perceptions of the nation's economy as a whole, dubbed "sociotropic" thinking (e.g., Alt & Lassen, 2013; Kinder & Kiewiet, 1979, 1981). Few Americans credit or blame the government for changes in their own personal economic circumstances. Therefore, most citizens do not evaluate the president based on the assumption that he has the potential to have notable impact on them, personally (Abramowitz et al., 1988). Instead, judgments about the national economy seem to shape political evaluations. Yet even here, voters were found to be very myopic, responding only to economic conditions over short periods of time rather than across a president's term in office (Achen & Bartels, 2004; Bartels, 2008).

Although there are many different (and sometimes divergent) indicators of the health of the nation's economy, past research on the relation between economic conditions and presidential approval has focused mostly on two statistics: the unemployment rate and the rate of price inflation. A citizen may learn about shifts in national unemployment or inflation rates from news coverage, and he/she may also make inferences about national rates based on his/her own personal employment experiences or experiences of people he/she knows who had a job, lost a job, or got hired (Sonderskov & Christiansen, 2013). National unemployment and inflation rates are routinely reported once a month, when new figures are released by federal statistical agencies. So unless a citizen is paying attention to the news that day, he/she may miss updates. This may explain why citizens do quite poorly at estimating the nation's unemployment rate (Ansolabehere et al., 2013; Conover et al., 1986; Holbrook & Garand, 1996).

But sometimes, e.g., when the unemployment rate broke the 10% mark in the early 1980s, media coverage of it was sustained, most likely calling it to the attention of many Americans. So the impact of macro-economic indications on presidential evaluations may increase with increased media attention to those statistics, in line with the priming hypothesis (Iyengar & Kinder, 1988). That is, when an economic indicator reaches especially bad levels, media coverage may spotlight the change and enhance its impact on presidential approval. Consistent with this notion of media influence, people's perceptions of the unemployment rate are significantly related to their media consumption patterns (Ansolabehere at al., 2012).

In contrast, most Americans can easily monitor retail gasoline prices because they are posted visibly at gas stations everywhere. And most Americans drive in cars (Chase, 2011), so they may see or pay those prices regularly.[2] Indeed, purchases of motor fuel account for 5% of all consumer expenditures (Anderson et al., 2013, p. 383). Not surprisingly, then, perceptions of gas prices are not significantly affected by an individual's media usage (Ansolabehere et al., 2012).

Although such prices vary across regions of the country, their increases and decreases are largely a function of producer prices, meaning that fluctuations over time impact most regions similarly ("Gasoline Prices by Formulation, Grade, Sales Type", 2014; "Petroleum Update: Gasoline and Diesel Fuel Update", 2014). Thus, Americans are likely to get fairly uniform signals about the dynamics of gasoline costs.

These dynamics are predictors of future economic conditions. For example, nearly all recessions in the modern history of the United States were preceded by sharp increases in the price of oil (Hamilton, 2011).[3] So Americans can readily infer that rising gas prices, though perhaps good for gasoline producers and retailers, are bad for individual and corporate consumers and signal relatively bad economic times ahead. And in fact, people seem to do just this. Specifically, people apparently use current gas prices to forecast future gas prices (Anderson et al., 2013) and to formulate perceptions of national economic conditions (Reeves & Gimpel, 2012).

Many observers have speculated that gasoline prices influence presidential approval (e.g. CNN, 2006; Walsh, 2011). And if people do use the price of gas to evaluate the president, they may do so in a sociotropic way (as indicators of the likely economic circumstances of the nation) or in a pocketbook way (as indicators of their own personal economic burdens). There is no requirement that such cognitive use of gas prices would be moderated by news media attention to gas prices, because people can and do observe those prices directly.

Consistent with this logic, rising gasoline prices coincided with dropping approval for George W. Bush over the course of his administration (see Figure 9.1). The same relation is apparent in the correlation between real (inflation adjusted) gas prices and presidential approval between 1977 and 2010: $-.52$ (Wood, 2011).[4] Furthermore, majorities of the public have said that a president can take steps to reduce gas prices in the short term (Gallup/USA Today, 2008; Times/SRBI, 2005),[5] and people who personally suffer from high gas prices the most are especially likely to disapprove of the president's performance (Mufson & Cohen, 2011). However, other observers have worried that the association between gas prices (and the economic burden they impose) with presidential approval may be spurious (e.g., Abramowitz, 2006).

To address this concern effectively, time series analysis is called for, controlling for the many known predictors of presidential approval and exploring the impact of gas prices. In this chapter, we report the results of just such analyses. Specifically, we describe tests of a multifaceted model of changes in presidential approval via a time series analysis of monthly data from January 1976 to July 2007. We gauged the extent to which gas prices influenced presidential approval directly and whether the impact of gas prices was moderated by the amount of media attention to those prices (as predicted by the priming hypothesis).

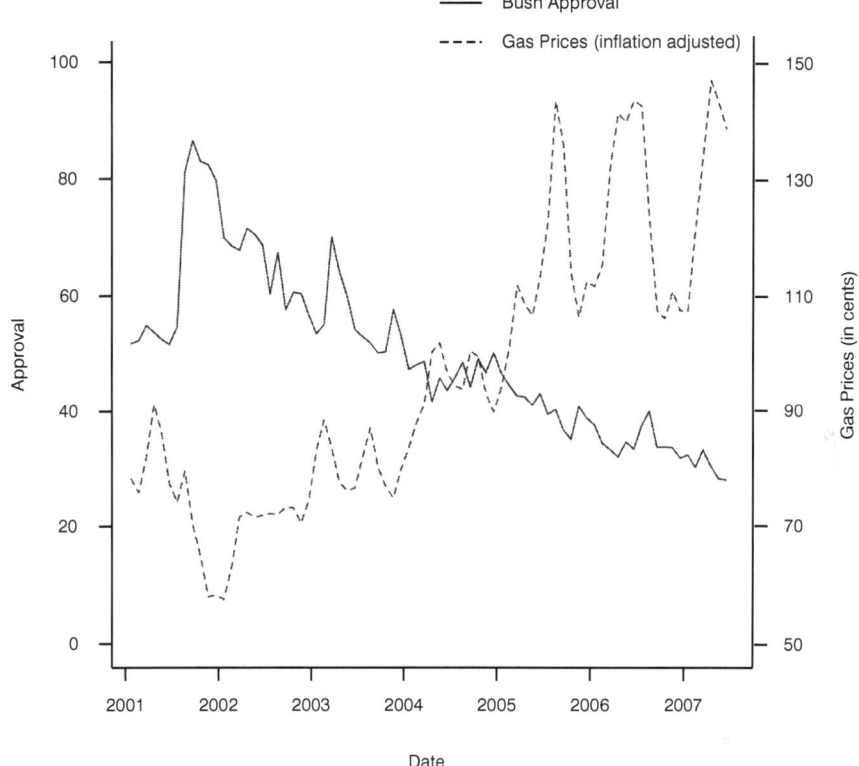

FIGURE 9.1 Trends of G. W. Bush Approval and Gas Prices (February 2001–July 2007)

We begin below by presenting a more detailed review of theories of presidential approval and the potential impact of various posited predictors of it. Then we describe the data sources and methodology we used. Section 4 reports our results, and the chapter concludes by discussing implications and possible extensions of this work.

A Review of Economic Voting

A rational individual can use many different pieces of information to assess presidential performance. One person might judge the president by his persuasiveness in public speaking and how the media portray him. Another person might use his or her assessment of bills that the president has shepherded through Congress. A third person might use perceptions of how other nations view the president. Or a person might use economic conditions, either his or her own economic position or the national economy.

Since the work of Mueller (1970) and Kramer (1971), a large body of work has indicated that presidential approval and congressional election results are influenced, in part, by a number of economic indicators, including inflation, real disposable income, and unemployment rates. There is less of a consensus, however, on whether voters use pocketbook or sociotropic factors as the basis for their political judgments. The key to answering this question may rest on who voters believe are responsible for changes in economic well-being.

The rational choice perspective of voting posits that individuals vote on the basis of a candidate's likely contribution to their utility (Downs, 1957). Although utility includes more than money, in practice, this self-interest has often meant that "pocketbook" issues are paramount. The pocketbook theory suggests that individuals base their political judgments on their own personal economic well-being, and how it has changed or is likely to change. These theories of self-interest seem plausible because of the ease of knowledge accumulation in this area. People know about their own financial situations in real time. Therefore, the information costs for pocketbook voting are small. In contrast, staying informed about the national economy seems to require a great deal of effort, perhaps more than most people are willing to devote to such a task.

Early literature on presidential approval and vote choice echoed this pocketbook theme (Kramer, 1971). Yet empirical tests focused mostly on aggregate measures of national economic conditions, despite the fact that the conceptual arguments were made at the individual level. The results obtained using aggregate measures, however, were compatible with a number of different individual-level models (Tufte, 1975). Scholars therefore began differentiating between personal economic conditions and national economic conditions.

The sociotropic model suggests that individuals make political judgments on the basis of national economic conditions rather than their own well-being. The difference between pocketbook and sociotropic evaluation can be thought of in terms of information used (Kinder & Kiewiet, 1981, p. 132). It may be largely a question of sophistication—"pocketbook politics requires little in the way of political expertise" (Kinder & Kiewiet, 1981, p. 130), whereas sociotropic voting requires slightly more political sophistication. Nonetheless, most scholars believe that even sociotropic voting only requires rough evaluations of the national economy, particularly since media coverage can easily supply this knowledge.

Those advocating the sociotropic perspective have suggested that problems with the early pocketbook literature included competing yet unrecognized predictions regarding unemployment vs. inflation and a reliance on cross-sectional analysis (Kinder & Kiewiet, 1981). Furthermore, also threatening to the pocketbook perspective is evidence that few people hold the president responsible for their own economic well-being, consistent with literature on American political culture and its emphasis on individualism and self-reliance (Abramowitz et al., 1988). Personal economic grievances are generally uncorrelated with collective economic judgments, and the former have little impact on congressional voting or evaluations of the president (Kinder & Kiewiet, 1979, 1981; Lau & Sears, 1981; Niemi et al., 1999).

The question of blame attribution has arisen in discussions of sociotropic models of presidential approval in other ways as well. For example, Lau and Sears (1981, p. 322) postulated that, "If the voter believes that rising inflation is due to factors beyond the president's control (energy shortages or OPEC)," then these sociotropic measures may not be related to presidential approval. And in fact, when voters do hold the president responsible for economic conditions, negative economic conditions translate into lower presidential approval (Peffley & Williams, 1985). Peffley and Williams (1985, p. 399) noted that responsibility includes three possibilities: "The president *caused* the conditions to occur; he is *morally or legally* responsible for them; or it is his *role* to correct them." Their empirical evidence offers support for each of these notions.

And some experimental evidence suggests that pocketbook voting may occur when an individual sees a direct connection between his or her economic circumstances and government policies (Sigelman et al., 1991). In general, however, the scholarly literature has come down on the side of sociotropic theories (Abramowitz et al., 1988; Kinder & Kiewiet, 1981, 1979; Lau & Sears, 1981; MacKuen et al., 1992). Interestingly, "Voters do not reward good economic performance as much as they punish mistaken policies" (Weatherford, 1986, p. 238). Thus, there may be an asymmetry in the operation of sociotropic thinking.

The connection between national economic conditions and presidential approval seems especially likely to be attributed to the news media. Given the limited knowledge that most Americans have about politics (Converse, 1964), media coverage of events seems especially likely to shape approval judgments. Brody (1991, p. 4) argued "that the American people form and revise their impressions of the quality of presidential performance on evidence contained in reports of politics and policy outcomes—political news—in the news media". Similarly, Shah et al. (1999) argued that campaign news coverage provides the cues necessary for voters to make "rough evaluations" of the national economy, which can then be used as the criteria for sociotropic voting. Weatherford summed up the role of the media as follows:

> The mass media provide the link between citizens and the world beyond the realm of personal experience, and as such, they are an indispensable source of information about economic conditions and government policies. Indeed, several of the most important studies of the influence of economic conditions on presidential popularity have been based on the assumption that the mass media provide the critical intermediate linkage in this multistage process.
>
> (Weatherford, 1986, p. 250)

It might seem that news media exposure is essential in order for sociotropic thinking to occur in a responsible way. That is, during most of the last 50 years, the only way that citizens could reliably learn about the state of the nation's unemployment or inflation rates (across all sectors of the economy) was through news stories. So in order for presidential evaluations to covary over time with those rates, as Kramer demonstrated, Americans seem most likely to have been learning about those rates from the media. Thus, real changes in economic conditions have had impact on presidential evaluations mediated by news coverage of those conditions.

However, this may be a misleadingly narrow portrayal of the sociotropic reasoning process, because of the literature's focus mostly on just two of the many indicators of national economic conditions: unemployment and inflation. Of course, people can learn about and think about the national economy in terms of other metrics as well, such as the performance of the stock market, the interest rates offered by banks on their checking accounts, and the prices people pay for retail goods such as gasoline. This is why our focus on gas prices has the potential to offer interesting insights into the psychology of presidential evaluations. Specifically, if gas prices drive presidential approval in part, that process need not involve the news media at all. People can and probably do learn about those prices directly at gas stations, so news coverage is not necessary.

But this is not to say that media coverage is necessarily irrelevant to the impact of gas prices on approval ratings. It is quite possible that this impact is moderated by news coverage. According to the news media priming hypothesis, extensive news coverage of gas prices (which may be spurred by unusually high prices) may cause Americans to choose to place more weight on those prices when evaluating the president. According to Miller and Krosnick (2000), this occurs because people perceive coverage of gas prices as a signal that news professionals believe that those prices are an important indicator for the nation. And citizens who trust the media follow the implication of that message by increasing the degree to which they use those prices to evaluate the president. Therefore, we might expect to see an interaction between gas prices and media attention to them, such that approval is depressed most by high prices when media attention is greatest. Thus, the role of the media would not be in affecting *perceptions* of gas prices but rather by increasing the weight that people choose to place on those prices when evaluating the president (see, e.g., Miller & Krosnick, 2000). We tested this hypothesis in various ways.

The presence or absence of this interaction can be viewed as signaling whether the impact of gas prices on presidential evaluations is pocketbook or sociotropic. If the impact of gas prices is the result of a pocketbook-focused evaluative process, then that would mean a citizen views those prices simply in terms of the economic burden they pose for him or her. The national importance of the issue is irrelevant to that reasoning process. Therefore, we should expect to see no interaction of gas prices with media attention. But if the impact of gas prices is sociotropic, then a signal (via news media attention) that the issue is important for the country should enhance the degree to which citizens evaluate the president on that basis. So we would expect to see the interaction.

Methodology

To assess if and how gas prices have affected presidential approval, we conducted a time series analysis using monthly data from January 1976 through July 2007. The dependent variable is monthly changes in presidential approval, measured by the percent of Americans answering "approve" to the questions, "Do you approve or disapprove of the way ___ is handling his job as president?" and variants of it.[6] Results were substantively similar when we used the percent approving of the president instead of the change in the percent approving.

To identify surveys that measured presidential approval, we searched the iPoll Databank maintained by the Roper Center for Public Opinion Research at the University of Connecticut (now housed at Cornell University). We searched their archive for all surveys done during the time period of interest with nationally representative probability samples of the American adult population. The number of polls in a single month ranged from 1 to 33. The smallest number of polls per month occurred during the Ford administration. The largest number of polls per month occurred in January 1998 during the Clinton administration. During the early years, only Gallup Organization surveys were available. But during the more recent years, data were collected by an array of survey firms in addition to Gallup. Tables 9.A1 and 9.A2 (in the appendix) list the survey firms whose data we analyzed. For each firm, we show their question wording, the date of the earliest poll of theirs that we used, the date of the latest poll of theirs that we used, and the number of polls that we used from the firm.

Three factors seem especially important to take into account when creating a monthly time series of presidential approval measurements in surveys: the temporal structure of approval (meaning the dependence of approval in one month on approval in the prior month), the number of respondents interviewed in each survey, and house effects. The more respondents who were interviewed in a survey, the more precise its measurements are, and the smaller should be associated standard errors. The notion of house effects refers to the fact that between-firm differences in results are thought to be attributable at least partly to so-called "house effects", presumably caused by differences between organizations in how they collect data.

A variety of statistical approaches for dealing with these issues have been used in the past. A Kalman filter, such as the samplemiser program (see Green et al., 1999), accounts for the dynamic structure of presidential approval over time (i.e., the temporal structure) and for variation in sample size from survey to survey. By accumulating information from many surveys, the goal of this approach is to distinguish random sampling error from real changes in public opinion (Green et al., 1999). In our case, this technique allows us to estimate a single approval number for each month. We identified each poll in our sample by the number of days between a president's inauguration and the last date when interviewing was done for the poll. By modeling the structure of opinion over time across these surveys, the Kalman filter provides an estimate of approval on the 15th of the month (i.e., the date we selected to represent average approval in that month). This method weights the polls by sample size and by the distance from the 15th of the month (incorporating time lags between polls), also taking into account the strong serial dependence in the monthly approval ratings. It also provides a standard error of each month's estimate of approval. However, this approach does not take into account house effects.

A second possible approach is to use Jackman's (2005) Bayesian estimation procedure for pooling across surveys and estimating house effects. Although this procedure is intended to take into account all three of the components we care about, in practice, we are unable to estimate house effects, because we lack a "true" measure of approval to which to compare, which is required by the method. In his analysis of surveys measuring two-party vote shares in the 2004 Australian federal election, Jackman used election results as the "true" measure of vote shares and based his calculations of house effects on this measure. Since no equivalent measure of presidential approval exists, Jackman's procedure is not suitable here.

A final possible estimation method is to use a hierarchical model to weight by sample size and include random effects to represent survey firms. There are two problems with this approach. First, it cannot easily account for serial dependence in presidential approval that is not accounted for by survey firm random effects. Second, in some months, there were almost as many or as many survey firms as there were polls, so there are limited observations with which to estimate parameters.

We therefore chose the Kalman filter method to estimate monthly presidential approval using the program developed by Green et al. (1999). The primary drawback of this approach is the lack of measurement of house effects. Including various polling houses in the analysis should not bias our estimates if the mix of houses remains constant over time. However, this is not the case, because the number of survey houses increased over time, and in the earlier years, most polls were done by the Gallup Organization. Although there is a negative correlation between gas prices during a month and the number of survey houses who measured approval during that month ($r = -.36$), including the number of survey houses per month as a predictor in the regression equations does not change the magnitude or significance of the gas prices variable. The resulting estimates of monthly approval and their standard error are presented in Figure 9.A1 (see the appendix).

To gauge gas prices, we used figures issued by the Energy Information Administration on U.S. city average retail price of unleaded regular gasoline, in cents. We adjusted these prices to correct for general inflation by dividing them by a consumer price index (the U.S. city average of all items other than food and energy), using 1982–1984 as the baseline (so that the average CPI across these three years is 100).

We also included a number of other predictors of presidential approval that have often appeared in the published literature. The first is the U.S. city average of food and beverages prices, thus capturing information about consumer prices for goods other than gasoline.[7] The second is the unemployment rate: the non-seasonally adjusted ratio of all persons over 16 years old who were unemployed and looking for a job divided by the number of persons over 16 years old who are in the labor force.[8]

Other predictors included dummy variables to identify times when presidential scandals occurred, when the Iran Hostage Crisis occurred, when the September 11th attacks occurred, when the first and second Gulf Wars occurred, and honeymoon periods just after a president was first elected. In addition, dummy variables identified each of the presidential administrations (with the Ford administration as the omitted comparison category). The presidential scandals included the Iran Contra Affair,[9] the White House Travel Office Firings (Travelgate),[10] Whitewater,[11] Filegate,[12] and the Valerie Plame Affair.[13] The September 11th dummy variable was coded "1" for September, October, and November 2001. The Iran Hostage Crisis dummy variable was coded 1 from November 1979 to January 1981. The Gulf War (*Desert Storm*) dummy variable was coded 1 from January and February 1991, and the Iraq War dummy variable was coded 1 from March to May 2003.[14] The honeymoon dummy variable was coded 1 for each of the first three months (February to April) of each new administration.

To measure the amount of media coverage of gas prices, we counted the number of articles (in 100s) in the New York Times and the Washington Post that included one or more of the following terms: gas(oline) price(s) and/or price(s) of gas(oline).[15]

Trends over time of the primary continuous variables are presented in Figure 9.A1 (see the appendix), along with the measure of presidential approval. As is apparent there, there is strong serial dependence in the presidential approval data. One issue of concern is whether the approval rate and gasoline prices have a so-called "unit root" in their time series representations, in which case spurious regression results becomes a concern. A second issue concerns how we should use the standard deviations generated from the Kalman filter in weighting the regression error. Finally, we must decide on the best way to account for dynamics, particularly for obtaining proper standard deviation of the regression coefficients to use for inference and confidence intervals.

The standard deviations obtained from the Kalman filter provide a measure of how much confidence we should have in each monthly approval rate. Therefore, we weighted the squared residuals in our regressions by using the reciprocal of the variance of the approval rate. This weighting appears to help correct the errors for heteroskedasticity. But when we computed standard errors, we did not assume that the weights entirely removed heteroskedasticity, for a couple of reasons. First, the standard deviations generated by the Kalman filter are for the approval rates themselves, not the errors in the regression. Second, the error variance may be related to many of the other explanatory variables, such as the prices of food and beverages, the unemployment rate, or various events for which we controlled. We found that using the weights improved the precision of the regression estimates, which provides justification for using weighted least squares (WLS) as long as our standard errors are adjusted to allow for a mis-specified variance function (see Wooldridge, 2013, Section 8.4, for further discussion about computing robust standard errors for OLS and WLS).

A second reason for preferring WLS to OLS is that scaling the approval rate and gas prices by the approval standard deviation produces time series processes that do not appear to have unit roots. Therefore, we can be more confident that our weighted least squares estimates are not subject to spurious regression problems.

To test for unit roots, we used the version of the Dickey-Fuller statistic (Phillips & Perron, 1988) that allows for general forms of serial correlation. Although we report results allowing for correlation in the errors up to 12 months apart, the findings are similar when we allow for up to 24 and 26 months of serial autocorrelation. For the weighted version of the approval rate, the estimated autocorrelation coefficient is .790, and the Phillips-Perron statistic is –7.04, which is well below the 1% critical value, –3.43 (Wooldridge, 2013, p. 640). For the inflation adjusted gas price, the estimated root is .862, and the unit root t-statistic is –4.61, another strong rejection of the unit root null.

Lastly, we must make a choice about how to account for the time series dependence in the approval rate when estimating the model predicting approval rates. The Phillips and Perron (1988) test shows that a unit root can be strongly rejected but that the weighted approval rates still manifest a fairly strong, positive serial correlation, as we would expect. One analytic option would be to use a purely static model, so that any relations of the approval rate with gas prices and other predictors is contemporaneous. Such an approach is justified when we rule out unit roots in the key variables or, if the variables do have unit roots, they satisfy a cointegrating relationship. We prefer a model that includes the lagged approval rate, which we call the "dynamic model," for a couple of reasons. First, including a single lag appears to clean up the substantial serial correlation in the static equation. Second, inference in a dynamic model is more robust than in a static model, in the sense that the inference is the same if the series are mean reverting or have a unit root and are cointegrated. With static regression, the way one performs inferences changes depending on which characterization holds (see Wooldridge, 1994).

In estimating the dynamic model, the change in the approval rating from one month to the next was the dependent variable, and the lagged approval rating was a predictor.[16] The other predictors were measured contemporaneously.[17] Because the prior month's approval rating is a predictor, we dropped the first observation of each presidency. Doing so prevents using the last month of one president's term to predict approval during the first month of the next president's term.

To check the robustness of the results, we estimated the parameters of equations in which the prices were subjected to a logarithmic transformation, and the obtained results are similar to those reported in the text (see Table 9.A3 in the appendix).

We also estimated static models in which the level of the approval was the dependent variable, and the lagged approval rate was not a predictor. This yielded much larger effects, because we did not hold the previous month's approval rating fixed when estimating the effects of gas prices and other variables.[18] For the technical reasons explained above, we have more confidence in the inference from the dynamic models.

Results

When predicting change in presidential approval from month to month using contemporaneous values of the economic measures (gas prices, unemployment, and food and beverage prices), the lagged effect of approval has the expected negative sign, suggesting regression to the mean, which is consistent with other literature on presidential approval over the course of an administration (see row 1 in column 1 of Table 9.1).[19] Also as expected, the unemployment rate, food and beverage prices, and presidential scandals all have significant negative effects on approval, and the Iran Hostage Crisis, the Gulf War and the Iraq War, and September 11th all had positive effects. Surprisingly, the honeymoon period is not marked by a significant increase in approval.

Gas prices had a significant and negative effect on change in approval (see row 4 in column 1 of Table 9.1). A 10 cent increase in gas prices led to a .60 percentage point drop in approval. When using the logarithm of gas prices instead, a 10 percent increase in real gas prices lowered approval by about .72 percentage points (see Table 9.A3 in the appendix).

As expected, gas prices and media coverage are positively correlated ($r = .43$, $p < 0.001$), so when gas prices increased, so did media coverage of gas prices. But according to the regressions, volume of news coverage of gas prices was not itself a significant predictor of approval when controlling for gas prices (see row 16 in column 1 of Table 9.1). This disconfirms the claim that the simple association of

TABLE 9.1   Weighted Least Squares Regression Parameter Estimates Predicting Change in Presidential Approval (1976–2007)

Predictor	Model 1	Model 2	Model 3	Model 4
Lagged approval	−0.23★★★	−0.23★★★	−0.23★★★	−0.22★★★
	(0.035)	(0.035)	(0.035)	(0.036)
Prices of food and beverages	−0.14★★★	−0.14★★★	−0.13★★★	−0.12★★★
	(0.046)	(0.046)	(0.045)	(0.046)
Unemployment rate	−1.37★★★	−1.38★★★	−1.37★★★	−1.34★★★
	(0.41)	(0.41)	(0.41)	(0.41)
Gas price	−0.060★★★	−0.057★★★	−0.055★★★	−0.055★★★
	(0.016)	(0.018)	(0.016)	(0.016)
Presidential scandal	−3.97★★★	−3.96★★★	−3.95★★★	−3.90★★★
	(1.34)	(1.34)	(1.32)	(1.32)
Honeymoon period	1.95	1.99	2.05	2.02
	(2.84)	(2.87)	(2.85)	(2.82)
Gulf War	12.7★★★	12.5★★★	13.2★★★	13.3★★★
	(2.16)	(2.14)	(2.09)	(1.93)
Iraq War	6.04	5.92	6.13	6.16
	(4.46)	(4.46)	(4.51)	(4.57)
9/11	13.0★★	12.9★★	12.9★★	12.8★★
	(6.41)	(6.42)	(6.40)	(6.50)
Iran hostage crisis	3.84★★	4.01★★	3.80★★	3.74★★
	(1.69)	(1.67)	(1.71)	(1.69)
Clinton Administration	9.83★★	10.2★★★	8.57★★	8.30★★
	(3.81)	(3.85)	(3.72)	(3.75)
Carter Administration	−1.49	−1.39	−1.47	−1.52
	(1.12)	(1.14)	(1.14)	(1.13)
Reagan Administration	8.48★★★	8.52★★★	8.01★★★	7.85★★★
	(2.20)	(2.21)	(2.20)	(2.23)
H. W. Bush Administration	8.84★★★	9.07★★★	8.06★★	7.81★★
	(3.26)	(3.30)	(3.19)	(3.23)

Predictor	Model 1	Model 2	Model 3	Model 4
G. W. Bush Administration	13.8★★★	14.2★★★	12.3★★	11.9★★
	(5.21)	(5.24)	(5.12)	(5.17)
Number of news stories (in 100s)	0.53	1.73		
	(0.48)	(1.67)		
Media × Gas price		−0.012		
		(0.017)		
Change in number of news stories (in 100s)			0.29	2.35
			(0.69)	(2.28)
Change in number of news stories × Gas price				−0.020
				(0.024)
Constant	36.3★★★	34.9★★★	35.0★★★	34.5★★★
	(6.88)	(7.25)	(6.85)	(6.97)
N	373	373	373	373
R^2	0.261	0.262	0.258	0.260

Note: Robust standard errors are in parentheses. The dependent variable is the change in presidential approval from the prior month. For Model 2, the count of media stories is centered about its mean in the interaction term so that the gas price coefficient is comparable across models.
★★★ $p<0.01$, ★★ $p<0.05$, ★ $p<0.1$

gas prices with presidential approval is mediated by media coverage of those prices, which causes changes in approval, rather than the prices themselves being the cause. The same conclusion is reached when examining change in media coverage of gas prices from month to month (see row 18 in column 3 of Table 9.1).

More importantly, media coverage volume did not interact significantly with gas prices in predicting approval (see row 17 in column 2 of Table 9.1). The same conclusion is supported when using change in media coverage of gas prices rather than using the number of news stories about gas prices (see row 19 in column 4 of Table 9.1). This suggests that the impact of gas prices on presidential approval does not depend on volume of media coverage of the topic. Moreover, the impact of gas prices on changes in approval does not substantially decline in magnitude when these interaction terms are added to the equation.

To gauge the robustness of this conclusion, we used several alternate measures of media coverage: (1) a count of the number of articles and that number squared, to permit a quadratic relation; (2) a dummy variable coded 1 when the number of stories was greater than the 75th percentile of monthly media stories and 0 otherwise, to permit a step function; and (3) a dummy variable coded 1 when the number of stories was greater than the 25th percentile of monthly media stories and 0 otherwise, permitting a different step function. None of the interactions of gas prices with these representations of media attention were statistically significant (see Table 9.2).

TABLE 9.2 Change in Approval (1976–2007), WLS, Additional Media Specifications

Predictor	Model 1	Model 2	Model 3	Model 4	Model 5	Model 6
Lagged approval	-0.23*** (0.035)	-0.23*** (0.035)	-0.23*** (0.035)	-0.23*** (0.035)	-0.23*** (0.035)	-0.23*** (0.036)
Prices of food and beverages	-0.14*** (0.047)	-0.14*** (0.046)	-0.13*** (0.045)	-0.13*** (0.045)	-0.14*** (0.046)	-0.13*** (0.046)
Unemployment rate	-1.38*** (0.42)	-1.37*** (0.41)	-1.38*** (0.41)	-1.38*** (0.41)	-1.37*** (0.41)	-1.39*** (0.42)
Gas price	-0.060*** (0.017)	-0.056*** (0.018)	-0.056*** (0.016)	-0.054*** (0.018)	-0.058*** (0.016)	-0.090** (0.038)
Presidential scandal	-3.97*** (1.34)	-3.94*** (1.34)	-3.96*** (1.32)	-3.94*** (1.31)	-3.99*** (1.36)	-3.92*** (1.36)
Honeymoon period	1.93 (2.85)	1.97 (2.83)	1.98 (2.79)	2.07 (2.72)	1.91 (2.88)	1.91 (2.85)
Gulf War	12.7*** (2.21)	12.6*** (2.19)	13.0*** (2.32)	12.8*** (2.38)	13.0*** (2.22)	13.1*** (2.22)
Iraq War	6.02 (4.47)	5.98 (4.49)	6.10 (4.49)	6.06 (4.53)	5.86 (4.47)	6.04 (4.47)
9/11	13.0** (6.42)	13.0** (6.41)	13.0** (6.37)	13.0** (6.37)	12.6** (6.37)	12.9** (6.36)
Iran Hostage Crisis	3.83** (1.69)	3.73** (1.79)	3.74** (1.72)	3.90** (1.82)	3.88** (1.69)	3.64** (1.69)

	(1)	(2)	(3)	(4)	(5)	(6)
Clinton Administration	9.94**	9.75**	8.92**	9.01**	9.70**	9.03**
	(3.91)	(3.91)	(3.74)	(3.78)	(3.90)	(3.87)
Carter Administration	-1.48	-1.48	-1.52	-1.49	-1.25	-1.27
	(1.12)	(1.17)	(1.14)	(1.16)	(1.16)	(1.16)
Reagan Administration	8.53***	8.35***	8.17***	8.17***	8.50***	8.36***
	(2.24)	(2.22)	(2.17)	(2.17)	(2.28)	(2.26)
H. W. Bush Administration	8.94***	8.75***	8.33***	8.38**	8.89***	8.50**
	(3.34)	(3.37)	(3.21)	(3.25)	(3.34)	(3.31)
G. W. Bush Administration	14.0***	13.7**	12.7**	12.8**	13.7**	13.0**
	(5.35)	(5.30)	(5.12)	(5.15)	(5.34)	(5.30)
Number of news stories	0.60	0.74				
	(0.81)	(3.17)				
Number of news stories × Gas prices		-0.0012				
		(0.035)				
Number of news stories squared	-0.043	0.61				
	(0.36)	(1.29)				
Number of news stories squared × Gas prices		-0.0064				
		(0.014)				
Number of news stories (>75th %)			0.23	0.95		
			(0.73)	(2.73)		
Number of news stories (>75th %) × Gas prices				-0.0067		
				(0.026)		

continued…

Table 9.2 continued…

Predictor	Model 1	Model 2	Model 3	Model 4	Model 5	Model 6
Number of news stories (>25th %)					0.68	-2.28
					(0.63)	(2.97)
Number of news stories (>25th %) × Gas prices						0.034
						(0.036)
Constant	37.0***	36.4***	35.6***	35.4***	35.5***	36.3***
	(7.08)	(7.01)	(6.79)	(6.80)	(6.92)	(6.90)
N	373	373	373	373	373	373
R^2	0.261	0.263	0.257	0.258	0.260	0.263

Note: Robust standard errors are in parentheses. The dependent variable is the change in presidential approval from the prior month. For models with interactions, the count of media stories is centered about its mean in the interaction term so that the gas price coefficient is comparable across models.
*** $p<0.01$, ** $p<0.05$, * $p<0.1$

Discussion

Analysis of changes in monthly presidential approval from 1976 to 2007 suggests that gas prices did exert an independent effect on presidential approval above and beyond traditional economic measures. As expected, an increase in gas prices led to a decline in approval. Because this effect is independent of the volume of news media coverage of gas prices, the effect seems to be a reflection of pocketbook thinking rather than sociotropic thinking. That is, gas prices did not have more powerful effects on approval when news media professionals signaled to the public that gas prices were an important challenge for the nation as a whole. Not only are public perceptions of gas prices uninfluenced by media coverage of them (Ansolabehere et al., 2012; Reeves & Gimpel, 2012), but the effect of gas prices on presidential approval is similarly independent of media coverage.

Consistent with the economic voting literature, contemporaneous values of unemployment and the prices of food and beverages had significant and negative impact on approval. Also, as expected, presidential scandals had negative effects on presidential approval. And as predicted, international rally events had significant and positive impacts on presidential approval. The Iran Hostage Crisis, the Gulf War, and the post-9/11 period all boosted presidential approval. The effects of the Gulf War and 9/11 events were much larger than that of the Iran Hostage Crisis, perhaps because of the apparent incompetence suggested by the Carter administration's failed attempt to rescue the hostages. These demonstrations are useful additions to the literature, because we have used a larger set of years than most other past investigations and employed different analytic methods, so the robustness of the observed effects is not surprising but is nonetheless reassuring, especially in the current period of concern about the replicability of scientific findings (see Makel et al., 2012; *Nature*, 2013).

Interestingly, the Clinton, Reagan, H. W. Bush, and G. W. Bush administrations all enjoyed higher levels of approval than did the Ford and Carter administrations, even when controlling for all other predictors. It would be interesting to investigate the explanations for this in future research. It is tempting to attribute Ford's lower approval ratings to the fact that he was not elected and took the reins from Richard Nixon. And it is tempting to attribute Carter's low levels of approval to the oil crisis that struck during his administration. But such post-hoc guesses are just that: guesses; so direct testing is merited.

Surprisingly, the honeymoon periods at the start of each administration did not evidence the expected statistically significant increase in approval ratings controlling for all other predictors. The weakness of the honeymoon effect may be due to the time period we analyze and the particular presidents in our series. Perhaps the 2000 post-election court case and contentious battle for the presidency meant that George W. Bush did not enjoy a honeymoon period, and this suppressed the test of that effect combined across presidencies.

Although our results are convincing with regard to the role of gas prices, there are a number of limitations with the data we used. For example, this analysis is done at the aggregate level, tracking the impact of gas prices and other real economic indicators on the nation's aggregate approval ratings. That is, we sought to predict changes over time in approval levels. Yet our interest here is in the impact of perceptions of gas prices on approval or disapproval by each individual citizen. Therefore, it would be interesting to supplement the current investigation with individual-level data analysis to explore the same hypotheses.

It would also be interesting for future work to explore whether the effects of gas prices are symmetric across increases and decreases. Macroeconomic research suggests that positive oil price shocks have impacts on the economy, but negative ones do not (Hamilton, 2011). Likewise, political science research suggests that the effect of the economy on public evaluations is larger when conditions deteriorate rather than when conditions are consistently bad over time (Ebeid & Rodden, 2006). Both findings suggest hypotheses worth testing with regard to gas prices in particular.

Nonetheless, the research reported here suggests that the public does use gas prices when evaluating the president and that the president might benefit by making efforts to reduce such gas prices, particularly before elections. This highlights a mutually beneficial alignment of political incentives for candidates with the public interest of citizens. However, although the public believes that the president can take actions to reduce gas prices (Gallup/USA Today, 2008; Times/SRBI, 2005), the actual ability of the president to influence gas prices may be minimal. For example, such prices usually move in response to events that occur abroad, well beyond a president's control. Therefore, it may be unfair for the public to use gas prices as a standard for judging presidents. Nonetheless, the linkage we observed between gas prices and approval certainly gives presidents an incentive to do whatever they can to reduce those prices.

Finally, our findings are especially provocative because of their implications regarding the sociotropic vs. pocketbook distinction and regarding news media priming. We proposed that if gas prices affect presidential approval via a sociotropic reasoning process, then their impact should be moderated by media attention to gas prices. But this hypothesis was disconfirmed over and over here. One implication of that result may be that gas prices influence presidential evaluations via a pocketbook reasoning process: people know what price they pay for gas and hold the president at least partly responsible for their gains or losses in this arena. Therefore, news media conferral of important on gas prices is not needed or consequential cognitively.

Interestingly, one might also view this finding as a failure to detect an instance of news media priming. That is, the priming hypothesis has been phrased generally, asserting that more media attention to any issue will increase its impact on presidential evaluations (e.g., Iyengar & Kinder, 1988). In their articulation of the theory, Iyengar and Kinder (1988) proposed that priming an issue will have no impact on presidential evaluations if the public does not hold the president responsible for performance in that domain. So one might be tempted to infer that our failure to find evidence of priming might be attributable to the public not holding the president responsible for gas prices. But if that were true, why would gas prices influence presidential evaluations at all? No answer seems readily obvious, so we are inclined to infer that the public does indeed hold the president at least partly responsible in this arena but does not require guidance from the news media about the national importance of gas prices when forming presidential evaluations. That is, when the public has ready access to prices that, in and of themselves, readily communicate the state of an economic indicator across the nation and are personally impactful, news media guidance is not needed. Thus, we may have identified another limiting condition of news media priming.

Finally, the absence of an interaction of gas prices with news coverage of them may reinforce the conclusion that media priming is not due to a mere increase in the cognitive accessibility of an issue that media coverage causes (e.g., Miller & Krosnick, 2000). Miller and Krosnick (2000) were the first investigators to explicitly test the presumption that news media coverage of an issue increases that issue's impact on presidential evaluations by increasing the accessibility of related knowledge in memory. Just as psychologists would expect, media coverage of an issue does indeed increase that accessibility immediately after exposure to news stories. But the increase in accessibility is not responsible for the increased impact of the issue sometime later, after time has passed and the accessibility fades. Instead, Miller and Krosnick (2000) showed, the mediator at work is judgments of the national importance of the issue—more news coverage leads to perceptions of greater national importance, which in turn increase the impact of an issue on presidential evaluations. If accessibility was in fact the mediator of news media priming, then our analysis should have produced evidence of moderation of the effect of gas prices on approval judgments. The absence of this moderation is therefore consistent with Miller and Krosnick's (2000) conclusion.

Appendix

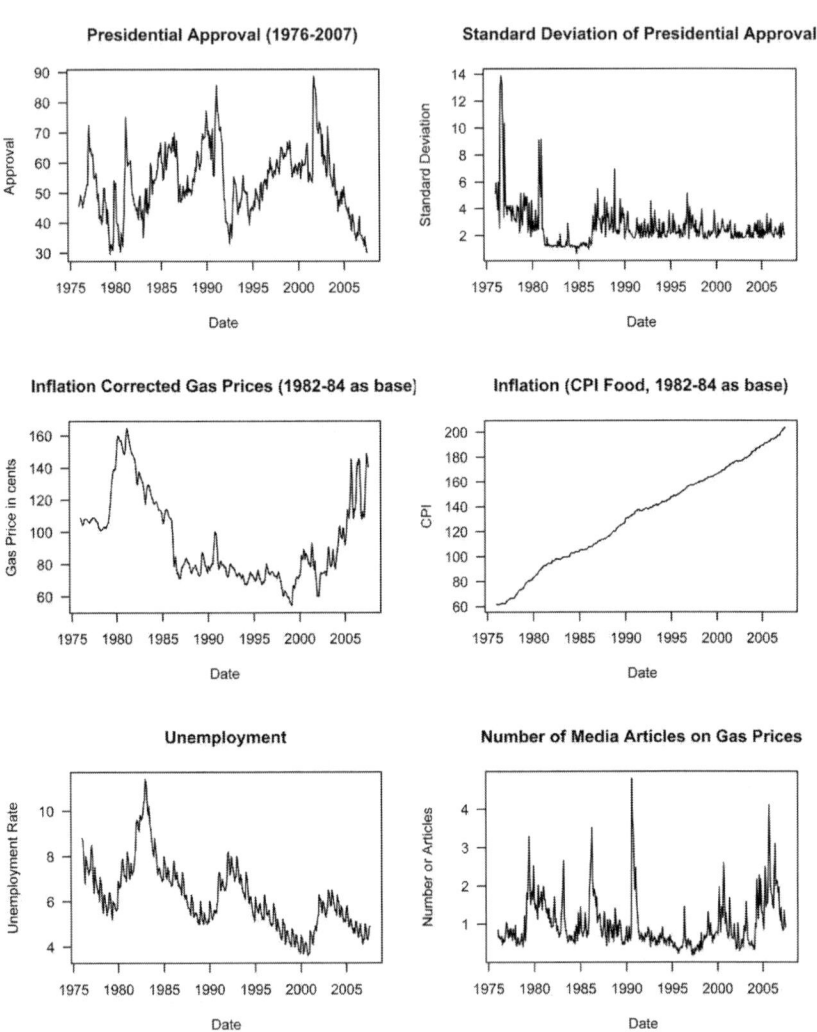

FIGURE 9.A1 Trends of Key Variables (Source: Calculated by the authors)

TABLE 9.A1 Presidential Approval Poll Summary

Survey House	Question Wording	Entry Date	Exit Date	Number of Polls
ABC News (also ABC News/ Washington Post beginning in 1981 and just Washington Post from Jan 1978)	Do you approve or disapprove of the way ____ is handling his job as President? (Occasionally—Do you approve or disapprove of the way ____ is handling his job as President? Is that approve/ disapprove strongly or somewhat?)	Jan 78	Jul 07	369
American Research Group	Do you approve or disapprove of the way ____ is handling his job as president?	Sep 01	Jul 07	70
CBS News (also CBS News/ New York Times)	Do you approve or disapprove of the way ____ is handling his job as President?	Apr 77	Jul 07	501
CNN: Opinion Research Corporation	Do you approve or disapprove of the way ____ is handling his job as president?	Apr 06	Jun 07	22
Gallup	Do you approve or disapprove of the way ____ is handling his job as President?	Jan 76	Jul 07	1022
Harris/Harris Interactive	In general, do you approve or disapprove of the way President (first name) ____ is handling his job as President?	May 01	Aug 06	30
IPSOS—Reid, Cook Poll	Overall, do you approve, disapprove or have mixed feelings about the way George W. Bush is handling his job as President?	Dec 01	Jul 07	171
Los Angeles Times	Do you approve or disapprove of the way ____ is handling his job as President? (If approve or disapprove) Is that (approve/ disapprove) strongly or (approve/disapprove) somewhat?	Apr 81	Jun 07	118
Market Strategies	Do you approve or disapprove of the way ____ is handling his job as President? (If approve/disapprove, ask: Would that be strongly (approve/disapprove) or just somewhat (approve/disapprove)?	Feb 90	Feb 99	11

continued…

Table 9.A1 continued…

Survey House	Question Wording	Entry Date	Exit Date	Number of Polls
NBC News (also NBC News/ *Wall Street Journal*)—Survey Organization is Hart and Teeter Research Associates	In general, do you approve or disapprove of the job _____ is doing as president?	Jun 88	Jun 07	180
Princeton Survey research Association	Do you approve or disapprove of the way _____ is handling his job as President?	Jan 91	Jul 07	365
Roper Organization	Do you approve or disapprove of the way _____ is handling his job as President?	Nov 81	Dec 87	10
Schulman, Ronca, & Bucuvalas	In general, do you approve or disapprove of the way President _____ is handling his job as President?	Jul 04	Apr 07	33
T.I.PP.—Technometrica Institute of Policy and Polling	In general, do you approve or disapprove of the way _____ is handling his job as president, or are you not familiar enough to say one way or the other?	Feb 01	Sep 04	38
Wirthlin Group	Do you approve or disapprove of the way _____ is handling his job as President?	Jun 91	Sep 01	41
Yankelovich Clancy Shulman	In general, do you approve or disapprove of the way _____ is handling his job as President?	May 82	Feb 01	163

TABLE 9.A2   Miscellaneous Polls Used in Calculating Average Approval

Survey house	Number of polls
America's Place In The World Survey	1
Campaign '92	1
Civic Services	1
Early January Political Communications Poll	1
Foreign Policy And Party Images Poll	2
Gordon S. Black Corporation	6
Greenberg Quilan	1
Health Pulse Of America	2
K.R.C. Research	1
Marttila and Kiley	3
Media Studies Center, Roper Center Unanchored Voter Poll	1
Media Survey	1
Mental Health Survey	1
Merit Report	1
National Earth Day Environment Poll	1
National Survey For R.N.C., N.R.C.C.	1
New Democratic Electorate Survey	1
Opinion Research Corporation	2
Peter D. Hart Research Associates	1
Pew	2
Quinnipiac University	5
New Models National Brand Poll	4
Scripps Howard News Service, Ohio University Poll	1
Social Trust And Volunteerism Survey	1

TABLE 9.A3 Change in Approval (1976–2007), WLS, Logged Prices of Food and Beverages and Gas Prices

Predictor	Model 1	Model 2
Lagged approval	–0.24★★★	–0.24★★★
	(0.037)	(0.037)
Log of the price of food and beverages	–19.0★★★	–19.2★★★
	(6.54)	(6.51)
Unemployment rate	–1.41★★★	–1.40★★★
	(0.42)	(0.42)
Log of gas price	–7.18★★★	–6.99★★★
	(1.76)	(1.84)
Presidential scandal	–3.79★★★	–3.79★★★
	(1.36)	(1.35)
Presidential honeymoon	1.79	1.83
	(2.73)	(2.77)
Gulf War	12.9★★★	12.7★★★
	(2.20)	(2.19)
Iraq War	6.39	6.25
	(4.46)	(4.46)
9/11	13.2★★	13.1★★
	(6.50)	(6.52)
Iran Hostage Crisis	4.86★★	5.06★★★
	(1.91)	(1.90)
Clinton Administration	13.1★★	13.5★★
	(5.32)	(5.27)
Carter Administration	–0.048	0.083
	(1.27)	(1.28)
Reagan Administration	12.2★★★	12.3★★★
	(3.55)	(3.55)
H. W. Bush Administration	12.8★★★	13.1★★★
	(4.79)	(4.77)
G. W. Bush Administration	16.7★★	17.1★★★
	(6.60)	(6.55)
Number of news stories (in 100s)	0.56	6.69
	(0.48)	(8.05)
Number of news stories × Gas price		–1.33
		(1.78)

Predictor	Model 1	Model 2
Constant	134.0★★★	127.0★★★
	(33.4)	(36.0)
N	373	373
R^2	0.257	0.259

Note: Robust standard errors are in parentheses. The dependent variable is the change in presidential approval from the prior month. For Model 2, the count of media stories is centered about its mean in the interaction term so that the gas price coefficient is comparable across models.

★★★ $p<0.01$, ★★ $p<0.05$, ★ $p<0.1$

Notes

1   The authors wish to thank Allison Denker for her work in starting this project and gathering the first round of data, Daniel Blocksom and the Political Psychology Research Group for gathering and proofing the data, and Richard Carson for pointing us toward economics research in this area. Jon Krosnick is University Fellow at Resources for the Future.

2   The number of times per week that people drive cars and the number of times they notice gas prices are positively correlated with the accuracy of their perception of gas prices (Ansolabehere et al., 2012).

3   The causal relation between the oil shocks and recessions, however, is less clear, as is the degree to which this relation is linear (Hamilton, 2011; Kilian, 2009).

4   However, when gas prices are low (i.e. less than US$2/gallon), this correlation is essentially zero.

5   The Gallup/USA Today poll (2008) asked, "Do you think there are—or are not—steps a president can take that would reduce gas prices significantly in the short term?" 68 percent of respondents answered affirmatively. The Time/SRBI poll (2005) asked, "How much do you think a President can do to keep gas prices down?" 39 percent of respondents said "a great deal," and another 36 percent of respondents said "some."

6   Some survey organizations asked the question, "Do you approve or disapprove of the way _____ is handling his job as President? (If approve or disapprove) Is that (approve/disapprove) strongly or (approve/disapprove) somewhat?" For these polls, we summed the responses for approve strongly and approve somewhat to get overall approval.

7   The correlation between inflation adjusted gas prices and food and beverage inflation is –0.41.

8   All measures of inflation and unemployment were collected from the Bureau of Labor Statistics website.

9   The Iran-Contra Affair dummy was coded as 1 from November 1986, when the scandal broke, until March 1987, when President Reagan apologized in a nationally televised press conference.

10   The Travelgate dummy was coded 1 for May 1993.

11   The Whitewater dummy was coded 1 from April 1994 until August 1994.

12   The Filegate dummy was coded 1 for June 1996.

13   The Valerie Plame Affair dummy was coded 1 from July 2003 to September 2003, when Novak asserted that no one in the Bush administration leaked the information.

14 Although the Iraq War continued in some forms for a more prolonged period, we coded the variable 1 when President Bush made his "Mission Accomplished" speech in May 2003.

15 Although we focus on the New York Times and Washington Post, we also ran the analysis with just the New York Times, since previous research suggests that that publication is a reasonable proxy for gauging changes over time in attention to issues in a variety of American news media outlets (Baumgartner & Jones, 1993; Terkildsen et al., 1998). The results were similar to those reported in the text. The media counts were obtained using Lexis Nexis.

16 Change in approval is measured as presidential approval$_t$ – presidential approval$_{t-1}$ where t indexes months.

17 Using change in approval as the dependent variable with a lagged approval rate as a predictor yields the same results as using the level of approval as the dependent variable with lagged approval as a predictor: the coefficient on the lagged approval changes, but the coefficients on the other explanatory variables are identical.

18 For instance, the effect of gas prices on the level of presidential approval is –.22 (p < 0.001).

19 Formal tests for unit root imply statistically significant mean reversion.

References

Abramowitz, Alan I. 2006. "Are Falling Gas Prices Boosting Bush?" Emory University. [accessed July 31, 2014]. Available at: http://www.emory.edu/news/Releases/GasPrices1159534460.html

Abramowitz, Alan I., David J. Lanoue, & Subha Ramesh. 1988. "Economic Conditions, Causal Attributions, and Political Evaluations in the 1984 Presidential Election." *Journal of Politics* 50(4): 848–863.

Achen, Christopher H., & Larry M. Bartels. 2004. "Musical Chairs: Pocketbook Voting and the Limits of Democratic Accountability." Presented at the Annual Meeting of the American Political Science Association in Chicago, IL.

Alt, James E., & Lassen, David Dreyer. 2013. "Information Differences and Economic Voting." EPSA 2013 Annual General Conference Paper 354. [accessed August 1, 2014]. Available at SSRN: http://ssrn.com/abstract=2224816.

Anderson, Soren T., Ryan Kellogg, & James M. Sallee. 2013. "What Do Consumers Believe About Future Gasoline Prices." *Journal of Environmental Economics and Management* 66(3): 383–403.

Ansolabehere, Stephen, Marc Meredith, & Erik Snowberg. 2012. "Sociotropic Voting and the Media." In J. H. Aldrich & K. M. McGraw (Eds.), *Improving Public Opinion Surveys: Interdisciplinary Innovation and the American National Election Study* (pp. 175–189). Princeton, NJ: Princeton University Press.

Ansolabehere, Stephen, Marc Meredith, & Erik Snowberg. 2013. "Asking About Numbers: Why and How." *Political Analysis* 21(1): 48–69.

Baumgartner, Frank R., & Bryan D. Jones. 1993. *Agendas and Instability in American Politics.* Chicago, IL: University of Chicago Press.

Bartels, Larry M. 2008. *Unequal Democracy: The Political Economy of the New Gilded Age.* Princeton, IL: Princeton University Press.

Bond, Jon R., & Richard Fleisher. 1990. *The President in the Legislative Arena.* Chicago, IL: University of Chicago Press.

Bond, Jon R., & Richard Fleisher. 2000. "Congress and the President in a Partisan Era." In J. R. Bond & R. Fleisher (Eds.), *Polarized Politics: Congress and the President in a Partisan Era* (pp. 1–8). Washington, DC: CQ Press.

Brody, Richard A. 1991. *Assessing the President*. Stanford, CA: Stanford University Press.

Canes-Wrone, Brandice. 2001. "The President's Legislative Influence from Public Appeals." *American Journal of Political Science* 45(2): 313–329.

Chase, Robin. 2011. "Car-Sharing Offers Convenience, Saves Money and Helps the Environment." ed. Bureau of International Information Programs. U.S. Department of State: You Asked: Does Everyone in America Own a Car?

CNN. 2006. Bush's Approval Ratings Slide to New Low. CNN.com, April 25, 2006 [accessed March 20, 2014]. Available from: http://www.cnn.com/2006/POLITICS/04/24/bush.poll/.

Conover, Pamela Johnston, Stanley Feldman, & Kathleen Knight. 1986. "Judging Inflation and Unemployment: The Origins of Retrospective Evaluations. *Journal of Politics* 48(03): 565–588.

Converse, Phillip E. 1964. "The Nature of Belief Systems in Mass Publics." In D. E. Apter (Ed.), *Ideology and Discontent* (pp. 206–261). New York: Free Press.

Downs, Anthony. 1957. *An Economic Theory of Democracy*. Boston, MA: Addison-Wesley.

Ebeid, Michael, & Jonathan Rodden. 2006. "Economic Geography and Economic Voting: Evidence from the US States." *British Journal of Political Science* 36(03): 527–547.

Gallup/USA Today. 2008. iPOLL Databank, The Roper Center for Public Opinion Research. University of Connecticut 2008 [accessed February 17, 2012]. Available from: http://www.ropercenter.uconn.edu/data_access/ipoll/ipoll.html

"Gasoline Prices by Formulation, Grade, Sales Type." 2014. In U.S. Energy Information Administration: Independent Statistics and Analysis [accessed August 1, 2014]. Available from: http://www.eia.gov/dnav/pet/pet_pri_allmg_a_EPM0_PTC_Dpgal_m.htm

Green, Donald P., Alan S. Gerber, & Suzanna L. de Boef. 1999. "Tracking Opinion Over Time: A Method for Reducing Sampling Error." *Public Opinion Quarterly* 63(2): 178–192.

Hamilton, James D. 2013. "Historical Oil Shocks," in Routledge Handbook of Major Events in Economic History, pp. 239–265, edited by Randall E. Parker and Robert Whaples. New York: Routledge Taylor and Francis Group.

Hamilton, James D. 2011. "Nonlinearities and the Macroeconomic Effects of Oil Prices." *Macroeconomic Dynamics* 15 (Supplement S3): 364–378.

Hobbes, Thomas. 2002. *Leviathan*. Edited by A. P. Martinich. Peterborough, Ontario: Broadview Press.

Holbrook, Thomas, & James C. Garand. 1996. "Homo economus? Economic information and economic voting." *Political Research Quarterly* 49(2): 351–375.

Iyengar, Shanto, & Donald R. Kinder. 1988. *News That Matters*. Chicago, IL: University of Chicago Press.

Jackman, Simon. 2005. "Pooling Polls over an Election Campaign." *Australian Journal of Political Science* 40(4): 499–517.

Kilian, Lutz. 2009. "Not All Oil Price Shocks Are Alike: Disentangling Demand and Supply Shocks in the Crude Oil Market." *The American Economic Review* 99(3): 1053–1069.

Kinder, Donald, & Roderick Kiewiet. 1979. "Economic Discontent and Political Behavior: The Role of Personal Grievances and Collective Economic Judgments in Congressional Voting." *American Journal of Political Science* 23(3): 495–527.

Kinder, Donald, & Roderick Kiewiet. 1981. "Sociotropic Politics: The American Case." *British Journal of Political Science* 11(2): 129–161.

Kramer, Gerald H. 1971. "Short-Term Fluctuations in U.S. Voting Behavior, 1896–1964." *American Political Science Review* 65(1): 131–143.

Lau, Richard R., & David O. Sears. 1981. "Cognitive Links Between Economic Grievances and Political Reponses." *Political Behavior* 4(3): 279–302.

Locke, John. 1948. "Essay Concerning the True Extent and End of Civil Government." In Sir E. Barker (Ed.), *Social Contract; Essays by Locke, Hume, and Rousseau* (pp. 1–143). New York: Oxford University Press.

MacKuen, Michael B., Robert S. Erikson, & James A. Stimson. 1992. "Peasants or Bankers? The American Electorate and the U.S. Economy." *American Political Science Review* 86(3): 597–611.

Makel, Matthew C., Jonathan A. Plucker, & Boyd Hegarty. 2012. "Replications in Psychology Research: How Often Do They Really Occur?" *Perspectives on Psychological Science* 7(6): 537–542.

Miller, Joanne M., & Jon A. Krosnick. 2000. "News Media Impact on the Ingredients of presidential Evaluations: Politically Knowledgeable Citizens Are Guided by a Trusted Source." *American Journal of Political Science* 44(2): 301–315.

Mueller, John E. 1970. "Presidential Popularity from Truman to Johnson." *American Political Science Review* 64: 18–34.

Mufson, Steven, and Jon Cohen. 2011. High Gas Prices Cutting Into Driving Habits—and Obama's Approval Rating [Online Newspaper]. *The Washington Post*, April 25, 2011 [accessed March 20, 2014]. Available from: http://www.washingtonpost.com/business/economy/high-gas-prices-curb-driving-habits--and-obamas-approval-rating/2011/04/25/AF9kdpkE_story.html.

Nature (2013). "Announcement: Reducing Our Irreproducibility." *Nature* April 25, 496(2): 398.

Neustadt, Richard. 1990. *Presidential Power and the Modern Presidents*. New York: Free Press.

Niemi, Richard G., John Bremer, and Michael Heel. 1999. "Determinants of State Economic Perceptions." *Political Behavior* 21(2): 175–1983.

Peffley, Mark, & John T. Williams. 1985. "Attributing Presidential Responsibility for National Economic Problems." *American Politics Quarterly* 13(4): 393–425.

"Petroleum Update: Gasoline and Diesel Fuel Update." 2014. In U.S. Energy Information Administration: Independent Statistics and Analysis [accessed August 1, 2014]. Available from: http://www.eia.gov/petroleum/gasdiesel/.

Phillips, Peter C.B., and Pierre Perron. 1988. "Testing for Unit Roots in Time Series Regression." *Biometrika* 75(2): 335–346.

Reeves, Andrew, & James G. Gimpel. 2012. "Ecologies of Unease: Geographic Context and National Economic Evaluations." *Political Behavior* 34(3): 507–534.

Shah, Dhavan V., Mark Watts, David Domke, David P. Fan, & Michael Fibison. 1999. "News Coverage, Economic Cues, and the Public's Presidential Preferences, 1984–1996." *Journal of Politics* 61(4): 914–943.

Sigelman, Lee, Carol K. Sigelman, & David Bullock. 1991. "Reconsidering Pocketbook Voting: An Experimental Approach." *Political Behavior* 13(2): 129–149.

Sonderskov, Kim Mannemar, & Martin Bisgaard Christiansen. 2013. "Local Experiences with Unemployment and Perceptions of the National Economy." Paper presented at the Annual Meeting of the Danish Political Science Association. Vejlefjord Hotel, Stouby, Denmark.

Terkildsen, N., F.I. Schnell, & C. Ling. 1998. "Interest Groups, the Media, and Policy Debate Formation: An Analysis of Message Structure, Rhetoric, and Source Cues." *Political Communication* 15: 45–61.

Times/SRBI. 2005. iPOLL Databank, The Roper Center for Public Opinion Research. University of Connecticut 2005 [accessed February 17, 2012]. Available from: http://www.ropercenter.uconn.edu/data_access/ipoll/ipoll.html

Tufte, E. R. 1975. "Determinants of the Outcomes of Midterm Congressional Elections." *American Political Science Review* 69: 812–826.

Walsh, Kenneth T. 2011. High Gas Prices could Hurt Obama in 2012. U.S. News and World Report, March 24, 2011 [accessed March 20, 2014]. Available from: http://www.usnews.com/news/articles/2011/03/24/high-gas-prices-could-hurt-obama-in-2012.

Weatherford, M. Stephen. 1986. "Economic Determinants of Voting." In S. Long (Ed.), *Research in Micropolitics* (pp. 219–269). Greenwich, CT: JAI Press.

Wood, Isaac. 2011. What Fuels Presidential Approval? The Link Between Gas Prices and Presidential Approval Ratings 2011 [accessed March 20, 2014]. Available from: http://www.centerforpolitics.org/crystalball/articles/ITW2011042801/.

Wooldridge, Jeffrey M. 1994. "Estimation and Inference for Dependent Processes." In R. F. Engle & D. L. McFadden (Eds.), *Handbook of Econometrics*, Vol. 4. Amsterdam: Elsevier, 2639–2738.

Wooldridge, Jeffrey M. 2013. *Introductory Econometrics: A Modern Approach* (5th ed.) Cincinnati, OH: South-Western.

10

THE IMPACT OF CANDIDATES' STATEMENTS ABOUT GLOBAL WARMING ON ELECTORAL SUCCESS IN 2008 TO 2015

Evidence Using Five Methodologies[1]

Bo MacInnis and Jon A. Krosnick

According to surveys conducted since 2008, large majorities of Americans have believed that the earth's temperature has been gradually increasing over the last 100 years, have believed that such warming is at least partly human-caused, have believed it is a threat, and supported government action to reduce future emissions of greenhouse gasses (what might be called a set of "green" opinions; see the first four rows of Table 10.1). Such majorities have also appeared among Independents (see rows 7 and 11 of Table 10.1) and might seem to suggest that political candidates could gain votes by staking out green positions on global warming and that taking not-green positions could cause candidates to lose votes.

However, according to the literature on issue publics in political science and to psychology's literature on attitude strength, gauging issue impact on voting should not be done by examining the entire electorate. According to these literatures, a policy issue such as global warming is unlikely to influence the votes of all citizens and will instead only influence the votes of people who consider it to be highly important to them personally (see, e.g., Anand & Krosnick, 2003; Krosnick, 1990; Visser, Bizer, & Krosnick, 2006). According to recent surveys, about 15% of America's adult population have considered the issue to be extremely personally important since 2008 (see row 5 of Table 10.1), and among these individuals, gigantic majorities have apparently taken green positions on the issue (see rows 9 and 13 of Table 10.1). This reasoning also suggests that candidates may have been able to win votes by taking green positions on climate and may have lost votes by taking not-green positions.

TABLE 10.1 Americans' Beliefs Regarding Global Warming and Personal Importance, 2008–2015

Belief	2008	2009	2010	2011	2012	2013	2015
The planet has probably been warming	80%	75%	75%	83%	73%	73%	69%
Humans have been at least partly responsible for the warming	77%	70%	75%	72%	77%	80%	81%
Global warming will be a very or somewhat serious problem for the U.S.	—	73%	75%	—	79%	80%	79%
The federal government should do more than it is doing now to address global warming	61%	56%	62%	—	61%	66%	61%
Global warming is extremely personally important	16%	16%	16%	15%	10%	18%	13%
The planet has probably been warming							
Among Democrats	87%	82%	87%	91%	86%	86%	82%
Among Independents	79%	74%	75%	84%	71%	73%	70%
Among Republicans	74%	67%	61%	66%	57%	57%	49%
Among people for whom global warming was extremely important personally	94%	92%	89%	89%	91%	90%	86%
The federal government should do more than it is doing now to address global warming							
Among Democrats	78%	71%	77%	—	76%	79%	78%
Among Independents	59%	54%	66%	—	60%	66%	62%
Among Republicans	39%	42%	35%	—	36%	49%	38%
Among people to whom global warming is extremely important personally	90%	86%	90%	—	81%	86%	91%

Notes: Question wording and coding and data collection methodologies for each survey are described in Appendix A.

This chapter describes eight studies carried out with five methodologies to test those hypotheses. Methodology 1 consisted of Studies 1 and 2, which were observational studies and focused on the 2008 and 2012 U.S. presidential election, respectively. Political scientists have routinely gauged the impact of a policy issue on vote choices by conducting statistical analyses using survey respondents' reports of their own positions on the issue and their perceptions of the candidates' positions on the issue. We used such measures to construct proximity scores (using various different methods) to quantify which candidate the respondent was closer to, and by how much. Vote choices were regressed on the proximity scores and other potential determinants of candidate preferences using data from a large national survey to look for evidence that global warming proximity might have shaped voting.

Methodology 2 consisted of Study 3, which employed a content analysis methodology and focused on votes cast during the 2010 Congressional elections. Speculating about the impact of global warming on those elections, some observers have claimed that supporting legislation to address global warming cost candidates victories (e.g., "Democrats who took risk and voted for climate bill pay price"; Hughes, 2010), whereas others disputed this claim (e.g., "Cap-and-trade didn't kill the Democrats"; Levi, 2010; see also Johnson, 2010; Taylor-Miesle, 2010). To test these speculations, we first conducted a content analysis of Congressional candidates' campaign websites and incumbents' Congressional websites to determine whether each candidate took a green position on global warming, took a not-green position, or was silent or mixed. Then, we conducted statistical analyses to assess whether these groups of candidates differed in their electoral success, while controlling for potential confounding factors. We also explored whether taking a green position paid off more when a candidate's opponent took a not-green position than when the opponent was silent and whether taking a not-green position hurt more when a candidate's opponent took a green position than when the opponent was silent.

Methodology 3, a mixture of methodologies of observational studies and content analysis, consisted of Study 4, which was an analysis relating statements made about global warming by candidates for the 2012 primary elections with respondents' intent to vote for them in hypothetical matchups. Study 4 involved a within-subject experiment embedded in a survey of a nationally representative sample of American adults (in September 2011) as well as content analysis of political candidates' stances on the issue of global warming. In the experiment, each respondent was asked the following five questions of hypothetical matchup voting questions with actual candidates (the order in which these questions were asked in each respondent was randomized): "If the 2012 presidential election were being held today and the candidates were Barack Obama, the Democrat, and [randomly selected: Mitt Romney / Jon Huntsman / Michele Bachmann / Ron Paul / Rick Perry], the Republican, for whom would you vote?" We used the standard method in political science to assess the potential impact of global warming beliefs and issue proximity on voting choice controlling for various other possible causes of vote choice. We employed a content analysis on the six candidates evaluated in the hypothetical matchup voting questions, and assigned each of them an index score on his/her stance on global warming.

Methodology 4, direct inquiry without manipulation, consisted of Study 5, which was an analysis of how various stances on global warming by hypothetical candidates would impact the likelihood of respondents' intent to vote for them. Study 5 involved a within-subject experiment embedded in a survey of a nationally representative sample of American adults (in January 2015). In the experiment, each respondent heard statements from three hypothetical candidates running for the U.S. Senate or the president of the United States. The three hypothetical candidates expressed a green position, a not-green position and a not-committal position on the issue of global warming. The order in which respondents heard the candidate with green, not-green, or not-committal position was randomized. After hearing the statement from each of the three candidates, respondents were asked that if a candidate says that statement, how this would affect how likely they would be to vote for the candidate. This experimental design allowed assessment of the electoral impact of a candidate's expressing a stance on global warming.

Methodology 5, experimental studies, consisted of Studies 6, 7, and 8. Studies 6 and 7 involved between-subject experiments embedded in surveys of representative samples of all American adults (in November 2010) and of adult residents of Florida, Maine, and Massachusetts (in July 2010), respectively. In both experiments, telephone interviewers read quotes from a hypothetical candidate said to be running for the U.S. Senate in the respondent's state, and the respondent indicated the likelihood that he or she would vote for the candidate. All respondents heard the candidate take positions on a series of issues other than global warming. For some respondents, the candidate took no position on global warming. Other respondents heard the candidate take a green position on global warming. And, in the national survey only, some respondents heard the candidate take a not-green position on global warming. This experimental design allowed assessment of the impact of adding a statement on global warming to a candidate's utterances.

Study 8 employed an experiment embedded in an Internet survey of Americans from a non-probability sample to assess the electoral impact of candidates' taking different stances on the issue of global warming. Study 8 used a different study design from Studies 5–7 in a number of aspects: (1) Study 8 used real candidates' real speeches in video as experiment stimuli; (2) Study 8 evaluated the electoral impact of a (real) candidate's taking different stances on the issue of global warming when that candidate was presented alone as if in a single candidate election, as well as when that candidate was presented with the opponent as in a two-candidates election; and (3) Study 8 explored the impact of a (real) candidate's taking different stances on the issue of global warming on measures of electoral outcomes, as well as others, such as effect and personality traits perception.

Study 1—An Observational Study about the 2008 Presidential Election

Study 1 employed traditional analytic methods to assess the impact on candidate choice in the 2008 U.S. presidential election of voter proximity to candidates on global warming policy.

Data and Method

Data Collection

The data used in this study is Face-to-Face Recruited Internet Survey Platform (FFRISP). Respondents in the FFRISP were recruited via face-to-face area probability sampling and were all given a free laptop (or its equivalent value in cash), high-speed Internet access at home (if they didn't have it already), and regular cash payments in exchange for completing monthly questionnaires for a year. The FFRISP began with 1,000 panelists, who were recruited between June and October 2008. The current study is based on data collected during the first, second, fifth, and seventh waves, initiated in October 2008, November 2008, February 2009 and July 2009, respectively. The response rate for panel enrollment was 47% (AAPOR RR4), and 989, 978, 970, 955 individuals completed the first, second, fifth and seventh wave questionnaires, respectively, yielding a cumulative response rate of 45%.

Following DeBell and Krosnick (2009), weights were constructed to adjust for unequal probability of household selection, household listing interview nonresponse, within-household selection of potential panel member, and non-coverage and nonresponse through post-stratification. In post-stratification, an iterative raking procedure implemented by Pasek (2010) was performed to closely match the FFRISP data to the population benchmarks of age, gender, educational attainment, race, Hispanic ethnicity, marital status, presence of children in household, household size, whether a language other than English was spoken in the household, region, type of housing unit, and whether internet connection had been available in the household in the previous two months. These benchmarks were the population estimates of non-institutionalized adults aged 18 years or older in American Community Survey in 2008, except that the benchmark of households with internet connections was based on the supplement on Computer and Internet Use in the 2009 Current Population Survey.

Table 10.2 displays unweighted and weighted distributions of demographics for the FFRISP respondents, as well as national benchmarks computed using the data from the 2008 American Community Survey. Before the weights were applied, the FFRISP respondents were similar to the American population, with a slight under-representation of males, people ages 65 and older, and people without a high school degree and high school graduates, and with a slight over-presentation of people aged 25–34, people with some college, and college graduates. After the weights were applied, the FFRISP respondents were nearly identical to the population.

TABLE 10.2   Study 1: Demographics of the Sample and the American Community Survey

Demographic	FFRISP (unweighted) (%)	FFRISP (weighted) (%)	American Community Survey (ACS) 2008 (%)	Difference: FFRISP (weighted)—ACS (%)
Gender				
Male	41.6	48.3	48.3	.0
Female	58.5	51.7	51.7	.0
Total	100.0	100.0	100.0	
	(N = 970)	(N = 970)	(N = 222,146,343)	
Age				
18–24	10.4	12.2	12.2	.0
25–34	22.4	17.7	17.7	.0
35–44	21.7	18.9	18.9	.0
45–54	22.0	19.7	19.7	.0
55–64	15.1	15.0	15.0	.0
65+	8.6	16.6	16.6	.0
Total	100.0	100.0	100.0	
	(N = 970)	(N = 970)	(N = 222,146,343)	
Ethnicity				
Hispanic	13.5	14.0	13.5	.5
Non-Hispanic	86.5	86.0	86.5	–.5
Total	100.0	100.0	100.0	
	(N = 970)	(N = 970)	(N = 222,146,343)	
Race				
Black	12.0	12.8	11.9	.9
Nonblack	88.0	87.3	88.1	–.8
Total	100.0	100.0	100.0	
	(N = 970)	(N = 970)	(N = 222,146,343)	

continued…

Table 10.2 continued...

Demographic	FFRISP (unweighted) (%)	FFRISP (weighted) (%)	American Community Survey (ACS) 2008 (%)	Difference: FFRISP (weighted)—ACS (%)
Education				
HS but no degree	8.4	14.9	14.9	.0
HS graduates	24.7	28.6	28.6	.0
Some college	27.9	23.3	23.3	.0
College or higher	39.0	33.2	33.2	.0
Total	100.0	100.0	100.0	
	(N = 970)	(N = 970)	(N = 222,146,343)	
Region				
Northwest	16.6	18.4	18.4	.0
Midwest	20.3	21.9	21.9	.0
South	38.5	36.6	36.6	.0
West	24.6	23.1	23.1	.0
Total	100.0	100.0	100.0	
	(N = 970)	(N = 970)	(N = 222,146,343)	

Measures

Question wording and coding of all the measures described below is available in Appendix B.

TURNOUT AND CANDIDATE CHOICE

The dependent measure is a four-category variable: voting for Mr. Obama, voting for Mr. McCain, voting for a non-major party candidate, or not voting at all. This measure was constructed using responses to questions asked of respondents in November 2008, about whether they voted in the Presidential Election and for whom they voted. Respondents who said they definitely or probably voted and said they voted for Obama, McCain, or someone else were coded "voting for Obama," "voting for McCain," "voting for a non-major party candidate," respectively. All respondents who said they definitely or probably did not vote in the Presidential Election were coded as "not voting at all." Question wordings and coding of this dependent variable and all other variables are described in Appendix B.

PROXIMITY ON GLOBAL WARMING POLICY

Proximity to the candidates on global warming policy was measured using three methods: Euclidean distance, and city block distance (Downs, 1957; Enelow & Hinich, 1984), and directional similarity (Rabinowitz, 1978; Rabinowitz & Macdonald, 1989). V_i and C_j denote voter i's own and his/her perception of candidate j's placement on the issue, where the neutral point is 0, and favoring and opposing with intensity are represented by positive and negative integers, respectively. That is, a positive value of self-placement V_i or candidate placement C_j indicates that the respondent is or the candidate is perceived to be green and supportive of global warming policies; greater positive values indicate more support for policies. $(V_i - C_j)^2$, $|V_i - C_j|$, and $V_i \star C_j$ are the Euclidean distance, city block, and directional measures of voter-candidate issue congruence, respectively.

We focused on two policy issues: the federal government lowering the amount of greenhouse gases that power plants were allowed to put into the air to reduce future global warming, and the federal government requiring automakers to build cars that use less gasoline. Global warming policy issue proximity score was averaged over the two polices. Regressions controlled for factors that might influence voting turnout and outcomes including political party identification, interest in politics, President Bush's job approval, perception of the health of the national economy, and demographics such as sex, age, race, ethnicity, education, income and region.

Measures of C_j were based on respondent reports of whether Mr. Obama and Mr. McCain favored, opposed, or neither favored nor opposed the following two policies: the federal government lowering the amount of greenhouse gases that power plants were allowed to put into the air to reduce future global warming, and the federal government requiring automakers to build cars that use less gasoline. Respondents who answered either "favor" or "oppose" then reported whether they thought Mr. Obama and Mr. McCain favored or opposed a great deal, moderately, or a little. This allowed us to place each candidate perception on a 7-point scale.

Measures of V_i were constructed in a similar way. Respondents were asked whether they favored, opposed, or neither favored nor opposed the same government policy, and the same follow-up question was asked, allowing placement on the same 7-point scale. The climate policy proximity score for each respondent was averaged over the two policies.

IDEOLOGICAL PROXIMITY

Political ideological congruence between the respondent and the candidates was computed in a similar way. Respondents were asked whether they would describe Mr. Obama and Mr. McCain as liberal, conservative, or neither liberal nor conservative. Respondents who said "liberal" or "conservative" were asked a follow-up question about whether the candidate was very liberal/conservative or somewhat liberal/conservative. Respondents who said "neither liberal nor conservative" were asked whether they thought the candidate was closer to liberals, closer to conservatives, or neither. This again allowed for placement on a 7-point scale, and respondents answered a pair of questions to place themselves on the same 7-point scale.

PERSONAL IMPORTANCE

Respondents were asked how important the issue of global warming was to them personally. People who said it was extremely or very important were treated as the high importance group, and all others were treated as the low importance group.

BELIEF IN ANTHROPOGENIC WARMING

Respondents who believed that the earth has been gradually warming over the last 100 years due to human activity were categorized as "green."

CONTROL VARIABLES

Respondents reported their political party affiliation, interest in politics, overall approval of President Bush's performance of his job, and perception of the health of the national economy. Demographics included sex, race, Hispanic ethnicity, age, education, income, and region.

Analysis

Multinomial logistic regression predicting polychromous outcomes is based on the assumption of Independence of Irreverent Alternative (IIA). The Hausman specification test revealed no evidence that this assumption was violated in our data. An alternative model for predicting polychromous outcomes is the multinomial probit specification, which makes an untestable assumption that the error terms for each category outcome are jointly normally distributed. Our results were similar whether conducted in multinomial logistic or multinomial probit regressions.

Another analytic approach we could take is modeling an individual fixed effect to capture all the factors that may have impacted each citizen's behavior, including variables that are observable and measured in the survey (e.g., the voter's political party affiliation), variables that are observable but were not measured in the survey (e.g., the citizen's positions on many other policy issues), and unobservable attributes of individuals. All these factors could have influenced voter's self-placements as well as candidate placements, so an appropriate estimation method would be conditional or individual fixed effect logistic regression, with a first-difference estimator. Similar results were obtained with this alternative estimation.

Results

A large majority, 81%, of respondents were green on the global warming issues (that is, the average global warming policy index score of self-placement was positive). A small minority, 13%, of respondents were not-green on the global warming issues (that is, the average global warming policy index score of self-placement was negative). The remaining 6% of respondents were neutral (that is, the average global warming policy index score was zero). A majority, 55%, of respondents perceived Mr. Obama to be greener than Mr. McCain on the global warming issues (that is, the average global warming policy index score of Mr. Obama's placement was greater than that of Mr. McCain's). Nearly half, 45%, of respondents said the issue of global warming was highly important to them personally (that is, they thought global warming was extremely important or very important personally). Among these high importance respondents, 86% were green on the global warming issues, 4% were not-green, and the remaining 10% were neutral. 60% of high importance respondents thought Mr. Obama was greener than Mr. McCain on the global warming issues. Because the vast majority of high importance respondents were green, and more high importance respondents saw Mr. Obama as being greener than Mr. McCain, these numbers suggest that Mr. Obama was advantaged overall by being perceived as greener than Mr. McCain.

Impact of Issue Proximity on Voting Behavior

Controlling for many other predictors of voting behavior, global warming issue proximity was a significant predictor in the expected direction using all three analytic methods (see Table 10.3). Matching Mr. Obama's position on global warming more closely than Mr. McCain's led people to be less likely to vote for Mr. McCain than for Mr. Obama (e.g., $b = -.39, p < .01$ with the city block measure; see row 1 in column (1) in Table 10.3; see row 1 in columns (4) and (7) in Table 10.3 for the results using Euclidian distance and directional models, respectively).

Other factors thought to influence candidate choice were also significant predictors in expected directions when using all three methods. People who matched Mr. Obama's ideology more closely than Mr. McCain's were less likely to vote for Mr. McCain. Democrats were less likely than were Independents to vote for Mr. McCain, and Republicans were more likely to do so than were Independents. People who approved of President Bush's performance were more likely to vote for Mr. McCain than were disapprovers. Blacks were less likely to vote for Mr. McCain than were non-blacks, and people in the South were more likely to vote for Mr. McCain than were people in the Northeast (see Table 10.3).

Also as expected, many factors thought to influence turnout had significant effects in expected directions (see Harder & Krosnick, 2008; Holbrook et al., 2001).

TABLE 10.3 Study 1: Multinomial Logistic Regression Coefficients Predicting Voting Behavior

Predictor	City block measures			Euclidian measures			Directional measures		
	Voted for McCain	Voted for other	Did not vote	Voted for McCain	Voted for other	Did not vote	Voted for McCain	Voted for other	Did not vote
Global warming Issue proximity	-0.39*** (0.09)	-0.30** (0.13)	-0.14* (0.09)	-0.07*** (0.02)	-0.06** (0.03)	-0.02 (0.02)	-0.15*** (0.03)	-0.12*** (0.04)	-0.06* (0.03)
Ideology proximity	-0.34*** (0.06)	-0.18*** (0.07)	-0.15*** (0.06)	-0.06*** (0.01)	-0.03*** (0.03)	-0.02** (0.02)	-0.13*** (0.03)	-0.08** (0.03)	-0.04* (0.02)
Democrat	-0.90** (0.37)	-1.24** (0.59)	-0.74** (0.29)	-0.92** (0.37)	-1.17** (0.57)	-0.76*** (0.29)	-0.90** (0.36)	-1.16** (0.58)	-0.75*** (0.29)
Republican	1.64*** (0.44)	-0.79 (0.80)	0.32 (0.43)	1.66*** (0.43)	-0.82 (0.80)	0.38 (0.42)	1.62*** (0.45)	-0.84 (0.82)	0.34 (0.434)
Attitudes toward Big government	-1.61*** (0.61)	-1.80** (0.82)	0.51 (0.61)	-1.73*** (0.61)	-1.78** (0.82)	0.46 (0.60)	-1.90*** (0.59)	-1.88** (0.84)	0.454 (0.60)
Bush approval	2.06*** (0.60)	-0.09 (0.82)	1.69*** (0.49)	2.17*** (0.58)	-0.18 (0.85)	1.79*** (0.48)	2.19*** (0.58)	-0.11 (0.80)	1.83*** (0.483)
Perception of the Economy	-0.09 (0.85)	2.61** (1.02)	-0.14 (0.63)	-0.02 (0.86)	2.74*** (1.02)	-0.07 (0.63)	0.08 (0.83)	2.78*** (1.01)	-0.08 (0.63)
Interest in politics	0.79 (0.67)	1.33* (0.78)	-1.93*** (0.51)	0.76 (0.65)	1.36* (0.78)	-1.95*** (0.50)	0.86 (0.65)	1.46* (0.77)	-1.91*** (0.50)
Female	0.15 (0.31)	-0.96* (0.52)	0.89*** (0.26)	0.20 (0.31)	-0.98* (0.53)	0.92*** (0.26)	0.19 (0.31)	-0.97* (0.52)	0.93*** (0.26)
Hispanic	-0.61 (0.55)	-0.42 (0.91)	0.13 (0.36)	-0.66 (0.57)	-0.41 (0.90)	0.14 (0.36)	-0.74 (0.56)	-0.45 (0.88)	0.10 (0.35)

	(1)	(2)	(3)	(4)	(5)	(6)	(7)	(8)	(9)
Black	-2.68***	-1.61**	-1.99***	-2.73***	-1.63**	-2.00***	-2.67***	-1.53**	-1.97***
	(0.70)	(0.77)	(0.52)	(0.69)	(0.79)	(0.52)	(0.69)	(0.75)	(0.52)
Age	0.01	-0.01	-0.02**	0.01	-0.01	-0.02**	0.01	-0.01	-0.02**
	(0.01)	(0.01)	(0.10)	(0.01)	(0.01)	(0.01)	(0.01)	(0.01)	(0.01)
Midwest	0.75	0.27	0.43	0.72	0.28	0.41	0.67	0.21	0.36
	(0.48)	(0.60)	(0.40)	(0.47)	(0.61)	(0.39)	(0.48)	(0.62)	(0.40)
South	1.18***	0.53	1.28***	1.19***	0.54	1.29***	1.14***	0.47	1.24***
	(0.41)	(0.59)	(0.34)	(0.41)	(0.59)	(0.34)	(0.42)	(0.59)	(0.34)
West	0.46	-1.05	0.45	0.46	-1.03	0.45	0.45	-1.07	0.42
	(0.43)	(0.80)	(0.34)	(0.42)	(0.80)	(0.34)	(0.43)	(0.82)	(0.34)
Education	1.95	4.58***	-0.78	1.70	4.42***	-0.93	2.01	4.70***	-0.87
	(1.29)	(1.61)	(0.94)	(1.24)	(1.61)	(0.93)	(1.32)	(1.64)	(0.95)
Income	-0.39	-1.37	-1.22***	-0.37	-1.41	-1.20***	-0.25	-1.39	-1.18***
	(0.55)	(1.06)	(0.44)	(0.57)	(1.08)	(0.44)	(0.56)	(1.06)	(0.44)
Constant	-2.67**	-3.68**	1.65*	-2.54**	-3.64**	1.69*	-2.54**	-3.64**	1.73**
	(1.15)	(1.72)	(0.87)	(1.08)	(1.70)	(0.87)	(1.16)	(1.74)	(0.88)

Note: N = 907. Standard errors are in parentheses.

***p<0.01, **p<0.05, *p<0.10

As compared to people who did vote, people who did not vote were more likely to be female ($b = .83$, $p < .01$) and more likely to be from the South and less likely to be from the Northeast ($b = 1.31$, $p < .01$), were less interested in politics ($b = -2.08$, $p < .01$), were younger ($b = -.02$, $p = .02$) and had lower incomes ($b = -1.21$, $p < .01$). Also, people who did not vote were less likely to be black than to be non-black ($b = -1.99$, $p < .01$).

Moderation by Personal Importance

As expected, when the interaction of high personal importance and global warming issue proximity was added as a predictor to the equations shown in Table 10.3, the impact of global warming issue proximity on candidate choice was strong and significant among respondents who attached high importance to the issue. The interaction of personal importance with global warming issue proximity was highly significant, and the main effect for global warming issue proximity was not. Thus, issue proximity only predicted voting behavior in the high importance group.

Study 2—An Observational Study about the 2012 Presidential Election

As in Study 1, Study 2 employed traditional analytic methods to assess the impact on candidate choice in the 2012 U.S. presidential election of voter proximity to candidates on global warming policy.

Data and Method

Data Collection

A random digit dial telephone survey of a national probability sample of U.S. adults ages 18 and older was conducted by Abt SRBI between June 13 and June 21, 2012. 603 respondents were interviewed on a landline phone, and 201 were interviewed on a cellular phone. Interviews were administrated in English only. Samples were drawn from both landline and cellular random digit dial (RDD) frames by Survey Sampling International. Numbers for the landline sample were drawn with equal probabilities from active blocks (area code + exchange + two-digit block number) that contained one or more residential directory listings. The cellular phone sample was drawn through a systematic sampling from 1000 blocks dedicated to cellular service according to the Telcordia database.

The data were weighted to ensure that the sample composition reflected the U.S. population in terms of demographics documented by figures from the U.S. Census Bureau. Weights were created to adjust for differential probabilities of selection due to the number of adults in the household, the number of voice-use landlines and cell phones, and the overlap of landline and cell phone RDD frames, as well as non-coverage and nonresponse through post-stratification. Post-stratification matched the population proportions of age and sex, education and sex, ethnicity and race, and region using targets from the 2010 American Community Survey conducted by the U.S. Census Bureau. The AAPOR Response Rate 3 for the survey was 15%.

Table 10.4 displays distributions of unweighted and weighted demographics along with national benchmarks computed using the data from the 2010 American Community Survey. Before the weights were applied, the sample was similar to the American population, with a slight under-representation of younger (aged 18–29) males and females and of males and female with no college education, and a small over-representation of older (aged 65 and older) males and females, non-Hispanic whites, and males and females with bachelor's degree or higher. After the weights were applied, the sample was nearly identical to the population in these regards. All results reported below were computed using the weights, although unweighted data produced comparable findings.

TABLE 10.4 Study 2: Demographics of the Sample and American Community Survey

	GW National Survey 2012 (unweighted) (%)	GW National Survey 2012 (weighted) (%)	ACS 2010 (%)	Difference: GW National Survey (weighted) – ACS (%)
Age and Gender				
Male 18 to 29	6.9	11.2	11.2	.0
Male 30 to 49	11.0	17.5	17.7	–.2
Male 50 to 64	15.6	12.4	12.2	.2
Male 65 and older	11.6	7.5	7.4	.1
Female 18 to 29	5.1	10.2	10.8	–.7
Female 30 to 49	14.9	18.1	18.0	.1
Female 50 to 64	17.7	13.2	12.9	.2
Female 65 and older	17.2	10.0	9.8	.2
Total	100.0	100.0	100.0	
	(N = 799)	(N = 799)	(N = 2,369,395)	

continued…

Table10.4 continued…

	GW National Survey 2012 (unweighted) (%)	GW National Survey 2012 (weighted) (%)	ACS 2010 (%)	Difference: GW National Survey (weighted) – ACS (%)
Race and Ethnicity				
Non-Hispanic White only	77.5	67.5	66.9	.6
Non-Hispanic Black only	8.8	11.6	11.7	−.1
Hispanic	6.7	13.7	14.3	−.6
Other race	7.0	7.3	7.2	.1
Total	100.0	100.0	100.0	
	(N =796)	(N =796)	(N =2,369,395)	
Education and Gender				
Male HS graduates or less	13.4	21.7	21.8	−.1
Male some college	12.0	14.4	14.3	.1
Male college graduates or more	19.9	12.7	12.4	.2
Female HS graduates or less	14.8	21.0	21.5	−.5
Female some college	17.3	16.8	16.7	.1
Female college graduates or more	22.7	13.6	13.3	.3
Total	100.0	100.0	100.0	
	(N =799)	(N =799)	(N =2,369,395)	
Region				
Northeast	18.2	18.5	18.2	.3
Midwest	21.6	21.8	21.6	.2
South	36.6	36.6	37.0	−.4
West	23.6	23.1	23.2	.0
Total	100.0	100.0	100.0	
	(N =804)	(N =804)	(N =2,369,395)	

Measures

CANDIDATE PREFERENCE

Respondents were asked: "If the presidential election were being held today and the candidates were Barack Obama, the Democrat, and Mitt Romney, the Republican, for whom would you vote?" The order of "Barack Obama, the Democrat" and "Mitt Romney, the Republican" was randomized across respondents. The dependent measure for our analyses was constructed to assign each respondent to one of the following categories: intent to vote for Mr. Obama, intent to vote for Mr. Romney, intent to vote for another candidate, and all other respondents, who were viewed as non-voters.

GLOBAL WARMING ISSUE PROXIMITY

Respondents were asked: "How much do you think the U.S. government should do about global warming—a great deal, quite a bit, some, a little, or nothing?" And respondents were also asked: "How much do you think the U.S. government is doing now to deal with global warming—a great deal, quite a bit, some, a little, or nothing?" The respondent's desired change in the government effort on global warming was constructed by assigning values of 1 through 5 to the responses to each question and then subtracting the amount of effort the government is doing from the amount of effort the government should do. The self-placement measure ranged from –4 to 4. The neutral point was 0, indicating that the respondent desired no change in government effort. Positive numbers indicated that the respondent wanted the government to do more; negative numbers indicated that the respondent wanted the government to do less.

Candidate placements were constructed similarly. Respondents were asked "In your opinion, how much government action does Barack Obama want on global warming—a great deal, quite a bit, some, a little, or nothing?" and the same question about Mitt Romney. The order in which the respondent was asked about the two candidates was determined randomly. The candidate placement measure was the candidate's desired change in government effort on global warming, which was constructed as subtracting the respondent's perceived amount of effort the government is doing from the respondent's perception on the amount of effort the candidate thought the government should do.

Respondents who said they didn't know or refused to answer any question of the three were excluded from the analysis.

Three methods were used to compute scores to represent respondent-candidate proximity on global warming: Euclidean distance, city block distance (Downs, 1957; Enelow & Hinich, 1984), and directional similarity (Rabinowitz, 1978; Rabinowitz & Macdonald, 1989). If V_i and C_j denote respondent i's and candidate j's placement on global warming belief, the calculation methods are as follows: (1) Euclidean distance: $-(V_i - C_j)^2$; (2) City block distance: $-|V_i - C_j|$; and (3) Directional similarity: $V_i \star C_j$.

Issue importance

Respondents were asked: "How important is the issue of global warming to you personally—extremely important, very important, somewhat important, not too important, or not at all important?" People who selected "extremely important" were assigned to the high importance group, and other respondents were assigned to the low importance group.

Attention to the election

Respondents were asked: "How closely are you following the 2012 presidential race: very closely, somewhat closely, not so closely, or not closely at all?" People who selected the top two responses were assigned to high attention to election group and the other respondents were assigned to low attention to election group.

Control variables

Control variables included political party affiliation, ideology, interest in the election campaign, sex, age, race, ethnicity, education, and region. All respondents were asked "Generally speaking, do you usually consider yourself as a Democrat, a Republican, an Independent, or what?" where the order of "a Democrat" and "a Republican" was randomized across respondents. Respondents who answered with "Democrat" and "Republican" were assigned to Democrats and Republicans, respectively, and all other respondents were assigned to Independents. Respondents were asked "Would you say your views on most political matters are liberal, moderate, or conservative?" Respondents who answered with "Liberal" and "Conservative" were assigned to liberals and conservatives, respectively, and all other respondents were assigned to moderates.

Respondents were asked "Are you of Hispanic origin or background?" People who answered positively were then asked "Are you White Hispanic or Black Hispanic?" People who said they were not of Hispanic origin or background were asked "Are you White, Black, or some other race." Using answers to these questions, respondents were coded as non-Hispanic white, non-Hispanic black, Hispanic, and other race for those who were white only and not Hispanic, black only and not Hispanic, Hispanic and the rest, respectively.

Respondents were asked "What was the last grade of school completed?" Respondents who did not graduate from high school were coded as "less than high school," those who graduated from high school were coded as high school graduates, those who attended some college or had associate degrees were coded as some college, and those who graduated from college were coded as college graduates.

Respondents were asked "Are you registered to vote at your present address, or not?" Respondents who answered affirmatively were coded as registered voters.

In the regressions, non-Hispanic whites, males, Independents, moderates, people who were ages 18–29, people who resided in the Northeast region, and people who had less than high school were the omitted base categories.

Analysis

The parameters of multinomial logistic regression equations were estimated to predict the polychromous outcome variable. An alternative approach is multinomial probit, which makes the untestable assumption that the error terms in determining each category outcome are jointly normally distributed. Our results were identical whether conducted with multinomial logistic regression or multinomial probit. The analyses were only of people who said they were registered to vote.

Results

Global Warming Issue Proximity and Candidate Preference

Global warming issue proximity predicted candidate choice among registered voters in the expected way (see Table 10.5, which displays the coefficient estimates from multinomial logistic regressions using voting for Mr. Obama as the omitted base category). The coefficient for global warming issue proximity was significant and in the expected direction in all three analyses. Matching Mr. Obama's position on global warming more closely than Mr. Romney's was associated with a lower likelihood to vote for Mr. Romney than to vote for Mr. Obama ($b = -.26$, $p = .01$ with the Euclidian measure; see row 1 in column (1) in Table 10.5). This was equally apparent using all three analytic methods for representing proximity (see row 1 in columns (4) and (7) in Table 10.5 for the measures of city block and directional models, respectively).

Other factors thought to influence candidate choice also had significant effects in the expected directions among registered voters. Using the Euclidian measures (see column 1 in Table 10.5), Democrats were less likely than Independents to intend to vote for Mr. Romney than for Mr. Obama ($b = -1.67$, $p = .01$). Republicans were more likely to do so ($b = 1.93$, $p = .00$). Hispanics and people of other races were less likely than non-Hispanic whites to intend to vote for Mr. Romney than for Mr. Obama ($b = -2.58$, $p = .02$; $b = -1.90$, $p = .03$). Females were less likely than males to intend to vote for Mr. Romney than for Mr. Obama ($b = -.87$, $p = .02$), and people in the South were more likely to do so ($b = 1.26$, $p = .06$). These effects were equally significant and in the expected directions when employing other measures of issue proximity (see columns 4 and 7 in Table 10.5 for measures of city block and directional models, respectively).

TABLE 10.5 Study 2: Multinomial Regressions of the Impact of Global Warming Issue Congruence on Intention to Vote among Registered Voters

Predictor	Euclidian Measure			City Block Measure			Directional Measure		
	Vote for Romney (1)	Vote for another candidate (2)	Not vote (3)	Vote for Romney (4)	Vote for another candidate (5)	Not vote (6)	Vote for Romney (7)	Vote for another candidate (8)	Not vote (9)
GW issue congruence	-0.26*** (0.09)	-0.13** (0.06)	-0.11 (0.07)	-0.89*** (0.26)	-0.34 (0.21)	-0.38* (0.21)	-0.49*** (0.09)	-0.27** (0.11)	-0.35*** (0.10)
Democrat	-1.67*** (0.61)	-2.27*** (0.76)	-2.21*** (0.82)	-1.60** (0.62)	-2.21*** (0.76)	-2.13*** (0.82)	-1.93*** (0.62)	-2.38*** (0.74)	-2.30*** (0.81)
Republican	1.93*** (0.62)	-0.28 (0.84)	-0.03 (0.84)	1.95*** (0.63)	-0.21 (0.85)	0.01 (0.85)	2.12*** (0.63)	-0.17 (0.82)	0.06 (0.83)
Liberal	-0.30 (0.64)	0.09 (0.71)	-0.86 (0.66)	-0.32 (0.63)	-0.01 (0.70)	-0.88 (0.64)	-0.22 (0.65)	0.13 (0.70)	-0.73 (0.65)
Conservative	0.83** (0.42)	0.99* (0.59)	-0.19 (0.60)	0.88** (0.43)	1.06* (0.60)	-0.17 (0.61)	1.12** (0.44)	1.16** (0.58)	-0.09 (0.60)
Female	-0.87** (0.38)	-1.14** (0.51)	-0.73 (0.48)	-0.87** (0.38)	-1.08** (0.50)	-0.71 (0.49)	-0.86** (0.39)	-1.10** (0.52)	-0.69 (0.52)
Age 30–39	0.02 (1.02)	-1.89* (1.05)	-0.23 (1.21)	-0.03 (1.00)	-1.81* (1.02)	-0.23 (1.21)	0.13 (1.05)	-1.83* (1.04)	-0.26 (1.27)
Age 40–49	-0.39 (0.96)	0.12 (0.75)	1.56 (1.04)	-0.48 (0.98)	0.07 (0.76)	1.49 (1.04)	-0.19 (0.87)	0.09 (0.76)	1.55 (1.05)
Age 50–64	-0.16 (0.67)	-0.99 (0.64)	0.45 (1.02)	-0.11 (0.68)	-0.95 (0.64)	0.46 (1.04)	0.03 (0.73)	-1.04 (0.68)	0.46 (1.04)

	(1)	(2)	(3)	(4)	(5)	(6)	(7)	(8)	(9)
Age 65 and older	-0.10	-0.17	1.06	-0.16	-0.20	1.03	-0.03	-0.29	1.02
	(0.72)	(0.69)	(1.01)	(0.73)	(0.69)	(1.05)	(0.76)	(0.71)	(1.03)
Non-Hispanic Black	-1.30	-33.31***	-33.82***	-1.29	-34.28***	-34.74***	-1.31	-34.21***	-34.62***
	(0.82)	(0.70)	(0.77)	(0.86)	(0.68)	(0.76)	(0.93)	(0.73)	(0.79)
Hispanic	-2.58**	0.40	-1.29	-2.63**	0.51	-1.19	-2.76**	0.22	-1.39
	(1.09)	(0.82)	(0.83)	(1.15)	(0.83)	(0.85)	(1.08)	(0.83)	(0.88)
Other race	-1.90**	-1.49	-1.36	-1.81**	-1.49	-1.33	-1.79**	-1.43	-1.33
	(0.84)	(1.00)	(0.97)	(0.86)	(0.99)	(0.97)	(0.74)	(1.01)	(1.02)
Midwest	-0.16	0.83	-0.53	-0.15	0.87	-0.51	-0.03	0.87	-0.54
	(0.67)	(0.74)	(0.74)	(0.69)	(0.74)	(0.74)	(0.68)	(0.75)	(0.74)
South	1.26*	1.02	-0.28	1.26*	1.06	-0.28	1.21*	0.93	-0.54
	(0.67)	(0.66)	(0.64)	(0.69)	(0.66)	(0.62)	(0.65)	(0.66)	(0.64)
West	0.72	0.07	-0.51	0.76	0.03	-0.53	0.85	0.10	-0.50
	(0.79)	(0.83)	(0.85)	(0.82)	(0.83)	(0.83)	(0.78)	(0.83)	(0.81)
High school graduate	1.48**	1.88*	0.19	1.52**	1.86*	0.19	1.72**	1.90*	0.30
	(0.73)	(1.03)	(1.06)	(0.74)	(1.05)	(1.06)	(0.85)	(1.00)	(1.09)
Some college	1.20	2.07**	0.86	1.15	1.94*	0.77	1.40*	2.04**	0.86
	(0.74)	(0.99)	(1.06)	(0.74)	(1.01)	(1.05)	(0.84)	(0.98)	(1.10)
College graduate	0.74	1.38	0.07	0.75	1.35	0.03	0.92	1.33	0.05
	(0.73)	(1.02)	(1.02)	(0.74)	(1.04)	(1.02)	(0.83)	(1.01)	(1.05)
N	528	528	528	528	528	528	528	528	528

Notes: Presented are the coefficients multinomial regression of intention to vote (with vote for Obama as the omitted base outcome) among registered voters. Standard errors are in parentheses. Omitted in the regressions are base categories of male, Independent, moderate, non-Hispanic white, age 18–29, Northeast, and less than high school.

*** p<0.01, ** p<0.05, * p<0.1

Moderation by Issue Importance and Election Engagement

As expected, when the interaction of high personal importance and global warming issue proximity was added as a predictor to the equations shown in Table 10.5, the impact of global warming issue proximity on candidate choice was strong and significant among registered voters who attached high importance to the issue. The interaction of personal importance with global warming issue proximity was highly significant, and the main effect for global warming issue proximity was not. Thus, issue proximity only predicted voting behavior in the high importance group.

Study 3—Content Analysis

Study 3 sought to assess the relation between what candidates in the 2010 Congressional elections said about global warming and their victory rates.

Data

Content Analysis

A content analysis of text on candidates' campaign websites (and congressional websites of incumbents) assigned each candidate to one of the four categories: "green" (if he/she made one or more statements that acknowledged the existence or human cause of global warming or endorsed the need for government actions, and did not make any "not-green" statements), "not-green" (if he/she made not-green statements and no green statements), "mixed" (if he/she made green and not-green statements), or "silent" (if he/she made no statements on the issue).

The procedures for the content analysis follow. A list of the names and campaign website addresses of all the candidates from Democratic and Republican Party in the 50 states and District of Columbia in the 2010 House and Senate elections was obtained from a directory created by Project Vote Smart, where the candidates registered their campaign information (www.votesmart.org). The campaign websites of incumbents were downloaded in October 2010. All the Congressional websites for the incumbent candidates were downloaded in December 2010.

All the webpages with text content were indexed, from which a list of webpages that contained any of four key terms ("climate," "global warming," "energy," or "cap") was generated for each candidate. Two coders (who were not aware of the research hypotheses being tested, and instructions to coders are available in Appendix C) independently read each website and answered a dozen yes/no questions following a set of detailed coding instructions (see Appendix C). Coders were able to answer "ambiguous" as well. The 12 coding questions asked coders to decide whether the candidate said each of the following ("GW/CC" below means global warming or climate change).

Q1. GW/CC has been happening.
- Global warming or climate change has been happening or will happen.
- There is scientific evidence indicating that GW/CC has been happening or will happen.

Q2. GW/CC has not been happening.
- Global warming or climate change has not been happening or will not happen.
- The candidate is not sure whether GW/CC has been happening or will happen.
- There is no, or little, or insufficient amount of scientific evidence indicating that GW/CC has been happening or will happen.
- The candidate is not sure whether there is (sufficient) scientific evidence that GW/CC has been happening or will happen.

Q3. GW/CC is man-made.
- Human actions, such as burning fossil fuels, are a cause of GW/CC.

Q4. GW/CC is not man-made.
- Human actions are not a cause of GW/CC.
- The candidate is not sure whether human actions cause GW/CC.

Q5. GW/CC is bad.
- Global warming or climate change will have one or more undesirable consequences.
- GW/CC is a serious problem.
- GW/CC is an important issue.

Q6. GW/CC is not bad.
- Global warming or climate change will not have undesirable consequences.
- The candidate is not sure whether GW/CC will have any undesirable consequences.
- GW/CC is NOT a serious problem.
- The candidate is not sure whether GW/CC is a (serious) problem.
- GW/CC is NOT an important issue.
- The candidate is not sure whether GW/CC is an important issue.

Q7. Producing energy by "green" methods is good.
- Passing laws that would encourage producing more energy from "clean" sources, such as wind, solar power, water, or nuclear power plants, would be a good idea.

Q8. Producing energy by "green" methods is not good.
- Passing laws that would encourage producing more energy from "clean" sources, such as wind, solar power, water, or nuclear power plants, would NOT be a good idea.

- The candidate is not sure whether passing laws that would encourage producing more energy from "clean" sources, such as wind, solar power, water, or nuclear power plants, would be a good idea.

Q9. Actions should be taken.
- Actions should be taken to reduce climate change or the effects of climate change.
- We should limit the amount of greenhouse gasses (carbon dioxide, CO_2) in the future.

Q10. NO actions should be taken.
- No actions should be taken about global warming or climate change.
- No actions should be taken to limit the amount of greenhouse gasses in the future.
- The candidate is not sure whether we should take actions about GW/CC.
- The candidate is not sure whether we should limit carbon emissions.

Q11. Support cap-and-trade.
- The candidate supports cap-and-trade or American Clean Energy and Security Act, or Waxman-Markey Bill, 2009.

Q12. Oppose cap-and-trade.
- The candidate opposes cap-and-trade.
- The candidate is not sure whether cap-and-trade is a good idea.

Agreement between the two coders was excellent: the coders agreed for 90% of candidates for question 1, 96% for question 2, 94% for question 3, 98% for questions 4 92% for question 5, 98% for question 6, 76% for question 7, 97% for question 8, 85% for question 9, 96% for question 10, 96% for question 11, and 88% for question 12. When the first two coders disagreed when answering a question, a third coder performed another round of independent coding of the candidate's entire website. The discrepancies in coding answers among the three coders were resolved by majority rule. The investigators resolved remaining discrepancies that arose when two coders answered a question with "ambiguous" and performed quality checks to confirm the accuracy of all final coding decisions.

A candidate was considered to have made "green statements" on climate change if he/she said any of the following: that global warming has been happening, that human activities are at least partly responsible for global warming, that global warming would be bad, that ameliorative actions about climate change should be taken; that he/she supported the cap and trade policy (i.e., a "yes" answer to questions 1, 3, 5, 9 or 11). A candidate was considered to have made "not-green statements" on climate change if he/she said any of the following: that global warming has not been happening, that human activities are not responsible for global warming, that global warming would not be bad, and that no ameliorative actions about climate change should be taken (i.e., a "yes" answer to questions 2, 4, 6 or 10).

Each candidate was assigned to one of the four categories. A candidate was categorized as "green" if he/she made one or more "green" statements and did not make any "not-green" statements. A candidate was categorized as "not-green" if he/she made one or more "not-green" statements and did not make any "green" statements. A candidate was categorized as "mixed" if he/she made "green" statements and "not-green" statements. A candidate was categorized as "silent" if he/she did not make any "green" statements or "not-green" statements.

Predicting Electoral Victory

One might imagine that a candidate's decision about what to say, if anything, about global warming is influenced by his or her perception of his or her chances of electoral success. For example, if candidates perceived taking a position on climate to be electorally risky, perhaps only "safe" candidates took such a position publicly. We addressed this issue by controlling for what we call the "party margin." For the House candidates, the party margin was the difference between the percent of votes cast for the Democratic candidate and the percent of votes cast for the Republican candidate in the same district during the 2008 elections. For the Senate candidates, party margin was the difference between the percent of votes cast for Barack Obama and the percent of votes cast for John McCain in the 2008 Presidential election in the State.

To explore whether a candidate's electoral success depended on his/her own position on global warming and that of his or her opponent, we estimated the parameters of logistic regression equations predicting victory by the Democratic candidate. The following were among the predictors.

- Two dummy variables for taking a green position and taking a not-green position by the Democratic candidate; being silent or mixed was the omitted category.
- Two dummy variables for taking a green position and taking a not-green position by the Republican candidate; being silent or mixed was again the omitted category.
- An interaction term, coded 1 when the Democrat took a green position and the Republican took a not-green position.
- Two dummy variables indicating whether the Democrat or the Republican was an incumbent running for reelection.
- The party margin in the 2008 Congressional elections.

Results

Candidates' Positions on Climate Change

Among the Democratic Senate candidates, more than half (57%) took a green position on global warming, and the remainder (43%) were silent or mixed (see

TABLE 10.6 Study 3: Congressional Candidates' Positions on Global Warming Expressed on Their 2010 Websites

Position expressed	Democratic candidates (%)	Republican candidates (%)
Senate Races		
Green	57.14	8.57
Silent/mixed	42.86	82.86
Not-green	0.00	8.57
Total	100.00	100.00
	(N = 35)	(N = 35)
House Races		
Green	59.56	6.13
Silent/mixed	39.71	78.30
Not-green	0.74	15.57
Total	100.00	100.00
	(N = 408)	(N = 424)
Senate and House Races		
Green	59.37	6.32
Silent/mixed	39.95	78.65
Not-green	0.68	15.03
Total	100.00	100.00
	(N = 443)	(N = 459)

Notes: 35 Democratic Senate candidates and 35 Republican Senate candidates were included in the analysis. Two Senate races run in 2010 were excluded: Nevada, because the campaign website of Sharron Angle could not be downloaded prior to the Election Day due to technical problems; and South Dakota, because only one candidate ran there. We treated the Alaska race as having just two candidates, Scott McAdams and Lisa Murkowski, and excluded Joe Miller so that the race could be included in the analyses that presumed only two major party candidates competed. 408 Democratic and 424 Republican House candidates were included in the analysis. A total of 412 Democratic candidates and 431 Republican candidates ran in the 2010 House races. A total of 11 House candidates—4 Democratic candidates and 7 Republican candidates—were excluded from the analysis because their campaign websites could not be downloaded due to technical problems.

Table 10.6). Among the Republican Senate candidates, a large majority (83%) were silent/mixed; half of the remaining candidates took a green position (9%), and half took a not-green position (9%).

Majorities of House candidates were also silent/mixed. Among the Democratic House candidates, more than half (60%) took a green position on global warming, almost all of the remaining candidates (40%) were silent/mixed, and a tiny proportion (1%) took a not-green position. Among the Republican House candidates, a large majority (78%) were silent/mixed, 6% took a green position, and 16% took a not-green position.

Combinations of Candidate Positions and Race Outcomes

Among the 430 two-candidate House and Senate races (see Tables 10.7 and 10.8):

- in 31% of the races, both candidates were silent/mixed; Democrats won 17% of these races
- in 49%, the Democrat was green, and the Republican was silent/mixed; Democrats won 69% of these races
- in 7%, the Democrat was green, and the Republican was not-green; Democrats won 68% of these races
- in 3%, the Democrat and Republican were both green; Democrats won 18% of these races
- in 4%, the Democrat was silent/mixed, and the Republican was green; Democrats won none of these races
- in 6%, the Democrat was silent/mixed, and the Republican was not-green; Democrats won 4% of these races.

Thus, when Republican opponents were silent/mixed or took a not-green position, Democrats were much more likely to win if they took a green position than if they were silent/mixed. When Democratic candidates were silent/mixed, Republicans were more likely to win if they took a green or not-green position than if they were silent/mixed.

TABLE 10.7 Study 3: Co-Occurrence of Positions on Global Warming Expressed by Democrats and Republicans

Democrat's position on global warming	Republican's position on global warming			
	Green	Silent/mixed	Not-green	Total
Green	2.56%	49.07%	7.21%	58.84%
Silent/mixed	3.95%	30.70%	5.81%	40.47%
Not-green	0.00%	0.47%	0.23%	0.70%
Total	6.51%	80.23%	13.26%	100.00%

Note: The total number of the races is 430.

TABLE 10.8 Study 3: Victory Rates for Democratic Candidates According to the Positions Expressed on Global Warming by the Democratic Candidate and the Republican Candidate

Democrat's position on global warming	Republican's position on global warming		
	Green	Silent/mixed	Not-green
Green	18.18% (N = 11)	69.19% (N = 211)	67.74% (N = 31)
Silent/mixed	0.00% (N = 17)	17.42% (N = 132)	4.00% (N = 25)
Not-green	N/A	N/A	N/A

Note: N/A indicates that the number of races was 0, 1, or 2 and was therefore too small to yield reliable numbers.

As expected, in a logistic regression predicting victory by the Democrat, the more the 2008 party margin favored the Democratic candidate, the more likely the Democrat was to win in 2010 (see row 10 and column 2 of Table 10.9). Also as expected, Democrats were more likely to win if they were incumbents than if they were not (see row 8 and column 2 of Table 10.9). Surprisingly, Republican candidates were not more likely to win if they were incumbents than if they were not (see row 9 in column 2 of Table 10.9).

When the Republican was silent/mixed, the Democrat had a 17 percentage point greater probability of winning ($p = .02$) when he/she took a green position rather than being silent/mixed (see row 1 in column 2 of Table 10.9). When the Republican was silent/mixed, the Democrat's probability of winning did not change depending upon whether he/she was silent/mixed or took a not-green position (row 2 in column 2 of Table 10.9). Thus, when the Republican was silent/mixed, going green apparently helped the Democratic candidate, and going not-green did not hurt.

When the Republican took a not-green position, the Democrat gained even more by taking a green position: he/she was 92 percentage points more likely to win ($p = .03$) than when he/she was silent/mixed (see rows 1 and 7 in column 2 of Table 10.9).[2] When the Republican took a green position, the Democrat gained more votes when taking a green position than when being silent/mixed ($b = .17, p = 02$, see row 1 in column 2 of Table 10.9).

When the Democrat was silent/mixed, the Democrat's probability of winning was the same regardless of whether the Republican took a green position or was silent/mixed (see row 4 in column 2 of Table 10.9). In other words, taking a green position did not help the Republican candidate when the Democrat was silent/mixed. However, when the Democrat was silent/mixed, the Democrat was 34 percentage points less likely to win ($p < .01$) when the Republican took

TABLE 10.9 Study 3: Regression Predicting Victory by the Democratic Candidate and Regression Predicting the Democratic Candidate's Margin of Victory in Races in which the Democrat's or Republican's Vote Share Was Between 40% and 60% in the 2010 House and Senate Races

Predictor	DV = Democratic victory		DV = Democratic candidate's margin of victory
	Coefficient (1)	Marginal Effect (2)	Coefficient (3)
Democrat: green	1.03** (.45)	.17** (.08)	.03* (.02)
Democrat: not-green	−.46 (1.45)	−.07 (.20)	.01 (.06)
Democrat: silent/ mixed (omitted)			
Republican: green	−.29 (1.36)	−.05 (.21)	−.03 (.04)
Republican: not-green	−4.27*** (1.58)	−.34*** (.07)	−.09** (.04)
Republican: silent/ mixed (omitted)			
Democrat: green × Republican: not-green	4.08** (1.67)	.75*** (.13)	.10** (.05)
Democrat: Incumbent	2.60*** (.71)	.42*** (.11)	.10*** (.02)
Republican: Incumbent	.42 (1.09)	.08 (.21)	.00 (.03)
2008 Party Margin	.06*** (.01)	.01*** (.00)	.00*** (.00)
R^2	.62		.47
N	430		195

Notes: Presented in column (1)-(2) are the coefficients and marginal probabilities (with standard errors in parentheses) of a logistic regression of predicting victory by the Democratic candidate. Two incumbency dummy variables were used, and one might imagine this occurred because the two incumbency predictors were nearly perfectly collinear, so their effects could not be separated. But in fact, 13% of the races we examined involved no incumbent at all, so statistical separation was possible. Presented in column (3) are the coefficients (with standard errors in parentheses) of an OLS regression of predicting the margin of victory by the Democratic candidate. The margin of victory was subjected to a natural log transformation after adding 1 because a Box-Cox analysis rejected the linear form of the dependent variable (likelihood ratio test statistic $\chi2 = 94.76$, $p = .00$) but failed to reject the natural log form—likelihood ratio test statistic $\chi2 = 0.79$, $p = .37$). ***$p < .01$, **$p < .05$, *$p<0.1$

a not-green position than when the Republican was silent/mixed (see row 5 and column 2 of Table 10.9). This is the one instance in which taking a not-green position apparently helped a candidate. That is, being silent in the face of a not-green Republican opponent was not wise for the Democrat. And by going green, the Democrat was able to eliminate the advantage that the Republican might have gained by being not-green. That is, in the face of a green Democrat, the Republican gained no votes by shifting from being silent/mixed to being not-green (see rows 5 and 7 in column 2 of Table 10.9, $b = .39, p = .76$).

Predictors of the Margin of Victory

Similar conclusions were supported by an OLS regression predicting the Democrat's margin of victory in races in which at least one candidate's vote share was within 10 percentage points of 50% (which are races whose outcomes could easily have been changed). Margin of victory was defined as the share of the votes cast for the Democrat minus the share of votes cast for the Republican. As expected, the more the party margin in 2008 favored the Democrat, the larger was the margin of victory for the Democrat in 2010 (see row 10 in column 3 of Table 10.9). Also as expected, Democrats had a larger 2010 margin of victory if they were incumbents than if they were not (see row 8 in column 3 of Table 10.9). Again, Republicans did not manifest a larger margin of victory if they were incumbents than if they were not (see row 9 in column 3 of Table 10.9). After accounting for the influences of party margin and of incumbency, the directions and statistical significances of the coefficients in column 3 of Table 10.9 were the same as those of the comparable coefficients in columns 1 and 2 of Table 10.9.

Simulation

To gauge the changes in the Democrats' electoral successes that might have occurred if the candidates had taken different positions on global warming, we conducted a simulation using the parameter estimates reported in column 3 of Table 10.9, focused on four types of races, as below.

1   Races in which the Democrat lost by a small margin, and both he/she and the Republican were silent/mixed. The positive coefficient for the Democrat taking a green position indicates that the Democrat's margin of victory would have increased if the Democrat had taken a green position instead of being silent/mixed. Therefore, the Democrats might have won seats if they had expressed green positions in these races.
2   Races in which the Democrat lost by a small margin, and he/she was silent/mixed while the Republican was not-green. The positive interaction between the Democrat expressing a green position and the Republican expressing a not-green position indicates that the Democrat's margin of

victory would have increased if the Democrat had taken a green position instead of being silent/mixed. Therefore, the Democrats might have won seats if they had expressed green positions in these races.

3   Races in which the Republican lost by a small margin, and both he/she and his/her Democratic opponent were silent/mixed. The negative coefficient for the Republican taking a not-green position indicates that the Republican's margin of victory would have increased if the Republican had taken a not-green position instead of being silent/mixed position. Therefore, the Republicans might have won seats if they had taken a not-green position in these races.

4   Races in which the Republican lost by a small margin, and he/she took a not-green position while his/her Democratic opponent took a green position. The negative coefficient for the Republican taking a not-green position was smaller in magnitude than the positive coefficient of the interaction between the Democrat taking a green position and the Republican taking a not-green position. Therefore, the Republicans might have won seats if they had been silent/mixed in these races.

The mechanics of the simulation are as follows. For race type (1), the Democratic candidate was hypothetically switched from silent/mixed to green, holding the Republican's silent/mixed position unchanged. The margin of victory for the Democrat was increased by 3 percentage points. For race type 2, the Democratic candidate was hypothetically switched from silent/mixed to green, holding the Republican's not-green position unchanged. The margin of victory for the Democrat was increased by 10 percentage points. For race type 3, the Republican candidate was hypothetically switched from silent/mixed to not-green, holding the Democrat's silent/mixed position unchanged. The margin of victory for the Republican was increased by 9 percentage points. For race type 4, the Republican candidate was hypothetically switched from not-green to silent/mixed, holding the Democrat's green position unchanged. The margin of victory for the Republican was increased by 10 percentage points.

We estimated how many election outcomes might have changed in two ways. First, using the coefficients presented in column 3 in Table 10.9, Democrats would have won 6 additional House races if the Democrat had taken a green position instead of being silent/mixed. Republicans would have won 7 additional House seats if the Republican had taken a not-green position instead of being silent/mixed.

Second, because the coefficients in column 3 in Table 10.9 are all estimated with uncertainty, and they each have a standard error, it is possible to generate a second set of simulation results treating each effect as being at the end of its 95% confidence interval that would yield the maximum plausible number of seat changes. Using this methodology, Democrats would have won a maximum of 15 additional seats (14 in the House and 1 in the Senate) if the Democrat had taken a green position instead of being silent/mixed. Republicans would have won a maximum of 26 additional Congressional seats if the Republican had been silent/ mixed instead of being not-green or if the Republican had been not-green instead of being silent/ mixed. Among these 26 seat gains, 10 (all in the House) would have been gained by the Republican taking a silent/mixed position instead of taking a not-green position, and 16 (2 in the Senate and 14 in the House) would have been gained if the Republican had taken a not-green position instead of being silent/mixed.

These simulations indicate that control of the House most likely would not have flipped to the Democrats even if the Democrats had all expressed strategically wise positions and the Republicans maintained the positions they expressed. Likewise, control of the Senate most likely would not have flipped to the Republicans if the Republicans had all expressed strategically wise positions while the Democrats maintained the positions they expressed.

Study 4—Content Analysis and Experimental Evidence from a National Survey in 2011

Study 4 employed a within-subject experiment embedded in a survey of a nationally representative sample of American adults (in September 2011) and content analysis of actual political candidates' stances on the issue of global warming. In the experiment, each respondent was asked the following five voting questions of hypothetical matchup between actual candidates where the order in which the five questions were asked was randomized. We used the standard method in political science to assess the potential impact of global warming beliefs and issue proximity on voting choice controlling for various other possible causes of vote choice. To construct the issue proximity between the actual candidates and respondents, we conducted a content analysis on the six candidates evaluated in the hypothetical matchup voting questions, and assigned each of them an index score on his/her stance on global warming.

Specifically, we set forth to explore the following two hypotheses. The first hypothesis concerns that Americans who believed in the existence and human cause of climate change preferred to vote for the Democratic candidate (President Obama) rather than to vote for any Republican candidate. Furthermore, among people who believed in the existence and human cause of climate change, their preference in the intent to vote toward President Obama was moderated by climate change beliefs strength and by political party identifications, with the preference being more pronounced among Democrats and people with high strength beliefs.

The second hypothesis probes further and directly tests for the presence of issue voting. It states that Americans would be more likely to vote for a candidate, Democratic or Republican, whose climate change belief matched their own than to vote for a candidate whose climate change belief differed from their own. Furthermore, evidence of climate change issue voting was moderated by climate change beliefs strength and by political party identifications, with the preference being more pronounced among Democrats and people with high strength beliefs.

Data and Method

Content Analysis

A content analysis of text on the CNN.com website assigned each candidate an index score of his/her stance on the issue of global warming based on 12 coding questions on fundamental beliefs about global warming.

The procedures for the content analysis follow. For each of the six candidates considered in the study: Barack Obama, Mitt Romney, Jon Huntsman, Michele Bachmann, Ron Paul and Rick Perry, a Google full-text search on the CNN.com website was conducted using search terms that indicate the candidate's last name and global warming or climate change, for example, "Obama AND ("global warming" OR "climate change") site://cnn.com." The search results were filtered for the time period between November 15, 2010 and September 12, 2011 (right before the survey used in this study was conducted) and then sorted by relevance; the resulting first 100 articles were used in the content analysis.

Three coders (who were not aware of the research hypotheses being tested, and instructions to coders are available in Appendix D) independently read each article for each candidate and answered a dozen yes/no questions following a set of detailed coding instructions. The 12 coding questions asked coders to decide whether the candidate said each of the following ("GW/CC" below means global warming or climate change).

Q1. GW/CC has been happening.
- Global warming or climate change has been happening or will happen.
- There is scientific evidence indicating that GW/CC has been happening or will happen.

Q2. GW/CC has not been happening.
- Global warming or climate change has not been happening or will not happen.
- The candidate is not sure whether GW/CC has been happening or will happen.
- There is no, or little, or insufficient amount of scientific evidence indicating that GW/CC has been happening or will happen.
- The candidate is not sure whether there is (sufficient) scientific evidence that GW/CC has been happening or will happen.

Q3. GW/CC is man-made.
- Human actions, such as burning fossil fuels, are a cause of GW/CC.

Q4. GW/CC is not man-made.
- Human actions are not a cause of GW/CC.
- The candidate is not sure whether human actions cause GW/CC.

Q5. GW/CC is bad.
- Global warming or climate change will have one or more undesirable consequences.
- GW/CC is a serious problem.
- GW/CC is an important issue.

Q6. GW/CC is not bad.
- Global warming or climate change will not have undesirable consequences.
- The candidate is not sure whether GW/CC will have any undesirable consequences.
- GW/CC is NOT a serious problem.
- The candidate is not sure whether GW/CC is a (serious) problem.
- GW/CC is NOT an important issue.
- The candidate is not sure whether GW/CC is an important issue.

Q7. Producing energy using "green" methods is good.
- Passing laws that would encourage producing more energy from "clean" sources, such as wind, solar power, water, or nuclear power plants, would be a good idea.

Q8. Producing energy using "green" methods is not good.
- Passing laws that would encourage producing more energy from "clean" sources, such as wind, solar power, water, or nuclear power plants, would NOT be a good idea.
- The candidate is not sure whether passing laws that would encourage producing more energy from "clean" sources, such as wind, solar power, water, or nuclear power plants, would be a good idea.

Q9. Actions about GW/CC should be taken.
- Actions should be taken to reduce climate change or the effects of climate change.
- We should limit the amount of greenhouse gasses (carbon dioxide, CO_2) in the future.

Q10. No actions about GW/CC should be taken.
- No actions should be taken about global warming or climate change.
- No actions should be taken to limit the amount of greenhouse gasses in the future.
- The candidate is not sure whether we should take actions about GW/CC.
- The candidate is not sure whether we should limit carbon emissions.

Q11. The candidate supported cap-and-trade.
* The candidate supports cap-and-trade or American Clean Energy and Security Act, or Waxman-Markey Bill, 2009.

Q12. The candidate opposed cap-and-trade.
* The candidate opposes cap-and-trade.
* The candidate is not sure whether cap-and-trade is a good idea.

Agreement between the three coders was excellent: the agreement was 88%, 90% and 93% of all the 12 yes/no coding questions among the six candidates between any two of the three coders. Any discrepancies in coding answers among the three coders were resolved by majority rule.

The "yes"/"no" to the 12 coding questions were then converted to numerical values. A "no" to any of the 12 questions gave the candidate a value of 0, a "yes" to each of questions 1, 3, 5, 7, 9, and 11 gave the candidate a value of 1 each, and "yes" to each of questions 2, 4, 6, 8, 10, and 12 gave the candidate a value of –1. Summing up these numerical values across the 12 coding questions and scaled to range between 0 and 1 with a higher value indicating a more positive attitude toward global warming yielded an index score for each candidate. The index scores were 1 (Barack Obama), 0.63 (Mitt Romney), 0.63 (Jon Huntsman), 0.13 (Michele Bachmann), 0.38 (Ron Paul) and 0 (Rick Perry).

Data Collection

The data used in this study is a random digit dial telephone survey of a national probability sample of U.S. adults aged 18 and older conducted by Ipsos Public Affairs of Washington, DC, between September 8 and September 12, 2011. 890 respondents were interviewed on a landline phone and 244 were interviewed on a cell phone. Interviews were administrated in English and Spanish.

Samples were drawn from both landline and cellular random digit dial (RDD) frames to represent people with access to either a landline or cell phone. The landline and cell phone samples were provided by Survey Sampling International, LLC. Numbers for the landline sample were drawn with equal probabilities from active blocks (area code + exchange + two-digit block number) that contained one or more residential directory listings. The cell phone sample was drawn through a systematic sampling from 1000 blocks dedicated to cellular service according to the Telcordia database.

The data were weighted to ensure that the sample composition reflects the U.S. population as documented by figures from the U.S. Census Bureau. Weights were created to adjust for differential probabilities of selection due to the number of adults in the household, the number of voice-use landlines and cell phones, and the overlap of landline and cell phone RDD frames, as well as noncoverage and nonresponse through post-stratification. Post-stratification matched the population proportions of age and sex, education, ethnicity and race, and region using targets from the May 2011 Current Population Survey conducted by the U.S. Census Bureau. The AAPOR Response Rate 3 was 8%.

Table 10.10 displays distributions of unweighted and weighted demographics along with a national benchmark computed using the data from the Current Population Survey from the U.S. Census Bureau in May 2011. Before the weights were applied, the sample was overall similar to the American population with a slight under-representation of younger (aged 18–34) males and females and people with no college education, and a small over-representation of older (aged 55 or more) males and females, white, and college graduates. After the weights were applied, the sample was nearly identical to the population except for a slight over-representation of people without college education and a slight under-representation of people who had some college but without college degree. All results reported below are adjusted for sampling weights, though unweighted data produced comparable findings.

TABLE 10.10   Study 4: Demographics of the Sample and Current Population Survey

	Ipsos Sept. 2011 (unweighted) (%)	Ipsos Sept. 2011 (weighted) (%)	CPS May 2011 (%)	Difference: Ipsos (weighted) – CPS(%)
		Gender and Age		
Male aged 18–34	9.3	15.4	15.5	–.1
Male aged 35–54	15.6	18.3	17.7	.6
Male aged 55 or more	24.7	14.7	15.2	–.5
Female aged 18–34	8.0	15.2	15.3	–.1
Female aged 35–54	14.3	18.8	18.4	.4
Female aged 55 or more	28.1	17.6	17.9	–.3
Total	100.0	100.0	100.0	
	(N = 1134)	(N = 1134)	(N = 230,805,929)	

	Ipsos Sept. 2011 (unweighted) (%)	Ipsos Sept. 2011 (weighted) (%)	CPS May 2011 (%)	Difference: Ipsos (weighted) – CPS(%)
		Race and Ethnicity		
Hispanic	10.1	13.7	14.0	–.3
White only	74.2	67.4	67.7	–.3
Black only	8.8	11.6	11.6	.0
Others	6.9	7.2	6.7	.5
Total	100.0	100.0	100.0	
	(N = 1134)	(N = 1134)	(N = 230,805,929)	
		Education		
No college	25.7	48.8	44.3	4.5
Some college	38.5	24.0	28.2	–4.2
College or higher	35.9	27.3	27.4	–.1
Total	100.0	100.0	100.0	
	(N = 1134)	(N = 1134)	(N = 230,805,929)	
		Region		
Northeast	19.3	18.5	18.4	.1
Midwest	21.8	21.9	21.8	.1
South	36.1	36.9	36.7	.2
West	22.8	22.6	23.1	–.5
Total	100.0	100.0	100.0	
	(N = 1134)	(N = 1134)	(N = 230,805,929)	

EXPERIMENTAL CONDITIONS

In this experiment, all the respondents were asked the following five questions where the order of the questions was randomized.

1 "If the 2012 presidential election were being held today and the candidates were Barack Obama, the Democrat, and Mitt Romney, the Republican, for whom would you vote?"

2 "If the 2012 presidential election were being held today and the candidates were Barack Obama, the Democrat, and Jon Huntsman, the Republican, for whom would you vote?"

3 "If the 2012 presidential election were being held today and the candidates were Barack Obama, the Democrat, and Michele Bachmann, the Republican, for whom would you vote?"

4   "If the 2012 presidential election were being held today and the candidates were Barack Obama, the Democrat, and Ron Paul, the Republican, for whom would you vote?"

5   "If the 2012 presidential election were being held today and the candidates were Barack Obama, the Democrat, and Rick Perry, the Republican, for whom would you vote?"

Measures

CANDIDATE PREFERENCES AS THE DEPENDENT MEASURES

Two dependent measures were used. First, in exploring whether the respondents who believed in global warming would vote for Barack Obama more often or vote for a Republican candidate, the dependent measure was the frequency of voting for Barack Obama, which is the number of times the respondent stated that he/she would vote for Barack Obama in the hypothetical 2012 presidential election when his Republican opponent was one of the five Republican candidates—Mitt Romney, Ron Paul, Rick Perry, Jon Huntsman, and Michele Bachmann. In each of the five questions, an indicator was constructed such that voting for Mr. Obama was coded 1 and 0 for all other answer.s The sum of the five indicators was the dependent variable measure, an integer ranging from 0 to 5. Question wording and coding for all measures are described in Appendix D.

Second, in assessing the preference for candidates whose global warming belief matched the respondent's global warming belief, the dependent measure for each voting choice occasion was dichotomous with a value of 1 indicating the respondent said he/she would vote for the candidate presented in the voting choice occasion and 0 otherwise. Six named candidates (Barack Obama, Mitt Romney, Ron Paul, Rick Perry, Jon Huntsman, and Michele Bachmann) plus the responses of voting for an unnamed candidate or "don't know" or refusal, all of which were voluntary responses, were measured in a numerical variable ranging from a value of 1 to 7. For each alternative/candidate in each voting choice occasion, one attribute was measured: a global warming belief proximity measure between the respondent and the candidate, the details of which are described below.

GLOBAL WARMING BELIEF AND BELIEF PROXIMITY AS INDEPENDENT MEASURES

Several independent measures were employed. First, the respondent's global warming belief—believing the existence and the human cause of global warming—was an indicator with a value of 1 indicating the respondent said that the world's temperature has been probably going up in the past 100 years and that the warming is caused mostly or partly by things people do, and 0 otherwise.

Second, the respondent-candidate proximity in global warming belief was measured using three methods: Euclidean distance and city block distance (Downs, 1957; Enelow & Hinich, 1984), and directional similarity (Rabinowitz, 1978; Rabinowitz & Macdonald, 1989). Let V_i and C_j denote respondent i's and candidate j's placement on global warming belief, $-(V_i - C_j)^2$, $-|V_i - C_j|$, $V_i \star C_j$ are the Euclidean distance, city block, and directional measures of respondent-candidate belief congruence, respectively. Each of the seven (potential) candidates mentioned in the survey questions was assigned to a number between 0 and 1, C_j, where 1 indicates most accepting of global warming and 0 most skeptical of global warming. C_j took the values of the index score generated from the content analysis above, specifically, they were 1 (Barack Obama), 0.63 (Mitt Romney), 0.63 (Jon Huntsman), 0.13 (Michele Bachmann), 0.38 (Ron Paul) and 0 (Rick Perry), respectively (Other/DFRF was assigned to be 0). Respondents' global warming belief, V_i, refers to a respondent's global warming belief—believing the existence and the human cause of global warming measure that is described above.

CERTAINTY OF GLOBAL WARMING BELIEF AS MODERATOR MEASURE

People who said they were "extremely sure" about their belief on whether the world's temperature has been going up in the past 100 years were coded as high certainty people, and the rest were coded as low certainty people. Other moderators such as personal importance of the issue of global warming were unfortunately not asked in the survey.

CONTROL VARIABLES

Two sets of control variables were constructed: political variables and demographics. Three political variables were employed: respondents' political party affiliation, overall job approval of President Obama, and the perception of the country going in the right direction. A standard set of demographics included sex, race, Hispanic ethnicity, age, marital status, education, income, and region.

Analysis

GLOBAL WARMING BELIEF AND CANDIDATE PREFERENCE FOR BARACK OBAMA

Two sets of analysis were conducted to explore the two research questions. The first addressed the following question: in a hypothetical presidential election that consisted of Mr. Obama and a Republican candidate, would respondents who believed global warming has been happening and believed the warming has been caused in part by human actions vote for Mr. Obama more often than vote for a Republican contender? To account for political party identification and other variables that are the usual suspects of modeling the voting behavior, ordered logistic regression, which is commonly used in predicting ordinal outcomes, was used to control for the influences of these variables. Our results were identical whether conducted in ordered logistic or ordered probit regressions.

Ordered logistic or ordered probit regression predicting ordinal outcomes is based on the proportional odds assumption where the odds have the same ratio for all independent variables. Upon the finding by the diagnostic procedures (Brant, 1990) that proportional odds assumption did not hold in our data, a generalized ordered logistic regression was employed to relax the proportional odds assumption. Our results were very similar whether conducted in ordered logistic regression or generalized ordered logistic regression.

GLOBAL WARMING BELIEF PROXIMITY AND CANDIDATE PREFERENCE

The second analysis examined the following question: in a hypothetical presidential election that consisted of Mr. Obama and a Republican candidate, would respondents prefer a candidate whose global warming belief was at a closer proximity to the respondent's own global warming belief? To test the statistical significance of the preference for the candidate to whom the respondent was closer in global warming belief, the data were analyzed using McFadden's conditional logit model for discrete choice data (McFadden, 1974). The conditional logit model, or alternative-specific conditional logit model, is designed for applications when a respondent is presented with two (or more) alternatives and selects one (or more) of them in each choice occasion. Selections are modeled as a linear function of alternative-specific characteristics and a random variable.

In the experiment embedded in the survey, a respondent encountered five voting choices occasions, and in each voting choice occasion, he/she was presented with two stated alternatives (two named candidates) and one implicit alternative (some other unnamed candidate or no response) and selected one of them. Characteristics potentially affecting selection of an alternative include respondent-candidate proximity on global warming belief, and respondents' demographics and political attitudes that are described in the control variables above.

Another analytic approach we could take is modeling an individual fixed effect to capture all the factors that may have impacted each citizen's behavior, including variables that are observable and measured in the survey (e.g., the voter's political party affiliation), variables that are observable but were not measured in the survey (e.g., the citizen's beliefs and attitudes on many other policy issues), and unobservable attributes of individuals. All these factors could have influenced the voter's beliefs on global warming, so an appropriate estimation method would be conditional or individual fixed effect logistic regression, with a first-difference estimator. When we carried this out, we observed the same results as shown below.

Results

Global Warming Belief and Candidate Preference for Mr. Obama

GLOBAL WARMING EXISTENCE/HUMAN CAUSE BELIEF AND CANDIDATE PREFERENCE

Americans were nearly equally divided on never or always voting for Mr. Obama: a plurality (38%) of Americans stated that they would not vote for Mr. Obama in any of the five hypothetical elections, and another plurality (40%) of Americans stated that they would vote for Mr. Obama in all five hypothetical elections; the remaining said they would vote for Mr. Obama in one to four times out of the five questions: 5% one time, 4% two times, 5% three times, and 8% four times. Respondents who believed global warming has been happening would vote for Mr. Obama for an average of 2.88 times, while respondents who believed global warming has not been happening would vote for Mr. Obama for an average of 1.23 times, and the difference was significant ($d = 1.75$, $p = .00$). This estimate clearly showed that global warming believers preferred Mr. Obama to any Republican contender, but the estimate was unadjusted and to account for the influence of other political attitudes and demographics, we turned to regression analysis.

In the full sample, believing that global warming has been happening and that it is caused by human actions influenced voting behavior in the expected way after controlling for party identification, perception of country going in the right direction, approval of President Obama, and demographics, and the influence was significant and in the expected direction (see Table 10.11, which displays the coefficient estimates from ordered logistic regressions). Believing in GW existence and human cause led people to vote for Mr. Obama more often than vote for a Republican candidate ($b = 0.74$, $p < .01$; see row 1 in column 1 in Table 10.11).

Other factors thought to influence candidate choice also had significant effects in the expected directions. Democrats voted more often for Mr. Obama than voted for a Republican candidate ($b = 1.52$, $p < .01$), and Republicans voted less often for Mr. Obama than vote for a Republican candidate ($b = -0.76$, $p = .01$). People who approved of President Obama's performance would vote more often for Mr. Obama than voted for a Republican candidate ($b = 5.46$, $p < .01$). Additionally, people who thought the country is going in the right direction would vote for Mr. Obama less often than vote for a Republican candidate ($b = -0.65$, $p = .01$); whites would vote for Mr. Obama less often ($b = -0.83$, $p < .01$).

These results held true when we ran the regression analysis among registered voters only. Among registered voters, believing in GW existence/human cause led them to vote for Mr. Obama more often than voting for a Republican candidate ($b = 0.58$, $p = .02$; see row 1 in column 2 in Table 10.11).

TABLE 10.11 Study 4: The Impact of Global Warming Belief on Candidate Preference for Barack Obama

Predictor	By party identification					By belief certainty	
	All sample (1)	Voters (2)	Democrats (3)	Republicans (4)	Independents (5)	High certainty (6)	Low certainty (7)
GW existence/human cause	0.74*** (0.22)	0.58** (0.25)	1.16** (0.51)	0.14 (0.56)	0.95*** (0.30)	1.87*** (0.62)	0.50* (0.26)
Democrat	1.52*** (0.25)	1.32*** (0.28)				1.28** (0.51)	1.69*** (0.31)
Republican	-0.76*** (0.27)	-0.86*** (0.29)				-1.84* (1.07)	-0.43 (0.32)
Country in right direction	-0.65** (0.26)	-0.37 (0.29)	-0.17 (0.48)	-1.57* (0.90)	-0.81** (0.38)	0.54 (0.61)	-0.86*** (0.31)
Approval of President Obama	5.46*** (0.38)	5.64*** (0.45)	5.76*** (0.83)	6.27*** (1.32)	6.00*** (0.54)	6.17*** (0.99)	6.04*** (0.49)
Male	0.12 (0.19)	0.14 (0.21)	-0.68* (0.40)	-0.13 (0.49)	0.51* (0.27)	0.39 (0.50)	0.12 (0.22)
White	-0.83*** (0.26)	-0.92*** (0.34)	-0.17 (0.63)	-0.75 (0.68)	-1.16*** (0.33)	-1.17 (0.94)	-0.78*** (0.30)
Hispanic	-0.48 (0.36)	-0.73 (0.49)	0.52 (0.81)	-1.39 (1.03)	-0.52 (0.54)	0.54 (1.02)	-0.61 (0.41)
Married	-0.26 (0.23)	-0.29 (0.26)	-0.30 (0.50)	-0.81 (0.79)	-0.25 (0.29)	-0.71 (0.67)	-0.33 (0.27)
Age: 25–34	-0.59 (0.39)	-0.33 (0.53)	0.24 (0.76)	-0.66 (1.11)	-0.86* (0.51)	0.90 (0.77)	-0.92* (0.53)
Age: 35–44	-0.28 (0.36)	-0.12 (0.50)	0.93 (0.71)	-1.92 (1.21)	-0.33 (0.47)	0.56 (0.80)	-0.17 (0.43)

Age: 45–54	−0.63 (0.40)	−0.31 (0.54)	0.55 (0.82)	−0.52 (1.21)	−0.96★ (0.54)	−0.62 (0.45)
Age: 55–64	−0.19 (0.38)	0.09 (0.53)	0.78 (0.74)	−0.90 (1.27)	−0.31 (0.50)	−0.37 (0.48)
Age: 65+	−0.01 (0.38)	0.34 (0.51)	0.93 (0.91)	−1.71 (1.04)	0.36 (0.54)	−0.02 (0.44)
High school graduate	−0.16 (0.39)	−0.64 (0.52)	−1.01 (0.75)	−1.46 (1.18)	0.33 (0.62)	−0.03 (0.49)
Some college	0.11 (0.38)	−0.04 (0.51)	−0.81 (0.75)	−0.71 (0.83)	0.48 (0.64)	0.35 (0.51)
College graduate	0.39 (0.41)	0.07 (0.56)	−0.95 (0.83)	−0.50 (0.96)	1.05 (0.67)	0.29 (0.56)
Region—Midwest	0.12 (0.30)	−0.26 (0.30)	−0.98 (0.64)	0.94 (0.81)	0.38 (0.44)	0.47 (0.37)
Region—South	−0.31 (0.26)	−0.51★ (0.27)	−1.03★ (0.57)	0.79 (0.75)	−0.13 (0.42)	−1.18★★ (0.54)
Region—West	0.12 (0.28)	0.10 (0.36)	−1.18★ (0.71)	0.82 (0.91)	0.30 (0.43)	0.13 (0.61)
Income: $15K–$25K	0.65 (0.43)	0.38 (0.49)	0.34 (0.64)	−0.02 (2.24)	0.86 (0.67)	0.53 (0.88)
Income: $25K–$40K	1.02★★ (0.47)	0.93★ (0.48)	0.26 (0.55)	1.28 (2.49)	0.68 (0.68)	−0.76 (0.89)
Income: $40K–$50K	0.96★★ (0.49)	0.77 (0.50)	1.49 (1.13)	−0.98 (2.43)	1.15★ (0.66)	1.10 (0.93)

continued…

Table 10.11 continued…

Predictor	By Party Identification					By Belief Certainty	
	All Sample (1)	Voters (2)	Democrats (3)	Republicans (4)	Independents (5)	High certainty (6)	Low certainty (7)
Income: $50K–$75K	0.54 (0.44)	0.52 (0.49)	0.75 (0.72)	0.63 (2.14)	0.20 (0.62)	0.26 (0.77)	0.70 (0.59)
Income: $75K–$100K	1.29*** (0.48)	1.32** (0.54)	1.50* (0.87)	−0.13 (2.69)	1.22* (0.62)	1.46 (1.05)	1.28** (0.58)
Income: $100K or higher	0.88* (0.45)	0.87* (0.49)	1.82 (1.11)	0.36 (2.50)	0.58 (0.57)	0.01 (1.07)	1.17** (0.53)
Constant (cutoff 1)	1.71*** (0.62)	1.35** (0.67)	0.21 (1.00)	0.18 (2.47)	2.53** (1.10)	1.98* (1.19)	2.29*** (0.85)
Constant (cutoff 2)	2.22*** (0.61)	1.90*** (0.66)	0.55 (0.99)	1.01 (2.56)	3.02*** (1.10)	2.52** (1.21)	2.84*** (0.84)
Constant (cutoff 3)	2.70*** (0.61)	2.30*** (0.66)	0.98 (0.96)	1.65 (2.62)	3.53*** (1.09)	3.14** (1.23)	3.35*** (0.84)
Constant (cutoff 4)	3.25*** (0.61)	2.95*** (0.67)	1.92* (0.98)	2.05 (2.68)	4.03*** (1.10)	4.00*** (1.23)	3.84*** (0.85)
Constant (cutoff 5)	4.20*** (0.64)	3.89*** (0.71)	2.70*** (1.03)	2.90 (2.79)	5.20*** (1.15)	5.02*** (1.31)	4.87*** (0.87)
N	1,071	893	341	278	452	275	771

Notes: Presented are the coefficients of ordered logistic regressions and standard errors in parentheses. Each column is a separate regression. Dependent variable in all columns is the number of times the respondent said he/she would vote for Mr. Obama against a Republican candidate in a hypothetical 2012 presidential election, an integer ranging from 0 to 5. *** $p<0.01$, ** $p<0.05$, * $p<0.1$

The positive relationship between global warming belief (on existence and human cause) and candidate preference for Barack Obama was apparent among Democrats and among Independents. Believing that global warming has been happening and that it is caused by human actions was associated with voting for Mr. Obama more often than voting for a Republican candidate ($b = 1.16$, $p = .03$ among Democrats, see row 1 in column 3 of Table 10.11; $b = 0.95$, $p < .01$ among Independents, see row 1 in column 5 of Table 10.11). However, the relationship between global warming existence/human cause belief and candidate preference was not significant among Republicans ($b = .14$, $p = .81$; see row 1 in column 4 of Table 10.11).

The positive relationship between GW existence/human cause belief and candidate preference was stronger among people with high certainty than among people with low certainty about their beliefs. Among low certainty people, believing in GW has been happening and that it is caused by human actions led them to vote for Mr. Obama more often than vote for a Republican candidate ($b = 0.50$, $p = .06$; see row 1 in column 7 of Table 10.11). But among high certainty people, believing in GW has been happening and that it is caused by human actions led them to vote for Mr. Obama more often than vote for a Republican candidate by a larger magnitude ($b = 1.87$, $p < .00$; see row 1 in column 6 of Table 10.11). In an alternative regression when the interaction term of GW existence/human cause belief and high certainty was included, this interaction was positive and significant ($b = 1.00$, $p = .06$) and the main effect of GW existence/human cause belief was also positive and significant ($b = 0.44$, $p - .07$).

Proximity on Global Warming Belief and Candidate Preference

Global warming belief proximity influenced candidate preference in the expected way after controlling for party identification, perception of country going in the right direction, approval of President Obama, and demographics, and the influence was significant and in the expected direction (see Table 10.12, which displays the coefficient estimates from alternative specific conditional logistic regression with voting for Barack Obama as the omitted base category). Matching the candidate's global warming belief closely with own global warming belief led people to be more likely to vote for the candidate ($b = .71$, $p < .01$; see row 1 in Table 10.12). The marginal effect of the global warming belief proximity on candidate preference was positive and significant (see row 2 in Table 10.12); the largest effect was in intent to vote for Barack Obama (m = .14 or 14 percentage points, $p < .01$), followed by intent to vote for Mitt Romney and Ron Paul ($m = .10$, $p < .01$ for both), then intent to vote for Rick Perry ($m = .08$, $p < .01$), and the smallest effect was intent to vote for Michele Bachmann and Jon Huntsman ($m = .07$, $p < .01$ for both).

Other factors thought to influence candidate choice also had significant effects in the expected directions. Democrats were less likely and Republicans were more likely to vote for any of the Republican candidates than for Mr. Obama (see rows 3–4 in Table 10.12). People who approved of President Obama's performance were less likely to vote for any of the Republican candidate than to vote for Mr. Obama (see row 6 in Table 10.12). Whites were more likely to vote for each of the Republican candidates than for Mr. Obama (see row 8 in Table 10.12).

The findings on the influence of global warming belief proximity on candidate preference were robust to alternative construction of proximity measures. In the city block or the Euclidian distance measure, matching the candidate's global warming belief closely with own global warming belief led people to be more likely to vote for the candidate ($b = .35$, $p < .00$ for both the city block and the Euclidian distance measure).

Moderation by political party

The positive relationship between global warming belief proximity and candidate preference in the full sample was apparent among Democrats and among Independents. Matching the candidate's global warming belief closely with own global warming belief led people to be more likely to vote for the candidate ($b = 1.07$, $p < .01$ among Democrats; $b = .99$, $p < .01$ among Independents). However, the relationship between global warming belief proximity and candidate preference was small among Republicans ($b = .19$, p-value was not available because of the failure to calculate the standard errors due to non-symmetry or high singularity of variance matrix).

Moderation by belief certainty

The positive relationship between global warming belief proximity and candidate preference was stronger among people with high certainty than among people with low certainty about their beliefs ($b = .96$, $p = .02$ among high certainty people; $b = .65$, $p < .01$ among low certainty people). The marginal effect of global warming belief proximity on intent to vote for Barack Obama was an increase of 24 percentage points ($p = .02$) among high certainty people compared to half of the amount, an increase of 12 percentage points ($p < .01$), among low certainty people.

TABLE 10.12 Study 4: The Impact of Global Warming Belief Proximity on Candidate Preference

Predictor	Vote for Barack Obama	Vote for Mitt Romney	Vote for Jon Huntsman	Vote for Michele Bachmann	Vote for Ron Paul	Vote for Rick Perry	Vote for other/ DKRF
GW belief proximity	0.71★★★ (0.15)	0.71★★★ (0.15)	0.71★★★ (0.15)	0.71★★★ (0.15)	0.71★★★ (0.15)	0.71★★★ (0.15)	0.71★★★ (0.15)
(Marginal effect of GW belief proximity)	0.14★★★ (0.03)	0.10★★★ (0.02)	0.07★★★ (0.02)	0.07★★★ (0.02)	0.10★★★ (0.02)	0.08★★★ (0.02)	0.04★★★ (0.01)
Democrat		−1.01★★★ (0.32)	−1.34★★★ (0.36)	−1.46★★★ (0.38)	−1.81★★★ (0.29)	−1.75★★★ (0.37)	−1.29★★★ (0.18)
Republican		1.62★★★ (0.34)	0.99★★★ (0.28)	0.62★★ (0.28)	0.78★★★ (0.30)	1.58★★★ (0.33)	−0.36★ (0.20)
Country in right direction		0.63 (0.40)	0.64 (0.44)	0.47 (0.41)	0.38 (0.36)	0.96★★ (0.40)	0.83★★★ (0.21)
Approval of President Obama		−6.11★★★ (0.49)	−5.85★★★ (0.51)	−5.38★★★ (0.47)	−4.96★★★ (0.40)	−6.49★★★ (0.51)	−4.28★★★ (0.26)
Male		0.17 (0.25)	−0.38 (0.25)	−0.11 (0.24)	−0.22 (0.22)	−0.11 (0.25)	−0.35★★ (0.15)
White		1.20★★★ (0.41)	0.93★★ (0.43)	1.33★★★ (0.49)	0.78★★ (0.34)	0.43 (0.44)	0.43★ (0.23)
Hispanic		0.31 (0.50)	0.03 (0.58)	0.82 (0.63)	0.13 (0.45)	−0.37 (0.55)	0.87★★★ (0.25)
Married		0.85 (0.54)	1.02★ (0.53)	−0.04 (0.56)	0.63 (0.50)	1.55★★★ (0.54)	1.31★★★ (0.27)

continued...

Table 10.12 continued...

Predictor	Vote for Barack Obama	Vote for Mitt Romney	Vote for Jon Huntsman	Vote for Michele Bachmann	Vote for Ron Paul	Vote for Rick Perry	Vote for Other/DKRF
Age: 25–34		0.39 (0.53)	0.94* (0.54)	0.65 (0.53)	0.30 (0.48)	1.12** (0.57)	0.27 (0.28)
Age: 35–44		0.65 (0.52)	0.63 (0.51)	0.44 (0.44)	0.31 (0.43)	1.14** (0.54)	1.39*** (0.27)
Age: 45–54		0.62 (0.58)	0.60 (0.51)	0.10 (0.45)	0.10 (0.46)	0.56 (0.58)	0.39 (0.27)
Age: 55–64		0.43 (0.50)	0.39 (0.49)	0.06 (0.45)	-0.02 (0.43)	0.29 (0.56)	0.37 (0.26)
Age: 65+		-1.01*** (0.32)	-1.34*** (0.36)	-1.46*** (0.38)	-1.81*** (0.29)	-1.75*** (0.37)	-1.29*** (0.18)
High school graduate		1.30* (0.69)	-0.24 (0.59)	-0.26 (0.59)	-0.18 (0.49)	0.71 (0.55)	0.69** (0.29)
Some college		1.25* (0.70)	-0.61 (0.57)	-0.33 (0.57)	-0.41 (0.50)	0.01 (0.53)	0.41 (0.29)
College graduate		1.08 (0.71)	-0.73 (0.58)	-0.89 (0.59)	-0.79 (0.51)	-0.18 (0.56)	0.09 (0.30)
Region—Midwest		0.52 (0.36)	0.13 (0.33)	-0.06 (0.37)	-0.20 (0.35)	0.57 (0.40)	-0.39* (0.24)
Region—South		0.58* (0.32)	0.19 (0.28)	0.17 (0.29)	0.31 (0.30)	0.96*** (0.35)	-0.02 (0.18)

	(1)	(2)	(3)	(4)	(5)	(6)
Region—West	0.45	0.41	0.02	-0.30	0.08	-0.14
	(0.37)	(0.36)	(0.34)	(0.33)	(0.40)	(0.20)
Income: $15K–$25K	0.27	-0.34	-0.50	0.53	0.22	-1.64***
	(0.53)	(0.55)	(0.58)	(0.48)	(0.60)	(0.29)
Income: $25K–$40K	-0.01	-1.08*	-0.65	0.02	0.36	-1.19***
	(0.57)	(0.58)	(0.60)	(0.50)	(0.61)	(0.32)
Income: $40K–$50K	-0.61	-0.15	-0.33	0.23	-0.06	-1.20***
	(0.57)	(0.65)	(0.58)	(0.52)	(0.63)	(0.31)
Income: $50K–$75K	0.02	-0.31	-0.13	0.92*	0.55	-0.91***
	(0.54)	(0.55)	(0.57)	(0.53)	(0.58)	(0.28)
Income: $75K–$100K	-0.03	-0.85	-0.66	0.58	-0.14	-1.82***
	(0.60)	(0.54)	(0.58)	(0.47)	(0.75)	(0.31)
Income: $100K or higher	0.35	-0.44	-0.76	0.82	0.49	-1.50***
	(0.57)	(0.54)	(0.60)	(0.51)	(0.65)	(0.28)
Constant	-0.51	1.89*	1.95*	1.81**	1.04	1.05**
	(0.96)	(1.02)	(1.12)	(0.73)	(0.92)	(0.50)
N	16,065	16,065	16,065	16,065	16,065	16,065

Notes: Presented are the coefficients (marginal probabilities of row 1 in row 2) of alternative specific conditional logistic regressions (standard errors in parentheses) of all respondents in the sample with Barack Obama as the base alternative. *** $p<0.01$, ** $p<0.05$, * $p<0.1$

There was a less consistent moderating effect by belief certainty in intent to vote for any of the Republican candidates. For example, the marginal effect of global warming belief proximity on intent to vote for Mitt Romney was an increase of 11 and 9 percentage points ($p = .04$; $p < .01$) among high and low certainty people, respectively; the marginal effect of global warming belief proximity on intent to vote for Rick Perry was an increase of 6 and 9 percentage points ($p = .09$; $p < .01$) among high and low certainty people, respectively.

Study 5—Experimental Evidence from a National Survey in 2015

Study 5 employed within-subject experiments with hypothetical elections in which a respondent heard three candidates in randomized order, one of whom took a green position, one took a not-green position, and one took a not-committal position. Our experiments explored the impact of taking green, not-green, and not-committal positions on voting and assessed whether this impact varied across Democrats, Independents, and Republicans.

Data

Data Collection

SSRS interviewed a representative national sample of 1,006 U.S. adults by telephone, 483 respondents were interviewed on a landline telephone, and 523 were interviewed on a cell phone. Interviews were conducted between January 7 and January 22, 2015, and were administrated in English and Spanish. The AAPOR Response Rate 3 was 12%.

Samples were drawn from both landline and cellular random digit dial (RDD) frames, with an overlapping frame design. The RDD landline sample was generated through Marketing Systems Group's GENESYS sampling system. The GENESYS RDD procedure produces an Equal Probability Selection Method sample of telephone numbers from all working. The sample was generated shortly before the beginning of data collection to provide the most up-to-date sample possible, maximizing the number of valid telephone extensions. Cell phone numbers were generated using the Telcordia database, which identifies 1,000-series telephone blocks dedicated to cellular devices. From the identified 1,000 series telephone blocks dedicated to cellular devices, MSG generates a random sample of possible telephone numbers.

For the landline sample, in households with two adults, one adult was randomly selected. In households with three or more adults, a first random selection was made to choose between the adult who answered the phone and the rest of the adults, and if the remaining adults were selected, one was randomly chosen using the last or next birthday method (whereby the adult with the most recent or the upcoming birthday was selected for interviewing; the use of next vs. last birthday for each household was determined randomly). For the cell phone sample, interviews were conducted with the person who answered the phone. Interviewers verified that the person was an adult and in a safe place before administering the survey. Cell phone sample respondents were offered a post-paid reimbursement of $10 for their participation.

Base weights were created to adjust for differential probabilities of selection due to the number of adults in the household, the number of voice-use landlines, and the number of cell phones. Final weights were computed through post-stratification to population proportions of age-by-gender, education, race, ethnicity, marital, phone status, Census region, a variable dividing U.S. counties into three based on the 2012 presidential election outcomes: Democratic-leaning counties; Republican-leaning counties; all other counties, using targets from the 2014 March Supplement of the Current Population Survey and telephone status parameters from the National Health Interview Survey for the time period between January and June 2014.

Table 10.13 displays distributions of unweighted and weighted demographics from the survey and national benchmarks from the 2014 March supplement of the Current Population Survey. These distributions show that the sample was similar to the American population before the weights were applied and, as expected, was more similar after the data were weighted. We report weighted results of the experiment, though unweighted data produced comparable findings.

Experimental Conditions

Each respondent heard statements from three hypothetical candidates purportedly running for Senate in their state or President of the United States; the three candidates expressed a green position, a not-green position and a not-committal position. The order in which respondents heard the candidate with green, not-green, or not-committal position was randomized. After hearing the statement, respondents were asked: "If a candidate says this, would this make you more likely to vote for this candidate, less likely to vote for this candidate, or would it not affect how likely you would be to vote for this candidate?"

The green statement was:

> "I believe that global warming has been happening for the past 100 years, mainly because we have been burning fossil fuels and putting out greenhouse gasses. Now is the time for us to be using new forms of energy that are made in America and will be renewable forever. We can manufacture better cars that use less gasoline and build better appliances that use less electricity. We need to transform the outdated ways of generating energy into new ones that create jobs and entire industries, and stop the damage we've been doing to the environment."

TABLE 10.13 Study 5: Distributions of Demographics of the Sample and the Current Population Survey

Demographic	GW National Survey—2015 (unweighted) (%)	GW National Survey—2015 (weighted) (%)	CPS— March 2014 (%)	Difference: GW Survey (weighted — CPS (%)
Age by Gender				
18–29 Male	7.4	11.0	10.9	.1
30–44 Male	11.5	12.6	12.5	.1
45–64 Male	20.5	16.8	16.7	.1
65 or older Male	12.8	8.5	8.3	.2
18–29 Female	5.7	10.4	10.6	–.2
30–44 Female	7.5	12.2	12.9	–.7
45–64 Female	21.0	17.9	17.8	.1
65 or older Female	13.7	10.5	10.3	.2
Total	100.0	100.0	100.0	
	(N = 1006)	(N = 1006)	(N = 100,633)	
Ethnicity				
Non-Hispanic	89.7	85.3	84.8	.5
Hispanic – U.S. born	7.0	7.2	7.2	.0
Hispanic – foreign born	3.4	7.5	8.0	–.5
Total	100.0	100.0	100.0	
	(N = 1006)	(N = 1006)	(N = 100,633)	
Race				
Non-Black	91.7	87.9	87.7	.2
Black only	8.4	12.1	12.3	–.2
Total	100.0	100.0	100.0	
	(N = 1006)	(N = 1006)	(N = 100,633)	
Education				
Less than HS	5.	11.7	12.3	–.6
HS graduate	25.3	30.0	29.6	.4

Demographic	GW National Survey—2015 (unweighted) (%)	GW National Survey—2015 (weighted) (%)	CPS— March 2014 (%)	Difference: GW Survey (weighted — CPS (%)
Some college	27.9	28.9	28.8	.1
College graduate	21.2	19.0	18.9	.1
Post college graduate	20.4	10.4	10.4	.0
Total	100.0	100.0	100.0	
	(N = 1006)	(N = 1006)	(N = 100,633)	
Region				
Northeast	18.9	18.1	18.2	−.1
Midwest	23.9	21.6	21.3	.3
South	35.4	37.3	37.1	.2
West	21.9	23.2	23.4	−.2
Total	100.0	100.0	100.0	
	(N = 1006)	(N = 1006)	(N = 100,633)	

The not-green statement was:

"The science on global warming is a hoax and is an attempt to perpetrate a fraud on the American people. I don't buy into the whole man-caused global warming mantra. We must spend no effort to deal with something that is not a problem at all. We should not invest in windmills and solar panels as alternative energy sources. Instead we should continue to focus on our traditional sources of energy: coal, oil, and natural gas. We should expand energy production in our country, including continuing to mine our coal and doing more drilling for oil here at home."

The not-committal statement was:

"When people ask me if I believe global warming has been happening, I'm not qualified to debate the science over climate change, because I am not a scientist. When people ask me if I believe human activity causes global warming, I don't know. There is significant scientific dispute about that. We can debate this forever. I am not qualified to make this decision. But I am astute enough to understand that every proposal to deal with climate change involves hurting our economy and killing American jobs."

Results

The Full Sample

In the full sample, taking a green position on global warming won votes for the candidate and taking not-green or not-committal position lost votes (see panel 1 of Table 10.14). 66% of respondents said hearing the green statement from the candidate would make them more likely to vote for the candidate, 12% said less likely to vote for the candidate and 21% said it had no effect, whereas 67% of respondents said hearing the not-green statement from the candidate would make them less likely to vote for the candidate, 13% said more likely to vote for the candidate and 19% said it had no effect.

TABLE 10.14 Study 5: Effects of Green, Not-Green and Not-Committal Statements on Voting Outcome for the Candidate in the 2015 Global Warming National Survey

Response	Respondents who heard the green statement on global warming (%) (1)	Respondents who heard the not-green statement (%) (2)	Respondents who heard the not-committal statement (%) (3)
Among full sample			
More likely to vote for the candidate	66	13	27
Less likely to vote for the candidate	12	67	44
Has no effect	21	19	27
Don't know/Refused	1	1	2
Total	100	100	100
N	1006	1006	1006
Among Democrats			
More likely to vote for the candidate	81	8	16
Less likely to vote for the candidate	3	78	58
Has no effect	15	13	22
Don't know/Refused	1	1	3
Total	100	100	100
N	307	307	307
Among Republicans			
More likely to vote for the candidate	48	24	37
Less likely to vote for the candidate	24	48	27
Has no effect	26	26	33

Response	Respondents who heard the green statement on global warming (%) (1)	Respondents who heard the not-green statement (%) (2)	Respondents who heard the not-committal statement (%) (3)
Don't know/Refused	2	1	3
Total	100	100	100
N	222	222	222
Among Independents			
More likely to vote for the candidate	64	10	30
Less likely to vote for the candidate	13	69	43
Has no effect	22	20	27
Don't know/Refused	1	1	0
Total	100	100	100
N	477	477	477
Among respondents attaching high personal importance to global warming			
More likely to vote for the candidate	85	4	18
Less likely to vote for the candidate	2	86	64
Has no effect	12	9	18
Don't know/Refused	1	1	0
Total	100	100	100
N	425	425	425
Among respondents attaching low personal importance to global warming			
More likely to vote for the candidate	51	19	35
Less likely to vote for the candidate	20	53	29
Has no effect	28	26	34
Don't know/Refused	1	1	3
Total	100	100	100
N	581	581	581
Among respondents who believe in man-made warming			
More likely to vote for the candidate	79	5	21
Less likely to vote for the candidate	4	81	54
Has no effect	17	14	24

continued…

Table 10.14 continued…

Response	Respondents who heard the green statement on global warming (%) (1)	Respondents who heard the not-green statement (%) (2)	Respondents who heard the not-committal statement (%) (3)
Don't know/Refused	1	0	1
Total	100	100	100
N	631	631	631
Among respondents who don't believe in in man-made warming			
More likely to vote for the candidate	45	26	37
Less likely to vote for the candidate	27	45	27
Has no effect	27	28	33
Don't know/Refused	2	2	3
Total	100	100	100
N	375	375	375
Among respondents who heard the question first			
More likely to vote for the candidate	61	17	30
Less likely to vote for the candidate	11	64	44
Has no effect	29	18	25
Don't know/Refused	0	1	1
Total	100	100	100
N	368	323	315
Among respondents who heard the question second or third			
More likely to vote for the candidate	69	11	26
Less likely to vote for the candidate	14	69	44
Has no effect	17	20	28
Don't know/Refused	1	1	2
Total	100	100	100
N	636	682	691

The same impact of the green statement was apparent among Democratic respondents and Independents (see panels 2 and 4 of Table 10.14). 81% of Democrats said the green statement would make them more likely to vote for the candidate, and 64% of Independents said so. The change brought about by the green statement in the intentions to vote was significantly different between Democrats and Independents ($p < .01$). The same impact of the not-green statement was also apparent among Democratic respondents and Independents (see panels 2 and 4 of Table 10.14). 78% of Democrats said the not-green statement would make them less likely to vote for the candidate, and 69% of Independents said so. The change brought about by the green statement in the intentions to vote was marginally significantly different between Democrats and Independents ($p = .06$). Among Republicans, taking a green or a not-green position caused a plurality of changes in intentions to vote for the candidate (see panel 3 of Table 10.14). 48% of Republicans said the green statement would make them more likely to vote for the candidate, while 48% of Republicans said the not-green statement would make them less likely to vote for the candidate.

Among respondents who heard the not-committal statement from the candidate, 44% of respondents said hearing that statement would make them less likely to vote for the candidate, 26% said more likely to vote for the candidate and 27% said it had no effect (see panel 1 of Table 10.14). A majority, 58%, of Democratic respondents reported the not-committal statement would make them less likely to vote for the candidate, compared to a plurality, 43%, of Independents who said so, and a minority, 27%, of Republicans did (see panels 2–4 of Table 10.14).

The Moderators of the Green, Not-Green, Not-Committal Statements

As expected, the finding among the full sample that taking a green position gained votes and taking a not-green or not committal position lost votes was greater among respondents who attached high personal importance than respondents who did not (see panels 5–6 of Table 10.14). Hearing the green statement invoked different reactions between respondents who did and who didn't consider global warming highly important personally ($p < .01$). For example, the green statement caused an increased likelihood to vote for the candidate among 85% of people who attached high personal importance to global warming, compared to 51% people who did not. Hearing the not-green statement also caused different responses between respondents who did and who didn't attach high personal importance to global warming ($p < .01$). For instance, the not-green statement caused a decreased likelihood to vote for the candidate among 86% of people who attached high personal importance to global warming, compared to 53% people who did not. Likewise, hearing the not-committal statement induced different reactions between respondents who did and who didn't consider global warming highly important personally ($p < .01$). For example, the not-committal statement caused a decreased likelihood to vote for the candidate among 64% of people who considered global warming highly important personally, compared to 29% people who did not.

As expected, the finding among the full sample that taking a green position gained votes and taking a not-green or not-committal position lost votes was stronger among respondents who believed in anthropogenic warming than respondents who did not (see panels 7–8 of Table 10.14). Hearing the green statement invoked different reactions between respondents who did and didn't believe in anthropogenic warming ($p < .01$). For example, the green statement caused an increased likelihood to vote for the candidate among 79% of believers in anthropogenic warming, compared to 45% non-believers in anthropogenic warming. Hearing the not-green statement also caused different responses between believers and non-believers in anthropogenic warming ($p < .01$). For instance, the not-green statement caused a decreased likelihood to vote for the candidate among 81% of people who believed in anthropogenic warming, compared to 45% people who did not. Likewise, hearing the not-committal statement induced different reactions between believers and non-believers in anthropogenic warming ($p < .01$). For example, the not-committal statement caused a decreased likelihood to vote for the candidate among 54% of believers in anthropogenic warming, compared to 27% of non-believers in anthropogenic warming.

Contrast Effect

In this experiment, each respondent was exposed to three hypothetical candidates making a green statement, a not-green statement, and a not-committal statement, respectively, and the order in which the three hypothetical candidates a respondent listened to was randomized. This design was referred to as a within-subject design. A within-subject design could induce a contrast effect for example, the positive effect in intention to vote of the green statement might be greater among respondents who heard the not-green or not-committal statement first than respondents who heard the green statement first. There was a contrast effect, the direction of which was as predicted, for the green statement ($p < .01$) (see panels 9–10 of Table 10.14). For instance, 61% of respondents who heard the green statement first said it would make them more likely to vote for the candidate, whereas 69% of respondents who heard the green statement second or third said so. There was a contrast effect, the direction of which was as predicted but marginally significant, for the not-green statement ($p = .08$). For instance, 64% of respondents who heard the not-green statement first said it would make them less likely to vote for the candidate, whereas 69% of respondents who heard the not-green statement second or third said so. However, there was no contrast effect for the not-committal statement ($p = .53$). For instance, 44% of respondents who heard the not-committal statement first said it would make them less likely to vote for the candidate, and the same percent, 44%, of respondents who heard the not-committal statement second or third said so.

Study 6—Experimental Evidence from a National Survey in 2010

Study 6 assembled the experimental evidence on the impact of candidates' taking a green or not-green position on electoral outcome in hypothetical elections, and experiments were based on between-subject design under which a respondent was randomly chosen to hear about a single candidate taking a green, not-green, or silent position. Our experiments explored the impact of taking green and not-green positions on voting and assessed whether this impact varied across Democrats, Independents, and Republicans.

Data

Data Collection

Abt SRBI interviewed a representative national sample of 1,001 U.S. adults by telephone, 671 respondents were interviewed on a landline telephone, and 330 were interviewed on a cell phone. Interviews were conducted between November 1 and November 14, 2010, and were administered in English and Spanish. The AAPOR Response Rate 3 was 17%.

Samples were drawn from both landline and cellular random digit dial (RDD) frames. Both samples were provided by Survey Sampling International, LLC, according to specifications from Abt SRBI. Landline telephone numbers were drawn with equal probabilities from active blocks (area code + exchange + two-digit block number) that contained one or more residential directory listings. The cell phone sample was generated through systematic sampling from 1,000-blocks dedicated to cellular service according to the Telcordia database.

A maximum of seven call attempts were made to each sampled telephone number. Refusal conversion was attempted with soft refusal cases in the landline sample. Calls were staggered over times of day and days of the week to maximize the chance of making contact with potential respondents. The sample was released for interviewing in replicates, which are representative subsamples of the full sample.

For the landline sample, in households with two adults, one adult was randomly selected. In households with three or more adults, a first random selection was made to choose between the adult who answered the phone and the rest of the adults, and if the remaining adults were selected, one was randomly chosen using the last or next birthday method (whereby the adult with the most recent or the upcoming birthday was selected for interviewing; the use of next vs. last birthday for each household was determined randomly). For the cell phone sample, interviews were conducted with the person who answered the phone. Interviewers verified that the person was an adult and in a safe place before administering the survey. Cell phone sample respondents were offered a post-paid reimbursement of $10 for their participation.

Abt SRBI created a base weight that adjusts for differential probabilities of selection due to the number of adults in the household, the number of voice-use landlines, and the number of cell phones. The base weight also adjusts for overlap of the landline and cell phone RDD frames. Final weights were computed using a raking algorithm (DeBell & Krosnick, 2009; Pasek, 2010) that accounted for unequal probabilities of selection and post-stratified to population proportions of age, sex, education, ethnicity, race, and Census region, using targets from the September 2010 Current Population Survey conducted by the U.S. Census Bureau. The weighting combined the interviews done on landlines and cell phones taking into account the rates of landline and cell phone usage documented by the 2009 National Health Interview Survey.

Table 10.15 displays distributions of unweighted and weighted demographics from the survey and national benchmarks from the 2010 March supplement of the Current Population Survey. These distributions show that the sample was similar to the American population before the weights were applied and, as expected, was more similar after the data were weighted. The weighted sample slightly over-represented females and people with some college or college graduates or more education and slightly under-represented Hispanics and people with some high school education but no high school degree, as well as high school graduates. We report weighted results of the experiment, though unweighted data produced comparable findings.

TABLE 10.15 Study 6: Distributions of Demographics of the Sample and the Current Population Survey

Demo-graphic	Global Warming National Survey— Nov 2010 (unweighted) (%)	Global Warming National Survey —Nov 2010 (weighted) (%)	Current Population Survey (CPS) —March 2010 (%)	Difference: Global Warming National Survey (weighted)— CPS (%)
		Gender		
Male	45.9	46.7	48.5	−1.8
Female	54.1	53.3	51.5	1.8
Total	100.0	100.0	100.0	
	(N = 808)	(N = 808)	(N = 149,071)	
		Age		
18–24	9.9	11.9	12.8	−0.9
25–34	11.3	18.7	17.9	0.8
35–44	13.4	17.4	17.6	−0.2
45–54	21.2	19.0	19.4	−0.4
55–64	18.0	16.0	15.4	0.6

Demographic	Global Warming National Survey— Nov 2010 (unweighted) (%)	Global Warming National Survey —Nov 2010 (weighted) (%)	Current Population Survey (CPS) —March 2010 (%)	Difference: Global Warming National Survey (weighted)— CPS (%)
65+	26.3	16.9	16.8	0.1
Total	100.0	100.0	100.0	
	(N = 769)	(N = 769)	(N = 149,071)	
Ethnicity				
Hispanic	11.0	12.6	13.9	−1.3
Non-Hispanic	89.0	87.4	86.1	1.3
Total	100.0	100.0	100.0	
	(N = 779)	(N = 779)	(N = 149,071)	
Race				
White only	74.0	81.6	81.0	0.6
Black only	9.9	12.1	11.9	0.2
Other race	16.1	6.3	7.1	−0.8
Total	100.0	100.0	100.0	
	(N = 808)	(N = 808)	(N = 149,071)	
Education				
Less than HS	6.9	10.5	13.7	−3.2
HS graduates	25.9	29.8	31.1	−1.7
Some college	24.9	30.2	27.9	2.3
College or higher	42.4	29.5	27.3	2.2
Total	100.0	100.0	100.0	
	(N = 788)	(N = 788)	(N = 149,071)	
Region				
Northeast	18.3	17.8	18.4	−0.6
Midwest	23.9	22.8	21.8	1.0
South	36.5	35.2	36.7	−1.5
West	21.3	24.2	23.1	0.8
Total	100.0	100.0	100.0	
	(N = 808)	(N = 808)	(N = 149,071)	

Experimental Conditions

After hearing each of a series of quotes from a hypothetical candidate purportedly running for Senate in their state, respondents reported whether they agreed or disagreed with the position expressed in the quote. After hearing all the quotes, respondents reported how likely they were to vote for or against the candidate. All respondents heard the candidate make statements on two issues other than global warming. For each respondent, these two statements were randomly selected from a set of six such statements (see Appendix E for the description of these issue statements). Respondents were randomly assigned also to hear the candidate express a green position on global warming, a not-green position on global warming, or no position on global warming (we refer to the latter individuals as the "control group" below). For a randomly selected half of the respondents who heard a global warming statement, it preceded the statements on other issues. For the remaining respondents who heard a global warming statement, it followed the statements on other issues.

The green statement was:

> "Like most Americans and most of the residents of our great State, I believe that global warming has been happening for the last 100 years, mainly because we have been burning fossil fuels and putting out greenhouse gasses. Now is the time for us to stop this by ending our dependence on imported oil and coal to run our cars and heat our houses. We need to begin using new forms of energy that are made in America and will be renewable forever. We can build better cars that use less gasoline. We can build better appliances that use less electricity. And we can make power from the sun and from wind. We don't have to change our lifestyles, but we do need to reshape the way our country does business. We need to end our long-term addiction to polluting the environment and instead let American genius do what it does best—transform our outdated ways of generating energy into new ones that create jobs and entire industries, and stop the damage we've been doing to the environment."

The not-green statement was:

> "There isn't any real science to say we are changing the climate of the earth. The science on global warming is a hoax and is an attempt to perpetrate a fraud on the American people. Climate science is junk science, and global warming is a manufactured controversy. I don't buy into the whole man-caused global warming, man-caused climate change mantra, and I believe that there's not sound science to back that up. We must spend no effort to deal with something that is not a problem at all. Yet that's exactly what's happening with the cap and trade bill that Congress has

considered. I oppose the cap and trade bill. Cap and trade is a job killer and damages our economy. We should not invest in windmills and solar panels as alternative energy sources. Instead we should continue to focus on our traditional sources of energy: coal, oil, and natural gas. We should expand energy production in our country, including by continuing to mine our coal, doing more drilling for oil here at home."

Results

As expected, the three experimental groups did not differ significantly from one another in terms of the distributions of demographic characteristics (see Table 10.16). Thus, it seems that random assignment to groups was done properly.

TABLE 10.16 Study 6: Distributions of Demographics of Experimental Conditions in the National Survey

Demographic	Green condition (%)	Control condition (%)	Not-green condition (%)	p-value
		Gender		
Male	42.9	47.2	50.1	
Female	57.1	52.8	49.9	
Total	100.0	100.0	100.0	$p = .45$
	($N = 266$)	($N = 266$)	($N = 276$)	
		Age		
18–24	14.2	11.0	10.4	
25–34	14.4	25.9	16.0	
35–44	19.6	14.3	18.3	
45–54	19.6	16.6	20.9	
55–64	15.4	16.9	15.7	
65+	16.7	15.4	18.7	$p = .45$
Total	100.0	100.0	100.0	
	($N = 259$)	($N = 247$)	($N = 263$)	
		Ethnicity		
Hispanic	17.4	8.3	11.5	
Non-Hispanic	82.7	91.7	88.5	
Total	100.0	100.0	100.0	$p = .07$
	($N = 266$)	($N = 266$)	($N = 276$)	

continued...

Table 10.16 continued…

Demographic	Green condition (%)	Control condition (%)	Not-green condition (%)	p-value
		Race		
White only	81.9	82.9	80.1	
Black only	11.4	11.5	13.3	
Other race	6.7	5.6	6.6	
Total	100.0	100.0	100.0	$p = .55$
	($N = 266$)	($N = 266$)	($N = 276$)	
		Education		
Less than HS	10.5	5.7	15.4	
HS graduates	34.9	30.5	27.9	
Some college	26.4	30.8	29.4	
College or higher	28.1	33.0	27.3	
Total	100.0	100.0	100.0	$p = .77$
	($N = 262$)	($N = 258$)	($N = 268$)	
		Region		
Northeast	16.2	19.8	17.4	
Midwest	19.9	23.6	24.7	
South	41.3	31.1	33.5	
West	22.6	25.6	24.4	
Total	100.0	100.0	100.0	$p = .77$
	($N = 266$)	($N = 266$)	($N = 276$)	

In the full sample, taking a green position on global warming won votes for the candidate, and taking a not-green position lost votes (see row 1 of Table 10.17). 65% of respondents said they would vote for the candidate who was silent on global warming, whereas 77% said they would vote for the candidate who took a green position on global warming, a significant 12 percentage point increase ($p = .01$). Among respondents who heard the candidate take a not-green position, only 48% said they would vote for him/her. The 17 percentage point difference between this group and the control group was also statistically significant ($p < .01$).

TABLE 10.17 **Study 6:** Effects of Green and Not-Green Statements on Predicted Voting for the Candidate in the National Survey

| Respondents | Percent of respondents who would vote for the candidate | | | | |
	Respondents who heard no statement on global warming (1)	Respondents who heard the green statement (2)	Respondents who heard the not-green statement (3)	Effect of the green statement (2)–(1)	Effect of the not-green statement (3)–(1)
Full sample	65.2% (N =266)	77.4% (N =266)	47.9% (N =276)	12.2%★★	−17.4%★★★
Democrats	53.0% (N =77)	74.3% (N =76)	37.4% (N =97)	21.3%★★	−15.5%★
Republicans	83.4% (N =71)	77.8% (N =68)	76.4% (N =59)	−5.6%	−7.1%
Independents	63.3% (N =118)	78.8% (N =122)	43.9% (N =120)	15.4%★★	−19.5%★★

Notes: One-tailed tests are reported for Democrats and Independents given strong a priori expectations of the directions of effects given the results in Table 10.1. Two-tailed tests are reported for Republicans because we had no such expectations.
★★★$p < .01$ ★★$p < .05$, ★$p < .10$

The same impact of the green statement was apparent among Democratic respondents and Independents (see rows 2 and 4 of Table 10.17). 53% of Democrats said they would vote for the candidate who was silent on global warming, whereas 74% said so when the candidate took a green position, a 21 percentage point increase ($p = .03$). Among Independents, 63% said they would vote for the candidate who was silent on global warming, and 79% said so about the candidate who took a green position, an increase of 15 percentage points ($p = .02$). The changes brought about by the green statement in intentions to vote were not significantly different between Democrats and Independents ($p = .65$).

Democrats and Independent were also similar to one another and to the full sample in terms of the impact of the not-green statement (see rows 2 and 4 of Table 10.17). 37% of Democrats said they would vote for the candidate who took a not-green position, a decline of 16 percentage points from the silent candidate ($p = .07$). 44% of Independents said they would vote for the candidate who took a not-green position, a decrease of 19 percentage points from the silent candidate ($p = .01$). The changes brought about by the not-green statement in intentions to vote were not significantly different between Democrats and Independents ($p = .77$).

Among Republicans, taking a green or a not-green position caused no significant change in intentions to vote for the candidate (see row 3 of Table 10.17). 83% of Republicans said they would vote for the silent candidate vs. 78% for the candidate who took a green position ($\Delta = 6\%, p = .43$). 76% of Republicans said they would vote for the not green candidate ($\Delta = 7\%, p = .38$). The impact of the green statement among Democrats and Independents combined was significantly greater than its impact among Republicans (the interaction of Democrats/Independents and the green statement was positive and significant, $b = .23, p = .01$). However, the impact of the not-green statement among Democrats/Independents was not significantly different from its impact among Republicans (the interaction was negative and insignificant, $b = -.12, p = .26$).

This last finding poses a small dilemma for interpretation. The most parsimonious conclusion to reach is that the not-green statement significantly decreased intention to vote for the candidate equally among Democrats, Independents, and Republicans. However, the observed magnitude of the effect among Republicans (7 percentage points, see the last column of Table 10.17) is smaller (though not significantly so) than the effects among Democrats and Independents (17 percentage points and 16 percentage points, respectively) and is also not significantly different from zero. Thus, one might be inclined to conclude that the not-green statement did not significantly alter voting intentions among Republicans. We are inclined instead to pay heed to the interaction test and to conclude that the not-green statement did indeed decrease voting intentions among Republicans.

Study 7—Experimental Evidence from Surveys in Florida, Maine and Massachusetts in 2010

Study 7 used the same experimental approach as in Study 6 to assess the impact of green statements among residents of Florida, Maine, and Massachusetts.

Data

Data Collection

The interviews were conducted by Abt SRBI between July 9 and July 18, 2010. In each state, approximately 400 respondents were interviewed on a landline telephone, and approximately 200 were interviewed on a cell phone. Interviews were conducted in English and Spanish.

The target population for the study is non-institutionalized persons age 18 and over, living in Florida, Massachusetts, and Maine. Samples were drawn from both the landline and cellular random digit dial (RDD) frames provided by Survey Sampling International. Numbers for the landline sample were drawn with equal probabilities from active blocks (area code + exchange + two-digit block number) that contained one or more residential directory listings. The cellular sample was drawn through a systematic sampling from 1,000-blocks dedicated to cellular service according to the Telcordia database.

A maximum of seven call attempts were made to numbers in the landline and cell phone samples. Refusal conversion was attempted on soft refusal cases in the landline sample. Calls were staggered over times of day and days of the week to maximize the chance of making contact with potential respondents. The sample was released for interviewing in replicates.

For the landline sample, the respondent was randomly selected from all of the adults in the household. For the cell phone sample, interviews were conducted with the person who answered the phone. Interviewers verified that the person was an adult and in a safe place before administering the survey. Cell sample respondents were offered a post-paid reimbursement of $5 for their participation.

Weights for the July 2010 surveys done in Florida, Maine, and Massachusetts account for unequal probabilities of selection, and post-stratify to population proportions of age, sex, education, ethnicity and race, using targets from the 2006–2008 American Community Survey for Florida, Maine, and Massachusetts. The weighting was also designed to combine interviews done on landlines and cell phones taking into account the rates of landline and cell phone usage from the NHIS.

AAPOR Response Rate 3 was 14%, 14% and 19% for the landline samples in Florida, Massachusetts, and Maine, respectively, and 10%, 9% and 12% for the cell phone samples in Florida, Massachusetts, and Maine, respectively.

Tables 10.18–10.20 display distributions of unweighted and weighted demographics of each of the three states' survey samples along with state-level benchmarks computed using data from the 2006–2008 American Community Survey for the three states. The unweighted samples under-represented younger adults, under-represented whites, and under-represented people with relatively little formal education. After weighting, the three samples closely resembled their corresponding populations.

Experimental Conditions

After hearing each of a series of quotes from a hypothetical candidate purportedly running for Senate in their state, respondents reported whether they agreed or disagreed with the position expressed in the quote. After hearing all the quotes, respondents reported how likely they were to vote for or against the candidate. All respondents heard the candidate make statements on two issues other than global warming (see Appendix E for the description of these issue statements). Respondents were randomly assigned to hear the candidate express a green position on global warming, or no position on global warming (we refer to the latter individuals as the "control group" below). The green statement was identical to that used in Study 6.

TABLE 10.18   Study 7: Demographics of the Florida Global Warming State Survey and the American Community Survey

Demographic	Florida Survey July 2010 (unweighted) (%)	Florida Survey July 2010 (weighted) (%)	Florida American Community Survey (ACS) 2006–2008 (%)	Difference: Florida State Survey (weighted)— ACS (%)
		Gender		
Male	48.8	49.4	48.5	0.9
Female	51.2	50.6	51.5	–0.9
Total	100.0	100.0	100.0	
	(N =600)	(N =600)	(N =442,524)	
		Age		
18–24	6.8	11.3	11.3	0.0
25–34	10.0	15.9	15.9	0.0
35–44	13.0	17.9	17.9	0.0
45–54	20.7	18.2	18.2	0.0
55–64	20.8	14.9	14.9	0.0
65+	28.7	21.9	21.9	0.0
Total	100.0	100.0	100.0	
	(N =571)	(N =571)	(N =442,524)	
		Ethnicity		
Hispanic	13.3	19.4	19.4	0.0
Non-Hispanic	86.7	80.6	80.6	0.0
Total	100.0	100.0	100.0	
	(N =579)	(N =579)	(N =442,524)	
		Race		
White only	77.2	80.2	80.2	0.0
Black only	11.2	14.3	14.3	0.0
Other race	11.7	5.5	5.5	0.0
Total	100.0	100.0	100.0	
	(N =574)	(N =574)	(N =442,524)	

Demographic	Florida Survey July 2010 (unweighted) (%)	Florida Survey July 2010 (weighted) (%)	Florida American Community Survey (ACS) 2006–2008 (%)	Difference: Florida State Survey (weighted)— ACS (%)
		Education		
Less than HS	5.5	15.5	15.5	0.0
HS graduates	28.0	31.3	31.3	0.0
Some college	21.2	29.6	29.6	0.0
College or higher	45.3	23.6	23.6	0.0
Total	100.0	100.0	100.0	
	(N =579)	(N =579)	(N =442,524)	

TABLE 10.19 Study 7: Demographics of the Massachusetts Global Warming State Survey and the American Community Survey

Demographic	Massachusetts Survey July 2010 (unweighted) (%)	Massachusetts Survey July 2010 (weighted) (%)	Massachusetts American Community Survey (ACS) 2006–2008 (%)	Difference: Massachusetts State Survey (weighted) — ACS (%)
		Gender		
Male	48.3	49.5	47.7	1.7
Female	51.7	50.6	52.3	–1.7
Total	100.0	100.0	100.0	
	(N = 600)	(N =600)	(N = 150,777)	
		Age		
18–24	8.2	13.1	13.1	0.0
25–34	10.3	16.3	16.3	0.0
35–44	14.3	19.4	19.4	0.0
45–54	22.4	19.7	19.7	0.0
55–64	22.8	14.4	14.4	0.0
65+	22.1	17.1	17.1	0.0
Total	100.0	100.0	100.0	
	(N = 575)	(N =575)	(N = 150,777)	

continued…

Table 10.19 continued…

Demographic	Massachusetts Survey July 2010 (unweighted) (%)	Massachusetts Survey July 2010 (weighted) (%)	Massachusetts American Community Survey (ACS) 2006–2008 (%)	Difference: Massachusetts State Survey (weighted) — ACS (%)
Ethnicity				
Hispanic	6.2	7.1	7.1	0.0
Non-Hispanic	93.8	92.9	92.9	0.0
Total	100.0	100.0	100.0	
	(N = 579)	(N =579)	(N =150,777)	
Race				
White only	85.4	85.4	85.4	0.0
Black only	6.2	6.6	6.3	0.3
Other race	8.4	8.0	8.3	–0.3
Total	100.0	100.0	100.0	
	(N = 577)	(N =577)	(N =150,777)	
Education				
Less than HS	4.6	11.7	11.7	0.0
HS graduates	22.6	27.8	27.8	0.0
Some college	18.1	25.7	25.7	0.0
College or higher	54.7	34.8	34.8	0.0
Total	100.0	100.0	100.0	
	(N = 592)	(N =592)	(N =150,777)	

TABLE 10.20 Study 7: Demographics of the Maine Global Warming State Survey and the American Community Survey

Demographic	Maine Survey July 2010 (unweighted) (%)	Maine Survey July 2010 (weighted) (%)	Maine American Community Survey 2006–2008 (%)	Difference: Maine State Survey (weighted)—ACS (%)
Gender				
Male	45.2	47.8	47.8	0.0
Female	54.8	52.2	52.2	0.0
Total	100.0	100.0	100.0	
	(N =600)	(N =600)	(N =30,153)	

Demographic	Maine Survey July 2010 (unweighted) (%)	Maine Survey July 2010 (weighted) (%)	Maine American Community Survey 2006–2008 (%)	Difference: Maine State Survey (weighted)—ACS (%)
Age				
18–24	6.4	10.7	10.7	0.0
25–34	9.5	14.5	14.5	0.0
35–44	13.9	18.1	18.1	0.0
45–54	22.5	21.2	21.2	0.0
55–64	24.2	16.7	16.7	0.0
65+	23.5	18.9	18.9	0.0
Total	100.0	100.0	100.0	
	(N =582)	(N =582)	(N =30,153)	
Ethnicity				
Hispanic	1.4	2.0	1.0	1.0
Non-Hispanic	98.6	98.0	99.0	−1.0
Total	100.0	100.0	100.0	
	(N = 583)	(N =583)	(N =30,153)	
Race				
White only	94.9	97.5	97.5	0.0
Black only	1.0	.7	.9	−0.2
Other race	4.1	1.8	1.6	0.2
Total	100.0	100.0	100.0	
	(N =582)	(N =582)	(N =30,153)	
Education				
Less than HS	6.7	11.1	11.1	0.0
HS graduates	26.3	36.1	36.1	0.0
Some college	21.0	29.2	29.2	0.0
College or higher	46.1	23.7	23.7	0.0
Total	100.0	100.0	100.0	
	(N =586)	(N =586)	(N =30,153)	

Results

Taking a green position won votes for the candidate (see Table 10.21). In Florida, 49% of respondents said they would vote for the candidate who was silent on global warming, whereas 73% said they would vote for the candidate who took a green position. This 24 percentage point increase was statistically significant ($p < .01$). In Maine, 64% of respondents said they would vote for the candidate who was silent on global warming, and 71% said so about the candidate who took a green position, an increase of 7 percentage points ($p = .08$). In Massachusetts, the effect was about 10 percentage points ($p = .02$); 67% and 77% of respondents said they would vote for the candidate who was silent and the candidate who took a green position, respectively.

The impact of the green statement was apparent among Democratic respondents (see row 4 of Table 10.21). 58% of Democrats said they would vote for the candidate who was silent on global warming, whereas 83% said so about the candidate who took a green position, a 25 percentage point increase ($p < .01$). Likewise, 57% of Independents said they would vote for a candidate who was silent on global warming, whereas 71% said so about the candidate who took a green position, an increase of 14 percentage points ($p < .01$). Among Republicans, taking a green position did not significantly alter intentions to vote for the candidate (71% for the candidate silent on climate vs. 63% for the

TABLE 10.21 Study 7: Estimations of the Green Effects and the Moderation of Party Affiliation in the States Survey

| Respondents | Percent of respondents who would vote for the candidate | | |
	Respondents who heard no statement on global warming	Respondents who heard the green statement	Difference
Florida	49.1% (N = 297)	72.7% (N = 302)	23.6%★★★
Maine	63.8% (N = 278)	70.5% (N = 318)	6.8%★
Massachusetts	67.2% (N = 288)	76.9% (N = 306)	9.7%★★
Democrats	58.18% (N = 257)	83.03% (N = 283)	24.9%★★★
Republicans	70.9% (N = 157)	62.7% (N = 162)	–8.1%
Independents	57.0% (N = 449)	71.2% (N = 481)	14.2%★★★

★★★$p < .01$ ★★$p < .05$ ★$p < .10$

candidate who took a green position, $\Delta=8\%$, $p = .34$). The impact of the green statement on voting intentions was different between Democrats/Independents and Republicans; the interaction of Democrats/Independents and the green statement was positive and significant ($b = .28$, $p < .01$).

Studies 6 and 7—Moderation by Belief in Anthropogenic Warming and by Personal Importance

According to reigning theories of voting, the effects seen so far should be particularly pronounced among individuals who themselves take a green position on global warming and who attached personal importance to the issue (e.g., Visser, Bizer, & Krosnick, 2006). To test these hypotheses, we pooled the data from the national survey and the state surveys to yield sufficiently large samples (see Appendix E for a description of the measures).

Moderators of the Green and Not-Green Statement Effects

As expected, the impacts of the green and not-green statements were much larger among respondents who believed that the Earth's temperature has been rising and that the temperature increase has been due to things people did than among respondents who did not hold these beliefs (see rows 1–2 of Table 10.22). 63% of respondents who believed in anthropogenic warming said they would vote for the candidate who was silent on global warming, whereas 80% said so about the candidate who took a green position, a 17 percentage point increase ($p < .01$). Among respondents who did not believe in anthropogenic warming, taking a green position did not significantly change intentions to vote for the candidate (57% for the silent candidate vs. 64% for the candidate who took a green position, $\Delta=7\%$, $p = .11$). The impact of the green statement was marginally significantly larger among respondents who believed in anthropogenic warming than among respondents who did not ($b = .09$, $p = .08$).

40% of respondents who believed in anthropogenic warming said they would vote for the candidate who made a not-green statement, a 24 percentage point decline as compared to the silent candidate ($p < .01$), whereas making a not-green statement did not significantly change intentions to vote for the candidate among respondents who did not believe in anthropogenic warming (62% for the candidate who took a not-green position, $\Delta=5\%$, $p = .53$). The impact of the not-green statements was significantly larger among respondents who believed in anthropogenic warming than among respondents who did not ($b = -.28$, $p < .01$).

Also as expected, the impact of the green and not-green statements was greater among respondents who attached more personal importance to the issue (see rows 3–4 of Table 10.22). 60% of high importance respondents said they would vote for the candidate who was silent on global warming, whereas 78%

TABLE 10.22 Studies 6 and 7: Moderation of the Effects of Green and Not-Green Statements on Predicted Voting for the Candidate by Belief in Anthropogenic Warming and by Personal Importance

Respondents	Percent of respondents who would vote for the candidate				
	Respondents who heard no statement on climate (1)	*Respondents who heard the green statement on climate (2)*	*Respondents who heard the not-green statement on climate (3)*	*Effect of the green statement (2)–(1)*	*Effect of the not-green statement (3)–(1)*
Believed in anthropogenic warming	63.1% (N =778)	79.7% (N =775)	39.6% (N =176)	16.6%★★★	–23.5%★★★
Did not believe in anthropogenic warming	57.1% (N =369)	64.3% (N =410)	61.9% (N =100)	7.2%	4.8%
High personal importance	60.0% (N =559)	78.3% (N =528)	37.7% (N =125)	18.3%★★★	–22.3%★★★
Low personal importance	62.2% (N =588)	71.2% (N =657)	57.9% (N =151)	9.0%★★★	–4.3%

★★★p < .01

said so about the candidate who took a green position, an 18 percentage point increase ($p < .01$). Among respondents low in personal importance, taking a green position caused a much smaller increase in intentions to vote for the candidate (62% for the candidate silent on climate vs. 71% for the candidate who took a green position, $\Delta = 9\%, p < .01$). The impact of the green statement was marginally significantly stronger among respondents who attached more personal importance to the issue ($b = .09, p = .06$).

38% of the high personal importance group said they would vote for the candidate who made a not-green statement, a 22 percentage point decline as compared to the candidate who was silent ($p < .01$). In contrast, making a not-green statement did not significantly alter intentions to vote for the candidate among respondents who were low in personal importance (58% for the candidate who took a not-green position, $\Delta = -4\%, p = .45$). The impact of the not-green statement was significantly larger among respondents who attached more personal importance to the issue ($b = -.18, p < .01$).

Evaluations of the Candidate's Green and Not-Green Statements

Consistent with the finding that a large majority of Americans believed in anthropogenic warming and supported ameliorative government action, 78% of respondents said they mostly agreed with the candidate's green statement, and this proportion varied significantly by party identification ($p < .01$): it was 86% among Democrats, 79% among Independents, and 64% among Republicans. Only a small minority of respondents, 22%, said that they mostly agreed with the candidate's not-green statement, and this proportion also varied by party identification: 44% among Republicans, 23% among Independents, and only 10% of Democrats said so ($p < .01$).

Study 8—Experimental Evidence From a National Survey in 2012

Study 8 employed an experiment embedded in an Internet survey of Americans from a non-probability sample to assess the electoral impact of candidates' taking different stances on the issue of global warming. Study 8 used a similar study design from Studies 6–7 but differed in three important ways: (1) Study 8 used real candidates' real speeches in video as experiment stimuli; (2) Study 8 evaluated the electoral impact of a (real) candidate's taking different stances on the issue of global warming when that candidate was presented alone as if in a single candidate election, as well as when that candidate was presented with the opponent as in a two-candidates election; and (3) Study 8 explored the impact of a (real) candidate's taking different stances on the issue of global warming on measures of electoral outcomes, as well as others, such as affect and personality traits perception.

Observational studies, particularly Study 3 which correlated Congressional candidates' electoral successes with their stances on global warming through content analysis of candidates' campaign (and government) websites (see Table 10.8), yielded the following hypotheses that were to be tested in Study 8.

Hypothesis 1a: When Democratic candidate (Mr. Obama) is silent (i.e., does not take a stance) on global warming, Republican candidate (Mr. Romney) may gain votes by going green from being silent on the issue.

Hypothesis 1b: When Democratic candidate (Mr. Obama) is silent on global warming, Republican candidate (Mr. Romney) may win votes by going not-green from being silent on the issue.

Hypothesis 2a: When Democratic candidate (Mr. Obama) takes a green stance on global warming, Republican candidate (Mr. Romney) may gain votes by taking a green stance from being silent on the issue.

Hypothesis 2b: When Democratic candidate (Mr. Obama) takes a green stance on global warming, Republican candidate (Mr. Romney) may not change votes by taking a not-green stance from being silent on the issue.

Hypothesis 3a: When Republican candidate (Mr. Romney) is silent on global warming, Democratic candidate (Mr. Obama) may win votes by going green from being silent on the issue.

Hypothesis 3b: When Republican candidate (Mr. Romney) takes a green stance on global warming, Democratic candidate (Mr. Obama) may win votes by going green from being silent on the issue.

Hypothesis 3c: When Republican candidate (Mr. Romney) takes a not-green stance on global warming, Democratic candidate (Mr. Obama) may win votes by going green from being silent on the issue.

Data and Method

Data Collection

Interviews were conducted with a national sample of 1492 American adults via the Internet by Toluna Corporate between November 2 and 4, 2012. The questionnaire was administered in English only.

Participants for this study were drawn randomly from Toluna's panel members. Most panel members were recruited from Toluna's social media space referenced as Toluna.com, and other panel members were recruited from multiple potential sample sources. When people joined the panel, Toluna collected demographic information such as sex, age, race/ethnicity, education, and income. Occasional e-mails inviting panel members to complete questionnaires were sent.

For this study, four respondent recruitment techniques were employed. (It is really three but one has two ways of notifying the respondent that a survey is waiting for them.) While a small proportion of participants entered the survey through theisroute, by far the most popular technique employed was via a direct invitation to the survey. Once a survey invitation was sent to a respondent, a notification was uploaded to an area of Toluna.com known as MySurveyCenter. The respondent entered the survey in two different ways: clicking on the link in the email invite or clicking on the link on their website notification.

The data for the survey were weighted to post-stratify in terms of age by gender, education, income, region, race, ethnicity and smoking status. Table 10.23 displays distributions of unweighted and weighted demographics of the survey sample and national benchmarks from the October 2012, Current Population Survey. These distributions show that the survey sample was similar to the American population before the weights were applied and was more similar after the data were weighted. Results reported in this chapterwere computed using weighted data.

TABLE 10.23 Study 8: Distributions of Demographics of the Sample and the Current Population Survey

Demographic	Global Warming Survey—2012 (unweighted) (%)	Global Warming Survey—2012 (weighted) (%)	Current Population Survey (CPS) —Oct. 2012 (%)	Difference: Global Warming Survey (weighted)—CPS (%)
		Gender		
Male	48.7	48.7	48.1	.6
Female	51.4	51.3	51.9	−.6
Total	100.0	100.0	100.0	
	(N = 2,000)	(N = 2,000)	(N = 101,289)	
		Age		
18–24	12.1	11.8	12.8	−1.0
25–34	19.0	18.3	17.5	.8
35–44	22.5	18.0	16.9	1.1
45–54	16.1	19.2	18.5	.7
55–64	13.1	15.7	16.4	−.7
65+	17.3	17.0	18.0	−1.0
Total	100.0	100.0	100.0	
	(N = 2,000)	(N = 2,000)	(N = 101,289)	
		Race and ethnicity		
Non-Hispanic White	78.7	70.0	66.2	3.8
Non-Hispanic Black	7.5	11.0	11.5	−.5
Hispanic	7.5	13.3	15.0	−1.7
Other race(s)	6.4	5.7	7.4	−1.7
Total	100.0	100.0	100.0	
	(N = 2,000)	(N = 2,000)	(N = 101,289)	
		Education		
High school graduate or less	28.1	44.7	42.3	2.4
Some college	30.1	27.5	28.9	−1.4
College graduate	27.1	17.2	18.8	−1.6
Post-college graduate	14.9	10.7	10.0	.7
Total	100.0	100.0	100.0	
	(N = 2,000)	(N = 2,000)	(N = 101,289)	

EXPERIMENTAL CONDITIONS

The experiment employed a 2x3 between-subjects design. Participants were randomly assigned to one of the two conditions: watching no Mr. Obama's video and watching a Mr. Obama's video. Participants were also independently and randomly assigned to one of the three conditions: watching none of Mr. Romney's videos, watching a Mr. Romney's green video and watching a Mr. Romney's not-green video). In sum, participants were randomly assigned to one of the following six experimental conditions and to watch 0, 1 or 2 short videos.

1   Control 1 (N = 228): Participants watched no video. This condition is the case when both Republican and Democratic candidates were silent on the issue of global warming.
2   Romney Green (N = 257): Participants watched a video whereby Mr. Romney expressed a green attitude toward global warming. This condition is the case when Democratic candidate (Mr. Obama) was silent on the issue of global warming and Republican candidate (Mr. Romney) took a green stance.
3   Romney Not-Green (N = 247): Participants watched a video whereby Mr. Romney expressed a not-green attitude toward global warming. This condition is the case when Democratic candidate (Mr. Obama) was silent on the issue of global warming and Republican candidate (Mr. Romney) took a not-green stance.
4   Control 2 (Obama Green) (N = 255): Participants watched a video whereby President Obama expressed a green attitude toward global warming. This condition is the case when Democratic candidate (Mr. Obama) took a green stance on global warming and Republican candidate (Mr. Romney) was silent on the issue.
5   Obama Green & Romney Green (N = 252): 4, plus participants watched a video whereby Mr. Romney expressed a green attitude toward global warming. This condition is the case when both Republican and Democratic candidates took a green stance on global warming.
6   Obama Green & Romney Not-Green (N = 253): 4, plus participants watched a video whereby Mr. Romney expressed a not-green attitude toward global warming. This condition is the case when Democratic candidate (Mr. Obama) took a green stance on global warming and Republican candidate (Mr. Romney) took a not-green stance.

After watching each of the assigned videos, participants reported three manipulation checks: how interesting the video was, how difficult the video was to understand, participants' agreement with what was said in the video.

Measures

Participants reported their intent to vote for the two presidential candidates, affect measures toward each candidate and perception of the personality traits of each candidate. The dependent measure, *electoral attitude favoring Mr. Romney index*, was an index of the following four measures or measure indices: intention to vote for Mr. Romney, like Mr. Romney relative to Mr. Obama, positive affect index distance, and personality perception index distance. A higher value of the dependent measure indicates more likely to vote for Mr. Romney and more favorable attitudes toward Mr. Romney than toward Mr. Obama. This dependent measure was used in assessing the electoral impact of Mr. Romney's taking a green or not-green stance on global warming.

INTENT TO VOTE FOR MR. ROMNEY

A randomly selected half of the respondents were asked: "If the 2012 presidential election were being held today and the candidates are Barack Obama, the Democrat, and Mitt Romney, the Republican, for whom would you vote if you were to vote?" And the other half of the respondents were asked: "If the 2012 presidential election were being held today and the candidates are Mitt Romney, the Republican, and Barack Obama, the Democrat, for whom would you vote if you were to vote?" Mitt Romney, the Republican = 1; Barack Obama, the Democrat = 0; refusal to answer = 0. Similarly, measure *intent to vote for Mr. Obama* was constructed as: Mitt Romney, the Republican = 0; Barack Obama, the Democrat = 1; refusal to answer = 0.

LIKE MR. ROMNEY DISTANCE

A distance between respondents' "like Mr. Romney" responses and those respondents' "like Mr. Obama" responses was constructed as: *like Mr. Romney distance = like Mr. Romney—like Mr. Obama*.

Like Mr. Romney

Respondents were asked "Do you like Mitt Romney, dislike him, or neither like nor dislike him?", and followed up with "Do you like Mitt Romney a great deal, a moderate amount, or a little?" or "Do you dislike Mitt Romney a great deal, a moderate amount, or a little?" like a great deal = 1; like a moderate amount =.83; like a little =.67; neither like or dislike = .5; dislike a little = .33; dislike a moderate amount = .17; dislike a great deal = 0; refusal to answer = 0.

Like Mr. Obama

Respondents were asked "Do you like Barack Obama, dislike him, or neither like nor dislike him?", and followed up with "Do you like Barack Obama a great deal, a moderate amount, or a little?" or "Do you dislike Barack Obama a great deal, a moderate amount, or a little?" like a great deal = 1; like a moderate amount =.83; like a little =.67; neither like nor dislike = .5; dislike a little = .33; dislike a moderate amount = .17; dislike a great deal = 0; refusal to answer = 0.

Similarly, a distance between respondents' "like Mr. Obama" responses and those respondents' "like Mr. Romney" responses was constructed as: *like Mr. Obama distance = like Mr. Obama—like Mr. Romney.*

AFFECT FOR MR. ROMNEY INDEX DISTANCE

A distance between respondents' affective responses to Mr. Romney and those to Mr. Obama was constructed as: *affect for Mr. Romney index distance = affect index for Mr. Romney—affect index for Mr. Obama*; each was an index of affective reactions to the candidate: how much respondents liked or disliked each candidate, and how hopeful, how proud, how afraid, and how angry respondents felt when thinking of each candidate. A participant's score on the index for each candidate, *affect index for Mr. Romney*, and *affect index for Mr. Obama*, was computed by averaging answers to the following questions coded as follows and therefore ranged from 0 (meaning the most negative affect) to 1 (meaning the most positive affect). Variables below were respondents' affective responses to Mr. Romney, and variables of respondents' affective responses to Mr. Obama were identically constructed.

Mr. Romney—hopeful

Respondents were asked "When you think of Mitt Romney, how hopeful does he make you feel—extremely hopeful, very hopeful, moderately hopeful, slightly hopeful, or not hopeful at all?" extremely hopeful = 1; very hopeful = .75; moderately hopeful = .5; slightly hopeful = .25; not hopeful at all = 0; refusal to answer = 0.

Mr. Romney—proud

Respondents were asked "When you think of Mitt Romney, how proud does he make you feel—extremely proud, very proud, moderately proud, slightly proud, or not proud at all?" extremely proud = 1; very proud = .75; moderately proud = .5; slightly proud = .25; not proud at all = 0; refusal to answer = 0.

Mr. Romney—angry

Respondents were asked "When you think of Mitt Romney, how angry does he make you feel—extremely angry, very angry, moderately angry, slightly angry, or not angry at all?" It was reversely coded; not angry at all = 1; slightly proud = .75; moderately proud = .5; very proud = .25; extremely angry= 0; refusal to answer = 0.

Mr. Romney—afraid

Respondents were asked "When you think of Mitt Romney, how afraid does he make you feel—extremely afraid, very afraid, moderately afraid, slightly afraid, or not afraid at all?" It was reversely coded; not afraid at all = 1; slightly afraid = .75; moderately afraid = .5; very afraid = .25; extremely afraid = 0; refusal to answer = 0.

Similarly, a distance between respondents' affective responses to Mr. Obama and those to Mr. Romney was constructed as: *affect for Mr. Obama index distance = affect index for Mr. Obama—affect index for Mr. Romney.*

Personality perception favoring Mr. Romney index distance

Related, a distance between respondents' personality traits perception of Mr. Romney and that of Mr. Obama was constructed as: *personality perception favoring Mr. Romney index distance = personality perception favoring Mr. Romney index—personality perception favoring Mr. Obama index*; each was an index of perception of personality traits about the candidate: how well did the word "moral," the word "intelligent," the phrase "really cares about people like you," and the phrase "strong leader" describe each candidate. A participant's score on the index for each candidate, *personality perception favoring Mr. Romney index*, and *personality perception favoring Mr. Obama index*, was computed by averaging answers to the following questions coded as follows and therefore ranged from 0 (meaning the most negative perception of personality traits) to 1 (meaning the most positive perception of personality traits). Variables below were respondents' personality traits perception of Mr. Romney, and variables of respondents' personality traits perception of Mr. Obama were identically constructed.

Mr. Romney—moral

Respondents were asked "How well does the word "moral" describe Mitt Romney—extremely well, very well, moderately well, slightly well, or not at all?" extremely well = 1; very well = .75; moderately well = .5; slightly well = .25; not well at all = 0; refusal to answer = 0.

Mr. Romney—intelligent

Respondents were asked "How well does the word "intelligent" describe Mitt Romney—extremely well, very well, moderately well, slightly well, or not at all?" extremely well = 1; very well = .75; moderately well = .5; slightly well = .25; not well at all = 0; refusal to answer = 0.

Mr. Romney—strong leader

Respondents were asked "How well does the phrase "strong leader" describe Mitt Romney—extremely well, very well, moderately well, slightly well, or not at all?" extremely well = 1; very well = .75; moderately well = .5; slightly well = .25; not well at all = 0; refusal to answer = 0.

Mr. Romney—care

Respondents were asked "How well does the phrase "really cares about people like you" describe Mitt Romney—extremely well, very well, moderately well, slightly well, or not at all?" extremely well = 1; very well = .75; moderately well = .5; slightly well = .25; not well at all = 0; refusal to answer = 0.

Similarly, a distance between respondents' personality traits perception of Mr. Obama and that of Mr. Romney was constructed as: *personality perception favoring Mr. Obama index distance = personality perception favoring Mr. Obama index— personality perception favoring Mr. Romney index.*

To summarize, two dependent measures were constructed. The dependent measure, *electoral attitude favoring Mr. Romney index*, which was used in assessing the electoral impact of Mr. Romney's taking a green or not-green stance on global warming, was constructed similarly as the average of these four indices: *intent to vote for Mr. Romney, like Mr. Romney distance, affect for Mr. Romney index distance*, and *personality perception favoring Mr. Romney index distance.* Similarly, the dependent measure, *electoral attitude favoring Mr. Obama index*, which was used in assessing the electoral impact of Mr. Obama's taking a green stance on global warming, was constructed as the average of these four indices: *intent to vote for Mr. Obama, like Mr. Obama distance, affect for Mr. Obama index distance*, and *personality perception favoring Mr. Obama index distance.*

Moderators

Two measures may moderate the electoral impact of candidates' taking a green or not-green stance on global warming.

Participants were asked "How important is the issue of global warming to you personally? Extremely important, very important, somewhat important, not too important, or not at all important?" extremely important = 1; very important = 1; somewhat important = 0; not too important = 0; not at all important = 0; refusal to answer = 0.

REGISTERED VOTER

Participants were asked "Are you currently registered to vote, or not?" registered to vote = 1; not registered to vote = 0; refusal to answer = 0.

LIKELY VOTER

Participants were asked seven questions that are used to assess the likely voter based on the Gallup model (Perry, 1960). Measure *likely voter* = 1 if the participant scored 1 on six or seven out of the following seven questions and *likely voter* = 0 if the participant scored 1 on five or fewer out of the following seven questions.

"How much have you thought about the upcoming election for President? Quite a lot or only a little?" quite a lot = 1; only a bit = 0; refusal to answer = 0.

"Do you happen to know where you who live in your neighborhood go to vote?" know where = 1; don't know where = 0; refusal to answer = 0.

"Have you ever voted in your precinct or election district?" have voted = 1; have not = 0; refusal to answer = 0.

"How often would you say you vote? Always, nearly always, part of time, or seldom?" always = 1; nearly always = 1; part of time = 0; seldom = 0; refusal to answer = 0.

"Do you plan to vote in the presidential election this November?" plan to vote = 1; not plan to = 0; refusal to answer = 0.

"In the last presidential election, did you vote for Barack Obama, John McCain, or someone else, or did things come up to keep you from voting?" voted for Barack Obama = 1; voted for John McCain = 1; voted for someone else = 1; things came up to keep me from voting = 0; refusal to answer = 0.

"If '1' represents someone who will definitely not vote and '10' represents someone who definitely will vote, where on this scale would you place yourself?" '1', '2', '3', '4', '5' or '6' = 0, '7', '8', '9' or '10' = 1, refusal to answer = 0.

Control variables

Participants reported their perceptions of the progress in the nation's economy, foreign relations and pollution, as well as job approval of President Obama as President, on handling the nation's economy, foreign relations and the environment. A randomly selected half of the respondents answered the job approval questions before the manipulation (watching the videos) and the other half did so after the manipulation. A dummy variable of question order was constructed and controlled for in the regressions testing the hypothesis.

PROGRESS ON ECONOMY

"Compared to two years ago, would you say that the nation's economy now is better, worse, or about the same?" IF BETTER, "Would you say much better or somewhat better?" IF WORSE, "Would you say much worse or somewhat worse?" much better = 1, somewhat better = .75, about the same = .5, somewhat worse = .25, much worse = 0; refusal to answer = 0.

PROGRESS ON FOREIGN RELATIONS

"Compared to two years ago, would you say U.S. relations with foreign countries are better, worse, or about the same?" IF BETTER, "Would you say much better or somewhat better?" IF WORSE, "Would you say much worse or somewhat worse?" much better = 1, somewhat better = .75, about the same = .5, somewhat worse = .25, much worse = 0; refusal to answer = 0.

PROGRESS ON POLLUTION

Compared to two years ago, would you say the amount of pollution in America is better, worse, or about the same?" IF BETTER, "Would you say much better or somewhat better?" IF WORSE, "Would you say much worse or somewhat worse?" much better = 1, somewhat better = .75, about the same = .5, somewhat worse = .25, much worse = 0; refusal to answer = 0.

APPROVAL OF PRESIDENT OBAMA

"Do you approve, disapprove, or neither approve nor disapprove, of the way Barack Obama has handled his job as President?" IF APPROVE, "Do you approve strongly or not strongly?" IF DISAPPROVE, "Do you disapprove strongly or not strongly?" approve strongly = 1, approve not strongly = .75, neither approve nor disapprove = .5, disapprove not strongly = .25, disapprove strongly = 0; refusal to answer = 0.

APPROVAL OF PRESIDENT OBAMA ON HANDLING THE ECONOMY

APPROVAL OF PRESIDENT OBAMA ON HANDLING THE ECONOMY

"Do you approve, disapprove, or neither approve nor disapprove, of the way Barack Obama has handled the U.S. economy?" IF APPROVE, "Do you approve strongly or not strongly?" IF DISAPPROVE, "Do you disapprove strongly or not strongly?" approve strongly = 1, approve not strongly = .75, neither approve nor disapprove = .5, disapprove not strongly = .25, disapprove strongly = 0; refusal to answer = 0.

APPROVAL OF PRESIDENT OBAMA ON HANDLING FOREIGN RELATIONS

"Do you approve, disapprove, or neither approve nor disapprove, of the way Barack Obama has handled U.S. relations with foreign countries?" IF APPROVE, "Do you approve strongly or not strongly?" IF DISAPPROVE, "Do you disapprove strongly or not strongly?" approve strongly = 1, approve not strongly = .75, neither approve nor disapprove = .5, disapprove not strongly = .25, disapprove strongly = 0; refusal to answer = 0.

APPROVAL OF PRESIDENT OBAMA ON HANDLING THE ENVIRONMENT

"Do you approve, disapprove, or neither approve nor disapprove, of the way Barack Obama has handled the environment?" IF APPROVE, "Do you approve strongly or not strongly?" IF DISAPPROVE, "Do you disapprove strongly or not strongly?" approve strongly = 1, approve not strongly = .75, neither approve nor disapprove = .5, disapprove not strongly = .25, disapprove strongly = 0; refusal to answer = 0.

PARTY IDENTIFICATION, IDEOLOGY AND DEMOGRAPHICS

Participants reported their political party identification, liberal/conservative ideology, sex, age, race, Hispanic ethnicity, education, income, and region of residence (see Appendix F for question wording and coding of control variables).

Mr. Romney's stance on global warming

Participants reported their perceptions of Mr. Obama's and Mr. Romney's stance on global warming. A stance index, *Mr. Romney's global warming stance index*, was constructed for Mr. Romney as an average over the following global warming belief measures, scaled from 0 to 1 with greater values indicating green stances and lower values indicating not-green stances. Variables below were respondents' perceptions of Mr. Romney's stance on global warming, and variables of respondents' perceptions of Mr. Obama's stance on global warming were identically measured and constructed. An index, *Mr. Obama's global warming stance index*, was similarly constructed.

MR. ROMNEY'S STANCE ON GLOBAL WARMING EXISTENCE

"If you had to guess, would you guess that Mitt Romney believes that the world's temperature has been going up over the past 100 years or that this probably has not been happening?" has been happening = 1; probably has not been happening = 0; refusal to answer = 0.

MR. ROMNEY'S STANCE ON GLOBAL WARMING CAUSE

"If you had to guess, would you guess that Mitt Romney believes that if the world's temperature has been going up over the past 100 years, that was caused [ROTATE THE ORDER: mostly by things people did, mostly by natural causes], or about equally by things people did and by natural causes?" mostly by things people did = 1; about equally by things people did and by natural causes = 1; mostly by natural causes = 0; refusal to answer = 0.

MR. ROMNEY'S STANCE ON THE GOVERNMENT EFFORT ON GLOBAL WARMING

"If you were to guess, how much would you guess Mitt Romney thinks the U.S. government should do about global warming? A great deal, quite a bit, some, a little, or none?" a great deal = 1; quite a bit = 1; some = 1; a little = 0; none = 0; refusal to answer = 0.

Analysis

OLS regressions were conducted to test the hypotheses by regressing the dependent measure, *electoral attitude favoring Mr. Romney index* in testing Hypothesis 1a, 1b, 2a and 2b, or *electoral attitude favoring Mr. Obama index* in testing Hypothesis 3a, 3b and 3c on the experiment condition that is pertinent to the hypothesis adjusting for sampling weights controlling for *progress on economy, progress on foreign relations, progress on pollution, approval of President Obama, approval of President Obama on handling the economy, approval of President Obama on handling foreign relations, approval of President Obama on handling the environment,* political party identification, liberal/conservative ideology and demographics. Additional analyses were conducted among subgroups of the sample: among Democrats, Republicans and Independents; among respondents who attached high personal importance to the issue of global warming and those who did not; among registered voters as well as among likely voters.

Results

The Impact of Mr. Romney's Taking a Green Stance In Absence of Mr. Obama

In the absence of Mr. Obama, Mr. Romney's taking a green stance on global warming, compared to being silent, yielded a higher score of respondents' *electoral attitude favoring Mr. Romney index* ($b = .04$, $p = .07$; see row 1 and column 1 in Table 10.24), lending evidence to Hypothesis 1a: when Democratic candidate is silent, Republican candidate may gain votes (favorable electoral attitudes) by taking a green stance on global warming compared to silence. This positive impact was concentrated among respondents who attached high personal importance to the issue of global warming ($b = .05$, $p = .09$; see row 1 and column 5 in Table 10.24) and among likely voters ($b = .05$, $p = .05$; see row 1 and column 1 in Table 10.24). Hypothesis 1a was supported.

The Impact of Mr. Romney's Taking a Not-Green Stance In Absence of Mr. Obama

In the absence of Mr. Obama, Mr. Romney's taking a not-green stance on global warming, compared to being silent, yielded a lower score of respondents' *electoral attitude favoring Mr. Romney index* ($b = -.04$, $p = .10$; see row 2 and column 1 in Table 10.24). With an exception of a negative impact among Independents ($b = -.10$, $p < .01$; see row 2 and column 5 in Table 10.24), there was no impact of Mr. Romney's taking a not-green stance among any of the subpopulations (see row 2 and columns 2–4 and 6–8 in Table 10.24), inconsistent with the prediction of Hypothesis 1b. The failure to support Hypothesis 1b was likely to be a result of the failure of the manipulation. If the manipulation had worked, respondents in the treatment condition (Condition 3: Romney Not-Green) would have had been more likely than respondents in the control condition (Condition 1: Control 1) to perceive Mr. Romney to take a not-green stance on the issue of global warming, however, perception of Romney's stance on global warming did not differ between the conditions ($m = .51$, $m = .57$ for the treatment and control condition respectively, $p = .14$), thus the treatment failed. The failure of the manipulation could be caused by the fact that Mr. Romney was well known for his not-green stance on global warming during his campaign and this study was conducted just days before the election, thus most people would be aware of Mr. Romney's not-green stance. To sum, Hypothesis 1b was not supported, possibly because of the failure of the manipulation.

TABLE 10.24 Study 8: Impact of Mr. Romney's Taking a Green or a Not-Green Stance In Absence of Mr. Obama

Predictor	All respondents	Democrats	Republicans	Independents	High personal importance	Low personal importance	Registered to vote	Likely voters
	(1)	(2)	(3)	(4)	(5)	(6)	(7)	(8)
Romney green =1 (Romney silence = 0)	0.04* (0.02)	0.02 (0.03)	0.01 (0.03)	0.02 (0.03)	0.05* (0.03)	0.04 (0.03)	0.03 (0.02)	0.05* (0.02)
Romney not-green =1 (Romney silence = 0)	-0.04* (0.02)	-0.01 (0.03)	-0.01 (0.04)	-0.10*** (0.03)	-0.05 (0.03)	-0.03 (0.03)	-0.04 (0.02)	-0.02 (0.02)
Progress economy	-0.11*** (0.04)	-0.17*** (0.06)	-0.14* (0.08)	-0.05 (0.06)	-0.09* (0.05)	-0.13** (0.05)	-0.13*** (0.04)	-0.12*** (0.04)
Progress foreign rel.	0.01 (0.04)	0.02 (0.05)	0.12 (0.08)	-0.01 (0.07)	0.06 (0.05)	-0.06 (0.05)	-0.00 (0.04)	0.01 (0.04)
Progress pollution	0.20*** (0.05)	0.10* (0.06)	0.12 (0.08)	0.21*** (0.08)	0.17*** (0.06)	0.14** (0.07)	0.19*** (0.06)	0.22*** (0.05)
Approval of Obama	-0.29*** (0.05)	-0.30*** (0.07)	-0.23** (0.11)	-0.33*** (0.07)	-0.26*** (0.06)	-0.36*** (0.09)	-0.28*** (0.05)	-0.31*** (0.06)
Approval on economy	-0.09* (0.05)	-0.13*** (0.05)	0.23 (0.15)	-0.13 (0.08)	-0.10* (0.05)	-0.09 (0.09)	-0.10** (0.05)	-0.06 (0.06)
Approval foreign rel.	-0.25*** (0.04)	-0.15*** (0.06)	-0.36*** (0.09)	-0.31*** (0.07)	-0.22*** (0.05)	-0.22*** (0.06)	-0.24*** (0.04)	-0.27*** (0.05)
Approval environ.	-0.02 (0.04)	-0.00 (0.05)	-0.12** (0.06)	-0.01 (0.07)	0.02 (0.05)	-0.04 (0.05)	-0.02 (0.04)	-0.03 (0.04)
Approval asked first	-0.00 (0.02)	-0.00 (0.02)	-0.04 (0.04)	0.00 (0.03)	-0.02 (0.03)	0.02 (0.02)	-0.00 (0.02)	-0.02 (0.02)

Democrat	−0.09*** (0.03)				−0.09** (0.04)	−0.10*** (0.03)	−0.10*** (0.03)
Republican	0.16*** (0.03)	0.11*** (0.04)		0.33*** (0.07)	0.09*** (0.02)	0.14*** (0.04)	0.14*** (0.04)
Liberal	−0.03 (0.03)	−0.25** (0.11)	−0.08* (0.04)	−0.03 (0.03)	−0.07* (0.04)	−0.03 (0.03)	−0.04 (0.03)
Conservative	0.09*** (0.02)	0.12*** (0.04)	0.07** (0.03)	0.07 (0.04)	0.07*** (0.02)	0.10*** (0.02)	0.10*** (0.02)
Female	−0.04** (0.02)	−0.09*** (0.02)	−0.03 (0.03)	−0.06*** (0.02)	−0.03 (0.02)	−0.04** (0.02)	−0.03 (0.02)
Married	0.00 (0.02)	−0.01 (0.03)	0.06** (0.03)	−0.03 (0.03)	0.05** (0.02)	−0.00 (0.02)	−0.01 (0.02)
Some college	−0.03 (0.02)	0.03 (0.03)	−0.05 (0.03)	0.02 (0.03)	−0.04 (0.03)	−0.04* (0.02)	−0.05** (0.02)
College graduate	−0.02 (0.02)	−0.00 (0.03)	−0.01 (0.03)	0.02 (0.03)	−0.03 (0.02)	−0.04* (0.02)	−0.03 (0.02)
Post college graduate	−0.01 (0.03)	0.05 (0.03)	−0.00 (0.04)	0.03 (0.04)	−0.02 (0.03)	−0.02 (0.03)	−0.03 (0.03)
Age 18 to 24	0.01 (0.03)	−0.02 (0.05)	−0.01 (0.05)	0.02 (0.05)	0.00 (0.04)	0.04 (0.03)	0.01 (0.04)
Age 25 to 34	0.05 (0.03)	−0.00 (0.04)	−0.04 (0.05)	0.07 (0.05)	0.02 (0.04)	0.06* (0.04)	0.06 (0.04)
Age 35 to 44	0.04 (0.03)	−0.01 (0.04)	0.01 (0.04)	0.06 (0.04)	−0.02 (0.04)	0.04 (0.03)	0.05 (0.03)

continued…

Table 10.24 continued...

Predictor	All respondents (1)	Democrats (2)	Republicans (3)	Independents (4)	High personal importance (5)	Low personal importance (6)	Registered to vote (7)	Likely voters (8)
Age 45 to 54	-0.04 (0.02)	-0.07** (0.03)	-0.00 (0.05)	-0.06 (0.04)	-0.03 (0.04)	-0.03 (0.03)	-0.03 (0.02)	-0.02 (0.03)
Age 55 to 64	0.00 (0.03)	-0.10*** (0.04)	0.04 (0.05)	0.03 (0.04)	-0.09** (0.04)	0.02 (0.03)	0.01 (0.03)	0.01 (0.03)
Having child <18	0.01 (0.02)	0.05* (0.03)	0.00 (0.04)	-0.00 (0.03)	0.03 (0.03)	-0.00 (0.02)	0.01 (0.02)	0.03 (0.02)
Having child 18+	0.09*** (0.02)	0.11*** (0.03)	0.07** (0.03)	0.08*** (0.03)	0.12*** (0.03)	0.04* (0.02)	0.09*** (0.02)	0.09*** (0.02)
Hispanic	-0.04 (0.04)	-0.02 (0.04)	-0.12** (0.05)	-0.05 (0.06)	-0.02 (0.04)	-0.08* (0.04)	-0.05 (0.04)	-0.02 (0.04)
White	0.02 (0.03)	0.05 (0.04)	0.17** (0.08)	-0.09* (0.05)	0.03 (0.04)	0.02 (0.05)	-0.01 (0.03)	0.04 (0.04)
Black	-0.00 (0.03)	0.01 (0.04)	0.02 (0.17)	-0.00 (0.06)	-0.04 (0.04)	0.05 (0.07)	-0.04 (0.04)	-0.01 (0.04)
Working	0.01 (0.02)	0.02 (0.02)	0.02 (0.04)	-0.01 (0.03)	0.02 (0.03)	0.01 (0.02)	0.00 (0.02)	0.01 (0.02)
Constant	0.55*** (0.06)	0.45*** (0.08)	0.60*** (0.11)	0.71*** (0.09)	0.38*** (0.10)	0.66*** (0.08)	0.61*** (0.07)	0.56*** (0.07)
N	732	288	184	260	347	385	646	584
R^2	0.796	0.641	0.575	0.744	0.730	0.826	0.808	0.823

Notes: Presented are OLS coefficient estimates of electoral attitudes favoring Mr. Romney index (standard errors in parentheses) adjusting for sampling weights.
Each column is a separate regression.
*** $p < 0.01$, ** $p < 0.05$, * $p < 0.1$

The Impact of Mr. Romney's Taking a Green Stance In Presence of Mr. Obama

In the presence of Mr. Obama's taking a green stance, Mr. Romney's taking a green stance on global warming, compared to being silent, yielded a higher score of respondents' *electoral attitude favoring Mr. Romney index* ($b = .04, p < .05$; see row 1 and column 1 in Table 10.25), supporting Hypothesis 2a: when Democratic candidate takes a green stance on global warming, Republican candidate may gain votes (favorable electoral attitudes) by taking a green stance compared to silence. This positive impact was concentrated among respondents who did not attach high personal importance to the issue of global warming ($b = .07, p < .01$; see row 1 and column 6 in Table 10.25) as well as among likely voters ($b = .03, p = .06$; see row 1 and column 8 in Table 10.25). Hypothesis 2a was supported.

The Impact of Mr. Romney's Taking a Not-Green Stance In Presence of Mr. Obama

In the presence of Mr. Obama's taking a green stance, Mr. Romney's taking a not-green stance on global warming, compared to being silent, did not alter respondents' score on *electoral attitude favoring Mr. Romney index* (favorable electoral attitude) (see row 2 and column 1 in Table 10.25), lending evidence to Hypothesis 2b: when Democratic candidate takes a green stance, Republican candidate may not change votes by taking a not-green stance on global warming compared to silence. Except among Independents ($b = .06, p = .06$; see row 2 and column 4 in Table 10.25) and respondents who did not attach high importance to the issue ($b = .06, p = .01$; see row 2 and column 4 in Table 10.25), there was no impact of Mr. Romney's taking a not-green stance with Mr. Obama's green stance among any other subpopulations (see row 2 and columns 2–3 and 5, 7–8 in Table 10.25). Hypothesis 2b was thus supported.

The Impact of Mr. Obama Taking a Green Stance In Absence of Mr. Romney

In the absence of Mr. Romney (i.e. Mr. Romney took a silence stance on the issue), Mr. Obama's taking a green stance on global warming, compared to being silent, led to an increase in respondents' scores on *electoral attitude favoring Mr. Obama index* (favorable electoral attitude) ($b = .04, p = .02$; see row 1 and column 1 in Table 10.26), lending evidence to Hypothesis 3a: when Republican candidate takes a silence stance, Democratic candidate may gain votes (favorable electoral attitudes) by taking a green stance on global warming compared to silence.

TABLE 10.25 Study 8: Impact of Mr. Romney's Taking a Green or a Not-Green Stance In Presence of Mr. Obama's Green Stance

Predictor	All respondents	Democrats	Republicans	Independents	High personal importance	Low personal importance	Registered to vote	Likely voters
	(1)	(2)	(3)	(4)	(5)	(6)	(7)	(8)
Romney green = 1 (Romney silence = 0)	0.04** (0.02)	0.02 (0.02)	0.01 (0.03)	0.05 (0.03)	0.02 (0.02)	0.07*** (0.02)	0.02 (0.02)	0.03* (0.02)
Romney not-green = 1 (Romney silence = 0)	0.01 (0.02)	0.01 (0.02)	-0.02 (0.03)	0.06* (0.03)	-0.02 (0.02)	0.06** (0.02)	0.02 (0.02)	0.03 (0.02)
Obama presented first	-0.04*** (0.01)	-0.04* (0.02)	-0.04 (0.02)	-0.05* (0.03)	-0.05** (0.02)	-0.03 (0.02)	-0.04** (0.02)	-0.03** (0.02)
Progress economy	-0.11*** (0.04)	-0.02 (0.05)	-0.10 (0.06)	-0.25*** (0.06)	-0.06 (0.05)	-0.19*** (0.05)	-0.11*** (0.04)	-0.11*** (0.04)
Progress foreign rel.	-0.07** (0.03)	-0.08* (0.05)	-0.13** (0.06)	-0.08 (0.07)	-0.02 (0.04)	-0.15** (0.06)	-0.07* (0.04)	-0.05 (0.04)
Progress pollution	0.15*** (0.04)	0.17*** (0.05)	-0.07 (0.06)	0.18*** (0.07)	0.14*** (0.04)	0.14*** (0.05)	0.13*** (0.04)	0.12*** (0.04)
Approval of Obama	-0.33*** (0.05)	-0.38*** (0.06)	-0.19** (0.09)	-0.21*** (0.08)	-0.31*** (0.06)	-0.38*** (0.08)	-0.36*** (0.05)	-0.39*** (0.05)
Approval on economy	-0.12*** (0.04)	-0.05 (0.04)	-0.27*** (0.09)	-0.19** (0.07)	-0.17*** (0.05)	-0.05 (0.06)	-0.11*** (0.04)	-0.10** (0.04)
Approval foreign rel.	-0.14*** (0.04)	-0.16*** (0.05)	-0.02 (0.05)	-0.15** (0.06)	-0.06 (0.05)	-0.16*** (0.05)	-0.14*** (0.04)	-0.14*** (0.04)
Approval environ.	-0.08** (0.03)	-0.02 (0.04)	-0.12** (0.05)	-0.18*** (0.05)	-0.04 (0.04)	-0.10** (0.04)	-0.07** (0.03)	-0.08*** (0.03)

Approval asked first	-0.02 (0.02)	-0.02 (0.02)	0.01 (0.02)	-0.04* (0.02)	-0.00 (0.02)	-0.01 (0.03)	-0.02 (0.02)
Democrat	-0.08*** (0.02)	-0.07*** (0.02)	-0.08** (0.03)	-0.07*** (0.03)			-0.04** (0.02)
Republican	0.14*** (0.03)	0.17*** (0.03)	0.14*** (0.03)	0.23*** (0.04)			
Liberal	-0.02 (0.02)	-0.03 (0.02)	-0.02 (0.03)	-0.04* (0.02)	-0.01 (0.04)	-0.10 (0.07)	0.03 (0.04)
Conservative	0.07*** (0.02)	0.04** (0.02)	0.05** (0.02)	0.03 (0.03)	0.06* (0.03)	0.04* (0.03)	-0.06*** (0.02)
Female	-0.03** (0.02)	-0.04** (0.02)	-0.02 (0.02)	-0.05** (0.02)	-0.03 (0.03)	0.03 (0.03)	0.09*** (0.03)
Married	-0.00 (0.02)	0.00 (0.02)	0.01 (0.02)	0.00 (0.02)	0.01 (0.03)	-0.04 (0.02)	0.02 (0.03)
Some college	0.03 (0.02)	0.03* (0.02)	-0.00 (0.02)	0.04* (0.02)	0.00 (0.03)	0.03 (0.03)	0.00 (0.03)
College graduate	0.06*** (0.02)	0.07*** (0.02)	0.04* (0.02)	0.06** (0.02)	0.10*** (0.03)	-0.01 (0.03)	0.03 (0.03)
Post college graduate	0.02 (0.02)	0.03 (0.02)	0.02 (0.03)	0.03 (0.03)	0.09** (0.04)	-0.06 (0.04)	0.02 (0.03)
Age 18 to 24	-0.03 (0.03)	-0.03 (0.03)	-0.06 (0.04)	0.03 (0.04)	-0.04 (0.06)	-0.03 (0.05)	0.00 (0.03)
Age 25 to 34	0.04 (0.03)	0.03 (0.03)	-0.01 (0.04)	0.05 (0.04)	0.05 (0.06)	0.05 (0.04)	-0.01 (0.04)
Age 35 to 44	-0.01 (0.03)	-0.00 (0.03)	-0.01 (0.03)	0.02 (0.04)	0.01 (0.05)	-0.07 (0.05)	0.00 (0.03)

continued…

Table 10.25 continued...

Predictor	All respondents (1)	Democrats (2)	Republicans (3)	Independents (4)	High personal importance (5)	Low personal importance (6)	Registered to vote (7)	Likely voters (8)
Age 45 to 54	-0.04 (0.03)	-0.05 (0.03)	-0.10★★★ (0.04)	-0.02 (0.06)	-0.03 (0.04)	-0.01 (0.03)	-0.05★★ (0.03)	-0.05★ (0.03)
Age 55 to 64	0.03 (0.02)	0.06 (0.04)	-0.04 (0.04)	0.03 (0.06)	0.04 (0.03)	0.04 (0.03)	0.02 (0.03)	0.02 (0.03)
Having child <18	0.00 (0.02)	0.02 (0.02)	0.00 (0.03)	0.01 (0.03)	0.01 (0.03)	0.01 (0.03)	0.01 (0.02)	0.01 (0.02)
Having child 18+	-0.01 (0.02)	0.02 (0.02)	0.03 (0.03)	-0.09★★★ (0.03)	0.02 (0.02)	-0.03 (0.02)	0.00 (0.02)	0.01 (0.02)
Hispanic	0.03 (0.02)	0.07★★ (0.03)	0.04 (0.05)	-0.02 (0.04)	0.00 (0.03)	0.03 (0.03)	0.04 (0.03)	0.04 (0.03)
White	-0.05★ (0.03)	-0.03 (0.03)	-0.10★★ (0.05)	0.08★ (0.04)	-0.04 (0.03)	-0.06 (0.04)	-0.06★★ (0.03)	-0.06★★ (0.03)
Black	-0.05★ (0.03)	-0.03 (0.03)	-0.26★★ (0.11)	-0.03 (0.05)	-0.06★ (0.03)	-0.03 (0.05)	-0.06★ (0.03)	-0.05 (0.03)
Working	0.02 (0.02)	0.01 (0.02)	0.04 (0.03)	-0.01 (0.03)	0.02 (0.02)	0.02 (0.02)	0.02 (0.02)	0.01 (0.02)
Constant	0.66★★★ (0.04)	0.47★★★ (0.06)	1.04★★★ (0.07)	0.62★★★ (0.08)	0.54★★★ (0.06)	0.73★★★ (0.06)	0.68★★★ (0.05)	0.70★★★ (0.05)
N	759	328	194	237	373	386	687	620
R^2	0.829	0.627	0.655	0.779	0.778	0.856	0.841	0.855

Notes: Presented are OLS coefficient estimates of electoral attitudes favoring Mr. Romney index (standard errors in parentheses) adjusting for sampling weights. Each column is a separate regression. ★★★ $p<0.01$, ★★ $p<0.05$, ★ $p<0.1$

TABLE 10.26 Study 8: Impact of Mr. Obama's Taking a Green Stance In Absence of Mr. Romney

Predictor	All respondents	Democrats	Republicans	Independents	High personal importance	Low personal importance	Registered to vote	Likely voters
	(1)	(2)	(3)	(4)	(5)	(6)	(7)	(8)
Obama green =1 (Obama silence = 0)	0.04** (0.02)	0.03 (0.02)	−0.03 (0.03)	0.11*** (0.03)	0.02 (0.03)	0.06*** (0.02)	0.06*** (0.02)	0.05*** (0.02)
Progress economy	0.16*** (0.05)	0.17*** (0.06)	0.16** (0.08)	0.09 (0.08)	0.05 (0.06)	0.23*** (0.05)	0.15*** (0.05)	0.17*** (0.05)
Progress foreign rel.	0.05 (0.05)	0.00 (0.06)	0.08 (0.07)	0.01 (0.09)	0.08 (0.06)	0.01 (0.07)	0.05 (0.05)	−0.01 (0.05)
Progress pollution	−0.16*** (0.05)	−0.10* (0.05)	−0.06 (0.07)	−0.28*** (0.09)	−0.14*** (0.05)	−0.11* (0.06)	−0.13*** (0.05)	−0.14*** (0.05)
Approval of Obama	0.31*** (0.06)	0.29*** (0.08)	0.09 (0.12)	0.44*** (0.09)	0.31*** (0.07)	0.33*** (0.08)	0.31*** (0.06)	0.36*** (0.06)
Approval on economy	0.14*** (0.05)	0.07 (0.06)	0.28*** (0.09)	0.17 (0.11)	0.15** (0.07)	0.09 (0.07)	0.14*** (0.05)	0.13** (0.05)
Approval foreign rel.	0.20*** (0.04)	0.24*** (0.07)	0.15*** (0.05)	0.23*** (0.08)	0.17*** (0.05)	0.24*** (0.06)	0.21*** (0.05)	0.21*** (0.05)
Approval environ.	−0.00 (0.04)	−0.02 (0.06)	−0.02 (0.06)	0.07 (0.07)	−0.08* (0.05)	0.08* (0.05)	−0.01 (0.04)	0.03 (0.04)
Approval asked first	0.01 (0.02)	0.00 (0.02)	−0.03 (0.03)	0.04 (0.03)	0.01 (0.02)	−0.01 (0.02)	0.00 (0.02)	0.01 (0.02)
Democrat	0.05** (0.02)				0.00 (0.03)	0.10*** (0.03)	0.06** (0.03)	0.05* (0.03)

continued...

Table 10.26 continued...

Predictor	All respondents (1)	Democrats (2)	Republicans (3)	Independents (4)	High personal importance (5)	Low personal importance (6)	Registered to vote (7)	Likely voters (8)
Republican	-0.18*** (0.03)				-0.28*** (0.06)	-0.13*** (0.03)	-0.18*** (0.03)	-0.16*** (0.03)
Liberal	0.04 (0.02)	0.02 (0.03)	0.18** (0.07)	0.02 (0.05)	0.02 (0.03)	0.07** (0.03)	0.03 (0.02)	0.03 (0.02)
Conservative	-0.06** (0.02)	-0.06 (0.04)	-0.05 (0.03)	-0.05 (0.04)	-0.09** (0.04)	-0.02 (0.03)	-0.05* (0.03)	-0.06** (0.03)
Female	0.04** (0.02)	0.06** (0.03)	-0.00 (0.03)	-0.00 (0.03)	0.08*** (0.03)	0.00 (0.02)	0.02 (0.02)	0.02 (0.02)
Married	-0.01 (0.02)	0.01 (0.03)	-0.04 (0.03)	-0.02 (0.03)	0.02 (0.03)	-0.09*** (0.03)	-0.02 (0.02)	0.01 (0.02)
Some college	-0.01 (0.02)	0.01 (0.03)	-0.02 (0.03)	-0.05 (0.04)	0.03 (0.03)	-0.02 (0.03)	0.00 (0.02)	-0.00 (0.02)
College graduate	-0.03 (0.02)	-0.02 (0.03)	-0.02 (0.04)	-0.06* (0.03)	0.01 (0.03)	-0.04 (0.03)	-0.02 (0.02)	-0.03 (0.02)
Post college graduate	-0.01 (0.03)	-0.01 (0.03)	0.04 (0.04)	-0.08 (0.06)	0.06 (0.05)	-0.03 (0.03)	-0.00 (0.03)	-0.00 (0.03)
Age 18 to 24	0.03 (0.04)	-0.01 (0.04)	-0.04 (0.06)	0.03 (0.08)	0.08 (0.05)	-0.05 (0.04)	0.02 (0.04)	0.06 (0.04)
Age 25 to 34	-0.06* (0.03)	-0.02 (0.04)	-0.16** (0.06)	0.02 (0.06)	0.01 (0.04)	-0.08** (0.04)	-0.07** (0.03)	-0.07** (0.03)

Age 35 to 44	0.01	0.04	-0.07	0.02	0.03	-0.01	0.01	-0.00
	(0.03)	(0.04)	(0.05)	(0.06)	(0.04)	(0.03)	(0.03)	(0.03)
Age 45 to 54	0.05★	0.05	0.04	0.06	0.04	0.03	0.05★	0.04
	(0.03)	(0.04)	(0.05)	(0.06)	(0.04)	(0.03)	(0.03)	(0.03)
Age 55 to 64	-0.02	0.06	-0.10★★★	-0.03	0.08★★	-0.06★	-0.01	-0.01
	(0.03)	(0.04)	(0.04)	(0.06)	(0.04)	(0.03)	(0.03)	(0.03)
Having child <18	0.01	-0.03	0.07★	0.05	-0.03	0.03	0.02	0.02
	(0.02)	(0.03)	(0.04)	(0.03)	(0.03)	(0.02)	(0.02)	(0.02)
Having child 18+	-0.05★★★	-0.07★★★	-0.07★★	-0.03	-0.05★	-0.05★	-0.05★★★	-0.07★★★
	(0.02)	(0.02)	(0.03)	(0.03)	(0.03)	(0.02)	(0.02)	(0.02)
Hispanic	-0.00	-0.10★★★	0.20★	0.13	0.02	0.02	-0.05	-0.06
	(0.04)	(0.04)	(0.12)	(0.08)	(0.04)	(0.05)	(0.05)	(0.05)
White	0.00	-0.07	-0.07	0.04	0.02	-0.08	0.03	-0.06
	(0.04)	(0.05)	(0.07)	(0.06)	(0.05)	(0.06)	(0.04)	(0.05)
Black	-0.02	-0.11★★	0.00	0.00	0.04	-0.16★★	-0.00	-0.07
	(0.04)	(0.05)	(0.00)	(0.07)	(0.05)	(0.07)	(0.05)	(0.06)
Working	-0.01	0.02	-0.02	-0.00	0.01	-0.04★	-0.01	-0.01
	(0.02)	(0.03)	(0.04)	(0.03)	(0.02)	(0.02)	(0.02)	(0.02)
Constant	-0.36★★★	-0.22★★	-0.38★★★	-0.46★★★	-0.32★★★	-0.29★★★	-0.40★★★	-0.34★★★
	(0.06)	(0.09)	(0.11)	(0.10)	(0.08)	(0.08)	(0.07)	(0.06)
N	482	222	120	140	236	246	439	398
R^2	0.845	0.651	0.750	0.828	0.779	0.887	0.853	0.871

Notes: Presented are OLS coefficient estimates of electoral attitudes favoring Mr. Obama index (standard errors in parentheses) adjusting for sampling weights. Each column is a separate regression.

★★★ $p<0.01$, ★★ $p<0.05$, ★ $p<0.1$

The positive impact of Mr. Obama's taking a green stance with Mr. Romney's silence stance was present among many subpopulations, including among Independents ($b = .11, p < .01$; see row 1 and column 4 in Table 10.26), among respondents who did not attach high personal importance to the issue ($b = .06$, $p < .01$; see row 1 and column 6 in Table 10.26), among registered voters ($b = .06, p < .01$; see row 1 and column 7 in Table 10.26) as well as among likely voters ($b = .05, p < .01$; see row 1 and column 8 in Table 10.26). Hypothesis 3a was supported.

The Impact of Mr. Obama Taking a Green Stance In Presence of Mr. Romney's Green Stance

In the presence of Mr. Romney's taking a green stance on the issue, Mr. Obama's taking a green stance on global warming, compared to being silent, led to no change in respondents' scores on *electoral attitude favoring Mr. Obama index* (favorable electoral attitude) (see row 1 and column 1 in Table 10.27), inconsistent with the prediction of Hypothesis 3b: when Republican candidate takes a green stance, Democratic candidate may gain votes (favorable electoral attitudes) by taking a green stance on global warming compared to silence. However, among registered voters and importantly, among likely voters, Mr. Obama's taking a green stance on global warming, compared to being silent, increased respondents' scores on *electoral attitude favoring Mr. Obama index* ($b = .05, p = .03; b = .04, p = .06$ among respondents registered to vote and likely voters, respectively; see row 1 and columns 7–8 in Table 10.27). Since Hypothesis 3a (and all other hypotheses in this study) was formulated based on the actual voting outcomes in Study 3, evidence among likely voters (which was a good approximation of actual voters) would be the most pertinent to testing this hypothesis, thus the evidence of positive electoral impact among likely voters led to the conclusion that Hypothesis 3b was supported.

The Impact of Mr. Obama Taking a Green Stance In Presence of Mr. Romney's Not-Green Stance

In the presence of Mr. Romney's taking a not-green stance on the issue, Mr. Obama's taking a green stance on global warming, compared to being silent, led to no change in respondents' scores on *electoral attitude favoring Mr. Obama index* (favorable electoral attitude) (see row 1 and column 1 in Table 10.28), inconsistent with the prediction of Hypothesis 3c: when Republican candidate takes a not-green stance, Democratic candidate may gain votes (favorable electoral attitudes) by taking a green stance on global warming compared to silence. There was no impact or no positive impact of Mr. Obama's taking a green stance among any of the subpopulations (see row 1 and columns 2–8 in

TABLE 10.27 Study 8: Impact of Mr. Obama's Taking a Green Stance In Presence of Mr. Romney's Green Stance

Predictor	All respondents	Democrats	Republicans	Independents	High personal importance	Low personal importance	Registered to vote	Likely voters
	(1)	(2)	(3)	(4)	(5)	(6)	(7)	(8)
Obama green =1 (Obama silence = 0)	0.03 (0.02)	0.03 (0.03)	0.03 (0.03)	0.05 (0.03)	0.04 (0.03)	0.01 (0.03)	0.05** (0.02)	0.04* (0.02)
Obama presented first	−0.02 (0.02)	0.05** (0.02)	−0.05** (0.03)	−0.02 (0.03)	−0.04 (0.03)	0.01 (0.02)	−0.03 (0.03)	−0.05 (0.03)
Progress economy	0.08* (0.04)	0.00 (0.06)	0.02 (0.08)	0.20*** (0.08)	0.05 (0.05)	0.12* (0.06)	0.10** (0.04)	0.09* (0.05)
Progress foreign rel.	−0.02 (0.05)	−0.05 (0.06)	−0.08 (0.09)	0.09 (0.08)	−0.08 (0.05)	0.12 (0.08)	−0.03 (0.05)	−0.06 (0.05)
Progress pollution	−0.24*** (0.05)	−0.18*** (0.07)	−0.11 (0.09)	−0.35*** (0.07)	−0.24*** (0.06)	−0.14* (0.07)	−0.24*** (0.06)	−0.23*** (0.06)
Approval of Obama	0.30*** (0.06)	0.42*** (0.07)	0.16 (0.10)	0.20* (0.11)	0.25*** (0.07)	0.41*** (0.10)	0.28*** (0.06)	0.33*** (0.07)
Approval on economy	0.13** (0.06)	0.15** (0.07)	0.04 (0.13)	0.18* (0.09)	0.19*** (0.07)	0.09 (0.09)	0.15** (0.06)	0.10 (0.07)
Approval foreign rel.	0.19*** (0.05)	0.18*** (0.06)	0.25*** (0.08)	0.18** (0.09)	0.17*** (0.06)	0.10 (0.07)	0.19*** (0.05)	0.22*** (0.05)
Approval environ.	0.09** (0.04)	0.01 (0.07)	0.15** (0.07)	0.19** (0.08)	0.08 (0.05)	0.10 (0.06)	0.10** (0.04)	0.09** (0.04)
Approval asked first	0.05** (0.02)	0.07*** (0.02)	0.11*** (0.04)	0.00 (0.04)	0.09*** (0.03)	0.00 (0.03)	0.06** (0.02)	0.07** (0.03)
Democrat	0.12*** (0.03)				0.05 (0.03)	0.13*** (0.04)	0.11*** (0.03)	0.12*** (0.04)

continued…

Table 10.27 continued...

Predictor	All respondents (1)	Democrats (2)	Republicans (3)	Independents (4)	High personal importance (5)	Low personal importance (6)	Registered to vote (7)	Likely voters (8)
Republican	-0.19*** (0.04)				-0.31*** (0.06)	-0.10*** (0.03)	-0.20*** (0.04)	-0.17*** (0.04)
Liberal	0.07** (0.03)	0.04 (0.02)	-0.01 (0.15)	0.11* (0.06)	0.08** (0.03)	0.00 (0.05)	0.05* (0.03)	0.06** (0.03)
Conservative	-0.03 (0.03)	0.02 (0.05)	-0.05 (0.03)	-0.04 (0.04)	0.01 (0.04)	-0.06** (0.03)	-0.03 (0.03)	-0.05* (0.03)
Female	0.01 (0.02)	0.08*** (0.03)	-0.09*** (0.03)	0.03 (0.04)	-0.00 (0.03)	0.04* (0.02)	0.02 (0.02)	0.01 (0.02)
Married	0.00 (0.02)	-0.00 (0.03)	0.05 (0.04)	-0.02 (0.04)	0.03 (0.03)	-0.02 (0.03)	0.00 (0.02)	0.01 (0.02)
Some college	0.01 (0.02)	-0.01 (0.03)	0.01 (0.04)	0.00 (0.04)	-0.04 (0.03)	0.02 (0.03)	-0.01 (0.02)	0.00 (0.03)
College graduate	-0.02 (0.03)	-0.03 (0.03)	0.09* (0.05)	-0.01 (0.05)	-0.05 (0.03)	0.01 (0.03)	-0.03 (0.03)	-0.02 (0.03)
Post college graduate	0.00 (0.03)	-0.03 (0.03)	-0.03 (0.05)	0.01 (0.06)	-0.03 (0.04)	-0.00 (0.04)	0.00 (0.03)	0.01 (0.03)
Age 18 to 24	0.05 (0.04)	0.07 (0.05)	0.06 (0.07)	0.10 (0.06)	-0.02 (0.05)	0.08* (0.05)	0.05 (0.04)	0.02 (0.04)
Age 25 to 34	0.02 (0.04)	0.11** (0.05)	-0.11* (0.06)	0.01 (0.07)	-0.01 (0.05)	0.11** (0.04)	0.02 (0.04)	-0.02 (0.04)

	(1)	(2)	(3)	(4)	(5)	(6)	(7)	(8)
Age 35 to 44	0.01	0.04	0.11**	-0.05	0.02	0.03	0.02	0.01
	(0.03)	(0.05)	(0.05)	(0.06)	(0.05)	(0.05)	(0.03)	(0.04)
Age 45 to 54	0.07**	0.08*	0.03	0.05	0.06	0.06	0.09***	0.06**
	(0.03)	(0.04)	(0.06)	(0.06)	(0.05)	(0.04)	(0.03)	(0.03)
Age 55 to 64	0.05	-0.04	0.39**	0.04	0.07	0.04	0.05	0.04
	(0.03)	(0.06)	(0.04)	(0.05)	(0.06)	(0.04)	(0.04)	(0.04)
Having child <18	-0.02	-0.01	-0.08**	-0.05	-0.03	-0.02	-0.03	-0.03
	(0.03)	(0.03)	(0.03)	(0.04)	(0.03)	(0.04)	(0.03)	(0.03)
Having child 18+	-0.01	-0.02	-0.05	0.02	-0.04	0.03	-0.02	-0.02
	(0.02)	(0.03)	(0.04)	(0.04)	(0.03)	(0.03)	(0.02)	(0.02)
Hispanic	-0.02	0.03	-0.01	-0.08	-0.02	-0.01	-0.02	-0.01
	(0.03)	(0.04)	(0.06)	(0.06)	(0.04)	(0.06)	(0.04)	(0.04)
White	0.03	0.00	0.37***	0.06	0.01	0.05	0.04	0.03
	(0.03)	(0.03)	(0.07)	(0.07)	(0.04)	(0.04)	(0.03)	(0.04)
Black	0.05	0.02	0.38***	0.06	0.08*	-0.06	0.05	0.01
	(0.04)	(0.04)	(0.10)	(0.08)	(0.05)	(0.05)	(0.04)	(0.04)
Working	-0.01	-0.07***	0.02	0.03	-0.04	0.02	-0.02	-0.00
	(0.03)	(0.03)	(0.04)	(0.04)	(0.03)	(0.03)	(0.02)	(0.03)
Constant	-0.44***	-0.37***	-0.95***	-0.52***	-0.28***	-0.61***	-0.45***	-0.44***
	(0.06)	(0.08)	(0.10)	(0.09)	(0.08)	(0.07)	(0.06)	(0.07)
N	509	204	130	175	243	266	457	410
R^2	0.800	0.707	0.484	0.730	0.792	0.821	0.816	0.827

Notes: Presented are OLS coefficient estimates of electoral attitudes favoring Mr. Obama index (standard errors in parentheses) adjusting for sampling weights.
Each column is a separate regression.
*** $p<0.01$, ** $p<0.05$, * $p<0.1$

TABLE 10.28 Study 8: Impact of Mr. Obama's Taking a Green Stance In Presence of Mr. Romney's Not-Green Stance

Predictor	All respondents (1)	Democrats (2)	Republicans (3)	Independents (4)	High personal importance (5)	Low personal importance (6)	Registered to vote (7)	Likely voters (8)
Obama green = 1 (Obama silence = 0)	-0.00 (0.02)	0.01 (0.03)	0.04 (0.03)	-0.08** (0.03)	0.02 (0.03)	-0.04* (0.02)	-0.00 (0.02)	-0.00 (0.02)
Obama presented first	0.02 (0.02)	-0.05* (0.02)	0.00 (0.03)	0.10*** (0.03)	0.03 (0.03)	0.02 (0.02)	-0.00 (0.02)	-0.01 (0.02)
Progress economy	0.14*** (0.05)	0.09 (0.07)	0.20** (0.09)	0.20*** (0.07)	0.15** (0.06)	0.14** (0.06)	0.16*** (0.05)	0.15*** (0.05)
Progress foreign rel.	0.03 (0.04)	0.08 (0.06)	0.04 (0.10)	-0.08 (0.08)	-0.06 (0.05)	0.18*** (0.07)	0.07 (0.05)	0.09* (0.05)
Progress pollution	-0.12** (0.05)	-0.16** (0.08)	0.00 (0.09)	-0.02 (0.07)	-0.07 (0.06)	-0.10* (0.06)	-0.11** (0.05)	-0.13** (0.05)
Approval of Obama	0.30*** (0.06)	0.31*** (0.10)	0.40** (0.16)	0.27*** (0.09)	0.23*** (0.07)	0.43*** (0.11)	0.40*** (0.06)	0.39*** (0.06)
Approval on economy	0.06 (0.05)	0.02 (0.06)	-0.23 (0.18)	0.17* (0.10)	0.09 (0.07)	0.04 (0.09)	0.03 (0.05)	0.02 (0.05)
Approval foreign rel.	0.22*** (0.06)	0.15* (0.09)	0.31*** (0.11)	0.24*** (0.08)	0.16* (0.09)	0.10 (0.07)	0.15*** (0.06)	0.17*** (0.06)
Approval environ.	0.06 (0.04)	0.04 (0.07)	0.21*** (0.08)	-0.04 (0.07)	-0.01 (0.06)	0.07 (0.06)	0.05 (0.04)	0.06 (0.04)
Approval asked first	-0.02 (0.02)	-0.00 (0.03)	-0.02 (0.04)	-0.05 (0.03)	-0.03 (0.03)	-0.01 (0.02)	-0.02 (0.02)	0.00 (0.02)
Democrat	0.05* (0.03)				0.07** (0.03)	0.01 (0.04)	0.05 (0.03)	0.07** (0.03)

	(1)	(2)	(3)	(4)	(5)	(6)	(7)	(8)
Republican	-0.15*** (0.03)				-0.26*** (0.07)	-0.12*** (0.03)	-0.12*** (0.04)	-0.09** (0.04)
Liberal	0.01 (0.03)	-0.01 (0.03)	0.15 (0.11)	0.04 (0.05)	-0.01 (0.03)	0.05 (0.05)	-0.01 (0.03)	-0.00 (0.03)
Conservative	-0.10*** (0.02)	-0.15*** (0.05)	-0.10*** (0.04)	-0.06 (0.04)	-0.07** (0.04)	-0.05* (0.03)	-0.09*** (0.03)	-0.10*** (0.03)
Female	0.05*** (0.02)	0.06** (0.03)	0.02 (0.04)	0.09*** (0.03)	0.08*** (0.03)	0.04* (0.02)	0.06*** (0.02)	0.05** (0.02)
Married	-0.00 (0.02)	-0.00 (0.03)	0.12*** (0.04)	-0.06 (0.04)	-0.01 (0.03)	-0.01 (0.03)	0.00 (0.02)	0.00 (0.02)
Some college	0.00 (0.03)	-0.03 (0.03)	0.02 (0.04)	0.05 (0.04)	-0.05 (0.03)	0.07** (0.03)	0.00 (0.03)	0.01 (0.03)
College graduate	-0.03 (0.02)	-0.04 (0.03)	0.02 (0.04)	-0.08* (0.05)	-0.03 (0.04)	0.02 (0.03)	-0.03 (0.03)	-0.01 (0.03)
Post college graduate	-0.05 (0.04)	-0.02 (0.05)	-0.04 (0.07)	-0.01 (0.06)	-0.06 (0.05)	0.01 (0.05)	-0.04 (0.04)	-0.01 (0.04)
Age 18 to 24	-0.01 (0.04)	0.01 (0.05)	-0.14 (0.09)	-0.08 (0.07)	-0.05 (0.05)	0.04 (0.05)	-0.04 (0.04)	-0.03 (0.05)
Age 25 to 34	-0.08* (0.04)	-0.02 (0.06)	-0.19*** (0.06)	-0.07 (0.07)	-0.11* (0.06)	-0.05 (0.05)	-0.09** (0.05)	-0.10** (0.05)
Age 35 to 44	-0.05 (0.03)	-0.05 (0.04)	-0.04 (0.05)	-0.02 (0.06)	-0.11** (0.05)	0.02 (0.04)	-0.06 (0.04)	-0.07* (0.04)
Age 45 to 54	0.02 (0.03)	0.08 (0.05)	0.02 (0.05)	-0.00 (0.07)	0.03 (0.04)	-0.02 (0.04)	0.01 (0.03)	0.02 (0.03)

continued…

Table 10.28 continued...

Predictor	All respondents (1)	Democrats (2)	Republicans (3)	Independents (4)	High personal importance (5)	Low personal importance (6)	Registered to vote (7)	Likely voters (8)
Age 55 to 64	-0.05 (0.03)	0.02 (0.05)	-0.06 (0.05)	-0.11* (0.06)	-0.04 (0.04)	-0.04 (0.04)	-0.05 (0.03)	-0.05 (0.03)
Having child <18	-0.03 (0.02)	-0.05 (0.04)	-0.02 (0.05)	-0.06 (0.04)	-0.03 (0.03)	-0.01 (0.03)	-0.04 (0.03)	-0.04 (0.03)
Having child 18+	-0.04* (0.02)	-0.09** (0.04)	-0.06 (0.04)	0.03 (0.04)	-0.08** (0.03)	0.03 (0.03)	-0.04* (0.02)	-0.04 (0.02)
Hispanic	0.05 (0.04)	-0.00 (0.04)	0.11** (0.05)	0.15** (0.08)	0.05 (0.05)	0.02 (0.04)	0.03 (0.05)	-0.01 (0.04)
White	-0.00 (0.03)	0.03 (0.05)	-0.01 (0.08)	-0.05 (0.05)	-0.02 (0.04)	0.03 (0.06)	0.02 (0.04)	0.03 (0.04)
Black	0.04 (0.04)	0.09* (0.05)	0.07 (0.16)	0.05 (0.07)	0.01 (0.04)	0.07 (0.08)	0.06 (0.04)	0.08* (0.04)
Working	-0.02 (0.02)	0.00 (0.03)	-0.03 (0.04)	0.00 (0.03)	-0.04 (0.03)	0.00 (0.03)	-0.01 (0.02)	-0.02 (0.02)
Constant	-0.30*** (0.07)	-0.16 (0.12)	-0.65*** (0.10)	-0.28** (0.12)	-0.07 (0.11)	-0.51*** (0.08)	-0.36*** (0.07)	-0.39*** (0.08)
N	500	190	128	182	241	259	437	396
R^2	0.795	0.557	0.703	0.748	0.708	0.841	0.812	0.830

Notes: Presented are OLS coefficient estimates of electoral attitudes favoring Mr. Obama index (standard errors in parentheses) adjusting for sampling weights. Each column is a separate regression. *** $p < 0.01$, ** $p < 0.05$, * $p < 0.1$

Table 10.28), not supporting Hypothesis 3c. As in the case of Hypothesis 1b that was not supported, the failure to support Hypothesis 3c was a result of the failure of the manipulation. If the manipulation had worked, respondents in the treatment condition (Condition 6: Obama Green & Romney Not-Green) would have had been more likely than respondents in the control condition (Condition 3: Romney Not-Green) to perceive Mr. Obama to take a green stance on the issue of global warming; however, perception of Mr. Obama's stance on global warming did not differ between the conditions ($m = .90$ and $m = .86$ for the treatment and control condition, respectively, $p = .15$), thus the treatment failed. To sum, Hypothesis 3c was not supported, possibly because of the failure of the manipulation.

Discussion

Methodology 1—Study 1

Study 1 used methodologies well-established in political science for exploring whether citizens might have used a policy issue as a basis for their candidate choice. As expected, greater relative proximity to Mr. Obama increased the likelihood of voting for him instead of for Mr. McCain in the 2008 presidential election. This held true in a wide range of analyses, using various different ways to represent issue proximity, and using various estimation techniques making different assumptions. Thus, the finding appears to be robust.

This study's limitations include reliance on only a single policy measure, controlling for a subset of the possible causes of vote choice, and assessing covariation among measures with no empirical handle to identify causal influence.

Methodology 1—Study 2

Study 2 employed methodologies well-established in political science for exploring whether citizens might have used a policy issue as a basis for candidate choice, and found evidence indicating that Americans used proximity to the candidates on global warming policy as a basis for choosing between the competitors in the 2012 U.S. Presidential election. The closer a person thought his or her desired change in the level of government action on global warming was closer to Mr. Obama's relative to Mr. Romney's, the more likely the person was to report an intent to vote for Mr. Obama. This held true in a wide range of analyses, using various different ways to represent issue proximity, using various estimation techniques making various different types of assumptions. Thus, the finding appears to be robust.

One methodological limitation of Study 2 involves the issue congruence measure employed: the proximity between the respondent's perception of the candidate's position and the respondent's own position on the same issue. Such issue proximity may be affected by two psychological processes: projection and persuasion (Krosnick, 2002). Persuasion occurs when a respondent shifts his or her own position toward his/her perception of a favored candidate's position on the same issue or away from the position of a disliked candidate. Projection occurs when the respondent shifts his/her perception of a favored candidate's position toward his/her own position on the same issue or shifts his/her perception of a disliked candidate's position away from his/her own.

Persuasion is most likely to occur among people who do not attach personal importance to an issue (see Boninger et al., 1995), so it is unlikely to explain the pattern of results we see here. Projection, if it occurs, may be more likely to occur among people who do attach importance to the issue and would therefore be troubled by agreeing with a disliked candidate or disagreeing with a liked candidate on that issue. However, the literature currently provides no convincing evidence that projection onto candidates actually occurs in the American context (see Krosnick, 2002). So although the relation documented in this study between global warming issue proximity and predicted vote are correlational and do not allow for unambiguous attribution to policy-based evaluation, these alternative explanations seem unlikely to be causing distortion of our conclusions. To estimate the effect of policy proximity on vote intent would require different types of data, such as panel data or experimental data. We look forward to seeing such research in the future.

Methodology 2—Study 3

Study 3 provided observational evidence suggesting that Congressional candidates' positions on global warming in 2010 might have influenced their electoral success. The results can be summarized as follows.

- The Democrat expressing a green position instead of being silent/mixed helped him/her win, regardless of whether his/her Republican was silent/mixed or not-green.
- When the Democrat expressed a green position, the Republican expressing a not-green position instead of being silent/mixed reduced his/her chances of victory.
- When the Democrat was silent/mixed, the Republican expressing a not-green position instead of being silent/mixed helped him/her win.

Put another way, when an opponent was silent/mixed, a candidate taking a position on global warming that was consistent with his/her political party's general tendency (a green position for Democrats, a not-green position for Republicans) won more often than if he/she was silent/mixed. However, in the face of a Democrat expressing a green position (in line with his/her party's general tendency), Republicans hurt their electoral chances by expressing a not-green position (in line with their party's general tendency) instead of being silent/mixed.

Simulations of possible election results if the candidates had taken different positions suggest that each party could have gained seats in 2010 if their candidates had taken different positions on global warming. But according to these simulations, control of the House most likely would not have flipped to the Democrats, even if the Democrats had all expressed strategically wise positions and the Republicans maintained the positions they expressed. Likewise, control of the Senate most likely would not have flipped to the Republicans if the Republicans had all expressed strategically wise positions while the Democrats maintained the positions they expressed.

These findings have simple implications for Democratic campaign strategies but tricky ones for Republicans. It appears that Democrats enhanced their chances of victory by taking a green position, regardless of what their Republican opponents said on the issue. But the optimal strategy for Republicans appears to have hinged on what their opponents said. If a Republican could be confident that his/her Democratic opponent would remain silent on global warming, then the Republican would have gained by expressing a not-green position. But once a Democrat expressed a green position, the Republican should not express a not-green position; being silent/mixed would have been better, and expressing a green position would have been even better than that.

We were not able to examine the impact on electoral victory of some strategies that candidates could have adopted, because too few people actually adopted them. Specifically, there were very few or no instances in which the Democrat expressed a not-green position, so we cannot offer speculations about the impact of them doing so.

Study 3 also has other limitations. First, our content analysis of campaign rhetoric was limited in some ways. For example, we ascertained candidates' positions on global warming via text on their websites. Some websites also included candidate expressions of their positions on issues via audio or video recordings, and we did not code these. Furthermore, candidates expressed positions on many issues during the course of their campaigns in ways that were not captured on their websites at all, such as in news interviews, at campaign rallies, in town hall meetings, and during debates. We assume here that the website analysis captures reasonably well what the candidates chose to articulate most often in these other settings, but we cannot know the plausibility of this assumption without further data collection and analysis.

It seems unlikely that a candidate expressed a green position on his/her website and expressed a not-green position regularly in other forums. And it seems unlikely that a candidate expressed a not-green position on his/her website and expressed a green position regularly in other forums. But it seems more possible that some candidates might have been silent about global warming on their websites but took green or not-green positions in other campaign settings. Thus, we may be overestimating the number of candidates who were silent. And if these candidates were to be re-coded in the analyses reported here, the results might change in ways we cannot anticipate.

Although we are inclined to look at the websites as indicators of what the candidates said throughout their campaigns, it is possible to view the websites differently: as the very medium of potential influence. When viewed in this way, the websites might be best analyzed taking into account the layout and accessibility of pieces of information there. For example, a candidate may have taken a green position on global warming on his/her website but done so on a page that citizens rarely saw when visiting the website due to the structure of links to it. Thus, although the information may have been publicly available, it may have been less influential in people's thinking than would have been the case if the information were easier to access. Our analysis did not take into account ease of accessing information on the candidates' websites, and doing so might have changed our findings.

A third limitation of Study 3 involves the coding of candidates' positions. We categorized each individual as being green, not-green, or silent/mixed. This approach ignores the fact that candidates differed in the intensity of their expressions on the issue. Some candidates were vociferous, whereas others were not. Perhaps we would have obtained different results if we had taken steps to take intensity of expression into account.

Fourth, because Study 3's results reported here are correlational, we cannot make strong statements about causal influence based on these results alone. That is, we cannot rule out spuriousness (e.g., candidates' decisions about what to say about global warming were influenced by factors that also independently influenced their electoral victories) or reverse causality (e.g., candidates' decisions about what to say about global warming were influenced by their apparent standing in pre-election polls). For example, a Democrat who thought she was leading in the polls might have chosen to express a green position on the grounds that doing so would be a safe way to increase enthusiasm among supporters. But that same candidate might have chosen to remain silent on global warming if she perceived herself to be at risk for losing the race and feared turning off potential supporters who were not-green.

Study 3's analyses did not take into account what the candidates said on issues other than global warming. Of course, the candidates said a great deal on a wide range of other policy matters during the campaign, and these statements may have been influential. If a candidate's expressed position on global warming was correlated with whether and what he/she said on other policy issues, then what might appear here to be an effect of global warming communications might instead be the result of statements on these other issues. Needless to say, a comprehensive analysis of all statements made by all candidates on all issues would be extremely challenging to implement for reasons of practicality. Nonetheless, future research might explore whether taking into account candidate utterances (or silence) on specific other, related policy issues might alter the findings reported above.

Another limitation of Study 3 is that the websites were downloaded just before the election and just after, but their content may have changed during the course of the primaries and the general election season. Therefore, we may not have fully captured what candidates said about global warming during this entire period.

Lastly, Study 3 was focused specifically on the 2010 Congressional elections, and there may be good reason to be cautious before generalizing these findings to other elections. Nonetheless, the results reported here are consistent with the conclusion that candidates may influence electoral outcomes via their statements or silence on global warming. Being strategically wise on this issue would require taking into account what both candidates say and could say, rather than simply examining one candidate's behavior at a time, ignoring the statements of his/her opponent.

Methodology 3—Study 4

Study 4 used methodologies well-established in political science for exploring whether citizens might have used a policy issue as a basis for their candidate choice as well as content analysis of political candidates' stances on the issue of global warming. Study 4 explored the extent to which the issue of climate change influenced voters' intent to vote. Consistent with the rational choice theory of voting, voters' greater relative proximity to the candidate increased the likelihood of their intent to vote for him/her instead of other candidates. This held true in a wide range of analyses, using various different ways to represent issue proximity, using various estimation techniques making various different types of assumptions. Thus, the finding appears to be robust.

Methodology 4—Study 5

Study 5 explored the extent various stances on global warming by hypothetical candidates would impact the likelihood of respondents' intent to vote for them. A hypothetical candidate's taking a green stance increased the likelihood that respondents would vote for the candidate, and taking a not-green or a non-committal stance reduced the likelihood that respondents would vote for the candidate. Consistent with the findings from Studies 1, 2, 3 and 4, that green stances gained votes and not-green or non-committal stances lost votes were apparent among respondents who believed global warming has been happening, who attached high personal importance to the issue of global warming, and who were Democrats and Independents.

Methodology 5—Studies 6, 7 and 8

Studies 6 and 7 yielded experimental evidence from representative national and regional samples of American adults suggesting Congressional candidates' positions on global warming influence Americans' voting behavior. Candidates who took a green position gained votes, and candidates who took a not-green position (or a non-committal position) lost votes. Confidence in these conclusions is justified by the fact that supportive results were obtained in five separate tests.

Like Studies 6 and 7, Study 8 produced experimental evidence that Mr. Romney, the Republican candidate in the 2012 presidential election, taking a green or a not-green position on global warming influenced Americans' voting behavior, supporting three of the four hypotheses generated from the results of Study 3. Mr. Romney's taking a green position on global warming compared to being silent on the issue yielded more votes for him and more favorable attitudes toward him, whether in absence or in presence of Mr. Obama, supporting the two hypotheses from the insights of Study 3. In presence of Mr. Obama, Mr. Romney's taking a not-green position on global warming compared to being silent on the issue led to no changes in votes for him and more favorable attitudes toward him, supporting another hypothesis from Study 3. However, in absence of Mr. Obama, Mr. Romney's taking a not-green position on global warming compared to being silent on the issue did vote gain votes for him and more favorable attitudes toward him, providing no evidence to another hypothesis from Study 3. The lack of support for this hypothesis might have resulted from that the fact that the experiment was conducted within 48 hours of the actual 2012 presidential election. Most people would have been familiar with Mr. Romney's stance on global warming, which was a not-green stance, thus diluting the experimental effect of exposing respondents to the video that Mr. Romney took a not-green stance on global warming.

These findings lend credibility to earlier surveys that used different methods to ascertain the attitudes and beliefs of Americans and to gauge the likely impact of these attitudes and beliefs on voting. Many studies suggest that the vast majority of people who attached great personal importance to global warming took green positions on the issue. This led us to expect exactly the effects shown in the present studies. Had these effects not been observed, we would have had reason to doubt the validity of past surveys' measurements. Therefore, the confirmation here of expected effects reinforces the portrait of public opinion that those past surveys paint.

These findings have interesting implications for candidates' campaign strategies. If we first assume that elections will be won and lost mostly by attracting the votes of Independent citizens whose votes cannot be predicted by party affiliations, our results suggest that candidates would do best to take green positions and hurt their electoral chances by taking not-green positions. Furthermore, the pattern of effects we observed among Democratic citizens suggests that candidates trying to capture a Democratic Party nomination or to inspire Democratic citizens to vote for them in general elections would be best off expressing a green position. Interestingly, Democratic candidates wishing to woo Republican voters during general elections apparently have nothing to gain or lose by the positions they take on global warming, leaving them free to take green positions in order to attract Independents.

According to our results, Republican candidates have even more to gain by taking green positions on climate. In addition to attracting Independent voters, Republican candidates who take green positions may have some success wooing Democratic citizens in general elections, especially if their Democratic opponents remain silent on global warming. Furthermore, taking a green position will apparently not hurt a Republican's standing with Republican voters, so this seems like a cost-free strategy. Consequently, Republican candidates are apparently free to take green positions even during primaries, perhaps thereby attracting early attention from Independent and Democratic citizens. Thus, according to our results, Republican candidates stand a good chance of gaining votes by taking green positions and should certainly not take not-green positions.

Studies 6, 7 and 8 have some limitations. First, because the analyses did not focus on the opinions of only likely voters, caution about generalizing the results on all citizens to voters in particular is merited. Furthermore, although we measured intentions to vote (rather than observing actual voting behavior), stated voting intentions are excellent predictors of actual voting behavior (e.g., Visser, Krosnick, Marquette, & Curtin, 1996). Another caution involves the fact that the hypothetical candidates took positions on just a few issues during a short period of time. Since real candidates take positions on many more issues, and because voters learn many other types of information about candidates, different influence might be observed in the course of a real election. Third, we tested one version of a green statement and one version of a not-green statement. The green statement was based partly on the opinions expressed by the American public about global warming in our past surveys, and partly on President Obama's statements about this issue. The not-green statement was based importantly on what Senator James Inhofe and other skeptical candidates said on their websites about global warming. These statements could have been written in other ways, and different results might be obtained with such alternative statements.

And in the simulated elections, only a single candidate was described, whereas contests normally involve competing candidates. Perhaps most importantly, we did not examine what would happen in voters' minds if a candidate took a green or not-green position and was then attacked by his or her opponent for doing so, which could certainly be studied in future experiments. It is conceivable that a candidate who takes a not-green position and is then attacked for doing so by his or her opponent would fare even worse with voters than a candidate who simply takes a not-green position that goes unchallenged. And perhaps a candidate who takes a green position would gain even more votes if his or her opponent attacked that position by taking a not-green position.

Conclusion

The data from all eight studies make a compelling case that Americans in 2008–2015 may have voted at least partly based on the candidates' positions on global warming. The evidence of moderation of such behavior by the personal importance that citizens attached to the issue is consistent with the issue publics theory of voting in contemporary American politics (see Krosnick, 1990).

Appendix A

Survey Methodologies and Measures in Table 10.1

Data Collection Methodologies of Surveys in Table 10.1

Data Collection Methodology of the 2008 Survey. The 2008 survey in Table 10.1 was a random digit dial landline telephone survey of a national probability sample of 1,000 U.S. adults ages 18 and older, conducted by TNS of Horsham, PA, between July 23 and July 28, 2008, commissioned by ABC News, Planet Green, and Stanford University. The sample was provided by Survey Sampling International, and interviews were conducted in both English and Spanish. The AAPOR Response Rate 3 was 29%.

Data Collection Methodology of the 2009 Survey. The 2009 survey in Table 10.1 was conducted by GfK Roper Public Affairs & Media, commissioned by Stanford University and the Associated Press. This telephone poll is based on a nationally representative probability sample of 1,005 adults age 18 or older. The interviews were conducted between November 17 and November 29, 2009, with 705 respondents on landlines and 300 on cellular telephones. Both the landline and cell phone samples were provided by Survey Sampling International. The survey sample included the contiguous 48 states, Alaska and Hawaii. Interviews were conducted in both English and Spanish. The AAPOR Response Rate 3 was 12%.

Data Collection Methodology of the 2010 Survey. The 2010 survey in Table 10.1 is a random digit dial telephone survey of a national probability sample of U.S. adults aged 18 and older conducted by Abt SRBI, November 1 and November 14, 2010. 671 respondents were interviewed on a landline phone and 330 were interviewed on a cell phone. Interviews were administrated in English and Spanish. Samples were drawn from both landline and cellular random digit dial frames to represent people with access to either a landline or cell phone. The landline and cell phone samples were provided by Survey Sampling International, LLC. The AAPOR Response Rate 3 was 17%.

Data Collection Methodology of the 2011 Survey. The 2011 survey in Table 10.1 is a random digit dial telephone survey of a national probability sample of U.S. adults aged 18 and older, which was conducted by Ipsos Public Affairs of Washington, DC, between September 8 and September 12, 2011. 890 respondents were interviewed on a landline phone and 244 were interviewed on a cell phone. Interviews were administrated in English and Spanish. The AAPOR Response Rate 3 was 8%.

Data Collection Methodology of the 2012 Survey. The 2012 survey in Table 10.1 is a random digit dial telephone survey of a national probability sample of U.S. adults aged 18 and older, which was conducted by Abt SRBI between June 13 and June 21, 2012. 603 respondents were interviewed on a landline phone, and 201 were interviewed on a cellular phone. Interviews were administrated in English only. The AAPOR Response Rate 3 for the survey was 15%.

Data Collection Methodology of the 2013 Survey. The 2013 survey in Table 10.1 is a random digit dial telephone survey of a national probability sample of U.S. adults aged 18 and older, which was conducted by Abt SRBI between November 20 and December 5, 2013. 521 respondents were interviewed on a landline telephone, and 280 were interviewed on a cell phone. Interviews were administrated in English only. The AAPOR Response Rate 3 was 13%.

Data Collection Methodology of the 2015 Survey. The 2015 survey in Table 10.1 is a random digit dial telephone survey of a national probability sample of U.S. adults aged 18 and older, which was conducted by SSRS between January 7 and January 22, 2015. 483 respondents were interviewed on a landline telephone, and 523 were interviewed on a cell phone. Interviews were administrated in English and Spanish. The AAPOR Response Rate 3 was 12%.

TABLE 10.A1   Global Warming Measures in Table 10.1

Measure	Survey question	Coding of the measure
Existence of global warming	You may have heard about the idea that the world's temperature may have been going up slowly over the past 100 years. What is your personal opinion on this—do you think this has probably been happening, or do you think it probably has not been happening?	1 if "Probably has been happening"; 0 if "Probably has not been happening", or Don't Know or Refused
Human causal influence on warming	[Added "Assuming it's happening" among those who were coded 0 in "The planet has probably been warming",] Do you think a rise in the world's temperature (is being/ would be) caused mostly by things people do, mostly by natural causes, or about equally by things people do and by natural causes?	1 if "Things people do" or "Both equally"; 0 if "Natural causes", or Don't Know or Refused
If nothing is done to stop it, global warming will be at least a moderately serious problem for the nation	2009–2015: If nothing is done to reduce global warming in the future, how serious of a problem do you think it will be for THE UNITED STATES—very serious, somewhat serious, not so serious or not serious at all?	1 if "Very serious" or "Somewhat serious"; 0 if "Not so serious", or "Not serious at all", or Don't Know or Refused
The federal government should do more than it is doing now to address global warming	2008: Do you think the federal government should do more than it's doing now to try to deal with global warming, should do less than it's doing now, or is it doing about the right amount? 2009 and 2010: A) How much do you think the U.S. government should do about global warming? A great deal, quite a bit, some, a little, or nothing? B) How much do you think the U.S. government is doing now to deal with global warming? A great deal, quite a bit, some, a little, or nothing?	1 if "Should do more" in 2008; 1 if the response in A) is greater than the response in B) in 2009 and 2010. 0 if "Should do less", or "Doing about the right amount", or Don't Know or Refused in 2008; 0 if the response in A) is equal to or less than the response in B) in 2009 and 2010, or "Don't Know" or Refuse in either 2009 and/or 2010.

Measure	Survey question	Coding of the measure
Members of global warming issue public	How important is the issue of global warming to you personally—extremely important, very important, somewhat important, not too important, or not at all important?	1 if "Extremely important"; 0 if "Very important", or "Somewhat important", or "Not too important", or "Not at all important", or Don't Know or Refused
Party identification	Do you consider yourself a Democrat, a Republican, an Independent, or none of these?	Respondents who said "Democrat" were coded as Democrats; respondents who said "Republicans" were coded as Republicans; respondents who said "Independent", "None of these", or Don't Know, or declined to answer were coded as "Independents".

Appendix B

Methodology of Study 2

Dependent Variable Measure: Turnout and Candidate Choice

Turnout and Candidate Choice. In the November 2008 wave of the FFRISP, all respondents were asked: "In the election held on November 4, Barack Obama ran on the Democratic ticket and John McCain ran on the Republican ticket. During the months leading up to the election for President, did you ever plan to vote in that election, or didn't you plan to do that?" and then asked: "Which one of the following best describes what you did in this election? Definitely did not vote; definitely voted in person at a polling place on Election Day; definitely voted in person at a polling place before Election Day; definitely voted by mailing a ballot to elections officials before election day; definitely voted in some other way; not completely sure whether you voted or not."

Respondents who said "definitely did not vote" and respondents who said "not completely sure whether you voted or not" and answered "probably did not vote" to the follow-up with the question "If you had to guess, would you say that you probably did vote in the election, or probably did not vote in the election?" were coded as not voting.

Respondents who said any of the "definitely voted" options and respondents who said "not completely sure whether you voted or not" and said "probably voted" to the follow-up with the question "If you had to guess, would you say that you probably did vote in the election, or probably did not vote in the election?"

were coded as voters. These respondents were asked in which state they voted, and then asked of their candidate choice through the following question "For whom did you vote for President and Vice President of the United States?" A complete list of candidates that was specific to the state in which they voted was displayed, including "BARACK OBAMA for President and JOE BIDEN for Vice President, Democrat," "JOHN MCCAIN for President and SARAH PALIN for Vice President, Republican," and other candidates who were listed on the ballot (e.g. "CHUCK BALDWIN for President and DARRELL L. CASTLE for Vice President, Independent"). Respondents who chose "BARACK OBAMA for President and JOE BIDEN for Vice President, Democrat" were coded as "voting for Obama," Respondents who chose "JOHN MCCAIN for President and SARAH PALIN for Vice President, Republican" were coded as "voting for McCain," and the respondents who chose others were coded as "voting for a nonmajor party candidate."

Issue Proximity

Self and Candidate Placements on Global Warming

In the November 2008 wave of the FFRISP, respondents were asked two global warming policy questions. First, they were asked: "Next, we'd like to ask whether Barack Obama favors, opposes, or neither favors nor opposes a series of ways that the federal government might try to reduce future global warming. Power plants put gases into the air that could cause global warming. Does Barack Obama favor, oppose, or neither favor nor oppose the federal government lowering the amount of these gases that power plants are allowed to put into the air?" Respondents who answered with "Favor" or "Oppose" were asked of a follow-up question "Does Barack Obama favor that a great deal, moderately, or a little?" or "Does Barack Obama oppose that a great deal, moderately, or a little?" (Favor a great deal = 3, Favor moderately = 2, Favor a little = 1, Neither favor nor oppose = 0, Oppose a little = –1, Oppose moderately = –2, Oppose a great deal = –3). Similar questions were asked about Mr. McCain.

A randomly selected half of the respondents were asked in October 2008 and the other were asked in February 2009 the identically worded questions (except that the questions were asked of their own placement): "Next, we'd like to ask whether you favor, oppose, or neither favor nor oppose a series of ways that the federal government might try to reduce future global warming. Power plants put gases into the air that could cause global warming. Do you favor, oppose, or neither favor nor oppose the federal government lowering the amount of these gases that power plants are allowed to put into the air?" The follow-up intensity questions were identically worded, and the coding of issue placement of global warming of the respondent himself/herself was done in the identical way.

The respondents were then asked, "Do you favor, oppose, or neither favor nor oppose the federal government requiring automakers to build cars that use less gasoline?", and then respondents were asked to report their perceptions of the candidates' positions on this issue as well. Coding was done as for the first question.

Ideological Proximity

Self and Candidate Placements of Liberal/Conservative Ideology

In the October 2008 wave of the FFRISP, all respondents were asked: "When it comes to politics, would you describe Barack Obama as liberal, conservative, or neither liberal nor conservative?" Respondents who chose "Liberal" or "Conservative" were then asked "Would you call Barack Obama very liberal or somewhat liberal?" or "Would you call Barack Obama very conservative or somewhat conservative?" Respondents who chose "Neither liberal nor conservative" were then asked "Do you think of Barack Obama as closer to liberals, or conservatives, or neither of these?" (Very liberal = 3, Somewhat liberal = 2, Closer to liberals = 1, Closer to neither liberals nor conservatives = 0, Closer to conservatives = −1, Somewhat conservative = −2, Very conservative = −3). Similar questions were asked about Mr. McCain.

Respondents were asked identically worded questions (except that the questions were asked of their own placement) in October 2008: "When it comes to politics, would you describe yourself as liberal, conservative or neither liberal nor conservative?" The follow-up intensity questions were identically worded, and the coding of political ideology placement of the respondent himself/herself was done in the identical way.

Party Identification and Other Political Variables

Party Identification

In the October 2008 wave of FFRISP survey, respondents were asked: "Do you consider yourself a Democrat, Republican, an Independent, or what?" A Democrat dummy variable was coded 1 for Democrats and 0 for all others. A Republican dummy variable was coded 1 for Republicans and 0 for all others.

Attitudes Toward Big Government

In the November 2008 wave of the FFRISP, respondents were asked three questions on size of government. First, they were asked: "Do you think the government should provide more services than it does now, fewer services than it does now, or about the same number of services as it does now?" Respondents who chose

"More" or "Fewer" were then asked: "Do you think that the government should provide a lot more services, somewhat more services, or slightly more services than it does now?" or "Do you think that the government should provide a lot fewer services, somewhat fewer services, or slightly fewer services than it does now?" (Coding: A lot fewer services = 0.00, Somewhat fewer services = .17, Slightly fewer services = .33, About the same = .50, Slightly more services = .67, Somewhat more services = .76, A lot more services =1.00)

Second, respondents were asked: "Do you think the U.S. federal government should have more effect on Americans' lives than it does now, less effect, or about the same amount of effect than it has now on Americans' lives?" Respondents who chose "More effect" or "Less effect" were then asked "A lot more, a moderate amount more, or a little more?" or "A lot less, a moderate amount less, or a little less?" (Coding: A lot less = 0.00, A moderate amount less = .17, A little less = .33, About the same = .50, A little more = .67, A moderate amount more = .76, A lot more =1.00)

Third, respondents were asked: "Do you think the U.S. federal government should do more to influence how businesses operate in this country, should the federal government do less to influence businesses, or should the government do about what it's doing now to influence businesses?" Respondents who chose "More" or "Less" were then asked "A lot more, a moderate amount more, or a little more?" or "A lot less, a moderate amount less, or a little less?" (Coding: A lot less = 0.00, A moderate amount less = .17, A little less = .33, About what it's doing now = .50, A little more = .67, A moderate amount more = .76, A lot more =1.00)

An index was computed by averaging the above three measures, ranging from 0 (favoring smaller government) to 1 (favoring big government).

Bush Job Approval

In the November 2008 wave of the FFRISP, respondents were asked: "Overall, do you approve, disapprove, or neither approve nor disapprove about the way George W. Bush is handling his job as President?" Respondents who chose "Approve" or "Disapprove" were then asked "Do you approve extremely strongly, moderately strongly, or slightly strongly?" or "Do you disapprove extremely strongly, moderately strongly, or slightly strongly?" (Coding: Strongly disapprove = 0.00, Somewhat disapprove = .17, Slightly disapprove = .33, neither approve nor disapprove = .50, Slightly approve = .67, Somewhat approve = .76, Strongly approve =1.00)

Perception of the Economy

In the October 2008 wave of FFRISP survey, respondents were asked: "Now thinking about the economy in the country as a whole, would you say that as compared to one year ago, the nation's economy is now better, about the same, or worse?" and then followed up with "Much better or somewhat better?" among respondents who chose "Better" and "Much worse or somewhat worse" among respondents who chose "Worse." (Coding: Much worse = 0.00, Somewhat worse = .25, About the same = .50, Somewhat better = .75, Much better = 1.00)

Interest in Politics

In the November 2008 wave of the FFRISP, respondents were asked: "How interested are you in information about what's going on in government and politics?" (Coding: Not interested at all = 0, Slightly interested = .25, Moderately interested = .50, Very interested = .75, Extremely interested = 1.00)

Personal Importance

In the April 2009 wave of the FFRISP, respondents were asked: "How important is the issue of global warming to you personally—not at all important, not too important, somewhat important, very important, or extremely important?" A dummy variable was coded 1 for respondents who said "Very important" or "Extremely important" and 0 for all other respondents.

A randomly selected half of the FFRISP respondents were asked the following question in October 2008, and the other half were asked in February 2009: "You may have heard about the idea that the world's temperature may have been going up slowly over the past 100 years. What is your personal opinion on this? Do you think this has probably been happening, or do you think it probably hasn't been happening?" Respondents who chose "Has probably been happening" were asked "Do you think a rise in the world's temperatures is being caused mostly by things people do, mostly by natural causes, or about equally by things people do and by natural causes?" A dummy variable was coded 1 for respondents who said "Things people do" or "About equally by things people do and by natural causes" and 0 for all others.

Demographics

Respondents in the FFRISP were asked the following demographic questions in September 2008.

Female. Respondents were asked: "Please enter whether you are male or female." A Female dummy variable was coded 1 for females and 0 for males.

Age. Respondents were asked: "Please enter your age." Age was measured in years.

Hispanic Ethnicity. Respondents were asked: "Are you of Spanish, Hispanic, or Latino descent?" A Hispanic dummy variable was coded 1 for those reporting Hispanic ethnicity and 0 for others.

Race. Respondents were asked to "check one or more categories" from a list in order to indicate what race(s) they considered themselves to be. A Black dummy variable was coded 1 for respondents who selected "Black or African–American" and 0 for all others.

Education. Respondents were asked: "What is the highest degree or level of school that you have completed?" (Coding: No schooling completed $= 0$, Nursery school to 4th grade $= .07$, 5th or 6th grade $= .14$, 7th or 8th grade $= .23$, 9th grade $= .30$, 11th grade $= .38$, 12th grade no diploma $= .46$, High school graduate $= .54$, High school diploma or the equivalent (GED) $= .62$, Some college, no degree $= .69$, Associate degree $= .77$, Bachelor's degree $= .85$, Master's degree $= .92$, Professional or Doctorate degree $= 1$)

Income. Respondents were asked: "The next question is about the total income of your household for the past 12 months. Please include your income plus the income of all members living in your household (including cohabiting partners and armed forces members living at home). Please count income before taxes, including income from all sources (such as wages, salaries, tips, net income from a business, interest, dividends, child support, alimony, and Social Security, public assistance, pensions, or retirement benefits). Was your total household income in the past 12 months?" (Coding: Less than $20,000 $= 0$, $20,000 to $34,999 $= .2$, $35,000 to $49,999 $= .40$, $50,000 to $74,999 $= .6$, $75,000 to $99,999 $= .8$, $100,000 or more $= 1$)

Region. Three dummy variables identified respondents in the Midwest, South, and West Census regions. Respondents living in the Northeast region constituted the omitted category.

Appendix C

Methodology of Study 3

Content Analysis: Instructions to Coders

You will answer 12 questions listed below for each candidate. Please answer each question based on the text in the spreadsheet for the candidate. Type your answer to each question in the column with the question's number at the top. Type "y" to answer a question yes, and type "n" to answer a question no. Type "a" for ambiguous if you are uncertain about whether to answer a question yes or no. You are to follow these general notes during the coding.

1   It is important that your coding be accurate, objective, and consistent. Please read and code at the pace that allows you to code accurately.
2   Please do NOT discuss the coding task AT ALL with anyone else besides the investigators of the study, especially the other coders. You must make your decisions completely independently—you must not influence or be influenced by others.
3   Please do NOT use information that you have learned about the candidates from other sources. Please rely only on what the candidate's website said and nothing else when making coding decisions.

12 Coding Questions

Please copy and paste the quote or quotes that form the basis for your answer "y" or "a" to EACH question about a candidate into the appropriate cell on that candidate's row. 12 Coding Questions are the following.

Q1. GW/CC has been happening.
 Type "y" if the candidate said something like:
1a   Global warming or climate change has been happening or will happen.
 OR
1b   There is scientific evidence indicating that GW/CC has been happening or will happen.

and paste all the quotes (in sentences, or parts of sentences) that are the basis for your code "y".
Type "n" if the candidate did not say anything like (1a) or (1b).
Type "a" if you are not sure and paste all the quotes that are the basis for your code "a".

Q2. GW/CC has not been happening.
 Type "y" if the candidate said something like:
1c   Global warming or climate change has not been happening or will not happen.
 OR
1d   The candidate is not sure whether global warming or climate change has been happening or will happen.
 OR
1e   There is no, or little, or insufficient amount of scientific evidence indicating that GW/CC has been happening or will happen.
 OR
1f   The candidate is not sure whether there is (sufficient) scientific evidence that GW/CC has been happening or will happen.

and paste all the quotes (in sentences, or parts of sentences) that are the basis for your code "y".

Type "n" if the candidate did not say anything like (1c), (1d), (1e), or (1f).

Type "a" if you are not sure and paste all the quotes that are the basis for your code "a".

Q3. GW/CC is man-made.

   Type "y" if the candidate said something like:

2a Human actions, such as burning fossil fuels, are a cause of GW/CC.

and paste all the quotes (in sentences, or parts of sentences) that are the basis for your code "y".

Type "n" if the candidate did not say anything like (2a).

Type "a" if you are not sure and paste all the quotes that are the basis for your code "a".

Q4. GW/CC is not man-made.

   Type "y" if the candidate said something like:

2d Human actions are not a cause of GW/CC.

   OR

2e The candidate is not sure whether human actions cause GW/CC.

and paste all the quotes (in sentences, or parts of sentences) that are the basis for your code "y".

Type "n" if the candidate did not say anything like (2d) or (2e).

Type "a" if you are not sure and paste all the quotes that are the basis for your code "a".

Q5. GW/CC is bad.

   Type "y" if the candidate said something like:

3a Global warming or climate change will have one or more undesirable consequences.

   OR

3b GW/CC is a serious problem.

   OR

3c GW/CC is an important issue.

and paste all the quotes (in sentences, or parts of sentences) that are the basis for your code "y".

Type "n" if the candidate did not say anything like (3a), (3b) or (3c).

Type "a" if you are not sure and paste all the quotes that are the basis for your code "a".

Q6. GW/CC is not bad.

    Type "y" if the candidate said something like:

3d Global warming or climate change will not have undesirable consequences.

    OR

3e The candidate is not sure whether GW/CC will have any undesirable consequences.

    OR

3f GW/CC is NOT a serious problem.

    OR

3g The candidate is not sure whether GW/CC is a (serious) problem.

    OR

3h GW/CC is NOT an important issue.

    OR

3i The candidate is not sure whether GW/CC is an important issue.

and paste all the quotes (in sentences, or parts of sentences) that are the basis for your code "y".

Type "n" if the candidate did not say anything like (3d), (3e), (3f), (3g), (3h), or (3i).

Type "a" if you are not sure and paste all the quotes that are the basis for your code "a".

Q7. Producing energy using "green" methods is good.

    Type "y" if the candidate said something like:

4a Passing laws that would encourage producing more energy from "clean" sources, such as wind, solar power, water, or nuclear power plants, would be a good idea.

and paste all the quotes (in sentences, or parts of sentences) that are the basis for your code "y".

Type "n" if the candidate did not say anything like (4a).

Type "a" if you are not sure and paste all the quotes that are the basis for your code "a".

Q8. Producing energy using "green" methods is not good.

    Type "y" if the candidate said something like:

4b Passing laws that would encourage producing more energy from "clean" sources, such as wind, solar power, water, or nuclear power plants, would NOT be a good idea.

    OR

4c The candidate is not sure whether passing laws that would encourage producing more energy from "clean" sources, such as wind, solar power, water, or nuclear power plants, would be a good idea.

and paste all the quotes (in sentences, or parts of sentences) that are the basis for your code "y".

Type "n" if the candidate did not say anything like (4b) or (4c).

Type "a" if you are not sure and paste all the quotes that are the basis for your code "a".

Q9. Actions about global warming should be taken.

   Type "y" if the candidate said something like:

5a   Actions should be taken to reduce global warming or the effects of global warming.

   OR

5b   We should limit the amount of greenhouse gasses (carbon dioxide, CO_2) in the future.

and paste all the quotes (in sentences, or parts of sentences) that are the basis for your code "y".

Type "n" if the candidate did not say anything like (5a) or (5b).

Type "a" if you are not sure and paste all the quotes that are the basis for your code "a".

Q10. NO actions about global warming should be taken.

   Type "y" if the candidate said something like:

5c   No actions should be taken about global warming or climate change.

   OR

5d   No actions should be taken to limit the amount of greenhouse gasses in the future.

   OR

5e   The candidate is not sure whether we should take actions about GW/CC.

   OR

5f   The candidate is not sure whether we should limit carbon emissions.

and paste all the quotes (in sentences, or parts of sentences) that are the basis for your code "y".

Type "n" if the candidate did not say anything like (5c), (5d), (5e), or (5f).

Type "a" if you are not sure and paste all the quotes that are the basis for your code "a".

Q11. The candidate supported cap-and-trade.

   Type "y" if the candidate said something like:

6a   The candidate supports cap-and-trade.

and paste all the quotes (in sentences, or parts of sentences) that are the basis for your code "y".

Type "n" if the candidate did not say anything like (6a).

Type "a" if you are not sure and paste all the quotes that are the basis for your code "a".

Q12. The candidate opposed cap-and-trade.

Type "y" if the candidate said something like:

6b   The candidate opposes cap-and-trade.

OR

6c   The candidate is not sure wheter cap-and-trade is a good idea.

and paste all the quotes (in sentences, or parts of sentences) that are the basis for your code "y".

Type "n" if the candidate did not say anything like (6b) or (6c).

Type "a" if you are not sure and paste all the quotes that are the basis for your code "a".

Appendix D

Methodology of Study 4—Ipsos

Question Wording, Response Options, and Coding

Candidate Preferences as the Dependent Variable Measures

All respondents were asked: "If the 2012 presidential election were being held today and the candidates were Barack Obama, the Democrat, and [INSERT CANDIDATE BELOW AND ROTATE LIST: Mitt Romney, Jon Huntsman, Michele Bachmann, Ron Paul, Rick Perry], the Republican, for whom would you vote?"

Frequency of voting for Barack Obama. The first dependent measure was the frequency of voting for Barack Obama, which is the number of times the respondent stated that he/she would vote for Barack Obama in the above five questions, in each of which an indicator was constructed such that voting for Mr. Obama was coded 1 and 0 for all other answers. The sum of the five indicators was the dependent variable measure, an integer ranging from 0 to 5.

Candidate choice. The second dependent measure was an indicator in each of the above five question with a value of 1 indicating the respondent said he/she would vote for the candidate presented in the voting choice occasion and 0 otherwise. Six named candidates (Barack Obama, Mitt Romney, Ron Paul, Rick Perry, Jon Huntsman, and Michele Bachmann) plus a composite fictional "candidate" that indicated the respondent would vote for some other unnamed candidate or gave a "don't know" answer or refusal to answer the question were measured in a numerical variable ranging from a value of 1 to 7.

Global Warming Belief and Belief Proximity as the Independent Measures

Believing in global warming existence/human cause. All respondents were first asked: "You may have heard about the idea that the world's temperature may have been going up slowly over the past 100 years. What is your personal opinion on this? Do you think this has probably been happening, or do you think it probably has not been happening?" Respondents who chose "Probably has been happening" were then asked "Do you think a rise in the world's temperatures is being caused mostly by things people do, mostly by natural causes, or about equally by things people do and by natural causes?" Respondents who chose "Probably has not been happening" or did not give an answer were asked "Assuming it's happening, do you think a rise in the world's temperatures is being caused mostly by things people do, mostly by natural causes, or about equally by things people do and by natural causes?" A dummy variable of Believing in Global Warming Existence/Human Cause was set to 1 for the respondents who chose "Probably has been happening" to the first question and chose "Things people do" or "About equally by things people do and by natural causes" to the second question and 0 for the rest.

Certainty of Global Warming Belief as Moderator Measure

Certainty of global warming belief. Respondents who answered with "Probably has been happening" to the existence of global warming were asked "How sure are you that the world's temperature has been going up—extremely sure, very sure, somewhat sure, or not sure at all?" Respondents who answered with "Probably has not been happening" to the existence of global warming were asked "How sure are you that the world's temperature has not been going up—extremely sure, very sure, somewhat sure, or not sure at all?" A High certainty dummy variable was coded to 1 if the respondents chose "Extremely sure" and 0 otherwise.

Party Identification and Other Political Variables Measures

Party identification

All respondents were asked: "Do you consider yourself a Democrat, Republican, an Independent, or none of these?" A Democrat dummy variable was coded 1 for Democrats and 0 for all others. A Republican dummy variable was coded 1 for Republicans and 0 for all others.

Approval of President Obama

All respondents were asked: "Overall, do you approve, disapprove, or have mixed feelings about the way Barack Obama is handling his job as President?" Respondents who chose "Approve" or "Disapprove" were then asked "Do you approve (disapprove) extremely strongly, moderately strongly, or slightly strongly?" (Coding: Strongly disapprove = 0.00, Somewhat disapprove = .17, Slightly disapprove = .33, neither approve nor disapprove = .50, Slightly approve = .67, Somewhat approve = .7583, Strongly approve =1.00)

Country in the right direction

All respondents were asked: "Generally speaking, would you say things in this country are heading in the right direction, or are they off on the wrong track?" A dummy variable Country in the right direction was coded 1 if the respondent chose "Right direction" and 0 otherwise.

Demographic Variables

Male. Interviewers recorded the gender of the respondent. A Male dummy variable was coded 1 for male respondents and 0 for female respondents.

Age. Respondents were asked: "In what year were you born?" Respondents who gave a valid range of answer between 1900 and 1993 to the birth year question were then asked "Have you already had a birthday this year?" Respondents who refused to answer the birth year question were asked "Are you ..." and asked to choose a 10-year age range such as "Under 25," "25–34," "35–44," "45–54," "55–64," "65–74," and "75 or older." Dummy variables were created for each of these age groups. Age group Under 25 was the omitted base category.

Hispanic Ethnicity. Respondents were asked: "Are you of Hispanic ethnicity?" A Hispanic dummy variable was coded 1 for those reporting Hispanic ethnicity and 0 for others.

Race. Respondents were asked: "Are you White, Black, or Asian?" A White dummy variable was coded for 1 for individuals who answered with "White" and 0 for others.

Education. Respondents were asked: "What is the last year of school you completed? Grade school or some high school, Completed high school, Some college but did not finish, Completed a two year college degree, Completed a four year college degree, Completed a post-graduate degree such as Master's or PhD?" A Less Than High School dummy variable was coded 1 if the respondent chose "Grade school or some high school" and 0 otherwise. A High School Graduate dummy variable was coded 1 if the respondent chose "Completed high school" and 0 otherwise. A Some College dummy variable was coded 1 if the respondent chose "Some college but did not finish" or "Completed a two year college degree" and 0 otherwise. A College Degree dummy variable was coded 1 if the respondent chose "Completed a four year college degree" or "Completed a post-graduate degree such as Master's or PhD" and 0 otherwise. Less Than High School was the omitted base category.

Income. All respondents were asked "Now, I am going to read a list of income ranges. When I get to the income range that best describes your household income from all sources in 2010, please stop me. Was your household income for 2010…?" A series of dummy variables were constructed for income under $15K, $15K–$25K, $25K–$40K, $40K–$50K, $50K–$75K, $75K–$100K, and $100K or higher. A dummy variable Income-DKRF was coded 1 if the respondent did not give an answer and 0 otherwise. Income Under $15K was the omitted base category.

Region. Was coded using a set of dummy variables representing three different census regions in the United States: Midwest, South, and West. Respondents living in the Northeast region constituted the omitted base category.

Content Analysis: Instructions to Coders

Coding Questions

You will answer 12 questions listed below for each candidate. Type your answer to each question in the column with the question's number at the top. For Q1–Q12, type "y" to answer a question yes, and type "n" to answer a question no. You are to follow:

1   It is important that your coding be accurate, objective, and consistent. Please read and code at the pace that allows you to code accurately.
2   Please do NOT discuss the coding task with anyone else besides the investigators of the study. You must make your decisions completely independently—you must not influence or be influenced by others.
3   Please do NOT use information that you have learned about the candidates from other sources. Please rely only on what you read about the candidate on this task and nothing else when making your coding decisions.

Important coding notes

1   You copy and paste the quote(s) and the webpage(s) address that contains(s) the quote(s) that form the basis for your answer "y" to EACH question

about a candidate into the appropriate cell on that candidate's row. E.g. your quote(s)/webpage(s) for Q1 should be entered in the column named "Q1—quotes/websites."

2   You use ANYONE's statements/quotes about the candidate, including the candidate himself/herself, to make the coding questions. That "ANYONE" includes the writers of the articles, an unnamed but identifiable identity (person(s) or organizations), such as:

"the public" or

"well-educated young Americans" or

"campaign advisers to or spokesmen of the candidate," or

"League of Conservation Voters."

A quote such as Obama says climate change is a threat to the world would allow you to code "yes" to "Q5 GW/CC is bad," but it does not allow you to code "Q6 GW/CC is not bad," because saying "GW/CC is bad" does not indicate saying "GW/CC is not bad."

In all coding questions, a coding decision of "yes" requires you to find (at least) one quote to support your decision however, a coding decision of "no" requires you to read all the articles you are asked to read for the candidate and find no evidence.

12 Coding Questions

Q1. GW/CC has been happening.

Type "y" if the candidate said or someone/organization said the candidate believed in something like:

1a   Global warming or climate change has been happening or will happen.
OR

1b   There is scientific evidence indicating that GW/CC has been happening or will happen.

and paste the quotes (in sentences, or parts of sentences), in column "Q1x quotes/websites," that are the basis for your code "y".

Type "n" if nobody said anything like (1a) or (1b) about the candidate's beliefs and attitudes.

Q2. GW/CC has not been happening.

Type "y" if the candidate said or someone/organization said the candidate believed in something like:

1c   Global warming or climate change has not been happening or will not happen.
OR

1d The candidate is not sure whether global warming or climate change has been happening or will happen.
OR

1e There is no, or little, or insufficient amount of scientific evidence indicating that GW/CC has been happening or will happen.
OR

1f The candidate is not sure whether there is (sufficient) scientific evidence that GW/CC has been happening or will happen.

and paste the quotes, in column "Q2x quotes/websites," that are the basis for your code "y".

Type "n" if nobody said anything like (1c), (1d), (1e), or (1f) about the candidate's beliefs and attitudes.

Q3. GW/CC is man-made.
Type "y" if the candidate said or someone/organization said the candidate believed in something like:

2a Human actions, such as burning fossil fuels, are a cause of GW/CC.

and paste the quotes, in column "Q3x quotes/websites," that are the basis for your code "y".

Type "n" if nobody said anything like (2a) about the candidate's beliefs and attitudes.

Q4. GW/CC is not man-made.
Type "y" if the candidate said or someone/organization said the candidate believed in something like:

2d Human actions are not a cause of GW/CC.
OR

2e The candidate is not sure whether human actions cause GW/CC.

and paste the quotes, in column "Q4x quotes/websites," that are the basis for your code "y".

Type "n" if nobody said anything like (2d) or (2e) about the candidate's beliefs and attitudes.

Q5. GW/CC is bad.
Type "y" if the candidate said or someone/organization said the candidate believed in something like:

3a Global warming or climate change will have one or more undesirable consequences.
OR

3b GW/CC is a serious problem.

OR

3c GW/CC is an important issue.

and paste the quotes, in column "Q5x quotes/websites," that are the basis for your code "y".

Type "n" if nobody said anything like (3a), (3b) or (3c) about the candidate's beliefs and attitudes.

Q6. GW/CC is not bad.

Type "y" if the candidate said or someone/organization said the candidate believed in something like:

3d Global warming or climate change will not have undesirable consequences.
OR

3e The candidate is not sure whether GW/CC will have any undesirable consequences.
OR

3f GW/CC is NOT a serious problem.
OR

3g The candidate is not sure whether GW/CC is a (serious) problem.
OR

3h GW/CC is NOT an important issue.
OR

3i The candidate is not sure whether GW/CC is an important issue.

and paste the quotes, in column "Q6x quotes/websites," that are the basis for your code "y".

Type "n" if nobody said anything like (3d), (3e), (3f), (3g), (3h), or (3i) about the candidate's beliefs and attitudes.

Q7. Producing energy using "green" methods is good.

Type "y" if the candidate said or someone/organization said the candidate believed in something like:

4a Passing laws that would encourage producing more energy from "clean" sources, such as wind, solar power, water, or nuclear power plants, would be a good idea.

and paste the quotes, in column "Q7x quotes/websites," that are the basis for your code "y".

Type "n" if nobody said anything like (4a) about the candidate's beliefs and attitudes.

Q8. Producing energy by "green" methods is not good.

Type "y" if the candidate said or someone/organization said the candidate believed in something like:

4b Passing laws that would encourage producing more energy from "clean" sources, such as wind, solar power, water, or nuclear power plants, would NOT be a good idea.
OR
4c The candidate is not sure whether passing laws that would encourage producing more energy from "clean" sources, such as wind, solar power, water, or nuclear power plants, would be a good idea.

and paste the quotes, in column "Q8x quotes/websites," that are the basis for your code "y".
Type "n" if nobody said anything like (4b) or (4c) about the candidate's beliefs and attitudes.

Q9. Actions should be taken to deal with GW/CC.
Type "y" if the candidate said or someone/organization said the candidate believed in something like:
5a Actions should be taken to reduce climate change or the effects of climate change.
OR
5b We should limit the amount of greenhouse gasses (carbon dioxide, CO_2) in the future.

and paste the quotes, in column "Q9x quotes/websites," that are the basis for your code "y".
Type "n" if nobody said anything like (5a) or (5b) about the candidate's beliefs and attitudes.

Q10. NO actions should be taken to deal with GW/CC.
Type "y" if the candidate said or someone/organization said the candidate believed in something like:
5c No actions should be taken about global warming or climate change.
OR
5d No actions should be taken to limit the amount of greenhouse gasses in the future.
OR
5e The candidate is not sure whether we should take actions about GW/CC.
OR
5f The candidate is not sure whether we should limit carbon emissions.

and paste the quotes , in column "Q10x quotes/websites," that are the basis for your code "y".
Type "n" if nobody said anything like (5c), (5d), (5e), or (5f) about the candidate's beliefs and attitudes.

Q11. Support cap-and-trade to reduce emissions contributing to GW/CC.

Type "y" if the candidate said or someone/organization said the candidate believed in something like:

6a The candidate supports cap-and-trade.

and paste the quotes , in column "Q11x quotes/websites," that are the basis for your code "y".

Type "n" if nobody said anything like (6a) about the candidate's beliefs and attitudes.

Q12. Oppose cap-and-trade to reduce emissions contributing to GW/CC.

Type "y" if the candidate said or someone/organization said the candidate believed in something like:

6b The candidate opposes cap-and-trade.

OR

6c The candidate is not sure whether cap-and-trade is a good idea.

and paste the quotes , in column "Q12x quotes/websites," that are the basis for your code "y".

Type "n" if nobody said anything like (6b) or (6c) about the candidate's beliefs and attitudes.

Appendix E

Methodologies of Studies 6 & 7

Study 6: Statements on Issues Other Than Climate Change

This part of the interview began by respondents hearing the following: "I'd like to read you a few things that a person running for U.S. Senate in your State might say. After you listen to each one, I'll ask you whether you mostly agree with it, mostly disagree with it, or neither agree nor disagree with it. First, what if the candidate said the following ..."

A first issue statement, randomly selected from six non-climate statements (the wording of these six statements is described below), was read to the respondent. Respondents were asked "Overall, do you mostly agree with what I just read, mostly disagree with it, or neither agree nor disagree with it?"

Respondents were then asked "Next, what if the candidate said this ..." A second issue statement, randomly selected from six non-climate statements (the wording of these six statements is described below), was read to the respondent. Respondents were asked "Overall, do you mostly agree with what I just read, mostly disagree with it, or neither agree nor disagree with it?"

Below are the six issues statements, from which two were randomly selected for each respondent.

1   "Our nation remains a target for terrorists. Terrorists are unrelenting in their desire to kill Americans. We cannot let down our guard, and we must continue to meet this ongoing threat with strength and resilience. During the past eight years, significant resources have been devoted to the prevention of a terrorist attack using a biological, chemical, or nuclear weapon. But the improvised explosive device remains the weapon of choice for terrorists. And terrorists can also choose to use firearms. For many Americans, including many families in our state, the right to own guns is part of their heritage and way of life. This right is protected by the Second Amendment. And so our government confronts a difficult issue today: how do we protect the constitutional right of Americans to bear arms, while preventing terrorists from using guns to carry out their murderous plans? None of us wants a terrorist to be able to purchase a gun. But neither should we want to infringe upon a constitutional right of law-abiding Americans."

2   "It makes no sense that the capital and risk standards for our nation's largest financial institutions are more lenient than those that apply to smaller depository banks, when the failure of larger institutions is much more likely to have a broad economic impact. Yet that is currently the case. We must give the regulators the tools and the direction to address this problem. I have proposed an amendment that will strengthen the economic foundation of these firms, increase oversight and accountability, and help prevent the excesses that contributed to the deep recession that has cost millions of Americans their jobs. Increasing capital requirements as firms grow provides a disincentive to their becoming "too big to fail" and ensures an adequate capital cushion in difficult economic times."

3   "When we are dealing with foreign-born suspects with known ties to terrorist organizations, and these people are carrying out plans to indiscriminately kill Americans, we need to NOT treat them like they're common criminals. Treating these people like common criminals is dangerous, and it limits the intelligence information that we can gather from suspects. The suspected Christmas Day bomber could have provided valuable information about potential terror plots. Instead, he was charged in the civilian court system where he got a lawyer and stopped talking. When someone is given Miranda rights and access to a lawyer, gathering valuable information about possible terrorist plots is greatly diminished."

4   "I believe that all Americans deserve quality, affordable health care, and that we must address the issues of rising health care costs and accessibility. Unfortunately, the recently enacted Federal health care legislation does not accomplish these goals and instead raises taxes on individuals and businesses, increases government spending, and will result in higher costs for consumers. I believe we must focus on fixing and replacing this law with common-sense

health care reforms that drive down costs, make it easier for people to purchase affordable insurance, and strengthen the existing private market system."

5   "I believe that terrorism is not a political issue; it is a national security issue. To win the war against terrorism, we must be able to quickly adapt to ever-changing terrorist tactics. Congress and the Administration must work together in a bipartisan fashion to continue support for all elements of national security, to increase information sharing and collective security efforts around the globe, and to expand vital law enforcement partnerships. Our Constitution and laws exist to protect this nation—they do not grant rights and privileges to enemies in wartime. In dealing with terrorists, our tax dollars should pay for weapons to stop them, not lawyers to defend them."

6   "I am an unwavering proponent of the Second Amendment to the United States Constitution and the right it confers on the people to keep and bear arms. As such, any attempts to deny this right violate both the letter and spirit of our Constitution. Enforcement, not new gun control laws, is the answer. To address concerns of gun crimes and criminal possession of firearms, the answer is not to create laws that deny law-abiding citizens the ability to defend themselves. Criminals will not be deterred by any such laws. Rather, the answer is proper and robust enforcement of appropriate gun laws now on the books. Furthermore, the proper way to combat crimes in our communities is to ensure that those who commit them are properly arrested, convicted and incarcerated for their crimes."

Study 7: Statements on Issues Other Than Climate Change

Florida

The follow-up questions were asked of all respondents in Florida when the issue statements unrelated to global warming were read to them. First issue statement was:

> "When we are dealing with foreign-born suspects with known ties to terrorist organizations, and these people are carrying out plans to indiscriminately kill Americans, we need to NOT treat them like they're common criminals. Treating these people like common criminals is dangerous, and it limits the intelligence information that we can gather from suspects. The suspected Christmas Day bomber could have provided valuable information about potential terror plots. Instead, he was charged in the civilian court system where he got a lawyer and stopped talking. When someone is given Miranda rights and access to a lawyer, gathering valuable information about possible terrorist plots is greatly diminished."

And the second issue statement was:

"Lifting the Cuba travel ban represents a blatant disregard of the human rights violations that the Castro regime commits against the Cuban people. This attempt to appease the Cuban dictatorship is wholly inconsistent with the United States' role as a beacon of freedom in this hemisphere, and around the world. This effort puts narrow corporate interests ahead of the need to protect the Cuban people from the Castro regime's brutal oppression. Canadian and European tourists have long made their way to Cuba, despite the fact that the Cuban regime has grown more repressive and living conditions for a majority of Cubans have declined to unprecedented low levels. The money they spend there is handed over to the Castro regime's desperate totalitarian machine. Americans cannot allow themselves to be caught in the same trap of funding brutality."

Massachusetts

The follow-up questions were asked of all respondents in Massachusetts when the issue statements unrelated to global warming were read to them. The first issue statement was:

"I believe that all Americans deserve quality, affordable health care, and that we must address the issues of rising health care costs and accessibility. Unfortunately, the recently enacted Federal health care legislation does not accomplish these goals and instead raises taxes on individuals and businesses, increases government spending, and will result in higher costs for consumers. I believe we must focus on fixing and replacing this law with common-sense health care reforms that drive down costs, make it easier for people to purchase affordable insurance, and strengthen the existing private market system."

The second issue statement was:

"I believe that terrorism is not a political issue; it is a national security issue. To win the war against terrorism, we must be able to quickly adapt to ever-changing terrorist tactics. Congress and the Administration must work together in a bipartisan fashion to continue support for all elements of national security, to increase information sharing and collective security efforts around the globe, and to expand vital law enforcement partnerships. Our Constitution and laws exist to protect this nation—they do not grant rights and privileges to enemies in wartime. In dealing with terrorists, our tax dollars should pay for weapons to stop them, not lawyers to defend them."

Maine

The follow questions were asked of all respondents in Maine when the issue statements unrelated to global warming were read to them. The first issue statement was:

"Our nation remains a target for terrorists. Terrorists are unrelenting in their desire to kill Americans. We cannot let down our guard, and we must continue to meet this ongoing threat with strength and resilience. During the past eight years, significant resources have been devoted to the prevention of a terrorist attack using a biological, chemical, or nuclear weapon. But the improvised explosive device remains the weapon of choice for terrorists. And terrorists can also choose to use firearms. For many Americans, including many Maine families, the right to own guns is part of their heritage and way of life. This right is protected by the Second Amendment. And so our government confronts a difficult issue today: how do we protect the constitutional right of Americans to bear arms, while preventing terrorists from using guns to carry out their murderous plans? None of us wants a terrorist to be able to purchase a gun. But neither should we want to infringe upon a constitutional right of law-abiding Americans."

The second issue statement was:

"It makes no sense that the capital and risk standards for our nation's largest financial institutions are more lenient than those that apply to smaller depository banks, when the failure of larger institutions is much more likely to have a broad economic impact. Yet that is currently the case. We must give the regulators the tools and the direction to address this problem. I have proposed an amendment that will strengthen the economic foundation of these firms, increase oversight and accountability, and help prevent the excesses that contributed to the deep recession that has cost millions of Americans their jobs. Increasing capital requirements as firms grow provides a disincentive to their becoming 'too big to fail' and ensures an adequate capital cushion in difficult economic times."

Studies 6 and 7: Question Wordings

After hearing all statements, respondents were asked, "Now based on all these things that you have heard the candidate say, how likely do you think you would be to vote for this candidate in an election for U.S. Senate? Do you think you definitely would vote for this candidate, probably would vote for this candidate, probably would not vote for this candidate, or definitely would not vote for this candidate?"

TABLE 10.E1 Measures of Beliefs and Attitudes about Global Warming and Personal Importance

Measure	Survey question	Coding of the measure
Existence of global warming	You may have heard about the idea that the world's temperature may have been going up slowly over the past 100 years. What is your personal opinion on this—do you think this has probably been happening, or do you think it probably has not been happening?	1 if "Probably has been happening"; 0 if "Probably has not been happening", or Don't Know or Refused
Human causal influence on warming	[Added "Assuming it's happening" among those who were coded 0 in "The planet has probably been warming",] Do you think a rise in the world's temperature (is being/ would be) caused mostly by things people do, mostly by natural causes, or about equally by things people do and by natural causes?	1 if "Things people do" or "Both equally"; 0 if "Natural causes", or Don't Know or Refused
Personal importance of global warming	How important is the issue of global warming to you personally – extremely important, very important, somewhat important, not too important, or not at all important?	1 if "Extremely important" or "Very important"; 0 if "Somewhat important", or "Not too important", or "Not at all important", or Don't Know or Refused
Party identification	Do you consider yourself a Democrat, a Republican, an Independent, or none of these?	Respondents who said "Democrat" were coded as Democrats; respondents who said "Republicans" were coded as Republicans; respondents who said "Independent", "None of these", or Don't Know, or declined to answer were coded as "Independents".

Appendix F

Methodology of Study 8

Question Wording and Coding

Party Identification and Demographic Variables

Party identification. Participants were asked: "Do you consider yourself a Democrat, Republican, an Independent, or none of these?" A Democrat dummy variable was coded 1 for Democrats and 0 for all others. A Republican dummy variable was coded 1 for Republicans and 0 for all others. An Independent dummy variable was coded 1 for participants who chose "Independent" or "None of these" and 0 for all others. A dummy variable was constructed for participants who refused to answer the education question. The Independent dummy variable was the omitted base category in the regression.

Ideology. Participants were asked: "Generally speaking, do you consider yourself liberal, moderate, or conservative?" A Liberal dummy variable was coded 1 for participants who chose "Liberal" and 0 for all others. A Conservative dummy variable was coded 1 for participants who chose "Conservative" and 0 for all others. A Moderate dummy variable was coded 1 for participants who chose "Moderate" and 0 for all others. A dummy variable was constructed for participants who refused to answer the education question. The Moderate dummy variable was the omitted base category in the regression.

Female. Participants were asked: "Please enter whether you are male or female." A Female dummy variable was coded 1 for females and 0 for males.

Age. Participants were asked: "Please enter your age." Age was measured in years. Dummy variables were constructed for age 18 to 24, age 25 to 34, age 35 to 44, age 45 to 54, age 55 to 64, and age 65 or older. Age 65 or older dummy variable was the omitted base category in the regression.

Race and Hispanic ethnicity. Participants were asked: "Are you of Spanish, Hispanic, or Latino descent?" A Hispanic dummy variable was coded 1 for those reporting Hispanic ethnicity and 0 for others. Participants were asked to "check one or more categories" from a list and were told to select what race(s) they considered themselves to be. A Non-Hispanic White dummy variable was coded 1 for participants who were not Hispanic and selected "White" and 0 otherwise. A Non-Hispanic Black dummy variable was coded 1 for participants who were not Hispanic and selected "Black or African–American" and 0 for others. A Non-Hispanic Other Race dummy variable was coded 1 for participants who were not Hispanic and selected a category other than "White" and "Black or African–American" and 0 otherwise. Non-Hispanic White dummy variable was the omitted base category in the regression.

Education. Participants were asked: "What is the highest grade of school that you completed?" and presented with the following response choices: Less than high school graduate, High school graduate, Technical/trade school, Some college, College graduate, Some graduate school, and Graduate degree. A dummy variable of "Less than high school or high school graduate" was constructed (1 for participants who chose "Less than high school," "High school graduate," or "Technical/trade school" and 0 otherwise). A dummy variable of "Some college" was constructed (1 for participants who chose "Some college" and 0 otherwise). A dummy variable of "College graduate" was constructed (1 for participants who chose "College graduate," "Some graduate school," or "Graduate degree," and 0 otherwise). A dummy variable was constructed for participants who refused to answer the education question. Less than high school or high school graduate dummy variable was the omitted base category in the regression.

Income. Participants were asked "Was your total income of you and all members of your family who lived with you in 2012, before taxes, less than $50,000, or $50,000 or more?" Participants who answered with "Less than $50,000" were asked to choose one of the following categories: Less than $10,000, $10,000 to $19,999, $20,000 to $29,999, $30,000 to $39,000, and $40,000 to $49,999. Participants who answer with "$50,000 or more" were asked to choose one of the following categories: $50,000 to $74,999, $75,000 to $99,999, $100,000 to $149,999, and $150,000 or more. A dummy variable was constructed for each of these income categories: less than $30,000, $30,000 to $49,000, $50,000 to $74,999, $75,000 to $100,000, and $100,000 or more. The lowest category, "Less than $30,000" was the omitted base category in the regression.

Region. Was coded using a set of dummy variables representing three different census regions in the United States: Midwest, South, and West. Participants living in the West region constituted the omitted base category in the regression.

Notes

1   This research was supported by National Science Foundation Grant 1042938 and by the Woods Institute for the Environment at Stanford University, California. Authors thank Ana Villar for her contribution to Study 7. Jon Krosnick is University Fellow at Resources for the Future. Address correspondence about this study to Jon A. Krosnick, McClatchy Hall, Stanford University, Stanford, CA 94305 (email: krosnick@stanford.edu).

2   We did not include an interaction to explore the case when the Democrat was not-green and the Republican was green, because no such instances occurred in 2010 (see row 1 column 1 in Table 10.7).

References

Anand, S., & Krosnick, J. A. (2003). The impact of attitudes toward foreign policy goals on public preferences among presidential candidates: A study of issue publics and the attentive public in the 2000 U.S. presidential election. *Presidential Studies Quarterly,* 33: 31–71.

Boninger, D. S., Krosnick, J. A., Berent, M. K., & Fabrigar, L. R. (1995). The causes and consequences of attitude importance. In R. E. Petty and J. A. Krosnick (Eds.), *Attitude Strength: Antecedents and Consequences*. Mahwah, NJ: Lawrence Erlbaum.

Brant, R. (1990). Assessing proportionality in the proportional odds model for ordinal logistic regression. *Biometrics*, 46: 1171–1178.

DeBell, M., & Krosnick, J. A. (2009). Computing weights for American National Election Study survey data. ANES Technical Report series, no. nes012427. Ann Arbor, MI, and Palo Alto, CA: American National Election Studies. Available at: http://www.electionstidies.org (accessed August 16, 2011).

Downs, A. (1957). *An Economic Theory of Democracy*. New York: Harper and Row.

Enelow, J., & Hinich, M. (1984). *The Spatial Theory of Voting*. Cambridge: Cambridge University Press.

Harder, J., & Krosnick, J. A. (2008). Why do people vote? A psychological analysis of the causes of voter turnout. *Journal of Social Issues*, 64(3): 525–549.

Holbrook, A. L., Krosnick, J. A., Visser, P. S., Gardner, W. L., & Cacioppo, J. T. (2001). Attitudes toward presidential candidates and political Parties: Initial optimism, inertial first impressions, and a focus on flaws. *American Journal of Political Science*, 45(4): 930–950.

Hughes, S. (2010). Democrats who took risk and voted for climate bill pay price. *Dow Jones Newswires* [accessed January 1, 2011]. Available at: http://www.automatedtrader.net/real-time-dow-jones/27739/democrats-who-took-risk-and-voted-for-climate-bill-pay-price.

Johnson, B. (2010). Ignore evidence, Politico spins climate vote as electoral loser. Think Progress [accessed January 1, 2011]. Available at: http://thinkprogress.org/green/2010/11/03/174834/politico-climate-midterms.

Krosnick, J. A. (1990). Government policy and citizen passion: A study of issue publics in contemporary America. *Political Behavior,* 12: 59–92.

Krosnick, J. A. (2002). The challenges on political psychology: Lessons to be learned from research on attitude perception. In J. H. Kuklinski (Ed.), *Thinking About Political Psychology*. New York: Cambridge University Press.

Krosnick, J. A. (2010). The climate majority. *New York Times*, June 9, sec. A.

Levi, M. (2010). Cap-and-trade didn't kill the Dems. *Council on Foreign Relations* [accessed January 1, 2011]. http://blogs.cfr.org/levi/2010/11/05/cap-and-trade-didnt-kill-the-dems.

McFadden, D. (1974). The measurement of urban travel demand. *Journal of Public Economics*, 3(4): 303–328.

Pasek, J. (2010). anesrake: ANES raking implementation. Comprehensive R Archive Network. Version 0.4 [accessed July 12, 2010]. Available from: http://cran.r-project.org/web/packages/anesrake/index.html.

Perry, P. (1960). Election survey procedures of the Gallup Poll. *Public Opinion Quarterly* 24(3): 531–542.

Rabinowitz, G. (1978). On the nature of political issues: Insights from spatial analysis. *American Journal of Political Science*, 22(4): 793–817.

Rabinowitz, G., & Macdonald, E. (1989). A directional theory of issue voting. *American Political Science Review*, 83(1): 93–121.

Taylor-Miesle, H. (2010). It's not the climate bill, stupid. *Huffington Post* [accessed January 1, 2011]. http://www.huffingtonpost.com/heather-taylormiesle/its-not-the-climate-bill_b_779012.html.

Visser, P. S., Bizer, G. Y., & Krosnick, J. A. (2006). Exploring the latent structure of strength-related attitude attributes. In M. Zanna (Ed.), *Advances in Experimental Social Psychology*. New York: Academic Press.

Visser, P. S., Krosnick, J. A., Marquette, J., & Curtin, M. (1996). Mail surveys for election forecasting? An evaluation of the Columbus Dispatch poll. *Public Opinion Quarterly*, 60: 181–227.

PART III

Challenging Conventional Wisdom about Politics

11

RACISM, CAUSAL EXPLANATIONS, AND AFFIRMATIVE ACTION

Theresa K. Vescio, Amy Cuddy, Faye Crosby, and Kevin Weaver

Social scientists have established a strong connection between racist attitudes and opposition to affirmative action (Crosby, Iyer, & Sincharoen, 2006). Study after study has found that opposition to affirmative action policies and practices is greatest among those who are the most racist (Arriola & Cole, 2001; Bobo, 1998; Bobo & Kluegel, 1993; Bobocel, Son Hing, Davey, Stanley, & Zanna, 1998; Brodish, Brazy, & Devine, 2008; Carmines & Layman, 1998; Hayes-James, Brief, Dietz, & Cohen, 2001; Hurwitz & Peffllcy, 1998; Katz & Hass, 1988; Lehman & Crano, 2002; Little, Murry, & Wimbush, 1998; Mack, Johnson, Green, Parisi, & Thomas, 2002; Nosworthy, Lea, & Lindsay, 1995; Oh, Choi, Neville, Anderson, & Landrum-Brown, 2010; Reyna, Henry, Korfmacher, & Tucker, 2005; Sawires & Peacock, 2000; Sears & Henry, 2003, 2005; Sears, Van Laar, Carrillo, & Kosterman, 1997; Shteynberg, Leslie, Knight, & Mayer, 2011; Sidanius, Pratto, & Bobo, 1996; Sniderman & Piazza, 1993; Stoker, 1998; Strolovitch, 1998; Tuch & Hughes, 1996). At least one major survey has found that modern or covert racism is an even stronger predictor of opposition to affirmative action than is old-fashioned racism (Williams et al., 1999). Similar associations have also been found for sexism and opposition to affirmative action, corroborating the predictive importance of prejudice (Kane & Whipkey, 2009; Tougas & Veilleux, 1990; Tougas, Brown, Beaton, & Joly, 1995; Tougas, Crosby, Joly, & Pelchat, 1995). Prejudice is not the only reason why Americans fail to support affirmative action (Crosby, 2004; Crosby, Iyer, Clayton, & Downing, 2003; Crosby et al., 2006), but it is a major reason (Harrison, Kravitz, Mayer, Leslie, & Dalit, 2006).

Several scholars have interpreted the association between racial attitudes and attitudes toward affirmative action in light of important social psychological theories like symbolic politics (Brandt & Reyna, 2012; Hughes, 1997; Kinder,

1998; Kinder & Sanders, 1996; Sears & Valentino, 1997), social dominance theory (Federico & Sidanius, 2000a, 2000b; Sidanius, Devereux, & Pratto, 1992; Sidanius, Pratto, & Bobo, 1996) and group conflict theory (Bobo, 1998; Bobo & Kluegel, 1993; Bobo & Smith, 1994; Bobo, Kluegel, & Smith, 1997; Tolbert & Grummel, 2003; see also Yogeeswaran & Dasgupta, 2014). Some researchers have examined associations among different ideological and practical factors to claim victory for one theoretical camp over other camps (Aberson, 2003; Glaser, 1994; Jacobson, 1985; Lehman & Crano, 2002; Strolovich, 1998). Others have cautioned that many different factors, variously interpreted, contribute to our understanding of why some privileged people support affirmative action, while others oppose it (Crosby, 2004; Crosby & Dovidio, 2008; Dawson, 2000; Hughes, 1997; Sidanius, Singh, Hetts, & Federico, 2000).

In this chapter, we seek to enlarge the discussion about the connection between racism and opposition to affirmative action by proposing that a major reason for the negative correlation between support for affirmative action and racist attitudes is that affirmative action challenges the underlying worldview of people who are high in racism. At the heart of our argument are two interconnected observations. First, as we show in the initial section of our chapter, the greater the racial prejudice among white people, the greater is the tendency to explain the disadvantages of black people in simplistic, dispositional terms and the less is the tendency to understand disadvantages in complex structural or situational terms. Second, as is clear from our descriptions of affirmative action, the policy calls for complex reasoning. Our description shows that affirmative action is a fair policy (perhaps, indeed, a fairer policy than equal opportunity). To see the fairness of the policy, however, requires cognitive work and requires a willingness to look at complicated causal factors. The worldview that includes simple explanations and valorizes personal or dispositional causality is consistent with the underlying premises of equal opportunity, but it is thus inconsistent with the underlying premises of affirmative action. The final section of our chapter touches briefly on some of the implications of our work.

The Worldview of the Contemporary Racist

Stereotypes are cognitive representations of social groups that describe how members of a given group are similar to one another and different from members of other groups. Stereotypes represent people's beliefs about a group's average standing. For instance, black Americans are stereotypically perceived as being poor, uneducated, unintelligent and unmotivated (among other things, see Devine, 1989; Lepore & Brown, 1997). Stereotypes also contain causal information that explains how the components are interrelated and linked to the social world (Wittenbrink, Gist, & Hilton, 1997). For instance, stereotypes describe the lower relative social status of black Americans (e.g., lower income, education) and explain the causes for those disadvantages.

There are two opposing kinds of causal beliefs that consistently have been linked to prejudice and brought to bear on theory and research on intergroup relations—dispositional causal beliefs and situational causal beliefs (see Bobo & Kluegel, 1993; Hewstone, 1990; Katz & Hass, 1988; Pettigrew, 1979; Vescio & Biernat, 1999; Wittenbrink et al., 1997). Considering the relative lower social status of black Americans than white Americans, high prejudice thought is characterized by dispositional causal explanations. Black individuals are perceived as lacking the dispositional material to succeed, such that the cause of blacks' lower social status (e.g., lower mean income and educational attainment) can be attributed to black individuals. By contrast, low prejudice whites tend to think in terms of situational causal explanations. Black individuals are perceived as being the targets of past injustices, situational barriers, and ongoing discrimination, which cause the lower social status of blacks (e.g., Wittenbrink et al., 1997).

Beyond being related to the causal focus of stereotypes (dispositional, situational), prejudice may be related to the complexity of stereotypic causal explanations. Perceptions of causation involve ideas about how energy is transmitted from an ultimate cause (or causes) to an event—"Events need to be linked via a causal chain so that the force can be transmitted from one link to the next" (Einhorn & Hogarth, 1986, p. 10). Therefore, when an observer initiates a causal search in the process of reaching an attribution, prior knowledge (e.g., stereotypic beliefs about the causes of group differences) and imagination are used to create a scenario or chain to link cause to effect. If X and Y can be directly connected then there is one causal link involved. For example, a flaw in the Pentium chip causes Intel stock prices to drop. However, the larger the gap between initial cause and the final effect, the more links that will be required to bridge the gap. To use Einhorn and Hogarth's (1986) example, consider the possibility that sunspots affect stock prices. One possible explanation for such an event might be the following: Sunspots lead to good weather, which in turn leads to increased crop production. Increased crop production affects the economy, which alters profits, and results in final price changes. There are six variables in this explanation—the ultimate cause (sunspots), the effect (price changes), and four intermediate variables (weather, agriculture, economy, and profits). The number of causal links in an explanation equals the number of intermediate variables plus one (five in this case).

If causal complexity is conceptualized in terms of the number of causal links that are needed to transmit energy from distal (and multiple) causes to the effect, then there may be differences in the causal complexity of the explanations that high and low prejudice whites generate for outcomes involving black Americans. The attributions that high, compared to low, prejudice whites make for the ambiguous and/or stereotype consistent behaviors of black Americans may be more simplistic and direct. For example, consider a black adolescent who behaves in a stereotypically aggressive manner. The attributional components of stereotypes (i.e., "the aggressiveness of blacks leads to increased contact with the criminal justice system") may direct attention toward the actor and his/her behavior. To use Heider's (1958) terms, "behavior engulfs the field" and dispositional factors provide the most ready and complete explanations for behavior—an aggressive disposition is a sufficient explanation for an aggressive act.

The attributional components of low prejudice people's stereotypes, however, focus on situational factors beyond the control of the actor (e.g., low SES, discriminatory practices of police) and require the inclusion of multiple causal factors and/or more distant ultimate causes. Whereas aggressiveness may lead directly to aggressive acts (i.e., high prejudice belief), being a member of a low-income family has effects on other variables that, in turn, produce aggressive behavior (i.e., low prejudice belief). For instance, low-income families reside in neighborhoods with few community programs for youth, which causes involvement with unsupervised groups of children, which may facilitate delinquent behavior that ultimately escalates into violent acts. In sum, the causal beliefs of low prejudice whites guide attention to belief consistent (and situational) aspects of the environment and result in more complex explanations.

Prior research from our lab has documented the linkages between white Americans, prejudice level and complex situational explanations for the relative lower social status of black Americans. For instance, in the first studies (Vescio, 1996) white Americans were asked to consider a series of statistical differences that reflect the lower social status of black Americans versus white Americans (e.g., differences in income and education level) and either (a) write open ended responses describing the primary causal factors or (b) rate the importance of the dispositional characteristics of black Americans, dispositional characteristics of white Americans, and characteristics of the situation or environment in producing the group difference. Participants across studies were also asked to draw causal diagrams connecting distal causes and concomitant causes to specific group differences. The findings showed a consistent pattern of correlations between prejudice (as measured by the Modern Racism Scale, MRS) and ratings of the importance of situational causes of group difference. Lower prejudice was related to a greater tendency to make situational attributions, but was also related to the complexity of the causal explanations generated (or the number of causal links participants used to explain group differences). These findings were replicated more recently, indicating the continued connection between contemporary forms of prejudice and attributions for racial differences, both in terms of the content and complexity of causal attributions.

If stereotypes contain causal components that, as a function of prejudice, vary in content and complexity (Vescio, 1996; Vescio & Biernat, 1999; Wittenbrink et al., 1997), then the attributional components of stereotypes should guide inferences and information seeking behaviors (or attention) in settings involving individual members of stereotyped groups. This is consistent with other findings in the stereotyping literature that demonstrate that perceivers display stereotype matching biases in information seeking strategies (Johnston & Macrae, 1994) and demonstrate general confirmatory hypothesis testing strategies (e.g., Evett, Devine, Hirt, & Price, 1994; Snyder & Swann, 1978; Snyder, Campbell, & Preston, 1982; for reviews see Klayman & Ha, 1987; Snyder & Gangestad, 1981).

To examine this possibility, we presented white participants with information about a black or white teenager who had engaged in aggressive delinquent behavior. The study participants had been pre-tested and selected on the basis of being either quite prejudiced or quite unprejudiced. We examined whether prejudiced participants would provide simplistic explanations for the aggressive behavior of a black delinquent but not of a white delinquent. We also wanted to see if prejudiced participants would gravitate toward dispositional rather than situational explanations.

Method

Participants

The experimental participants were 50 white undergraduates at a Midwestern university who were chosen from a larger sample of 630 introductory psychology students based on their responses to the Modern Racism Scale. Among the pre-testing sample, scores on the Modern Racism Scale (MRS) could, and did, range from 7 to 35, with a mean of 14 and a standard deviation of 5.39. Participants for this study were chosen from the upper and lower quartiles of the MRS distribution. We classified 14 males and 10 females as high prejudice. All of our prejudiced participants had MRS scores greater than 19. We classified 10 males and 18 females, all with MRS scores less than 11, as low prejudice.

Procedure

Upon arrival, participants were greeted by a white experimenter who was unaware of the participants' prejudice level. After signing an informed consent statement, participants were told that they would be taking part in a law and psychology study and were given information about one of several possible cases that had been heard by juvenile court. All participants were presented with the same information with one exception—we manipulated the race of the juvenile.

Following the introduction, participants were given time alone to look over a one page description of a vandalism case. The race of the target was manipulated by the presence of an identification photo, which was attached to the upper left hand corner of the case description. Pre-testing indicated that the black and white targets were equivalent in terms of attractiveness and that the photos accurately conveyed the race and age of the target. To assure that target race was successfully manipulated, however, participants completed a brief offender identification form under the guise of helping us keep track of which case they had read about. One of the questions on the information sheet asked the race of the juvenile, which all correctly answered.

Participants were then presented with four files containing reports about various aspects of the adolescent's environment and disposition, contained in different color binders and labeled as follows: (1) School Environment; (2) Home Environment; (3) Academic Ability and Achievement; and (4) Personality and Psychological Evaluation. The files were constructed such that the school and home environment files contained situational causal information (e.g., information about neighborhood SES, busing status, family composition) and the academic ability and personality files contained dispositional causal information (e.g., I.Q., scores on standardized achievement test, personality profiles). The content of the four folders was balanced for the amount and valence of information provided, as well as controlling for presentational style. All reports contained a cover page and five pages of information with equal numbers of words and were described as psychological reports (or prepared by psychologists) to control for potential differences in perceived status of the source of the information. Finally, each report was typed in a different font and format to enhance believability in the authenticity of the reports. Clearly labeled folders were placed on a table in a random order and participants were left alone to read through the information in the folders. Participants opened the door of the experimental room when they were finished looking at the materials.

The participants were then presented with questions about the causes and controllability of the delinquent act. First, participants reported their perceptions of the important causal role of different potential contributors to the delinquent act, the likelihood that the adolescent will engage in further delinquent behavior and their impression of the controllability of the delinquent act. Second, participants wrote a free-form description of the primary causes of the adolescent's delinquent behavior and were asked to diagram how those primary causes led to the delinquent behavior of the adolescent. More specifically, participants were asked to write a detailed description of their beliefs about the factors that caused the adolescent's delinquent behavior. They were then asked to think about what they had written and to draw a causal diagram. To create a causal diagram, participants arranged causes to display the relation among distal and proximal causes to the group difference. This task was modeled on Einhorn and Hogarth's (1986) discussion of causal chains and Antaki's (1988) causal diagramming task and required that respondents diagram the transmission of energy from the ultimate cause(s) to the effect.

Dependent Measures

We summed the number of causal factors included in participants' descriptions of the causes of the adolescent's delinquent act to create a *situational attribution* variable and a *dispositional attribution* variable. We also created a *causal complexity score* by counting the number of arrows respondents used in their diagrams. A raw count was used because it included the distance of the ultimate cause from the outcome, multiple causes, and interactions between situational and dispositional variables (e.g., situational barriers cause learned helplessness and laziness, which produce differences in mean income). Complexity scores do not simply equal the sum of the total number of situational and dispositional causes mentioned. Instead, complexity takes into account all the causal linkages between distal and proximal variables.

Results and Discussion

Attributional Focus

Attributions were submitted to an attribution type (situational, dispositional) × participant prejudice level (high, low) × race of juvenile (black, white) mixed model Analysis of Variance. Type of attribution was a within-participants variable in this analysis, whereas participant prejudice level and juvenile race were between-participants variables. Three significant patterns of findings emerged from this analysis. Overall, participants' explanations of the juvenile's delinquent act contained a greater number of situational causal factors ($M=3.74$) than dispositional causal factors ($M=1.46$), as evidenced by a main effect of attribution type, $F(1,46)=43.12$, $p<.001$, $\eta_p^2=.48$. This tendency was also stronger among low prejudiced participants ($Ms=4.19$ and 1.35, respectively) than high prejudiced participants ($Ms=3.09$ and 1.64), as evidenced by the significant attribution type × prejudice level interaction, $F(1,46)=4.51$, $p=.039$, $\eta_p^2=.09$. These effects were, however, qualified by a three way interaction, $F(1,46)=8.25$, $p=.006$, $\eta_p^2=.15$.

The means associated with the predicted attribution type × juvenile race × participant prejudice level interaction are shown in Table 11.1. A series of simple effects tests and subsequent comparisons were performed to interpret the interaction, which revealed three critical differences in the responding of high prejudiced participants versus low prejudiced participants. First, compared to high prejudiced participants, low prejudiced participants included more situational (but not dispositional) attributions when the juvenile was black, $F(1,24)=12.52$, $p=.002$, $\eta_p^2=.36$. Second, focusing on situational attributions across prejudice level and juvenile race, low prejudiced participants included more situational attributions when the juvenile was black than white, $F(1,26)=3.66$, $p=.069$, $\eta_p^2=.12$.

TABLE 11.1 Attributional Focus of the Explanations Generated for the Adolescents' Delinquent Act and a Function of Participant Prejudice Level and Juvenile Race

	Juvenile race			
	Black		White	
	Situational Causes	Dispositional causes	Situational causes	Dispositional causes
High prejudiced participants	2.36 (.59)	1.64 (.30)	3.82 (.58)	1.64 (.30)
Low prejudiced participants	5.00 (.50)	1.00 (.26)	3.38 (.54)	1.69 (.28)

By contrast, high prejudiced participants included *fewer* situational attributions when the juvenile was black rather than white, $F(1,20)=5.04$, $p=.036$, $\eta_p^2=.20$. Third, focusing on dispositional attributions across prejudice level and juvenile race showed an opposite pattern. Low prejudiced participants' included fewer dispositional attributions when the juvenile was black versus white, $F(1,26)=4.18$, $p=.051$, $\eta_p^2=.138$, whereas high prejudice participants focus on dispositional causes did not vary as a function of the juvenile's race, $F<1$.

In addition, within prejudice level × juvenile race conditions, the greater focus on situational than dispositional attributions was reliable in all but one condition. Low prejudiced participants included significantly more situational causes than dispositional causes when explaining the delinquent act of both a black juvenile, $F(1,14)=31.11$, $p<.001$, $\eta_p^2=.69$, and a white juvenile, $F(1,12)=8.16$, $p=.014$, $\eta_p^2=.405$. Likewise, high prejudiced participants included more situational causes than dispositional causes when explaining the delinquent act of a white juvenile, $F(1,10)=12.58$, $p=.005$, $\eta_p^2=.56$. This difference did not, however, reach acceptable levels of statistical significance when high prejudiced people were explaining the delinquent act of a black juvenile, $F<1$. No other comparisons approached significance.

Causal Complexity

Complexity scores were submitted to a participant prejudice level × juvenile race between participants ANOVA. Two effects emerged from analysis of complexity. First, there was a significant main effect of participant prejudice level, $F(1,46)=4.24$, $p=.045$, $\eta_p^2=.084$. Low prejudiced participants ($M=5.64$) offered more complex causal explanations than did high prejudiced participants ($M=4.41$). Second, there was a marginally significant interaction between participants' prejudice level and target race, $F(1,46)=3.25$, $p=.078$, $\eta_p^2=.078$.

TABLE 11.2 Causal Complexity as a Function of Participants' Prejudice Level and Juvenile Race

	Target Race	
	Black	White
High prejudiced participants	3.82[a]	5.00[b]
Low prejudiced participants	6.13[b]	5.15[b]

As can be seen in the bottom panel of Table 11.2, low prejudiced participants offered non-significantly more complex explanations when the target was black rather than white. High prejudiced participants did the opposite; high prejudiced participants offered more complex explanations when the target was white than black. Interestingly, the interaction was driven by the less complex explanations that high prejudiced participants offered for the behavior of a black target.

In addition, participants' greater inclusion of situational determinants in their explanation of the delinquent act were highly related to causal complexity ($r=.81$, $p<.001$). Stated differently, an emphasis on situational causes was associated with complex attributions. Conversely, an emphasis on dispositional causes was associated with a non-significant tendency toward more simplistic thinking ($r= -.22$, $p=.129$).

In sum, we predicted that high and low prejudiced whites would differ in their responding toward a black individual who engaged in a negative behavior. When the target was black, low (vs. high) prejudiced participants were expected to show preference for situational causal explanations and make more complex attributions. Consistent with predictions, when presented with the aggressive behavior by a black teen, low prejudiced whites were more likely than high prejudiced whites to explain the behavior in terms of situational causes than dispositional causes, and to construct more complex causal explanations.

These findings further highlight the relation between whites' prejudice and their causal explanations. Whereas prior research has suggested that prejudice is related to the content and complexity of whites' explanations for the disadvantaged status of blacks in society (e.g., lower income and education), this is the first work to link prejudice to the complexity of whites' explanations for events involving black individuals. Low prejudiced beliefs are associated with complex, situational explanations for negative outcomes involving blacks, whereas high prejudiced beliefs are associated with simpler and more dispositionally focused explanations. These differences are argued to be a result of the different worldviews, or stereotypes, of high versus low prejudiced whites. Importantly, differences in both the content and complexity of high and low prejudiced beliefs have implications for reactions to affirmative action.

Affirmative Action

Affirmative action is not America's favorite policy (Crosby et al., 2006). Although attitudes tend to be more positive than negative, endorsement of the policy is both variable and easily influenced by the wording of questions (Crosby, 2004). Affirmative action seems to mean different things to different people, and it is certainly true that people's understanding of the policy influences their support for it (Golden, Hinkle, & Crosby, 2001).

In this section of the chapter, we describe affirmative action, explaining the philosophy behind the policy and how the policy operates. We then consider the effectiveness of the policy for improving the situation of people of color and of women. Next we draw out the distinctions between affirmative action and equal opportunity and note the implications of the distinctions.

Description of the Policy

Whenever an organization undertakes efforts that are designed to equalize opportunities afforded people of color and white people or afforded women and men, the organization engages in affirmative action (Crosby & Cordova, 1996). Affirmative action is deliberate. Affirmative action expends resources, both in terms of time and in terms of money.

In addition to the general definition of affirmative action, there are specific definitions, often of a rather technical nature. The principles underlying affirmative action in employment are the same as those underlying affirmative action in education (Crosby, 2000). Yet, the specific mechanisms of affirmative action in employment differ from the specific mechanisms of affirmative action in education, as described below.

Affirmative Action in Employment

In 1965, President Lyndon Johnson signed an Executive Order (EO) intended to help promote his vision of "the great society." EO 11246 required the federal government itself and any federal contractor above a certain small size doing more than a minimal amount of business with the federal government to be "an affirmative action employer." Employers with less than 50 employees were exempt from the requirement, as were organizations with contracts under $50,000. Any organization with 50 or more employers that did not wish to become an affirmative action employer was not required to do so, but such a decision would disqualify the organization from doing business with the federal government.

What does it mean to be an affirmative action employer? Certain procedures need to be followed, which generally involve a two-step process. In the first step, the organization keeps track of the proportion of employees who are members of targeted gender groups (i.e., women) and ethnic groups (i.e., African Americans, Hispanic Americans, Asian Americans, and Native Americans). One might note that white males comprise the only non-targeted group, that is, the only group for which the organization need gather no statistics.

Once an organization knows what proportion of its work force belong to targeted groups, it must compare those figures with the proportion of workers in different job categories who might potentially come from the targeted groups. Figures for actual workers are called "utilization figures" or "incumbency figures." Figures for the potential workers are called "availability figures." The core process in the first step of affirmative action in employment, as dictated by EO 11246, is to look at the match between utilization and availability.

Determining availability is a more arduous task than determining utilization, and it involves more subjectivity. Yet, certain practices have evolved to ease the burden of compliance. To determine availability for each job category, the organization must decide if candidates for that job are sought locally, regionally, or nationally. In a university, for example, professorial and other professional jobs are usually filled from a national pool; while jobs like administrative assistant are filled from a local pool. The organization then uses published information to calculate availability. At a university, availability figures for professorial positions might be calculated by the affirmative action office by using national statistics on the numbers of Ph.D.s who are African American, Latino, Asian American, or Native American in the humanities, the sciences, the social sciences, engineering, and so on. Availability figures for administrative assistants may be calculated by computing the number of African Americans, Latinos, Asian Americans, and Native Americans who live within 35 miles of the university.

If an organization discovers that its utilization of ethnic minority talent or of female talent falls short of availability, then the organization must initiate the second step of the process. Importantly, initiating the second step requires no inference of prejudice or discrimination. No one need admit to or be found guilty of intentional discrimination. No aggrieved victims need step forward on their own behalf, and no one needs to certify that there is a class of wronged persons.

The second step of the affirmative action process centers on correction of the documented problem(s). Following established practices, organizations devise a plan or set of plans to remedy an imbalance discovered in the first step of the process.

An example may illustrate. Imagine that University X discovers that it underutilizes women in the professoriate of the social sciences. It must then devise a plan to correct the underutilization. The plan should be sensible and cannot trammel the rights of men. Thus University X might project the retirements of faculty over the next decade and also specify any plans for expansion. The university might set goals for replacing retiring male faculty with new female faculty members. The university might, further, analyze the factors in its past and current hiring and promotion practices that might have contributed to the gender imbalance. Perhaps the hiring committees were all male. Perhaps feminist journals were not counted as "scholarly" when assessing productivity of faculty at the point of tenure. Perhaps the university lacked family friendly policies and was, therefore, unattractive to women with alternate offers.

What happens if an organization fails to realize the improvements specified in its affirmative action plan? As long as the organization can document that it is making good-faith efforts to meet its goals and to correct the problems, no sanctions can be applied. But if the organization flouts the corrective plans and flagrantly persists in its discriminatory ways, the federal government can take punitive action (e.g., impose fines, bar receipt of federal contracts).

The institution charged with monitoring federal contactors as they monitor themselves is the Office of Federal Contract Compliance Programs (OFCCP). During the presidency of George W. Bush, the OFCCP had become reduced in size. Currently there are about 700 employees nation-wide working for the OFCCP. Together the various district and regional offices oversee affirmative action programs in over 200,000 organizations. Approximately one-quarter of the American labor force is covered by affirmative action, by virtue of working for the federal government, a federal contractor, or a large and covered sub-contractor.

Affirmative action in employment has sometimes taken the form of preferential treatment in procurement, as opposed to monitoring and correction in hiring and promotions. At various points in the past, a program administered by the Small Business Administration gave preference to minority-owned businesses and to women-owned businesses. Such procurement programs were generally credited with helping to increase the numbers of successful minority-owned businesses (Bendick & Egan, 1999). Nonetheless, several legal challenges led to an overhaul of the set-aside programs. In the case of *Adarand v Pena Construction Company*, the Supreme Court declared that it was unconstitutional to grant preferences of the sort in *Adarand*.

Affirmative Action in Education

The logic of the affirmative action programs in higher education follows the logic of affirmative action in employment. Educators make estimates about the number of women and ethnic minority students who would be admitted to and graduate from college or university programs. When the actual number of women and ethnic minority students who attend and graduate from institutions of higher education falls short of what one would expect, given the talent pool, then the institutions develop programs designed to correct the imbalances.

Looking at the state of California provides a window into the issues of affirmative action in higher education. Access to higher education has long been an issue of import to Californians. Since the promulgation of the Master Plan for Higher Education in California in the 1960s the state has sought to provide access to higher education to all youth. Any graduate of a California high school has the right to attend a community college. The top 33% of the graduating high school students are entitled to attend one of the 23 California State Colleges, provided that they have fulfilled certain requirements (e.g., taken a certified course in California history). Although they are not guaranteed admission to the campus of their choice, the top 12.5% of high school graduates are entitled to take a seat at one of the 10 campuses of the University of California.

A desire to fulfill their historic mission in the face of mounting costs and demographic pressures has made administrators at the University of California particularly sensitive to questions of access. Studies undertaken at the Office of the President of the University of California showed that Latino students constituted a higher proportion of the "top" students graduating from California high schools than of students matriculated at the University. Questions arose about why Latinos were not selecting to attend at UC, and it was discovered that Latinos were not being guided into the proper sequence of courses in high school. Even though their grades and scores on standardized tests placed them in the top one-eighth of graduating high school students, a disproportionate number of Latinos had not taken the complete set of required courses and had thus not fulfilled the eligibility requirement (Crosby, 2004).

Having begun to monitor its behavior and performance with respect to access to education, the University of California continued its self-scrutiny in some very interesting ways. A study by Geiser and Studley (2001), two statisticians working at the Office of the President, revealed that scores on the SAT I provided very inadequate predictions of college performance, as indexed by freshman year grade-point average. The report also demonstrated that the SAT II, while much better than the SAT I, had quite limited predictive power concerning performance in college. "Each 100-point increase in SAT II," said the report, "adds about .18 of a grade point to predicted GPA, whereas a 100-point increase in SAT I scores adds only .05 of a grade point" (Geiser & Studley, 2001, p. 9). On average, the group scoring the worst (African Americans, with an average of 1041) averaged about 200 points less on the two-test SAT II than did the group scoring the best (whites, with an average of 1213).

The implications of the Geiser and Studley analysis were clear. The 200-point difference in SAT scores serves to eliminate most blacks from the pool of those admitted to the University of California. As a result, the SATs end up eliminating people who might obtain a B-minus GPA rather than a solid B GPA. Given the importance of having visible paths to achievement open to students from all backgrounds, it seemed advisable to some, including the then-president, of the University of California, Richard Atkinson, to jettison the uninformative tests and use alternative means of selecting applicants. Indeed, taking action to affirm equality of opportunity, Atkinson publicly promised to help eliminate the reliance on SAT scores for admissions unless the tests were changed. Perhaps coincidentally, the Educational Testing Service soon ramped up its efforts to make significant changes in the SAT.

Another public university that has paid great attention to issues of accessibility and affirmative action is the University of Michigan. In June 2003, the Supreme Court rendered decisions on two cases involving the University of Michigan: *Gratz v Bollinger* and *Grutter v Bollinger*. In *Gratz*, two white applicants (Jennifer Gratz and Patrick Hamacher) who had been denied admission to the University of Michigan sued the university when they discovered that black applicants with lower grades and test scores had been admitted. A similar scenario occurred in *Grutter* when a white woman (Barbara Grutter) was rejected from the law school. Although the claims of the plaintiffs were quite similar in *Gratz* and in *Grutter*, the decisions of the Supreme Court differed. In *Gratz*, Chief Justice Rhenquist wrote the majority opinion, and the Court found that the University had violated the rights of the applicants. Meanwhile, Sandra Day O'Connor wrote the majority opinion in *Grutter*, deciding that the university's law school had not erred in its admissions policies.

What accounts for the differences? The central difference concerned the nature of the admissions processes: in the law school, applicants received individualized scrutiny, but the undergraduate college had relied on a more mechanistic system of points. Importantly, even though the Court found against the university in the case of *Gratz*, Rhenquist's majority opinion made a point of stating explicitly that the state has a compelling interest in creating a diverse study body. Race-conscious policies were declared to be in accord with both the constitution and the statutes in both the *Gratz* and the *Grutter* cases; but the specific race-conscious methods deployed by the University of Michigan struck the Court as being sufficiently narrowly tailored in the law school and not narrowly tailored enough in the case of the undergraduate college.

Effectiveness of Affirmative Action

Scholars have used three research strategies, outlined below, for gauging the effectiveness of affirmative action as established by EO 11246. All three strategies indicate that affirmative action in employment has been effective. The evidence concerning the policy's effectiveness in higher education has been hotly contested; but, on balance, it too shows that affirmative action has produced documented positive results.

Effects of EO 11246

The first strategy used by some social scientists to gauge the effects of EO 11246 is to compare the federal government with other employers. Such comparisons show that slow but steady progress has been made by African Americans, Latinos, and women (of all ethnic groups) since 1965 when affirmative action was created (Reskin, 1998). One study showed, for example, that the number of African American managers and professionals in the employ of the federal government rose 200 percent from 1970 to 1980 while the number of white managers and professionals rose only 29% (Konrad & Linnehan, 1995a,b). Another study showed that years after the inauguration of affirmative action in the federal government, college educated African American men had ten times more chance of working as a manager in a public sector job than in a job in the for-profit sector (Smith, 1976).

A second research strategy for gauging the success of EO 11246 is to compare hiring and employment patterns of federal contractors, on the one hand, and non-federal contractors on the other. Adjusting for market sector (e.g., manufacturing or retail), the statistics show that federal contractors have hired, retained, and promoted more women and people of color than comparable companies that are not federal contractors. (For a review see, Crosby, 2004). One study looked at over 40,000 firms in 1966 and 1970, and found that federal contractors had a much greater chance than other firms of moving from an all-white work force to an integrated work force (Ashenfelter & Heckman, 1976).

The final strategy for gauging the effectiveness of EO 11246 is to conduct surveys where the self-report of employees are used to identify affirmative action employers (Holzer & Neumark, 1999). Despite the problems with self-reported data, such a method improves over the other two methods because many organizations establish voluntary affirmative action plans.

Organizations with voluntary plans would be classified as "non-contractors" in the second method, and could thus make the non-contractors appear to be more vigorous in the hiring of people of color and of women than they actually are. One such study involving comparisons based on survey data found that 33% of the employees who worked for a firm that was not an affirmative action employer declared that no African Americans worked at their companies while only 7% of those working for affirmative action employers said the same (Herring & Collins, 1995). The same investigators also found that people of color earned more at affirmative action companies than at other companies.

Education

The weight of the evidence indicates that in higher education, vigorous affirmative action programs have helped augment the numbers of students of color at colleges and universities (Bowen & Bok, 1998). Some analyses question whether the augmentation has occurred equally at all levels of the educational hierarchy and whether the apparent increase has been artificially inflated by a failure to distinguish between, say, community colleges and elite universities and between the matriculation figures and the graduation figures (Renner & Moore, 2004). But other scholars show that even when one takes into account such factors, there are measurable positive effects of affirmative action in education.

Given the importance of the *Grutter v Bollinger* case, and given the strong influence of lawyers on legal and social realities, much attention has been focused on the effects of race-sensitive admissions programs for law schools. A detailed study of the law school at the University of Michigan documented the increase in ethnic minority matriculants and graduates as a result of race-sensitive admissions policies (Lempert, Chambers, & Adams, 2000a, 2000b).

Recently, a study of 27,000 law students who matriculated in accredited law schools in 1991, challenged the effective conclusion that race-sensitive admissions policies benefit blacks. Indeed, law professor Richard Sander (2004) claims that race-sensitive admissions plans have outlived their effectiveness for law school and now contribute to a shortage of African Americans who graduate from law school and also pass the bar. Sander's study, published in the prestigious *Stanford Law Review*, generated a firestorm of interest. A number of prominent researchers have published rebuttals to the Sander's article (Ayres & Brooks, 2005; Chambers, Clydesdale, Kidder, & Lempert, 2005; Wilkins, 2005) questioning Sander's assumptions, methods, and conclusions.

To date, no one has conducted the statistical analysis by which one could determine the validity of Sander's claim that black law students are harmed by being given a boost in the quality of the law schools they attend. The data are clear that many black applicants are given a boost in their applications and are admitted to law schools of a higher tier than would be true were they white. Yet, the proof that such a boost proves detrimental resides in a comparison of the outcomes (graduation rates, rates of passing the bar) of those who were given a boost and those who were given no boost. Such an analysis nowhere appears in Sander's article.

Reasons

Some of the reasons for the effectiveness of affirmative action are clear. Racism continues to affect the treatment of people of color in the United States (e.g., Neville, Awad, Brooks, Flores, & Bluemel, 2014). So-called "equal opportunity" does not, therefore, operate in the way it would operate absent prejudicial attitudes and discriminatory behavior. Given the hurdles that people of color face in the United States, it is only logical that positive consequences derive from the taking of actions ensuring the elimination of racial biases of those who hire or promote employees and those who devise and implement admissions policies.

Another reason for the effectiveness of affirmative action is that affirmative action, unlike "equal opportunity," helps diminish what the sociologist Christopher Jencks calls "selective system bias." According to Jencks, "selective system bias [arises] whenever the standardized racial gap in job performance is smaller than the standardized racial gap in test performance" (Jencks, 1998, p. 77). Oftentimes people of color do much less well than white people on the entrance exam, or have credentials that appear to be much less impressive than those of whites, and yet do only a little less well or no different than white people on the job or at the school. Jencks notes that, for example, a reliance on the SAT tests, when such tests predict only a tiny amount of the variance in college performance, is unfair because such a reliance "forces blacks to pay for the fact that social scientists have unusually good measures of a trait on which blacks are unusually disadvantaged" (Jencks, 1998, pp. 14–15).

Not only is selective system bias unfair; it is also impractical: by using gating mechanisms that exclude one group without providing highly accurate information about future performance, selective system bias deprives schools of a source of potentially successful students and provides businesses of sources of potentially successful workers. When the bias is eliminated, not only do those who were previously excluded benefit; so do the organizations that admit or select them (Holzer & Neumark, 1999).

The final reason that affirmative action has proven so effective is that it is the only mechanism for reducing or eliminating sex discrimination that does not require aggrieved parties to come forward. People are not allowed to bring lawsuits on behalf of others, unless they themselves have "standing" in the case. Thus, social activists can use the courts to redress racial discrimination, but only if there is at least one aggrieved party who is willing to serve as plaintiff. Very few people are willing to submit to the cost, time, trouble, and the social ostracism of publicly complaining about situations in which they feel that they have been the victims of discrimination (Rhode & Williams, 2007). In fact, most people do not even wish to acknowledge that they have been placed at a disadvantage because of their sex or ethnic background. Instead, there is strong evidence indicating the "denial of disadvantage" (Crosby, 1984), which is the tendency to minimize the extent to which one is personally harmed by the prejudice and discrimination that affects one's membership group.

Research has also shown that when a victim who has been in denial has an epiphany about the extent to which they are disadvantaged, the results can be quite explosive (Crosby & Ropp, 2002). With the policy of affirmative action, an affirmative action officer scrutinizes data looking for patterns of discrimination (without considering intent) so that corrective actions can be taken without arousing feelings of disgruntlement among people in organizations.

Equal Opportunity

The end goal of affirmative action is to enhance true equality in the United States. The general definition of affirmative action makes clear that the philosophical basis of affirmative action is wholly consistent with seeing affirmative action as a non-passive way to assure that people from all ethnic backgrounds are fairly treated. In some senses, affirmative action is simply one form, and a very vigorous one, of the time-honored American policy of equal opportunity. On the issue of equality, opponents of affirmative action have made a simple distinction. They contrast equality of opportunity and equality of outcome (Sowell, 2004). Affirmative action, they say, tries to guarantee equality of outcome, something that seems vaguely un-American (Connerly, 1995). At first glance, it is very hard to see any fault in the reasoning of the opponents of affirmative action.

A moment of reflection, however, allows us to differentiate between things that are mechanistically identical and things that are substantively similar. Imagine that John and Susan are going to run a foot race. Should they not have the same shoes? Would not it be unfair to require Susan to wear high-heeled shoes while John wears sturdy wing-tips? But, even as we decide that John and Susan should wear the same shoes, we decide what we mean by "the same." In a purely mechanistic view, the shoes should be the same in every way: if John gets canvas running shoes, so must Susan; and if Susan is given a size 5 shoe, then so must John be given a size 5 shoe. However, it is much more sensible to strive for substantive similarity, by which both John and Susan will be issued shoes that fit their feet (large for John and small for Susan). An additional athletic metaphor is useful for those who wish to compare the fairness of affirmative action and of "equal opportunity." Imagine that you wish to select members of the track team without regard to sex or ethnic origin, but only on the basis of how quickly people run. Someone who runs a mile in 5 minutes should be admitted to the team ahead of someone who runs a mile in 6 minutes. If there are a limited number of spaces on the team, the 6-minute runner should be eliminated. That is how "equal opportunity" works. But what if you learn that the slower runner was running a mile up a mountain while the faster runner was running a mile downhill? Is it still sensible and fair to bring the 5-minute runner on the team ahead of the 6-minute runner? Like the coach who looks not only at performance (e.g., the time to run a mile) but also at the circumstances (e.g., the terrain), those who implement affirmative action are forced to look beyond the simple appearances and must instead engage in more thoughtful and difficult determinations.

If "equal opportunity" is unreflective about issues of similarity, it also makes naïve assumptions about power. Specifically, policies of equal opportunity assume that it is equally easy for people to voice complaints as it is to voice compliments. Equal opportunity policies also implicitly assume that all individuals have equal access to hiring and promotion agents and have equal credibility. Opportunities, in other words, are assumed to be equal unless one can identify someone who has intentionally made them unequal.

Affirmative action also differs from "equal opportunity" in the degree to which the former emphasizes structures and the latter emphasizes individuals

(Crosby, 1994). According to "equal opportunity," people create and maintain fair systems simply by their intention to do so. Affirmative action, in contrast, acknowledges that many times unfairness can occur even though no one in the current situation is prejudiced.

An example of a highly effective affirmative action program involved an intervention made on behalf of women who had a desire to be fighter pilots. The army had forbidden women from flying expensive planes because they genuinely believed the evidence that women regain consciousness after a plunge through space less quickly than men do. The evidence had been produced by the apparently objective means of spinning individual women and men, wearing anti-gravity suits, in a simulation machine and measuring the time (in milliseconds) that they required to regain consciousness after a simulated loss of altitude. Although no one had intended to discriminate against the female flyers, a discriminatory practice had occurred as a result of cost-consciousness and thoughtlessness about gender issues. Specifically, the anti-gravity suits worn by the women had been made for men, not women. Thus, for instance, a 5'10" woman who was tested wore an anti-gravitational suit made for a 5'10" man. Anti-gravitational suits help people regain consciousness through the use of pressure on the leg. As the average woman has longer legs than the average man of the same height, the anti-gravitational suits literally fit the women less well than they fit the men. The apparently slower recovery time of women turned out to be the fault of the ill-fitting suits, but until someone affirmatively acted on behalf of the women, the fault appeared to lie in the physiology of the female body (Crosby, 1996).

An extension of the debate over equality is the debate over race consciousness and race blindness. Race blindness is an approach that is theoretically possible for those who endorse equal opportunity. In theory, with equal opportunity, one can simply let everyone apply for the job or seek admission, and the decisions about hiring or admitting candidates can be made without knowing whether the candidates are male or female, black, brown, or white. Race blindness is not possible, even in theory, with the policy of affirmative action. One cannot monitor to see that people from targeted ethnic groups are represented in proper proportion unless one takes cognizance of people's ethnic groups.

Proponents of affirmative action often acknowledge the awkwardness of endorsing race-consciousness, given the end goal of establishing equality among all ethnic groups. Proponents also note the salutary effects of marking everyone's ethnicity. No longer should Americans differentiate between "people" and "ethnic minority people," with the unstated implication that real "people" are all white. By marking some people as "ethnic minority" and others as "ethnic majority," we begin to make it possible to acknowledge white privilege. Recognition of the advantages that are automatically granted to whites in America—a recognition that is fostered by the policy of affirmative action and often impeded by policy of equal opportunity—is essential if we are to devise methods of measuring and rewarding merit.

In short, affirmative action, as contrasted with simple equal opportunity policies, is effortful not only in a practical sense but also in terms of cognition. Affirmative action is more effective than equal opportunity, but it takes some reflection to see why. To appreciate the policy of affirmative action, one has to devote some thought to issues of equality, differentiating between mechanistic formations and substantive ones. The appreciation of affirmative action, furthermore, rests on a sophisticated understanding of the role of race in America and on attention to structural and situational factors that affect performance and that influence how much one can use present performance as a prediction for further performance.

Making the Connection

Given the contrast between affirmative action and "equal opportunity," it is not at all surprising that affirmative action should be unpopular among those who think about the disadvantages and problems of ethnic minority people in simplistic terms. Nor is it surprising that affirmative action sits poorly with those who explain the disadvantages and problems of ethnic minority individuals in dispositional, rather than situational, terms. As simplistic and dispositional explanations of black disadvantage and of black misbehavior increase among whites as racial prejudice increases, the link between racial prejudice and opposition to affirmative action seems almost inevitable.

Several authors have wondered what might be done to increase the endorsement of affirmative action among Americans. Pratkanis and Turner (1996, 1999), for example, have identified a set of practices that might increase the popularity of affirmative action plans among employees of companies. Among other things, Pratkanis and Turner urge employers to let it be known when a person of color or a white woman is promoted to high position that standards were not lowered by advertising the accomplishments of the person who was promoted.

One clear implication of our work is that strong acceptance of affirmative action will be limited as long as people harbor prejudices and as long as they gravitate toward simplistic outlooks and dispositional explanations. Thoughtful and clever strategies such as the ones proposed by Pratkanis and Turner are likely to have little impact on employees who long for simple slogans, who shy away from situational explanations, and who harbor racial prejudices.

Our work also suggests an interesting possibility. Perhaps it is possible to train people to think more complexly. Perhaps, people can learn to eschew simplistic explanations and be trained to think in structural or situational terms. Some would say that such training should be at the core of a college education.

But, whether training in cognitive complexity is or is not an essential feature of the college curriculum, it may hold the key to some related processes, helping both to increase the endorsement of affirmative action policies and to decrease the persistence of racism.

References

Aberson, C. L. (2003). Support for race-based affirmative action: Self-interest and procedural justice. *Journal of Applied Social Psychology, 33*, 1212–1225.

Adarand Constructors v. Pena (93-1841), 515 U.S. 200 (1995).

Antaki, C. (1988). Structures of belief and justification. In C. Antaki (Ed.), *Analyzing everyday explanation* (pp. 60–73). London: Sage publications.

Arriola, K. R. J., & Cole, E. R. (2001). Framing the affirmative action debate: Attitudes toward out-group members and white identity. *Journal of Applied Social Psychology, 31*, 2462–2483.

Ashenfelter, O., & Heckman, J. (1976). Measuring the effect of an anti-discrimination program. In J. Blum & O. Ashenfelter (Eds.), *Evaluating the labor market effects of social programs* (pp. 47–89). Princeton, NJ: Princeton University Press.

Ayres, I., & Brooks, R. (2005). Does affirmative action reduce the number of Black lawyers? *Stanford Law Review, 57*, 1807–1855.

Bendick, M. Jr., & Egan, M. L. (1999). Adding testing to the nation's portfolio of information on employment discrimination. In M. Fix & M. A. Turner (Eds.), *A national report card on discrimination in America: The role of testing* (pp. 47–68). Washington, D.C.: The Urban Institute.

Bobo, L. (1998). Race, interests, and beliefs about affirmative action: Unanswered questions and new directions. *American Behavioral Scientist, 41*, 985–1003.

Bobo, L., & Kluegel J. R. (1993). Opposition to race-targeting: Self-interest, stratification ideology, or racial attitudes? *American Sociological Review, 58*, 443–464.

Bobo, L., & Smith, R. A. (1994). Antipoverty policy, affirmative action, and racial attitudes. In S. H. Danziger, G. D. Sandefu, & D. H. Weinberg (Eds.), *Confronting poverty: Prescriptions for change* (pp. 365–395). Cambridge, MA: Harvard University Press.

Bobo, L., Kluegel, Jr., & Smith, R.A. (1997). Laissez-faire racism: The crystallization of a kinder, gentler, antiblack ideology. In S. A. Tuch & J. K. Martin (Eds.), *Racial attitudes in the 1990s: Continuity and change* (pp. 15–42). Westport, CT: Praeger.

Bobocel, D. R., Son Hing, L. S., Davey, L. M., Stanley, D. J., & Zanna, M. P. (1998). Justice-based opposition to social policies: Is it genuine? *Journal of Personality and Social Psychology, 75*, 653–669.

Bogardus, E. (1925). Measuring social distance. *Journal of Applied Sociology, 9*, 299–308.

Bowen, W. G., & Bok, D. (1998). *The shape of the river: Long-term consequences of considering race in college and university admissions.* Princeton, NJ: Princeton University Press.

Brandt, M. J., & Reyna, C. (2012). The functions of symbolic racism. *Social Justice Research, 25*, 41–60.

Brodish, A. B., Brazy, P. C., & Devine, P. G. (2008). More eyes on the prize: Variability in White Americans' perceptions of progress toward racial equality. *Personality and Social Psychology Bulletin, 34*, 513–527.

Carmines, E. G., & Layman, G. C. (1998). When prejudice matters: The impact of racial stereotypes on the racial policy preferences of Democrats and Republicans. In J. Hurwitz & M. Peffley, *Perceptions and prejudice: Race and politics in the United States* (pp. 100–134). New Haven, CT: Yale University Press.

Chambers, D. L., Clydesdale, T. T., Kidder, W. C., & Lempert, R. O. (2005). The real impact of eliminating affirmative action in American law schools: An empirical critique of Richard Sander's study. *Stanford Law Review, 57,* 1855–1898.

Connerly, W. (1995, May 3). U.C. must end affirmative action. *San Francisco Chronicle.*

Crandall, C. S. (1991). Multiple stigma and AIDS: Medical stigma and attitudes toward homosexuals and IV-drug users in AIDS-related stigmatization. *Journal of Applied Social and Community Psychology (formerly Social Behaviour),* [Special Issue on AIDS, D. Abrams (Ed.)], *1,* 165–172.

Crosby, F. J. (1984). The denial of personal discrimination. *American Behavioral Scientist, 27,* 371–386.

Crosby, F. J. (1994). Understanding affirmative action. *Basic and Applied Social Psychology, 15,* 13–41.

Crosby, F. J. (1996). A rose by any other name. In K. Arioli (Ed.), *Quoten und gleichstellung von frau und mann* (pp. 151–167). Basel, Switzerland: Helberg & Lichtenhan.

Crosby, F. J. (2000). Introduction. In F. J. Crosby & C. VanDeVeer (Eds.), *Sex, race, and merit: Debating affirmative action in education and employment* (pp. 1–10). Ann Arbor, MI: University of Michigan Press.

Crosby, F. J. (2004). *Affirmative action is dead; long live affirmative action.* New Haven, CT: Yale University Press.

Crosby, F. J., & Cordova, D. (1996). Words worth of wisdom: Toward an understanding of affirmative action. *Journal of Social Issues. 52,* 33–49.

Crosby, F. J., & Dovidio, J. F. (2008). Discrimination in America and legal strategies for reducing it. In E. Borgida & S. Fiske (Eds.), *Psychological science in court: Beyond common knowledge* (pp. 23–43). Boston, MA: Blackwell.

Crosby, F. J., & Ropp, S. (2002). Awakening to discrimination. In M. Ross & D. T. Miller, *The justice motive in everyday life* (pp. 382–396). New York: Cambridge University Press.

Crosby, F. J., Iyer, A., Clayton, S., & Downing, R. A. (2003). Affirmative action; Psychological data and the policy debates. *American Psychologist, 58,* 93–115.

Crosby, F. J., Iyer, A., & Sincharoen, S. (2006). Understanding affirmative action. *Annual Review of Psychology. 57,* 585–611.

Dawson, M. C. (2000). Slowly coming to grips with the effects of the American racial order on American policy preferences. In D. O. Sears, J. Sidanius, & L. Bobo (Eds.), *Racialized politics: The debate About racism in America* (pp. 344–357). Chicago, IL: University of Chicago Press.

Devine, P. G. (1989). Stereotypes and prejudice: Their automatic and controlled components. *Journal of Personality and Social Psychology, 56,* 5–18.

Einhorn, H. J., & Hogarth, R. M. (1986). Judging probable cause. *Psychological Bulletin, 99,* 3–19.

Evett, S. R., Devine, P. G., Hirt, E. R., & Price, J. (1994). The role of the hypothesis and the evidence in the trait hypothesis testing process. *Journal of Experimental Social Psychology, 30,* 456–481.

Federico, C. M., & Sidanius, J. (2002a). Racism, ideology, and affirmative action revisited: The antecedents and consequences of "principled objections" to affirmative action. *Journal of Personality and Social Psychology, 82*, 488–502.

Federico, C. M., & Sidanius, J. (2002b). Sophistication and the antecedents of whites' racial policy attitudes: Racism, ideology, and affirmative action in America. *Public Opinion Quarterly, 66*, 145–176.

Geiser, S., & Studley, R. (2001). *UC and the SAT: Predictive validity and differential impact of the SATI and SAT II at the University of California*. Retrieved November 11, 2003 from: http://www.ucop.edu/sas/research/.

Glaser, J. M. (1994). Back to the black belt: Racial environment and white racial attitude in the South. *Journal of Politics, 56*, 21–41.

Golden, H., Hinkle, S., & Crosby, F. J. (2001). Reactions to affirmative action: Substance and semantics. *Journal of Applied Social Psychology, 31*, 73–88.

Gratz v. Bollinger, 539 U.S. 244, 123 S. Ct. 2411. 2003.

Gross, K., Aday, S., & Brewer, P. R. (2004). A panel study of media effects on political and social trust after September 11, 2001. *The Harvard International Journal of Press/Politics, 9*(4), 49–73.

Grutter v. Bollinger, 529 U.S. 306, 123 S. Ct. 2325. 2003.

Harrison, D. A., Kravitz, D. A., Mayer, D. M., Leslie, L. M., & Dalit, L. A. (2006). Understanding attitudes toward affirmative action programs in employment: Summary and meta-analysis of 35 years of research. *Journal of Applied Psychology. 95*(1), 1013–1036.

Hayes-James, E., Brief, A. P., Dietz, J., & Cohen, R. R. (2001). Prejudice matters: Understanding reactions of whites to affirmative action programs targeted to benefit blacks. *Journal of Applied Psychology, 86*, 1120–1128.

Heider, F. (1958). *The psychology of interpersonal relations*. Hillsdale, NJ: Erlbaum.

Herring, C., & Collins, S. M. (1995). Retreat from equal opportunity? The case of affirmative action. Crisis. In M. P. Smith & J. R. Feagin (Eds.), *The bubbling cauldron: Race, ethnicity, and the urban crisis* (pp. 163–181). Minneapolis, MN: University of Minnesota Press.

Hewstone, M. (1990). The "ultimate attribution error"? A review of the literature on intergroup causal attribution. *European Journal of Social Psychology, 20*, 311–335.

Holzer, H., & Neumark, D. (1999). *Assessing affirmative action*. National Bureau of Economic Research, Inc.

Hughes, M. (1997). Symbolic racism, old-fashioned racism, and Whites' opposition to affirmative action. In S. A. Tuch & J. K. Martin (Eds.), *Racial attitudes in the 1990s: Continuity and change* (pp. 45–75). Westport, CT: Praeger.

Hurwitz, J., & Pefflley, M. (1998). *Perception and prejudice: Race and politics in the United States*. New Haven, CT: Yale University Press.

Johnston, L. C., & Macrae, C. N. (1994). Changing social stereotypes: The case of the information seeker. *European Journal of Social Psychology, 24*, 581–592.

Islam, M. R., & Hewstone, M. (1993). Intergroup attributions and affective consequences in majority and minority groups. *Journal of Personality and Social Psychology, 64*, 936–950.

Jacobson, C. K. (1985). Resistance to affirmative action: Self-interest or racism? *Journal of Conflict Resolution, 29*, 306–329.

Jencks, C. (1998). Racial bias in testing. In C. Jencks & M. Phillips (Eds.), *The Black-White test score gap* (pp. 55–85). Washington, D.C.: Brookings Institution.

Kane, E. W., & Whipkey, K. J. (2009). Predictors of public support for gender-related affirmative action: Interests, gender attitudes, and stratification beliefs. *Public Opinion Quarterly, 73*, 233–254.

Katz, I., & Hass, R. G. (1988). Racial ambivalence and American value conflict: correlational and priming studies of dual cognitive structures. *Journal of Personality and Social Psychology, 55*, 893–905.

Kinder, D.R. (1998). Attitudes and action in the realm of politics. In D. T. Gilbert, S. T. Fiske, & G. Lindzey (Eds.), *The Handbook of Social Psychology* (4th ed., Vol. 2) (pp. 778–867). Boston, MA: McGraw-Hill.

Kinder, D. R., & Sanders, L. (1996). *Divided by color: Racial politics and democratic ideals.* Chicago, IL: University of Chicago Press.

Klayman, J., & Ha, Y-W. (1987). Confirmation, disconfirmation, and information in hypothesis testing. *Psychological Review, 94*, 211–228.

Konrad, A. M., & Linnehan, F. (1995a). Formalized HRM structures: Coordinating equal employment opportunity or concealing organizational practices? *Academy of Management Journal, 38*, 787–820.

Konrad, A.M., & Linnehan, F. (1995b). Race and sex differences in line managers' reactions to equal employment opportunity and affirmative action interventions. *Group and Organization Management, 20*, 409–439.

Lehman, B. J., & Crano, W. D. (2002). The pervasive effects of vested interest on attitude-criterion consistency in political judgment. *Journal of Experimental Social Psychology, 38*, 101–112.

Lempert, R. O., Chambers, D. L., & Adams, T. K. (2000a). Michigan's minority graduates in practice: The river runs through law school. *Law and Social Inquiry, 25*, 395–505.

Lempert, R. O., Chambers, D. L., & Adams, T. K. (2000b). Law school affirmative action: An empirical study of Michigan's minority graduates in practice: Answers to methodological queries. *Law and Social Inquiry, 25*, 585–597.

Lepore, L., & Brown, R. (1997). Category and stereotype activation: Is prejudice inevitable? *Journal of Personality and Social Psychology, 72*, 275–287.

Little, B. L., Murry, W. D., & Wimbush, J. C. (1998). Perceptions of workplace affirmative action plans: A psychological perspective. *Group and Organizational Management, 23*, 27–47.

Mack, D. A., Johnson, C. D., Green, T. D., Parisi, A. G., & Thomas, K. M. (2002). Motivation to control prejudice as a mediator of identity and affirmative action attitudes. *Journal of Applied Social Psychology, 32*, 934–964.

McConahay, J. B., Hardee, B. B., & Batts, V. (1981). Has racism declined in America? It depends on who is asking and what is asked. *Journal of Conflict Resolution. 25*(4), 563–579.

Neville, H. A., Awad, G. H., Brooks, J. E., Flores, M. P., & Bluemel, J. (2013). Color-blind racial ideology: Theory, training, and measurement implications in psychology. *American Psychologist, 68*, 455–466.

Nosworthy, G. J., Lea, J. A., & Lindsay, R. C. L. (1995). Opposition to affirmative action: Racial affect and traditional value predictors across four programs. *Journal of Applied Social Psychology, 25*, 314–337.

Oh, E., Choi, C., Neville, H. A., Anderson, C. J., & Landrum-Brown, J. (2010). Beliefs about affirmative action: A test of the group self-interest and racism beliefs models. *Journal of Diversity in Higher Education, 3*, 163–176.

Peterson, C., Semmel, A., von Baeyer, C., Abramson, L., Metalsky, G. I., & Seligman, M. (1982). The attributional style questionnaire. *Cognitive Therapy and Research, 6,* 287–300.

Pettigrew, T. F. (1979). The ultimate attribution error: Extending Allport's cognitive analysis of prejudice. *Personality and Social Psychology Bulletin, 5,* 461–476.

Pratkanis, A. R., & Turner, M. E. (1996). The proactive removal of discriminatory barriers: Affirmative action as effective help. *Journal of Social Issues, 52,* 111–133.

Pratkanis, A. R., & Turner, M. E. (1999). The significance of affirmative action for the souls of White folk: Further implications of a helping model. *Journal of Social Issues, 55,* 787–815.

Regan, D. T., & Totten, J. (1975). Empathy and attribution: turning observers into actors. *Journal of Personality and Social Psychology, 32,* 850–856.

Renner, K. E., & Moore, T. (2004). The more things change, the more they stay the same: The elusive search for racial equity in higher education. *Analyses of Social Issues and Public Policy, 4,* 227–241.

Reskin, B. F. (1998). *The realities of affirmative action in employment.* Washington, D.C.: American Sociological Association.

Reyna, C., Henry, P. J., Korfmacher, W., & Tucker, A. (2005). Examining the principles in principled conservativism: The role of responsibility stereotypes as cues for deservingness in racial policy decisions. *Journal of Personality and Social Psychology, 90,* 109–128.

Rhode, D. L., & Williams, J. C. (2007). Legal perspectives on employment discrimination. In F. J. Crosby, P. Stockdale, & A. Ropp (Eds.), *Sex discrimination in the workplace: Multidisciplinary perspectives* (pp. 235–270). London: Blackwell.

Sander, R. H. (2004). A systemic analysis of affirmative action in American law schools. *Stanford Law Review, 57,* 367–483.

Sawires, J. N., & Peacock, M. J. (2000). Symbolic racism and voting behavior on proposition 209. *Journal of Applied Social Psychology, 30,* 2092–2099.

Sears, D. O., & Henry, P. J. (2003). The origins of symbolic racism. *Journal of Personality and Social Psychology, 85,* 259–275.

Sears, D. O., & Henry, P. J. (2005). Over thirty years later: A contemporary look at symbolic racism. In Mark Zanna (Ed.), *Advances in Experimental Social Psychology, 37,* 95–150. San Diego, CA: Elsevier Academic Press.

Sears, D. O., & Valentino, N. A. (1997). Politics matters: Political events as catalysts for pre-adult socialization. *American Political Science Review, 91,* 45–65.

Sears, D. O., Van Laar, C., Carrillo, M., & Kosterman, R. (1997). Is it really racism? The origins of White Americans' opposition to race-targeted policies. *Public Opinion Quarterly, 61,* 16–53.

Shteynberg, G., Leslie, L. M., Knight, A. P., & Mayer, D. M. (2011). But affirmative action hurts us! Race-related beliefs shape perceptions of white disadvantage and policy unfairness. *Organizational Behavior and Human Decision Processes, 115,* 1–12.

Sidanius, J., Devereux, E., & Pratto, F. (1992). A comparison of symbolic racism theory and social dominance theory as explanations for racial policy attitudes. *Journal of Social Psychology, 132,* 377–395.

Sidanius, J., Pratto, F., & Bobo, L. (1996). Racism, conservatism, affirmative action, and intellectual sophistication: A matter of principled conservatism or group dominance? *Journal of Personality and Social Psychology, 70,* 476–490.

Sidanius, J., Singh, P., Hetts, J. J., & Federico, C. M. (2000). It's not affirmative action, it's the Blacks: The continuing relevance of race in American politics. In D. O. Sears, J. Sidanius, & L. Bobo (Eds.), *Racialized politics: The debate about racism in America* (pp. 191–235). Chicago, IL: The University of Chicago Press.

Smith, S. P. (1976). Government wage differentials by sex. *Journal of Human Resources, 11,* 185–199.

Sniderman, P. M., & Piazza, T. (1993). *The Scar of Race.* Cambridge, MA: Harvard University Press.

Snyder, M., & Gangestad, S. (1981). Hypothesis-testing processes. In J. H. Harvey, W. Ickes, & R. F. Kidd (Eds.), *New directions in attribution research* (Vol. 3) (pp. 171–198). Hillsdale, NJ: Erlbaum.

Snyder, M., & Swann, W. B., Jr. (1978). Behavioral confirmation in social interaction: From social perception to social reality. *Journal of Experimental Social Psychology, 14,* 148–162.

Snyder, M., Campbell, B. H., & Preston, E. (1982). Testing hypotheses about human nature: Assessing knowledge. *Journal of Personality and Social Psychology, 39,* 222–234.

Sowell, T. (2004). *Affirmative action around the world: An empirical study.* New Haven, CT: Yale University Press.

Stoker, L. (1998). Understanding whites' resistance to affirmative action: The role of principled commitments and racial prejudice. In J. Hurwitz & M. Peffley (Eds.), *Perception and prejudice: Race and politics in the United States* (pp. 135–70). New Haven: Yale University Press.

Strolovitch, D. Z. (1998). Playing favorites: Public attitudes toward race- and gender-targeted anti-discrimination policy. *NWSA Journal, 10,* 27–53.

Tolbert, C. J., & Grummel, J. A. (2003). Revisiting the racial threat hypothesis: White voter support for California's proposition 209. *State Politics and Policy Quarterly, 3,* 183–202.

Tougas, F., & Veilleux, F. (1990). The response of men to affirmative action strategies for women: The study of a predictive model. *Canadian Journal of Behavioural Science, 22,* 424–432.

Tougas, F., Brown, R., Beaton, A. M., & Joly, S. (1995). Neosexism: Plus ça change, plus c'est pareil. *Personality and Social Psychology Bulletin, 21,* 842–849.

Tougas, F., Crosby, F. J., Joly, S., & Pelchat, D. (1995). Men's attitudes toward affirmative action: Justice and intergroup relations at the crossroads. *Social Justice Research, 8,* 57–71.

Tuch, S. A., & Hughes, M. (1996). Whites' racial policy attitudes. *Social Science Quarterly, 77,* 723–745.

Vescio, T. K. (1996). The attributional underpinnings of prejudice. Unpublished dissertation. The University of Kansas. Lawrence, KS.

Vescio, T. K., & Biernat, M. (1999). When stereotype-based expectations impair perceivers' performance: The effect of prejudice, race, and target quality on judgments and perceiver performance. *European Journal of Social Psychology, 29,* 961–969.

Weiner, B. (1979). A theory of motivation for some classroom experiences. *Journal of Educational Psychology, 71,* 3–25.

Weiner, B. (1986). *An attributional theory of motivation and emotion.* New York: Springer-Verlag.

Wilkins, D. B. (2005). A systematic response to systemic disadvantage: A response to Sander. *Stanford Law Review, 57,* 1915–1961.

Williams, D. R., Jackson, J. S., Brown, T. N., Torres, M., Forman, T. A., & Brown, K. (1999). Traditional and contemporary prejudice and urban Whites' support for affirmative action and government help. *Social Problems, 46,* 503–527.

Wittenbrink, B., Gist, P. L., & Hilton, J. L. (1997). Structural properties of stereotypic knowledge and their influences on the construal of social situations. *Journal of Personality and Social Psychology, 72,* 526–543.

Yogeeswaran, K., & Dasgupta, N. (2014). The devil is in the details: Abstract versus concrete construals of multiculturalism differentially impact intergroup relations. *Journal of Personality and Social Psychology, 106,* 772–789.

12

"FOREVER CHANGED?"

Some Surprising Findings About U.S. Public Opinion After the Attacks of 9/11/2001 on the U.S.

Randall K. Thomas, Jon A. Krosnick, Natalie J. Shook, and I-Chant A. Chiang

> Nearly nine months have passed since the day that forever changed our country. Debris from what was once the World Trade Center has been cleared away in a hundred thousand truckloads. The west side of the Pentagon looks almost as it did on September the 10th. And as children finish school and families prepare for summer vacations, for many, life seems almost normal. Yet we are a different nation today—sadder and stronger, less innocent and more courageous, more appreciative of life, and for many who serve our country, more willing to risk life in a great cause.
>
> (President George W. Bush, Television Address to the Nation, June 6, 2002)

On September 11, 2001, terrorist attacks on US soil left a permanent scar on the land and in our everyday lives. Americans turned their full attention to understanding what happened and why. In addition to the immediate military response in Afghanistan and Iraq, many changes in domestic policies resulted from the terrorist attacks, ranging from the creation of the Department of Homeland Security to added security measures in airports. The 9/11 terrorist attacks are widely believed to have had a profound and long-lasting effect on public opinion in the United States. In a now-familiar phrase, political leaders often evoke the tragedies of that day to emphasize that "everything changed"[1] after the attacks. Conventional wisdom dictates that because Americans lost loved ones, their jobs, and their collective sense of safety, so too changed their political opinions about national security and counterterrorism. It is clear from the proliferation of polls following the attacks that there was an increase in support for American policies and symbols, perhaps most notably in the public approval of President Bush's job performance, which soared to unprecedented levels of enthusiasm.[2] However, as we write this more than a decade after 9/11, is there any evidence that American public opinion was fundamentally transformed? Despite anecdotal evidence that our lives have changed, what evidence do we have that American attitudes toward government policies have changed in any permanent manner? In this chapter we explore how public opinion regarding counterterrorism and foreign affairs changed over time and how this change compares to other policy areas, both related and unrelated to the key area of terrorism.

Pre-Post 9/11 Public Opinion Polling

Because of the unique nature of an event such as 9/11, an immediate shift in public opinion can certainly be expected. But how did it change? One challenge we often face in tracking public opinion change over time and events is obtaining consistent measurement—polling immediately following a powerful event is often conducted post-hoc and, as a result, with unique question and response wording focused on the particular event. Additionally, public opinion polls are often sponsored by news media that are looking to use polls as background for stories and analysis, helping provide a social norming and comparison function, as well as an attempt to draw more readership interest (selling more newspapers or getting more hits on websites). As a consequence, however, this often leads to substantial data in multiple waves *following* the event, but with limited or no similar data collected *prior* to the event, making pre-post comparisons difficult and limiting our ability to discern which factors most affect public opinion change. Rarely do we find that the same questions with the same responses, which are sufficiently specific and relevant to the event, have been administered prior to and immediately following the event of interest. And, when there are relevant questions administered before and after the event, the items are often worded more generally or about related topics, rather than items targeted specifically to the event itself. There are examples of similar items that are administered over time (like the American National Election Study—ANES), but due to the fielding constraints the studies are fielded at time intervals that cannot pick up the immediate and profound change in public opinion as a result of events that may take place between fielding waves.

Changes in perceptions of threat and risk of terrorist actions are related to changes in support for actions to fight terrorism (Gadarian, 2010), most likely through the increased importance attached to the topic, which can lead to public opinion shifts that would be predicted to be relatively stable (Krosnick, 1990). Among the relevant items administered before the events of 9/11 and immediately after, Jenkins-Smith and Herron (2005) found that the perceived terrorist threat rose from a value of 6.60 (on a 0 to 10 scale) in 1997 to 8.27 in the two months following 9/11 and then dropped to 8.00 in 2002 (the 2002 data were from a subset of respondents who were recontacted from the 9/11 wave). ABC News administered an item related to the perceived threat of terrorism which was reported from 1995 to 2009—"How concerned are you about the possibility there will be more major terrorist attacks in this country? Is that something that worries you a great deal, somewhat, not too much, or not at all?"[3] While 21% indicated "A great deal" in 1997, 49% selected this response immediately following the attacks of 9/11. Further, 22% indicated "A great deal" in September 2002 and 18% selected this response in September 2008.

The *Washington Post* (in conjunction with the Pew Research Center and ABC News for different waves) administered a question related to prevention of terrorist attacks in 1997, immediately following the events of 9/11, and through 2013.[4] To the question, "How much confidence do you have in the ability of the U.S. government to prevent further terrorist attacks against Americans in this country?" 10% of respondents indicated "A great deal" in 1997, while 35% indicated "A great deal" immediately following 9/11, and 17% indicated "A great deal" in November 2001, with a low of 12% reported in September 2002, and most recently 15% in April 2013. *Perceptions of threat* and *confidence in preventing terrorist attacks*, however, are precursors to action (Huddy, Feldman, Taber, & Lahav, 2005) but are not equivalent to supporting or opposing increased action directed at eliminating terrorism.

There were a number of polls assessing specific actions that could be used to fight terrorism. Sullivan and Hendriks (2009) reviewed a number of studies conducted before and after 9/11 that asked Americans about their willingness to sacrifice civil liberties to fight terrorism. They found a strong increase in their willingness to sacrifice immediately following 9/11, but then observed a noticeable decline in their willingness in the years following. As an example, a CBS News Poll found that 74% of Americans supported giving up some of their personal freedoms to make the country safe from terrorist attacks in September 2001 and rose to 79% in October 2001, but this number dropped to 65% in January 2006.[5] However, Jenkins-Smith and Herron (2005) did not detect much change in support for curtailing freedom of speech (one specific aspect of civil liberties) when they compared a survey from 1995 with one conducted immediately after 9/11. These findings indicate that events such as 9/11 may have differential effects on giving up civil liberties, depending on the nature of the specific types of freedoms (e.g. freedom of speech, of assembly, of unwarranted search, etc.) held as a core belief in the foundation of the United States (cf. Davis & Silver, 2004).

Somewhat less related to taking action to fight terrorism, in a series of Gallup polls, the belief that the U.S. should take a leading role in world affairs rose following 9/11 then dropped in the following years (starting at 16% in February 2001, rising to 26% in February 2002, dropping to 16% in February 2011[6]). Similarly, the NBC News/Wall Street Journal found a related change—37% felt that the U.S. should become more active in world affairs in September 2001 dropping to 19% in April 2014.[7] In addition, Gallup found that satisfaction with the U.S. in the world today reached a peak of 71% in February 2002 to a low of 30% in February 2008 and then rising slightly to 35% in February 2010.[8]

Though somewhat tangential, all polls tracking presidential approval picked up an immediate and strong increase in presidential approval following 9/11 (this "rally around the President" effect, or more generally "rally around the flag" effect, had been observed in earlier polling following attacks or sudden external challenges to the U.S.—Chapman & Reiter, 2004; Kam & Ramos, 2008; Mueller, 1970). These same polls also showed significant declines in presidential approval in the years following 9/11. In addition, this approval corresponded to significant changes in perceptions that the rest of the world respected Bush, with a peak in February 2002 of 75% following 9/11 and dropping to 33% by February 2006.[9] This further generalized to confidence in the U.S. to handle international problems, with a peak of 83% saying "A great deal/Fair amount" in October 2001 to a low of 59% in February 2006.[10]

Post-Only 9/11 Public Opinion Polling

As we indicated, there were a larger number of studies that fielded periodically in the post-9/11 period, and though they had no pre-9/11 baseline levels with which to compare results, they employed the same methodology and questions across the waves following 9/11. Most of these studies obtained similar results to those obtained in the pre-post 9/11 studies in the period following 9/11, with a peak immediately following 9/11 and then a drop-off at different rates over waves subsequent to 9/11. Around the precursors of the central issue (taking action to stop terror attacks), a number of polling organizations found similar results about perceived likelihood of terrorist attacks—there were higher levels immediately following 9/11 with a decline over time (Davis & Silver, 2004). The USA Today/Gallup poll also found that 40% of respondents perceived the likelihood of acts of terrorism in the next several weeks as "very likely" in October 2001, which then dropped to a low of 4% in June 2005.[11] CBS News found similar results for a question about likelihood of another terrorist attack within the next few months—a peak of 53% of respondents indicated "very likely" in October 2001 dropping to a low of 5% in January 2009.[12] And polling by ABC News/Washington Post found that those concerned "a great deal" about the possibility of more major terrorist attacks in the U.S. dropped from a high of 41% in October 2001 to 18% in October 2008. They also found that 32% thought that the U.S. campaign against terror was going "very well" in January 2002, which dropped to 7% in September 2006.[13]

Related to how authorities were handling terrorist threats, a number of polls indicated a gradual but dramatic decline. CBS News found that approval for President George W. Bush's handling of the war on terror reached a peak of

90% approval in December 2001 and dropped to a low of 39% in June 2007.[14] With a similar item, ABC News/Washington Post found a peak in October 2001 of 92% approval, dropping to a low of 40% in September 2007.[15] In addition, those thinking the U.S. and its allies were winning the war on terror peaked at 66% in January 2002 and dropped to a low of 29% in June 2007, according to the Gallup Poll.[16] Further, ABC News found that 71% of respondents felt that the United States was doing all it reasonably could do to try to prevent further terrorist attacks in October 2001, which dropped to a low of 38% in September 2006.[17] CBS News/New York Times found that respondents' confidence in the ability of the U.S. government to protect its citizens from future terrorist attacks "a great deal" peaked in September 2001 at 35% and dropped to a low of 16% in June 2002.[18] The Pew Research Center likewise found that 38% thought that the job that the U.S. government was doing to reduce the threat of terrorism was "very well" in October 2001 and dropped to a low of 16% in June 2002.[19]

In post-only 9/11 studies, the highest values were obtained in measures most proximal to the 9/11 attacks with declines in subsequent waves (e.g., measures of trust—Gross, Aday, & Brewer, 2004). Jenkins-Smith and Herron (2005) examined support for using conventional military force and found that it was higher immediately following 9/11 followed by a significant decline one year later (4.37 to 3.49 on a 0 to 6 scale). Similarly, in Fox News/Opinion Dynamics polling from October 2001 to April 2004, approval for reinstituting the military draft to help fight terrorism declined from a high of 76% to 41% across 5 waves.[20]

Background for Current Study

As we have seen, across a number of different issues, and for both polls that tracked the same items pre-9/11 and post-9/11, as well as those that measured post-9/11 only, there appeared to be a peak in public opinion immediately following 9/11. This was followed with a decline, for some issues relatively rapidly, whereas for others the decline took place over a much longer period of time.

One of the difficulties with the number of polls cited is that the items are often singular and hard to compare across polling organizations, with varying item and response wording, uneven time intervals for the different items, and varying sampling methodologies. The study we report here used the same set of items, same methodology, and same sample source administered over the Internet over a series of waves before and after 9/11 to help determine more accurately the effects of the events of 9/11 on public opinion across a wider range of issues, some centrally related to the central issue (stopping terrorist groups), some less related (e.g. making the U.S. the most powerful nation), and some unrelated (e.g. education) to determine shifts in public opinion due to the attacks of 9/11.

Methodology

We administered web-based questionnaires in 16 waves over an eight-year period from June 2000 to October 2007. Samples were randomly drawn from a large national pool of American adults recruited by Harris Interactive, which had developed a multi-million member non-probability panel of respondents who had volunteered to participate in web-based surveys when sent an email invitation. Samples drawn from this non-probability panel have yielded results comparable to those obtained by telephone with probability-based samples (Thomas, Krane, Taylor, & Terhanian, 2008). As one example, tracking presidential approval using the panel from 2000 to 2008 showed a correlation of .98 with aggregated results obtained by telephone interviews with RDD samples (Figure 12.1), comparable to results obtained in other polls conducted using RDD methods (e.g. AP, Fox, Quinnipiac, Time) with aggregated poll results (cf. Heatherington & Nelson, 2003).

For each wave of this study, respondents were drawn on a stratified random basis by gender (male and female), age group (18–29, 30–39, 40–49, 50 or over), and region of the country (Northeast, South, Midwest, West) to resemble proportions obtained in the U.S. Census Bureau's Current Population Survey (March supplement for each year). Having volunteered to participate in surveys on a regular basis, respondents were sent email invitations with a web link to complete the web-based questionnaire. The first wave fielded in July 2000. Table 12.1 summarizes the fielding periods and number of respondents for each wave.

FIGURE 12.1 Comparison of Harris Poll Online Presidential Evaluation with RDD Polls (values along the horizontal axis represent weeks from June 1, 2000 through May 31, 2008)

TABLE 12.1 Summary of Data Collection Wave Periods

Wave	N	Begin Field	End Field
1	1541	7/20/00	7/31/00
2	1664	10/4/00	10/17/00
3	2366	9/20/01	9/27/01
4	2202	10/8/01	10/16/01
5	2334	10/30/03	11/10/03
6	2909	11/29/03	12/12/03
7	2043	5/24/04	6/3/04
8	2470	7/22/04	7/31/04
9	3473	8/27/04	9/9/04
10	2388	10/8/04	10/21/04
11	4527	10/27/04	11/2/04
12	4715	10/11/05	10/31/05
13	2647	11/1/05	11/15/05
14	6676	7/25/06	8/8/06
15	5136	10/18/06	11/2/06
16	3871	10/24/07	11/8/07

The questionnaire had items designed to measure support for federal government policies and also asked how important respondents considered these policies. For some of the opinion questions, respondents answered using a 7-point rating scale, with response options "very good," "good," "somewhat good," "neither good nor bad," "somewhat bad," "bad," and "very bad" (see the Appendix for all question wordings). Other policy opinion questions asked respondents to indicate their preferred level of government effort to address problems, on a 5-point rating scale with response options "a lot more," "a little more," "about the same," "a little less," and "a lot less."

Policy Issue Grouping

While a larger set of policy issues was asked of respondents in Waves 1 and 2 in 2000, immediately following the attacks of 9/11, due to constraints on interview length, we reduced the number of policy issues and divided them into five groups (though the items themselves were randomly ordered in their presentation to respondents and not grouped by these issue groups). The items composing each category are listed below. The first group consisted of the "focal issue" fighting terrorism. The second group consisted of "directly protective" issues, which are clearly associated with the focal issue and are opinions concerning issues that can be directly protective of the U.S. As a consequence, changes in opinions on the focal issue would likely lead to changes in these issues. The "indirectly protective" group had issues that may be associated with the focal issue due to their long-term, and potentially indirect, relevance to protect the U.S. The fourth group, "foreign involvement" issues, reflected opinions about the involvement of the U.S. in the affairs of other nations. The final group, "domestic issues," included issues that were unassociated with terrorism or foreign affairs and more related to policies internal to the U.S. and were unlikely to be conceptually connected to the focal issue or international affairs generally. The policy issues measured by group were as follows.

Focal Issue
- Fighting Terrorism

Directly Protective Issues
- Military Spending
- Preventing the Spread of Nuclear Weapons
- Making the U.S. the Most Powerful Nation
- Building a Missile Shield
- Immigration Control
- Weakening Militaries of Our Enemies

Indirectly Protective Issues
- Strengthening the Militaries of Our Allies
- Protecting Democracies
- Changing Non-democracies into Democracies

Foreign Involvement Issues
- Giving Humanitarian Aid to Poor Countries
- Protecting Citizens of Countries from Abuse by Their Government
- Resolving Disputes Between Other Countries
- Preventing People in Other Countries from Killing Each Other
- Preventing Other Countries from Polluting

Domestic Issues
- Improving U.S. Exporting of Commercial Goods
- Outlawing Capital Punishment
- Education Spending

- Gun Control
- Fighting Crime
- Limiting Imports into the U.S.

After each question about respondents' attitudes on an issue, they were asked, "How important is this issue to you personally?" Responses were on a 5-point rating scale, with options "not important at all," "somewhat important," "important," "very important," and "extremely important."

We also asked respondents about their political party identification and political ideology. The political party identification question asked "Generally speaking, do you usually think of yourself as a/an ...?" with responses of "Republican," "Democrat," "Independent," and "Other" (with "Republican" and "Democrat" randomly alternated in order of presentation). To measure political ideology, respondents were asked: "When it comes to politics, would you describe yourself as ...?" with responses of "a liberal," "a conservative," and "neither" (the responses "liberal" and "conservative" were randomly ordered). Both the party identification and political ideology questions were subsequently branched to measure gradations of response.

Results

Weighting Methodology

Comparing data across waves presented us with some options with regard to data adjustment—did we want to represent the general population using known demographic characteristics (e.g. age, sex, region of country, education, ethnicity, and income), or did we want to compare change across time, controlling for variations in sample demographic proportions without regard to external population proportions? In the first case, weighting to U.S. demographic targets can lead to an approximation of the dynamics of the larger population of the U.S. However, because we did not have quotas for sample proportions within the survey nor did we select sample based on proportions of strata within the variables of education, income, and ethnicity, the weights we would develop could be quite extreme in order to bring the sample in line with demographic targets when using these additional variables to develop the weights. This stretching of the weights can inflate the variance of point estimates and significantly reduce the sensitivity in testing differences across waves. In addition, the demographic targets changed year over year (e.g. from 2000 to 2007 the proportion of Hispanics increased 2.8%, the proportion of those with high school or less education declined 3.1%, those having a household income greater than $100,000 increased 10.3%), and these demographic changes could result in an apparent change due to underlying demographic change rather than change in opinions due to external events. To control for demographic changes over time, we could use an analysis of covariance to partial out demographic variables after weighting (somewhat reducing even further the sensitivity of detecting differences between waves when the data were weighted) or we could weight to U.S. demographic targets based on the averages for the entire period of fielding. An alternative weighting scheme would be to weight to a sample-based common weight target (averaged over waves) to control for differences from wave to wave, but without an attempt to project to the larger U.S. population. This would lead to a minimum of inflation of the variance for point estimates and a higher sensitivity in testing differences. In comparing these weighting alternatives, we found that the point estimates based on raw data correlated with weighted point estimates over .99 for all weighting algorithms (all $ps < .0001$), and all weighted point estimates had correlations of over .99 with each other as well (all $ps < .0001$). The differences between point estimates based on raw data and those based on common demographic targets (across all waves) averaged 1.6% lower for issues and .3% lower for importance for full weights and 1.2% less for issues and .1% less for importance when weights were trimmed at .2 and 5. As a result of these analyses, and with our desire to represent the larger U.S. population, we decided to use weights using U.S. demographic targets based on the averages for the entire period of fielding and trimmed weights at .2 and .5 (out of 50,962 total respondents across all waves, 1,310 respondents—2.6%— had their weights trimmed at .2 while 1,121 respondents—2.2%—had their weights trimmed at 5). The proportions of the sample by demographic group, along with weighted proportions (employing trimmed common weights), and demographic targets by group are presented in Table 12.2. Trimming weights improved weighting efficiency to 47.2%, compared to an efficiency of 34.5% without trimming, which improved the sensitivity of significance tests as a result (since the effective base size is larger with more efficient weights).

Changes in Political Party Identification and Political Ideology

First, we were interested in any core political identity and ideology changes that may have taken place over time. Controlling for demographic differences across waves (using the trimmed average demographic weights), we saw some changes in political party identification across waves when employing the categorical measure (i.e., asking people to classify themselves as one category) as reflected in Figure 12.2. Specifically, there was an upward drift in those indicating "Other" over the waves (rising from 8.6% in July 2000 to 13.1% in October 2007) and a drop in those identifying as "Republican" (from 33.4% in July 2000 to 27.7% in October 2007), with a particularly notable drop from October 2004 to October 2005. Specifically, there was a significant reduction in the number of people who identified themselves as Republicans from 2004 to

TABLE 12.2 Average Proportions of Sample, Weighted Sample, and Demographic Targets for 2000–2007

Group	N	Sample	Trimmed demographic weight	Demographic target
Age–Sex Combination				
Male 18–29	4923	9.7%	10.6%	11.0%
Male 30–39	4895	9.6%	9.7%	9.6%
Male 40–49	5374	10.5%	10.3%	10.2%
Male 50–64	7098	13.9%	11.0%	10.6%
Male 65+	3221	6.3%	7.0%	6.9%
Female 18–29	5151	10.1%	10.5%	10.9%
Female 30–39	4788	9.4%	9.8%	9.8%
Female 40–49	4829	9.5%	10.6%	10.5%
Female 50–64	7245	14.2%	11.9%	11.3%
Female 65+	3438	6.7%	8.7%	9.2%
U.S. Region				
East	11454	22.5%	22.2%	22.2%
South	15960	31.3%	32.6%	32.8%
Midwest	12288	24.1%	23.1%	22.6%
West	11260	22.1%	22.2%	22.4%
Education				
High school grad or less	8286	16.3%	44.4%	47.9%
Some college	20862	40.9%	29.0%	27.3%
College grad—4 year	10739	21.1%	17.5%	16.7%
Postgraduate	11075	21.7%	9.1%	8.1%
Income				
Less than $15,000	3651	7.2%	9.0%	9.3%
$15,000 to $24,999	4895	9.6%	9.4%	9.3%
$25,000 to $34,999	6071	11.9%	9.7%	9.5%

Group	N	Sample	Trimmed demographic weight	Demographic target
$35,000 to $49,999	7672	15.1%	13.3%	13.0%
$50,000 to $74,999	10004	19.6%	17.8%	17.4%
$75,000 to $99,999	5546	10.9%	11.3%	11.1%
$100,000 or more	5930	11.6%	15.5%	16.3%
Decline to answer	7193	14.1%	14.0%	14.1%
Ethnicity/Race				
Hispanic	2923	5.7%	9.8%	12.0%
Black (non-Hispanic)	2643	5.2%	9.6%	11.3%
All others	45396	89.1%	80.5%	76.7%
Total N	50962			

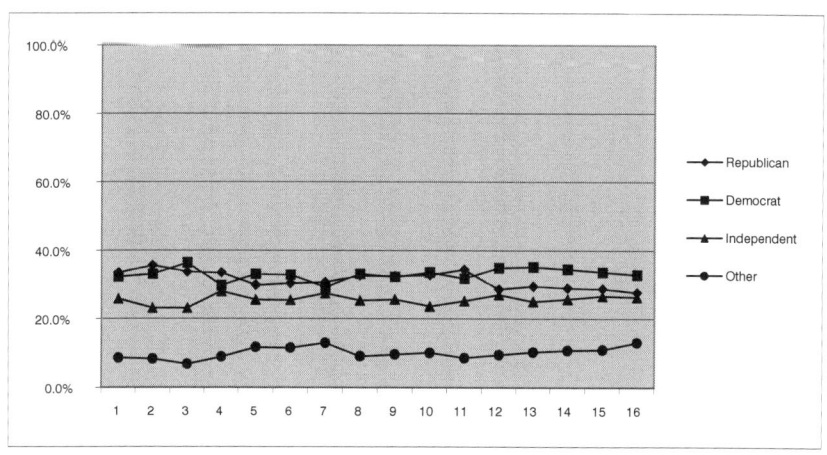

FIGURE 12.2 Proportion Identifying with Political Parties (Wave of fielding is shown as the horizontal axis, Wave 1 was June 2000, Wave 3 was September 2011, Wave 16 was October 2007. A full listing of waves and dates is in Table 12.1)

2005 (going from 34.4% in Wave 11 immediately prior to the 2004 election to 28.6% in Wave 12 one year later), which continued through the end of the study (Wave 16). Regarding specifically the events of 9/11, from October 2000 to September 2001 the net difference between Republicans and Democrats shifted 5.3% (Republicans going down from 35.6% to 33.7% and Democrats going up from 33.0% to 36.4%), which seems somewhat paradoxical in that support for President Bush rose dramatically following the events of 9/11. However, there appeared to be somewhat of a snap-back going from September 2001 to October 2001, with those identifying as "Democrat" dropping from 36.4% to 29.7% and those identifying as "Independent" going from 23.1% to 28.0% (no shift for those identifying as "Republican"—33.7% vs. 33.4%).

Looking at the branched 7 category measure of political party identification showed a small but significant shift over time (Figure 12.4). These results paralleled the significant drop in identification with "Republican" as reflected in the mean political party ID scale (going from 3.92 in Wave 11 to 4.19 in Wave 12), but there were no significant differences pre-post 9/11.

Regarding shifts in political ideology (Figure 12.3), we saw increases in those indicating "Conservative" going from July 2000 to October 2000 (33.9% to 37.1%) and a drop from October 2001 to October 2003 (34.0% to 28.8%; with an increase in "Neither" going from 45.2% to 49.8%). The average political ideology as measured on the branched 7 category scale, however, showed no changes over the waves (Figure 12.4).

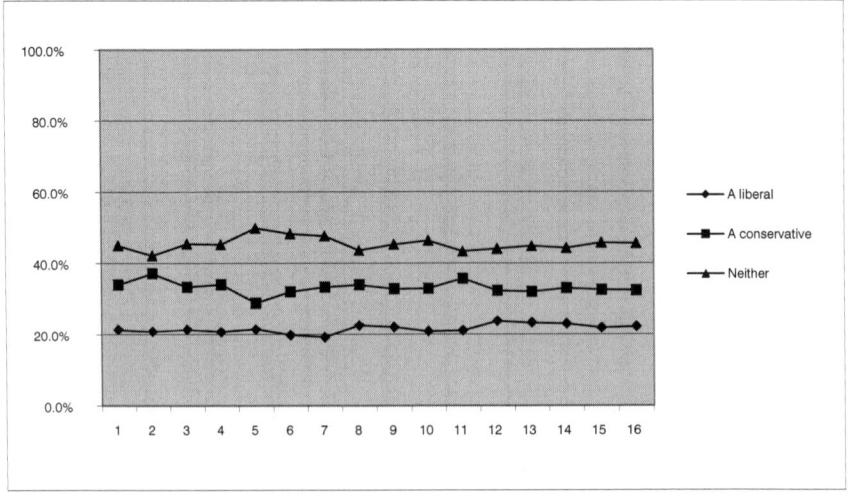

FIGURE 12.3 Proportion Identifying Conservative, Liberal, or Neither (Wave of fielding is shown as the horizontal axis, Wave 1 was June 2000, Wave 3 was September 2011, Wave 16 was October 2007. A full listing of waves and dates is in Table 12.1)

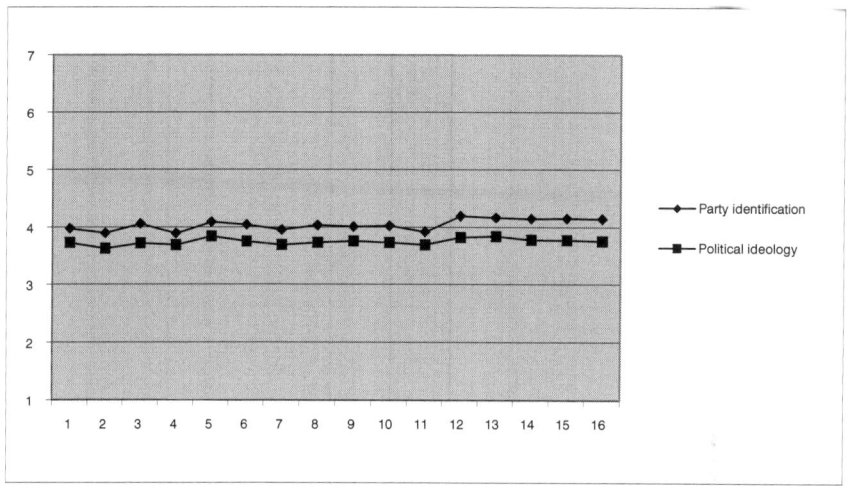

FIGURE 12.4 Mean Value for Party ID and Political Ideology over Waves (Note: Party Identification—1 = Very Strong Republican; 7 = Very Strong Democrat and Political; Ideology—1 = Extremely Conservative; 7 = Extremely Liberal. Wave of fielding is shown as the horizontal axis, Wave 1 was June 2000, Wave 3 was September 2011, Wave 16 was October 2007. A full listing of waves and dates is in Table 12.1)

Distributions of Attitudes

Focal and Directly Protective Issues

For ease of presentation, the analyses reported here focus on the proportion of respondents who said a policy was a "very good" idea or that government effort concerning an issue should be increased "a lot."[21] Figure 12.5 summarizes the proportions supporting the actions or policies for the focal and directly protective issues while Figure 12.6 summarizes the proportions of those rating the same issues as either "Very important" or "Extremely important." Since the issues and wave-over-wave tests were quite numerous, we will focus on the overall trends and selected wave-over-wave comparisons. Key waves to focus on are Waves 2, 3, 5, 11, and 15 (Wave 2 = immediate pre-2000 election, Wave 3 = immediate post 9/11, Wave 5 = October 2003, Wave 11 = immediate pre-2004 election, Wave 15 = immediate pre-2006 election).

With regard to the focal issue of fighting terrorism, from October 2000 to September 2001, there was an immediate and sharp increase in the proportions of Americans thinking that stopping terrorist groups was "Very good" for the federal government to do (rising from 75.9% to 89.4%). In addition, those considering the issue "Extremely important" to them personally also rose from 67.2% to 90.9%. Reflecting results from other polls, we found a significant decline in those rating it "Very good" from October 2001 to October 2003 (from 86.6%

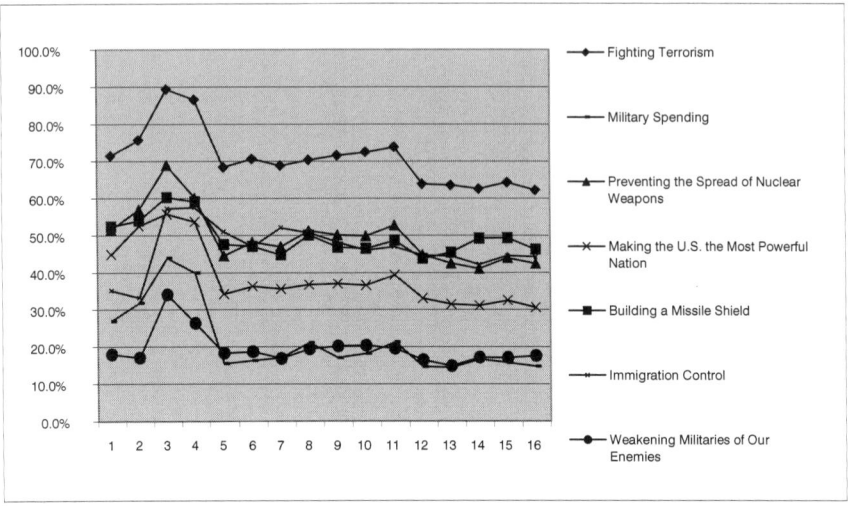

FIGURE 12.5 Support for Focal Issue and Immediate Protective Responses (Wave of fielding is shown as the horizontal axis, Wave 1 was June 2000, Wave 3 was September 2011, Wave 16 was October 2007. A full listing of waves and dates is in Table 12.1)

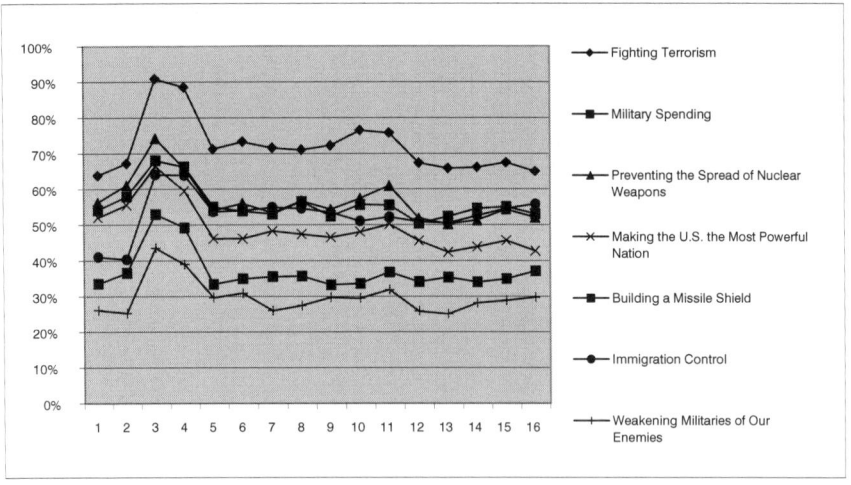

FIGURE 12.6 Importance of Focal Issue and Immediate Protective Responses (Wave of fielding is shown as the horizontal axis, Wave 1 was June 2000, Wave 3 was September 2011, Wave 16 was October 2007. A full listing of waves and dates is in Table 12.1)

to 68.4%) as well as a decline in considering it "Extremely" or "Very" important from 88.5% to 71.3%. Rather than plateauing back to pre-9/11 levels however, there appeared to be a distinct drop in issue support following the 2004 election (i.e., following Wave 11), dropping to a new low—averaging 63.3% support for stopping terrorist groups as "Very good" in the final 5 waves. Rated importance dropped, but then returned to levels from pre-9/11 (averaging 66.4%).

Most of the other directly protective issues showed similar patterns in issue support—rising immediately following 9/11, then falling to at or below pre-9/11 levels by October 2003, and then falling further to levels even further below pre-9/11 levels: "Military spending," "Preventing the spread of nuclear weapons," "Building a missile shield," and "Making the U.S. the most powerful nation." "Weakening the Militaries of Our Enemies," though similar, fell to pre-9/11 levels, but did not fall to a level lower than pre-9/11. Rated importance for all issues also showed similar patterns. The one distinctive issue that did not follow the same pattern was support for immigration control. It rose dramatically from October 2000 to September 2001 (33.1% to 57.2%) and dropped to an average of 44.1% over the last 5 waves, but never returned to its original support level. Ratings of importance for the immigration issue paralleled these results, reflecting a sustained increase in public concern about immigration control.

Indirectly Protective Issues

Among the three issues we identified as indirectly protective all showed modest increases in support following 9/11 (see Figures 12.7 and 12.8). Two returned back to pre-9/11 levels by October 2003 ("Protecting Democracies" and "Changing Non-democracies into Democracies"). The rated importance of these issues rose following 9/11 and dropped back slightly, but remained higher in importance post-9/11 compared to pre-9/11. Support for "Strengthening the Militaries of our Allies" rose somewhat following 9/11 and dropped back by October 2001 to pre-9/11 levels, which was also reflected in ratings of importance.

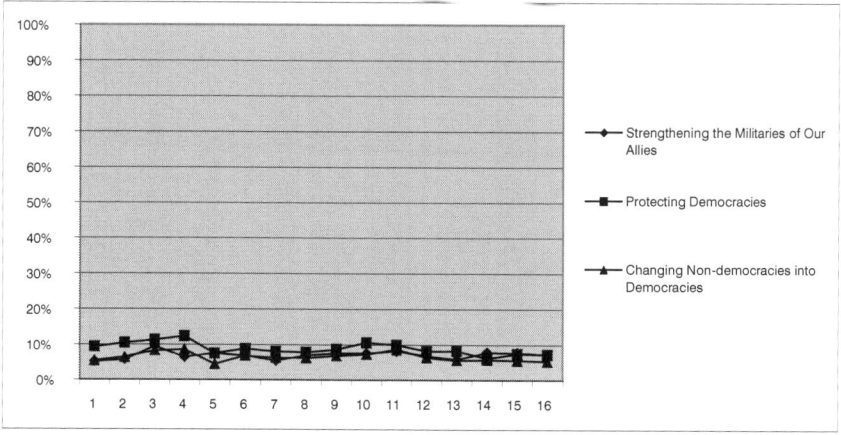

FIGURE 12.7 Support for Indirectly Protective Issues (Wave of fielding is shown as the horizontal axis, Wave 1 was June 2000, Wave 3 was September 2011, Wave 16 was October 2007. A full listing of waves and dates is in Table 12.1)

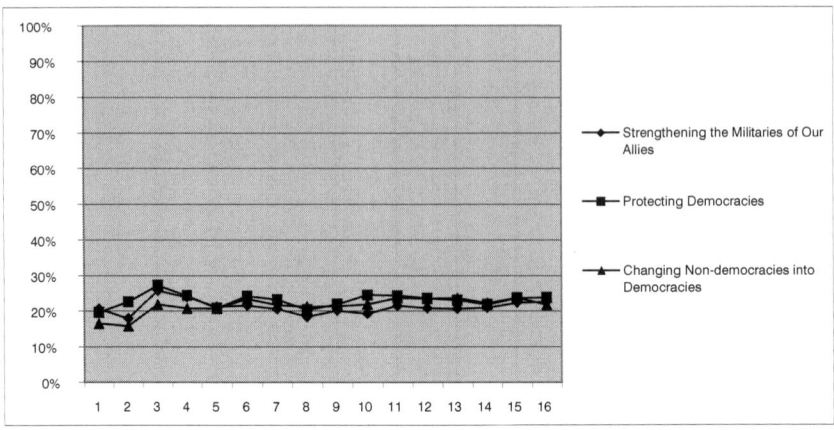

FIGURE 12.8 Importance of Indirectly Protective Issues (Wave of fielding is shown as the horizontal axis, Wave 1 was June 2000, Wave 3 was September 2011, Wave 16 was October 2007. A full listing of waves and dates is in Table 12.1)

Foreign Involvement Issues

Among the general foreign involvement issues (see Figures 12.9 and 12.10), only one showed a significant post-9/11 increase in support—"Giving Humanitarian Aid to Poor Countries" (averaging 11.7% in the 2 pre-9/11 waves to an average of 15.7% in the final 5 waves). The issue's importance also paralleled the increase in support. While support for "Resolving disputes between other countries" did not increase following 9/11, ratings of its importance did increase, but then declined by October 2003, as did support for the issue.

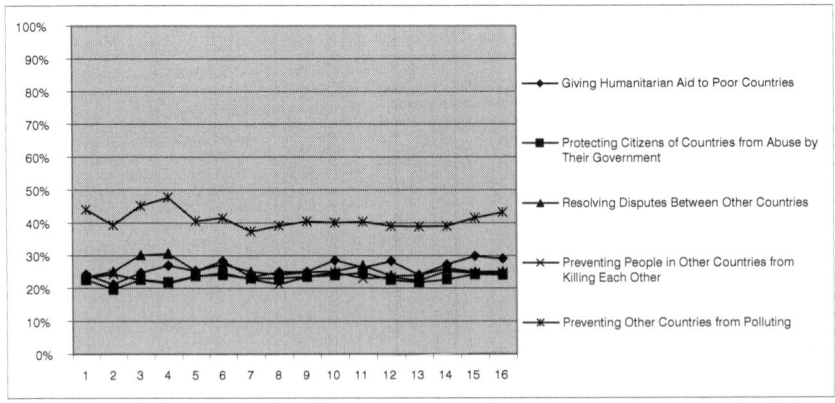

FIGURE 12.9 Support for General Foreign Involvement Issues (Wave of fielding is shown as the horizontal axis, Wave 1 was June 2000, Wave 3 was September 2011, Wave 16 was October 2007. A full listing of waves and dates is in Table 12.1)

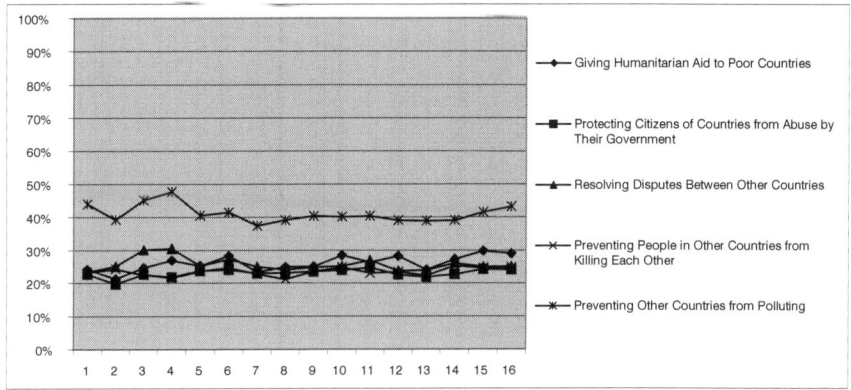

FIGURE 12.10 Importance of General Foreign Involvement Issues (Wave of fielding is shown as the horizontal axis, Wave 1 was June 2000, Wave 3 was September 2011, Wave 16 was October 2007. A full listing of waves and dates is in Table 12.1)

Domestic Issues

Among the domestic issues, support did not substantially change from pre- to post-9/11 (Figure 12.11). Beginning in Wave 5 (October 2003), we saw a significant rise in support for spending for education and a significant drop in support for helping American companies sell things to other countries. As contrasted to changes over time in the support for these issues, four of the issues showed substantial drops in rated importance over waves—spending on education, gun control, controlling crime, and capital punishment (Figure 12.12).

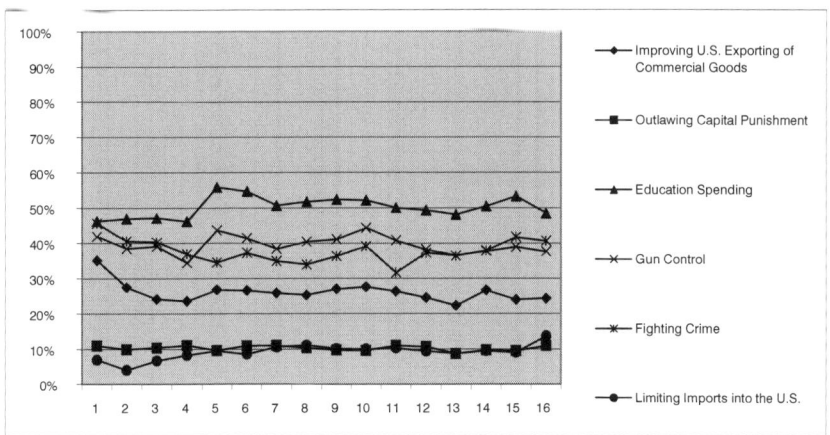

FIGURE 12.11 Support for Domestic Issues (Wave of fielding is shown as the horizontal axis, Wave 1 was June 2000, Wave 3 was September 2011, Wave 16 was October 2007. A full listing of waves and dates is in Table 12.1)

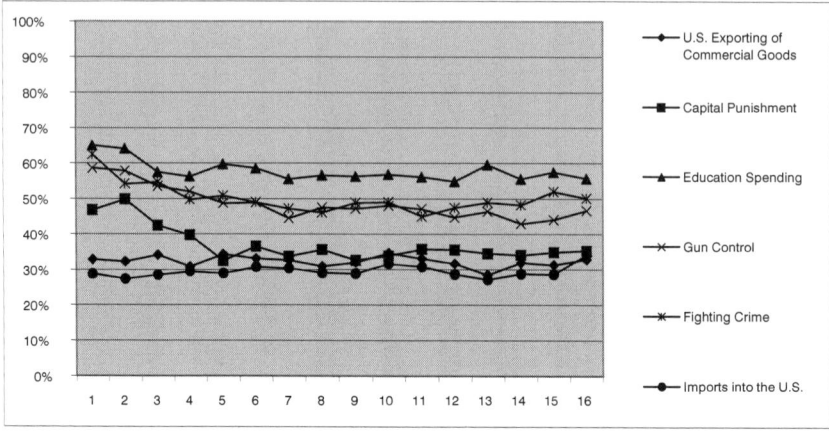

FIGURE 12.12 Importance of Domestic Issues (Wave of fielding is shown as the horizontal axis, Wave 1 was June 2000, Wave 3 was September 2011, Wave 16 was October 2007. A full listing of waves and dates is in Table 12.1)

Attitude Structure Change

Except for attitudes toward immigration, most measures directly related to responding to the attacks of 9/11 returned to pre-9/11 levels, and many dropped to even lower levels of support than existed before 9/11. Though these changes did not support evidence of permanent opinion change, it may be that the attitudinal structures of the people changed over this period. To examine this, we looked at the correlations between issue support (full range measures) and political party identification and political ideology (based on the full 7 category scales resulting from branching). Based on the major changes we saw over waves, we created four time periods—combining the two waves prior to 9/11 to form the first period, the two waves following 9/11 (September and October 2001) for the second period, combining the waves from October 2003 to October 2004 (Waves 5 to 11) for the third period, and combining the waves from October 2005 to October 2007 (Waves 12 to 16) for the final time period. Table 12.3 summarizes the correlations between political issue support and political party identification by time period, while Table 12.4 summarizes the correlations between issue support and political ideology. Focusing on political party ID, we can see that for the two post-9/11 periods there were significant changes in rated support for the issues. Except for support for military spending, which did not substantially change in its correlation with party ID (which was correlated with being Republican before 9/11), the focal measure of terrorism, the immediate protective issues, and long-term protective issues, all moved to become more closely identified.

TABLE 12.3 Correlations of Item Support with Party Identification by Time Periods

Item	Party identification			
	Pre-9/11	Sept–Oct 2001	Post 9/11	Post 2004
Fighting terrorism	0.01	−0.03	−0.16	−0.15
Military spending	−0.32	−0.25	−0.35	−0.35
Preventing the spread of nuclear weapons	0.00	0.03	−0.15	−0.15
Making the U.S. the most powerful nation	−0.16	−0.14	−0.24	−0.22
Building a missile shield	−0.20	−0.21	−0.27	−0.22
Immigration control	−0.13	−0.08	−0.18	−0.16
Weakening militaries of our enemies	−0.07	−0.03	−0.18	−0.18
Strengthening the militaries of our allies	−0.03	−0.04	−0.14	−0.14
Protecting democracies	0.01	−0.05	−0.18	−0.18
Changing non-democracies into democracies	0.04	−0.02	−0.25	−0.23
Giving humanitarian aid to poor countries	0.16	0.11	0.11	0.13
Protecting citizens of countries from abuse by their government	0.19	0.08	−0.09	−0.02
Resolving disputes between other countries	0.13	0.02	−0.06	−0.06
Preventing people in other countries from killing each other	0.22	0.11	−0.02	0.03
Preventing pollution	0.17	0.19	0.13	0.15
Improving U.S. exporting of commercial goods	0.02	−0.04	−0.07	−0.06
Outlawing capital punishment	0.31	0.25	0.25	0.26
Education spending	0.37	0.31	0.34	0.35
Gun control	0.38	0.32	0.32	0.29
Fighting crime	0.14	0.09	0.11	0.10
Limiting imports into the U.S.	0.02	0.04	0.00	0.00
N	3205	4568	20144	23045

Note: For this study, Strong Republican was "1" and Strong Democrat was "7" so a positive correlation indicated more support by Democrats and a negative correlation indicated more support by Republicans.

TABLE 12.4 Correlations of Items with Political Ideology by Time Periods

Item	Political ideology			
	Pre-9/11	Sept–Oct 2001	Post 9/11	Post 2004
Fighting terrorism	0.00	–0.08	–0.19	–0.19
Military spending	–0.33	–0.31	–0.35	–0.36
Preventing the spread of nuclear weapons	–0.02	0.01	–0.16	–0.18
Making the U.S. the most powerful nation	–0.19	–0.20	–0.28	–0.29
Building a missile shield	–0.20	–0.27	–0.30	–0.27
Immigration control	–0.17	–0.20	–0.25	–0.24
Weakening militaries of our enemies	–0.07	–0.10	–0.22	–0.23
Strengthening the militaries of our allies	–0.06	–0.08	–0.15	–0.19
Protecting democracies	0.03	–0.05	–0.19	–0.19
Changing non-democracies into democracies	0.01	–0.07	–0.27	–0.26
Giving humanitarian aid to poor countries	0.18	0.16	0.13	0.15
Protecting citizens of countries from abuse by their government	0.24	0.13	–0.05	–0.01
Resolving disputes between other countries	0.10	0.03	–0.05	–0.04
Preventing people in other countries from killing each other	0.22	0.12	0.00	0.03
Preventing pollution	0.18	0.21	0.14	0.16
Improving U.S. exporting of commercial goods	0.01	–0.02	–0.07	–0.06
Outlawing capital punishment	0.27	0.26	0.26	0.24
Education spending	0.36	0.32	0.33	0.35
Gun control	0.39	0.27	0.28	0.26
Fighting crime	0.08	0.00	0.02	0.00
Limiting imports into the U.S.	–0.01	–0.08	–0.08	–0.08
N	3205	4568	20144	23045

Note: For this study, Very Conservative was "1" and Very Liberal was "7" so a positive correlation indicated more support by Liberals and a negative correlation indicated more support by Conservatives.

Except for humanitarian aid (which remained associated with Democrats across periods), support for the Foreign Involvement issues appeared to be more closely identified with being Democrat in the pre-9/11 period, but in the 9/11 period and post-9/11 periods thereafter, support was not correlated with party ID. The domestic issues of "Outlawing Capital Punishment" and "Gun Control" reduced their association with being Democrat over the time periods as well.

Many of the results for Party ID were also found for Political Ideology. So, while support for directly protective measures may have significantly reduced over time, returning to levels that were at or below pre-9/11 levels, there did appear to be a more substantial polarization of attitudes following 9/11 as issues became more identified as Republican or less identified as Democrat (and similarly for political ideology, more identified as conservative or less identified as liberal).

To further examine these results for issues by political party identification, we examined the top box endorsement ("Very good" for the federal government to do or "A lot" in terms of increased support) by political party across the major time periods. Tables 12.5, 12.6, 12.7, and 12.8 summarize the results for the categorical identification (Republican, Democrat, Independent, Other).

We present some selected comparisons next resulting from this examination of political parties and issue support over time. For the focal issue of fighting terrorism, Figure 12.13, we discovered some of the political party dynamics underlying the changes. While all groups rose in parallel in their support of fighting terrorism following the attacks of 9/11, following 9/11, all groups dropped in their support, but Democrats, Independents, and Others did not parallel the results for Republicans, they dropped more than Republicans in their support to below pre-9/11 levels, while Republicans dropped to pre-9/11 levels. For support for military spending (Figure 12.14), we saw basic parallelism—all groups rising and dropping in parallel, and dropping to levels below pre-9/11 levels by the first post-9/11 period. For immigration control (Figure 12.15), we found that Democrats rose more in their support in the 9/11 period, nearly matching Republican support, rising above both Independents and Others. Democrats also fell furthest in their support in the post-9/11 periods, but all groups ended significantly above the pre-9/11 levels in their support except for those identifying themselves as "Other." For support for education spending (Figure 12.16), both Democrats and Independents increased their support in the post-9/11 periods, but the Republicans and Others did not show any significant changes across the periods.

TABLE 12.5 Issue Support by Major Time Period—Republican

Issue	Pre–9/11	Sept–Oct 2001	Post 9/11	Post 2004
Fighting terrorism	74.2%	89.9%	84.8%	77.1%
Military spending	46.3%	57.5%	28.4%	22.4%
Preventing the spread of nuclear weapons	55.9%	65.1%	59.7%	53.6%
Making the U.S. the most powerful nation	60.0%	67.1%	50.6%	45.2%
Building a missile shield	64.4%	69.3%	61.6%	60.1%
Immigration control	39.8%	61.5%	56.3%	51.9%
Weakening militaries of our enemies	21.4%	33.4%	24.8%	22.9%
Strengthening the militaries of our allies	7.1%	7.1%	9.0%	9.1%
Protecting democracies	11.2%	14.6%	13.9%	11.7%
Changing non-democracies into democracies	6.5%	10.4%	12.1%	9.9%
Giving humanitarian aid to poor countries	6.6%	11.5%	9.3%	9.2%
Protecting citizens of countries from abuse by their government	7.9%	8.9%	15.3%	11.1%
Resolving disputes between other countries	12.7%	13.6%	11.7%	11.3%
Preventing people in other countries from killing each other	4.6%	5.2%	6.6%	5.9%
Preventing pollution	23.5%	24.9%	22.0%	18.9%
Improving U.S. exporting of commercial goods	33.9%	25.8%	31.0%	28.0%
Outlawing capital punishment	6.7%	6.7%	6.0%	6.2%
Education spending	31.4%	32.9%	35.7%	31.1%
Gun control	24.6%	24.0%	25.7%	24.8%
Fighting crime	39.4%	35.7%	28.6%	33.3%
Limiting imports into the U.S.	6.6%	6.4%	8.7%	8.7%
N	1107	1532	6472	6618

TABLE 12.6 Issue Support by Major Time Period—Democrat

Issue	Pre-9/11	Sept–Oct 2001	Post 9/11	Post 2004
Fighting terrorism	75.4%	88.4%	65.5%	56.8%
Military spending	16.1%	33.8%	11.7%	11.0%
Preventing the spread of nuclear weapons	55.7%	68.5%	44.8%	38.7%
Making the U.S. the most powerful nation	42.7%	52.5%	28.8%	26.1%
Building a missile shield	46.8%	55.9%	38.1%	40.3%
Immigration control	28.1%	57.7%	42.9%	38.1%
Weakening militaries of our enemies	16.5%	30.2%	16.2%	14.1%
Strengthening the militaries of our allies	5.1%	7.4%	6.7%	7.2%
Protecting democracies	10.5%	12.6%	6.4%	5.4%
Changing non-democracies into democracies	7.4%	9.3%	4.0%	4.6%
Giving humanitarian aid to poor countries	19.0%	19.8%	20.5%	21.1%
Protecting citizens of countries from abuse by their government	14.4%	12.4%	11.5%	12.0%
Resolving disputes between other countries	20.2%	17.5%	13.2%	13.4%
Preventing people in other countries from killing each other	8.8%	7.7%	7.8%	9.1%
Preventing pollution	38.3%	40.6%	33.9%	33.0%
Improving U.S. exporting of commercial goods	30.9%	23.1%	25.3%	23.6%
Outlawing capital punishment	14.2%	12.8%	13.7%	13.5%
Education spending	62.8%	59.3%	68.1%	65.7%
Gun control	59.7%	50.5%	58.4%	51.9%
Fighting crime	54.3%	44.5%	42.8%	45.1%
Limiting imports into the U.S.	4.7%	8.6%	11.1%	10.8%
N	1045	1515	6499	7887

TABLE 12.7 Issue Support by Major Time Period—Independent

Issue	Pre-9/11	Sept–Oct 2001	Post 9/11	Post 2004
Fighting terrorism	73.0%	87.2%	66.6%	60.2%
Military spending	26.8%	37.8%	15.8%	15.0%
Preventing the spread of nuclear weapons	51.4%	59.1%	47.7%	40.6%
Making the U.S. The most powerful nation	45.8%	47.9%	33.6%	28.5%
Building a missile shield	47.6%	50.7%	45.1%	46.0%
Immigration control	32.7%	53.7%	48.4%	44.0%
Weakening militaries of our enemies	14.7%	24.4%	17.4%	14.2%
Strengthening the militaries of our allies	3.7%	7.5%	6.8%	5.9%
Protecting democracies	8.5%	10.1%	7.1%	6.4%
Changing non-democracies into democracies	4.3%	5.6%	5.1%	4.2%
Giving humanitarian aid to poor countries	8.7%	14.9%	14.2%	16.7%
Protecting citizens of countries from abuse by their government	8.8%	8.9%	11.0%	9.9%
Resolving disputes between other countries	16.9%	15.3%	13.6%	13.4%
Preventing people in other countries from killing each other	4.6%	3.8%	6.9%	6.5%
Preventing pollution	32.5%	29.6%	28.9%	26.9%
Improving U.S. exporting of commercial goods	29.1%	22.2%	24.5%	23.9%
Outlawing capital punishment	9.7%	13.5%	10.4%	9.5%
Education spending	44.1%	44.4%	51.4%	49.6%
Gun control	35.6%	33.8%	41.0%	35.5%
Fighting crime	34.0%	36.7%	33.7%	36.7%
Limiting imports into the U.S.	5.2%	7.2%	10.2%	9.9%
N	782	1162	5112	6930

TABLE 12.8   Issue Support by Major Time Period—Other

Issue	Pre-9/11	Sept–Oct 2001	Post 9/11	Post 2004
Fighting terrorism	65.6%	80.1%	58.1%	54.6%
Military spending	19.6%	24.1%	13.9%	12.0%
Preventing the spread of nuclear weapons	50.9%	52.5%	38.0%	33.5%
Making the U.S. the most powerful nation	35.6%	42.7%	26.7%	21.8%
Building a missile shield	48.5%	52.9%	39.0%	38.3%
Immigration control	37.8%	46.9%	42.5%	40.5%
Weakening militaries of our enemies	13.0%	21.1%	15.3%	15.3%
Strengthening the militaries of our allies	4.9%	9.8%	5.7%	6.4%
Protecting democracies	6.7%	6.5%	5.9%	4.1%
Changing non-democracies into democracies	2.2%	4.3%	4.1%	3.2%
Giving humanitarian aid to poor countries	13.3%	24.0%	16.0%	16.1%
Protecting citizens of countries from abuse by their government	14.6%	8.2%	11.5%	9.7%
Resolving disputes between other countries	13.9%	14.2%	9.9%	9.1%
Preventing people in other countries from killing each other	8.9%	5.4%	9.1%	7.5%
Preventing pollution	33.6%	33.2%	28.3%	27.8%
Improving U.S. exporting of commercial goods	26.4%	23.2%	21.1%	21.4%
Outlawing capital punishment	13.0%	14.8%	13.3%	9.8%
Education spending	53.9%	55.1%	57.2%	53.9%
Gun control	40.8%	41.2%	38.4%	35.0%
Fighting crime	39.7%	36.5%	34.2%	39.7%
Limiting imports into the U.S.	4.7%	5.1%	10.4%	11.1%
N	271	358	2060	2510

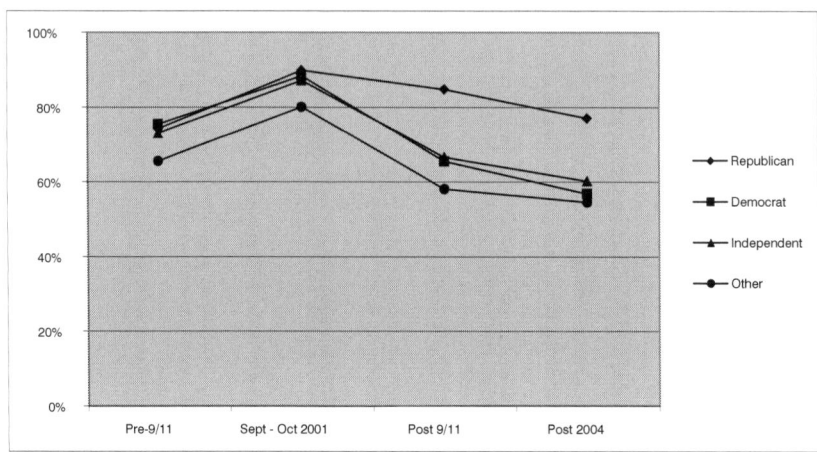

FIGURE 12.13 Support for Fighting Terrorism by Political Party Identification

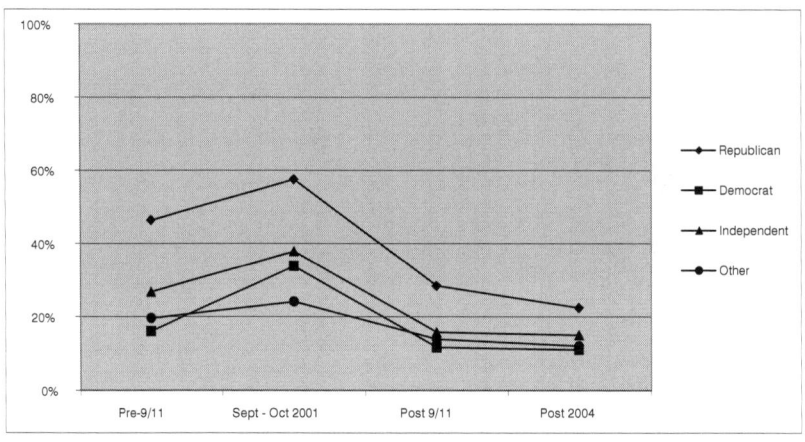

FIGURE 12.14 Support for Military Spending by Political Party Identification

Discussion

The goal of this research was to determine what effects the events of September 11, 2001 had on Americans' attitudes toward government policy options and the personal importance of such issues. To this end, we examined the results of repeated cross-sectional surveys asking citizens questions on a wide range of issues, involving foreign and domestic affairs, environmental protection, capital punishment, education, gun control, and crime.

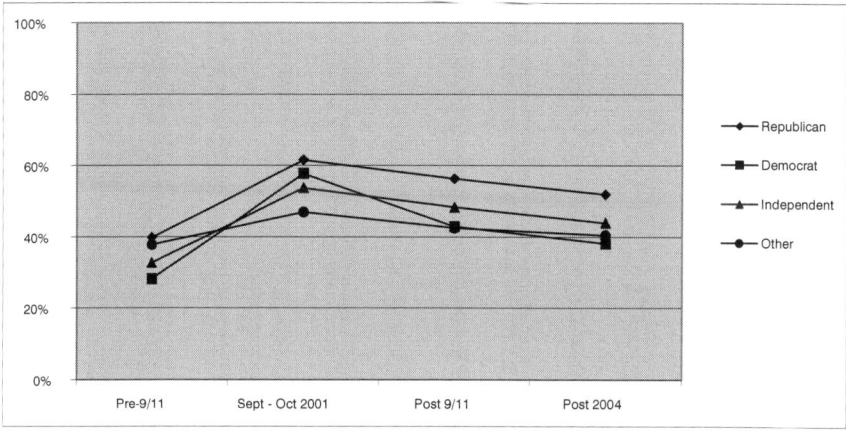

FIGURE 12.15 Support for Immigration Control by Political Party Identification

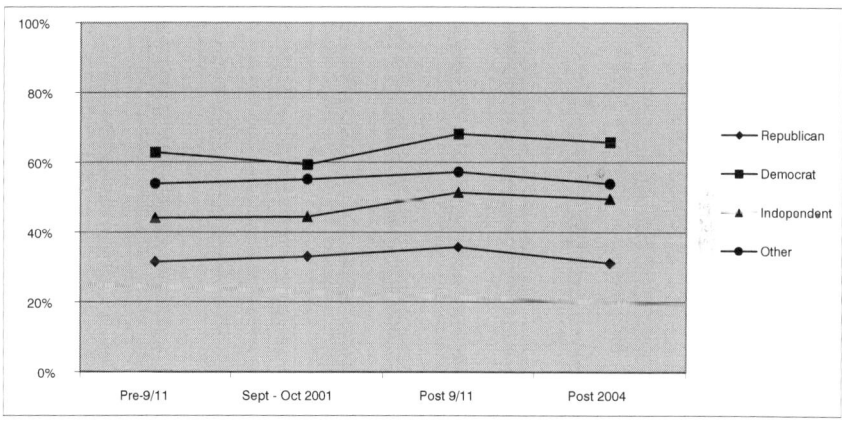

FIGURE 12.16 Support for Education Spending by Political Party Identification

We found that, while public opinion about counterterrorism experienced a substantial increase in support immediately following the attacks, public opinion returned to pre-attack levels by October 2003 (Wave 5). In other words, the increase in support for the issue area most closely related to terrorism experienced a surge in public salience for slightly over two years following the attack—the length of the actual surge could be far less, but we were unable to measure it more precisely due to limitations of the data.[22] However, we can conclude that support for "stopping terrorism in other countries" dropped to pre-9/11 levels within twenty-five months following the 9/11 attacks. The conventional wisdom that "everything has changed" appears to be incorrect, at least as it related to opinions concerning counterterrorism. We next review a number of theoretical perspectives that might be helpful in organizing our understanding of our results.

Theoretical Perspectives—Parallel Publics

Page and Shapiro's (1992) theory of the rational public argues that "For the most part the preferences of the many small parallel publics that make up the general public stay in tandem—moving in parallel or standing still together" (p. 319). For a number of issues we studied, those identifying with different political parties moved in parallel. However, for a number of other issues there was not parallelism. As one example, Republicans were the only subgroup who did not return to pre-9/11 levels on the counterterrorism question. In fact, following the attacks, Republicans consistently reported that stopping terrorism in other countries was "very important" at higher levels than both Democrats and Independents. And Republicans, through the last wave of our study, dropped very slowly in their level of support—back to 77.1% in the most recent waves compared to their pre-9/11 levels of 74.2%, while those with other party identifications dropped to much lower levels than their pre-9/11 levels. However, Page and Shapiro (1992) recognized that there are some possible exceptions to the simple version of their thesis. They argued that there were some instances of publics which diverge from the main thesis. Of particular interest to our study is party identification. Page and Shapiro found that the parties generally behaved in a parallel fashion, but they also found cases of divergent movement of party opinion, with the parties becoming more dissimilar over time, and hypothesized this is due to party leadership. So some of the divergence we obtained may have been due to the emergence of party leadership advocating significantly different emphases for particular issues following 9/11. It may well be that fighting terrorism became a core differentiator for Republicans achieving a higher level of importance that then became part of a core value, hence sustaining support for anti-terrorist action (Krosnick, 1990). That this issue differentiated Republicans and seemed to organize responses to related issues (and may have continued to have an influence on beliefs and opinions—in 2011, 46% still believed that Iraq was providing support to al Qaeda and 47% believed that Iraq either had a WMD program or actual WMDs at the time of the 2003 invasion, with the majority of those holding these beliefs being Republican[23]). As a result, these data may indicate that at least one opinion public became more polarized with a longer lasting effect across time and issues for a large group within the U.S. (cf. Converse, 1964 where he indicated that most people do not have strong coherent belief systems).

Theoretical Perspectives—Elastic Opinion Shift

Rather than permanent and "forever changed," most of the opinion changes we found and the polling results we reviewed appeared to last, at most, 1 to 6 years before returning to pre-9/11 levels (when there were pre-9/11 measures upon which to compare). This apparent elasticity of opinion change is one way to help understand 9/11 reactions. Cialdini, Levy, Herman, Kozlowski, and Petty (1976) found that students would shift their attitude to be more moderate about personally relevant topics when they believed they were going to discuss the topic with some opponents immediately. This attitude shift was temporary and only occurred when the participants thought they were engaging in a cognitive task where the attitude shift might be useful or strategic. Their attitudes shifted back to original when they were told that the discussion with an opponent would not happen. Therefore, Cialdini et al. suggested that these shifts in attitude were elastic and strategic in nature, due to the situation of expecting to discuss an opinion with an opponent. Similar studies have also found that attitude shifts are often situational in nature (Cialdini, Levy, Herman, & Evenbeck, 1973; Hass & Mann, 1976). Factors associated with these elastic shifts have been inducing the desire to appear consistent (from the theory of impression management) and reducing cognitive load, such as arguing a moderate position in a discussion. That these attitudes "snap back" may indicate that true attitudes are not easily subject to long-lasting change. However, this elasticity appeared to be true only for the low-personal relevance topics. When the topics were high in personal relevance, the attitudes were found to be less susceptible to snapping back.

In the aftermath of the September 11 attacks, there may have been strong situational factors that fostered attitude change in a widespread, systematic manner. These situational factors include a desire to appear unified as citizens of the United States in the face of adversity or a fear of expressing unpopular opinions that may solicit unwanted attention by appearing "unpatriotic." After the largest terrorist attack ever on U.S. soil, Americans rallied behind President Bush to fight the war on terror (Kam & Ramos, 2008), developing an "us" versus "them" mentality that increased the strength of those situational factors. While it is tempting to believe that the events of September 11 had such a profound impact, leaving a permanent scar on American public opinion, Cialdini et al.'s (1976) research would suggest otherwise. Elastic opinion shifts are in direct opposition to the belief that attitudes are relatively stable and durable and if, by some great force, they do change, the changes appeared not to be permanent. This apparent conflict is acknowledged by discussing the temporary nature of these changes and calling them "position shifts" which are quite different from a true attitude change. The participants in the Cialdini et al. study had their opinion shift back to original levels within a matter of minutes. Based on our review of other polling data, we did not expect the position shifts after September 11 to be that ephemeral, but what is a reasonable amount of time to expect attitudes to snap back, and for what attitudes? The results we obtained indicated that while all protective attitudes dropped following 9/11, some remained at higher levels than pre-9/11 (and did not "snap back"), yet others dropped below pre-9/11 levels. Both of these findings would be difficult to explain if situational events led to only temporary change and left little permanent change, since the attitudes did not snap back to their original position.

Shifts in support occurred for some other issues, but not apparently related to the events of 9/11—one issue that exemplified this was support for increase in education spending beginning in October 2003. Other foreign involvement issues and domestic issues manifested no notable changes in proportions of support after September 11. However, the personal importance of many of these issues decreased for some issues (e.g. spending on education, gun control, capital punishment, fighting crime) but did not change for others, indicating that shifts may have been due to shifting attention of the electorate and politicians, but these shifts again indicated more long-term trends rather than elastic shifts due to passing events in the domestic arena.

Theoretical perspectives—Elite Opinion Leadership

According to Zaller (Zaller, 1994; Zaller & Feldman, 1992), public opinion most often results from individual choices of response options that reflect the preponderance of ideas and situational influences at the time of the response selection. These often include considerations of what opinion elites (e.g., party leaders) may have said, as the person interpreted and remembered. Relevant and accessible considerations are then combined in some form of calculus (akin to Anderson, 1971) to formulate response selection for a given issue. Further, Zaller (1994) argues that because the public is particularly poorly informed about foreign policy issues, the public is especially likely to rely on elite opinion leadership to determine acceptable opinions. According to Zaller, an individual's level of political awareness and the level of discord in elite opinion will determine how much support exists for a particular policy. When elite opinion is of one voice, politically aware citizens will tend to support a policy more strongly than non-aware citizens. When elite opinion is divided, however, politically aware Americans are more likely to side with their party's position on the issue in question. Zaller claimed that elite opinion leadership should be at its height during times of national emergency and providing uniform direction, and, under conditions of non-threat (or lower threat), diverges with a consequent divergence in those with different party identification. The one issue that may not have behaved in ways desired by the elite opinion leadership of the different political parties may have been support for immigration control. In addition, support for many of the direct protective issues dropped below pre-9/11 levels for all groups other than the Republicans. This finding appeared to be in opposition to what the elite opinion leadership was supporting for the Democrats during this period. This may mean that the central core values that distinguish Democrats and Independents (or possibly for the party or groups out of power) from Republicans and upon which they formulate their opinions for specific issues became more influential in guiding opinion than those espoused by leaders.

Conclusions Concerning Theoretical Perspectives

One difficulty with theories of public opinion stability and change is that they appear more descriptive of observations and can be modified to fit the facts, making them hard to test and difficult to disprove. The elastic opinion change theory (Cialdini et al., 1976) was not fully confirmed in a number of ways—some opinions did not snap back to their original levels (though others did, or did so for specific groups but not others). The elite opinion leadership theory (Zaller) may not have been confirmed since some issues did not appear to follow elite opinion leadership (and issues like immigration may be following more a "bottom-up" rather than "top-down" influence strategy—akin to the "wisdom of the crowd" whereby leaders try to discern what the voters want). Further research relating public statements and influence attempts of public leaders across time needs to be conducted to determine if elite opinions were leading or following the crowd on some of the issues we observed. Finally, the parallel publics theory (Page and Shapiro) is much more difficult to derive testable hypotheses that are falsifiable with our observations (cf. Greenwald & Ronis, 1981).

Conclusions

To what extent can these results be generalized to the American public as a whole? Certainly, the survey samples examined here were more educated and wealthier than the nation's general population and most likely more politically interested and engaged than the population as well. However, weighting these data to resemble the general population in terms of demographics did *not* notably alter our results (as also observed by Thomas et al., 2008). It is possible that the impact September 11 had on some opinions among our respondents may have been muted among less attentive and less engaged citizens, which may have left other segments of the public less affected than our data suggest, though our results parallel findings from other polls of the general U.S. population. We hope this work will inspire other studies in the future, taking advantage of pre-existing data to try to explore these issues anew in other samples.

Taken together, our results help to flesh out the portrait of contemporary democratic citizens as responsive to unfolding events and open to change, both in their attitudes toward policies and in their psychological investments in matters of government strategy. Opinions on a particular issue can apparently move quite easily without disrupting the balance of citizens' cognitive systems, while being more closely tied to ideological orientation for other issues. How such polarization takes place, and the consequences of it for political influence, are ripe areas for future research and theories to help understand both stability and change within public opinion.

Appendix

Wordings of Attitude Measures

1   Do you think stopping terrorist groups in other countries from hurting or killing Americans is or would be ...? [Response options: Very good, good, somewhat good, neither good nor bad, somewhat bad, bad, very bad] (fighting terrorism)
2   Do you think the federal government should spend more money on the military than it does now, less money on the military, or about the same amount as it spends now? [Response options: A lot more, a little more, about the same, a little less, a lot less] (military spending)
3   Do you think preventing countries that do not have nuclear weapons now from getting them is or would be ...? [Response options: Very good, good, somewhat good, neither good nor bad, somewhat bad, bad, very bad] (preventing the spread of nuclear weapons)
4   Do you think making sure the U.S. is the most powerful nation in the world is or would be ...? [Response options: Very good, good, somewhat good, neither good nor bad, somewhat bad, bad, very bad] (making the U.S. the most powerful nation)
5   Do you think building weapons to blow up missiles that have been fired or might be fired at the U.S. is or would be ...? [Response options: Very good, good, somewhat good, neither good nor bad, somewhat bad, bad, very bad] (building a missile shield)
6   Do you think the federal government should make it more difficult for people from other countries to move to the U.S. than it is now, make it easier for them to move to the U.S., or keep these rules about the same as they are now? [Response options: A lot more, a little more, about the same, a little less, a lot less] (immigration control)

7   Do you think weakening the militaries of countries that might threaten the
     U.S. is or would be …? [Response options: Very good, good, somewhat
     good, neither good nor bad, somewhat bad, bad, very bad] (weakening
     militaries of our enemies)

8   Do you think strengthening the militaries of countries that are friends
     of the U.S. is or would be …? [Response options: Very good, good,
     somewhat good, neither good nor bad, somewhat bad, bad, very bad]
     (strengthening militaries of U.S. allies)

9   Do you think that preventing democratic governments in other countries
     from being turned into governments that are not democratic is or would
     be …? [Response options: Very good, good, somewhat good, neither good
     nor bad, somewhat bad, bad, very bad] (protecting democracies)

10   Do you think that changing governments in other countries that are
     not democratic into governments that are democratic is or would be
     …? [Response options: Very good, good, somewhat good, neither good
     nor bad, somewhat bad, bad, very bad] (changing non-democracies into
     democracies)

11   Do you think helping poor countries provide food, clothing, and housing
     for their people is or would be …? [Response options: Very good, good,
     somewhat good, neither good nor bad, somewhat bad, bad, very bad]
     (giving humanitarian aid to poor countries)

12   Do you think preventing governments of other countries from hurting
     their own citizens is or would be …? [Response options: Very good, good,
     somewhat good, neither good nor bad, somewhat bad, bad, very bad]
     (protecting citizens of other countries from their governments)

13   Do you think helping to resolve disputes between two other countries is
     or would be …? [Response options: Very good, good, somewhat good,
     neither good nor bad, somewhat bad, bad, very bad] (resolving disputes
     between other countries)

14   Do you think preventing people in other countries from killing each other
     is or would be …? [Response options: Very good, good, somewhat good,
     neither good nor bad, somewhat bad, bad, very bad] (preventing people
     in other countries from killing each other)

15   Do you think preventing other countries from polluting the environment
     is or would be …? [Response options: Very good, good, somewhat good,
     neither good nor bad, somewhat bad, bad, very bad] (preventing other
     countries from polluting)

16   Do you think helping American companies sell things to other countries
     is or would be …? [Response options: Very good, good, somewhat good,
     neither good nor bad, somewhat bad, bad, very bad] (improving U.S.
     exporting of commercial goods)

17 Do you think preventing states from executing people who have been convicted of murdering someone is or would be …? [Response options: Very good, good, somewhat good, neither good nor bad, somewhat bad, bad, very bad] (outlawing capital punishment)

18 Do you think the federal government should spend more money on public schools than it does now, less money on public schools, or about the same as it spends now? [Response options: A lot more, a little more, about the same, a little less, a lot less] (education spending)

19 Do you think the federal government should make it more difficult for people to buy a gun than it is now, make it easier for people to buy a gun, or keep these rules about the same as they are now? [Response options: A lot more, a little more, about the same, a little less, a lot less] (gun control)

20 Do you think the federal government should do more to fight crime than it does now, less to fight crime than it does now, or about the same amount as it does now? [Response options: A lot more, a little more, about the same, a little less, a lot less] (fighting crime)

21 Do you think making it hard for foreign companies to sell things in the U.S. is or would be…? [Response options: Very good, good, somewhat good, neither good nor bad, somewhat bad, bad, very bad] (limiting imports into the U.S.)

Endnotes

1 See, for example, Vice-President Dick Cheney's interview with Tim Russert on MSNBC, September 14, 2003. Says Cheney, "And in a sense, sort of the theme that comes through repeatedly for me is that *9/11 changed everything*." http://msnbc. msn.com/id/3080244/. Accessed 22 August, 2014.

2 For a listing of many such poll results, see http://www.pollingreport.com/BushJob. htm. Accessed 22 August, 2014.

3 http://www.pollingreport.com/terror12.htm and http://www.pollingreport.com/ terror3.htm. Accessed 22 August, 2014.

4 See http://www.pollingreport.com/terror.htm. Accessed 22 August, 2014.

5 See http://www.pollingreport.com/terror5.htm and http://www.pollingreport. com/terror11.htm. Accessed 22 August, 2014.

6 See http://www.pollingreport.com/defense.htm. Accessed 22 August, 2014.

7 ibid.

8 ibid.

9 http://www.gallup.com/poll/21595/majority-dissatisfied-us-position-world.aspx. Accessed June 24, 2016.

10 http://www.gallup.com/poll/21595/majority-dissatisfied-us-position-world.aspx. Accessed June 24, 2016.

11 http://www.pollingreport.com/terror3.htm. Accessed August 22, 2014.

12 ibid.

13 ibid.

14 ibid.

15 ibid.

16 See http://www.pollingreport.com/terror4.htm. Accessed August 22, 2014.
17 ibid.
18 ibid.
19 ibid.
20 ibid.
21 Though we report using top box endorsements, results using means and full range variance of measures reflected similar patterns.
22 That is, our data were collected in waves. Public opinion on counterterrorism returned to pre-9/11 levels sometime between Wave 4 in October 2001 and Wave 5 in October 2003.
23 http://www.brookings.edu/research/reports/2011/09/08-opinion-poll-telhami. Accessed 8/22/2014.

References

Anderson, N. H. (1971). Integration theory and attitude change. *Psychological Review, 78*, 171–206.

Chapman, T. L., & Reiter, D. (2004). The United Nations Security Council and the Rally 'Round the Flag Effect. *Journal of Conflict Resolution, 48*, 806–909.

Cialdini, R. B., Levy, A., Herman, C. P., & Evenbeck, S. (1973). Attitudinal politics: The strategy of moderation. *Journal of Personality and Social Psychology, 25*, 100–108.

Cialdini, R. B., Levy, A., Herman, C. P., Kozlowski, L. T., & Petty, R. E. (1976). Elastic shifts of opinion: Determinants of direction and durability. *Journal of Personality and Social Psychology, 34*, 663–672.

Converse, P. E. (1964). The nature of belief systems in mass publics. In D. E. Apter (Ed.), *Ideology and discontent* (pp. 75–169). New York: Free Press.

Davis, D. W., & Silver, B. D. (2004). Civil liberties vs. security: Public opinion in the context of the terrorist attacks on America. *American Journal of Political Science, 48*, 28–46.

Gadarian, S. K. (2010). The politics of threat: How terrorism news shapes foreign policy attitudes. *Journal of Politics 72*, 469–483.

Greenwald, A. G., & Ronis, D. L. (1981). On the conceptual disconfirmation of theories. *Personality and Social Psychology Bulletin, 7*, 131–137.

Hass, R. G., & Mann, R. W. (1976). Anticipatory belief change: Persuasion or impression management? *Journal of Personality and Social Psychology, 34*, 105–111.

Hetherington, M. J., & Nelson, M. (2003). Anatomy of a rally effect: George W. Bush and the war on terrorism. *Political Science and Politics, 36*, 37–42.

Huddy, L., Feldman, S., Taber, C., & Lahav, G. (2005). Threat, anxiety, and support of antiterrorism policies. *American Journal of Political Science, 49*, 593–608.

Jenkins-Smith, H. C., & Herron, K. G. (2005). United States public response to terrorism: Fault lines or bedrock? *Review of Policy Research, 22*, 599–623.

Kam, C. D., & Ramos, J. M. (2008). Joining and leaving the rally: Understanding the surge and decline in Presidential approval following 9/11. *Public Opinion Quarterly, 72*, 619–650.

Krosnick, J. A. (1990). Government policy and citizen passion: A study of issue publics in contemporary America. *Political Behavior, 12*, 59–92.

Mueller, J. (1970). Presidential popularity from Truman to Johnson. *American Political Science Review, 64*, 18–34.

Page, B. I., & Shapiro, R. Y. (1992). *The rational public: Fifty years of trends in Americans' policy preferences*. Chicago, IL: University of Chicago Press.

Sullivan, J. L., & Hendriks, H. (2009). Public support for civil liberties pre- and post-9/11. *Annual Review of Law and Social Science, 5*, 375–391.

Thomas, R. K., Krane, D., Taylor, H., & Terhanian, G. (2008). Phone and web-based interviews: Effects of sample and weighting on comparability and validity. Paper presented at ISA-RC33 7th International Conference, Naples, Italy.

Zaller, J. (1994). Elite leadership of mass opinion: New evidence from the Gulf War. In W. L. Bennett & D. L. Paletz (Eds.), *Taken by storm: The media, public opinion, and U.S. foreign policy in the Gulf War* (pp. 186–209). Chicago, IL: University of Chicago Press.

Zaller, J. & Feldman, S. (1992). A simple theory of the survey response: Answering questions versus revealing preferences. *American Journal of Political Science, 36*, 579–616.

13

TRUST IN SCIENTISTS' STATEMENTS ABOUT THE ENVIRONMENT AND AMERICAN PUBLIC OPINION ON GLOBAL WARMING

Bo MacInnis and Jon A. Krosnick

Scientists have the potential to have tremendous influence on contemporary societies. Theory-based and empirically validated understanding of physical, social, and psychological processes can set the stage for practical interventions, improve quality of life, and help people manage profound challenges. Yet in order for scientists to have such impact, they must enjoy the public's trust in the integrity and motives of scientists as well as in the methods of investigation and the competence to employ such methods by scientists (Hardwig, 1991; Luhmann, 1979; Resnik, 2009).[1] Such trust justifies funding of research efforts, large-scale adoption of practices based on scientific principles, and young people's decisions to pursue scientific careers (Resnik, 2011; Siegrist et al., 2007).

In light of the importance of trust in science for society, it is interesting to consider the recent history of the issue of global warming in America. During the last decade, this issue has joined others (e.g., the creationism/evolution debate and its implications for public education, and the question of when life begins, with its implications regarding abortion and stem cell research) as raging public controversies with considerable political significance. Some politicians, including Barack Obama, John McCain, and others, asserted their views that global warming is real and a threat that should be addressed by government, while others (e.g., Mitt Romney) have expressed skepticism about whether global warming has been occurring, the degree to which warming has been caused by human activity, and the appropriateness of action at the time of a national recession.

Skepticism about climate science may be an important driver of the growing division between citizens who call themselves Republicans and who call themselves Democrats on the issue of global warming (Kahan et al., 2012;

McCright & Dunlap, 2011). Such skepticism has also been a source of great frustration for some in the natural science community and is seen by some observers to be evidence of a larger campaign being waged against science generally (Mooney, 2005, 2012; Mooney & Kirshenbaum, 2009; Oreskes & Conway, 2010). As a result, scientists have, understandably, expressed concern about the trajectories of their place in contemporary society and their potential to make positive contributions (Mooney, 2005).

These concerns were expressed often in late 2009 when the news media accorded coverage to two events thought to threaten the public's confidence in scientific research on global warming (Montford, 2010). The first was the so-called "Climategate" episode: emails among climate scientists were released to the public and characterized as revealing corruption: a mission to suppress the voices of researchers who were skeptical about whether global warming has been happening or who believed that it does not pose a significant threat. The second involved errors in a report published by the Intergovernmental Panel on Climate Change (IPCC). Both of these events were perceived by some observers to reduce the public's confidence in climate scientists and in their findings and perhaps to threaten the public's trust of scientists more generally. As a result, significant efforts have been devoted to repairing the damage thought to have occurred (Curry, 2010a, 2010b; IPCC, 2010a; Lempinen, 2010; Ward, 2010).

In this chapter, we explore the impact of those events on public trust in and public acceptance of natural scientists' findings about global warming. We begin by describing the two controversies and then describe the methods and findings of a new investigation gauging the impact that these events have had on public beliefs about global warming and on the public's trust in scientists' statements about the environment. We describe evidence suggesting that few people recalled hearing or reading something in the news about the controversial events months later, and at most, an extremely small number of Americans changed their views about global warming as the result of the news about these events. Furthermore, we show that changes in public beliefs about global warming after 2008 might have resulted from annual changes in the world's average temperature among people who didn't trust scientists and not from changes in perceptions of the national economy or in the total volume of news media coverage on global warming. And we describe an experiment showing that the greatest impact of information from a mainstream scientist and from a skeptical scientist occurs among people who trust scientists' statements about the environment highly, while the impact of information from a mainstream scientist and from a skeptical scientist was minimal among people who do not trust scientists' statements about the environment highly. The latter finding that discredits the claim that change in the opinions of people who do not trust scientists' statements about the environment highly after 2008 was due to changes in the prominence of messages from mainstream scientists.

Climategate and the IPCC Report Errors

Climategate broke onto center stage in the national news media on November 19, 2009. Someone hacked into the computer system at the Climatic Research Unit of the University of East Anglia and released to the public thousands of emails and documents related to global warming research. Within days of the revelation, some people asserted that the emails revealed scientific misconduct within the climate science research community and that climate scientists should not be trusted; a firestorm of debate resulted (Norton, 2010).

Between the revelation of Climategate on November 19, 2009, and June 30, 2010, the emails were discussed in at least 506 articles in U.S. print newspapers and at least 348 U.S. television news programs, according to searches using Lexis Nexis.[2] Broadcast television networks (ABC, CBS, and NBC) aired 11 stories about Climategate on their national news programs. Fox News featured 75 stories, and mainstream cable news outlets (CNBC, MSNBC and CNN) featured 92 stories.[3] The majority of the coverage occurred within the month after the initial release of the emails: about 80% of coverage by CNN/CNBC/MSNBC combined, about 70% by ABC/NBC/CBS combined, and 65% by Fox News. The greatest coverage of Climategate by these television news outlets occurred during the two weeks between November 30, 2009, and December 14, 2009. The same over-time pattern was manifested in Google searches for information related to Climategate (Norton, 2010).

The British government investigated the emails and rejected criticisms of climate scientists in reports issued in March and July 2010, concluding that there was no evidence of misconduct by the scientists at the Climatic Research Unit of the University of East Anglia. Consequently, some news media organizations then referred to Climategate as a "manufactured controversy" (*New York Times*, 2010).

On the heels of Climategate, in December 2009, a small number of alleged errors were found in the Fourth Assessment Report issued by the Intergovernmental Panel on Climate Change. The only real error in the report was the projected date of melting of Himalayan glaciers—it should have been 2350 instead of 2035 (IPCC, 2010b). Nonetheless, between December 2009, and June 30, 2010, 209 articles in U.S. print newspapers and 85 U.S. television news programs covered the alleged errors.[4]

Some observers claimed that Climategate and IPCC report errors cast doubt on the credibility of climate scientists and of scientific evidence on global warming (Curry, 2010a, 2010b; IPCC, 2010a; Lempinen, 2010; Ward, 2010). Describing those doubters, Ralph Cicerone, President of the National Academy of Sciences, said in a February 5, 2010 editorial in *Science* that:

> [T]his incident … has raised concern about the standards of science and has damaged public trust in what scientists do … Public opinion has moved

toward the view that scientists often try to suppress alternative hypotheses and ideas and that scientists will withhold data and try to manipulate some aspects of peer review to prevent dissent. This view reflects the fragile nature of trust between science and society, demonstrating that the perceived misbehavior of even a few scientists can diminish the credibility of science as a whole.

Impact of These Events

Was Dr. Cicerone right? Did Climategate (and perhaps the IPCC report errors) actually decrease public confidence in climate science and in the findings of climate scientists? One sort of evidence taken as support for this view came from public opinion polls, some of which indicated a decline after 2008 in the proportion of Americans who said they thought the earth has been warming (Pew Research Center, 2010; PollingReport, 2012). However, this sort of evidence is hardly conclusive because other events that occurred during this time could have produced the shifts in public opinion.

Impact With Awareness

We assessed whether Climategate and the IPCC report errors might have reduced public confidence in climate science and scientists in a number of different ways. One method we employed explored whether the American public was so powerfully struck by the revelations that people remembered the revelations months later and drew a specific implication of the news regarding the trustworthiness of scientists. To do so, we first asked the following question to a nationally representative sample of 1,000 American adults in June 2010 (the methodology of the survey is described in the Appendix A):

> *During the last six months, do you remember hearing or reading anything in the news about emails that were sent by scientists who study the world's climate, or do you not remember hearing or reading anything in the news about that?*[5]

About one-third (32%) of the respondents said they remembered hearing or reading something. Thus, a majority of the respondents, 68%, said they had no memory of this event at all. However, a respondent saying that he or she remembered hearing or reading something does not mean that he or she could recall the specifics of the content of the news stories.

Respondents who said they remembered were asked the following open-ended question:

What do you remember hearing or reading about that?

Interviewers were instructed to record verbatim the answer exactly as the respondent said it, and probed with "What else do you remember hearing or reading about that?" until the respondent said "nothing." We conducted a content analysis on respondents' answers to the open-ended question. Each respondent was coded "yes" or "no" for nine questions (see Appendix B for methodology details).[6]

1   Emails were hacked or stolen.
2   Research was inaccurate or invalid.
3   There was disagreement among scientists.
4   There was scientific misconduct.
5   There was misinterpretation by opponents or the media.
6   There were statements about polar bears, arctic, glaciers, ozone, volcanoes, oceans and other naturals.
7   There were statements about global warming.
8   Respondents didn't remember.
9   Respondents said something substantive other than 1–8.

Many of these recollections were not a basis for doubting the credibility of climate science: 6% of respondents remembered that the emails made statements about polar bears, the arctic, glaciers, ozone, volcanoes, or other natural phenomena. 4% remembered the emails showing that there was disagreement among scientists. 3% remembered that the emails were hacked. 1% said that the emails made statements about global warming. And 1% said that the emails were misinterpreted by the media or others.

Only 12% of the respondents were both aware of the emails and reported that they indicated that scientific misconduct had occurred or that research findings had been inaccurate. Thus, if the emails were ever prominent in the minds of large numbers of Americans, the emails faded from people's consciousness six months after the event broke off.

Respondents who said they remembered were also asked:

Do these emails indicate to you that scientists who study the world's climate should be trusted, indicate to you that these scientists should not be trusted, or do they not indicate to you anything about whether these scientists should be trusted?

Only 9% of all survey respondents said that the emails suggested that climate scientists should not be trusted.[7]

To explore the impact of the IPCC report errors in a similar fashion, we asked the 1,000 respondents in the June 2010 survey:

During the last six months, do you remember hearing or reading anything in the news about mistakes in scientific reports that were written by the Intergovernmental Panel on Climate Change, or do you not remember hearing or reading anything in the news about that?

About one-quarter (24%) of the respondents said they remembered hearing or reading something in the news about the IPCC report errors. Thus, a majority of the respondents, 76%, said they had no memory of this event at all. Furthermore, a respondent saying that he or she remembered hearing or reading something does not mean that he or she could recall the specifics of the content of the news stories.

Respondents who said they remembered were asked the following open-ended question:

What do you remember hearing or reading about that?

Interviewers were instructed to record verbatim the answer exactly as the respondent said it, and probed with "What else do you remember hearing or reading about that?" until the respondent said "nothing." We conducted a content analysis on respondents' answers to the open-ended question. Each respondent was coded "yes" or "no" for six questions (see Appendix C for methodology details).[8]

1   There was disagreement.
2   There were mistakes or inaccuracies.
3   There was scientific misconduct.
4   There were statements about natural phenomena.
5   Respondents didn't remember.
6   Respondents said something substantive other than 1–5.

Many of these recollections were not a basis for doubting the credibility of climate science: 8% of respondents remembered that there were mistakes in the reports. Four percent remembered that there was disagreement among scientists. Five percent remembered nothing specific. Two percent remembered that there were some statements about polar bears, arctic, glaciers, ozone, volcanoes, oceans and other naturals. Only 4% of the full survey sample said they had heard that the errors indicated scientific misconduct.

Respondents who said they remembered were also asked:

Does what you heard or read about mistakes in these reports indicate to you that reports written by the Intergovernmental Panel on Climate Change should be trusted, indicate to you that these reports should not be trusted, or do you not indicate to you anything about whether these report should be trusted?

Only 13% of all survey respondents reported that they remembered hearing or reading about the mistakes and that the mistakes indicated that the IPCC reports should not be trusted.

Among the very small groups of people who said that the Climategate emails or the IPCC report mistakes raised questions about the trustworthiness of climate scientists, these pieces of news may have changed opinions about global warming or climate scientists. But it is also possible that the news had no impact on these people, because they may have distrusted scientists' statements about the environment and held skeptical views of global warming even before exposure to these news stories. To gauge the maximum possible effects of the Climategate and IPCC report error stories, we examined the distributions of beliefs and attitudes about global warming among respondents who thought that Climategate and the IPCC report errors raised doubts about the integrity of climate scientists.

Of the 9% of respondents who said that Climategate raised questions about the trustworthiness of climate scientists, 43% said that they trusted scientists' statements about the environment highly even after learning the news (4% of the full survey sample). Therefore, news of Climategate did not convince these people to become skeptical about these statements. The remainder, 57% of the 9% (5% of the full survey sample) is an upper bound estimate on the number of people who report having been influenced to become skeptical of scientists' statements about the environment by Climategate. A similar calculation indicates that 6% or less of the full survey sample report having been influenced to deny the existence of global warming. And a maximum of 5% report having been influenced to believe that past warming was not caused by humans.

Similar figures appeared with regard to the IPCC report errors. Of the 13% of respondents who said that the IPCC report errors raised questions about the trustworthiness of climate scientists, 41% said that they trusted scientists' statements about the environment highly even after learning the news (5% of the full survey sample). Therefore, news of the IPCC report errors did not convince these people to become skeptical about these statements. The remainder, 59% of the 13% (7% of the full survey sample) is an upper bound estimate on the number of people who report having been influenced to become skeptical of scientists' statements about the environment by the IPCC report errors. A similar calculation indicates that 8% or less of the full survey sample report having been influenced to deny the existence of global warming. And a maximum of 7% report having been influenced to believe that past warming was not caused by humans.

Of the people who believed that the news of Climategate or the IPCC report errors called scientists' trustworthiness into question and did not trust scientists' statements about the environment after the news broke, if a considerable number did not trust those statements before they heard about Climategate and the IPCC report errors, then the upper bound estimates in the prior two paragraphs may be substantial over-estimates of the numbers of people who were induced to think that scientists' statements about the environment should not be trusted, to doubt the existence of global warming, and to doubt the role of human activity in causing past warming.

However, it is also possible that all the above figures are underestimates of the numbers of people who were induced by the controversies to adopt skeptical views of scientists' statements about the environment and about global warming. Our analytic approach so far hinges on the assumption that people were not influenced unless they remembered the events and considered its implications to be damaging to climate scientists months after the news broke in the press. But perhaps some members of the public were influenced at the time the news was first disseminated and held onto their new skeptical views months later, even though these people could not recall Climategate or the IPCC report errors. Next section addressed this concern.

Impact Without Awareness

One may be concerned that we did not address the attitude change among people who did not remember exposure to news coverage of these events but whose trust in scientists was in fact influenced by these events. This seems a legitimate concern as numerous studies demonstrated that behavioral changes were induced to subjects without their awareness; that is, people were unaware of stimuli that affected their behavior (Nisbett & Wilson, 1977; Adams, 1957). In the traditional stimulus-response methodology whereby a response is predicted after exposure to stimulus, three sets of literature might pertain to our present study in terms of the perceptibility of stimulus of the exposure, the degree of attending to stimulus during the exposure, and cognitive process models of generating the response.

First set of literature pertains to subliminal stimulus, of which subjects could not conceivably be aware (Bornstein & D'Agostino, 1992; Bornstein, Leone, & Galley, 1987; Greenwald & Draine, 1997). The effect of subliminal stimuli was found to be mainly on affect, such as people's moods (Hawkins, 1970) and liking for objects (Bornstein, Leone, & Galley, 1987; Zajonc, 1968). While this literature shows that subliminal stimuli could influence behaviors, its applicability to our present study is limited for a number of reasons. The influence seemed to manifest on affect, but not on attitudes such as trust in scientists. The duration of the influence to subliminal stimuli was unspecified (Bornstein, Leone, & Galley, 1987), though many subliminal perception studies measured immediate influence while our survey asked people about the events that occurred six months ago. Another important difference was that reading news stories or watching news programs is unlikely to be exposure to subliminal stimulus.

Second set of literature is concerned with the effect of exposure to perceptible stimulus without attending to it; that is, influence from learning without involvement, such as in television advertisements (Krugman, 1965; Pechmann & Stewart, 1988). With repeated exposure, various behavioral outcomes, such as people's attitudes toward, intent to purchase and actual purchase of a brand in advertisements, were changed regardless of whether people were able to recall the brand, in an immediate or delayed fashion (Pechmann & Stewart, 1988). Attitudinal changes without remembering the exposure in advertisements are related to our study: people voluntarily exposed themselves to news coverage of these events, many of them may have multiple exposures with variations of news stories about these events. While it is possible that people who had been exposed to news coverage of these events were influenced by the exposure but failed to recall the exposure when probed as asked in our survey months later, this literature suggests few people would fall into this scenario, though a quantitative upper bound was infeasible to obtain given that studies in this literature involved non-representative samples of the American adult population.

Third set of literature pertains to the cognitive processing model of forming judgment—online versus memory-based judgment—when stimulus is perceptible and attention is paid to it (Hastie & Park, 1986; Lavine, 2002). It could be that when news media covered these events, some people were aware of and attended to the coverage, the information in the news coverage affected their attitudes toward these events and climate scientists and their trust in scientists more generally, and these people formed or updated these attitudes during their exposure to the coverage of these events. As time progressed, these people subsequently forgot about their attending to news coverage of these events, but the influence of the news coverage on their trust in scientists remained, making it an online judgment. When asked in our survey about their trust in scientists, these people would perform an online judgment by directly retrieving their summary opinion without retrieving or processing the information upon which the summary opinion was initially formed and/or subsequently updated. In our case, these people reported their trust in scientists through an online task while the trust judgment had been influenced by their exposure to news coverage of these events, which they did not remember.

Of interest is to gauge who might be those people and how to characterize them; that is, what proportion of the respondents might have performed online judgment in responding to our survey questions. Ability and motivation are hypothesized to be factors determining which processing model—online or memory-based—that people engage in for their political attitudes; online processing requires more of both ability and memory than memory-based processing because directly retrievable summary opinions require that people possess both the willingness and ability to attend to politics and to form evaluative responses toward political objects (Lavine, 2002). We employed personal issue importance measure to delineate people who might be most likely to undertake online processing (Bizer et al., 2006). All respondents were asked:

How important is the issue of global warming to you personally—extremely important, very important, somewhat important, not too important, or not at all?

We considered respondents who said "extremely important" or "very important" as people likely to engage in online judgment. Thirty-two percent of the survey sample fell into this category and reported that they did not remember reading or hearing news coverage on Climategate; among these people, less than one-fourth, 24%, did not trust scientists' statements about the environment. Assuming that all these low-trust people had been high trust before Climategate and became low trust because of Climategate, an upper bound of the trust-reducing effect of Climategate through online processing and failure to remember would be 8% of the survey sample.[9,10]

Trends in High Trust in Scientists and Global Warming Existence Belief

To overcome possible ambiguity in our results so far in this regard, we capitalized on two aspects of our survey data collection. First, since 2006, our annual national surveys have measured public trust in scientists' statements about the environment by asking:

How much do you trust the things scientists say about the environment— completely, a lot, a moderate amount, a little, or not at all?

As consistently throughout the chapter, high-trust people or people who trust scientists' statements highly are defined as people who gave response "completely," "a lot" or "a moderate amount" to the trust question, and low-trust people or people who do not trust scientists' statements highly are defined as people who gave response "a little," or "not at all" to the trust question. The 2009 interviewing was done immediately after the Climategate news broke (November 17–29), and the 2010 interviewing occurred seven months later. Comparison of our 2008, 2009, and 2010 surveys allowed us to assess whether the aggregate distribution of Americans' opinions changed after news of the controversies broke. The observed fluctuations in percentages estimate the net change in opinions of (1) people whose opinions changed and who were aware of the Climategate or IPCC error report news months later, and (2) people whose opinions changed as the result of exposure to the news but later forgot these events.

Public trust in scientists' statements about the environment did not decline from 2008 to 2009 or from 2009 to 2010. The percent of high-trust people— respondents who said they trusted scientists' statements about the environment completely, a lot, or a moderate amount was equivalent in 2008 and 2009 (69% in 2008 vs. 70% in 2009; design effects adjusted $F = .16, p = .69$), in 2008 and 2010 (69% in 2008 vs. 71% in 2010; design effects adjusted $F = 1.17, p = .28$), and in 2009 and 2010 (70% in 2009 vs. 71% in 2010; design effects adjusted $F = .23, p = .63$).[11] This evidence is inconsistent with the claim that Climategate and the IPCC errors decreased the public's trust in scientists' statements about the environment.

Consonant with the same conclusion is another type of evidence: changes in public opinion about the existence of global warming. If news stories about Climategate and the IPCC errors reduced trust in scientists' statements about the environment, the percent of Americans saying that global warming has been occurring might have declined as a result. To test this possibility, we examined the measurements obtained by various survey organizations that asked a question either directly or indirectly indicating respondents' beliefs about the existence of global warming (1) before Climategate and the IPCC report errors were publicized, and (2) after they were publicized.

Perhaps the most informative data were collected by NBC and the *Wall Street Journal*. In their October 2009 survey, conducted just before the news stories broke, 56% of respondents either said that "global climate change has been established as a serious problem and immediate action is necessary" or said that "there is enough evidence that climate change is taking place and some action should be taken." In a survey in December 11–14, 2009, just after the news stories broke, that figure was about the same: 54%. And seven months after the news stories broke, in June 2010, the figure was back to 56%. Neither of these shifts is statistically significant, suggesting that no real change in the distribution of opinions occurred.

The same conclusion is supported by data collected by the Pew Research Center. In their October 2009 survey, just before the news stories broke, 57% of respondents said that from what they had seen or heard, there was solid evidence that the earth's temperature had been rising during the last few decades. Eleven months after the news stories broke, another Pew survey found this figure to be 59%, not significantly different from the 57%. Thus, again, this evidence is consistent with the conclusion that the events caused no lasting change in the distribution of opinions.

Other surveys did register statistically significant changes over longer time periods, but they were small. For example, in March 2009, eight months before the news stories broke, 83% of Gallup Organization survey respondents said they believed that effects of global warming had already begun to occur or will occur in the future. That figure was 79% in March 2010, four months after the news stories broke, a significant but small 4 percentage points lower. Likewise, in May 2009, six months before the news stories broke, 69% of respondents in a Fox News survey said that they believed global warming existed. In December 8–9, 2009, just after the news stories broke, that percentage was 63% in another Fox News poll, a significant six percentage point decline.

Our own surveys revealed a similar pattern. In our July 2008 survey, 80% of respondents said they thought that the earth's temperature has probably been going up slowly over the past 100 years. That figure was 75% in our survey conducted just after the news stories broke (a significant decline) and was 74% seven months later, in June 2010.

Only one survey organization produced a different pattern of results. In a survey done in April 2009, CNN found that 81% of respondents said that global warming was a proven fact. That figure dropped to 68% in a survey done in December 2–3, 2009, and dropped a little more to 64% in May 2010. The drop from 81% to 68% was statistically significant, though the drop from 68% to 64% was not.

Averaging across all of the nine pre-November 2009 to post-November 2009 comparisons that these surveys permit, the drop potentially attributable to Climategate and the IPCC report errors is six percentage points. Because other events occurred during the time period between each pair of surveys, we cannot know with confidence what caused this apparent decline. But it does seem reasonable to conclude that at most, the impact of these events was very small.[12,13]

The Impact of Trust in Scientists' Statements about the Environment

Every one of the surveys reviewed above showed that a majority of Americans believed that global warming was real, and some surveys documented huge majorities holding that belief. Is this evidence that most Americans have been persuaded by the scientific evidence on this point? We believe not. The reason is that Americans can come to believe that the earth has been warming by a variety of different routes, some of which do not involve scientists at all.

Conceptually, what might shape public perception of the existence of global warming and what might account for the variability of such perception? Weber (2010) proposed two learning models through which beliefs about global warming are formed: learning from personal experience and learning from a statistical description. Learning from a statistical description involves cognitive processes that require analytical processing skills that need to be acquired as well as cognitive efforts, while learning from personal experience involves associative and affective processes that are automatic, provided by the basic human ability and require neither acquired analytical processing skills nor cognitive efforts. While climate scientists formed their perceptions of global warming based primarily on analytic processing, nonscientists or laypersons typically rely more on associative and affective processing of climate-related information that they are exposed to.

When laypersons rely on external sources of scientific evidences and scientific expertise to form their opinions about global warming, the effectiveness of this reliance depends on attention to and trust in external sources, i.e. scientists who study the world's climate. This route hinges on trust in an expert source. According to a great deal of theory and empirical evidence in social psychology, people are more likely to accept a person's assertion if that person is perceived to be expert on the topic (Hovland, Janis, & Kelley, 1953; Petty & Cacioppo, 1986; Petty, Cacioppo, & Schumann, 1983; Sternthal, Phillips, & Dholakia, 1978). Trust in the source of a message has been shown to regulate attitude change in this way in many domains, such as social capital formation (Putnam, 1993), the impact of the news media on evaluations of presidents (Miller & Krosnick, 2000), and vote choice (Heatherington, 1999). Therefore, when deciding whether the earth has been warming over the last 100 years, relying on scientific research findings is likely to occur among citizens who trust the scientists who generated the evidence (Malka, Krosnick, & Langer, 2009).

But about one quarter of Americans are low-trust people, people who have trusted scientists' assertions about the environment only a little or not at all?[14] Unable or unwilling to rely on external sources of scientific evidences and expertise provided by climate scientists, how should such a citizen decide whether the earth has been warming over the last 100 years? According to some recent research, these individuals might execute experiential processing (Marx et al., 2007) and generalize from their own personal experiences observing what they believe to be the effects of global warming (Myers et al., 2013) or with changes in local temperatures (Borick & Rabe, 2012; Deryugina, 2013; Egana & Mullina, 2012; Joireman, Truelove, & Duell, 2010; Li, Johnson, & Zava, 2011). That is, low-trust people tend to form perceptions about global warming based on some personal experience; for example, low-trust people who believe they have seen effects of global warming or who believe that temperatures have been warmer recently or who are warm at the time of answering a survey question might therefore be especially inclined to report that long-term warming has been occurring.

In summary, these theories and empirical evidences suggest that laypersons who trust external sources of scientific evidences and expertise form science-related beliefs such as whether global warming has been happening based on assertions from these sources, while those who do not form theirs based on their own personal experience. That trust in scientific sources regulates how laypersons form their beliefs about scientific constructs not only sheds light on what route laypersons take to form their perceptions of global warming, but also provides predictions on what accounts for the variability of such beliefs. First, the moderating role of scientific trust predicts between-route variations in perceptions formed from the two routes. For beliefs about the existence of global warming whereby there is a strong consensus among scientists that the warming is unequivocal, people who trust scientists and rely on scientists' findings would be more likely to believe in the warming than people who do not trust scientists and rely on their own personal experience such as witnessing climate events that might be manifested by global warming. Drawing from anecdotal evidence and general observations that suggest a pattern of generally underweighting small-probability climate events, Weber (2010) stated that judging whether global warming has been happening based on personal experience will lead to judgments that are low. This prediction also sheds light on the role of personal experience of high-trust people in forming science-related beliefs. Having not assumed that high-trust people would completely ignore their own personal experience, it follows from this prediction that high-trust people who have a higher level of judgment about global warming existence would supersede any judgment drawn from personal experience which is lower.

Second, the moderating role of scientific trust also predicts within-route variation in perceptions formed from each of the two routes. For beliefs about the existence of global warming whereby scientific evidences supporting the occurrence of warming has been consistent over time, people who trust scientists and rely on scientists' findings would be consistent in their perceptions about global warming and there will be thus little variations in their perceptions over time, while people who do not trust scientists and rely on their own personal experience would show large variations in their perceptions over time because personal experience is more variable and volatile (Weber, 2010).

Here, we propose another possible reasoning strategy that low-trust individuals might implement. Rather than generalizing from their own personal experiences to the entire planet, low-trust people could rely on planet-level data that are not collected or analyzed by scientists. Specifically, low-trust citizens might rely on reports of trends in world temperatures. We suspect that many people believe that temperature measurements are not complex scientific assessments subject to controversy and are instead objective facts that can be obtained indisputably with a thermometer, with no scientific competence necessary. And low-trust individuals might be inclined to base their beliefs about long-term warming of the planet on such data.

In fact, news media stories published in recent years have routinely trumpeted the prior year's average world temperature (Banerjee, 2013), because the National Oceanic and Atmospheric Administration has issued a report on this annually, accompanied by a press release (NOAA, 2012a), and headlines have often made claims that the world's temperature has been unusually high or low (Banerjee, 2013; Durando, 2013; Samenow, 2013). Advocates of concern about global warming have often encouraged using the prior year's global temperature to make inferences about long-term planetary warming. For example, such advocates were quick to point out in 2011 that 2010 was the warmest year on record and that this should be viewed as evidence that global warming is real (Eilperin, 2010). By the same token, 2011 was the coolest year worldwide between 2001 and 2011, which was viewed by some skeptical observers as evidence questioning global warming (NOAA, 2012b). Because average world temperature has gone up and down from year to year in small increments, perhaps the proportion of low-trust citizens who believed in the existence of global warming has risen and fallen in parallel, because these individuals have over-generalized from the most recent year.

To test for this possibility, we separated our survey samples into people high in trust in scientists' statements about the environment and people low in such trust[15]. As shown in Figure 13.1, among high-trust people, the proportion who believed that the earth has been gradually warming held relatively steady between 2006 and 2012. It was highest in 2007 (88%) and lowest in 2010 (81%), a statistically significant difference. However, among low-trust people, the percent who thought that gradual warming had been occurring dropped from a high of 77% in 2006 to a low of 55% in 2009, a much more dramatic and statistically significant shift, three times the size of the drop among high-trust people.

The pattern among low-trust people matches remarkable closely the world's average temperature over those years, lagged by one year (so 2006's temperature appears in the column labeled 2007), shown in Figure 13.1.[16] From 2006 to 2007, the world's temperature (lagged) declined (by almost one-tenth of a degree Celsius), and so did the percentage of low-trust people who believed in the existence of global warming (a decrease of 6 percentage points). A similar pattern occurred from 2008 to 2009: world temperature declined (by nearly

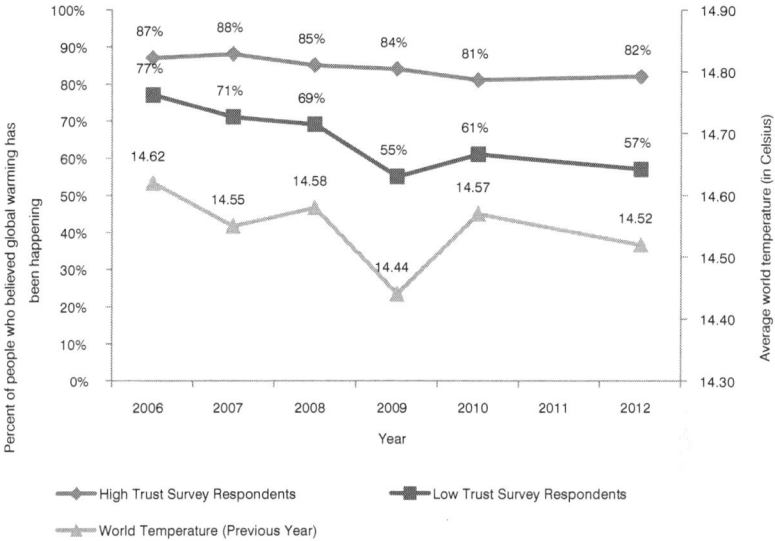

FIGURE 13.1 Public Opinion about the Existence of Global Warming and Recent World Temperatures (Notes: Data on the average world temperature were compiled by the Earth Policy Institute using information from the National Aeronautics and Space Administration, the Goddard Institute for Space Studies, and the "Global Land-Ocean Temperature Index in 0.01 Degrees Celsius," available at: data.giss. nasa.gov/gistemp/tabledata/GLB.Ts+dSST.txt, updated January 2012. Data on trust in scientists and global warming were obtained from national surveys conducted by Stanford University and affiliates.)

one and half tenths of a degree Celsius), and this was accompanied by a large reduction (14 percentage points) in the fraction of low-trust people who believed that global warming had been happening. Conversely, when world temperature increased (e.g., from 2008 to 2009), the proportion of low-trust people who believed in global warming's existence also increased.

Consistent with this logic are results of regressions predicting belief in the existence of global warming. Among low-trust people, for every one-tenth degree increase in the previous year's average temperature, belief that global warming had been happening increased by a significant 10 percentage points ($b = .10, p < .01$). This relation was absent among high-trust people ($b = .01, p = .26$). This is consistent with the notion that the dynamics of low-trust people's opinions about the existence of global warming were partly driven by recent world temperatures.

Time series data of this sort are routinely used to evaluate the plausibility of causal propositions (e.g., Shumway, 1988). The fact that temperature changes in one year anticipated changes in public opinion the next year rules out the possibility of reverse causation or simultaneity. Nonetheless, the decline in existence beliefs in 2009 might be attributable to other causes, such as the substantial drop in news media coverage of global warming that occurred then (Boykoff & Nacu-Schmidt, 2013). According to the agenda-setting hypothesis, when news stories devote considerable attention to an issue, the issue becomes more salient to the public, and the public infers that more salient problems are more nationally significant (McCombs & Shaw, 1972). If the public infers the existence of the problem (i.e., whether the planet has been warming) from the frequency with which they've heard it discussed in news stories, then public belief about the existence of long-term warming might covary with the extent of news coverage of global warming.

However, the available data do not confirm this claim. The total volume of mainstream U.S. news media coverage of global warming increased substantially from 2006 to 2007 and then decreased in 2008 and decreased more in 2009, increased a bit after that, and declined thereafter until 2011 (Boykoff & Nacu-Schmidt, 2013). This pattern (even with a one-year lag) does not match the dynamics of opinions shown in Figure 13.1: although news media coverage of global warming was dramatically greater in 2007 than in 2006, public belief in the existence of global warming did not rise between those years—indeed, the proportion of low-trust people who believed in the existence of long-term warming declined.

Another hypothesis that might explain the drop in existence beliefs in 2009 involves Americans' perceptions of the economic health of the nation. Perhaps when economic conditions are tough, people are motivated to deny the significance of environmental threats, so that public energy can be focused on improving the economy without distraction by environmental issues. Therefore, perhaps recession-induced economic hardships that began in late 2008 created economic insecurity and dampened confidence in the economy, which in turn led to a decline in the proportion of people who believed that global warming had been occurring, so as to rationalize non-attention to that issue (Brulle, Carmichael, & Jenkin, 2012; Kahn & Kotchen, 2010; Scuggs & Benegal, 2012; Shum, 2012).

To test this hypothesis, one might be tempted to use objective indicators of the health of the economy, such as the unemployment rate, the inflation rate, average stock prices, or many others. However, we see no obvious conceptual grounds to select among the numerous possible such indicators for use in analysis. More importantly, such indicators seem likely to influence public judgment only to the extent that people use them to make inferences about the health and trajectory of the economy. We therefore measured such perceptions directly via assessments of consumer confidence, which are individual-level perceptions of and optimism about the state of the national economy. The Index of Consumer Sentiment (measured monthly in the University of Michigan's Survey of Consumers) increased from 2006 to 2007, declined smoothly until late 2008, remained low in 2009, and rose in 2010 and 2011 (Consumer Sentimental Index, 2013). In contrast, among low-trust Americans, the proportion who believed in the existence of global warming declined from 2006 to 2007, remained steady from 2007 to 2008, dropped in 2009, rose in 2010, and dropped by 2012. Thus, the two time series do not exhibit matching trajectories.

Furthermore, even if it were true that the changes in public beliefs about the existence of global warming shown in Figure 13.1 are attributable to changes in the volume of news coverage of the issue or to the 2008 economic recession, there is no strong theoretical rationale for why such impact would be confined to people low in trust in scientists' statements about the environment. In fact, one might anticipate the opposite relation: mainstream news media coverage of global warming has been dominated by coverage of claims by natural science experts that the earth has been warming and has rarely devoted attention to claims by such experts that global warming has not been happening (Boykoff & Boykoff, 2004; Boykoff & Roberts, 2007). Therefore, changes in the volume of such coverage would presumably influence highly trusting people more than low-trust people.[17]

Yet another possible explanation for the decline in the number of people who believed in global warming's existence in 2009 is Downs' "Issue Attention Cycle" (Downs, 1972). According to Downs, controversial issues often progress through five stages: (1) the pre-problem stage, before the public is aware of its seriousness; (2) a dramatic event (such as the *Exxon Valdez* Oil Spill) suddenly calls people's attention to a highly undesirable situation and causes elites to commit to solving the problem, which in turn causes a surge in public concern about it; (3) people begin to realize that solving the problem won't be easy; (4) people begin to feel threatened by solutions or to become bored with the topic; and (5) public concern disappears. This perspective might explain the decline in existence beliefs in Figure 13.1 from 2008 to 2009 if that was a time period when the public became especially aware of the difficulties that would be entailed by trying to address global warming, became bored with the issue, and sought to rationalize inattention by denying the existence of the problem. But this theory would not predict, nor could it explain, the increase in existence belief that occurred between 2009 and 2010, nor does this theory anticipate that over-time changes would be concentrated among people low in trust in scientists.

The argument we have made so far is that among people high in trust in scientists' statements about the environment, opinions about the existence of global warming were constant over time because these people were especially likely to rely on these scientists' statements, whereas low trust individuals were not. Support for this general perspective comes from an experiment we conducted. The experiment was embedded in a survey of American adults who signed up with a firm to complete surveys regularly via the Internet in exchange for cash or prizes and completed our questionnaire during January 2009 (see Appendix D for the data collection methodology of the survey).[18] Respondents were randomly assigned to watch one of four television news stories, and then answered questions reporting their opinions on global warming. The four news stories were as follows.

1 **Existence without Skeptic** (1 min., 45 sec.): An ABC News story describing IPCC-endorsed research suggesting that the earth's temperature has been increasing due to human activity.

2 **Existence with Skeptic** (2 min., 23 sec.): The **Existence without Skeptic** story plus an additional 38 seconds featuring a skeptical scientist arguing that current carbon emissions are not influencing global temperature.

3 **Consequences without Skeptic** (1 min., 20 sec.): A PBS news interview with a natural scientist describing the likely harmful consequences of global warming, including floods and hurricanes, harm to a variety of plant and animal species, and undesirable economic consequences.

4 **Consequences with Skeptic** (2 min., 14 sec.): The **Consequences without Skeptic** story plus an additional 54 seconds of an interview with a skeptical economist arguing that more carbon dioxide will produce more plants, will produce more food for animals, and will favorably impact the American economy.

Upon watching one of the above four new stories, respondents answered questions reporting their opinions on global warming: global warming has been happening and certainty of this belief, five degrees Fahrenheit warming in 75 years would be bad, global warming will be a serious problem for the world, and desired amount of government action to deal with global warming (see Appendix D for question wording and response coding).

Comparisons across these conditions allowed us to explore two issues.

1 Does exposure to someone presented as an expert expressing skeptical views about climate change increase acceptance of those skeptical views?

2 Does the impact of exposure to a message from someone portrayed as a skeptical expert have more impact on the opinions of people who place more trust in scientists?

Adding a skeptic to the mainstream science messages reduced expression of the mainstream scientific views by the survey respondents. Compared to respondents who watched the mainstream scientific message without a skeptic, exposure to the skeptic led to an 8 percentage point decrease in the percent of people who believed that global warming had been happening with high certainty ($d = -.08$, $p < .01$), as well as decreases in the percent of people who said global warming would be bad ($d = -.07$, $p < .10$), who said that global warming is a globally serious problem ($d = -.05$, $p < .05$), and who supported more federal government action on global warming ($d = -.05$, $p < .05$).

Furthermore, the impact of the skeptics was greater among people who trusted scientists' statements about the environment. For example, exposure to the skeptics reduced belief in the existence of global warming among people who were highly trusting of scientists' statements about the environment ($d = -.05$, $p < .05$), but no change in this proportion occurred among people who were low in trust in scientists' statements about the environment ($d = .03$, *n.s.*). The same pattern of moderation by trust appeared with judgments of the seriousness of global warming and in policy support: the decrease was apparent among people who trusted scientists' statements about the environment but not among those who did not (global warming is a globally serious problem: $d = -.08$, $p < .01$; $d = .06$, *n.s.*, respectively; desire for more government actions about global warming: $d = -.09$, $p < .05$; $d = .04$, *n.s.*, respectively). Thus, not surprisingly, people who were more trusting of scientists' statements about the environment relied more on their opinions, including the opinions of people portrayed as scientific experts who expressed skepticism.

The Origins of Trust in Scientists' Statements about the Environment

Next, we explored the causes of trust in scientists' statements about the environment (Critchley, 2008; Das & Teng, 2004; Siegrist, 2000; Siegrist & Cvetkovich, 2000; Slovic, 1993). We hypothesized that more formal education might cause more exposure to the scientific method and that such exposure may engender more trust in that method. Furthermore, because younger adults' exposures to science in school, in the news across their lifetimes, in their work settings are likely to have illustrated more sophisticated research methods and findings, these individuals may end up with more confidence in science and scientists. Furthermore, because trusted leaders can persuade citizens to adopt their views, visible attacks on the credibility of science by prominent Republicans during the last decade might have induced citizens who think of themselves as Republicans or conservatives to express more skepticism about scientists (Zaller, 1992). Likewise, more exposure to conservative-leaning presentations of news (e.g., by Fox News) might have reduced trust in scientists' statements, whereas more exposure to mainstream news might entail more sympathetic portrayals of science and therefore increase trust.[19]

Results consistent with these predictions emerged from a logistic regression predicting trust using our 2010 survey data (see Appendix A for the data collection methodology of the survey; see also Table 13.1). The more educated an individual was, the more likely he or she was to express trust. Also as expected, younger adults were more trusting than older adults. Third, Democrats were expectedly significantly more trusting than Independents, whose trust levels were equal to those of Republicans (Mooney & Kirshenbaum, 2009). And conservatives were significantly less trusting than moderates, whose trust levels were equal to those of liberals (Gauchat, 2012).

TABLE 13.1   Predictors of High Trust in Scientists' Statements about the Environment (Survey Data Collected in November 2010)

Predictor	Marginal Effect
Democrat	0.13★★★
Republican	–0.03
Liberal	0.05
Conservative	–0.09★★
Female	0.11★★★
Having child(ren)	0.06
Hispanic	0.06
African American	–0.11
Asian and other races	0.08
Married	–0.01
High school graduate	0.11★
Some college	0.12★★
College graduate	0.19★★★
Age 25–34	–0.17
Age 35–44	–0.18
Age 45–54	–0.25★★
Age 55–64	–0.28★★
Age 65 and older	–0.31★★★
Midwest	–0.07
South	–0.06
West	–0.11
(10) Days viewing Fox News	–0.10★★★
(10) Days viewing TV News	0.07★★★
N	1001

Notes: Presented are the marginal effects from a logistic regression predicting high trust in scientists' statements about the environment adjusting for sampling weights. Omitted categories are Independent, moderate, non-Hispanic, White, non-married, having no child, less than high school education, ages 18–24, and lived in the Northeast. Dummy variables identifying people with missing values for each predictor were included in the regression but are not shown here. The dependent variable was coded 1 for respondents who trusted what scientists say about the environment completely, a lot, or a moderate amount, and 0 for respondents who said they trusted what scientists said about the environment a little or not all or did not answer (excluding the five people who did not answer did not change the results).
★★★ $p<0.01$ ★★ $p<0.05$ ★ $p<0.1$

As expected, more exposure to Fox News was associated with lower levels of trust in scientists' statements about the environment.[20] And more exposure to non-Fox television news was associated with more trust in scientists' statements about the environment (for similar findings, see Hmielowski et al., 2012).[21]

Trust did not vary across racial groups, between parents and non-parents, or across regions of the country. However, women were more trusting of scientists' statements about the environment than were men.

Our finding regarding sex contrasts with some evidence in other domains finding no differences between men and women in other sorts of trust (Croson & Buchan, 1999; Scott, 1983) or finding that women were less trusting of scientific research than were men (e.g. Siegrist, 2000, in the domain of gene technology). Therefore, the gender gap in trust in science or scientists might be domain-dependent, and what was observed here might be specific to global warming.

Our results are in line with other findings discovered in previous studies and are sometimes strikingly different. For example, a survey of residents of the Milwaukee area did show that older people and more politically conservative people trusted university scientists' statements about the environment less (as did we) but revealed no relation of trust with sex or education, and showed African-Americans to be less trusting than Whites (Brewer & Ley, 2013). As did we, Hmielowski et al. (2012) found that trust in scientists as a source of information about global warming was greater among more educated people, among people who were less exposed to conservative television news and talk radio, among people who were more exposed to non-conservative news media, and among people with more conservative political ideologies, and found no relation of trust with race (Hmielowski et al., 2012). Perhaps like us, these authors also found trust in scientists' statements about global warming to be significantly related to sex, but the authors did not explain how sex was coded in their regressions, so it is not possible to tell whether men or women manifested higher levels of trust. However, Hmielowski et al. (2012) found no relation of trust with age. Another study revealed that trust in scientific statements about offshore oil drilling were lower among people who were more conservative but did not vary with political party identification (Carlisle et al., 2010). Gauchat (2011) found that trust in science was higher for more educated people but lower for non-whites than for whites and unrelated to age or sex or political conservatism (Gauchat, 2011). Gauchat (2012) found, as did we, that trust in science increased with education, decreased with increasing age, and was lower among conservatives and moderates than among liberals (Gauchat, 2012). But unlike us, Gauchat (2012) found that women trusted science less than did men, that Southerners trusted science less than people in other regions, and that Republicans were no less trusting than Democrats. Thus, findings regarding the correlates of trust in science and scientists have been quite inconsistent across studies and therefore seem to merit further investigation.

In summary, some of these findings match those in past studies of predictors of trust in scientists, but other findings do not, so it appears that more research in this area is needed to clarify these inconsistencies.

Differentiating Types of Scientists

In our past surveys, we have routinely measured trust by asking respondents about their trust in scientists' statements about the environment. One might imagine that the public differentiates scientists' statements about the environment from scientists' statements about global warming in particular. To investigate this possibility, we asked all the respondents in our June 2012 survey two questions about trust:

> How much do you trust the things scientists say about the environment—completely, a lot, a moderate amount, a little, or not at all?
> and
> How much do you trust the things scientists say about global warming—completely, a lot, a moderate amount, a little, or not at all?

(See Appendix A for the data collection methodology of the survey.) These two trust questions were spaced out during the survey administration; the first trust question was asked of respondents at the beginning of the survey while the second one was asked toward the end of the same survey.

The distributions of responses to the two questions were nearly identical. As consistently throughout the chapter, high-trust people or people who trust scientists' statements highly are defined as people who gave response "completely," "a lot" or "a moderate amount" to the trust question, and low-trust people or people who do not trust scientists' statements highly are defined as people who gave response "a little," or "not at all" to the trust question. When asked about scientists' statements about the environment, 64% said completely, a lot, or a moderate amount.[22] That number was 61% when asked about scientists' statements about global warming. A paired *t*-test showed these proportions not to be significantly different from one another.

Furthermore, answers to the two questions matched for the vast majority of the respondents. Among respondents who trusted scientists' statements about the environment highly, an overwhelming majority (81%) trusted scientists' statements about global warming highly. And among respondents who did not trust scientists' statements about the environment highly, nearly as large a majority (75%) did not trust scientists' statements about global warming highly. In total, only 21% of respondents offered different opinions in response to the two questions (high trust to one, low trust to the other). And of these individuals, 62% did so because their ratings differed by the very small distance of only one point on the 5-point rating scale (from a moderate amount to a little or from a little to a moderate amount). Thus, there is no notable difference between the public's trust in scientists' statements about the environment generally and in scientists' statements about global warming in particular. These survey questions did not differentiate subgroups of scientists from one another. We asked respondents about trust in what "scientists" say about the environment or global warming; we did not ask about "scientists who specialize in studying the earth's climate," for example. Therefore, our questions presumably referred both to statements made by such scientists and statements made about the environment or global warming by scientists who do not specialize in the latter issue. Future research might explore whether asking about "scientists who specialize in studying the earth's climate" yields different results than do the questions we have asked to date.

Conclusion

More than a decade of public opinion research on global warming supports three conclusions. First, only a very small portion of Americans were aware of the Climategate and IPCC error controversies and maintained the view that these controversies raised questions about the integrity of climate science. Second, most Americans have trusted scientists' statements about the environment at least moderately, and public trust did not decline after the two controversies hit the front pages of newspapers. Third, the percent of Americans who believed in the existence of global warming was lowered by a very small amount after publicity of these controversies. All this suggests that these controversies, which captured the attention of many natural scientists and many observers of science, had little if any measurable impact on relevant opinions of the nation as a whole.

We saw evidence suggesting that trust in scientists' statements about the environment has been consequential in the process of opinion formation, just as social psychologists would anticipate. Among people who did not trust scientists' statements about the environment, opinions about the existence of global warming rose and fell since 2006 in ways paralleling the prior year's average world temperature, suggesting that that signal may have been a basis for those opinions. No such relation was apparent among people who did trust scientists' statements about the environment—these individuals were more likely to believe that global warming has been occurring than were less trusting people. This suggests that public acceptance of scientific research findings was not notably affected by Climategate, nor by the IPCC report errors.

Furthermore, we saw that the impact of scientists who are climate skeptics is regulated by trust in scientists' statements about the environment. People who trust scientists' statements about the environment were more persuaded by skeptical experts than were people who do not. There is no small amount of irony in this finding. Some mainstream scientists may be disappointed to learn that the credibility of their profession generally lends credibility to all members of the community, regardless of whether an individual scientist's views are in line with the majority or not. This raises the intriguing notion that perhaps future surveys should measure public trust in research findings of scientists who believe global warming is real and human-caused vs. research findings of scientists who do not express these views. Our data suggest that efforts to enhance the public's trust in scientists' statements about the environment may increase the degree to which people accept the views of mainstream climate scientists and of climate skeptics.

Finally, our findings suggest that as Americans receive increasing amount of formal education, exposure to scientific training may become more widespread, and national trust levels may rise as a result. But if climate skepticism becomes more prominent on Fox News and/or if people's exposure to such news outlets rises in the future while their content remains the same as it has been, and if national exposure to mainstream news media continues to decline while its content remains the same, this may cause a decrease in public trust in scientists' research findings about the environment. If such a decline does occur, then the influence on global warming beliefs of signals such as annual world temperatures may rise.

Appendix A

Data Collection Methodology for National Global Warming Surveys

Data Collection Methodology of the Stanford 2006 Survey

The 2006 survey was a random digit dialing telephone survey that involved calling landline telephone numbers of a national probability sample of 1,002 U.S. adults ages 18 and older, conducted by TNS of Horsham, PA, between March 9 and March 14, 2006, commissioned by ABC News, Time, and Stanford University. The sample was provided by Survey Sampling International, and interviews were conducted in both English and Spanish. The results have a 3-point margin of error.

Data Collection Methodology of the Stanford 2007 Survey

The 2007 survey was a random digit dial landline telephone survey of a national probability sample of 1,002 U.S. adults ages 18 and older, conducted by TNS of Horsham, PA, between April 5 and April 10, 2007, commissioned by ABC News, Washington Post, and Stanford University. The sample was provided by Survey Sampling International, and interviews were conducted in both English and Spanish. The results have a 3-point margin of error.

Data Collection Methodology of the Stanford 2008 Survey

The 2008 survey was a random digit dial landline telephone survey of a national probability sample of 1,000 U.S. adults ages 18 and older, conducted by TNS of Horsham, PA, between July 23 and July 28, 2008, commissioned by ABC News, Planet Green, and Stanford University. The sample was provided by Survey Sampling International, and interviews were conducted in both English and Spanish. The AAPOR Response Rate 3 was 29%.

Data Collection Methodology of the Stanford 2009 Survey

The 2009 survey was conducted by GfK Roper Public Affairs & Media, commissioned by Stanford University and the Associated Press. This telephone poll involved interviews with a nationally-representative probability sample of 1,005 adults age 18 or older. Interviews were conducted between November 17 and November 29, 2009, with 705 respondents on landlines and 300 on cellular telephones. The landline and cell phone samples were provided by Survey Sampling International. Interviews were conducted in both English and Spanish. The AAPOR Response Rate 3 was 12%.

Data Collection Methodology of the Stanford June 2010 Survey

The Stanford June 2010 survey was a random digit dial telephone survey of a national probability sample of 1,000 U.S. adults aged 18 and older conducted by GfK Custom Research North America between June 1 and June 7, 2010, with 699 respondents on landlines and 301 on cellular telephones. Both landline and cell phone samples were provided by Survey Sampling International. Data were weighted to account for probabilities of selection due to varying numbers of telephone lines that could reach the respondent and varying numbers of adults living in each household, and then post-stratified on age, sex, education and race, using targets from the March 2009 supplement of the Current Population Survey. The weighting also took into account the patterns of land and cell phone usage by region from the 2009 fall estimates provided by Mediamark Research Inc. The survey had margin of error of plus or minus 4.4 percentage points.

Data Collection Methodology of the Stanford November 2010 Survey

The November 2010 survey, sponsored by Stanford University, was a random digit dial telephone survey of a national probability sample of U.S. adults aged 18 and older conducted by Abt SRBI, November 1 and November 14, 2010. Some 671 respondents were interviewed on a landline phone, and 330 were interviewed on a cell phone. Interviews were administrated in English and Spanish.

Samples were drawn from both landline and cellular random digit dial (RDD) frames to represent people with access to either a landline or cell phone. Both samples were provided by Survey Sampling International, LLC, according to specifications from Abt SRBI. Numbers for the landline sample were drawn with equal probabilities from active blocks (area code + exchange + two-digit block number) that contained one or more residential directory listings. The cellular sample was drawn through a systematic sampling from 1000-blocks dedicated to cellular service according to the Telcordia database.

The data were weighted to ensure that the sample composition reflected the U.S. population in terms of demographics documented by figures from the U.S. Census Bureau. Weights were created to adjust for differential probabilities of selection due to the number of adults in the household, the number of voice-use landlines and cell phones, and the overlap of landline and cell phone RDD frames, as well as non-coverage and nonresponse through post-stratification. Post-stratification matched the population proportions of age, sex, education, ethnicity, race, and Census region, using targets from the September 2010 Current Population Survey conducted by the U.S. Census Bureau. The weighting combined the interviews done on landlines and cell phones taking into account the rates of landline and cell phone usage documented by the 2009 National Health Interview Survey. The AAPOR Response Rate 3 was 17%.

Data Collection Methodology of the Stanford 2012 Survey

The Stanford 2012 survey was a random digit dial telephone survey of a national probability sample of 804 U.S. adults aged 18 and older conducted by Abt SRBI, between June 13 and June 21, 2012. 603 respondents were interviewed on a landline phone, and 201 were interviewed on a cellular phone. Interviews were administered in English only.

Samples were drawn from both landline and cellular random digit dial (RDD) frames by Survey Sampling International. Numbers for the landline sample were drawn with equal probabilities from active blocks (area code + exchange + two-digit block number) that contained one or more residential directory listings. The cellular phone sample was drawn through a systematic sampling from 1000 blocks dedicated to cellular service according to the Telcordia database.

The data were weighted to ensure that the sample composition reflected the U.S. population in terms of demographics documented by figures from the U.S. Census Bureau. Weights were created to adjust for differential probabilities of selection due to the number of adults in the household, the number of voice-use landlines and cell phones, and the overlap of landline and cell phone RDD frames, as well as non-coverage and nonresponse through post-stratification. Post-stratification matched the population proportions of age and sex, education and sex, ethnicity and race, and region using targets from the 2010 American Community Survey conducted by the U.S. Census Bureau. The weighting combined the interviews done on landlines and cell phones taking into account the rates of landline and cell phone usage documented by the 2009 National Health Interview Survey. The AAPOR Response Rate 3 for the survey was 15%.

Appendix B

Instructions for Content Analysis of Survey Responses on Climategate

You will read answers that survey respondents gave to an open-ended survey question and make nine coding decisions about what each person said. Survey respondents—nationally representative sample of American adults—were asked, on phone interviews, the following question:

During the last six months, do you remember hearing or reading anything in the news about emails that were sent by scientists who study the world's climate, or do you not remember hearing or reading anything in the news about that?

The respondents who answered "yes" to the above question were asked the following question:

What do you remember hearing or reading about that?

And their answers are for you to read and make six coding decisions. Please do your work completely independently. Do NOT talk with anyone other than the study investigators about anything you do on this project. Please read the text very carefully and follow the instructions below.

9 Coding Questions

Note: The pronoun "they" in responses can be interpreted to be referring to scientists.

Q1. "emails were hacked"
   Type "yes" if the respondent said anything that indicates *any* of the following:
a   someone hacked or stole emails OR
b   someone leaked emails OR
c   emails scientists wrote about their research (data, figures, methods, results) OR
d   emails where scientists made comments on others (other scientists).

   Type "no" if the respondent said none of the above.

Q2. "inaccuracy of research"
  Type "yes" if the respondent said anything that indicates *any* of the following:
a   research, including data, methods, and findings, or other information, was
    not accurate OR
b   research, including data, methods, and findings, or other information, was
    not valid OR
c   research, including data, methods, and findings, or other information, was
    exaggerated or overestimated OR
d   research, including data, figures, methods, findings, or other information,
    was questionable or was questioned OR
e   research findings show that climate change is not as serious a problem as
    some scientists have claimed.

  Type "no" if the respondent said none of the above.

Q3. "disagreement among scientists"
  Type "yes" if the respondent said anything that indicates *any* of the following:
a   there was disagreement among scientists OR
b   some scientists said one thing, and other scientists said the opposite OR
c   there was an argument among scientists OR
d   there is controversy about what scientists' findings mean.

Type "no" if the respondent said none of the above.

Q4. "scientific misconduct"
  Type "yes" if the respondent said anything that indicates *any* of the following:
a   one or more scientists did something unethical in their research OR
b   one or more scientists did something unethical with their data—they
    withheld the data, or they manipulated or falsified the data OR
c   one or more scientists did something unethical in their statistical analysis—
    they skewed the analysis or biased their results OR
d   one or more scientists should not be trusted OR
e   one or more scientists did research for their own personal or financial gains
    (including to get more funding for their research) OR
f   one or more scientists did research for political reasons.

Type "no" if the respondent said none of the above.

Q5. "misinterpretations of the content of the emails"
  Type "yes" if the respondent said anything that indicates *any* of the following:
a   the content of emails was described in a misleading way by taking quotes
    out of context (by opponents, or by the media), or people misinterpreted
    the emails OR

b   controversies or disagreement among scientists were exaggerated by the news media.

Type "no" if the respondent said none of the above.

Q6. "polar bears, arctic, glaciers, ozone, volcanoes, oceans, or other natural phenomena"
Type "yes" if the respondent said anything that indicates *any* of the following:
a   about polar bears or other animals OR
b   about arctic icebergs or glaciers melting or receding OR
c   about ozone, or volcanoes, or oceans, or storms, or other natural phenomena.

Type "no" if the respondent said none of the above.

Q7. "green or not-green statements"
Type "yes" if the respondent said anything that indicates *any* of the following:
a   the emails were about global warming or climate change OR
b   the emails were about the evidence on or causes of global warming or climate change OR
c   the emails said that global warming or climate change has been happening, or has been caused by human actions OR
d   the emails indicate that actions should be taken to mitigate the effects of global warming or climate change OR
e   the emails indicate that global warming or climate change has NOT been happening, or is NOT caused by human action OR
f   the emails indicate that no actions should be taken to mitigate the effects of global warming or climate change

Type "no" if the respondent said none of the above.

Q8. "don't remember"
Type "yes" if the respondent said anything that indicates *any* of the following:
a   don't or can't remember, or don't or can't remember the specifics OR
b   don't know the specifics OR
c   not sure about the specifics.

Type "no" if the respondent said none of the above.

Q9. "other"
Type "yes" if the respondent said anything in addition to 1a–1d, 2a–2e, 3a–3d, 4a–4f, 5a–5b, 6a–6c, 7a–7f, 8a–8c.
Type "no" otherwise.

Appendix C

Instructions for Content Analysis of Survey Responses on IPCC Report

You will read answers that survey respondents gave to an open-ended survey question and make six coding decisions about what each person said. Survey respondents—nationally representative sample of American adults—were asked, on phone interviews, the following question:

During the last six months, do you remember hearing or reading anything in the news about mistakes in scientific reports that were written by the Intergovernmental Panel on Climate Change, or do you not remember hearing or reading anything in the news about that?

The respondents who answered "yes" to the above question were asked the following question:

What do you remember hearing or reading about that?

And their answers are for you to read and make six coding decisions. Please do your work completely independently. Do NOT talk with anyone other than the study investigators about anything you do on this project. Please read the text very carefully and follow the instructions below.

6 Coding Questions

Note: The pronoun "they" in responses can be interpreted to be referring to scientists or members of IPCC committee.

Q1. "disagreement"

Type "yes" if the respondent said anything that indicates *any* of the following:
a   there was disagreement, or argument, or debate OR
b   some conflicting or contradictory reports with some saying one thing while others saying the opposite OR
c   there was a controversy.

Type "no" if the respondent said none of the above.

Q2. "mistakes or inaccuracies"

Type "yes" if the respondent said anything that indicates *any* of the following:
a   the IPCC reports contained any statements that were incorrect or based any statements on other research reports that themselves were not credible OR
b   the IPCC reports, including data, methods, and findings, were not accurate OR
c   the IPCC reports, including data, methods, and findings, were not valid OR
d   the IPCC reports, including data, methods, and findings, were exaggerated or overestimated OR

e   the IPCC reports, including data, figures, methods, findings, were questionable or was questioned.

Type "no" if the respondent said none of the above.

Q3. "scientific misconduct"
Type "yes" if the respondent said anything that indicates *any* of the following:
a   one or more scientists (or members of IPCC committee) did something unethical in their research OR
b   one or more scientists (or members of IPCC committee) did something unethical with their data—they withheld the data, or they manipulated or falsified the data OR
c   one or more scientists (or members of IPCC committee) did something unethical in their statistical analysis—they skewed the analysis or biased their results OR
d   one or more scientists (or members of IPCC committee) should not be trusted OR
e   one or more scientists (or members of IPCC committee) did research for their own personal or financial gains (including to get more funding for their research) OR
f   one or more scientists (or members of IPCC committee) did research for political reasons.

Type "no" if the respondent said none of the above.

Q4. "natural phenomena"
Type "yes" if the respondent said anything that indicates *any* of the following:
a   about polar bears or other animals OR
b   about arctic icebergs or glaciers melting or receding OR
c   about ozone, or volcanoes, or oceans, or storms, or other naturals phenomena.

Type "no" if the respondent said none of the above.

Q5. "don't remember"
Type "yes" if the respondent said anything that indicates *any* of the following:
a   don't remember the specifics, or not sure about the specifics.

Type "no" if the respondent said none of the above.

Q6. "other"
Type "yes" if the respondent said anything in addition to 1a–1c, 2a–2e, 3a–3f, 4a–4c, 5a.
Type "no" otherwise.

Appendix D

Methodology of January 2009 Non-probability Survey

Data Collection Methodology of January 2009 Non-probability Survey

The participants were 2,885 members of Luth Research's SurveySavvy panel. Most of the members of this panel volunteered to complete surveys in exchange for a chance to win prizes, so this panel is not a representative sample of American adults. The panel members were recruited in several ways. Initially, random digit dialing phone calls were made to invite some American adults to sign up to receive email invitations to complete surveys via the Internet. Similar recruitment phone calls were made to professionals working in the information technology sector who were listed in professional directories. These initial panel members (a total of approximately 5,000) were then offered a chance to win cash or gift certificates in exchange for referring other people to join the panel. Referred panel members were offered the same incentives to refer other people. Panel members were also recruited through online advertisements (posted on the Luth Research website, news sites, blogs, and search engines) and through emails sent by businesses and non-profit organizations with which prospective panelists were affiliated. Panel members were rewarded when one of their referrals, or one of their referrals' referrals, completed a survey.

A total of 89,918 SurveySavvy panelists were invited to complete there surveys between January 15 and 18, 2009. Invitees were selected to maximize the match of the participants to the nation in terms of the distributions of some demographic variables. A total of 3,013 people completed the 12–15 minute survey, 2,885 of whom indicated that they were able to see and hear a test streaming video and were therefore included in the analyses reported here. Five respondents were dropped because their reported age was under 18, resulting in a usable sample size of 2,880 for the analysis.

Global Warming Measures in January 2009 Non-probability Survey

Upon watching one of the above four new stories, respondents answered questions reporting their opinions on global warming as follows.

Global warming existence. "You may have heard about the idea that the world's temperature may have been going up slowly over the past 100 years. What is your personal opinion on this—do you think this probably has been happening, or do you think it probably hasn't been happening?" Answers were coded 1 and 0, respectively.

Certainty about global warming existence. Participants who said that global warming has been happening were then asked, "How sure are you that the world's temperature has been going up – extremely sure, very sure, somewhat sure, or not sure at all?" Participants who said that global warming has not been happening were asked the same question with the word "hasn't" substituted for the word "has." Participants who said that they were extremely sure or very sure were coded 1, and all other participants were coded 0.

Attitude toward global warming. "Scientists use the term 'global warming' to refer to the idea that the world's average temperature may be about five degrees Fahrenheit higher in 75 years than it is now. Overall, would you say that global warming would be good, bad, or neither good nor bad?" Participants who said that global warming would be bad were coded 1, all others were coded 0.

Global seriousness. Participants who thought global warming had been happening were asked, "If nothing is done to reduce global warming in the future, how serious of a problem do you think it will be for the world—very serious, somewhat serious, not so serious, or not serious at all?" Participants who thought global warming had not been happening were asked, "Assuming it's happening, how serious of a problem do you think it will be for the world—very serious, somewhat serious, not so serious, or not serious at all." Participants who said that global warming would be very serious were coded 1, and all others were coded 0.

Support for government action. "Do you think the federal government should do more than it's doing now to try to deal with global warming, should do less than it's doing now, or is it doing about the right amount?" Participants who said the government should do more were coded 1, and all others were coded 0.

Notes

1 A great deal of research has explored trust more generally, and this construct has been defined in many different ways (see, e.g., Das & Teng (2004)). In line with much of that work, we define trust in scientists as having two components: (1) a belief in competence; and (2) a belief that motives are well-intentioned.

2 The search results were obtained from Lexis Nexis as follows: time span was between November 17, 2009 and June 30, 2010; full-text search terms were "climategate" OR "climate gate" OR "Climatic Research Unit" OR CRU; sources were U.S. Print Newspapers and "TV & Radio News Transcripts" for the two searches, respectively.

3 These search results were obtained from Lexis Nexis as follows: time span was between November 17, 2009 and June 30, 2010; full-text search terms were "climategate" OR "climate gate" OR "Climatic Research Unit" OR CRU; sources were "Fox News Network"; "ABC News", "CBS News", and "NBC News"; and "CNBC News", CNN", and "MSNBC", under the category of "TV & Radio News Transcripts", respectively.

4 The search results were obtained from Lexis Nexis as follows: time span was between November 17, 2009 and June 30, 2010; full-text search terms were (IPCC OR "Intergovernmental Panel on Climate Change") AND (error OR mistake OR errors OR mistakes); sources were U.S. Print Newspapers and "TV & Radio News Transcripts" for the two searches, respectively.

5· This question wording is called "balanced" because it acknowledges both sides of the issue equally saliently and thereby avoids acquiescence response bias (Krosnick & Fabrigar, forthcoming).

6 The agreement level between coders was 93% and 81% for questions 1 and 2, respectively; 87% and 82% for questions 3 and 4, respectively; 97% and 96% for questions 5 and 6, respectively; 96% and 96% for questions 7 and 8, respectively; and 76% for question 9. For respondents for whom the two coders gave different answers to at least one coding question, a third coder performed another round of coding independently using the same coding process the first two coders followed. The discrepancy in coding answers among three coders was resolved by the majority rule.

7 Another 9% said that the emails suggested that climate scientists should be trusted, and 11% said that these emails did not indicate anything to them about whether climate scientists should be trusted. These findings are broadly consistent with the results of a national survey done in January 2010 (Leiserowitz et al., 2012), in which 29% of respondents said they had heard of news stories about Climategate (similar to the 32% found in our study) and about 15% of respondents said they had heard of the stories and thought these stories caused them to trust climate scientists less (53% of the 29% of all respondents), not very different from the 9% of the respondents in our survey who remembered the stories and thought the emails indicated that scientists should not be trusted.

8 The agreement level between coders was 91% for question 1, 83% for question 2, 85% for question 3, 97% for question 4, 94% for question 5 and 80% for question 6. For respondents for whom the two coders gave different answers to at least one coding question, a third coder performed another round of coding independently using the same coding process the first two coders followed. The discrepancy in coding answers among three coders was resolved by the majority rule.

9 If we considered people who thought the issue of global warming was extremely important to them personally, the upper bound of the trust-reducing effect of Climategate through online processing and failure to remember would be 2% of the survey sample. If we required people likely to engage in online processing to have high ability by imposing the assumption of college graduate, the upper bound of the trust-reducing effect of Climategate through online processing and failure to remember shrank to less than 1% of the survey respondents.

10 We employed an alternative measure—opinion strength—to characterize people likely to engage in online processing as follows, and all respondents were asked: "How strong are your opinions on the issue of global warming—extremely strong, very strong, somewhat strong, not too strong, or not at all strong?" We obtained similar estimates of upper bounds of the trust-reducing effect of Climategate through online processing and failure to remember as the estimates using the issue importance measure.

11 The same conclusion is reinforced if we dichotomize trust differently or if we treat it as a continuous variable.

12 One might imagine that the effect of the focal events was very short-lived, so surveys done months after November 2009, would fail to document this effect on public beliefs. However, the NBC/Wall Street Journal sequence of polls challenges the notion of an immediate effect of the revelations (during December 11–14, 2009) or an effect that emerged more slowly over the next few months.

13 An alternative approach to assessing the impact of Climategate and the IPCC report errors could be to ask survey respondents whether news of these events changed their opinions (see, e.g., Leiserowitz et al. (2012)). However, a huge literature in psychology suggests that this is unlikely to yield valid results. Hundreds of studies

reviewed by and inspired by Nisbett and Wilson's (1977) landmark paper show that people are not aware of the forces that shape their thinking and action. And dozens of studies show that people cannot accurately describe changes that occurred in their opinions in the past (for a review, see Krosnick & Fabrigar (forthcoming)). Another approach one might take is asking people to agree or disagree with various statements about the Climategate and IPCC report errors (see, e.g., Leiserowitz et al. (2012)). But dozens of studies have shown that answers to agree/disagree questions are biased by acquiescence response bias (Krosnick & Fabrigar, forthcoming).

14 As consistently throughout the chapter, high-trust people or people who trust scientists' statements highly are defined as people who gave response "completely," "a lot" or "a moderate amount" to the trust question: "How much do you trust the things scientists say about the environment—completely, a lot, a moderate amount, a little, or not at all?", and low-trust people or people who do not trust scientists' statements highly are defined as people who gave response "a little," or "not at all."

15 Consistently throughout the chapter, we use the response to the trust question: "How much do you trust the things scientists say about the environment—completely, a lot, a moderate amount, a little, or not at all?" to categorize respondents as high-trust and low-trust people, respectively, with the former defined as respondents who gave response "completely," "a lot" or "a moderate amount" and the latter defined as respondents who gave response "completely," "a lot" or "a moderate amount" to the trust question, respectively. The terms "high trust people" and "people who trust scientists' statements highly" are used interchangeably, and so are the terms "low-trust people" and "people who do not trust scientists' statements highly."

16 This one year lag is sensible because the public typically learns about a year's average world temperature in news stories disseminated early the following year.

17 Brulle, Carmichael, and Jenkins (2012) reported evidence that might seem to offer a series of alternative explanations for the changes in public opinion shown in Figure 13.1. But there are many reasons to hesitate before reaching such a conclusion. First, Brulle et al. (2012) did not predict changes over time in beliefs about whether the earth has been warming during the last 100 years, as we did. Instead, they predicted an index that they dubbed "concern about the threat of climate change," which was measured by responses to a wide variety of survey questions on many different topics. Second, the over time dynamics of that index did not parallel the over-time changes in our (or others') measures of belief in global warming's existence— Brulle's index rose from 2006 to 2007, whereas our surveys showed no such increase in existence beliefs. And although our surveys documented a decrease in existence beliefs between 2008 and 2009, Brulle et al. (2012) reported an increase in concern during that time. Third, from Brulle et al.'s (2012) regressions, it is impossible to tell which of their predictors would anticipate an increase in concern from 2009 to 2010, because the annual values of the predictors are not reported. And reports of annual world temperatures were not among the predictors those investigators examined. So we do not see a basis for concluding that Brulle et al.'s (2012) findings conflict with those reported here or suggest alternative explanations for the patterns we observed.

18 Because the participants were not randomly sampled from the American adult population, this should not be viewed as a nationally representative sample.

19 Consistent with the notion that Fox News coverage of global warming was more skeptical, Hart (2008) found that between 1998 and 2004, Fox News was notably more skeptical about climate change than was CNN (Hart, 2008). Likewise, in an analysis of editorials, columns, and commentators from all newspapers and television stations owned by News Corp in the U.S., Britain, and Australia between 1997 and 2007, McKnight (2010) found that Fox News program hosts regularly expressed skepticism about climate change. And Feldman et al. (2011) found that during 2007

and 2008, Fox News took a more dismissive tone toward climate change than did CNN and MSNBC (Feldman et al., 2011).
20 Respondents reported the number of the last 30 days on which they watched a Fox news program and the number of days on which they watched a non-Fox television news program.
21 Because these regressions reveal cross-sectional partial correlations, the coefficients might reflect the influence of media exposure on trust and/or the effect of trust in scientists on choices of media exposure.
22 Similar patterns are observed when dichotomizing in different ways.

References

Adams, J. K. (1957). Laboratory studies of behavior without awareness. *Psychological Bulletin*, 54(5): 383–405.
Banerjee, N. (2013). 2012 was among the 10 hottest years on record globally. *Los Angeles Times*, January 15, 2013.
Bizer, G. Y., Tormala, Z. L., Rucker, D. D., & Petty, R. E. (2006). Memory-based versus online processing: Implications for attitude strength. *Journal of Experimental Social Psychology*, 42(5): 646–653.
Bornstein, R. F., & D'Agostino, P. R. (1992). Stimulus recognition and the mere exposure effect. *Journal of Personality and Social Psychology*, 63(4): 545–552.
Bornstein, R. F., Leone, D. R., & Galley, D. J. (1987). The generalizability of subliminal mere exposure effects: Influence of stimuli perceived without awareness on social behavior. *Journal of Personality and Social Psychology*, 53: 1070–1079.
Borick, C. P., & Rabe, B. G. (2012). Weather or not: Examining the impact of meteorological conditions on public opinion regarding climate change. The American Political Science Association Annual Meeting 2012 Paper.
Boykoff, M. T., & Boykoff, J. (2004). Bias as balance: global warming and the US prestige press. *Global Environmental Change*, 14(2): 125–136.
Boykoff, M. T., & Nacu-Schmidt, A. (2013). 2000–2013 US Newspaper Coverage of Climate Change or Global Warming. University of Colorado. Accessed in April 2013 at http://sciencepolicy.colorado.edu/media_coverage/us/graph.jpg.
Boykoff, M. T., & Roberts, J. T. (2007). *Media Coverage of Climate Change: Trends, Strengths and Weaknesses*. New York: UN Human Development Report Office.
Brewer, P. R., & Ley, B. L. (2013). Whose science do you believe? Explaining trust in sources of scientific information about the environment. *Science Communication*, 35(1): 115–137.
Brulle, R. J., Carmichael, J., & Jenkin, J. C. (2012). Shifting public opinion on climate change: An empirical assessment of factors influencing concern over climate change in the U.S., 2002–2010. *Climatic Change*, 114(2): 169–188.
Carlisle, J. E., Feezell, J. T., Michaud, K. E. H., Smith, E. R. A. N., & Smith, L. (2010). The public's trust in scientific claims regarding offshore oil drilling. *Public Understanding of Science*, 19(5): 514–527.
Consumer Sentimental Index (2013). University of Michigan. Accessed in April 2013 at http://www.sca.isr.umich.edu/documents.php?c=tr.
Critchley, C. R. (2008). Public opinion and trust in scientists: the role of the research context, and the perceived motivation of stem cell researchers. *Public Understanding of Science*, 17: 309–327.

Croson, R., & Buchan, N. (1999). Gender and culture: International experimental evidence from trust games. *The American Economic Review*, 89(2): 386–391.

Curry, J. (2010a). On the credibility of climate research, part II: Towards rebuilding trust. Accessed in April 2013 at http://curry.eas.gatech.edu/climate/towards_rebuilding_ trust.html.

Curry, J. (2010b). Opinion: Can scientists rebuild the public trust in climate science? Accessed in April 2013 at http://icecap.us/images/uploads/Opinion_Curry.pdf.

Das, T. K., & Teng, B. S. (2004). The risk-based view of trust: A conceptual framework. *Journal of Business and Psychology*, 19(1): 85–116.

Deryugina, T. (2013). How do people update? The effects of local weather fluctuations on beliefs about global warming. *Climatic Change*, 118: 397–416.

Downs, A. (1972). Up and down with ecology: The "issue-attention" cycle. In D. L. Protess, & M. E. McCombs (Eds.), *Agenda Setting: Readings on Media, Public Opinion, and Policymaking* (pp. 48–59). Hillsdale, NJ: Lawrence Erlbaum Associates.

Durando, J. (2010). NOAA: Global temperature in 2010 ties for hottest on record. *USA Today*, October 15, 2010.

Egana, P. J., & Mullina, M. (2012). Turning personal experience into political attitudes: The effects of local weather on Americans' perceptions about global warming. *The Journal of Politics*, 74(3): 796–809.

Eilperin, J. (2010). Hottest climate year on record, NASA says. *Washington Post*, December 10, 2010.

Feldman, L., Maibach, E. W., Roser-Renouf, C., & Leiserowitz, A. (2011). Climate on cable: The nature and impact of global warming coverage on Fox News, CNN, and MSNBC. *The International Journal of Press/Politics,* 17(1): 3–31.

Gauchat, G. (2011). The cultural authority of science: Public trust and acceptance of organized science. *Public Understanding of Science*, 20(6): 751–770.

Gauchat, G. (2012). Politicization of science in the public sphere: A Study of public trust in the United States, 1974–2010. *American Sociological Review*, 77(2): 167–187

Greenwald, A. G., & Draine, S. C. (1997). Do subliminal stimuli enter the mind unnoticed? Tests with a new method. In J. D. Cohen & J. W. Schooler (Eds.), *Scientific Approaches to Consciousness* (pp. 83–108). Mahwah, NJ: Erlbaum.

Hardwig, J. (1991). The role of trust in knowledge. *Journal of Philosophy*, 88(12): 693–708.

Hastie, R., & Park, B. (1986). The relationship between memory and judgment depends on whether the task is memory-based or online. *Psychological Review*, 93: 258–68.

Hart, P. S. (2008). Market influences on climate change frames in CNN and Fox News climate change broadcasts. Presented at the International Communication Association Annual Meeting, Montreal, Quebec, Canada.

Hawkins, D. (1970). The effects of subliminal stimulation on drive level and brand preference. *Journal of Marketing Research*, 7: 322–326.

Heatherington, M. J. (1999). The effect of political trust on the presidential vote, 1968–96. *American Political Science Review,* 93 (June): 311–326.

Hmielowski, J. D., Feldman L., Myers, T. A., Leiserowitz, A., & Maibach, E. (2012). An attack on science? Media use, trust in scientists, and perceptions of global warming. *Public Understanding of Science*, 22(3): 1–18.

Hovland, C. I., Janis, I. L., & Kelley, H. H. (1953). *Communication and Persuasion: Psychological Studies of Opinion Change*. New Haven, CT: Yale University.

Intergovernmental Panel on Climate Change (IPCC) (2010a). Statement of the IPCC chairman on the establishment of an independent committee to review IPCC procedures. Accessed in April 2013 at http://www.ipcc.ch/pdf/press/PA_IPCC_Chairman_Statement_27Feb2010.pdf

Intergovernmental Panel on Climate Change (IPCC) (2010b). IPCC statement on the melting of Himalayan glaciers. Accessed in August 2012 at http://www.ipcc.ch/pdf/presentations/himalayastatement-20january2010.pdf.

Joireman, J., Truelove, H. B., & Duell, B. (2010). Effect of outdoor temperature, heat primes and anchoring in belief in global warming. *Journal of Environmental Psychology*, 30(4): 358–367.

Kahan, D. M., Peters, E., Wittlin, M., Slovic, P., Ouellette, L. L., Braman, D., & Mandel, G. (2012). The polarizing impact of science literacy and numeracy on perceived climate change risks. *Nature Climate Change*, 2: 732–735.

Kahn, M. E., & Kotchen, M. J. (2010). Environmental concern and the business cycle: The chilling effect of recession. National Bureau of Economic Research Working Paper No. 16241.

Krosnick, J. A., & Fabrigar, L. R. (forthcoming). *The Handbook of Questionnaire Design*. New York: Oxford University Press.

Krugman, H. E. (1965). The impact of television advertising: Learning without involvement. *Public Opinion Quarterly*, 29(3): 349–356.

Leiserowitz, A., Maibach, E., Roser-Renouf, C., Smith, N., & Dawson, E. (2013) Climategate, public opinion, and the loss of trust. *American Behavioral Scientist,* 57(6): 818–837.

Lempinen, E. W. (2010). Science leaders urge new effort to strengthen bonds with public. *Science*, 327(5973): 1591–1593.

Lavine, H. (2002). Online versus memory-based process models of political evaluation. In K. R. Monroe (Ed.), *Political Psychology* (pp. 225–247). Mahwah, NJ: LEA.

Li, Y., Johnson, E. J., & Zava, L. (2011). Local warming: daily temperature change influences belief in global warming. *Psychological Science*, 22(4): 454–459.

Luhmann, N. (1979). *Trust and Power*. New York, NY: John Wiley and Sons.

Malka, A., Krosnick, J. A., & Langer, G. (2009). The association of knowledge with concern about global warming: Trusted information sources shape public thinking. *Risk Analysis*, 29: 633–647.

Marx, S. M., Weber, E. U., Orlove, B. S., Leiserowitz, A., Krantz, D. H., Roncoli, C., & Phillips, J. (2007). Communication and mental processes: Analytical and experiential processing of uncertain climate information. *Global Environmental Change*, 17: 47–58.

McCombs, M. E., & Shaw, D. L. (1972). The agenda-setting function of mass media. *Public Opinion Quarterly*, 36(2): 176–187.

McCright, A. M. & Dunlap, R. E. (2011). The politicization of climate change and polarization in the American public's view of global warming, 2001–2010. *The Sociological Quarterly*, 52: 155–194.

McKnight, D. (2010). A change in the climate? The journalism of opinion at News Corporation. *Journalism* 11(6): 693–706.

Miller, J. M., & Krosnick, J. A. (2000). News media impact on the ingredients of presidential evaluations: Politically knowledgeable citizens are guided by a trusted source. *American Journal of Political Science*, 44(2): 301–315.

Montford, A. W. (2010). *The Hockey Stick Illusion: Climategate and the Corruption of Science (Independent Minds)*. London, UK: Stacey International Publishers.

Mooney, C. (2005). *The Republican War on Science*. New York: Basic Books.

Mooney, C. (2012.) *The Republican Brain: The Science of Why They Deny Science and Reality*. Hoboken, NJ: Wiley Press.

Mooney, C., & Kirshenbaum, S. (2009). *Unscientific America*. New York: Basic Books.

Myers, T. A., Malibach, E. W., Roser-Renouf, C., Akerlof, K., & Leiserowitz, A. A. (2013). The relationship between personal experience and belief in the reality of global warming. *Nature Climate Change*, 3: 343–347.

National Oceanic and Atmospheric Administration (NOAA) (2012a). National Climatic Data Center, "State of the Climate", accessed in April 2013 at http://www.ncdc.noaa.gov/sotc/; "News", accessed in April 2013 at http://www.ncdc.noaa.gov/news/2012-global-temperatures10th-highest-record.

National Oceanic and Atmospheric Administration (NOAA) (2012b). State of the climate, global analysis, annual 2011. Accessed in August 2012 at http://www.ncdc.noaa.gov/sotc/global/2011/13.

New York Times (2010). A climate change corrective. Editorial, *New York Times*, July 10, 2010.

Nisbett, R.E., & Wilson, T.D. (1977). Telling more than we can know: Verbal reports on mental process. *Psychological Review*, 84(3): 231–259.

Norton, D.W. (2010). Constructing "Climategate" and tracking chatter in an Age of Web n.0. Working Paper, American University. Accessed in April 2013 at http://www.centerforsocialmedia.org/sites/default/files/documents/pages/david_norton_climateate.pdf.

Oreskes, N., & Conway, E. M. (2010). *Merchants of Doubt: How a Handful of Scientists Obscured the Truth on Issues from Tobacco Smoke to Global Warming*. London, UK: Bloomsbury Press.

Pechmann, C., & Stewart, D. W. (1988). Advertising Repetition: A critical review of wearin and wearout. *Current Issues and Research in Advertising*, 11(1–2): 285–329.

Petty, R. E., & Cacioppo, J. T. (1986). *Communication and Persuasion: Central and Peripheral Routes to Attitude Change*. New York: Springer-Verlag.

Petty, R. E., Cacioppo, J. T., & Schumann, D. (1983). Central and peripheral routes to advertising effectiveness: The moderating role of involvement. *Journal of Consumer Research*, 10 (September): 135–146.

Pew Research Center (2010). Wide partisan divide over global warming. Accessed in August 2012 at http://pewresearch.org/pubs/1780/poll-global-warming-scientists-energy-policiesoffshore-drilling-tea-party.

PollingReport (2012) Environment. Accessed in August 2012 at http://www.pollingreport.com/enviro2.htm.

Putnam, R. D. (1993). *Bowling Alone*. New York: Simon and Schuster.

Resnik, D. B. (2009). *Playing Politics with Science*. New York: Oxford University Press.

Resnik, D. B. (2011). Scientific research and the public trust. *Science and Engineering Ethics*, 17(3): 399–409.

Samenow, J. (2013). Earth had third warmest May on record (tie with 1998 and 2005). *The Washington Post*, June 20, 2013.

Scott, D. (1983). Trust differences between men and women in superior and subordinate relationships. *Group and Organization Studies*, 8(3): 319–336.

Scuggs, L., & Benegal, S. (2012). Declining public concern about climate change: Can we blame the great recession? *Global Environmental Change*, 22(2): 505–515.

Shum, R. Y. (2012). Effects of economic recession and local weather on climate change attitudes. *Climate Policy*, 12(1): 38–49.

Shumway, R. H. (1988). *Applied Statistical Time Series Analysis*. Englewood Cliffs, NJ: Prentice Hall.

Siegrist, M. (2000). The influence of trust and perception of risks and benefits on the acceptance of gene technology. *Risk Analysis*, 20(2): 195–203.

Siegrist, M., & Cvetkovich, G. (2000). Perception of hazards: The role of social trust and knowledge. *Risk Analysis*, 20(5): 713–719.

Siegrist, M., Keller, C., Kastenholz, H., Frey, S., & Wiek, A. (2007). Laypeople's and experts' perception of nanotechnology hazards. *Risk Analysis*, 27: 59–69.

Slovic, P. (1993). Perceived risk, trust, and democracy. *Risk Analysis*, 13(6): 675–682.

Sternthal, B., Phillips, L. W., & Dholakia, R. (1978). The persuasive effect of source credibility: A situational analysis. *Public Opinion Quarterly,* 42 (Fall): 285–314.

Ward, B. (2010). A reputation in tatters. *New Scientists*, 206(2762): 26–27.

Weber, E. U. (2010). What shapes perceptions of climate change. *WIREs Climate Change*, 1 (May/June): 332–342.

Zajonc, R. B. (1968). Attitudinal effects of mere exposure. *Journal of Personality and Social Psychology,* 9(2): 1–27.

Zaller, J. (1992). *The Nature and Origins of Mass Opinion*. Cambridge, UK: Cambridge University Press.

INDEX